# *URBAN DESIGN AND PEOPLE*

# URBAN DESIGN AND PEOPLE

MICHAEL DOBBINS

John Wiley & Sons, Inc.

This book is printed on acid-free paper.



Published by John Wiley & Sons, Inc., Hoboken, New Jersey

Published simultaneously in Canada



For general information about our other products and services, please contact our Customer Care Department within the United States at (800) 762-2974, outside the United States at (317) 572-3993 or fax (317) 572-4002.

Wiley also publishes its books in a variety of electronic formats. Some content that appears in print may not be available in electronic books. For more information about Wiley products, visit our web site at www.wiley.com.

*Library of Congress Cataloging-in-Publication Data:*

Dobbins, Michael, 1938-
Urban design and people / by Michael Dobbins.
p. cm.
Includes bibliographical references and index.
ISBN 978-0-470-13816-8 (cloth : alk. paper)
1. City planning. 2. Urban ecology. I. Title.
HT166.D58 2009
307.1'216--dc22

Printed in the United States of America

10 9 8 7 6 5 4 3 2 1

*To Peggy, Jeb, and Clem, who keep me going;*

*To all citizen activists who work tirelessly to improve their public environment; and*

*To all public servants who keep the faith*

# CONTENTS

# Preface

*Urban design* is a diffuse and abstract term. It means different things to different people. For those not directly involved in its practice or aware of its effects on their daily lives, it may not mean much, if anything at all. I first heard the term in architecture school, but I didn't really think much about what it might mean until my schoolmate Jonathan Barnett started using it to describe his aspiration to put together with some of his colleagues a design capability in the New York City government. That opportunity had come up after the election of John Lindsay as mayor in 1966. Lindsay, concerned about deterioration in the public environment, empanelled a study commission on design, chaired by William Paley, chair of CBS. The commission's report asserted that the quality of design was of utmost importance, that the city government should take the lead in advancing a public design agenda, and that, among other measures, it should recruit and employ trained designers toward that end.

I am honored to have been the first hired by the design group initiators (which in addition to Jonathan, included Jaquelin Robertson, Myles Weintraub, Richard Weinstein, and Giovanni Pasanella). They had negotiated with the Lindsay team and settled on placing the group in the City Planning Department. We set up shop in April 1967 in an "eye-ease" green-walled, gray linoleum–floored space on the 14th floor of 2 Lafayette Street where the city planning department was housed. So began for me a total redirection of my career, from an architect worrying about finding the next commission to devoting my energies and whatever were my design capabilities to improving the quality of the public environment. I came to a whole new concept of the *client,* from single patron to the city's 7.5 million citizens. I've been a public servant ever since.

For me, *urban design* came to describe the design and functionality of all urbanized places—how they looked and how they performed. Furthermore, the emphasis in urban design is on *public* places—the streets, parks, plazas, the open spaces that everyone shares. These are the places that provide the interface with and connection to the *private* places—the home, the workplace, the mostly enclosed spaces where people carry on their more personal and private life activities. Urban design is the design of the public environment, the space owned by all, as it connects to, frames, and is framed by the private environment—that space owned by individuals or corporate entities. Urban design is the public face and public base of human settlements. People proud of their places are the mark of good urban design.

In 40 years of practice as a public sector urban designer, in addition to the usual base of urban design theory and practice, I have identified at least three important themes that get short shrift or are ignored altogether. First, people are the core of successful urban places. If a place looks good, feels comfortable, and meets its functional expectations, it will attract people and engender their embrace, ongoing interaction, and stewardship. Such a happy outcome is more likely to occur if representatives of the people who are or will be in the place play an active role in guiding the design and development decisions and priorities that make places happen. I've never met anyone who didn't want to live in a better place.

Second, urban design work does not and cannot happen without the integration of all the interests that together regulate, build, and use the public realm. Whether conscious of the role each plays or not, every public place reflects and exhibits the government, which owns it; the private sector, whose buildings frame it; and everyday citizens, who need it to get around and to come together. Where the relationships between the three spheres are often more important than the spheres themselves, a conscious and positive partnership is a key factor for making places better.

Third, the disciplines responsible for designing public places must integrate and synthesize their activities in an informed, thoughtful, and respectful way—the opposite of what usually happens. Civil engineers in their various subdisciplines are most responsible for the design of the public right-of-way. Architects design the private buildings that frame and connect to the public space. Landscape architects are more and more involved in designing streetscapes, public parks, and plazas. And city planners design and administer the public policies and rules that determine the activities and sizes of buildings and their relationships with the public realm. Other design forces are in play as well, but these big four must come together around common design visions if places are to get better.

I write this book because much of the information that my colleagues and I have gained in carrying out wide-ranging urban design and development initiatives was not sufficiently covered in existing texts. Pieces of what constitutes urban design practice are covered in many books, often in elegant forms. But the substance of mine and others' day-to-day work experience, what really happens and how to get the job done, I have not found. Furthermore, while most of us agree that urban design is mainly about design of the public realm, I find little that covers the three themes noted above, which I believe to be vital to successful urban design and development outcomes.

The book is organized in five parts: Background, Content, Principles, Processes, and Strategies. The text draws on experience, mine and others'. It is an exposition more of practices that work than a product of academic research. Accordingly, the reader will note that most references and many examples are presented as sidebars. In addition, as a comprehensive treatment, the text suggests many references in the form of websites, and the reader is encouraged to use Google or Yahoo search engines to probe subjects in depth and to gain other perspectives. It is for students, for teachers, and for practitioners across the spectrum of disciplines who come together to design and build the public environment. Maybe most importantly, though, I have written it as a guide for everyday citizens who are concerned about their public environment and who want to (and work to) make it better. If it's successful, it should provide a general roadmap to design and development in the public environment and a starter kit of tools for effectively engaging these processes. Further, it should prepare people in their various roles to understand and embrace the role of everyday citizens as stewards of the public environment, at all scales.

Finally, a word about civil service and government: Usually, city planning and urban design administrators working for the local government are in the best position to understand and help facilitate the necessary, but often left out, interactions among all those who make public places happen. And they are often the "point person" responsible for bringing together all parties in the more complicated of the private-public-community development initiatives. Committing to public service generally is an uphill battle in the privatizing societal and economic structure and culture that began with the Reagan years, first in California and then nationally. Civil servants became easy to attack and hard to defend, and both government and the numbers of service-minded citizens who might be drawn to it went into a protracted state of decline. People are now awakening to the effects of this decline on their daily lives, in public institutions, parks, infrastructure, services, the quality and functionality of the public environment, and, most recently, in the impacts of deregulation on the finance industry. I hope this book will serve as a useful reference for citizens pushing to shift American priorities toward public service, toward government meeting citizens' day-to-day needs and improving their quality of life, a role that privatization has not fulfilled.

I have worked for a few local governments and with government agencies at all levels. I find that my fellow workers are good people, committed to making things better in their various spheres of activity, and they generally work on an ethical plane usually above their private sector counterparts. When I talk to students, I remind them that as they look for work in the private sector they will have to be valued more for the revenue they generate minus salary, than for making places better, the reason why most of them went into urban design and planning in the first place. Then I ask them where else could they work twice as hard for half the pay but have 10 times the impact—local government. And I leave them with the thought that if they want to take back their government, the best way is to work for it. Some of them do.

# Acknowledgments

Everyone I have ever worked with to make places better—neighborhood people, businesspeople, city planners, engineers, architects, landscape architects, civil servants, elected officials, my colleagues at city halls, teachers, students, colleagues at universities, developers, contractors, homebuilders, attorneys, lenders—has contributed to this book.

My wife, Peggy, has contributed the most, sustaining me through 40 years of practice with ideas and analyses, providing a rich theoretical base, only some of which I have so far been able to put into practice. So I have a way to go. My son Jeb, a writer, early on reminded me that writing something that is readable requires a kind of attention different from that of bureaucrats writing memos—and he marked up parts of the text to make his point. At least the text is better than it might have been. My son Clem, a neuroscientist who was finishing his PhD while I was working on this, kept my head up, looking forward, as I tried to do for him.

A whole string of colleagues, public, private, and community leaders, have guided me into and through my quests for the better design of places. Bill Gilchrist, my collaborator in saving Birmingham's Civil Rights Institute as a building of distinction and my successor there as planning director, has steadfastly encouraged me to put my experience into print. My Atlanta City Hall urban design colleagues, Alycen Whiddon, Aaron Fortner, Caleb Racicot, Enrique Bascunana, Renee Kemp Rotan, and Beverly Dockeray-Ojo, worked with me to infuse the city with urban design guidance and influence. More recently, my Georgia Tech colleagues in the City and Regional Planning Department and the Architecture Department have provided valuable feedback and encouragement as I pushed along. The work of my urban design colleagues at Georgia Tech is reflected throughout the text, whether noted or not. Doug Allen, Ellen Dunham-Jones, Richard Dagenhart, Randy Roark, David Green, and John Peponis have all contributed significantly to the rich dialogue that we share in Atlanta with communities, government agencies, and private sector practitioners and developers. More generally, colleagues whose voiceprints have guided me include the late dean, Tom Galloway, who figured out how to provide me a home in academe; behavioral psychologist Craig Zimring; and city planning professors Michael Elliott and Catherine Ross. All of my other city planning, architecture and building construction colleagues have encouraged me along my way, as well. Mike Meyer in the Civil and Environmental Engineering Department and Eric Dumbaugh, now at Texas A&M University, gave me good feedback and advice on how to incorporate transportation and traffic engineering considerations into the context of the book. Georgia Tech students Renato Ghizoni, Chelsea Arkin, and Jared Yarsevich all contributed valuable research on various aspects of the content, as well as examples from which some of the illustrations are drawn.

Paul Drougas at Wiley somehow thought that I would be able to write this book, or something like it, thus giving me both the confidence and the structure to persist, for which I am most grateful. And his colleagues have borne with me as a newcomer to the publishing world.

# PART I

# BACKGROUND

## Setting the Stage

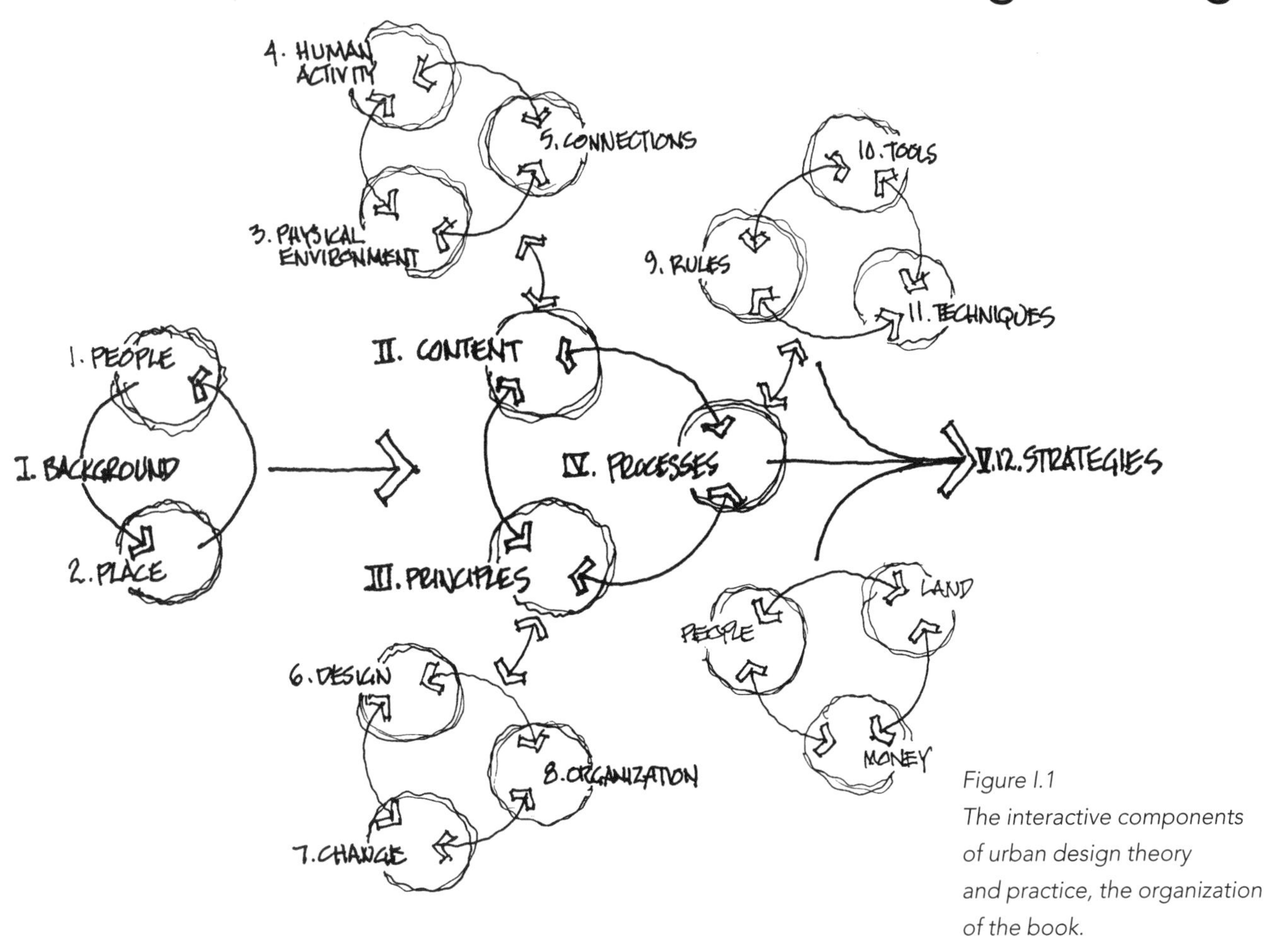


*Figure I.1*
*The interactive components of urban design theory and practice, the organization of the book.*

# Overview

I base this text on two overarching premises:

- People want to live in better places
- Urban design can make places better

*Places* refers to the civic environment, generally the publicly owned space shared by all for public activities like walking, biking, driving, riding, parking, getting on and off transit, going in and out of buildings, sitting, dining, picnicking, hanging out, getting together, playing, relaxing, having festivals, partying, congregating, parading, marching, demonstrating—in short, the full range of public activities as provided for under the Constitution and the Bill of Rights. These activities occur in such places as streets, sidewalks, parks, plazas, and squares in neighborhoods, districts, towns, cities, suburbs, regions, and natural areas all over the country. Sometimes, these kinds of activities may occur in privately owned spaces of similar physical character, but in these cases the private owner controls the range of activities permitted. Public spaces and the activities they support represent the points of interconnection, the seam between the public and the more private activities that occur within the buildings and yards that typically provide the borders of the public realm. Altogether, the public spaces and the private activities that frame them make up the physical component of what gives places their character, their memorability, and their identity.

In recent years, finding the places that define their public identity unattractive or dysfunctional or both, people have been initiating civic improvement activities all over the country. Civic leadership for these initiatives may come from all walks of life, and it spans the full scale of urban territory, from neighborhood to region. The numbers of such initiatives and the range of initiators, along with the sophistication and effectiveness of their efforts, have been accelerating. A decided increase in organized citizen leadership marks this drive for change and the progress it is making. Government and the relevant private sector development interests are increasingly having to react and respond, either positively or not. Part of the purpose of this book is to support citizen activism for better places with experiences and observations across a career dedicated to listening and trying to respond to the citizen voice.

Urban design in its current incarnations is a relatively new field, now growing fairly rapidly. People are coming to understand the need for synthesis as they realize how much that is dysfunctional in their daily civic environment is attributable to the dominance of any one discipline to the exclusion of the others. In the room where the decisions affecting place design and development are made, the seat for someone who understands how it all comes together, the urban designer, has been empty. Urban design focuses on the public realm, the quality and workability of the public spaces that connect and engage buildings and other activities (some may occur on private property), at all scales. Urban design addresses the whole of these places, how they look and how they work as the continuum of experience for the citizens who depend on them to connect with each other and with the activities that make up daily life.

To do this, urban design must consider all of the individual design disciplines and interests typically at work in the public realm and it must synthesize these in order to fulfill visions shared by citizens to achieve the

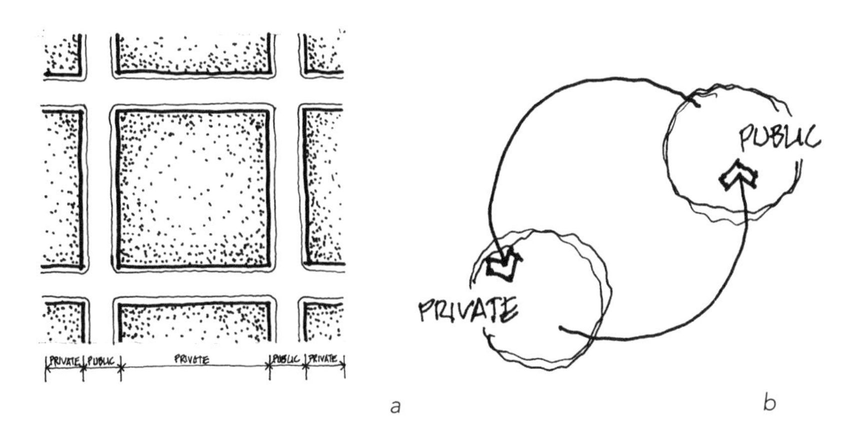


*Figure I.2*
*Plan diagram of public (blank) and private (stippled) spaces in urbanized setting (a) and how the two are in constant interaction (b).*

desired improvements. Further, urban design needs to incorporate and contribute to both the regulatory and financial processes that combine with design to develop the civic environment. In service to citizens' aspirations for better places to live their lives, urban design thus functions as a nexus for the disciplines and interests that build places. Supporting urban design's drive to strengthen this nexus is the other core purpose of this text. In the business of improving places, people matter in ultimately judging the success of public places by their presence and embrace, and design matters in making places that attract, that work, and that last.

The relationships and interactions between people and the places they occupy have varied widely over time and space. In the United States, in varying proportions, there are always three recognizable spheres of interest in the civic environment: the *private sector,* the *government,* and the *community.* The private sector—businesses, corporations, developers, realtors, and investors—designs and builds most of what frames the civic environment that provides access and foreground for the private activity beyond. The government—in urban places local government, for the most part—owns the public realm and it controls what and how much can be built on the private property to which its public holdings provide access. The community—everyday citizens as well as neighborhood-, business-, or issues-based groupings—experience the result and, as the greatest numbers of people affected, can exercise their voice through civic and political action.

As the diagram in Figure I.3 suggests, the relationships among these three spheres are interactive, not linear. That is, initiatives can arise from any one of them, along with their responses, in any order and in ways that are not necessarily predictable. Often the links between the spheres (the arrows) are more important than the spheres themselves. These interactive relationships define a process through which people make the places they occupy, a process that tends not to have a beginning or an end. Urban design is not a project or even a series of projects, but rather a kind of guidance system whose goal is to contribute to places where the people who inhabit them ultimately determine their success and long-term viability.

In the post–World War II years, most of the big decisions about how and where people would live, work, and travel were made primarily through interactions between the private sector and government spheres, in which the community sphere had little role. Failures in this system, like urban renewal, massive dislocation of people and places by infrastructure projects, the public and private investment that combined to build the

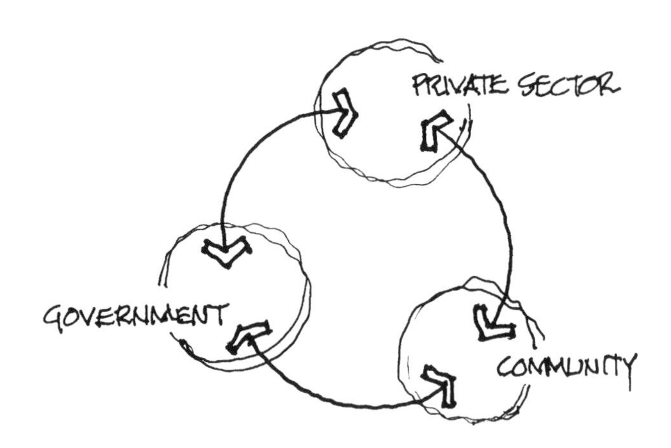


*Figure I.3*
*The interactive relationships among the private sector, the government, and the community, visible in any public place.*

settlement patterns now known as sprawl and its attendant environmental havoc, combined to call for an accounting and the consideration of other choices.

Beginning in the 1960s, people started to question claims of technological and technocratic expertise about how to make places and settle territory, and organized to push themselves onto the stage where these decisions are made. Beyond the dissatisfaction so many have with so much about the appearance and workability of the places that frame their daily lives, access to information for how to do things better and how other places have done it seems to be fueling this move for a bigger role. Over the last 40 years or so, citizen participation mandates have improved the ability for everyday citizens to influence how design and development decisions get made. In addition, particularly over the last 10 years with the explosion of information available through the Internet, citizens have gained much better access to the information necessary to guide these decisions. Greater and greater numbers of people, eager to overcome the negative impacts of both harsh and threatening cityscapes and the congestion and disconnectedness of suburbanscapes, are using these resources to shape positive changes. They are working from the local scale of building, block, street, neighborhood, and district up to the scale of towns, cities, and metropolitan settlement patterns.

Examples abound where citizen action has changed things for the better, from the neighborhood to the regional scale. To mention a few of the more familiar from the 1960s and 1970s, San Franciscans blocked the Embarcadero Freeway from proceeding along the waterfront from the Oakland Bay Bridge to the Golden Gate Bridge and then succeeded in removing the parts that had already been built. A movement that included professionals, academics, and, more important, masses of ordinary citizens generated enough influence to restore the city's foremost amenity and character-defining natural feature: its visual and physical connection between the hills and the bay. In the same timeframe, another group of citizens, led and inspired by three intrepid women, saved San Francisco Bay from being significantly filled in for private development, were instrumental in the creation of the Bay Conservation District Commission, and succeeded in ensuring that most of the whole bay frontage would remain accessible to the public.

Beginning in 1961, Sylvia McLaughlin, Catherine Kerr, and Esther Gulick, with amazing energy, broad-based organizing, and connections with the University of California, overcame all odds and daunting opposition to assure the success of the Save the Bay movement and, at the same time, put the word *environmentalism* into the mainstream vocabulary.

Staten Islanders rallied to remove a planned Robert Moses freeway from running along the spine of its treasured greenbelt. New Orleanians organized the resistance that prevented the highway department from building the Riverfront Expressway, which would have severed any connectivity between the French Quarter and the Mississippi River. Just a couple of years later, a somewhat differently constituted group succeeded in blocking the planned construction of a massive new bridge that would have ripped through uptown neighborhoods along Napoleon Avenue. Atlantans dismembered the Georgia Department of Highways' plan to lace its older neighborhoods with a freeway grid, and then later forced the abandonment of a planned freeway, a project that instead became a linear park and parkway from downtown to the Carter Center and beyond. A downtown Birmingham public housing community succeeded in stopping the destruction of their neighborhood by a proposed freeway, obliging the highway department instead to relocate it to bypass them.

I was directly involved in supporting the citizens' initiatives in the Staten Island, New Orleans bridge, and Birmingham cases.

Virtually every town and city has such stories to tell, at all scales, where the government and leaders in the private sector have been thwarted from carrying out projects that are certain to degrade the quality of life for the many, usually for some short-term and short-sighted economic or political gain for a few. All of the above examples depended on alliances of people across all classes and interests to mount political pressure that, usually after long and contentious struggle, in the end could not be denied. All of them succeeded in creating alternatives to the initial proposal in a way that whatever merits may have been attached to the original proposal were achieved in a different way or different location. The resulting projects met their narrowly defined need and purpose and still managed to preserve and enhance cherished environments to the benefit of the whole citizenry.

Those in government and the private sector are taking note of the trend toward greater influence of citizen activists. The reality is that to make attractive and functional places that are meaningful and lasting, it takes all three spheres working in cooperation and ultimately collaboration to make it happen. The focus needs to shift away from what separates the spheres to where they might come together. In design and development practices, it is the interactions among these spheres that determine how the places people share look and work—interactions that are going through a period of dynamic and positive change.

To respond to this new reality, the people who plan, design, and build places at all scales are recognizing the vital need from the very beginning to include, listen, coordinate, cooperate, and collaborate, both with each other and in citizen participation processes. To understand these dynamics better, it is worthwhile to provide the background and context of the two intertwined themes of this book: the evolution of people's roles in shaping civic design and the design traditions that have shaped settlement patterns and urban form in the United States.

We are at the point where a convergence between planning, design, and development conceptualizations can be stripped of their mysteries. The shift toward this transparency and the legitimacy of more democratic processes has four principal causes:

- Some of the old ways have not succeeded in making our built places better than they were before; in fact, some have devastated previously functioning and appreciated communities and the urban places they created and occupied.
- The explosion of access to information has armed growing numbers of untrained people with a reasonable working knowledge of the concepts and values of planning, design, and development as it affects their public realms.

- Common sense often trumps abstract, technocratic, one-size-fits-all, uni-disciplinary design conceptualizations.
- People are increasingly aware of, and chary of, the motives of the principal beneficiaries of many design and development initiatives.

The role of ordinary citizens, while still a theoretical and practical battleground, continues to move forward in influence, advocating for, shaping, and leading to better places to live. The fast-moving evolution of *citizen participation,* a new concept in the 1960s, is reaching the point where the citizen voice, the citizen aspiration for better communities can no longer be ignored. The four shifts mentioned above are all citizen driven, often over the objections of many in the planning, design, and development fields, the government, and many private sector interests.

The following two chapters frame the context for the rest of the text. The first describes what citizens and urban designers actively engaged in the improvement of their places have been doing about it. The second provides a theoretical and historical framework for reading and understanding the principal design approaches and outcomes that have shaped our places over the last few decades. The goal is to provide a background for people to get together to create a better foreground.

*Figure 1.1*
*People gathered to envision their future spaces.*
*Georgia Conservancy*
*Photo by Chelsea Arkin*

# 1

# *PEOPLE & PLACE...*

## How People Have Shaped Their Worlds

• • •

*"Where's the voice of the people?"*

*"The city is the people."*

• • •

*Figure 1.2*
*Diagram showing the interaction between people and place—each shapes the other.*

My earliest direct experience with the concepts and potential of citizen participation occurred when I was the director of the Office of Staten Island Planning of the New York City Planning Department in 1969. A small and earnest group of Staten Island citizens, supported by nascent environmental groups including the Sierra Club, raised concerns with me about the future of the Staten Island Greenbelt. This was a wonderful and for the most part undisturbed ridge of forested and spring-fed land running some five miles from southwest to northeast in the middle of the island. Including Latourette Park and other semi-protected lands, this swath was the designated path for a ridge-top highway planned by Robert Moses as part of his "circle the islands and drive a cross through the middle of it" highway planning mantra. We were successful in relocating the parkway into an already degraded existing travel corridor, which served the travel need, was more cost effective, and saved the greenbelt. The effort was successful by almost any terms one might use to evaluate it, and it began to become clear to me that citizens' good sense, coupled with values larger than those usually found in government and certainly the private sector, held great promise for making places better.

# Introduction

Design and development practices determine how the places people share look and work. The relationship between these practices and the people who experience the result is going through dynamic and positive change. Over the last 40 years, citizen participation mandates have improved the ability for everyday citizens to influence how design and development decisions get made. In addition, particularly over the last 10 years, citizens have gained much better access to the information necessary to consider these decisions.

Greater and greater numbers of people, eager to overcome the negative impacts of harsh and threatening cityscapes on the one hand and congestion and disconnectedness of suburbanscapes on the other, are using these resources to shape positive changes. They are working from the scale of building, block, street, and neighborhood to the scale of metropolitan settlement patterns.

The idea of widespread citizen participation as an integral part of the planning, design, and development process for projects in the public realm is relatively new. For the hundred years or so leading up to the 1960s, private developers, corporations, institutions, and governments made the moves that built places. These served their usually linked interests—governments acting with more or less integrity to fulfill the goals of public policies and the private sector acting to fulfill its return-on-investment goals, occasionally with a little flair or pride of self-expression. Yet, beyond the physical presence of government and private investments, virtually every civic space reflects the citizens who use it and put their mark on it too, one way or the other. Until the 1960s, though, access for ordinary citizens to play a before-the-fact shaping role in the policies and processes that create the civic environment was difficult and limited. The idea of actually influencing public and private development activities was foreign (except in the most affluent neighborhoods, which always have access).

Unrest in the 1960s, tracing from the civil rights movement and the mass movements that followed it, called forth sweeping federal legislative

*Figure 1.3*
*Staten Island Greenbelt, the path of an unbuilt freeway.*
*Photo by Andy Cross*

actions to relieve mounting popular pressure for reform and to restore stability. Some of the many federal responses were designed to improve the civic environment through legislation and programs that addressed housing and community development, transportation, and the environment. Most of these programs required citizen participation processes to afford people affected by programs or projects receiving federal funding the right to speak. Just as the physical design of places is a dynamic and multidisciplinary enterprise, the new legislation and programs recognized that social, economic, political, and cultural forces directly shape the civic environment. So began a significant shift in the relative relationships

In the 1820s and 1830s for example, Frances Wright, a Scottish woman with radical ideas (and a confidante of the aging American Revolutionary War hero, the Marquis de Lafayette), in particular pursued ideals of equality, promulgating "workingmens' associations," promoting public education for all, and pointing out the obviously anti-democratic status of women and people of African descent. Her gender and some of her more iconoclastic views began to gain ground among ordinary people, threatening people in power who successfully attacked her and diminished her influence. She succeeded, though, in adding an effective voice to the movement for the abolition of slavery, to the idea that workers had a right to organize, to advocacy for the equality for women, and to the call for education for all. Americans who believed that the republic needed to be open and responsive to the needs and contributions of the whole of the population viewed all of these efforts as essential for the advance of an aspirant democratic republic.

In this experience I began to learn several key lessons that provided foundations for future practice and principles:

- The community holds key information about almost any issue affecting its future, information that is likely not to show up in conventional databases and information that is likely to be crucial for framing sound strategies.
- The community is likely to care more than anyone else what happens (except specific project investors).
- There are always some number of community leaders who are prepared to work hard for better results—from their point of view (not necessarily in agreement with prevailing public or political policies and more often not in agreement with private sector development aspirations).
- The need and commitment to listen is critical.
- Most significant, organized community initiatives can be a powerful force in achieving major change, both in government policy and in resetting the framework for private sector activities.

One of our initiatives of that time was the preparation of the "Plan for New York City," borough-by-borough plans introduced by a city-wide plan. Applying my new insights in preparing the Staten Island volume, I leaned on the services of my wife, a sociologist, to randomly survey ordinary citizens about what they liked and didn't like about emerging development patterns and incorporated the feedback into some of the analyses and recommendations that we made.

among the three spheres of interest—private, public, and community—that create and use civic space at all levels, a shift that continues to evolve.

The sections below trace the evolution of citizen participation as it affects civic space. It is important to understand the context in which place design at the urban scale is evolving—what opportunities and obstacles it faces—and how citizens are becoming empowered to respond to and initiate positive change. I seek to address key questions, like: How did people figure in place design leading up to the 1960s? How did the 1960s launch citizen participation? How has citizen participation evolved since? What challenges have some of the citizen participants encountered? Where does citizen participation stand now and where might it be going?

# Antecedents

The idea of the interests of the broad citizenry having anything to do with place design and development in this country picks up from its birth. Benjamin Franklin and Thomas Jefferson, among others, put high stock in two ideas for making a democracy work: direct and sustained citizen involvement and people with means giving back. They felt that these two faces of civic responsibility were essential for the U.S. experiment in democracy to succeed.

Responding to these revolutionary visions, exhilarated by the opportunities of a new country, and eager to explore the paths that freedom and equality seemed to offer, people with new ideas set out to test the young nation's potential. Utopianists like Robert Owen, Frances Wright, Henry George, John Humphrey Noyes, and others imagined both social organizations and physical places that might provide better living situations for people than the old forms permitted. They built experimental communities, like New Harmony in Indiana, Fairhope in Alabama, and Oneida in New York. Out of these experiments other ideas, perhaps more practical and lasting, began to set the course for the waves of settlement that were under way.

Later, from the 1840s onward, two kinds of movements affecting the general population and relevant to settlement patterns and the civic environment gained momentum. Labor organizations were able to form and build up strength, fighting to overcome appalling and exploitative workplace conditions. And civic reformers, often well-placed in society, shone the spotlight on the abysmal shelter conditions in the neighborhoods where most of those same workers and their families lived.

These early movements reflected two approaches to citizen activism. Labor was a broad-based movement generated and supported by workers that focused most of its energy on striving to bring living wages, safer working conditions, fairer measurements of productivity, and limitations on hours of work to some humane standard. The labor reform movement established that labor, both in industry and in trades, could organize in the interest of workers for the purpose of protecting their life and livelihood interests, using the refusal to work as a powerful tool to get the attention of the bosses. The writings of Karl Marx, Friedrich Engels, and a number of others contributed to the labor movement's base. Particularly relevant to the discussion here were the advances in theories and actions that reflected the interests and values of the whole citizenry, the other way around from acceding to an elite the right to make the big decisions about qualities and priorities for civic life and its physical environment.

The labor movement's effect on settlement patterns and the civic environment, while mostly indirect, leaves at least two lasting legacies. At the small scale, a number of places represent pivotal moments in labor history, whose visual traces may stimulate the struggle, memorialize losses, or proclaim success. At the larger scale, the ability for immigrants, the poor, and working people to move from tenement to flat to duplex to single-family house with a yard, by the millions, marks labor's contribution to building a society where wealth was shared to an unprecedented extent.

Well-educated and caring civic reformers, often church-based, represent a second approach to activism in the civic environment, in their case initially largely focusing on housing reform. By their own lights they undertook to improve living conditions for the urban poor, both at the habitation and the neighborhood scale. Often in the same or higher economic class as their slumlord targets, they made progress with more peaceable struggles than labor, whose gains came at a significant cost in strife and human life. Workers were acting directly in their own interests. Civic reformers apparently were motivated by that "certain social sentiment" described by Adam Smith in his landmark analysis and formulation of the tenets of capitalism as necessary to curb the excesses of greed and exploitation that are intrinsic in the economic system.

The civic reformers' initiatives, while not so much a broad-based citizens' movement, were comprehensive and did directly affect the design of cities and their places. They established that the patterns and conditions of housing and the neighborhood environment were a public interest and that government should moderate its laissez-faire ways and step in to advance that interest. In the 1890s, Jacob Riis, a Danish immigrant and police reporter, wrote extensively and compellingly on the subject, and in his book of the same name coined the concept of learning and caring about "how the other half lives." The classic and familiar outcomes were tenement laws in New York City. First the "old law" (in 1867) and then the "new law" (1901) regulations were enacted, mandating higher levels of access to light, air, and sanitation facilities.

More broadly, as it was discovered that sources of disease, epidemics, and social unrest could be traced directly to the tenement housing quadrants of the city, these reformers took on larger public health and safety issues. They pressed for building codes, water and sewer standards, and roadway and other public works standards, many of which were either instituted or improved. They promulgated these reforms as necessary to improve public health for all, not just the immediate victims.

Both movements, interacting with the growing progressive movement, achieved successes against powerful arrays of deeply rooted interests. They laid the foundation for government regulation of both private industry and private development to incorporate minimum measures to safeguard basic health, safety, and welfare priorities for the community as a whole. It is important to emphasize that regulation did not come out of the blue. It came as a reaction and a response to periodic fiascos, some of them catastrophes—building fires, building collapses, neighborhood pollution and disease, and so on—causing death and injury here and there around the country. While most industry acted more or less responsibly within the standards of the day, the tragic exceptions represented all too frequent lapses of responsibility and accountability that could be traced to private sector greed, callousness, or ignorance.

Until recently, labor's achievements of the 40-hour work week; minimum wages (at one time pegged as "livable" wages); workplace safety; and health, pension, and other benefits reforms became the basis on which the United States was able to build a middle class. For several decades, the labor movement was able to lift up the majority of working people to higher standards of living than each previous generation. It became possible for most Americans to begin to at least imagine a truly working democracy that could interact with its capitalist economic system to perform better for more and more people.

*Figure 1.4*
*Vista of Mayor Robert Speer's City Beautiful vision for Denver's Civic Center.*
*Courtesy Brokers Guild, Denver*

For many years, civic leaders found it easy to ignore the victims of these fiascos, mostly from the working and immigrant classes. But as progressive civic values, and particularly as the link between the conditions of the poor and disease affecting the rich was established, the reformers gained growing and organized popular support. Religious institutions that took their service missions seriously stepped up and, believing that rough conditions in the community led to moral transgressions, they also saw a fertile ground for conversions to their faiths.

The reform movements broadened and spread across the country. They shared a general call for civic betterment that joined economic, political, and community leadership to produce civic movements reaching for expressions of civic pride. In terms of city and space design, these movements, experienced by most cities beginning around the turn of the century, gave rise to what is widely referred to as the City Beautiful movement. This period often expressed itself in grand and sweeping terms—great parks, boulevards, and focal axes, framed by street-fronting buildings with regular bay spacings that marked an orderly progression of the street environment. This formal, classical, even monumental frame was often mixed and softened by the picturesque, romantic landscapes of the garden city traditions, particularly in parks and parkways. A few of the more famous of these initiatives included Chicago's Columbian Exposition (1893), Daniel Burnham and Edward Bennett's Plan for Chicago (of "make no small plans" fame, 1909), San Francisco's World's Fair (1915), St. Louis's Jefferson Park (the venue for the World's Fair of 1904), and Denver Mayor Robert Speer's civic center, parks, and boulevards (1904 on).

Traditional corporate and civic leadership structures, in which women and wives usually played an unsung but significant role, led the City Beautiful movement. Its focus on the quality of the public environment marked a shift toward balancing private interests with some broader sense of the common good. The recognition of the essential interdependence among everybody inhabiting the urban landscape led directly to federal legislation enabling states and, through states, local jurisdictions to establish zoning and subdivision regulations, city plans, and the administrative structures to administer both.

The community reform movements that improved the quality of the civic environment certainly represented advances in good government and for the most part did more good than harm. But their tools and processes were centered in local government, were manipulated by private real estate and development interests, and were not directly accessible to most neighborhoods or their citizens. Always an exception, affluent neighborhoods had and used the tools to their advantage, achieving significant place improvements in the areas they cared most about through their knowledge, resources, and access. It took the upheavals of the 1960s and 1970s to begin to extend this access to the middle class and lower-income people so that they too could influence development and the civic environment in their neighborhoods and districts.

Planning, zoning, and subdivision have been around in most urbanized places from their inceptions, with the first zoning ordinance enacted in New York City in 1916. As publicly controlled processes, with public notification requirements, these rules created thresholds for communities to begin to have a say in the shape of what is to come. Since the citizen participation climate changed in the 1960s, everyday citizens have been crossing the thresholds in growing numbers. As such, one might consider zoning among the first of the processes that enabled people to have a significant say over the quality and appearance of their neighborhoods and districts. The new rules began to modulate the use of private property in the context of larger community values. The sphere of the community began to take a more active form, rising out of its formerly passive role as the receiver, sometimes the victim, of untrammeled private initiative. In some ways, subdivision rules are even more directive of the shape of the civic environment than zoning, particularly in residential areas, both urban and suburban, as described in some detail in Chapters 9 and 10. Typically, though, citizens have less access to the creation and administration of subdivision rules.

From the beginning, proponents and detractors have debated zoning and subdivision rules in an up and down trajectory, marked by successions of court cases and uneven outcomes. Land and development regulation lies at the very seam of public and private, let out at one moment and taken in at the next as the uneasy dialectic between public good and private gain plays its unending game. Development-regulating processes are always in a state of flux, both in theory and in practice, with a wide range of local responses. The debate will persist, on political, philosophical, and practical grounds, and citizens' influence in that debate is likely to keep growing.

Planning, zoning, and subdivision regulations have certainly been helpful tools for governments and increasingly communities to curb some of the more flagrant excesses projected by private initiatives. The effectiveness of that check has depended on cities' commitment and ability to

*Figure 1.5*
*Affluent Brooklyn Heights citizens banded together in the early 1950s to block a freeway that would have cut off their view of the East River and Lower Manhattan. The result produced their famed esplanade, completed in 1954, which hung over the freeway lanes, which themselves are hung off the cliffs below.*
*Photo by Lucius Kwok ©*

properly reflect their citizens' concerns and represent their interests in the development process. In recent years, citizens themselves are exercising greater direct influence on the processes. The private sector, meanwhile, with its vaunted scent for opportunity, has found and continues to find ways to shape the application of zoning and subdivision tools to advance their narrower, project-by-project interests over broader community or civic interests. The tensions in the system usually challenge the trust among the three spheres of private, public, and community. The interactions among the three, therefore, must always aim at finding areas of overlapping interest to establish the trust necessary to make places better.

## The 1960s

What was it about the 1960s that so fundamentally altered access so that ordinary citizens could develop meaningful roles in the planning, design, and development of their everyday places? The following discussion puts this historical moment into perspective.

Leading into and through the 1960s, the civil rights movement made a great leap in closing the gap between what the United States claimed to be and what it was. With the Voting Rights Act of 1964 highlighting a whole string of policy, legislative, and legal advances for racial equality, this period marked progress toward democratization more dramatically

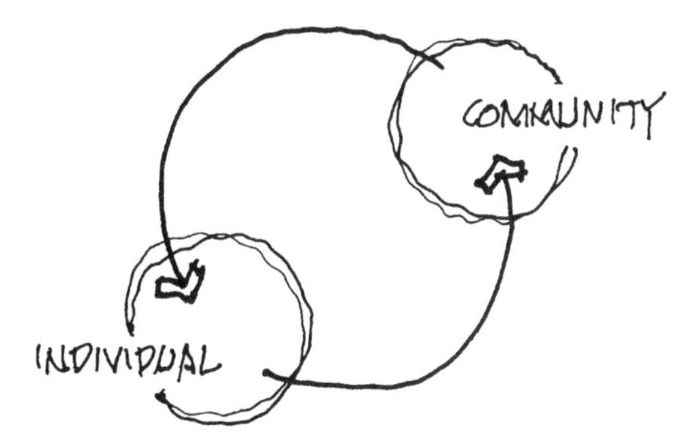


*Figure 1.6*
*The individual and the community, where the values of the one are in continuous interaction with the values of the many.*

than anything since the decades-long suffragette movement that finally gave women the vote with the Nineteenth Amendment in 1920. Under leadership epitomized by Martin Luther King Jr. for numbers of local civil rights leaders committed to justice through nonviolent means, there came an insistence to be heard that marked a new day, including a dawning of the idea of citizen participation. The movement had profound implications for spatial and settlement patterns, as we shall see.

Dovetailed into the civil rights movement and indeed increasingly central to Dr. King's message came the widening dissension over the Vietnam War. Citizens became more and more disillusioned about the "public purpose" of a war so costly in lives and money and waged on ever more transparently questionable premises. First the free-speech movement and then the anti-war movement ultimately succeeded in tilting the politics to defeat the war's advocates and in bringing about U.S. withdrawal.

The women's movement, finding that the vote by itself did not establish equality, sought redress for the second-class status of more than half of the nation's citizens. At their most creative and ambitious, women envisioned a society where values of nurturing would become more central in guiding the United States' future, or at least in balancing the prevailing values that resisted civil rights and waged war. The prevailing message of their movement, however, placed women in positions to assimilate into and compete more effectively in the dominant, male-value economic structure, where glass ceilings for a few were a more important target than a stable floor for the many. Neither the anti-war movement nor the women's movement had particularly profound effects on settlement patterns or place design, although the latter did either introduce or support a range of access initiatives shared by civil rights, child care, people with disabilities, and pedestrian advocates.

All of these movements represented people rising against authority—on the face of it governmental authority—at all levels. Many in the movements also understood that those same governments were thoroughly intertwined with, and generally bending to the will of, powerful private sector interests, again at all levels, collectively referred to as "the establishment." For their part, the participants in the various movements, while diffuse, collectively referred to themselves as "the movement." There was sufficient alarm, particularly at the federal level, where both government and private sector interests placed stability over other values, in crafting a strategy to meet the threat, real or perceived. Surely the climate called for bending toward democratization, or at least appearing to do so.

In the realm of the civic environment, the vigorous expressions of dissent accompanying the anti-war and other movements of the day led directly to the walling up of previously windowed banks and businesses and even more pervasively the construction of windowless school buildings all over the country.

One could argue that the memorial to the Vietnam War, Maya Lin's hushingly successful D.C. monument, marked a radical shift away from the heroic individual war vision, like, for example, the Iwo Jima statue nearby, toward the reality of the masses who experience the result. This is, perhaps, another way of viewing the advance of citizen participation.

My contemporaries from that time are unlikely to ever forget President Nixon, a candidate for reelection in 1972, raising his hands over his head, pointing his forefingers to the heavens and bellowing out the Black Panthers' rallying cry: "Power to the people."

Also energized by the climate of the 1960s and early 1970s, but with deeper roots, consumer activism broadened its scope and concern, seeking accountability across the whole of the economy for the kinds of narrower reforms it had demanded and achieved in earlier decades. The ever more powerful impacts of sophisticated marketing accelerated the growing realization that consumers could be exploited and knowingly and cynically exposed to all manner of health- and life-threatening products in the pursuit of profit for their makers. Industry's emphasis accelerated a shift toward producing what they could sell most effectively and away from linking production to basic needs. The ripples of consumer advocacy continue to wash up on the not-so-friendly shores of the current not-so-civic era. While consumer advocacy did not generally seek to alter or advocate for place-based civic improvement, its goals were complementary and it accounted for one of the most remarkable improvements in the civic environment: the widening ban on smoking in public places.

# The "Movement" and the Civic Environment

The different movements that represented a sharp increase in citizen participation in matters that concerned them had profound and lasting effects on settlement patterns and civic space. While primarily about voting, public access, public education, and just plain justice, fairness, and decency, the civil rights movement had direct impacts on city form, on city planning, on citizen participation, and on place design. The movement's human rights successes triggered a whole range of spatial consequences, some anticipated, some not; some intended, some not.

Rather quickly after the passage of the range of civil rights measures, whites began to run away from cities, fleeing school and neighborhood integration in an expression both of historic patterns of white race–based antipathy to blacks and marking the superior economic means and choices available to whites. These "white flight" patterns coincided with, and were reinforced however purposefully by, the auto/petroleum industry assaults on public transportation coupled with federal subsidies for the white out-migration through VA and FHA financing, mortgage interest deductions, and public road and highway building. So began the heavily marketed and hyped real estate and road-building bonanza that many now call "sprawl," with impacts that physically separate people from each other by class, race, and even age; and separate people from their work, their schools, and their shopping and service needs.

Meanwhile, black businesses, no longer constrained by their imposed historic boundaries, moved to new locations in search of greater success, often depopulating once-thriving community retail and institutional centers. Black families moved into neighborhoods that were previously barred to them. All the while, the dislocational impacts of modernist urban renewal initiatives compounded the assault on what had been close-knit and viable, economic- and age-diverse neighborhoods of all ethnicities in cities across the land. In more recent years, African Americans and other ethnic minorities have been joining whites in identifying moving to the suburbs as the mark of having "made it." But as cities gentrify, the first-ring suburbs are becoming the nearest affordable housing to major job and service centers, and as their tenancy shifts from owner to renter and their structures succumb to age and substandard construction another significant urban out-migration seems to be well underway, this time led by lower-income families and including a significant proportion of growing Latino and Asian populations.

The mass white move to the suburbs, unintentionally fueled by civil rights advances, did not include in its agenda building or retaining places that attracted a diversity of people to share in civic purposes. As has been pointed out for years now, tracing from Gertrude Stein's famous characterization, in the suburbs "there's no there there," and the house–car–cul de sac cells of suburban geography are intentionally and effectively isolating. Some argue that these broad movements were citizen-driven, reflections of how and where people chose to live—in short, the exercise of free choice in a free market. These arguments are accurate up to a point. On the other hand, one could argue that the realistic choices for middle-class white Americans were actually quite limited. Driving the suburban settlement patterns were legacies of ever more sophisticated marketing, projecting "must-have" images built around the private car, the private house, the private street. These interacted with deep subsidies and racially influenced behavior to induce the suburban choice. In this sense, the "demand" was "socially engineered," to borrow a phrase, by a powerful partnership between the auto, petroleum, real estate, and road-building industries, fully supported by both fiscal and monetary policy at all levels of government. The above is not the only analysis of how settlement patterns came to be what they are. Yet to be effective in making things better than they are, it should demonstrate how important it is for urban designers and community activists to have some understanding of the forces that dealt the hand they must now play.

Out of the civil rights movement came the beginnings of the concepts of community development and community economic development. One of the first of these that put in place grassroots structure and local citizen empowerment was the Model Cities Program, part of President Johnson's War on Poverty, a part of the "butter" half of his "guns and butter" strategy for deflecting or defusing growing unrest over racism, sexism, and opposition to the Vietnam War. This program, launched in 1966 as part of the Demonstration Cities and Metropolitan Development Act, sought to defuse unrest in urban renewal–afflicted and poverty-stricken urban areas. Citizens in the selected areas, by now mostly occupied by minorities, were able to create local governance structures for administering significant sums of federal block grant funding, aimed at catalyzing housing and economic development. Part of the purpose for these organizational structures was to endow grassroots organizations with the authority and the funding to conduct their own community renewal efforts.

To some extent these federally devised structures, which had direct lines of communication to the Department of Housing and Urban Development (HUD), obligated the cooperation of local government. The program educed a lot of cynical "you're so smart, you figure it out" responses from professionals, developers, and local government officials. Occasional transgressions led skeptics or more affluent citizens who felt they were left out (an unaccustomed experience) to describe activists in the movement as "poverty pimps." The effectiveness of these experiments was probably not so different than the other established development practices of the day, but the beneficiaries certainly were different.

Nonetheless, it established in the minds of many for the first time that people in America's most distressed communities existed, and their needs became somewhat known. In fact, what these communities needed to be successful were the resources, experience, technical expertise, public policy commitments, and private investment patterns that their histories had denied them. Many Model Cities Programs structured their organizations on models that they had some familiarity with, like local city councils or school boards, building in all the obstacles that such organizations face in trying to reach fair and balanced decisions. So while not as effective in jump-starting community redevelopment as some had hoped, from the community perspective the Model Cities Program was certainly better than either the neighborhood-razing urban renewal programs that preceded it or the market forces that ignored these neighborhoods. Overall, the program varied and evolved from place to place, did some good, had some failures, but most importantly for this discussion, introduced the heretofore unthinkable notion that poor people should have a voice and

---

In Birmingham, for example, David Vann, first as a city council member and later as mayor, used the provisions for citizen participation in the CDBG program—which the city had earlier rejected because they didn't want any of "that tainted federal money" with its anti-segregation provisions—to establish an extensive neighborhood-based citizen participation program. Vann, his staff, and citizens all over town worked to create some 100 neighborhoods, organized into communities, and a city-wide advisory board, each level electing its leadership bi-annually. These neighborhood associations debate the issues of the day, weigh in on zoning and other development initiatives, and in a remarkable commitment to the democratic experiment, allocate capital funds set aside for them to civic improvement projects—the amounts based on population and median income. Thus in a few short years Birmingham went from being one of the most repressive cities in the country to one of the most progressively experimental, at least in the area of citizen participation. While Vann stepped up to formally launch these initiatives, they would not have happened without the support of civil rights veterans and social progressives, both black and white. Not every decision taken at the neighborhood level has been the wisest, but the program has produced a lot more successes than failures, and the tasting and exercising of democracy has broadened the base from which citizens elect their city council members and on which the city makes its policies and decisions.

---

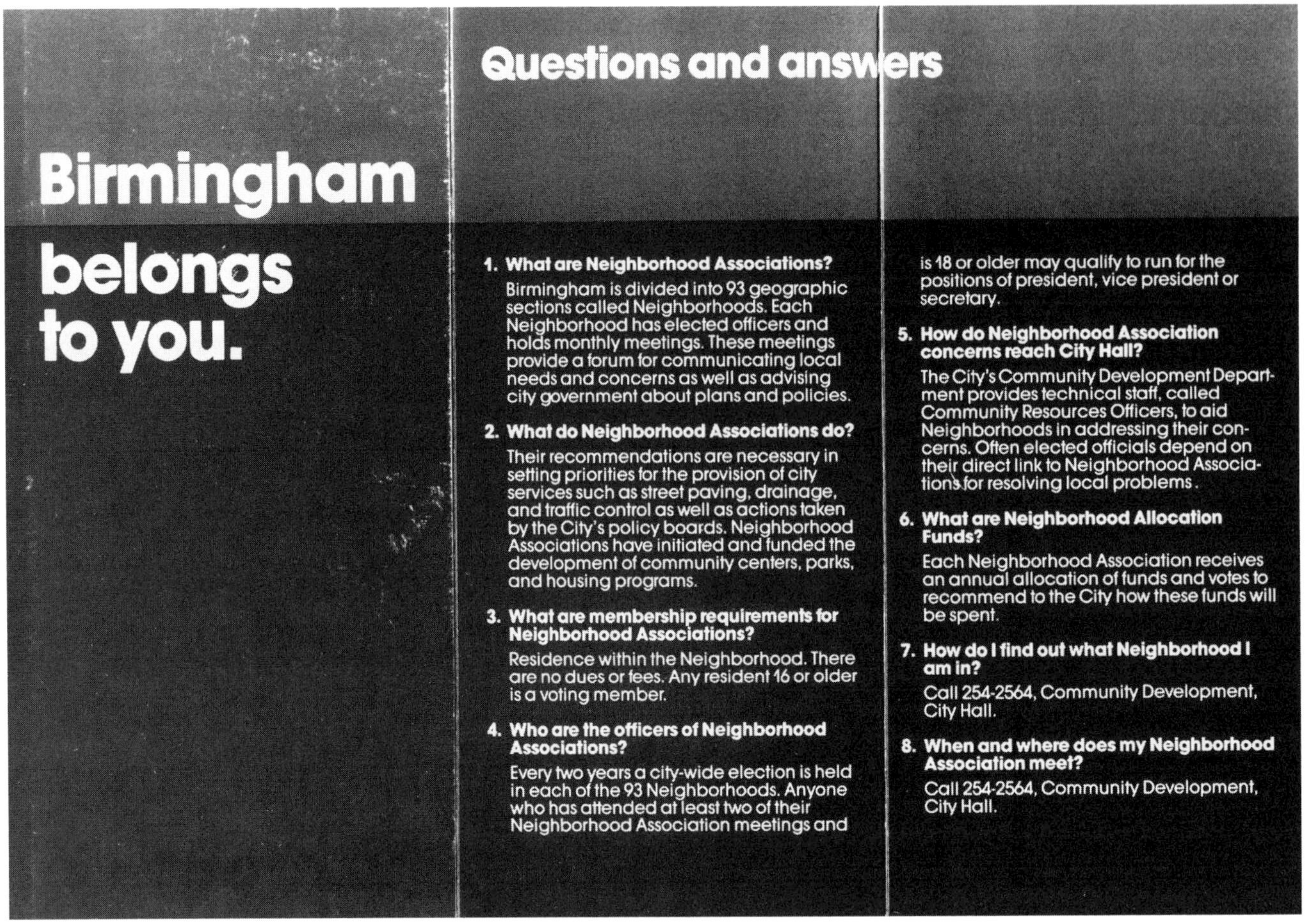

**Birmingham belongs to you.**

**Questions and answers**

1. **What are Neighborhood Associations?**
   Birmingham is divided into 93 geographic sections called Neighborhoods. Each Neighborhood has elected officers and holds monthly meetings. These meetings provide a forum for communicating local needs and concerns as well as advising city government about plans and policies.
2. **What do Neighborhood Associations do?**
   Their recommendations are necessary in setting priorities for the provision of city services such as street paving, drainage, and traffic control as well as actions taken by the City's policy boards. Neighborhood Associations have initiated and funded the development of community centers, parks, and housing programs.
3. **What are membership requirements for Neighborhood Associations?**
   Residence within the Neighborhood. There are no dues or fees. Any resident 16 or older is a voting member.
4. **Who are the officers of Neighborhood Associations?**
   Every two years a city-wide election is held in each of the 93 Neighborhoods. Anyone who has attended at least two of their Neighborhood Association meetings and is 18 or older may qualify to run for the positions of president, vice president or secretary.
5. **How do Neighborhood Association concerns reach City Hall?**
   The City's Community Development Department provides technical staff, called Community Resources Officers, to aid Neighborhoods in addressing their concerns. Often elected officials depend on their direct link to Neighborhood Associations for resolving local problems.
6. **What are Neighborhood Allocation Funds?**
   Each Neighborhood Association receives an annual allocation of funds and votes to recommend to the City how these funds will be spent.
7. **How do I find out what Neighborhood I am in?**
   Call 254-2564, Community Development, City Hall.
8. **When and where does my Neighborhood Association meet?**
   Call 254-2564, Community Development, City Hall.

*Figure 1.7*
*This widely disseminated brochure explained Birmingham's citizen participation program, with maps showing the neighborhood and community boundaries, descriptions of programs available, and telephone numbers to call for more information.*
*Courtesy of City of Birmingham*

some authority in their home places and that that voice should be institutionalized.

Coming out of the "Great Society" or "War on Poverty" concepts of the Johnson administration, with Model Cities experiences both good and bad under its belt, the housing advocacy community rose with new force in this period. It was able to marshal the support necessary to secure the passage of the Housing and Community Development Act of 1974 (HCDA) with its Community Development Block Grant (CDBG) program, a major source of flexible federal funding tied to supporting low- and moderate-income communities. The act institutionalized citizen participation as a requirement for access to the funds, thus providing the basis on which communities could extend their influence over this important funding source.

The program, at the time joining the federal revenue-sharing program as ways of returning federal tax dollars to state and local jurisdictions, carried two purposes that characterized the federal response to troubled times: (1) recognition of the desperate straits of core cities and towns caused by the disinvestment patterns of suburban development subsidies and white flight; and (2) an effort to empower citizens experiencing these circumstances to have a significant role in doing something about it. The mandates for citizen participation, while providing broad flexibility for local jurisdictions to determine the funds' use, also required targeting the funds to improve conditions for people of low and moderate income, to mitigate slums and blighting conditions, and to assist in meeting urgent unmet needs.

Leading toward the formal codification of citizen participation in federal policy or most local governments, beyond the Model Cities experiment there were a number of issue-focused movements that coalesced and were emboldened by the fermentation of the times, some directly affecting the future of our physical places, some not. Some, however, did and still do have profound effects both on how places are designed and on the expanding roles of citizens to influence the process. These advocacy communities represent issues involving housing and community development, the environment, historic preservation, Americans with Disabilities, and other movements focused on improving the quality of various aspects of civic space, altogether constituting the citizen participation movement.

Housing advocacy activity remains strong and generally focuses on improving housing and neighborhoods of people with lesser means. In the dynamic interactions between public and private, however, the current market-driven ideologies and power alignments that suffuse the federal government do not seem to accept as a goal the aspiration first stated in the 1949 Housing Act: "a decent home and a suitable living environment for every American." Backing off from policies that defined the 1960s and 1970s underscores the ascendancy of the private sector in setting government priorities. Nonetheless, the sector continues to take full advantage of heavy subsidies in the form of publicly provided roads, infrastructure, and tax and lending programs. Current policies, therefore, make the job of those advocating for housing affordability and decency particularly difficult.

In the same timeframe, the environmental movement coalesced, gained momentum, and focused its demands on a more conscious and sustainable stewardship of the earth's resources. It directly affected, and continues to affect, regional, city, and place design. Environmentally driven spatial analyses and initiatives are a major theme throughout the text. The sweep of environmentalism lies at the root of concepts like "sustainability," "growth management," "smart growth," "green building," "green communities," and legislation like the National Environmental Policy Act (NEPA), the Clean Water Act, the Clean Air Act, and countless state and local initiatives to measure environmental impact and mandate mitigation of negative impacts.

Among all of these, related to broadening citizen participation, NEPA was perhaps most sweeping and effective. Adopted in 1969, it required citizen involvement processes for providing input in all federal or federally funded actions. And it required some conscious level of environmental analysis on any such federal actions, with progressive analysis required based on the level of impacts identified. It sought to be comprehensive, requiring consideration of a full range of possible impacts—on air and water quality, habitat, land use, soils, historic and cultural resources, and official planning policy where the proposed action would occur.

The environmental movement too lies at the base of a range of local and regional interest groups pressing for more sustainable planning, design, and development policies and practices. Such groupings spread across a wide range, including smart growth movements, transit advocacy, bicycle and pedestrian advocacy, ecology commissions, tree commissions, creek "daylighting" initiatives, storm drainage management districts, conservation subdivision initiatives, farmland preservation movements, organic and "slow" food movements, and recycling programs, to name several.

Considered in its broader social context, sustainability raises issues of fairness and equity as necessary underpinnings of any truly sustainable approach to community design. Environmental sustainability is not conceivable without socio-economic sustainability, which cannot be achieved reliably without the willful participation of citizens at all levels. Environmental justice, for example, entered the lexicon of criteria for consideration for federally funded projects with President Clinton's 1994 Executive Order 12898. Acknowledging that environmentally degrading facilities tended to concentrate in lower-income neighborhoods, the order at least obligated processes to face the problem and look for alternatives that would more equitably spread the impacts of the many environmentally undesirable activities and facilities necessary to sustain communities.

Another concurrent movement with direct impacts on place design and city form was the historic preservation movement. With roots in class-based efforts to preserve the mansions, cathedrals, banks, and plantations of patrician ancestors, the movement rather quickly opened its doors to broader and broader bases of citizens. These were appalled by the wholesale destruction of history and more importantly the destruction of the character of place caused by modernist urban renewal interventions in core cities. Many of the victims of these assaults, indeed, lay at the opposite end of the stick from the movement's progenitors. The work of Jane Jacobs helped popularize what had been a sometimes sleepy but well-defended sentiment for the preservation of heritage. It has galvanized all sorts of people to consider and honor their physical past, whether that past evoked glory or symbolized survival in conditions of race and class discrimination. In addition, the movement progressed quickly from buildings and landmarks to neighborhoods and precincts. Both public and nonprofit initiatives provided resources and support for communities, ultimately across class, race, and geographic lines, to resist wrong-headed private sector and public urban renewal practices.

A later movement that has and will continue to shape the public realm is the demand for equal access for people with physical disabilities. The Americans with Disabilities Act, or ADA, enacted in 1990, succeeded in putting in place standards at both the larger place and the individual building scales that improve the likelihood that people with disabilities will not be barred from habitations or public places because of their inability to get into or use such resources. Ramps, landings, elevators, wheelchair ramps, beeping traffic signals, disability access routes, and specified parking spots are some of the most ubiquitous manifestations of the outcome of this movement. More broadly, the ADA has affected site selection for public facilities and the basic design organization of countless parks and public buildings across the country.

In summary, the 1960s and 1970s movements and their ensuing legislation and implementation, beyond the specific thrust of each separate act, began the process of codifying citizens' participation as a requirement for actions contemplating the use of federal funds. Among those most directly affecting design and development in the public sphere were NEPA and the HCDA, both of which, however nominally, mandated public comment processes. Granted, the requirements were pretty rudimentary, often just requiring public hearings on contemplated plans or actions with duly published notification thereof. But they began and sanctioned processes that allowed democratic reform–minded local officials, like David Vann in Birmingham and Maynard Jackson, the first African American mayor of Atlanta, to push for genuinely progressive experimentations in democracy.

# Organizational Responses to the Rise of Citizen Participation

The legitimization and rise of citizen participation began to unsettle established ways of doing business in government and in the private sector. At one level the initial moves in support of empowerment were those of a federal administration trying to smooth over unrest, placate the most vocal, and nip in the bud any sustained protest. At another level, though, many people in government service—in all positions—were legatees of the Kennedy "ask what you can do for your country" era, and these actively pushed for broader democratization. The federally sanctioned gesture toward empowerment encouraged citizen participation and spread demands for more involvement to the local and state levels. These change forces had a direct impact on the design and development of urbanized places as well.

## The Public Sector

Cities responded in different ways to the new empowerment language written into federal statutes and programs. Some took a dim view of this unsettling foray into the established turf. Some politicians viewed mandated citizen involvement as a breeding ground for aspirant challengers to their seats. Many public agencies, on the one hand, were pretty sure they knew better and didn't want to open themselves up to second-guessing, and on the other, were nervous about their report card results that could be spotlighted by greater transparency and public accountability. These tended to take the minimum route—small, buried advertisements for public hearings to be held at times inconvenient for most working citizens, a perfunctory reporting, and usually dismissal of whatever comments the minimum public process produced. NEPA-related activities evolved to require a written response from the sponsoring agency to every comment that the mandated citizen participation process required. The responses mandated by the Housing and Community Development Act, while less rigorous, still provided for some degree of transparency and accountability.

As the mandates for community development and citizen participation in particular were spreading, though, some cities' planning agencies embraced community development as a goal generally consistent with good city planning practice and positioned themselves to tap the resources that HUD was focusing into housing and community development. These agencies tended to be both philosophically and functionally committed to pushing the limits for democratization, and so became those cities' frontline community interface agencies. Other cities, however, viewed the housing and community development mission more narrowly, as a production function more than as part of comprehensive renewal strategies, and were less concerned with how CDBG fit into the bigger picture. Both paths had successes and failures, and both paths represented measurable steps forward in effective citizen involvement. Still others resisted the whole premise and did the minimum necessary to secure the federal largesse. Some cities kept their city planning and community development functions separate, while others combined them, an indication of how comprehensively they viewed their opportunity.

Under Maynard Jackson's leadership, the City of Atlanta set up a system of Neighborhood Planning Units (NPUs), 24 in all, each of which provided an umbrella for a handful of geographically associated neighborhoods. This system was recognized in the city charter, thus giving each NPU the voice to render advisory opinions on zoning and variance proposals as well as other public actions affecting the civic environment of their neighborhoods. The NPUs receive planning support from the Bureau of Planning, by which a planning staffer attends each monthly meeting of each NPU to give an update on activities relevant to it and to hear the NPU's position on issues as well as process requests for information. Typically, staff from the public works, parks, and police and fire departments may also be in attendance with reports and information as called for. NPUs typically have their own committee structure, covering such issues as land use and zoning, transportation, the environment, and public safety. It is not a perfect system, yet the NPUs' formal status ensures that all neighborhoods in the city—black, white, poor, rich—have a seat at the table of local governance.

Some cities, like Birmingham, Dayton, Atlanta, and Seattle, moved forward more quickly than others to embrace and activate citizen participation processes. In these, local political leadership committed to actively test and extend the institutions of democracy to a broader population than had been active or encouraged before. Because I worked for jurisdictions that were more committed to taking this path, most of my observations stem from that experience. The examples I use to put a face on citizen participation may presage what could be turning out to be a profound shift. Broadening bases of citizens to exercise more control over the government and private sector actions that affect them in their immediate civic environment could prove to be a model that works. If so, informed and committed citizens and their organizations could join or even surpass private sector and government agencies as places to look for leadership in making the day-to-day world a better place to live.

## The Private Sector

That part of the private sector most directly affected by the new stirrings for broadening the base of decision-making were developers, including the lawyers, lenders, design consultants, accountants, and real estate team members likely to come under the developer umbrella. Needless to say, most developers took a dim view, even though not many of them were building in the low-income areas where the shift toward citizen participation was having its greatest transformative impact. The developers' calculus depends so much on time and money that anything that could threaten to take more time or cost more money is a red flag.

The other side of the developer picture, though, is that there is usually an indefatigable, resolute aspect to the industry that accounts for its ability to maintain momentum by adjusting and persisting—it takes what it takes. From this perspective, coupled with the singularly project-centered focus that it takes to get the job done, developers were more oriented toward finding what would work out of these new mandates than what would not. The local control aspect of the CDBG program, for example, provided the potential of access to new sources of funding that could be attractive. From the point of view of start-ups and minority business enterprises, CDBG, however laced with accountability provisions, offered access to capital that white-controlled finance did not offer at the time.

Furthermore, development is an intrinsically interdisciplinary enterprise, calling on lots of different people to play one role or another as projects proceed from conceptualization to completion. Adding one more dimension to this process was not so off-putting. The industry's home base, the Urban Land Institute (ULI), had already been running an early form of community engagement process, the panel advisory. This program brought to cities and places all over the country interdisciplinary resources and knowledge to work on development problems identified by the community, albeit usually the development community. Its processes tended to engage a larger representation of affected citizens than the more traditional client-consultant way of developing projects. This program is described in more detail in Chapter 10, Tools.

Over the years, perhaps through the community-serving panel advisory program, and particularly now, developers are moving to more tolerant positions on community input. Many have benefited through taking a cooperative and participatory approach, not just as a way of easing approvals, thus saving time and money, but also in terms of improved product. The ULI for some years has provided leadership in encouraging positive steps toward community involvement among its members. Even the more specialized homebuilders and industrial and office park associations are softening their historic oppositional positions to engaging the local community in their policies and practices.

Just as cities, communities, and developers responded to the new empowerment movements, so did the professions. Architects, at least a few, acted on the need to better support the physical space needs of neighborhoods and communities around the country. In New York, Richard Hatch worked with low-income neighborhood activists to put together the Architects Renewal Committee for Harlem (ARCH). Young architects in New York, responding to the tenor of the times for addressing poverty and substandard housing and living environments, formed the Architects Technical Assistance Committee, a loosely organized effort to provide direct services to low-income families. One idea, concretized by a group that called itself Operation Move In, was to assist people to move back into buildings long abandoned in the Upper West Side urban renewal area, an early case of the squatter movement. They took direct action, hooking up turned-off electricity, gas, and water (usually bypassing the meter), doing minor home improvements, making the structures reasonably habitable for "illegal" tenants—in short, paying attention to the overwhelming unmet housing needs across a city with a considerable inventory of relic buildings from the urban renewal era.

## The Professions

A few members of the American Institute of Architects (AIA) began to respond to the call for technical assistance from communities around the country. First, in 1966, they created a program that evolved into the Regional/Urban Design Assistance Team or R/UDAT. Later the AIA provided some support for community-driven efforts at local revitalization in the form of Community Design Centers. These programs have been supported by architects who are urbanists, who heard the call of Jane Jacobs on the importance of reflecting peoples' needs and cultures in any urban strategy, who saw what architecture's stand-alone trophy buildings were doing to urban places, and who were determined to explore other paths to apply their design skills to improve the civic environment.

From early in the R/UDAT program, these architects developed processes in which a charrette structure provided for citizen participation and interdisciplinary teams. The charrette brought together professionals (architects, planners, landscape architects, civil engineers, developers, economists, sociologists, and public officials, to name a few) with local civic leadership and ordinary citizens to consider complex urban design and development problems. With a typical pre-charrette preparation period of six months or so, the charrettes themselves take place over a very intense five-day period, the outcome of which is a public presentation of the findings, usually with a supporting document. The charrette as a way to gather people into a consensual visioning process has continued to expand, mature, and by now dominates how jurisdictions, and even some developers, structure their public processes to consider district-wide civic improvement planning, design, and development approval initiatives. In fact, managing such processes has become a mainstream offering of many design firms. The program is described in more detail in Chapter 10, Tools.

*Figure 1.8*
*Brochure describing how the R/UDAT program helps communities develop a vision for their future. Courtesy American Institute of Architects*

City planners, by this time reacting to the negative consequences of urban renewal in which they had been complicit, had left the fold of the physically dominated city-shaping forces of the post–World War II era and instead oriented themselves toward policy, information management, land use, development regulation, economic development, transportation, and other more specialized pursuits. At the same time, many had joined the War on Poverty commitment to the under-represented, under-resourced populations spotlighted by such community organizing and advocacy pioneers as Saul Alinsky and Paul Davidoff. In fact, of all the professions involved in the business of planning, designing, and building our urban environments, only planners reached toward the new democratization opportunities in any great numbers. They became, mostly either as public or nonprofit workers, the professional force that set about seeking to assist communities and cities in structuring citizen participation. Unfortunately, some of their bosses tended to be not as enthusiastic, and not all cities stepped up to the opportunity.

Interestingly, though being in the forefront of advocating the democratization of planning processes, the American Planning Association has never developed a program for offering direct technical and organizational assistance to help communities in the way that the AIA's R/UDAT or ULI's panel advisories have done. Perhaps the whole idea of the charrette and its intense focused effort are more in the character of architects and developers, while planners, so many of whom are working in and for the public sector, know that the long haul of sustained effort is where the difference in making places better is going to actually happen. Perhaps, too, the decline of physical planning after the 1960s has discouraged such skills from being developed within the profession. At the same time, however, it is clear that charrette-type activities can focus a cross section of citizen interest on generating a vision about new directions that can build consensus. As planners realize that how places and cities look and work in physical terms is a major impetus behind community interest and demand for making their places better, the profession is beginning to reintegrate urban design into its professional and academic arsenal.

Landscape architecture has made great strides in extending its contribution from the affluent showplaces that lie in its history to engage the landscape of the everyday. The field and its practitioners find their leadership in these new directions in the writings of J. B. Jackson and Grady Clay, who always sought to urge the profession into a conscious social, economic, and political context. Even so, landscape architects, with a few exceptions, have not been in the forefront of assisting citizen participation processes. Fortunately though, landscape architects are increasingly represented in the team that goes about designing civic places. As they engage urban territories more holistically, landscape architects are making major contributions in support of devising, designing, and implementing sustainable practices on the one hand, and on the other, in restoring or interjecting natural and ecological values into the urban fabric in what has become a movement of sorts, called "landscape urbanism."

Transportation planners and engineers have stepped up their processes for responding to the broad public, moving from little public exposure of their activities before the 1960s to rather quickly having to ramp up to meet the minimum NEPA and U.S. Department of Transportation (USDOT) mandated citizen participation processes. NEPA too has greatly broadened civil engineering practice through its requirements for environmental assessment. These began a still-evolving process for ever more interdisciplinary approaches to the infrastructure projects that are the bread and butter of the profession.

As an example of an "out there" city planner, Christopher Tunnard, director of Yale's City Planning Department, took especially articulate and forceful stands against the Vietnam War in terms of its allocation of federal resources and its social inequities. As a director, tenured professor, and esteemed member in the profession and the academy at the time, Tunnard caused Yale's leaders a good bit of worry for a time over what to do about his unruly advocacy. They decided to simply abolish the department altogether, which is why Yale does not have a city planning program today (though Alex Garvin teaches courses in the subject).

# Growing Pains—The Challenges of Citizen Participation

Citizen empowerment has been difficult and halting from the beginning. Important advances have been made, yet it's still, like democracy itself, a messy work in progress. The first line of resistance is predictable: People whose traditional powers were being impinged upon were unwilling to share. Then there are the internal challenges: How do traditionally marginalized people rise to trust the opportunity to participate? Too often their efforts have been ignored or rebuffed, resulting in oppositional activism at best or apathetic resignation at worst.

Initially, citizen organizations modeled themselves after the democratic institutions with which they were most familiar, the city council or the school board. In making this choice, they imported some of the culture and behavior that came with it. They had to deal at the local scale with divergent perspectives, power struggles, jockeying for position, tradeoffs, impulses to exclude those who didn't agree, and so on. These organizational growing pains from the beginning tended to slow down action. For those whose projects may be slowed, neighborhood processes have prompted calls for streamlining or dismantling citizen participation structures. While such a position may be understandable from their point of view, it applies equally to other democratically constituted processes, which they typically leave alone.

As the formal and traditional barriers against just anyone having a voice in private or public development processes began to break down, the challenge was to adjust to the new realities. Community activists were thrust from positions of agitation and advocacy to figuring out how to implement a working structure of inclusion and partnership, moving from "stop" to "start." As is often the case across a range of change movements, advocates don't always make the best implementers. Advocates may start by trying to implement full-blown, sloganized visions—what galvanizes people to take the risk for change—without realizing all of the steps and partnerships that are necessary to move in the direction of the vision. They may be impatient and unsympathetic to detail. Their stridency, effective in getting people's attention, may risk the support they need to begin to shift from demanding to delivering a sustainable and effective citizens' guidance structure.

Implementers, on the other hand, may not have seen the vision initially, coming later to acknowledge that its direction made sense. They are likely to be more attuned to the mechanics and associations necessary for concrete progress. The divergence in the roles between agitation and implementation may cloud the baseline of shared understanding of the need and direction for change. They may even become antagonistic toward each other, instead of uniting to overcome the forces resisting the change. Forces resistant to change in the first place have been successful in blocking it by recognizing and placing wedges between the advocates and the implementers. When this happens, the change effort most likely fails. For change both to become possible and to be managed properly, however, both skill sets and both orientations are essential. The dynamics of change and organization are addressed more fully in Part Three, Principles.

In considering private and even public development proposals and how to exercise their newfound voice, at the beginning citizens often went with their initial impulse, which was, like Nancy Reagan's in a different context, to "just say no." After all, the experience in many neighborhoods has been that new development projects, both private and public, have made things worse, not better, for the people living there, from their perspective. Often, this deterioration is exacerbated by a project being represented one way and turning out another way. Frequently, well-informed and thoughtful neighborhood activists predict the actual outcome and so are vindicated, further eroding trust for the next outside initiative that comes along. In the decision-making environment in which citizens newly found themselves, then, almost any initiative had to be viewed with suspicion—people's responses reflect their experience.

As it affected the design of the civic realm, what citizen participation meant was that the voice of the people immediately impacted should be heard, understood, and respected. The process for reviewing programs and projects affecting their civic environment challenged people at the local level to develop their own knowledge base and leadership structure and to act responsibly, or risk having their opinion go unheard up the approval ladder.

Another challenge that community-based organizations face is the phenomenon of posturing, which may be observed in older, more established organizations as well. There is always one individual, sometimes more, who will be so driven, or so certain of his or her correctness, as to try to dominate the debate. Without structures to balance participation, such individuals, however well-meaning, may have the effect of restricting the fair exchange of ideas, sometimes to the point of reaching bad decisions or putting off curious newcomers from returning. At the same time, posturing may simply be an expression of passion for the subject at hand, and caring is a fundamental criterion for effective citizen participation.

One must keep in mind that citizens showing up at a neighborhood or community meeting are using discretionary time to do so. They should always be made to feel welcome, their views should be respected, and their lack of background in whatever is the subject at hand should be patiently filled in, on the side if necessary. If they are of the community, they should not be made to feel like outsiders. Good neighborhood leadership, in fact, is always looking around the room to see who in the community is not there, even people with contrary viewpoints. Effective leadership makes a point of reaching out to these for the next meeting. On the subject of leadership: a word of caution. Neighborhoods are just as prone as other democratic structures to the ironic contradiction that occurs in the discourse between participation and politics: that is, that once you are elected to office your desire to stay there may trump your support for participation for others who might challenge you.

Internal stresses of citizen participation are exacerbated by constant pressures from outside. From the perspective of a private developer, or sometimes even an elected official or a public servant, the idea of having to listen to neighborhood opinion in the already contentious approval gauntlet posed by city planning commissions, zoning committees, and councils is not always a pleasant prospect. So the new empowerment was resisted by all those organizations both public and private, usually powerful, for whom the old ways were certainly familiar and from their perspective better. Citizen participation experiences continuous attacks for its inefficiency, its demands, and its cost in time and money. It is challenged as to its effectiveness in achieving better outcomes. The effort to dismiss, avoid, attack, or dismember local citizens and their organizations in the development approval process is an ever-present challenge to those committed to including the neighborhood voice.

These kinds of criticisms and attacks are certainly understandable from the perspective of their sources, yet the people there are the ones who finally judge whether a project or initiative makes things better or worse. The larger-scale approval bodies, often more closely tied to the people proposing a development initiative than to the people living and working where it is to occur, simply cannot always be counted on to hear the local perspective, let alone seriously factor it into their decision-making. Having to include this perspective in the partnership that plans, designs, builds, and then uses the resulting civic space, in my experience, however, usually improves the outcome from the community and government perspective and most often from the developer's perspective as well. Developers figure out how to "pencil out" a development, or they don't do it. Cases of developers going belly-up over acceding to broader community values seem few and far between.

There is an ominous side to the rise of influence of citizen participation. Some communities use their new empowerment to exclude and limit the very democratic purposes that the programs enabled. Often affluent and white, such communities seek to keep out people of other races, classes, sometimes even ages, often using zoning as their tool of choice. They may require lot size or house size minimums as their exclusionary tool, or they may establish private communities with exclusionary membership requirements. While there are fair housing and anti-discrimination laws on the books that can address some of these situations, the people who create such communities are pretty adept at dodging, meanwhile usually sopping up more than their fair share of infrastructure and tax advantage support to achieve their goals. The split between rich and poor represented by these kinds of communities tends to fragment the urban region and threaten the quest for a shared vision.

The movements toward broad-based empowerment in shaping neighborhoods, centers, regions, and their places have certainly advanced democratization in how local government has worked over the last 40 or so years. More people and more different kinds of people have gained access to information and influence than could have been imagined before the uprisings of the 1960s. If democracy is about more people being involved to make things better for more people, then citizen participation is certainly moving along a useful path.

## Citizen Participation—Where We May Be Heading

Stresses that challenge citizen participation, while daunting, are beginning to take a new turn. The old and predictable "NIMBY" response is giving way to a reach for partnership. Citizens' organizations are beginning to internalize the fact that private developers are likely to be the ones to initiate almost anything that will happen in their neighborhoods and places. They control the lion's share of investment capital and development know-how. Citizen leaders need to be looking for ways to bend that investment toward serving community needs as part of the process. "Just say no" as a tactic to confront almost any untrusted change initiative is moving in the direction of saying "maybe, if." As the citizen participation movement proceeds, little by little its maturity begins to build a new openness to partnership with the private sector and government. Citizens are realizing that private investment can be shaped to better address and incorporate community needs and that government can play an honest broker role as well as facilitate regulatory and sometimes financial support for a consensually developed initiative or project. Threads of trust can be woven into a stronger fabric.

Countless examples of this change in position are cropping up around the country, often making use of what is often called a community benefit agreement, or CBA. In these, community organizations working through a legal entity they have established may pledge support for expediting the approval process for a prospective development that addresses community needs in some way. In most cases, this approach is yielding better results, usually both for the community and the developer, where in the best cases the policy and regulatory framework of local government becomes an active and enabling partner to the enterprise.

In essence, community participatory experience can evolve from stop to go. More and more examples of these kinds of outcomes, what MBA types might call "win-win-win" in business negotiations, are occurring around the country. These kinds of partnerships promise projects or initiatives that have a tripod under them—they profit their investors, they fulfill public policy goals, and they provide values in their communities that leave things better than they were before. While these partnerships do not remedy inequities that seem endemic in the market economy, they could broaden the base of informed, active, and committed citizens necessary to exercise growing leadership in how the fruits of the economic system can expand its beneficiary pool. The improvement in the quality and functionality in civic environment across all urban settings could stand as encouraging markers that the great effort required to bring about these improvements can pay off. Such an outcome, in turn, could spread to other sectors where the community's voice is muted.

From the professional response point of view, both the R/UDAT and the panel advisory programs have had significant successes in helping communities to envisage possibilities for better futures. In many cases these focused charrettes have set in motion lasting and positive changes in planning, design, and development directions. And the R/UDAT program can rightly claim distinction as one of the earliest formalized design assistance processes to insist, or try to, on full and broad-based citizen input as a critical and integral part of its charrette process. Now, the AIA has launched another citizen-responsive program, adding the Sustainable Design Assessment Team (SDAT) to the R/UDAT as a tool available to communities around the country.

As one of several examples in Atlanta, the Lindbergh City Center project developers entered into an agreement to mitigate new traffic generated by their project by installing streetscape improvements to calm traffic along three streets through the existing neighborhoods. Leaders of four of the five affected neighborhoods advocated both for the necessary development approvals and for the use of a reserve of impact fees to help defray the costs. Individuals from the fifth neighborhood sued, slowing the development process until their case lost in court.

Over the last decade or so, too, the ULI has led its members away from skepticism and resistance to be more open to participatory processes. Recently, for example, the ULI has taken the lead in bringing the dynamics of planning, design, and development into the grassroots through its "Urban Plan" tool kit. ULI members and other supportive professionals and civic leaders bring the processes for development decision-making into mock processes for high schools and citizen organizations around the country. The program conveys the lessons that private development is most development, that it is complicated, and that it must profit.

In many communities, public agencies or developers themselves have begun to craft citizen participation processes to inform and, on a good day, actually listen to and reflect community values in their proposals, usually using a consulting firm versed in the process to assist them. Although there is no mistaking the underlying profit motive to engage in such activities, the facts that local jurisdictions are putting more and more weight on the community voice in their approval processes and that most development proposals going through such a process are improved along the way are measures of the greater influence of ordinary citizens on development that affects them.

Many public planning agencies, in the early days sometimes resistant to R/UDATs or panel advisories, have by now strengthened their public interaction processes to be able to convene and manage charrette-type processes on their own, often better than those of developers or consultants, since their agenda is more service than profit oriented. The public agencies, moreover, are in for the long haul. They are able to establish and institutionalize policy-informing dialogue with their constituent neighborhoods and districts. And they are the ones charged with actually carrying out the good ideas that such processes invariably come up with. Further, there is no doubt that some of the experiences and lessons of effective citizen empowerment have valuable transferability from one community to the next. The lessons from these experiences, some of which are addressed later in Part Four, Processes, should provide input for any community-guided participation endeavor.

At the same time, citizens need to be aware of and concerned about the sophistication with which the now-standard community engagement tools are currently being employed. To put it perhaps a little cynically, developers usually and governments sometimes are no less interested in working their will on neighborhoods and communities than they were before they had to mess with "citizen participation." Accepting that citizen participation in some form is probably here to stay, they are finding new ways to minimize questions or disruptions so that they can control the timing and outcomes of their proposals.

There has emerged a veritable industry of citizen participation facilitators, hired by developers or government agencies to bring in their packaged tool kits and ultimately deliver a result. Sometimes the process is sincere, where there is a genuine openness to community guidance, and sometimes it is not, where the intended outcome has been predetermined. The commitment of the client or the provider to understand and deal with the substance of the issues accompanying a proposal, as well as the ethics guiding the effort, runs the gamut from straight up, honest, and open to devious, deceitful, and clandestine. Through charrettes, focus groups, and other devices, the clients and their facilitators may be inclined to define who the "community" is and what values the "community" espouses, to pick a leadership to work with, to present pleasing images, and to make nods to the most persistent questioners. In short, consultants are often hired to manufacture citizen participation that works—for their clients and themselves. Citizen activists need to be alert to all possibilities, while at the same time taking advantage of any crack in the door to influence the process to the community's advantage.

To filter out the genuine from the purely self-serving, always an issue when design proposals come before the community, people need to insist on identifying and comparing alternatives and remember to ask the questions of who gains and who loses and what are the costs and benefits of the alternatives before them. It takes time for such processes to properly run their course, potentially a conflict for paid citizen participation managers who are on a clock and whose contracts usually stipulate the number of meetings that they will be paid for. This is information that should be disclosed from the beginning.

Under these circumstances, then, citizen participation remains a fragile beginning with lots of impediments to reaching the goal advanced in the 1960s of lifting the citizen voice into some semblance of parity with the private sector and government in shaping the civic environment. The inequities built into the nation's economic structure threaten "citizen participation" with all the anti-democratic features of present-day mainstream politics; whoever has the most money usually wins—a kind of market democracy.

Beyond external impediments, even within the ranks of citizen participation there is a tendency for citizens to splinter away from focus on overlapping interests to diverge on smaller points and thus cloud agreement on the shared larger purpose. Dissension, lack of trust, or lack of solidarity within citizen organizations open them up to further erosion from outside.

People intent on working their will with enough money can manipulate and accentuate differences in the community to support their desired outcomes. Altogether, though, in making things better than they were before, messy neighborhood politics is better than slick and efficient manipulation.

A central hope for more representative and community-serving citizen participation is the recent explosion of access to information. It turns out that most neighborhoods house people with skills, resources, understandings, and capabilities that can be effective in joining the planning and development partnership if they have access to the same information that the more focused private or government proponents possess. Through the Internet, rapid advances in GIS, and other relational databases, ordinary citizens can test their own assumptions and advance their own understandings of impacts associated with going one way or another on a development proposal.

The technical mystification that has provided cover for developers, their consultants, and government professionals is beginning to melt away. Citizens are beginning to realize that the complexities of urban planning and development stem from quantity, not from quality. The individual components in a civic design environment—the street, utilities, landscape, light, activities, building scale, and placement—by themselves are fairly understandable to almost anyone who takes an interest in learning about them. It is in the number and interactive effects between these components where complexity arises. Even so, people can grasp and relate to the planning and development dynamics of initiatives in their community. Unlike astrophysics, it is not a "hard" science.

# Summary

Citizen participation has come a long way since arriving on the scene some 40 years ago. It already has achieved much success in the quest to make things better than they were before, and greater success than most projects of the private sector or government that lack community partners. It holds promise to continue along this progressive path, promise that could burgeon if the proliferation of citizen-based movements can find and build bridges to common purposes. It faces constant threat from vested and powerful interests resistant to community-serving change through co-optation, subversion, or direct attack, as well as, regrettably, from its own internal stresses. When patterns of private sector and government deception and exploitation do arise that make things worse in the community, one hopes that they are exposed through better citizen organization and access to information. For citizen participation to meet the promise born of its origins in protest and resistance among the broad citizenry, it must always put community success above individual success. Place is about what people share. Home is about selves.

# 2

# *URBAN DESIGN TRADITIONS*

Design and People—Spatial Models in the Built World

# Introduction

*Figure 2.1*
*Diagram showing the interaction between place and people.*

Human settlements are many and complex, yet all have some mix of civic space and private space. This book focuses on public spaces, the property that the public usually owns and controls through its government. Public spaces—streets, sidewalks, parks, plazas, squares, and public buildings—provide access to the private spaces and buildings that usually frame the public realm. Public spaces connect people with each other and with their activities across the urban landscape.

What have been the major themes guiding place design in recent decades? What have been the contexts out of which these themes have developed? How do they relate to current contexts? How can the design disciplines coordinate their contributions to making better places and regions? What role do everyday people play in the processes through which places get built? How can people develop sufficient planning, design, and development knowledge to influence the processes for making places better? These are some of the questions addressed in this chapter.

Public places have existed since humans began making settlements, perhaps 10,000 years ago. People have created these spaces to support all those activities that occur in the civic realm—markets, exchange, discourse, defense, pageantry, sports, and leisure. They are where people get together. The publicly shared parts of cities and towns connect the private activities that occur in the home with the activities by which people gain their livelihood and meet their other daily needs. The forms that places take tend to work best when they reflect the nature of the activities they support—like walking, gathering, sitting, or accommodating cars, transit, and parking—usually flexibly across time and space, and scaled to the human form and how people move about. These forms both reflect and support the diversity of people's activities.

Over the last few decades of the nineteenth century, into the twentieth century and up to the present, one can characterize the design themes that largely describe American urban and metropolitan landscapes as fitting in three general traditions. These themes have emerged in economic, political, and social contexts that relate them to their sources and their suitability to support civic activity. They need to be understood as reflecting and to some extent shaping relations between people, their civic environment, and their social structures, between centers of power and the broad citizenry.

The first two traditions are ancient in their roots. The oldest, which we call *organic,* derives from an interactive relationship between people and local natural forces in shaping urban places. The next one, which we call *formalist,* derives from geometric order as the organizer of a place's activities upon the natural landscape. The third, which we call *modernist,* came into being in the early part of the twentieth century as a conscious and radical break from the first two, originally and nominally conceived to use a new technological order to advance the quality of people's urban existence.

These characterizations are perhaps too sweeping, yet they should be helpful for understanding how and why places tend to look and perform like they do. They provide a spatial context for considering different approaches and frameworks for making places better. They should aid in getting at the core questions about the public environment's success in serving people's needs, both functional and aesthetic. Later chapters will cover design considerations in detail.

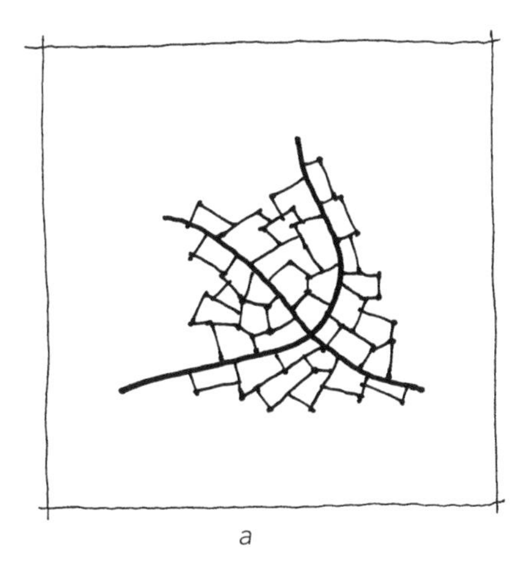


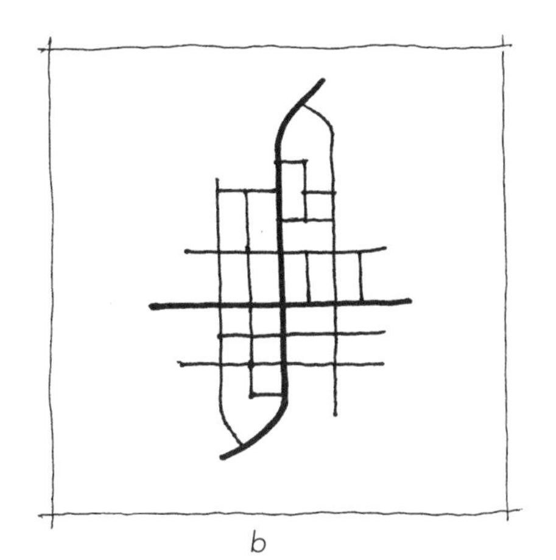


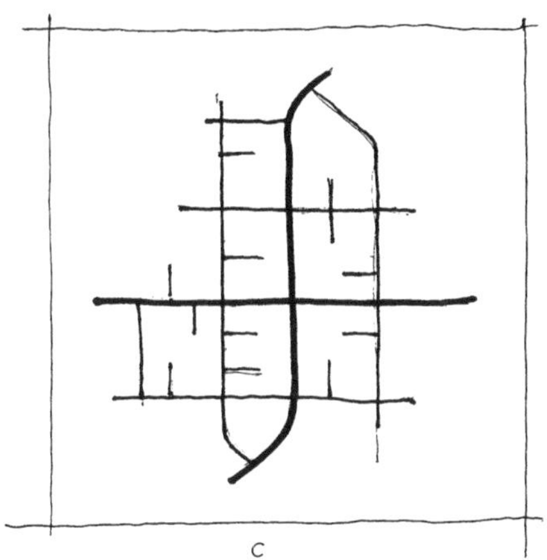


*Figure 2.2a–2.2c*
*Diagrams of settlement patterns typical of the three traditions: the organic (2.2a), the formalist (2.2b), and the modernist (2.2c).*

# The Organic Tradition

The first tradition for how settlements have been arranged could be thought of as belonging to the organic family, with extended family members being variously called *naturalistic, indigenous, vernacular, incremental, informal, romantic,* or *picturesque*. The antecedents to these themes for organizing urban space trace back to the first settlements, when people arranged their activities and their connections largely according to natural systems, like water courses, land contours, arable soils, orientation, and climate. These were people who discovered the utility of grouping themselves into more permanent, larger-than-clan clusters, whether for defense, economic productivity, or cultural needs. Ordinary people were doing the best they could to fulfill their life needs, adapting to physical environments and social structures that imposed clear limitations on materials and resources. The outcomes of these endeavors, work done by ordinary people cooperating with each other and using the means at hand across a wide variety of landscapes, continue to be visible in settlements whose forms, shapes, materials, and decorative expressions somehow communicate an honoring of the human spirit, the spirit of everybody. This tradition has persisted ever since and, of the three, interacts most comfortably with the ranges of natural environments that people have inhabited.

There are well-known examples of the organic way of building settlements all over the world and throughout time. Ancient towns in all continents followed this tradition, most familiar of which to American travelers perhaps might be the myriad types and ages of villages around the Mediterranean—Greece and Turkey, the Trulli villages of southeast Italy, villages throughout the Middle East and in North Africa. Medieval towns all over Europe show this tradition as well. Once the bishop and the prince got their defensive wall built around the town and the cathedral and the castle done right, the physical manifestations of their power and stature, the people who were their builders and providers were relatively free to organize their own living environments. These artisans accommodated themselves to the topography, climate, and other compelling natural features to build their shops and houses, using whatever time they had left over and known and readily available materials to build a suitable living situation. Houses and shops of various sizes and shapes, stuck one to the other,

*Figure 2.3*
*Ancient organic pattern still functioning at Taos, New Mexico.*

define the streets and travel ways that connect them to each other, their workplaces, and their shared civic spaces. As long as access was provided, there was no particular commitment to straightness or standard widths or lengths of the ensuing blocks or streets. The buildings and their activities shaped the streets more than the other way around. Most such towns maintained near their middle a market square as well as sometimes a church plaza to focus social survival activities, like trade and cultural expression.

Whether ancient, medieval, or modern, from the evolution from kin to class society when settlements began to organize themselves, the power structure requires fulfillment of a top-down agenda, whether ecclesiastical, noble, military, or economic. Thus settlements' organization and priorities usually produce buildings that symbolize that power structure, whether the castle, the church, the palace, the town hall, or the corporate headquarters. For all of these the street, square, plaza, and other civic open space provides the physical and social connection. In this tradition until the arrival of mass production, the habitations, shops, and other work spaces were more casual, more bottom-up, built by the people who lived in them, and more interactive with their natural and social world in their implementation.

Closer to home, mound villages in the Southeast and Midwest, like Cahokia just across the Mississippi River east of St. Louis, Mesa Verde, or Taos are all examples of precolonial organic towns, each with different responses to their different settings and all sharing the essential goal of providing a social living environment for anywhere from a few hundred to, in the case of Cahokia, a few thousand souls. The pueblos in the Southwest predate the arrival of the Europeans and continue as exemplars of this tradition, where the societal structure is less hierarchical than the European, and the defining space is often the ceremonial and market square and the later European-induced church.

Exemplars of this tradition, pretty much wherever they are found, persist as picturesque urban settlements in the organic tradition, just as much a draw for tourism as the iconic structures that their townspeople built for the power elites. The resonance of these villages and pieces of city, with

*Figure 2.4a–2.4b*
*Figure-ground maps of Boston and Lower Manhattan, with buildings in black, open space in white, and the earliest (the organic) patterns shown darker.*
*Base map courtesy of Office of Geographic and Environmental Information (MassGIS), Commonwealth of Massachusetts Executive Office of Environmental Affairs; graphic enhancement by Renato Ghizoni*

*a*

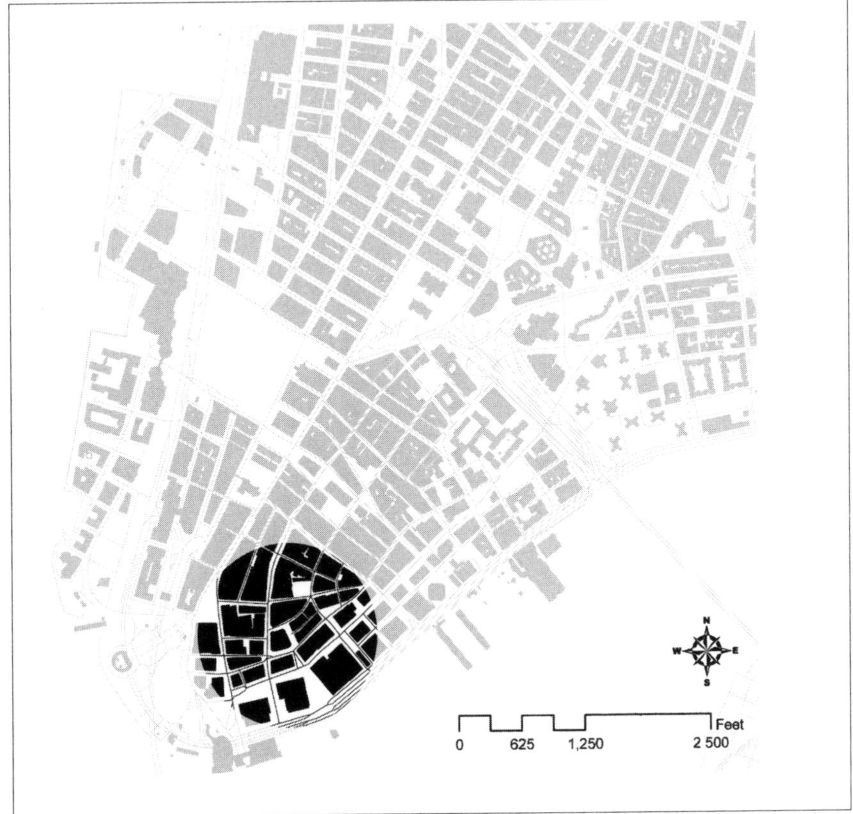


Urban designers and others in the design disciplines use figure-ground maps to contrast built spaces, usually buildings, to unbuilt spaces, usually streets and yards. They provide a useful way to "read" city form in terms of "solid" and "void."

*Base map copyrighted by the New York City Department of Information Technology and Telecommunications. All rights reserved. Graphic enhancement by Renato Ghizoni*

*b*

indigenous counterparts of widely varying physical appearance around the globe and across the ages, could reflect an instinctive sense of connection and respect from their visitors and viewers. These places' meaning is embedded in their physical presence—work done by ordinary people cooperating with each other and using the skills and materials at hand to fulfill their life needs by shaping their particular physical environments to their common purpose in the context of demanding social and economic structures. Always with the intention and the drive to make their places better, the outcomes of these endeavors are visible in forms, shapes, and decorative expressions that somehow communicate an honoring of the human spirit, the spirit of everybody, not just the domination of the hierarchy up on the hill beyond. Maybe that's why these townscapes show up on so many postcards, from all over the world.

More recently than the pueblo villages, cities like Boston and New York found their beginnings in the organic tradition. Irregular topography and lots of navigable river and bay shoreline shaped early Boston, while the lower tip of Manhattan afforded a similar access to the navigable waterfront. The somewhat cranky twists and bends of these early responses to settlement in the new country impart a special character and in some ways anchor the later dominant grid patterns and the even later modernist inserts into these cities' spatial character.

For the most part, as a way of creating settlements in the United States the formalist, mostly grid approach to laying out towns and cities pushed aside the organic tradition as the decisive model from the turn of the nineteenth century until post–World War II suburbanization. From the National Land Survey begun in 1785 at the urging of Thomas Jefferson through the laying out of countless railroad towns all across the country, the grid, usually aligned with the compass points, became the default position for town and city making.

The organic tradition, however, was by no means dead. As the Industrial Revolution transformed core cities into manufactories of all kinds, they became sumps of air and water pollution, and urban quality of life deteriorated all through the nineteenth and well into the twentieth century. The longstanding tradition of rich people having a country home away from the hurly burly began to proliferate into the upper middle classes and finally to the middle class. The wealth generated by the workers in the industrial economy and its multiplier effects provided the means for more and more people to move out, first as a retreat and later the home place as rail and then cars provided access. As responses to human need, the naturalistic tradition that shaped first the exurban and later suburban settlement patterns implicitly and explicitly rejected the city of that day as a fit place for human habitation. It seemed to draw from a yearning for a life that is more in balance with nature. It shows up in romanticized follies from Marie Antoinette's grotto at Versailles to the mansions that dot the Colorado mountains.

This yearning for nature, then, represents a persistent counterpoint to the dominant theory and practice of building cities on the grid. Central Park in Manhattan, for example, interrupts the resolute grid pattern established by the Commissioner's Plan of 1811 (which did not contemplate park space) and introduces a slice of evocatively romantic nature artfully manufactured by Frederick Law Olmsted and Calvin Vaux. This introduction of romance into an otherwise resolute order was one of a number of similar efforts in Europe and the United States to provide some degree of

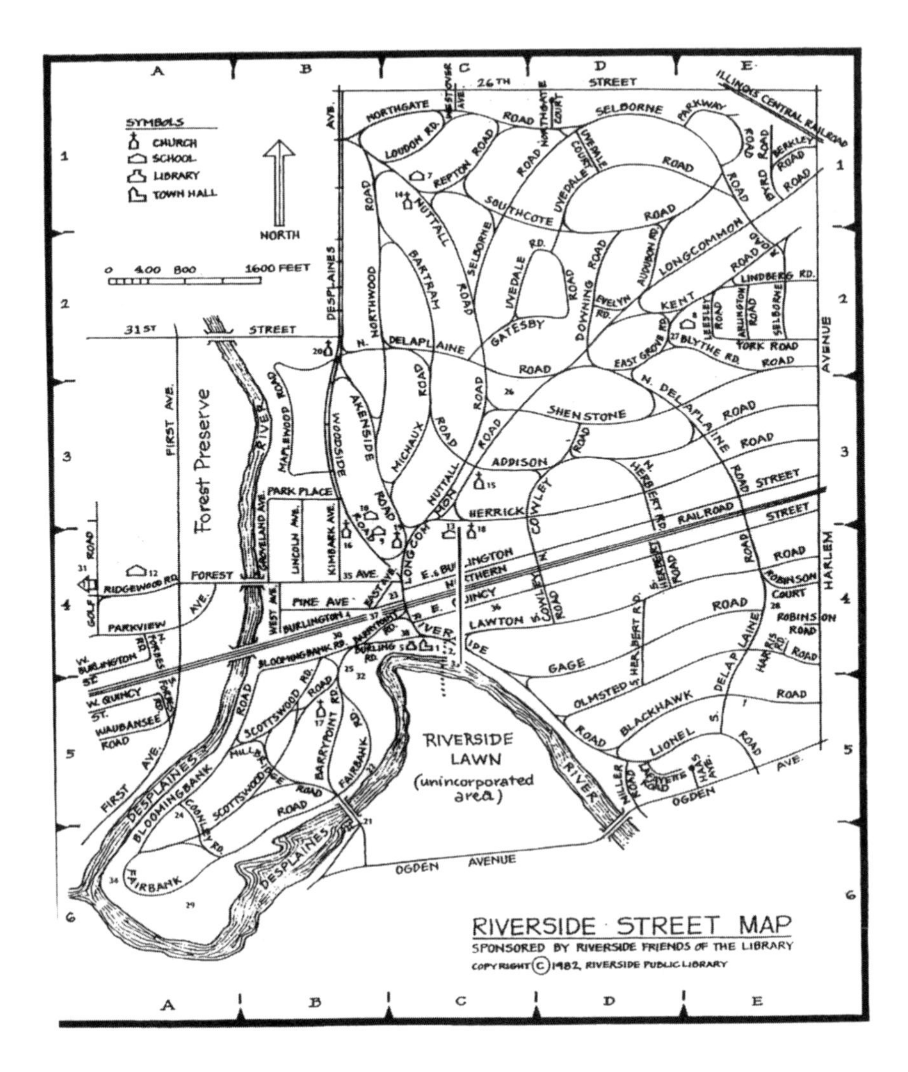


*Figure 2.5*
*One of the earliest subdivisions laid out in the organic tradition, Olmsted and Vaux's 1857 Riverside Plan shows a studied break from the gridiron plan that had come to dominate town geometry at the time. Courtesy of Riverside Friends of the Library*

humanitarian relief from the unremitting forms, spaces, and environments that characterized the production side of the capitalist city. Paris's Parc Buttes-Chaumont of about the same time as Central Park gave Baron Haussmann's landscape architect, Alphonse Alphand, the chance to create a naturalistic, romantic, totally artificial in-town landscape. The park transformed a gallows site from an earlier era into a picturesque scene that afforded Parisians some feeling of an increasingly distant countryside. Brooklyn's Prospect Park, also crafted by Olmsted, the earlier Boston Common, St. Louis's Forest Park, and later San Francisco's Golden Gate Park all represent a growing sense of the need for civic action to balance with grand open spaces the inexorable swallowing up of all urban land for profit-making purposes. These civic stirrings led directly into the City Beautiful movement, a concerted effort to reverse the decline in the quality, and the healthiness, of urban life.

If one way to balance benign nature and the foul city was to bring nature into the city, a tradition that is finding new form nowadays as "landscape urbanism," another way was to provide for those who could afford it a naturalistic setting to move to beyond the city's grip. Olmsted and Vaux again combined forces to design Riverside, an early exclusive suburb of Chicago, in 1869. Using their flair for the picturesque, they created a

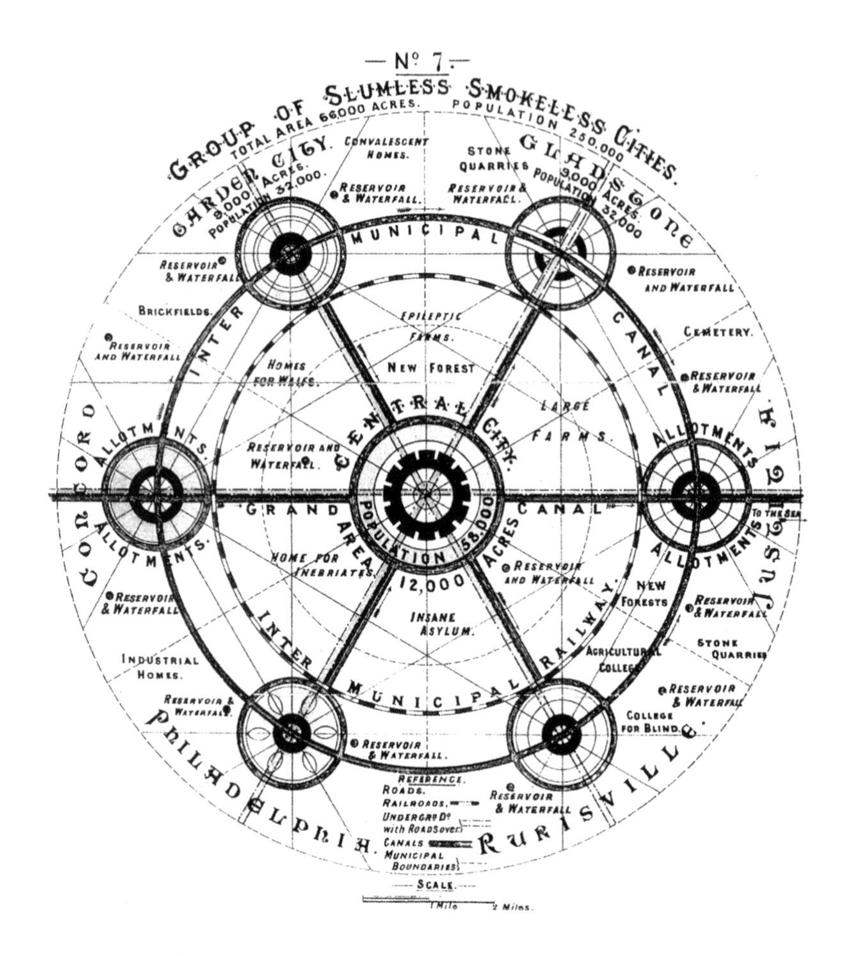


*Figure 2.6*
*One of a series of diagrams prepared by Ebenezer Howard to illustrate ways of planning for settlement patterns that were more environmentally sustainable and socially equitable.*
Garden cities of tomorrow *(1902), Ebenezer Howard*

romantic naturalism on a treeless plain by introducing tree-lined curving streets and undulating topography in a setting and for a purpose that became a model for later suburbanization. Earlier protosuburbs had tended to extend the rigor of the grid radially outward from the center, a pattern that seemed dull and perhaps too evocative of the urban pattern from which people increasingly wanted to escape. The idea of a "naturalistic" setting for people "just like us" living in the must-have single-family home with its own yard set the table for generations of repetitions throughout the country that persist today. Olmsted and his successor firms continued to most familiarly and famously mark this new direction in urban settlement patterns, but they were joined by many other less ballyhooed practitioners of the emerging field of landscape architecture and suburb design.

A breakthrough and more comprehensive response to the grim, environmentally degraded industrial cities symbolically associated with the grid forms came from an English court reporter named Ebenezer Howard in the late nineteenth century. Howard's transcendent purpose was to create an urban setting that would be better for everyone, not just the landowner, lender, and developer. His garden city proposals in their diagrammatic abstractions projected a new way for conceptualizing cities, which picked up from utopianist notions of embodying both physical and social content as the drivers for new forms. First titled "To-Morrow, a Peaceful Path to Social Reform" in 1898, they were reissued under the title of "Garden Cities of To-Morrow" in 1902. One of his famous diagrams is titled "Group of Slumless Smokeless Cities," presaging aspirations that remain challenging today for those who stand for "smart growth," a title that encompasses mixed income, compact, walkable, and environmentally sustainable cities.

Howard had in mind a model that recognized and responded to the activities and needs of the whole population, the integration of the natural and the built worlds, and strategies for planning transportation and other infrastructure to connect the garden city, both internally and with towns and cities beyond. He represented his ideas as diagrammatic abstractions that were clear and legible. These were geometric formulations that could be adapted to the natural setting to assure an appropriate balance and connectivity between landscape and cityscape. His idea was to provide an antidote to the congested, often environmentally foul core cities where the industrial labor force was then concentrated.

His diagrams showed a larger central city surrounded by greenspace, through which radial connections from the center penetrated to satellite cities, connected to each other circumferentially. Each of these was to be more or less self-sufficient—that is, to include jobs, shops, services, housing, and some agricultural production, with densities intensifying at centers surrounded by transit and transected by roads. In this respect the concept is actually anti-suburban, even though it arose from a similar, but more civically motivated, desire to alleviate the stresses of industrial core cities. While the settlement pattern proposed is certainly different from early exclusionary suburban developments, the principal difference is the commitment to social equity that lies at the core of his proposal, almost the antithesis of the vision for Olmsted's Riverside from 30 years earlier.

As impulses, Howard's ideas reflect recognition of the essential interactions between people and their physical environment; as diagrams, they seek to rationalize these interactions into formalist, geometric schema. The diagrams first found form in interpretations by Raymond Unwin and Barry Parker in Letchworth, England, which was built beginning in 1904, and later new town efforts. Patrick Geddes, a Scot and adherent of much of Howard's theory, took a different emphasis coming out of Howard's comprehensive vision. Before Howard's work, Geddes had been advocating the importance of understanding and honoring what was already there, both physical and cultural, in approaching city design problems, and he maintained this emphasis in his practice after absorbing Howard's contribution. In so doing, he is a purer advocate for the organic, indigenous, incremental approach, including the essential link between people and their places. The comprehensive and inclusive underpinnings of these twentieth-century urban design pioneers, both in theory and practice, had and still have great impact on thinking about settlement patterns. Together, they have been used to support in different ways not just organic but also formalist and modernist interpretations as well as mixes of the three.

The organic tradition for laying out inner suburbs continued to spread through the work of Frederick Law Olmsted Jr. and his brother in their national practice, notably in their layout (along with Grosvenor Atterbury) of Forest Hills Gardens in Queens in 1915 and the development by J. C. Nichols of the Country Club District in Kansas City. These kinds of designs gained steam as a sharply different approach from the grid, viewed in this time, particularly by the growing affluent, as stultifying and ungracious. So began a growing proliferation of designers and developers, adapting naturalistic forms to promote the development advantages flowing from a rapidly growing—and spreading—population.

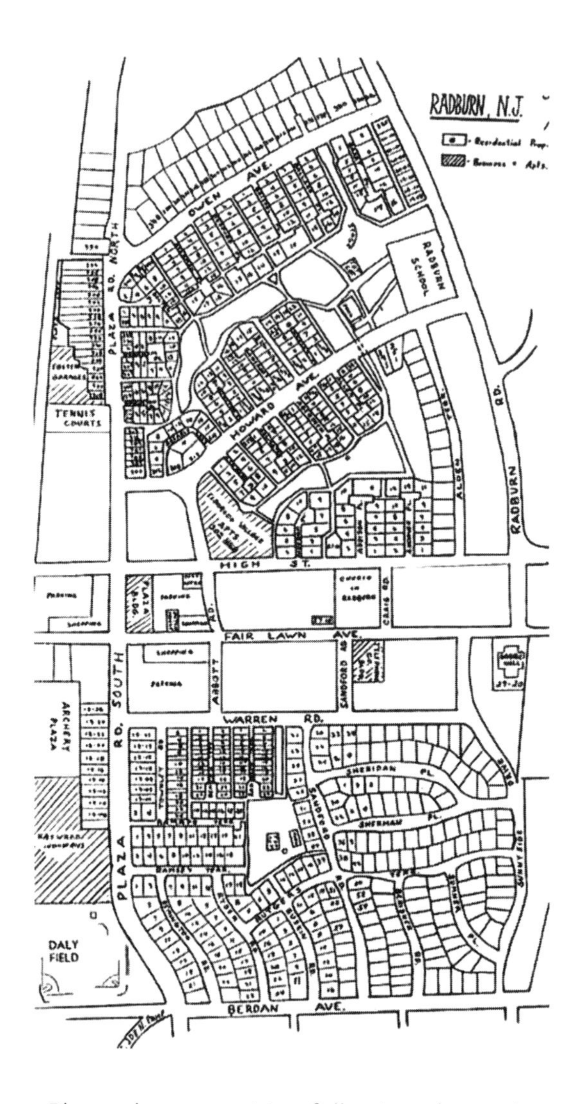


*Figure 2.7*
*Plan for Radburn, New Jersey, often cited as a model for the garden suburbs that later proliferated. Courtesy of the Radburn Association*

Planned communities following the various permutations of the organic tradition began to proliferate all over the country from this period into the 1930s, most of them commissioned by real estate and development interests, most of these aimed at the more affluent, nuclear family demographic. Overall, it is likely that most of these designed communities worked out better than undesigned areas, at the least because they were conceived holistically and carried out by trained and skilled people commissioned to do the job.

Radburn, New Jersey, designed by Clarence Stein and Henry Wright in 1929, is often cited as a model village for the impending diasporas of suburban development. The design incorporated themes from Howard's garden city, like creating work places, shops, schools, and mixed densities associated with the access system. It warped the grid to bend around natural features and interrupt cross-street continuity, pursuing the goal of a picturesque, naturalistic setting. It reflected the growing influence of modernism (see later) in creating superblocks, larger than usual tracts for development with less expense for streets than a grid system would produce, and by separating pedestrian walkways from auto travel ways, creating bridges and underpasses to accomplish that goal. In these latter moves, Radburn sought to design for the advancing car age and in so

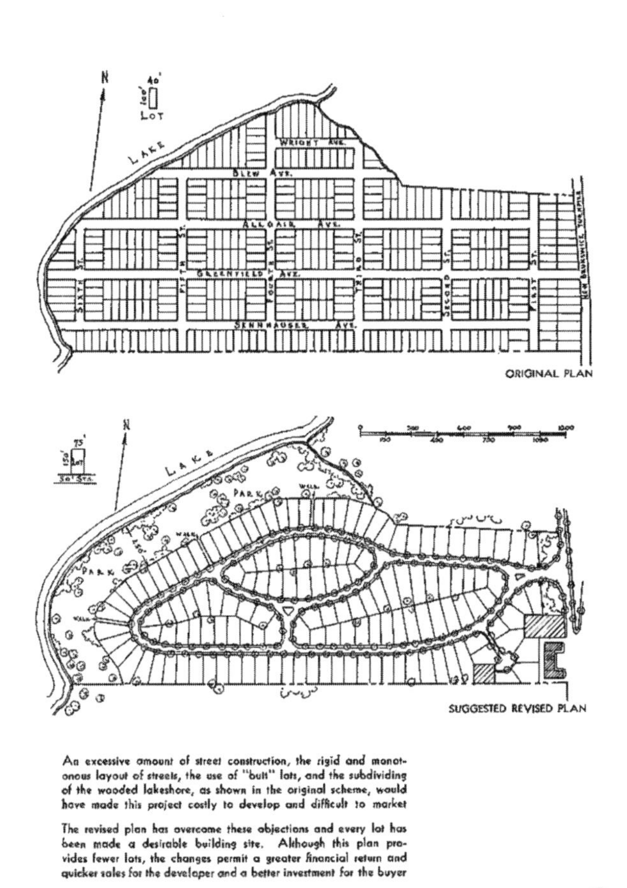


An excessive amount of street construction, the rigid and monotonous layout of streets, the use of "butt" lots, and the subdividing of the wooded lakeshore, as shown in the original scheme, would have made this project costly to develop and difficult to market

The revised plan has overcome these objections and every lot has been made a desirable building site. Although this plan provides fewer lots, the changes permit a greater financial return and quicker sales for the developer and a better investment for the buyer

25

*Figure 2.8*
*The Federal Housing Administration and the Urban Land Institute put out manuals on how to do subdivisions right, as shown here in the FHA's "Planning for Profitable Neighborhoods," showing bad practice as having straight streets with greater potential connectivity and good practice as having curving ones more self-contained.*
*Courtesy of the U.S. Department of Housing and Urban Development*

doing defined the car as antithetical to and incompatible with a walkable environment, carefully relegating it to its own separate hierarchy of access. The idea was to accommodate the car's space-gobbling needs and at the same time downplay its presence in the otherwise picturesque environment where people were walking to and from their nominal front doors. The result embodied the uneasy confusion that persists about how and where to deal with the car in relation to the walk; in Radburn's case, the design produced two "front doors," one from where the car parked, where most people came and went, and the other where the walkway was, where people were "supposed to" come and go.

As is often the case with prototypes, the adapters who followed (in this case the onset of hordes of suburban speculators, developers, and homebuilders) picked and chose the most affordable, approvable, and marketable features, in which swervy streets, larger blocks, and in many instances the elimination of sidewalks instead of separated sidewalks became the norm. In short, the parts of the model that could turn more profit remained and the parts that made less or no profit disappeared, reasserting the value system on which U.S. settlement patterns depend. For the next several decades, these early models and their knockoffs dominated new residential development across the country. This variant of the organic tradition, in fact, even became official U.S. policy after the Federal Housing Administration was established in 1934. In documents with titles like "Planning for Profitable Neighborhoods" or the Urban Land Institute's "Community Builders' Handbook," the public and private imprimatur, with tangible regulatory and financial content, virtually assured the rejection of the grid in favor of the more naturalistically conceived subdivision projects that now make up a sizeable portion of every urban area's residential landscape.

These early efforts promised a picturesque setting for settlements for the emerging middle classes that were just beginning to respond to the distance and distribution freedoms that the car was on the way to establishing. At the same time, the garden suburb tradition showed new ways for building in densifying urban regions, as alternatives to the orthogonal grid norms applied to most such areas before. The economic, cultural, and class-based factors that fueled the growth and proliferation of suburbia persist as one of the major development themes of today, that is, that outside of the city—the suburbs, as it turns out—is better than inside. The garden suburb became the model of choice for the rising middle- and upper- middle-income classes. The separation of living from working as well as from all the other facilities that centers provided ran apace, fueled by the anti-urban aspiration of each family to its own separate house, yard, and garage as the pinnacle symbol of attainment, a vision celebrated famously in Frank Lloyd Wright's "Broadacre City" proposals.

Suburban America has reflected the garden suburb's romanticized tradition ever since. Winding streets, lots of cul-de-sacs, a range of lot sizes and shapes, often generously sized, create blocks, already large in the Radburn model, that are usually much larger than those of the more formalist grid tradition. And block sizes continued to grow as their car-dominated access systems largely eliminated or suppressed the need for a walking environment. The idea of walking access to shops, schools, parks, and community facilities disappeared. Instead, in many ways reflecting the emergent modernist passion for separation of land uses and travel hierarchies, shops, services, and jobs are sprinkled along major arterial corridors. Meanwhile, heavier concentrations of commercial activity find their homes in office parks as clusters of "single-family office buildings" often cushioned from their parking fields with "naturalistic" berms, flowers, shrubs, trees, and winding paths; and every now and again one finds an enclosed shopping mall floating in a sea of asphalt parking, usually with no landscape cushion.

Through the agency of boatloads of homebuilders, developers, and real estate speculators, deeply subsidized by mortgage lending programs, public roadways, and other infrastructure and tax incentives, suburban America continues to reinvent the romantic or garden suburb tradition. Indeed, a strong case could be made that the "market" actually constrains the options for conceptualizing how the built world could or should be, by passing all ideas first through the accepted baseline screen of profitability. The advantages of the car, the house, the yard became the well-marketed impetus to create the dominant model for housing the U.S. population after World War II. This movement, with an assist from racist sentiment and white flight in the wake of desegregation, left the whites' old neighborhoods to minorities who faced the block-busting discriminatory real estate, lending, and insurance practices that further destabilized core cities, often even including their commercial centers.

Figure 2.9
*An example of the suburban environment of today, where about half of the nation's population lives. Copyright Craig L. Patterson 2007*

These patterns and the street hierarchies put in place to provide access to them reflect incremental development, where older streets may track preexisting rural roads, and properties may represent ad hoc breaking up of old agricultural holdings. The street hierarchies, often referred to as "dendritic" because in layout they resemble the form of a tree or a leaf, begin with a trunk, spread into limbs, branches, and finally twigs. The corresponding street names for this "tree" are arterials, collectors, local streets, and finally cul-de-sacs. While such a pattern might seem sensible enough—and it certainly corresponds well with the elemental, largely unplanned breakup of rural landholdings—it carries with it the flaw of each "tree" being disconnected from the next one. In many ways, this disconnectedness accounts for growing congestion across the suburban landscape, for if the collector or arterial experiences a blockage, the traffic behind has no alternative travel path. This pattern contrasts sharply with the grid (see later), which always provides the possibility for another travel route. For all the informal willy-nilly, incremental, hopscotch patterns typical of suburbia, the results show a remarkable sense of sameness—no matter where I am in suburbia, I feel like I've been there before.

Beyond its physical predictability, suburbanization has produced other drawbacks. It has tended to segregate people by income, age, and ethnicity, as each subdivision was targeted to a single demographic market. Family time and civic time are replaced with driving time, and now the

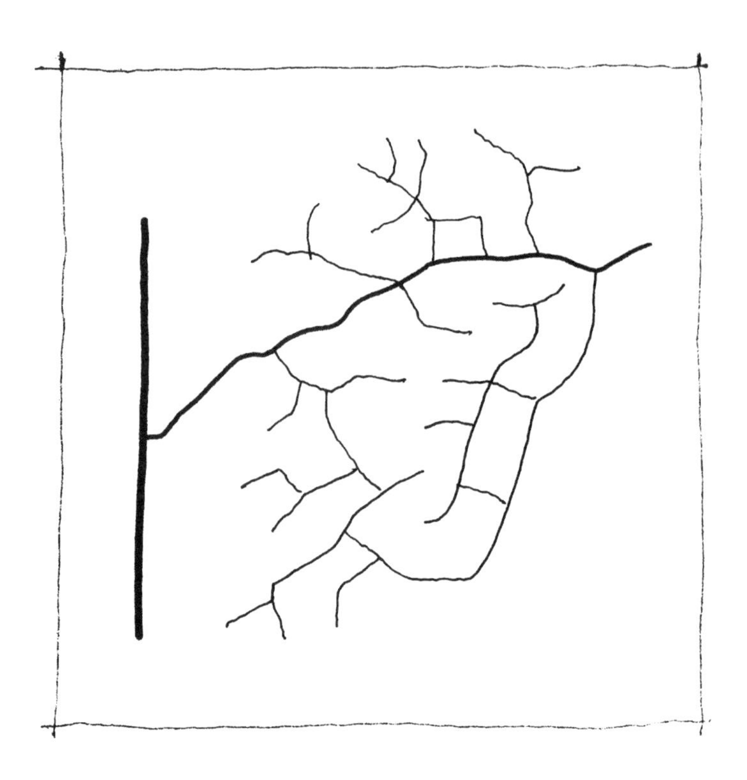

*Figure 2.10*
*Diagram of dendritic street pattern, showing dependence on collector and arterial streets to gain access to otherwise nearby neighbors.*

cost of driving is nudging past the cost of housing as the major budget item for many middle- and lower-income families. The breakdown of the extended or intergenerational family unit has interacted with the sameness of both price and physical product characteristic of suburbanization—"just like us" tends not to include parents, grandparents, or even children as they become independent. Costs of infrastructure and services increase on a per unit basis the farther out they are from centers and major travel corridors, while many suburban areas continue to rely on septic tanks, ultimately fouling groundwater. In short, there is a widely reported litany of problems facing suburbia that were not considered or considered and rejected as long-term problems in a short-term, fast-buck subdivision environment.

As the spread of population across old city-centered regions continues, limitations of this pattern are becoming more evident, and alternatives are beginning to be more attractive in the marketplace. Now some of the block patterns established under this tradition, which for all their sinuosity are not particularly flexible, are beginning to face the strains of adaptation for different populations and activities, circumstances ripe for urban design assistance. Should and can one retrofit the suburban pattern and if so, how?

My colleague at Georgia Tech, Ellen Dunham-Jones, and June Williamson explore these questions in some detail in their book, *Retrofitting Surburbia.*

In an increasingly recognized turnabout, it is likely that the problems of suburbia will only compound as their forms, cultures, governments, and revenue bases are called upon to accommodate the proportions of population that are shifting from higher- to lower-income people. Meanwhile, the choice for more-urban environments is becoming more attractive for the middle and upper-middle classes, a phenomenon that on the one hand is producing "new urbanist" development projects on greenfield sites in the suburbs, and on the other is interacting with towns and cities rearranging their regulatory and financial priorities to respond to this new market.

All of these new settlement pattern dynamics, not really anticipated even 10 or 15 years ago, call for the active involvement and consideration of both citizen leaders, with their leavening of increasingly well-informed common sense, and urban designers, as synthesizers of the processes that can create better living environments. Historically, neither the victims of urban renewal nor the aspirants to the suburban utopia were particularly involved or represented in the large public policy deliberations that produced the patterns with which all are grappling today. Instead, private sector priorities, whether real estate, auto industry, petroleum, road building, development, or finance and their law, planning, engineering, and increasingly sophisticated and effective marketing consultants engineered policies to maximize return on investment. The production side of suburbanization drove a rapidly evolving consumer/marketing culture: What sold quickest and at highest profit was most hyped and soon most irresistible. Marketing, in the name of offering choice, swamped people with many options of house style, color, kitchen, bathroom, cabinets, gadgets, and fixtures, essentially denying choice on big-picture life-choice issues.

Now as cracks are appearing in the suburban juggernaut and gentrification becomes an issue in older towns and cities, the citizen voice needs to be put forward—and listened to. And the people trained in design who understand the consequences of design choices at this scale need to step up and get active, even if their typical clients or government positions constrain them. The old patterns, beyond their private sector impetus, traded on two linked circumstances: there not being enough people in the greenfields to worry about—at least until the environmental movement picked up momentum—and the ability to ignore lower-income, often minority, populations in urban centers most affected by the demographic and investment shifts. The design professions whose services enabled the old patterns, meanwhile, were fragmenting one from another, talking with each other less and each claiming an "expertise," the fruits of which turn out not to be so sweet.

The recognition and advocacy for integrating citizen guidance and the design disciplines into strategies for making better places is not new. The work and thought of Patrick Geddes, the recognition of the need for community-based checks and balances embodied in the State Zoning Enabling Act and the State City Planning Enabling Act, the programs of the New Deal that sought to include the whole population, not just those with the greatest financial investment, as beneficiaries of government policy and action—all these led into the positive and progressive sides of the turbulence of the 1960s.

The inclusion, even the celebration, of the everyday citizen in determining the quality of civic spaces, figures prominently in the work of Jane Jacobs and other writers and thinkers since. One of the more articulate and persuasive contemporary advocates for the organic tradition is Christopher Alexander, whose *Pattern Language* and *The Timeless Way of Building* have evoked and inspired that subconscious desire for connectedness among ordinary people, from urban centers to communes. Similarly, Margaret Crawford, in her book *Everyday Urbanism*, explores people's yen to connectedness with regular people, not just *oohing* and *aahing* over the lives of the inaccessible rich and famous.

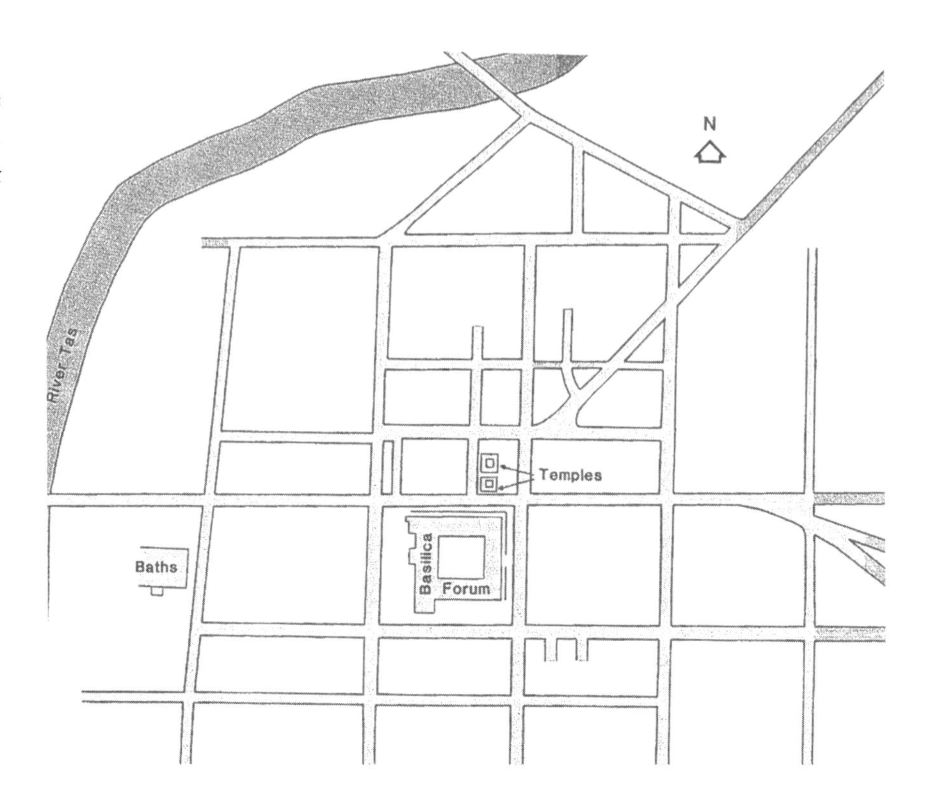


*Figure 2.11*
*The grid, here in its simplest form, was repeated dozens of times throughout the Roman Empire. Courtesy of Norfolk Archeology Trust*

# The Formalist Tradition

The *formalist* tradition is the family heading under which I group such other related tendencies as *planned, classical or classicist, the grid, monumental, beaux arts, the grand manner,* and particularly in the United States, *City Beautiful* 100 years ago and *the New Urbanism* now. This tradition as reshaped in the United States has ancient antecedents in Egypt, Greece, and China, with their most systematic formalization shaping the towns of the Roman Empire with lasting influence in North Africa and throughout Europe. The tradition flowered during the Renaissance and Baroque periods and projected itself forward to produce such palace grounds as Versailles in France; the grand boulevards in Paris, Berlin, and other cities; and church plazas like St. Peter's in Rome. It shaped new cities in the United States as well as reshaped older cities in Europe.

This tradition has purposeful and studied geometry at its formalistic base, often an orthogonal grid of hierarchically arranged street systems, sometimes sweeping diagonals across whatever pattern existed before, as well as formal parks, squares, and plazas. Buildings or monuments deemed important by the power structure of the time—like churches, triumphal arches, obelisks, parks, courthouses, palaces, capitols, or corporate headquarters—often punctuate or terminate the vistas of major, sometimes almost ceremonial boulevards.

The tradition established formal, monumental, axial, or symmetrical urban forms, often as a conscious move to express and exercise the power and authority of the state or church. For the Roman conquerors, it put a stamp on countless new colonial settlements, at once showing who was in

*Figure 2.12a–2.12b*
*Figure-ground maps of Boston and Lower Manhattan, with buildings in black, open space in white, and the formalist grid patterns shown darker. Base map courtesy of Office of Geographic and Environmental Information (MassGIS), Commonwealth of Massachusetts Executive Office of Environmental Affairs; graphic enhancement by Renato Ghizoni*

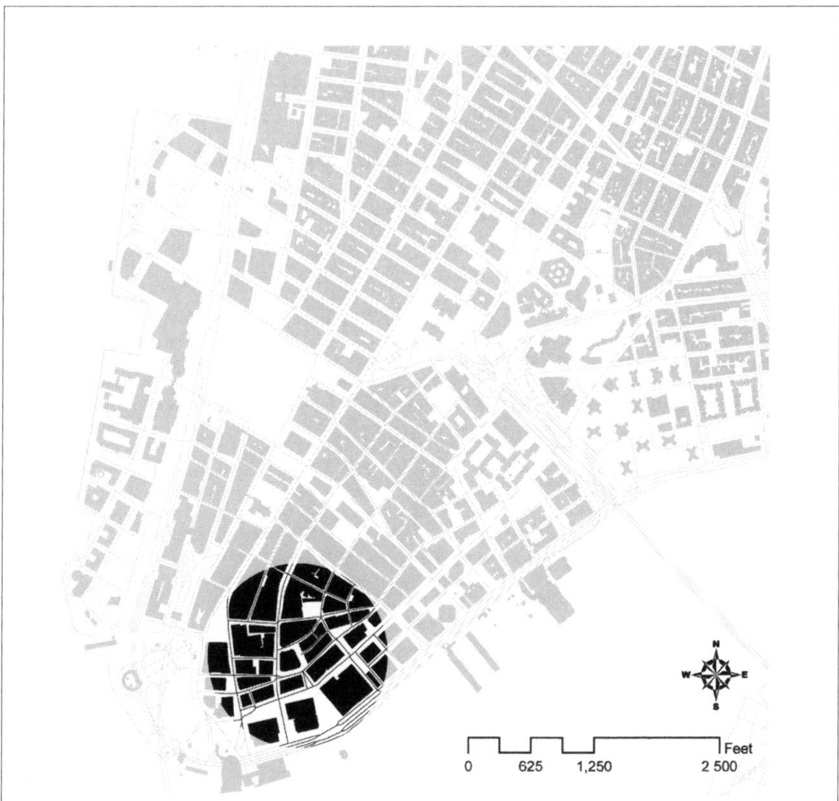


*Base map copyrighted by the New York City Department of Information Technology and Telecommunications. All rights reserved. Graphic enhancement by Renato Ghizoni*

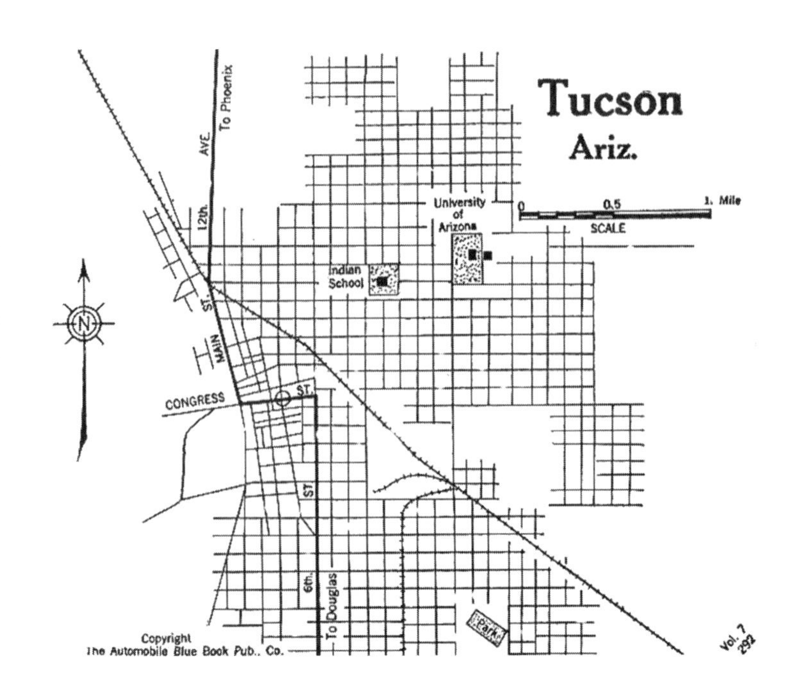


*Figure 2.13*
*Springing from the Land Ordinance as the proper way to subdivide territory, "railroad towns" like this one were mapped all over the country as ways of punctuating rail corridors with planned settlements.*
*The Automobile Blue Book Publishers (no longer in business)*

charge and how things were going to be. It communicated hierarchy, order, and power, both visually and operationally. The grid provided not just superior street and other infrastructure connectivity between the various functions of the town but also a way to quickly control any disorder that might arise. It provided a consistent way for organizing buildings along the street, most often lined up pretty evenly to define the streetscape, blockfront activities, and points of ingress and egress. Louis XIII and his urban designers in seventeenth-century Paris, for example, used formalistic devices to begin to control the cross-sectional relationships between building heights and street widths to assure that sunlight could reach the sidewalk.

Formalism was the tradition that influenced James Oglethorpe in laying out Savannah, William Penn in laying out Philadelphia, and Pierre L'Enfant in laying out Washington, D.C. It was also the tradition adopted by Boston when filling in the Back Bay and by the New York City Commissioners in 1811 for Manhattan above 14th Street. This tradition, with the simple, powerful, and functional grid system as its core geometry, accounts for how most of the towns and cities in the United States were laid out during the nineteenth and early twentieth centuries. The grid, whether rectangular, square, or modified by radials as in Paris or Washington, is functionally very efficient. It provides the best connectivity of any form both for travel ways and for utilities, a direct result of its providing choice and redundancy for the full range of systems necessary to achieve access to the activities housed along the blocks that the travel ways serve.

Accordingly, Jefferson persuaded the Continental Congress to adopt the Land Ordinance of 1785, which established the grid as the way to subdivide land across the country. Already established cities and towns, as well as those to come, most prominently railroad-generated towns, used the grid as their baseline organizing device for fast-growing settlements. The grid, usually framing rectangular or square blocks, provided the most practical and functional way to lay out the future town and expanding city.

It provided a rational way for managing ownership patterns. Its structure had been proven flexible and serviceable enough to accommodate the wide variety of activities necessary to support town life within reasonable walking distances. The grid dominated most city building traditions in the United States as the major form-generating force in urban form from early in the nineteenth century up until the garden suburb and modernist traditions kicked in during the early twentieth.

Later, when Napoleon III wanted to reshape Paris to exalt his Second Empire, he called on Baron Haussmann to impose an order that would symbolize his reign, building on the moves of the last Bourbon kings and his emperor uncle with grand, ornately landscaped boulevards slicing through the still largely medieval forms of Paris. These moves are largely credited for Paris's leap forward as a model for other cities' transformations, and not just in visual terms. Beneath the dramatic visual impacts, the work-over created a workable water delivery and sewer and storm water control network that directly affected the locations and layouts of the boulevards above. The new systems greatly enhanced transportation connectivity, service delivery, water supply, sewage treatment, public health, and crowd control. The private-public partnerships created to build the structures lining the boulevards presaged practices that flourish today.

These improvements propelled Paris into the forefront of large European cities in the areas of health, safety, and welfare that improved the quality of life for most people in the city, across a scale where those with more benefited more. People in the upper and ruling classes generally favored formalism and its expressions as consonant with their vision of a stable and impressive world and the sense of their status in it. Not coincidentally, broad, straight boulevards provided quick and easy access for security forces and so functioned as a bulwark against the challenges or changes that broader-based social and labor movements might bring forth. Patrons for this tradition have included nobility, clerics, bankers, merchants, mayors, presidents, dictators, and, in the case of Paris, emperors.

In its grandest incarnations, the City Beautiful movement around the turn of the twentieth century adopted the formalist tradition to express its values of confidence and the pride of an ascendant civic order. The forms adopted imparted the monumental feeling of the grand manner adopted by Paris, Berlin, and Vienna, beginning with the Columbian Exposition in Chicago in 1893, followed in the same city by its perhaps most transcendent expression in Daniel Burnham and Edward Bennett's Chicago Plan of 1909. The City Beautiful movement and its contemporaneous municipal art movement saw that the quality of the public realm was both functionally and symbolically important for fostering pride and identity among the broad citizenry. The spread of consciously designed streets, squares, and parks with their symbolic stability and practical serviceability did indeed create frameworks that approached that goal. The City Beautiful movement's strategy for integrating the ever-growing presence of the car, for example, tried to create a balanced geometry that could accommodate the car and its travel ways so that they did not overwhelm the rest of the urban landscape. In their grandest boulevards they framed streets with building fronts and created a streetscape environment of trees, lights, benches, and wide enough sidewalks to balance what the car required—or so they thought.

While the City Beautiful movement swept across the country with grand and rationalistic attention to form in city centers, at the smaller scale Clarence Perry, a sociologist working for the Russell Sage Foundation in

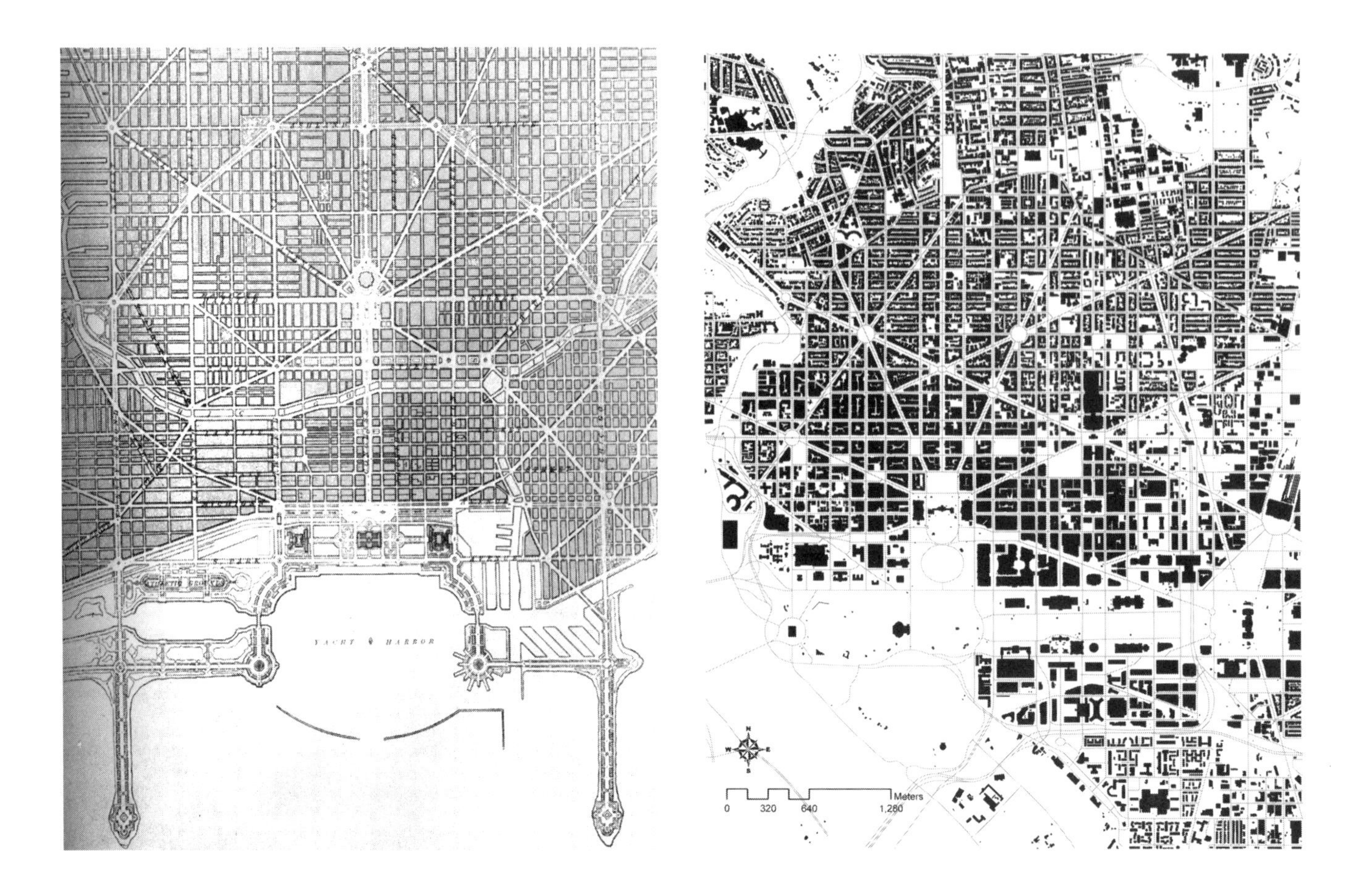


*Figure 2.14a–2.14b*
*Perhaps the fullest expression of the City Beautiful pattern at the scale of the city, Burnham and Bennett's plan for Chicago (2.14a) shows the formalist grid punctuated by strategic diagonals, not unlike L'Enfant's plan of 100 years earlier for Washington (2.14b).*
*2.14a: Commercial Club of Chicago, 1909*
*2.14b: Courtesy of District of Columbia Geographic Information Systems—Office of the Chief Technology Officer*

New York in the 1920s, conceptualized a formalized way to plan neighborhoods. Picking up on the rational side of Ebenezer Howard's diagrams for designing settlements, he formulated a comprehensive design approach at the scale of where people live. The outcome of his work, which he called the "neighborhood unit," showed new ways for building in denser urban settings, flexing up on the by then tired unending grid to introduce some curving but still connected street patterns.

As Perry envisaged it, the neighborhood unit fit into the larger urban grid and provided for the integration of needs and activities necessary to provide a cohesive and definable neighborhood. While it had parallels with the Radburn model and other such efforts, Perry's approach was more systematic and, like Howard's work, almost formulaic. He described neighborhoods in terms of size (about 160 acres, or a half mile square), walking distance (about a quarter mile), connectivity (a hierarchy of streets that discouraged cut-through traffic), and appropriate levels and locations of shops, schools, park spots, and other community facilities. He suggested how bounding streets should engage the neighborhood unit and how the blocks, streets, and sidewalks should be laid out internally to accommodate the full range of anticipated neighborhood activities. He did not propose to disassociate pedestrian from auto travel ways, as Stein and Wright did in Radburn, nor did he propose the superblock concept, evident in both Radburn and modernist practice.

As the idea of neighborhood was supplanted with subdivisions and as the realities of capitalist market forces weeded out ideas like shops, parks,

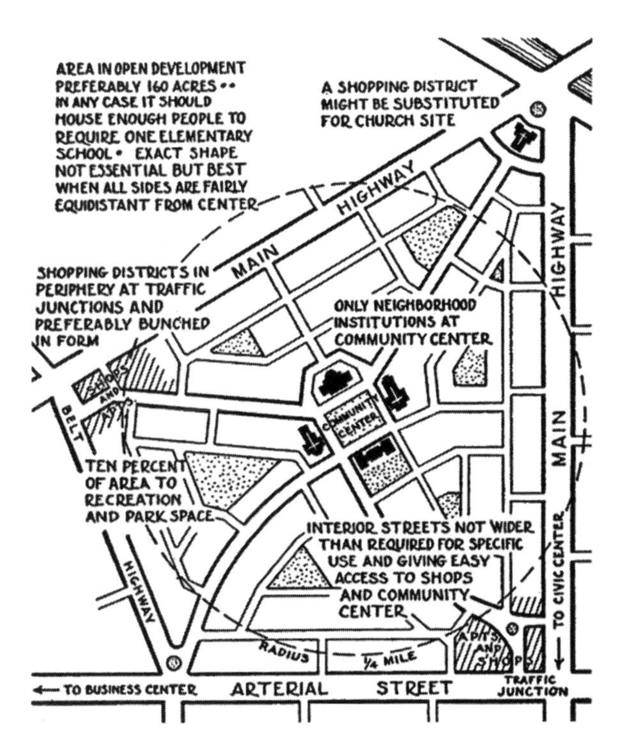


*Figure 2.15*

*Clarence Perry's idea of a planned neighborhood, mixing housing types, retail and workplaces, civic buildings and parks, which he called the "neighborhood unit," foreshadows current ideas like traditional neighborhood development, new urbanism, and smart growth.*

*Courtesy of Treasure Coast Regional Planning Commission*

schools, or community centers within walking distance, along with diversity of housing type and small connected blocks, Perry's ideas receded. Over the last 20 or so years, however, these ideas have been picked up and given new life by urban designers and community leaders.

The new urbanists of the present day have proclaimed a return to classical, punctuated grid forms supporting a mix of activities as their idea of the right way to build new suburbs or retrofit urban redevelopment sites. These patterns evoke middle- and upper-class neighborhoods developed from the Civil War into the period when the suburban organic models began to dominate settlement patterns. The traditional neighborhood and "new urbanist" models thus seek to reestablish the lost features from the Perry model. Coinciding with the gradually dimming luster of the suburban model, new urbanist designers and developers have been effective marketers of the model, adding to its growing popularity. This new marketing vector appears to be tapping a latent desire for something different, something better, something that at least appears to reflect civic values, diversity, walkability, living, working, and shopping close together. The message, beyond the practical advantages of compactness, walkability, and mixed-use, mixed-density patterns, plays on a nostalgia for a time when civic and social values retrospectively may seem, rightly or wrongly, to be more community supportive than what the sweep of suburbanization and modernism brought after the 1920s. In terms of building places with ostensible civic values, new urbanist models appear clearly superior to commercial strips.

Predating and feeding into the new urbanist model has been a more comprehensive yet more abstract and less form-based response to the compounding shortfalls of the suburban model. With its origins in the 1960s' rise of environmental consciousness and activism, this movement has developed through successive stages of seeking a better balanced way

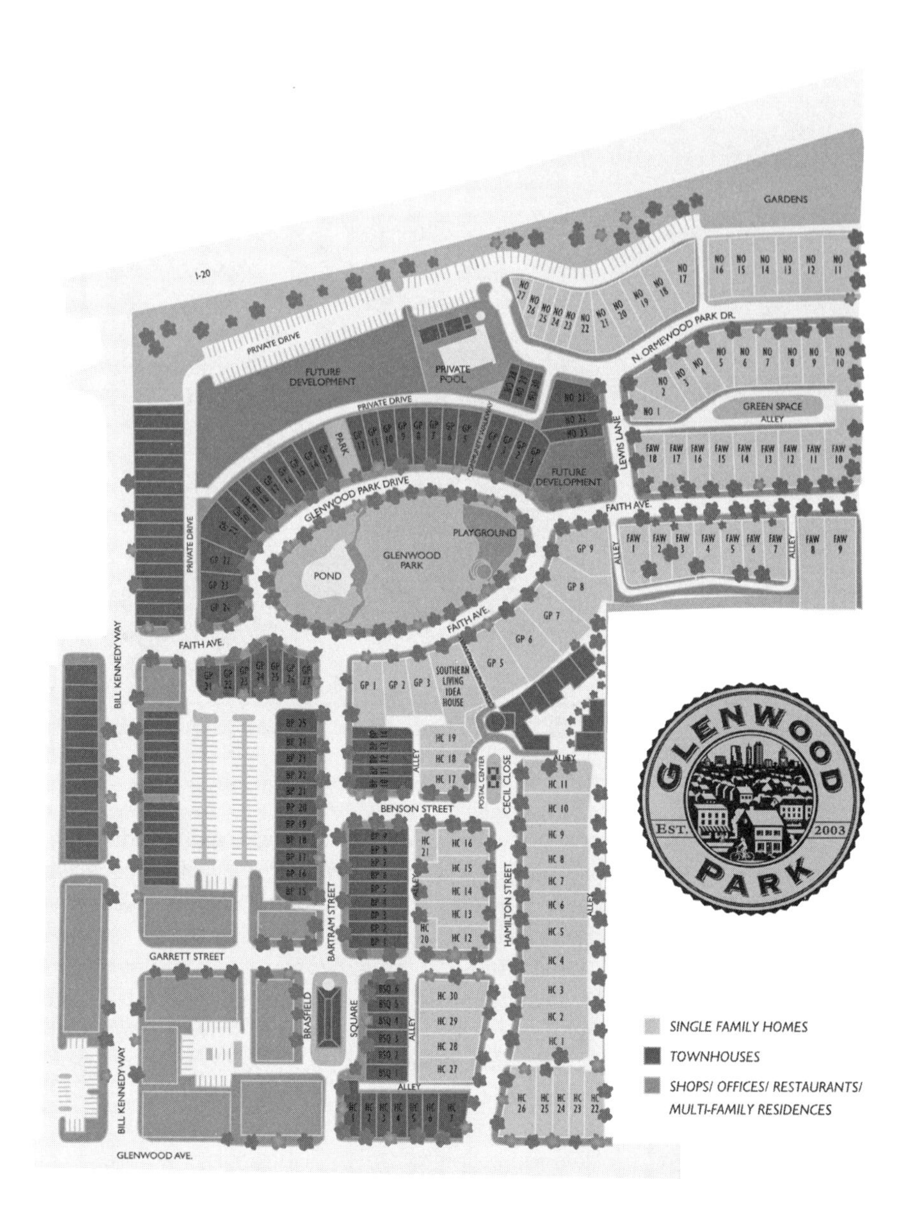


*Figure 2.16*
*An urban infill new urbanist project in the formalist tradition, Glenwood Park in Atlanta, won the Congress of New Urbanism's top award in 2004. Courtesy of Greenstreet Properties*

of accommodating population growth and environmental sustainability. In its current iteration this movement is usually called "smart growth," whose formalist base envisions more compact, walkable, transit-able, and environmentally sustainable use of the land and water, along with a more conscious inclusion of energy conservation and climate change concerns.

From its origins, the smart growth movement has antecedents in the National Environmental Policy Act and subsequent state legislation that sought to address concerns about the environment in a comprehensive way. Then in the 1970s the oil crisis raised concerns about the energy component of settlement patterns. Programs variously called "growth control" or "growth management" proposed such devices as urban growth boundaries and the linkage of public infrastructure priorities with environmentally desirable development patterns. Smart growth's priorities are now intertwined with the fast-growing green building movement, which itself is converging with smart growth in seeking to understand and promote green communities. As these tendencies multiply and their market share increases, government, most often local government, and private sector consultants and developers are moving to take advantage of a relatively untapped market—good news for the smart growth movement.

The formalist implications of smart growth are increasingly emphasizing repopulation of older, more compact towns and cities, many of whose cores eroded in the wake of suburbanization. A large and growing number of local governments, eager to tap the growing market for new housing, jobs, and services and the investment energy that can reinvigorate their centers and corridors, are revising their codes to both permit and encourage the rediscovered forms. Before postwar zoning "reforms," most of these core places were organized under the formal traditions of the grid with the attributes noted earlier. On the private side, while new urbanism has provided an attractive, usually formalist visual representation of what smart growth might look like, it is largely a project-based practice where many of the projects are in the suburbs or on greenfield sites and thus not necessarily consonant with the goals of smart growth, since they may add densities to travel and other infrastructure that is already overburdened.

Further reinforcing the prospects for smart growth are demographic shifts in which seniors and empty nesters find their traditional suburban environment isolated, hard to maintain, and with growing travel times that make meeting their needs increasingly difficult. Similarly, at a time when more people under 30 grew up in suburban environments than not, staying in that environment is less and less their preferred choice. In some ways, indeed, smart growth has come to mean anything that is not cul-de-sac and strip commercial living. What this really seems to mean is that Americans have come to realize that there are choices in where and how to live and work as well as in how to travel between. The return to the formal, classical, even monumental traditions has emerged as a positive alternative to the informal, incremental, naturalistic traditions that have dominated the suburban living, working, and traveling patterns of the last 50 years. It is clear that this alternate market depth has just begun to be plumbed.

# The Modernist Tradition

The third tradition, *modernism*, carries under its umbrella such terms as *functionalist, rationalist, technological, utilitarian, systematic,* and *efficient.* The modernist movement initially represented bold efforts to use technology and notions of a regimented democracy to recast how and where people should live and work and how they should get around. As a city design movement, modernism rejected centuries of urban accretions, with their interplay of organic and classical forms, as simply being incapable of measuring up to the task of providing a fair and functional city for all. Its impulse was to start over, with remarkable and hubristic confidence that its precepts implemented through modern technology were the only reliable path for meeting the needs of twentieth-century urban society.

Beginning after World War I, early exponents of this counter-romantic, counter-monumental or beaux arts tendency, like Le Corbusier and Ludwig Mies van der Rohe, saw technical breakthroughs and the forms they were devising as the best way to reduce the costs of decent habitation.

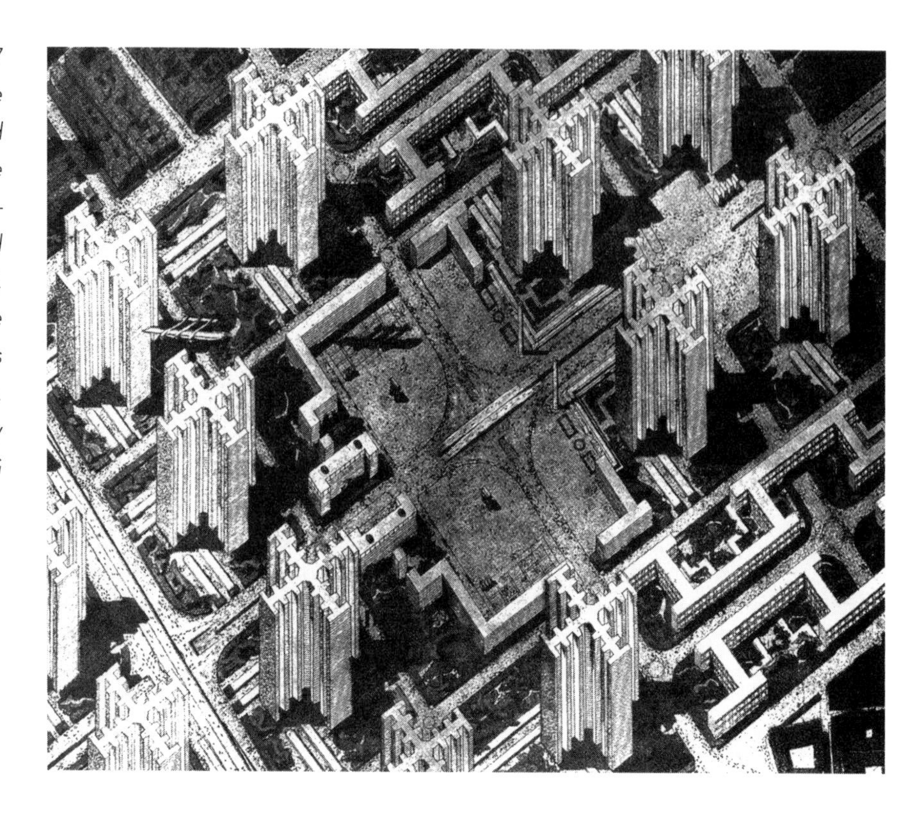

*Figure 2.17*
*Le Corbusier's visions for the "Ville Radieuse," or radiant city, projected what became the model for the modernist vision for rebuilding cities—clean, rational, mechanical, functional maybe, but simple-minded, vapid, one-size-fits-all, and unresponsive to the diverse needs and patterns of real people for sure.*
*Copyright 2002 Artists Rights Society (ARS), New York/ADAGP, Paris/FLG*

They saw it as a way to improve health, to introduce light and air into both habitations and workplaces, and to bring parks and cultural institutions more affordably within reach of ordinary citizens. Furthermore, modernism purported to meet head-on the demands of the newly emerging, soon-to-become-dominant form of transport, the car.

Modernists' approaches put a high value on mechanically defined efficiency, replacing the details and adornments of the past with a machine aesthetic, as the way to provide for life's minimal needs and barest essentials, as the movement's proponents defined them. Part of the motivation for this drive was to use resources in a way that lifted life's amenities for city- and industry-bound masses. Le Corbusier defined the house as a "machine for living in," and he carried this mindset and conceptualization into his sweeping visions for cities of the future. His drive was to raze the urban fabric of the past, created by layers of people, tradition, culture, and time, and replace it with a singular "solution" hatched out of a single mind. He was not the only one who took this radical view of how cities should be, but rather one of a school of European modernists who seized on technological advances and waves of sentiment for democratization to propose whole new arrangements for living, working, and getting around.

Common to all of these functional, clean, efficient, rationalist, technological approaches was the absence of any dialogue with the people who were the intended beneficiaries of all this high-level thinking. The theorists bypassed direct interaction with the broad citizenry that was supposed to live in the places they were designing, disrespecting their cultural traditions, leaving out an understanding of the connection of transportation and other infrastructure to land use, and ignoring the social, economic, and political structures upon all of which the very purpose of cities depends. Uninformed by or dismissive of how people really live or what they really value (what we might call "evidence-free" design today), these precepts began to sweep across the architecture and planning professions, burying the messy but richly textured and accessible past with efficient but arrogant and sterile upper-middle-class visions for a better future—as they saw it. While modernism did achieve improvements for many people, particularly in the areas of infrastructure, the movement suffered from its omission of consideration of all those human values that fall outside of technical problem solving.

Modernists generalized individuals as they did most problems. In their quest for single sweeping solutions, they proposed one-size-fits-all ideas. Buildings were either single-purpose or self-contained. Connections became diagrammatic. Most of the urban character of walkable, mixed-use places was supplanted by giant "superblocks" ringed with generic, hierarchical travel ways for cars or transit with a separated and disconnected system for pedestrian paths. The idea of a shop or building entrance–defined streetscape environment fell off the palette of options for modernists along with functional and visual connectedness between pedestrians and their daily needs. Here too began the mantra of the separation of uses, whose activities were abstractly judged to be mutually incompatible—residential, commercial, and industrial each in their own pristine zone. This theory without much analysis found its way into most of the nation's zoning ordinances from the 1930s into the 1980s, which in many ways have dictated the patterns and character of development in urbanized areas all over the country.

Probably because they were at least thinking of cities' physical problems holistically, albeit leaving out the people, Le Corbusier and the other modernists of the Congres Internationaux d'Architecture Moderne (CIAM), were very persuasive. As propagandists for a new way, they seemed to offer promise for a world emerging first from World War I, the "war to end all wars," and a series of democracy-seeking revolutions. The 1920s were turbulent times, people celebrating after the catharsis of World War I, experiencing the reality and illusions of wealth garnered by rebalancing the economy from war to consumerism, reacting to the bold new experiment launched by Lenin in the Soviet Union, and succumbing to the inclination among many vanquished Germans to rediscover their pride in Hitler.

After World War II, compelling rebuilding needs in Europe joined with slum clearance sentiments in the United States to set off sweeping transformations of the living environment. These affected the habitation, the workplace, public places, travel ways, and whole cities. Paralleling these events were democratization movements, a gradual broadening of concern for the choices and living standards for working people who were forming a growing middle class—not poor, but not rich either. Most of the models for how to rebuild had to face the challenge of how best to integrate the car into suitable living environments.

As the country shifted from a pumped-up war production economy into a consumer economy, the ideas and proponents of modernism represented the most coherent strategy to follow in accommodating new growth as well as disinvested and deteriorating core cities. Technology held such promise that it achieved an iconic status. This period saw a rise in public esteem for the notion, even a certain mystique, that somehow "experts" held the key, and that ordinary citizens couldn't possibly grasp the intricacies of the new world rolling out before them. Lacking access to where the decisions were being made, people either reduced their trust in

a

Figure 2.18a–2.18b
Figure-ground maps of Boston and Lower Manhattan, with buildings in black, open space in white, and the modernist urban renewal areas shown darker.
Base map courtesy of Office of Geographic and Environmental Information (MassGIS), Commonwealth of Massachusetts Executive Office of Environmental Affairs; graphic enhancement by Renato Ghizoni

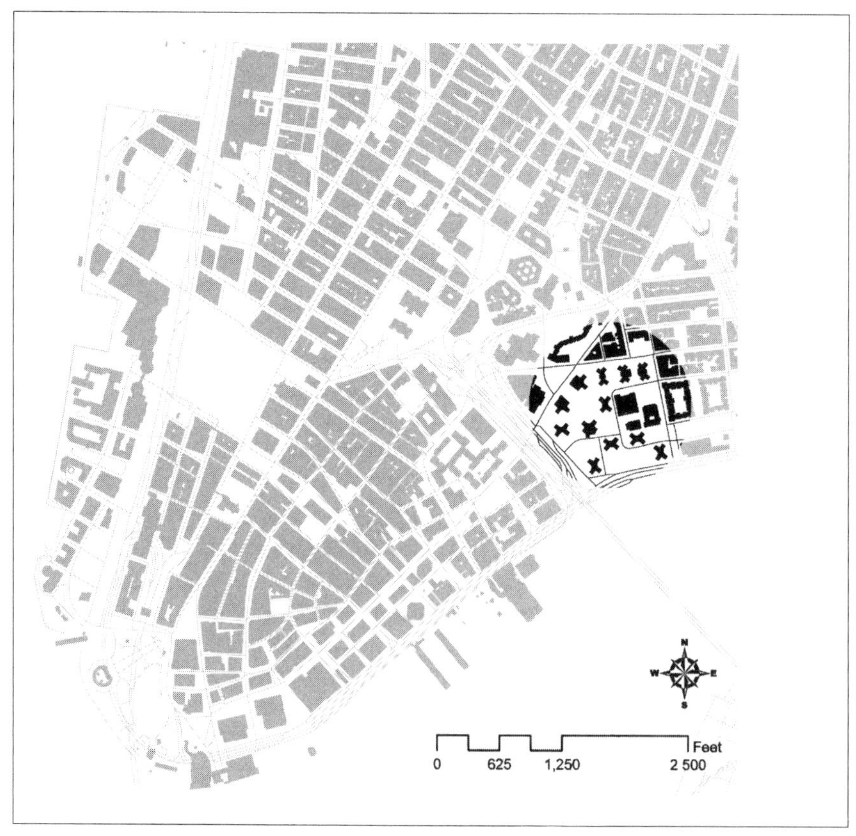


b

Base map copyrighted by the New York City Department of Information Technology and Telecommunications. All rights reserved. Graphic enhancement by Renato Ghizoni

their own instincts and experience or they glorified the "experts," or both. Most of the architects and city designers building in the CIAM tradition rode on this wave, being dubbed, and dubbing themselves, the "man with the plan." In many ways, ordinary citizens became more separated than ever before from the process of shaping their environment, bowled over by the scale, the newness, and the glitter of the new, unapproachable, and singular visions emerging from modernism.

The most brilliant of architects, however, was limited by the visions containable in a single mind, losing from the very beginning of the conceptualization process the very richness and diversity of experience, vision, aspiration, and commitment to a better life that any handful of people unlike themselves could provide. A new order of elitism had arrived, and its top-down theory and practice sent cities reeling, from Moscow to Paris to New York to Chicago. Out of this automatonic vision of homogenous, albeit "equalized," humanity, theories applied mainly to the larger-scale scene, losing sight of the particulars that dominate the concerns of most of us. Much of what didn't work from these narrow spectrum concepts of city building stemmed from "experts" deciding the "right way" for people to live. Most of these brought values derived from highly educated, upper-middle-class value systems, with presumptions about what "should" work from the point of view of either a deterministic technology or a single "big idea" architectural expression. Thus the modernist visions of cities were often simplistic and one-dimensional, leaving out how humans actually behave in both physical and social or cultural settings in favor of mass-produced uniformities.

In order to understand the shortcomings of these urban visions, which are visible, recognizable, and for the most part leaving stains all over our present-day world, it is important to put these circumstances into the context of the dominant architectural traditions, since architecture more than any other discipline accounted for the way modernism unfolded in city design. Architecture among all the arts is the most dependent on patronage for its existence—without patrons architects as defined in their critical literature would have no work to do. Buildings cost a lot of money, way more than paintings, sculpture, music, or even giant landscapes. In order to carry forward a vision or aspiration, architects need to find a compliant client with lots of money. Needless to say, the architect's view of the world is filtered through the lens of the patron, a world view from a lofty perch with a clear sense of social order, in which the patron sits at the top. Architects who espouse this aspiration are inclined not to consider buildings "architecture" unless they are driven by such patrons, and this culture of elitism, however unconsciously, is likely to carry over into their conceptualizations of the city.

Frank Gehry, one of the preeminent trophy architects of the patronage culture, stated this attitude clearly to a convention of neuroscientists in Atlanta on October 14, 2006: "Only five percent of buildings are architecture, the other ninety-five percent are just buildings." Cities are more about the 95 percent than the 5.

A second and equally important factor in understanding modernism—or architecture in general—is to remember that architects are schooled in building design for individual clients and carry that limitation into their understanding of the city. Architects tend to conceptualize the city as a singular building problem to solve, either in repetitive units or just as one great big building or megastructure. Architects are not trained in the design of connections between buildings, the civic space that defines the public environment, and they are not trained to respond to the broader public as their client. For the modernists, their rather simplistic approach, under the cloak of making the city more efficient, left out huge blocks of information about how cities really work, most important of which was bypassing any guidance or information from the broad citizenry.

*Figure 2.19*
*Harrison and Abramovitz's grandiose modernist scheme for housing many of the functions of the New York state government—a space that works well for large concerts and demonstrations, otherwise pretty cold.*
*Photo by Grant Jun Otsuki*

# Interactions and Overlaps of the Three Traditions

We have presented the recurring characteristics of urban form and practice under the headings of three traditions: the organic, the formalist, and the modernist. For the sake of clarity these expositions focused on the salient and easily recognizable features of each so that one might "read" a town, city, or suburb typologically. In fact, the three traditions are in continuous interaction with each other so that the forms one encounters, while usually dominated by one of the three, may show tendencies from one or both of the others as built and evolved over time. These combinations sometimes result in a city's or a district's most memorable images, points of orientation, or creative development responses. This section gives a few examples of how these interactions might look in common experience.

To begin with, it is worth reiterating some of the key relational aspects of the three traditions, in which each has its pros and cons. The organic tradition tends to reflect the features of the natural world, like topography, water courses, and orientation. At the same time, as an incremental and accretive schema, it builds on historic travel and trade routes, accounting for curving and often dendritic, disconnected street systems. Formalism is most closely associated with the grid for its superior flexibility and accessibility on the one hand, and its assertion of physical and social order on the other. Modernism combines its quest for abstract efficiency with the exigencies of modern real estate development practices to reorder the built world into superblocks, separated vehicle and pedestrian systems, and separated functional activity zones.

While it is beyond the scope of this work to substantiate the traditions' relationships with social, economic, political, and cultural orders, there do

Modernism's already compromised commitment to a better world for all eroded further as the art world's critical acclaim of modernism's forms obscured the purported original purpose. When Henry Russell Hitchcock and Phillip Johnson curated a show at the Museum of Modern Art in New York in 1932, they produced a catalog entitled *The International Style*, and modernism passed from a movement seeking substantive advances in democratization and the provisions for a better life to the latest style rage among well-heeled avant garde collectors. Whatever were the progressive intentions of modernism and many of its adherents waned as their efforts began to attract the collectors of architecture who had only recently become jaded by baroque knock-offs churned out by the beaux arts tradition.

seem to be some recurrent themes. The organic family of traditions originates and thus to some extent derives from people making their own choices on where and how to live in the interplay between human activity and the natural environment—initially to survive. From the smallest scale, the family or even the individual, people in their more primitive states had less access to resources and had to live more interactively with the natural world. Individuals in early emerging societies were close to the decision-making process. Yet as we have seen, most types of societal structures over the centuries have adopted forms of the organic tradition, either by necessity or choice, from people scrabbling out a hand-to-mouth living to ordinary people wanting to live on their own plot in their own house in the suburbs to the rich seeking visions of pre-urban country bliss—the romantic landscape, curving roads, picturesque and changing views, a studied informality, the simple life.

The formalist tradition, with its classic, sometimes monumental forms, is usually associated with hierarchically layered, sometimes authoritarian societal structures. It takes a central authority to impose a grid or other prospective form on a city-to-be, and it takes concentrated resources to rein in the vagaries of the natural world to serve that society with infrastructure systems that make life better. At the same time, the undifferentiated grid can be thought of as egalitarian from a formal perspective, since as a public network it nominally affords equal access to the blocks, if not the buildings, that it encompasses.

The modernist tradition, while tracing its roots to visions of egalitarianism, in fact seems to depend even more on central power and authority to actualize itself than does the formalist tradition. Most of the visions of modernist urbanism, as overarching, often one-dimensional concepts, depend on concentrated wealth, major infrastructure, land clearance, and large-scale development projects to take actual form. As we have seen, modernism tends to leave both ordinary people and the natural environment out of its equations, instead looking for magic bullet solutions for narrowly defined technical or aesthetic problems. Modernism creates scaleless constructs to which both people and nature have to conform. At the same time, however, the precepts and practices of modernism raised the bar on expectations that all should be able to live at a higher level, including adequate shelter, working water and sewer systems, decent workplaces, and accessible parklands.

In their most imageable forms, we can see many examples of how the traditions mix with each other all along their histories. Thomas Jefferson, one of this country's great civic-scale designers and a staunch proponent of the grid as the base for city design, melded geometry and nature in the great University of Virginia mall, with its orthogonal order connecting to the natural world and aimed at the natural horizon. His flair for the picturesque similarly shows in his siting of Monticello. Ebenezer Howard's model, while responding to the need for people to reconnect with the healthful aspects of nature as a relief from foul industrial cities, created diagrams that could be and have been interpreted in the forms of all three traditions.

Focusing on more recent practice, Radburn, while an exemplar of the garden suburb in terms of interplay between built and natural worlds, shows the influence of modernism in its superblock framework and its rigid separation between vehicular and pedestrian travel systems. Clarence Perry's neighborhood unit diagrams, while a model for the planned city, again places the "ideal" neighborhood within a larger-scale

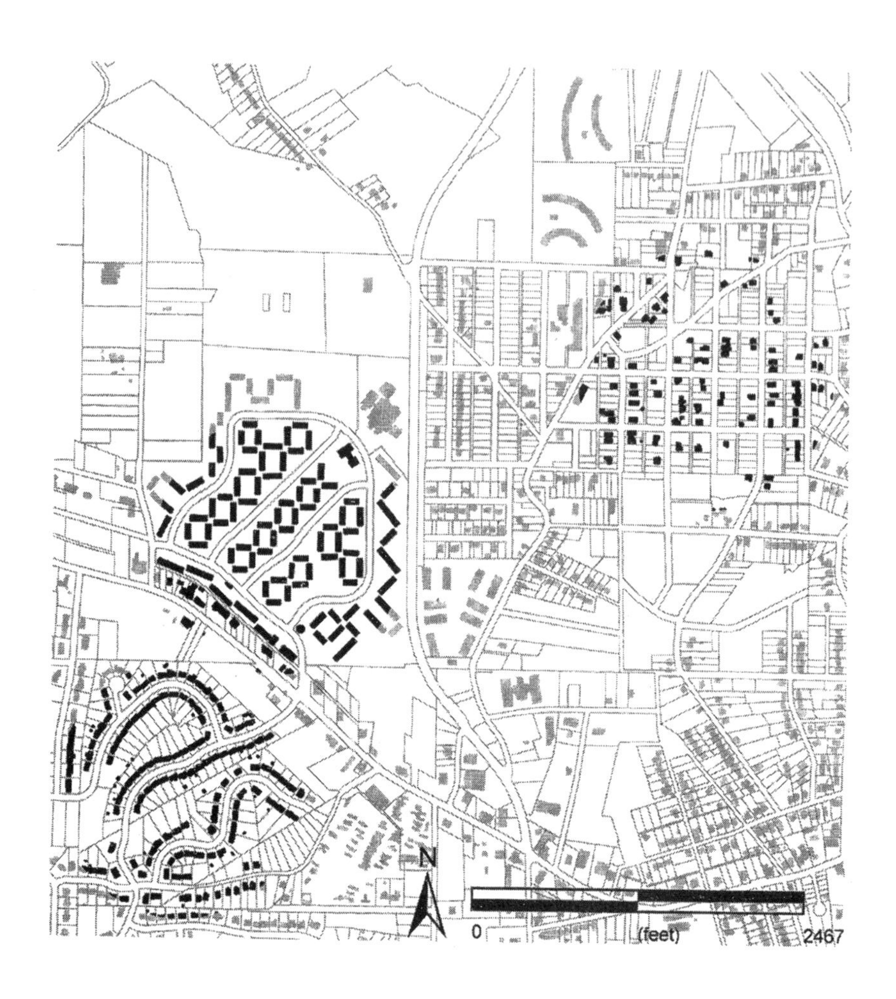


*Figure 2.20*
*Figure-ground map of a random slice of Atlanta, showing the coexistence of the three traditions (darkened areas show from lower left to upper right organic, modernist and formalist), typical of patterns found in most cities' spatial form.*

grid that could be termed a superblock, and it bends its internal grid systems in a gesture toward the picturesque.

Robert Moses, who had a significant role in shaping New York City and broad influence on high-handed approaches in other cities, drew on all three traditions. Moses reshaped the city with freeways that took advantage of the technical efficiencies of following the waterfronts or ripping through poor people's neighborhoods, where land was cheaper and people less able to resist. People were thus essentially disconnected from the city's most powerful natural features, and urban renewal "took care of" the poor people. At the same time, he created systems of grand parks that were genuine and beloved picturesque and functional amenities. His manner reflected his work, evoking both the formal assertiveness of the monumental tradition as well as the expression of singular power associated with it.

Meanwhile, suburbs, while overall responding to a kind of incremental, back-to-nature logic and seemingly laissez-faire—though in fact heavily subsidized—market forces, display modernism's stringent separation-of-use principles. There are usually no shops in subdivisions. There are usually no houses on commercial strips. Offices are penned up in office parks. Malls are centered on shimmering asphalt superblocks.

On another front, cities laid out on the grid may spice up their geometry by preserving a street or two laid down according to the organic tradition, like the curving, pre-grid Broadway in Manhattan, which creates an exciting tension wherever it crosses the grid. Grids may also clash, like one oriented north-south jamming into one that was laid out according to preexisting orientations or natural features, like Market Street in San Francisco or Broadway in Denver. In New Orleans, the French Quarter establishes a grid on a bend of the Mississippi River, setting up subsequent efforts to meld grids with the sinuosness of the river and the topography of the historic natural levees. Olmsted's Central Park, the lungs for a dense city, gains naturalistic symbolic power from its juxtaposition with the rigidly formalist grid that encloses it. Reflecting Ebenezer Howard's garden city model, Reston, Virginia, blends formalism in its original town square, more properly horseshoe, anchoring a suburbanscape beyond. In the formalist, self-contained design for the model new urbanist Seaside project, street axes executed in the grand manner engage the picturesque, connecting the eye to the Gulf or other natural landscapes beyond.

# Getting to Where We Are Today

What are the current dynamics between the forces now designing and building urban places? How do these affect place design at all scales? How have the traditions evolved in practice? What role have people played in influencing how urban design traditions have progressed? And how have the professions that play key roles in designing cities evolved? The following observations bring the history of urban design up to date and prepare the way for considering the Content, Principles, and Processes—the remaining three parts of the book—that students, professionals, and citizens may consider as they engage their urban issues.

To begin with, what happened to modernism as a major determinant of the form and function that have shaped so many urbanized areas over the last 50 years? Modernism took root in the interwar period and dominated thinking about how to go about the massive rebuilding after the smoke cleared to reveal the refuse of war in Europe and how to level America's visible expressions of poverty—urban slums. Modernism's role as a guiding theory for city design was not seriously challenged until people began to figure out that, while modernists designed some keen and elegant buildings, their designs at the scale of cities simply didn't work. Lewis Mumford had been railing against many of its impacts since the 1920s, and others from the local to the national level were building up similar messages.

The effective pushback against this movement's influence came from three sources. First, there was a growing outcry against the destruction of places of familiar and treasured cultures coupled with their replacement with palpably inferior forms. Jane Jacobs epitomized this source of resistance and became its best-known spokesperson, most notably in her book *The Death and Life of Great American Cities* in 1961.

Second, the stirrings of environmentalism, while not particularly aimed at modernist urbanism, began to lay the basis for understanding the inescapable interactions between nature and the form of human settlements. That nature could—and should—be overcome, controlled, or engineered into irrelevance, the modernist attitude, ran up against powerful assertions to the contrary. In a way paralleling Jacobs, the nascent

---

Post-modernism in its reaction to modernism looked back stylistically to the artifacts of the classical traditions: ersatz columns, pediments, ornamentation, bay spacing, and roofs pitched and vaulted in various ways instead of being flat. San Francisco in the 1970s, for example, had a veritable revolution against what was characterized as "Manhattanization," a proliferation of "cereal box" towers that destroyed the profile of the city's treasured seven hills. An early practitioner of the newly emerging field of urban design, Richard Hedman, an employee of the city, was instrumental in crafting new zoning and development rules that effectively barred flat-tops and at the same time assured that the sun could reach the street. (Somehow, while modernism emphasized solar orientation as a key component of its theory, in the rough and tumble of real estate–driven projects such obvious criteria as sun angles had left the lexicon of many modernist designers; real light and air were replaced with artificial light and air technology.)

At one end of the scale, post-modernism reincorporated scale, proportion, and detailing that evoked earlier times, probably more for their incorporation of the scale of the human body into design than for the details themselves. Strip shopping centers and malls began to sprout Dryvit* pediments, cornices, columns, arcades, and other details, usually painted a shade of beige.

*(continues on the next page)*

** Dryvit was a brand name describing a Styrofoam-based material that was easy to mold and apply to an underlying structure, both for insulation and adaptability for various decorative motifs.*

*(continued from the previous page)*

At the other end of the scale, post-modernists like Robert Venturi, took it upon themselves to celebrate the physical urban artifacts of market capitalism—both the form and the meaning. Whatever was made in the mass market should be extolled as models for form in our times. This tendency seemed to accept that whatever was produced at a profit must be what people wanted, that the forms generated by the "free" market must be the marker of what people value and the kinds of places where they want to live, missing the link that profit drives product in a market economy more than need or desire. In the pop art movement, however, exemplified by Andy Warhol, attitudes were able to shift to satire while in architecture, probably because buildings are so expensive, any satirical subtexts were muted at best. Post-modernism, while never really developing a cohesive urbanist position, contributed to the groundwork out of which ideas like Traditional Neighborhood Development and New Urbanism arose.

Ominously, the formal precepts of modernism are reemerging at the larger-than-building scale among richly patronized, neo-modernist, neo-expressionist architects. These practitioners hold considerable sway among the collector class, many of whose members have the power and authority to assert their values over larger urban territories. The results threaten, like modernism, a new wave of urbanscapes that are neither responsive nor respectful of ordinary people's needs or cultures.

1960s' most influential popularizer of this view was Rachel Carson, whose *Silent Spring* in 1962 both resonated with widespread uneasiness about development practices and affirmed taking a whole different approach to understanding the environment and humans' effect on it.

Finally, the unrest over how "the establishment" was mismanaging the people's business across a spectrum of issues—civil rights, the Vietnam War, gender equity, consumer protection, environmental degradation—in the area of urban form spotlighted failings of the modernist experiment, as epitomized by urban renewal with its assaults on both space and culture. This point of attack against modernism's design and development tenets reflected Jacobs' positions to some extent as well as a broader, more diffuse cross section of U.S. citizens concerned about empowerment—their ability to participate in the form of their future, as addressed in more detail in the prior chapter.

Physical design responses to the pushback took different forms. Jacobs reintroduced people, their life patterns, and their scale to the mainstream of city planning and design, and, it seemed, buried modernism and its precepts as a way to approach city and place design. Historic preservation rose up as a powerful counterforce, first in preserving the artifacts of earlier social orders but then sweeping into the preservation of the vernacular neighborhoods and cross sections of American culture. Architecture in the aftershocks of Jacobs' commonsense revelations, as is its wont, exhibited stylistic as much as substantive responses, moved into post-modernism, deconstructivism, and new urbanism. Of these, only new urbanism puts forward a civic-scaled vision, drawing in many ways on Jacobs-oriented visions of what settlements should look like. Landscape architecture, meanwhile, began to link its practice to the emerging environmental movement, as its reaction against the technocratic failings of modernism.

It took some years and a growing litany of voices supporting Jacobs's theses and environmental sustainability precepts to turn the tide of modernism. Its underlying flaws as a form-giving concept continued apace, destroying pieces of existing towns and cities through urban renewal and creating new one-dimensional suburban barrens around cities throughout the United States and Europe. The most effective challenges to modernist theories of city design come from the dual prongs of environmentally sustainable and urban form alternatives. Smart growth provides a promising framework for reordering urban growth patterns around the underlying themes of environmental sustainability, energy conservation, and community health, which many associate with compact, transit-served, walkable urban patterns and forms of any style. New urbanism—actually, returning to old, pre-modernist urbanism—provides for more human-scaled patterns that are showing increasing strength in interaction with changing development and investment markets.

# Environmentalist Responses—From Exploitation to Balance

More and more people have become alarmed at the degradation of the natural world wrought by land-eating, air- and water-polluting development practices. The "rational," technocratic approaches to overcoming the constraints that nature puts on development have revealed their flaws. Linear, nonintegrated technological "solutions" for car-based transportation, water, sewer, storm water runoff, along with deforestation, regrading, leveling, loss of farmland, species extinction, depletion of natural resources, topped by polluting the atmosphere by generating electricity, manufacturing, and ever-growing car use simply aren't working. Rachel Carson's haunting scenarios of a dying planet both made the case and confirmed anxieties that people all over the country were beginning to have about the state of the natural world and our dependence on it. These sentiments tap many of the same roots that characterize the naturalistic tradition, a desire to interact positively with the natural world, a yen for harmony.

Ian McHarg's *Design with Nature* in 1969 posited a whole different way of developing, in essence beginning with the natural world, honoring and respecting its morphology, ecology, and climate and accordingly developing patterns that had the least negative impacts on gradations of ecologically sensitive territory. Many other practitioners in a revived landscape architecture profession worked along similar lines to good effect here and there, though for the most part the offending market-driven development practices continued right along into the present day and certainly will continue (one hopes at a diminishing pace). In many ways, McHarg's work moved toward understanding and objectifying some of the tendencies in the "naturalistic" design tradition and advancing those values. The evolved pattern in this tradition, however, applied mainly to the tussle of how to build in greenfield locations, the ever-spreading rings around the core city and the sub-cities absorbed by the sprawl. More recently, ideas of how to better reintroduce the values of ecology into core cities, often on abandoned tracts, have been making a move that some call "landscape urbanism."

It was in the 1970s era that the concept of sustainability took root. Out of interactions among concerned professionals and academics, groupings in the United States and elsewhere in the world began to face the fact that the earth's resources were limited. The U.N. subsequently adopted a charge to call upon people to give back at least as much as they took from the natural world. In design and development practices, the idea is that development should aim for a goal of balancing natural resources removed with natural resources returned, a sort of "do no harm" default position on how to develop.

Environmental consciousness has caught on in most quarters by now, not just here but worldwide, and the movement toward a sustainable future continues to push forward. The Kyoto Protocol in 1997 and the Nobel Peace Prize award to Al Gore in 2007 are dramatic examples of the international embrace of sustainability as a concept. From growth management to linking private development with public infrastructure availability, to growth boundaries to smart growth, the new strategies call for settlement pattern trajectories that are different from those that have built the suburbs. The goal is to take less heavy tolls on the natural environment and to use less energy. Now, public health professionals are taking seriously the links between public health and settlement patterns, noting that individual health is in many ways linked to community health, citing walking and exercise as a basic indicator for any number of public health concerns (obesity, heart and lung conditions, depression, and so on). These concerns add to evolving notions of what smart growth is and the steps necessary to make it happen.

The Congress for the New Urbanism (CNU), beginning with its founders, have contributed greatly to the relegitimation of the formalist, classical tradition in the exploration of form, marketing, and regulation. Yet it represents but one of several explorations into this territory. Its inclination to "brand" the movement, perhaps reflecting the architectural culture out of which its part of the movement grew, facilitates its entry into mainstream marketing culture but perhaps runs the risk of the conceptual error of CIAM—that is, proclaiming magic bullet solutions based mainly on form to complex problems.

The U.N., following the recommendation of the Brundtland Commission in 1987, put it this way: Development should "meet the needs of the present generation without compromising the ability of future generations to meet their own needs."

Even in the face of on-again off-again official attitudes about whether people need to worry about the environment, encouraging signs of community consciousness and activism have helped launch such initiatives as the U.S. Green Building Council. This organization has shown remarkable progress in reforming designer and developer practices. From just a nice idea 10 or 15 years ago, the practice of designing and building LEED-certified buildings (Leadership in Environmental and Energy Design) has become a marker to which more and more practitioners in the design and development world aspire. Confirming the position of this text, the leadership and success of this movement have depended on widespread, growing, and seemingly randomly organized sentiments among people at all levels—environmentalists, young architects, academics, and lots of everyday citizens—where the commonsense logic of sustainability overrides the esoteric debates it engenders. It has not been an initiative of government (although a few local governments jumped on the idea pretty early) and certainly not from the development industry. The movement is now searching for how to extend its sustainability philosophy to the scale of neighborhoods and larger territories, perhaps the current best representation of which is in Douglas Farr's *Sustainable Urbanism: Urban Design with Nature*.

My colleague Andy Euston, who along with Jane Harkness and others mounted a campaign for sustainability in the early 1970s, tried to incorporate this aspirational idea by recasting "urban design" as "urban environmental design." Probably because in the 1970s urban design itself was not a mainstream term or concept, the insertion of "environmental" into the concept, itself a word still suspect in the general population, the term UED has never caught on.

# Design Responses—Old Urbanism to New Urbanism, or Forward to the Past

While the environmentalist approaches are more consistent with the organic tradition, design-trained professionals seem to be more interested in formalist or modernist approaches. The new urbanist movement, for example, in its essence derived from formalist classical traditions, returns to the punctuated grid as its form-giving concept. Yet it begins to assert diversity as a conscious and positive theme, not just something that tended to happen as in the earlier City Beautiful city forms. Thus, mixing housing densities, types, and costs; introducing commercial and retail activity (jobs and goods); and taming the car's dominance by building alleys, narrowing streets, and otherwise putting the car out of sight are all characteristics of this new and popular interpretation of the City Beautiful tradition.

Many of the applications of new urbanism, however, are to be found as developers' projects in suburban and greenfield locations, supported by their developer-friendly attribute of increasing densities on single-family-priced land. This pattern may bode ill for solving problems of transportation, congestion, and other infrastructure that is not sized nor conveniently retrofittable to the new, denser pattern. It is not yet clear whether the provision of mixes of housing types and provisions of some jobs will help the underlying problems of sprawl or simply introduce a new, harder-to-serve form into the amorphous overall suburban mix. The nominal commitment to the provision of some affordable units in new urbanist developments has largely evaporated as their market has heated up, pushing new urbanism into a high-end, high-profit development environment.

Atlantic Station in Atlanta, which I was involved with as the Commissioner of Planning, Development, and Neighborhood Conservation, and Stapleton in Denver are large-scale examples of the application of mixed-use, mixed-density approaches. Both aimed at replacing obsolete facilities—in Atlanta an abandoned steel mill and in Denver Stapleton Airport. In the Atlanta case, in addition, traffic reduction was a central purpose for public support. The project's approvals depended on meeting car traffic reduction goals, which it satisfied by its mix of housing, inclusion of affordable housing units, shopping, and employment and by connecting itself by shuttle to adjacent Midtown Atlanta and the Arts Center MARTA station. The goal for this provision was to reduce predicted vehicle miles traveled (VMT) to about a third of the regional average, a goal which has been significantly exceeded in practice.

The new urbanist way of developing small towns, suburbs, and greenfields has less impact on developed cities, probably because most of these already have in their origins many of the principles that new urbanism espouses. Atlanta and Denver, for example, have seen their fair share of new mixed-use, mixed-density, walkable developments designed and built. They have modified their zoning codes and practices and have prioritized capital funding to support public infrastructure to encourage the new—or really old—urbanist approach. Several new in-town developments are taking advantage of this flexibility and encouragement, from the infill lot scale to developments of large acreages.

For the most part, reflecting their zoning and street design guidance, these seem to dovetail well with their surroundings. They are working well in the marketplace (see Figure 2.16, Glenwood Park). Yet providing adequate levels of affordability remains a serious challenge, in some ways exacerbated by their very market success and attendant land value inflation.

In a climate of growing realization that interdisciplinary collaboration is fundamental to the business of making people's places better, there are encouraging signs that two of the better defined counter-modernist tendencies, smart growth and new urbanism, can better coordinate their activities toward that common end. Furthermore, the Urban Land Institute, the theory and practice home of the development industry and thus focused on "getting it done," has moved its membership toward better integration of both tendencies into their thought processes. Such syntheses, as with all interdisciplinary work, require listening first, respecting all positions, and checking ownership at the door. Emerging alternative patterns should continue to provide choices on settlement patterns, for many people better choices than what is generally more available.

Watch out, though. Modernism, now neo-modernism, has been making a comeback over the last several years, and in architecture at least it presently has reasserted its dominance on the collectible scene. Coupled with architects' never-ending love affair with creating new forms just because they can, now with ever more exotic digital design and construction technologies, the mystique of technology again threatens to keep decisions about how cities want to be out of the hands of citizens at large. The lingering hope that technology can overcome both nature and culture is always in service to those with the means and thus the motives to control it. There is another side to the technology picture, however, which is very encouraging for citizen advocates working to improve their public environment. Technology can and should serve better living environments for people. Access to and the ability to widely share information is supporting the proliferation of activism around processes and decisions that affect the design and development of places, acting at once to advance publicly held values and scrutinize and if necessary put the brakes on designs and projects that don't measure up.

The architectural side of modernism, after a dip in the 1970s and 1980s, has reemerged as a leading focus of critical and patronage attention. The "wow" factor of technology, not unlike what was beginning to happen a hundred years ago, has once again shown its ability to sweep people off their feet. Frank Gehry has been among the leaders of this latest modernist ascension (sometimes termed deconstructivism or neo-expressionism, but all rooted in the modernist tradition) with big-name patron trophy buildings, like the Guggenheim Museum in Bilbao, the Disney Concert Hall in Los Angeles, or the computer science building at MIT.

## Citizen Participation and Urban Design—From Receiver to Transmitter

None of the design traditions as they have developed over the last 150 years began by including the idea of engaging a fair representation of citizens in the decisions to be made. (Hence my enthusiasm for the growing use of charrettes and other participation devices by urban designers, which is opening the doors of decision to a broadening base of citizens.)

Trophy buildings are, in fact, very important symbols of the globalizing world, and people should reflect on their messages. Through banks, corporate headquarters, kingdoms, private equity funds, elite universities, luxury condos, mega-mansion retreats, foundations, and museums, they assert the order that holds and exercises power. They mark the time in history where excess combines with technology to express in in-your-face form the widest-ever gap between the few rich and the many poor. They can be breathtakingly dramatic. Ironically, many of them are fragile, possibly even ephemeral, as the push to technological limits either demands ever-rising levels of maintenance or results in accelerating deterioration. They are marketed and sometimes accepted as symbols of civic pride, but this architecture is not where to look for any expression of democracy.

Neo-modernists, extrapolating from building-as-art-object architecture like their modernist forebears, propose scales of city form that do not relate to human form. Rather they are scaleless, vast, costly expressions, which as buildings may satisfy those who pay for them, but as models for everyone else are chilling. Their progenitors seem to forget that most people get up in the morning, put on their clothes, maybe drink a cup of coffee, and step out the door, go to work or school, usually somewhere else, just like they've always done. Dutch architect Rem Koolhaas, for example, has illustrated a number of scaleless and chilling follies that seem to seek excitement and exhilaration in playing with the chaotic forms that market forces create, one of which was partially executed in Lille, France. Cool for houses maybe, but cold for cities.

On the environmental side, a longer history of citizen activism, often confrontational activism, is giving way to the recognition of the need for collaboration between citizens, the government, and the private sector to get things done in the common interest. In both cases, though, the citizen voice, as the ultimate judge of whether or not the quality of places is getting better, must be lifted into parity with private sector resources and government authority. The substance, relationships, and forms that account for cities and civic places should flow from some representation of everyone, and people working together must assert this role. Successful city and place design "solutions" can never flow out of a single head.

The dynamic between traditional narrowly held centers of control and the forces of democratization continues, slowly and unevenly tilting in the direction of more inclusive values—politically, economically, socially, and culturally. This dynamic cuts across the whole of the design world as well, and here the focus is on civic design, which includes planners, civil engineers, architects, and landscape architects. The urban design consequences of making representation, along with fairness and equity, an underlying tenet of community sustainability are significant and sweeping in their reach.

Remembering that urban design, civic design, or community design is mainly directed at public property, the public realm, good public policy would aim for its improvement throughout any jurisdiction without respect to class, race, or culture. People ultimately judge the success or failure of their public environment by how they interact with it, and it's in the jurisdiction's interest to foster positive response and buy-in from its whole citizenry. Civic improvements are all publicly funded, everyone pays taxes, everyone is supposed to have an equal vote, and so evening up the quality of the public realm across the town or city can only foster the kind of pride and confidence in the civil order that allows people to attain a better living environment. Obviously though, if equitable treatment of the public realm across communities is a reasonable standard, both urban designers and society as a whole have a conceptual distance to travel before this picture can come into focus.

Growing activism and sophistication among citizen leaders and urban designers present opportunities for engaging the particular design issues they may face. People active in the endeavors of improving places are certain to encounter forms and circumstances reflective of all three design traditions. Recalling their source, symbolism, and forms should assist in providing guidance for achieving better results.

While organic tradition began with people interacting with each other and nature to make places that worked for them, and thus had "citizen participation" engrained in its roots, the other traditions were never conceived as opportunities for ordinary people to engage in giving form to their public environment. Whatever role citizens might have played in shaping their places along the way, their influence waned as building practices were narrowed by mass production on the one hand and profit margins to mass developers on the other. As the stresses of suburbia mount, the attraction of more compact patterns grows, and access to information about all the alternatives multiplies, expect citizen engagement to increase. In addition, environmentalism is certain to reassert values of sustainability, with impacts on both urban form and societal structure, as the successors to the Bush administration are forced to deal with ominous portents on the environmental front, from climate change to urban environmental quality.

Regardless of which tradition is dominant, citizen involvement and active guidance, as shown in examples in the first chapter, can and should shape urban design thinking on formal responses to city design and development circumstances. Indeed, the interactions between citizens and professionals in the various place-making fields have galvanized the emergence, purpose, and content of urban design over the last 40 years. As a discipline directed at highlighting and proving the value of good-quality urban environments, most urban design practitioners by now are eager for widespread citizen input in their processes. Communities that function well and are able to sustain themselves often exhibit their social and cultural make-up positively in the physical places they occupy. This means that the stamp of the people, their footprints on their places, must show in their streets, their houses, where they gather, shop, work, and relax. On the other hand, the more the design of a place is prescribed and commoditized, the less likely people will be able to or want to make it their own.

The growing popularity of the older urban forms designed and built whether before modernism or reincarnated in new urbanism could be reflecting such places' interactivity and adaptability with the people who live and work there. The demand for better places suggests that, despite the waves of suburbanization and urban renewal, people have a yen for something more satisfying than the scaleless technological artifacts of modernism or the endless seas of subdivision that otherwise define urban America.

For those enthralled by the building forms that float across this scaleless landscape as somehow being free expressions of unrestrained market forces, it is worth remembering that the market is not "free." Anything built at the scale of places or regions costs a lot, is usually heavily subsidized, and is functionally and financially intertwined with public money, that is, people's taxes.

# The Place Design Disciplines—From Divergence to Convergence

In the course of designing the civic environment in the wake of World War II, the main participants—planners, civil engineers, architects, and landscape architects—have experienced changeable relationships even though at the end of the day their fingerprints (except for landscape architects, who entered the scene more recently) show on most of what people see and experience in their public places. The specific roles of each are dealt with in considerable detail in later chapters. Since their relationships are critical to achieving optimum results, though, these are worthy of some attention here in the context of the three traditions.

While physical design visions of how to live better at various civic scales were being promoted from all three traditions' design fonts, other observers and activists on the urban scene were laying the base for a more egalitarian vision of what American democracy might look like and how it might work in policy terms. Out of these broader policy-based initiatives, aimed at the whole of the living environment, city planning became a central discipline, with all its subsets—land use, zoning and subdivision, transportation, environment, community and economic development, housing, historic preservation, information management, and now again, urban design.

The relationship between city planning and related physical design disciplines has fluctuated through the years. Architecture and city planning were closely allied at the turn of the twentieth century, when attention converged on the plight of urban dwellers as a highly exploited, largely immigrant labor army and the realization that formal options existed for housing urban populations. Indeed, city planning as a field emerged out of the commitment and purpose to understand the source of the problems and do something useful to remedy them.

Planning and architecture, however, both got caught up in the momentum of modernism, planners succumbing to the flaws of "rational planning," a concept largely born of modernism's overwrought confidence in technocratic, oversimplified solutions, which manifested as a "we know better," paternalistic attitude toward people. Urban renewal planning coupled with modernist architectural assaults, along with brazen slum-removing road and highway projects, attacked virtually every city. These left legacies of uprooted communities and cultures, expressions of state and corporate arrogance, and laid bare the fundamental contradictions between the ideas of democracy and the realities of the market economy.

The disciplines that had been more or less working in concert in the wake of the City Beautiful movement diverged after World War II as people converged on cities. Each discipline set about trying to solve the urgent large-scale technical problems of urban renewal and of suburbanization, focusing on their own specialization to carry out these radical transformations. The civil and transportation engineers planned and built water and sewer infrastructure and roads and bridges to the countryside and to replace transit and slum housing in the cities. The architects, by now fully caught up in the modernist tradition, started building towers, blocks and bars of buildings on superblocks (with an occasional iconic trophy building). The landscape architects, not yet having regained the prestige that the Olmsted legacy had promised nor yet having discovered environmentalism, created landscapes at best in the effort to soften the harsh edges laid down by their engineering and architecture counterparts. The planners did the best they could to relate this wave of building to some kind of people-serving policy guidance, but they too had been swept up in modernism's thrall, and so the great proliferation of master plans and zoning and subdivision ordinances had the effect of codifying some of the more destructive tendencies within the modernist movement.

In the wake of the patent failures of urban renewal, planners, appalled at the impacts of their best-intentioned efforts, ran away from physical planning, redirecting their interests toward policy, regulation, and information systems, hoping to achieve through words what their participation in pictures had so disappointed. Planning became more about policy and less about place, losing the essential connectedness between the two. Civil and transportation engineering, using its own "rational" methods, kept on building roads, widening and straightening streets, narrowing sidewalks, accelerating storm water run-off and flattening hills and landscape. The engineering discipline was set on solving crucial but narrowly conceived problems, like how to get as many cars as quickly and safely by any point as possible, with little consciousness or concern about larger consequences to the overall living environment. Architecture backed off its Corbusian muse as the providers of vision at the scale of places and cities but stayed on its ever-aspiring course to create signature buildings for powerful patrons. Landscape architecture found its way to ecology, morphology, and hydrology, gradually gaining larger-scale influence from its previous site-specific-dominated practice.

This period of disciplines going their separate ways left deeply engrained professional cultures about how to do things, where the very divergence between them became badges of pride—and sources for finger pointing when things didn't turn out right. While this divergence contributed its fair share to degradation of urban form and the public environment, the reality is that each of these expressly place-building design disciplines does have expertise, and a lot of it. The job to do now, though, is to bend each toward conceptualizing a unifying vision of the best future, from the neighborhood square to the region. For this to happen each must listen and learn from the other, contribute mutually toward conceptualizing the big picture. Just as important, they must listen to the citizens there, whose interests will be most affected by any action, and whose vital knowledge base does not exist within any of the disciplines. Jane Jacobs pointed out the now obvious, that in city design the "experts" could not be counted on to know what they were doing. Her observations began the process of breaking down the walls that modernism's divisions and urban miscalculations had erected, creating grounds for citizens to more actively and confidently intervene in development processes and for urban designers to help the process along.

In the last several years has come the realization that all the disciplines share space at every level of urban place and how helpful it would have been to interact before construction instead of trying to make do afterward. Until recently each of these disciplines continued to function somewhat independently from the other, each with its own culture, certain in its job and expertise, rarely stopping to reflect upon the overarching interrelatedness of their endeavors. Now each is paying more attention to the common purpose that they all serve—that is, the overall improvement of the living environment (not just the driving or the aesthetic or the policy environment). Only now, in the last few years, after urban evisceration and regrowth, increasing ethnic and class strife, sprawl, energy and environmental crises, manifest failures to produce better places for people to share, people expressing their "fed up-ness," is serious attention being given to reintegration of the place-building disciplines. Urban design has emerged, albeit unevenly and haltingly, as a place where planning- and design-oriented people can explore what might happen if the basic tenets of the separate place-building disciplines could be brought together.

# Summary

We have seen that there are three loosely defined but generally recognizable patterns that account for much of the built space in urban areas in the United States: the organic, the formalist, and the modernist. Interacting with the people and forces that built them through public policies and private markets, these forms take on meanings that help us to understand where they came from, where they could be going, and how people can shape them to meet the goal of improving the civic environment. The forms of urban design reflect a complex interplay of societal, economic, political, and cultural forces. Whether they actually work toward improving quality of life for citizens across the board is a related question; how well they work, for whom, and to what end are crucial measures of their success or failure. It should be clear, then, that the forms of urban settlement itself do not determine the answer to these questions. Instead, the people who built them, who use them, and who live their lives in them ultimately hold those answers. The key to interpreting space is to understand people's roles in creating, adapting, embracing, or rejecting the spatial forms that emerge.

People's involvement in and reactions to the spaces they build and use may fluctuate just as interactive relationships among people fluctuate. Yet, there are enduring places, places that seem to largely transcend the vicissitudes of time and fortune, and as it happens, these may fall into any of the three traditions or their mixes. Much more analysis needs to be done to understand the meanings of place more reliably, but I expect that people will be found to be more important in imparting that meaning than the forms they create. Part Two explores in some detail the content of urban design, the ingredients from which those involved in place design and development create places that, however unconsciously, do mean something.

# PART II

# CONTENT

## The Elements of Urban Design

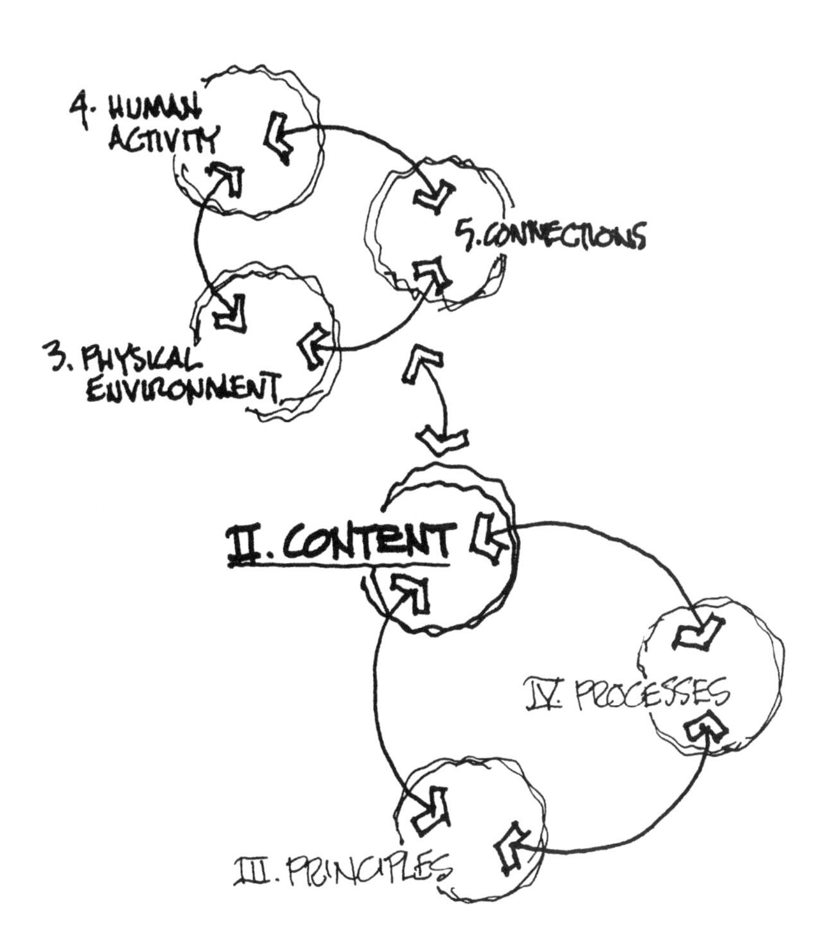


*Figure II.1*
*The elements of urban design, grouped into three spheres, each of which is in continuous interaction with the other.*

# Overview

In the broadest sense the elements of urban design may be organized in three spheres, each of which is interactive with the other: the **physical environment**, **human activity**, and the **connections** between.

Under each of these headings is a lengthy list of characteristics, all familiar to people in their daily experience. Those most relevant to public places, urban design, and citizen engagement are described in this part.

The **physical environment** for those involved in the urban design process consists of the ***natural world*** and the ***built world***.

The natural world was here first, and people have built their way into accommodation with it, for better or worse, ever since their emergence a million or so years ago. For our purposes, the natural world includes:

- Topography
- Geology
- Soil
- Location
- Climate
- Water
- Air
- Ecosystems

The built world includes the succession of spaces that people have built to shelter and shape the full range of their activities across time, place, and culture and across social, economic, and political structures:

- Buildings
- Lots
- Blocks
- Streets
- Parking
- Utilities
- Neighborhoods
- Districts
- Towns and cities
- Regions

**Human activity** is what people do, pretty much have always done, and will probably keep on doing. Typical activities are listed first with locations and kinds of places in parentheses.

- Living, sleeping, eating, procreating (home, housing—residences)
- Working, making a living, producing (office, factory, outdoors—workplaces)
- Shopping, trading, exchanging (shop, mall, market, marketplace—commerce)
- Learning and meeting other functional needs (school, health center, service centers generally—institutions)
- Relaxing, playing, entertaining (leisure, culture, sports, time off—recreation)
- Driving, riding, walking, biking, moving about, communicating (travel ways, communication channels—infrastructure)

**Connections** facilitate the flow of human activity and tie humans to each other and to the physical environment. These connections are the infrastructure that distinguish the urban world from the frontier and include:

- Transportation
- Utilities
- Communications

At one level, the elements that make up the content of the civic environment seem obvious. They are the ingredients that almost anyone who stops to think about it would identify as essential considerations in describing a setting or a place. It is remarkable, though, how frequently crucial aspects of a planning, design, or development process simply overlook one or a combination of these elements and thereby flaw the conceptualization of how to frame or solve a problem.

In my practice, I have found it useful to continuously remind myself of the range and scale, the purposes and meaning of the elements of urban design, almost like a checklist a pilot uses before taking off. In this way, even though only a few elements may play a decisive role in any particular urban design problem, a review of what *could* be involved gives some confidence that nothing important will be left out. In fact, such a review often does uncover an element, maybe not so obvious upfront, that is or becomes an important consideration as the process unfolds.

Synthesizing these elements to meet human needs in space and time accounts for the functionality and form of the built world and the sustainability of the natural world. People generally seek to improve the quality of their lives, to make things better than they were before for themselves and for their children. The interactions between human activity, the physical environment, and the connections between are what produce the forms and the workings of human settlement, from rural lands to the urban core, throughout time, across cultures and organizational systems, around the world. People everywhere get up in the morning, go outside, get where they need to get, do what they need to do, and return home on a daily basis. They experience the hills, plains, and rivers, the quality of the air, the buildings, the streets, the blocks, the landscape, the travel—and they have thoughts and ideas about how this physical environment might work better for them. People have the will and the capability to make changes that will improve their environment, complicated as that may be.

The interactive quality of these elements is the primary cause of their complexities. Whenever any element in any of the three categories changes, in fact or perception, it is likely to alter the substance or the priority of other elements. For example, the car has caused profound shifts in human activity, what people do with their day, and where and how they spend their time. And the car has irrevocably altered the physical world: the location, shape, and form of the built world and the character, quality, and sustainability of the natural world. At the local scale, accommodating the car has diminished other travel choices, like walking, biking, or riding transit. This shift has been both a conscious move on the part of car-related industries that stand to gain from it, and as a result of the almost magical attraction the car holds for most people, and the massive claims on space that the car requires. For six decades, government at all levels has prioritized spending on roadways, while relatively reducing funding for the alternatives. Pavement accounts for more than a quarter of all urbanized lands. New roads get built. Old roads usurp sidewalks with more and wider lanes. Parking lots proliferate or replace former buildings. Now many are questioning the inevitability, sustainability, and wisdom of the patterns established by and for the car. They are beginning to propose new "what ifs," new choices. It seems likely that the demand for alternative travel, with its associated living and working choices, will change the patterns of the last 50 years, to an extent still unknown.

People in every society have roles and responsibilities for these interactive processes. However consciously, effectively, or accountably, people exercise their influence and power through investment decisions as well as planning, design, and development policies, laws, and regulations. In the United States, the policies and regulations that shape the content of the world people live in include comprehensive development plans, general plans, land use plans, zoning ordinances, subdivision regulations, public works standards, building codes, fire codes, transportation plans, public facilities plans, economic development plans, environmental plans, and housing policies and programs, among others. These policies and regulations furthermore show up in more tangible form in capital improvement plans that identify sources and uses of the funds necessary to implement the plans and provide the basis for the adoption of budgets to do so.

The physical and organizational systems directing the urban design and development process are also interactive and therefore complex. People experience and come to understand each piece of each system every day—people walk out the door, hop in the car, pull through a drive-through coffee place, get on the freeway, exit, park, pass through the workplace door, and interact with other people in the organization to do or make something so that they can get paid. The interactive qualities of such a sequence of events are complicated more by the sheer numbers of their pieces and possible interactions than the events themselves. Over the centuries, people have met the challenges for achieving continued improvement overall, despite significant economic and political obstacles, occasional setbacks, and sometimes discouraging patterns of uneven progress. With all the ups and downs, as time moves along there are more people, living longer, with better prospects overall, eager to improve the functionality and quality of the places that cradle their lives.

People persist in seeking and finding better ways to accommodate and support their activities, to adapt these across widening varieties of physical circumstances, and to improve the connections that are the lifelines to a better future. This endeavor and its importance to human survival intensify as population grows. The premise of this book is that more and more of that population must be involved in improvement strategies at all levels if the challenge is to be satisfactorily met. The links between the world we have, how it got that way, and what people can do about it are decisions for everyone to make, not just the "experts." Therein lies the hope for doing better, and therein lies the potential for the trust between people and institutions without which effective strategies cannot be carried out. There are no magic bullets. The opportunity to do better is extraordinary: In the United States, for example, half of the built world where people will be living and working in 2030 will be built between now and then.

The widely reported projection of Chris Nelson anticipates that more than half of the built space people will occupy by 2030 in the United States will be built between now and then.

The following chapters describe in more detail the content of the places where people live. The particular context for the discussion is those public spaces where people share social and economic activity and opportunities for their improvement. Analysis of these elements and their interactions with each other provide the basis for the principles guiding their combinations in Part Three, the processes necessary for getting better places built in Part Four, and representative strategies for how to move forward in Part Five.

# 3

# THE PHYSICAL ENVIRONMENT

## The Places People Occupy

# The Natural World

## Introduction

*"In Wilderness is the preservation of the world." —Henry David Thoreau*

Before people, there was the earth. No place—urban, suburban, or rural—can happen in the absence of its physical setting. Natural world factors all figure fundamentally in the designing and making of places and must be on every urban designer's and every citizen activist's checklist. They will be more or less important depending on the particular situation. Professionals from the various disciplines participating in urban design activities will know a lot about one or another of the factors. The urban designer's job is to know enough to be able to synthesize a comprehensive picture that recognizes the importance of natural world factors and their interactive effects on each.

In recent years, citizens have driven the focus on responsible stewardship of the natural world. While scientists, academics, and professionals are playing significant roles in identifying, analyzing, communicating, and making recommendations, the coalescence of forces that has lifted environmental sustainability to a central issue happens because people, ultimately millions of people, treasure their natural world. These forces are achieving landmark legislative and regulatory advances, beginning in the 1960s with legislation like the National Environmental Policy Act (NEPA) in 1969 and proceeding at the federal, state, and local levels, albeit unevenly, ever since. More and more, approval processes require consideration of natural world factors, both for zoning, subdivision, and public works approvals and for consideration of use of public funds. While federal commitment and leadership has receded in recent years, there is no doubt that federal attention will have to ramp up, as underlying issues of environmental degradation and especially those swirling around energy escalate.

Over the last 10 years, for example, citizens, professionals, and now developers are increasingly embracing the U.S. Green Building Council's LEED program (for Leadership in Environmental and Energy Design) as a way of reducing buildings' carbon footprint. The program measures and rates building projects on their use of sustainable design features and technologies and energy conservation. The movement is now extending its measures to the design of places and communities.

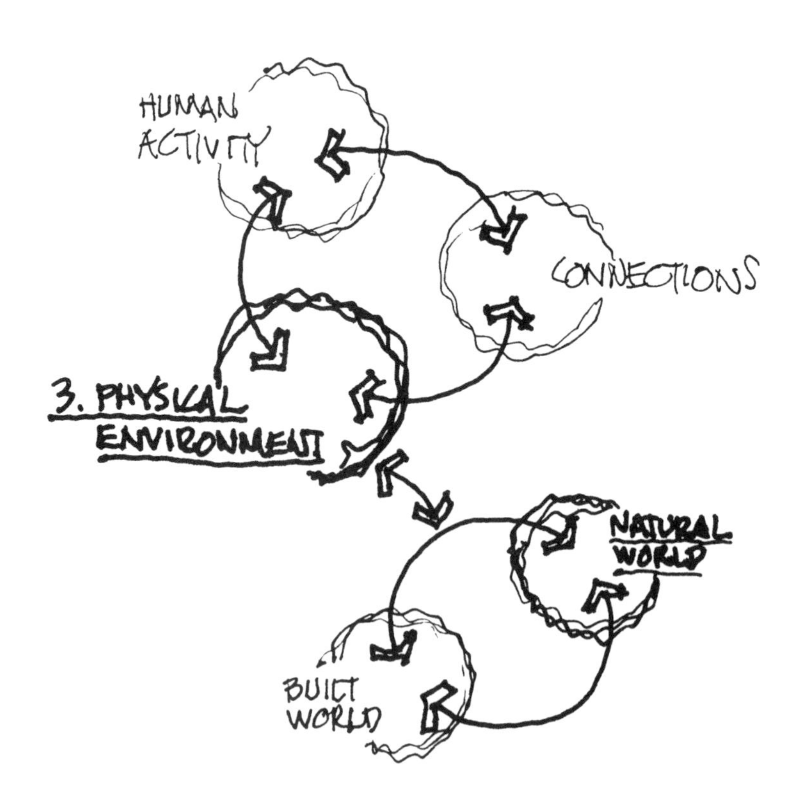


*Figure 3.1
The natural world interacting with the built world.*

Meanwhile, the citizens' awareness and attention to the concerns that prompted environmental legislation and regulation in the first place is now leading to the promulgation of higher standards to safeguard natural assets at all jurisdictional levels. Many of the people advocating for awareness and action to build more responsibly in the natural world are not credentialed "experts" in one or another of the disciplines that together build the world we live in. Yet it is the growing cross section of aware and committed citizens who do something else for a living that get the lion's share of credit for what is now a groundswell of support for more sustainable and healthy development practices.

## The Elements

How does this picture affect the work of urban designers and community activists? How do sustainable design measures figure into the design of places, from the neighborhood to the region? The following sections provide a sampling of how natural environment issues bear on the urban design and development of the civic environment.

### *Topography*

*"Over in them thar hills..."*

How does the land lie? Is it hilly or flat? Is there water? How does the sky meet the ground? Human activity upon the land has provided a range of answers with a range of results. A few generally familiar outcomes include San Francisco's grid laid across its seven hills; hundreds of earth-flattening shopping malls all over the country; Mesa Verde's cliff villages with fields on the mesas above; Seattle's "Denny Regrade," which flattened hills to make "development" easier; low-lying New Orleans and Amsterdam trying to control the water; way up there in Mexico City and La Paz surviving with less oxygen. Every settlement sits on the ground, yet how and why people have accommodated that circumstance stretches the limits of imagination.

The wide range of taming approaches is a fundamental urban design consideration, from the regional to the local-scale. Topography directly affects the particulars of local scale design work. From how buildings,

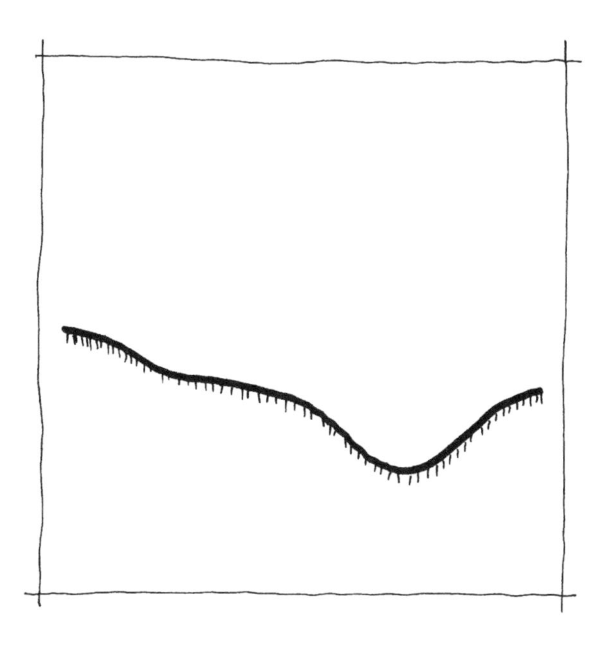

*Figure 3.2*
*Topography—the hills and valleys.*

blocks, and roadways meet the ground to how to manage storm water run-off are questions that affect virtually every place building activity. People's responses to these circumstances run the gamut from brilliant and enduring to uninspired and ephemeral, or even ultimately destructive. Knowledge and the willingness to incorporate topography in positive ways seem to account for the difference. The body of knowledge accumulated from centuries of trial and error is the best safeguard against the negative risks of unpredictable, unforeseen, changing circumstances or just plain bad luck.

Lessons learned from the mythic Atlantis, to Pompeii, to twice hurricane-flattened Indianola, Texas, in the nineteenth century, to challenges facing New Orleans, Venice, or coastal cities generally in the twenty-first, should be informing decisions about how best to make region-wide settlement pattern decisions in these times. At the other end of the scale, in an era that shows less tolerance for the negative ripple effects of willy-nilly land disturbance, urban designers must consider using land forms positively to shape street layouts, parks, civic spaces, and building siting.

In order to realize better futures, people working together across jurisdictions, disciplines, and interests need to remind themselves of these big-picture geographical and morphological problems, compounded by the underlying context of global social, economic, and political complexities and disparities.

## *Geology*

*"House built on a rock foundation—it will stand, oh yes, oh yes…"*

The most dramatic geological impacts on settlement patterns are earthquakes, tsunamis, and volcanoes. The knowledge base for understanding these threats has expanded exponentially. Yet the historic, cultural, and capital investment made in places at risk seems to have an inertial power that induces people to continue to build on fault lines, close to the shore, and in the shadow of volcanoes. Sentiment sometimes trumps good sense. At the regional scale, geologic factors are playing a bigger role in shaping communities' visions of their best future. At the local scale, questions come up all the time. What are we building on top of? How much

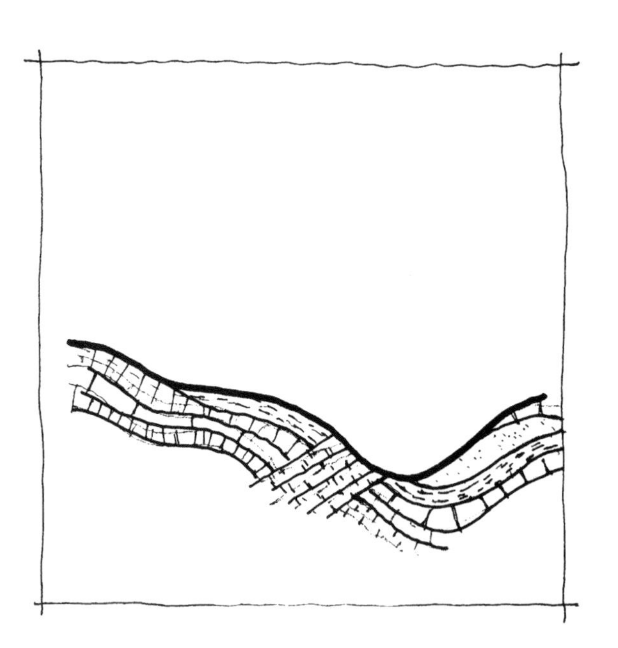

*Figure 3.3*
*Geology—the substrate that supports what people build.*

weight will it support? Or, just as important: Where's the water? How deep is it? Can we use it? Does it pose threats?

Along with these direct constructability criteria, it is worth reflecting that geologic formations account in significant measure for the building materials and fossil fuel energy sources at hand to shape building activities at the global scale. Rock and concrete and their availability directly shape the character and technologies of settlements, even now in the era of global transportation access. Iron, steel, and more exotic metallic materials are all transformed out of rock. And for the moment at least fossil fuels energize both the building processes and the connectivities on which the modern world depends. Oil, gas, and coal, all carbon compounds, account for most of the world's current energy sources. Renewable energy advocates suggest that geothermal sources could begin to join other renewable energy sources like solar, hydro, and wind power to shoulder some part of the ever-growing energy load on which people depend for improving their quality of life. More controversial, some alternative energy advocates tout the advantages of uranium and its derivatives as a necessary future energy source. While perhaps not yet, energy availability, cost, and environmental impacts will figure heavily into how we design our future settlement patterns.

Geology remains tricky, even now with our ever more sophisticated information-gathering systems and drilling and sounding devices. Yet we see sinkholes in multimillion-dollar highway projects, big change orders in construction contracts to account for the empty pocket found where rock was supposed to be, or to excavate rock where it wasn't supposed to be. For urban design, geologic issues are reflected in the built environment at both ends of the scale, consideration of which is essential and knowledge of which should reinforce design and development approaches. Urban designers need to be able to synthesize the geologic factors with others to help design the comprehensive framework to support community and project design and development. At the local place design scale, for example, incorporating materials found beneath the surface into park or plaza design is a way to make conscious the connection people have to what holds them up, a building block for the authenticity that people respond to.

## *Soils*

*"The worm has turned."*
*"Dirt, the skin of the earth."*
*"We are losing ground."*

Soil has always been a critical element in determining where people settle, stemming from food production needs. Soil along with climate largely determines the nature and quantity of agricultural production. Less considered in these days of corporate agriculture and dominant urban settlement patterns, soil nonetheless should remain on every urban designer's checklist. Increasingly affecting regional settlement patterns, farmland protection ordinances are cropping up with increasing frequency. Driving the movement to seek a better balance in regional settlement patterns is the likely slowing of sprawl patterns of development coupled with the threat of development on some of our most agriculturally productive lands.

Soils, like geology, also may supply basic building materials that shape the nature and character of the built world. Thus clayey soils provide the base for brick, its structural characteristics and its colors, or in dryer climates for adobe or other earthen structures. Similarly, stucco, plaster, and other materials typically combine clayey soils with gypsum or limestone-derived cement to provide weather-resistant or decorative surfaces to

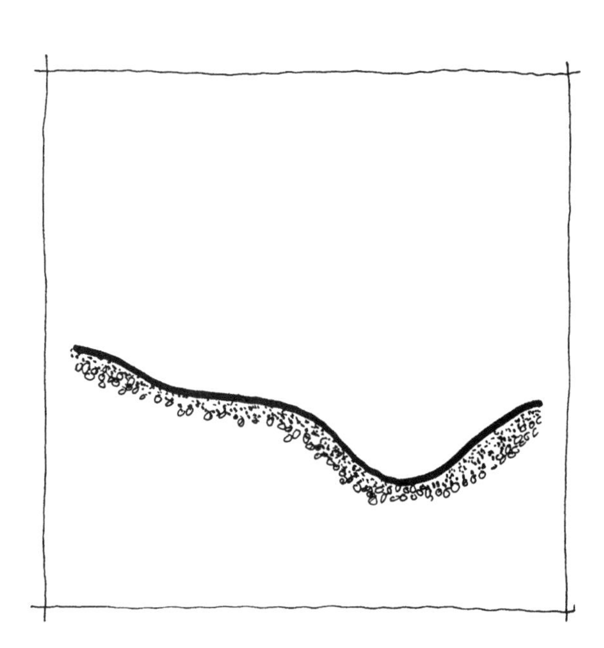

*Figure 3.4*
*Soils—where what grows.*

structures. These together link the character of the built world to its natural setting, reflecting the cultures that have forged these links for an improved living environment. Transportation and building technologies have blurred these links and their cultural expressions, as people can build adobe houses in Seattle or log homes in the desert, yet the links usually persist in defining the character of places.

At the scale of place design, urban designers generally find themselves working on previously built sites. What are the subsurface soil characteristics? Is there adequate bearing capacity for structures, roadways, or sidewalks? Is there contamination and if so what kind? What is the range of possible reuses of "brownfield" sites or areas? Is there a high clay content whose shrink-swell characteristics would discourage permanent structures? What soil conditions will support tree and other landscape plantings? For example, an abandoned gas station or dry cleaner whose contaminated soils are prohibitively costly to clean up in the middle of a streetscape improvement program may thwart the typical urban design goal of building civic space continuity. Similarly, soil conditions may dictate park locations or landscape enhancements. Better to know early in the process.

## Location

*"Where the hell are we?"*

Where on earth are you? For centuries people have had ways of specifically locating the spot they occupy on earth by latitude, longitude, and altitude. First depending on a succession of astronomic, navigational, surveying, and cartographic devices, the picture of where we are has taken a great leap forward in the digital communications era. Now, through global positioning systems (GPS), we can know precisely where we are on earth at any moment. By itself, this information is useful for documenting and measuring places. It constitutes a datum on which we all buy and sell property and design and build roads, utilities, and buildings. But it is an abstraction that says nothing about the character of the place. Each point on earth has been and will be the same for all time, but what's happening on the ground there is always subject to change. Think of a

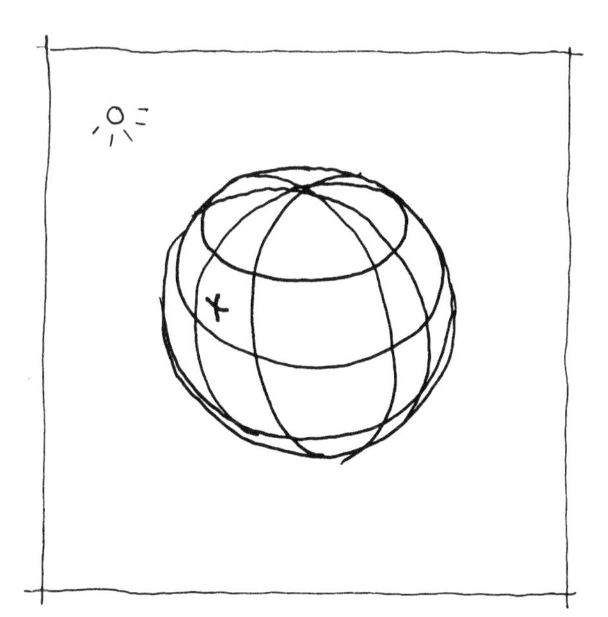

*Figure 3.5*
*Location—the latitude, longitude, and altitude unique to each spot on earth.*

point on earth from the geologic time perspective of water to land to water again caused by plate tectonics. Or, in the experience of many, the forest that became a farm that became a subdivision that became an apartment building. Or the sidewalk that got rebuilt to add car travel lanes, or the wetland that got turned into a parking lot—all the biographies of points on earth. These and countless other possibilities may alter radically—or not at all—any point on the globe.

For urban designers, the most direct and constant impacts on conceptualizing places driven by location on earth are the more particular orientation factors, like sun angles and prevailing winds, their changes through the seasons, and their impacts on both human comfort and energy consumption. This factor is much more widely considered than it was 20 or 30 years ago. Even so, it is remarkable the extent to which urban design and building siting processes are oblivious to this obvious and everyday information. The simple consideration of where the sun is at noon in the summer and the winter with associated wind characteristics can make a place swing from being hot and unpopulated to cool and pleasant. Or the opposite: A cold barren place in the shade can become tolerable and cheery if it is sun-washed. Altitude should always be noted as well, though it is less likely to be ignored since it is reflected in climate: The higher you are above sea level the more your climate warps to reflect more northerly climates (or southerly if you're in that hemisphere).

## Climate

*"T'ain't a fit night out for man nor beast."*
*"Oh, what a beautiful morning."*

Temperature, wind, and precipitation significantly shape the planning and design of regions, cities, and their places. People can affect but not control the climate of natural settings at the global and the local scale. Planners and urban designers have responsibility for assuring climate's consideration as an intrinsic condition in their activities. Wherever on earth one finds oneself, whether on the ocean front, in the forest, on the plains, or in the mountains, local places must be designed to reflect their climate. The technological responses to climate known as climate control have done wonders at overcoming climate-driven barriers. Air conditioning, heating, humidification, and dehumidification have enabled cities like Phoenix or Atlanta or Anchorage or Dubai to exist in much the same way that the Colorado River enabled Los Angeles. Yet what it takes to overcome natural climatic conditions calls into question the wisdom of planning and development strategies that depend on the commitment to bear those costs, a commitment that could become unpalatable or even impossible over time.

At the largest scale, the climatic impacts of and responses to the present climate change phenomenon appears more and more likely to fundamentally change the premises on which many settlements have been established. There continues to be much debate about the nature, direction, and global differential impacts of climate change, but less and less debate that the phenomenon is real, and now (or last year?) is the time to start planning for it. It's a problem whose solution will require a change in attitude and values, maybe even societal structures, not just technology—turning on more air conditioning won't work.

At the micro scale, working knowledgeably with climate can improve human comfort and contribute to environmental sustainability. Integrating urban design decisions with appropriate technology can increase comfort and lessen discomfort. The micro climate is a key factor in determining whether design and development forces make a place better or worse. If we fail to understand and apply climatic factors to our processes of modifying places, we are setting ourselves up for likely failure.

Think of empty windswept or sun-baked or shadowy "plazas" that deaden cities' office buildings or residential environments, or the ubiquitous asphalted urban parking lots, all of which add up to create urban "heat islands" where the temperature may be 5 or 10 degrees warmer than nearby greenfields. Or iced-up sloping sidewalks. Or, on the other hand, leafy garden settings in the deep South fanned by cooling breezes. Or bright, sun-warmed (though maybe space-heater supplemented) decks in ski towns. The opportunity for improving quality of life and quality of places through naturally complementary climate modification is great, and more and more planners and urban designers are picking up

*Figure 3.6*
*Climate—the ranges of sunshine, temperature, wind, and precipitation.*

the knowledge to make such strategies work. Managing design for climate poses a fundamental and essential challenge for advancing the integration of intrinsic natural world qualities and technological prowess. There are extensive knowledge bases for both, yet the knowledge gap threatening sound and sustainable decisions stems from the holders of one knowledge set not listening to the holders of the other.

## Water

*"Water, water, everywhere? Really?"*

Fluid as water is, it is a static resource, and so how and where it is located, distributed, and used is a major factor in determining settlement patterns. Should people be settling where water is scarce? Should water use be rationed? Controlled through pricing? What to do about drought and its cycles? How much infrastructure investment should be made to bring water where it is scarce, or, conversely, to keep water from flooding low-lying coastal areas? How much can technology safely overcome present water quantity and quality issues? Will purification tablets work well enough to allow settlement regardless of water quality? Are there technologies that will allow significant increases in the use of water as a renewable energy source, and how might this affect settlement choices? Predicting and planning for the answers to these questions are certain to reshape human settlement, particularly as the impacts of climate change become more compelling and better understood.

Water, like most of the other factors in the natural world, was a taken-for-granted, used and abused resource until the people-based movements of the 1960s began to call for environmental stewardship as a national priority. Concern about water quality and quantity, whether in oceans, lakes, streams, or aquifers, and concern about wastewater discharge, whether industrial, sanitary, or storm, fueled both the popular movements and scientific inquiry that led to the establishment of first the Federal Water Pollution Control Act of 1972 and more familiarly in 1977 the Clean Water Act. It set forth a sequence that prioritized cleaning up "point sources" and then "nonpoint sources." Federal mandates and federal funding jump-started meaningful initiatives, reforms, and regula-

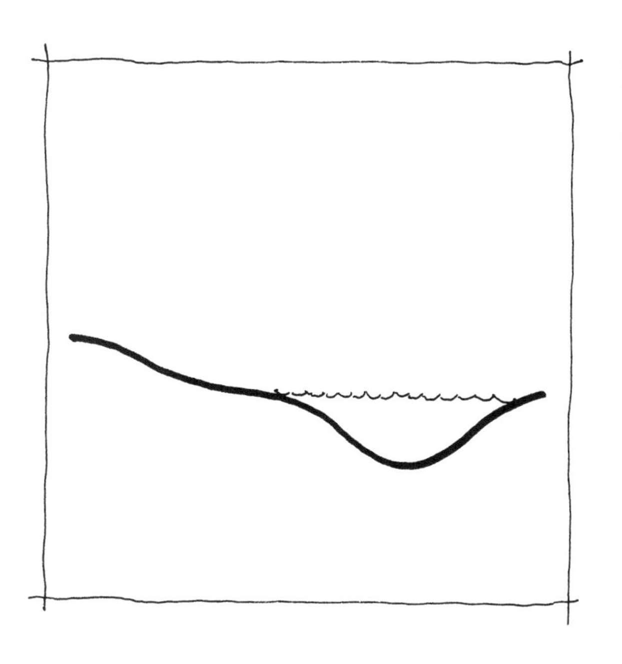

*Figure 3.7*
*Water—the fluid of life, finite and essential.*

tions that have slowed substantially the curve toward water quality degradation. As populations continue to grow overall, and as they concentrate in areas that may or may not have adequate available water sources, issues of quantity and equity among neighboring jurisdictions, always hot, seem to be getting hotter.

While forces working at the large-scale national and regional levels will try to address some of these issues, smaller-scale water issues have a major effect on local economies, settlement patterns, and even neighborhoods and centers. Planners and urban designers must incorporate good water design and management practices from the regional to the very local scale. Water is precious and finite. The more people spew it over the landscape or through their pipes, the more trash people dump into it, all out of ignorance or for short-term convenience or profit, the harder and more expensive it is to provide for demand or to get it cleaned up to a usable condition. Planners, designers, citizens, and developers face issues daily that they must resolve increasingly with the overriding purpose of preserving and protecting this vital resource. How to limit pavement so that water can cleanse itself through percolation, how to design and build permeable hardscape surfaces, how to discharge storm water, how to collect and reuse water, how to reduce water usage, how to incorporate water positively and visually into place and streetscape design are all questions for which interdisciplinary planning and design teams need to supply better answers.

## *Air*

*"...leaves me gasping for breath."*
*"I need room to breathe."*

Air quality affects both regional settlement patterns and individual and community health. Widespread citizen concern and increasing concern among health professionals about palpably deteriorating air quality was another of those flowers that bloomed in the 1960s. Pittsburgh and Birmingham, for example, both steel manufacturing cities, had reached the point in the 1950s that the sun never shined, and the birds and squirrels (and the people who had the means) moved out, leaving the cities to the people whose labor built the steel wealth to suffer the environmental consequences. The realization that urban environments were becoming uninhabitable obliged a change in national policy and national resources.

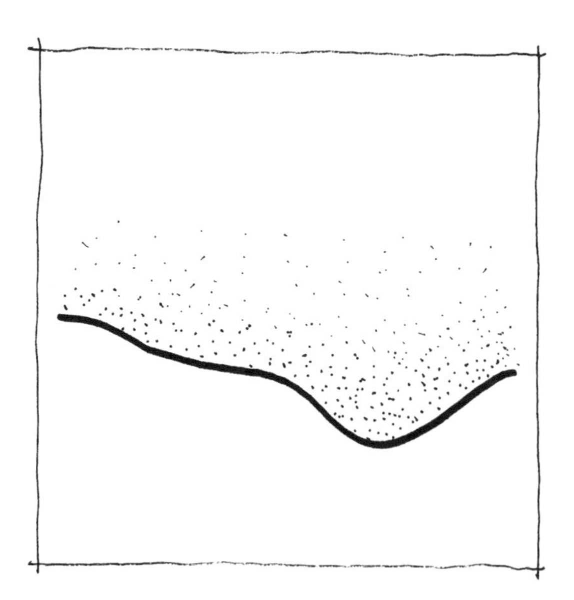

*Figure 3.8*
*Air—the breath of life.*

Citizen activism backed by science led the nation to establish ways to measure, analyze, control, and mitigate fossil fuel emissions, first brought together as federal law with the Clean Air Act of 1963, which was greatly strengthened in 1970. Health impacts of poor air quality were amply documented, and government at all levels acted to turn the course. Pittsburgh and Birmingham began to clean their air. In Denver, car-driven settlement patterns had fouled the air people breathed, and as a further affront shrouded the views of the city's iconic mountain range. The defining issue inducing the citizens of Denver to tax themselves to establish transit was air quality, not transportation balance.

Ground has been lost in recent years as federal-level leadership has favored narrower corporate priorities over broadly held citizen values. In this vein, it is important for planners and designers to remember that the private sector is rarely in the forefront of legislation aimed at environmental protection or enhancement. Think of the cigarette industry. Nonetheless, because of the 1960s movement, air quality in most settled regions is significantly better than it was 40 years ago.

For urban designers, the impact of air quality on the livability of our places and on regional settlement patterns is a matter of fundamental concern. Our choices have a direct bearing on whether air quality gets better or worse. Think of all the restaurants in Atlanta where, perhaps bowing to the deep Atlanta yearning for cars, outdoor dining decks often overlook parking lots, not gardens. Think of settlement patterns whose mix can reduce the average miles driven in cars and the move to green building that will reduce emissions. Think of odors wafting up from aging combined sewer mains. Think of the high incidence of asthma in lower-income inner-city neighborhoods, a health burden among all the others that restrains whole populations from reaching their self and community improvement goals. Think of the few furtive souls huddling around the service entry of downtown office buildings, puffing cigarettes through their 10-minute break before returning to work; 25 years ago they would have been blissfully blowing real smoke over their cubicles. Breezes, air flow, orientation, and landscape treatments can all improve the quality of the air we breathe in our public places.

## *Ecosystems*

No matter how natural or how wasted a piece of territory is, something lives there: flora and fauna, sometimes just bacteria. The quality and trend line for ecosystems at both the regional and local scale is another baseline consideration for urban design. Building on the legacy of the country's great naturalists from the nineteenth and early twentieth centuries and galvanized by Rachel Carson's *Silent Spring* in 1962, citizens and the scientific community sounded an alarm that couldn't be ignored. Scrutiny of growing threats to habitat led to waves of federal legislation and regulation aimed at reversing calamitous downward trends. While some of that momentum has dissipated, partly because the rules generally have shown results that have dampened urgency and partly because of the antipathy of the Bush administration, the underlying issues of habitat stewardship remain.

*"Where have all the flowers gone?"*
*"Save the Gunnison sage grouse."*

At the regional scale, for example, habitat continuity is a device that can shape settlement and infrastructure patterns that promote "live and let live" ethics in regional patterns. Knowledge of the species with which people share the environment is the first step for planning for the diversity that seems to characterize healthy communities, healthy for both people

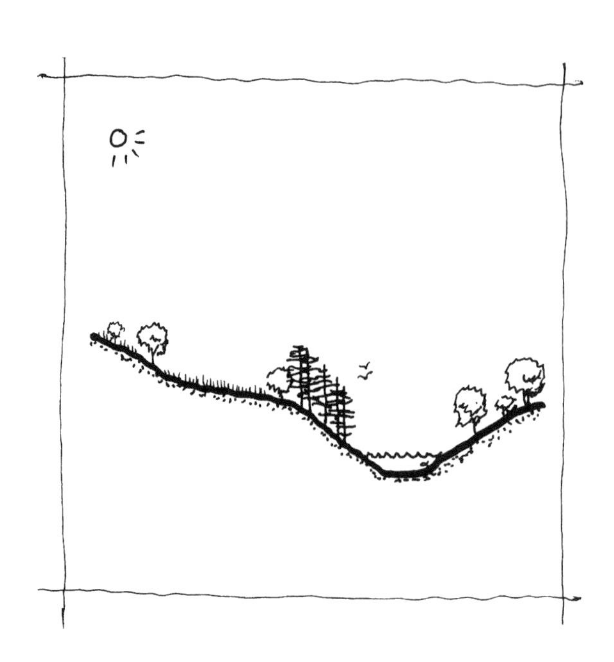

*Figure 3.9*
*Ecosystems—life in all its forms, across the natural world.*

and all the other species out there. At the local level, movements to "daylight" streams, restore wetlands, and bring nature back in the city generally are meeting with growing success and growing popular support.

Most fundamentally, ecosystem management directly affects food supply. What people eat, the sustainability of that food source, adaptability to changing climate, or poor stewardship practices all determine the character and longevity of societies. Similarly, ecosystems provide much of the material of which the built world is made. Most kinds of wood and even some grasses are ubiquitous throughout the built world, again reflecting and to some extent shaping the cultures that depend on these materials for shelter, from simple to elaborate. Stewardship of these resources becomes crucial to the sustainability of societies as well, with many waxing and waning as a direct function of their knowledge and responsibility for these resources. Finally, ecosystems provide significant energy sources, from wood to ethanol, where again a balance must be struck between production and consumption if these resources are to be reliably renewable.

At the place scale, where the existing or proposed environment is committed to focused human activity, ecosystems may not always play a significant role. It is nonetheless useful to be on the lookout for opportunities to bring the "natural" into the human setting. This is truer for flora than fauna, where the needs of plant types, from trees to shrubs to flowers to herbs, must be well understood before introducing them into the place setting. Ever just luxuriate in an urban garden with seasonal successions of blossoms and scents, under the flecked, filtered sun of a graceful tree canopy? Or, more ominously, ever see a dead tree, shrub, or weed lot degrade and even make undesirable a place that you might otherwise like to be in or pass by? But even animal life can have a profound effect on a place. Ever marvel at the twittering and rapping of birds in the middle of an otherwise mostly built-out urban environment? Or the other side of the fauna question: Ever see a rat, cockroach, mosquito, or maybe the trace of a pigeon that diminished your enjoyment of a place? What we do in designing places directly affects what is going to live there, including whether people desire to be there or not.

## Summary

As plain as the features of the natural world may be, as a practitioner, client, and teacher I have found it remarkable how frequently designers, developers, and community leaders omit one or another of the above factors as key considerations in their designs, proposals, or aspirations. Sometimes, these omissions actually get reflected in built projects, and a whole lot of hand-wringing and calls for common sense ensue. For us in the place-building disciplines, whether at the local or the regional scale, we simply must demand of ourselves and of others that we always pay attention to natural world factors. In the city and regional planning world, many jurisdictions require a "land suitability analysis" for larger scale land use planning and development initiatives. This is one way to assure consideration of these natural world factors. Places work better, feel better, and look better when we take these factors into account, and they may turn out as disasters or just plain foolish when we don't.

Facing the now generally accepted reality called "climate change," in which the interactions between all of the above factors play some role, those involved with the design of the civic environment will play a central role in coming up with strategies to deal with its challenges. One among several design responses to this challenge that is gaining ground is called "landscape urbanism," in which the sharp edge between natural and built is being supplanted with the interpenetration of the two.

# The Built World—What People Have Done with It

## Introduction

What kinds of civic environments have people built to support their daily activities in the physical environment? How have they engaged civic space to survive and even prosper in widely varying natural and societal settings? Who makes the decisions about how to design and develop, and what are recurrent themes for organizing the built environment? Why and how did it get like it is and what can urban designers and community leaders do now to improve it? These are a few of the questions that this chapter seeks to address.

Just like the activities that generate them, the types of civic spaces that people have built to meet their needs are in their essence neither particularly numerous nor complicated. The territory of the built world is made up of buildings, properties, blocks, travel ways, parks, parking, and utilities whose multiples form neighborhoods, districts, towns, cities, and regions. These pieces are designed and built to support the range of activities that make up civic life. Their infinite combinations in a variety of natural, social, economic, political, and cultural circumstances account for their complexity.

Yet people continuously synthesize these complexities and make choices about them, both on a daily basis and over time, however reflexively or forethoughtfully. Thus people decide what route to take to get to work on the one hand and decide where to live next on the other—short-term, right-now kinds of choices and looking-down-the-road kinds of

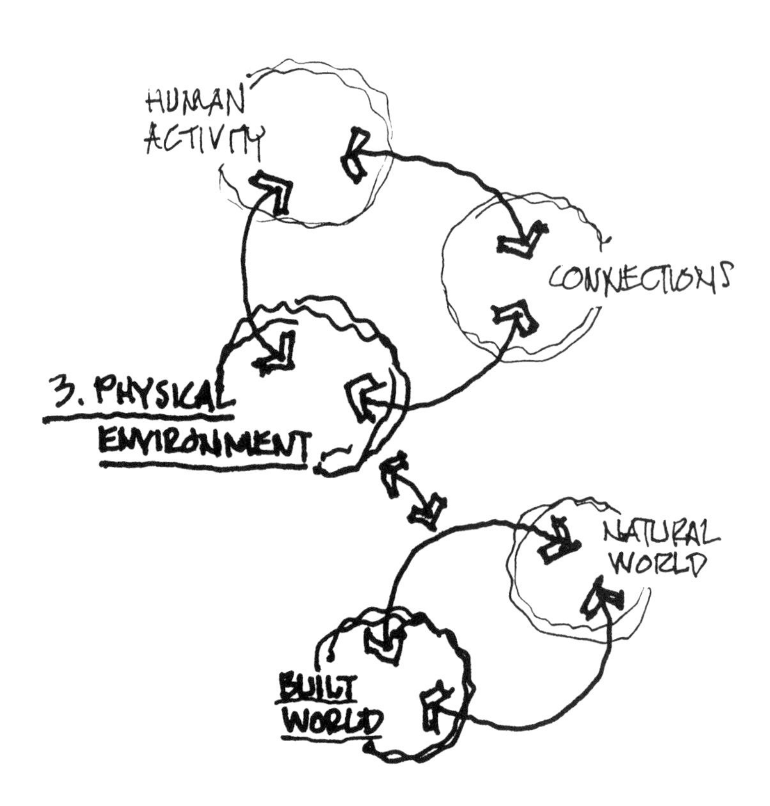


*Figure 3.10*
*The built world interacting with the natural world.*

choices. These are decisions that require processing factors whose interactions are complex, based on the best information available, screened through cultural lenses that in our times are dominated by marketing. Available information, what works best, what is most effective and doable from cost, time, and quality of life considerations are the senses that guide these choices. People then decide based on their experience and their values whether the choices made left them better off than they were before and what to do next. These choices occur at the scale of the individual, the family, and the community, and they form the basis for building community cohesion and leadership at the larger scales.

Urban designers bring to this daily and long-term synthesizing process a studied consciousness of traditional organizational frameworks and the more detailed physical parameters involved in making these choices. Their knowledge base includes all those physical factors at work and as much information as possible about the likely outcomes of interactions between them. In the built world, this means breaking down the whole into discrete, understandable subsets so that at least imagining the interactions between them begins from knowable baseline information. Based on these exercises, the whole is reassembled conceptually with the intent of making a place work and look better.

Along a commercial street, for example, relating block size to the activities along the block front and to the character of the street traffic along the block will join with economic, social, and cultural factors to describe a place. The mix of these separate elements will determine its character: Are the sidewalks wide enough and pleasantly walkable? Are the building fronts and their contents visible and accessible? Is there on-street parking? Is there an appropriate balance of space given to cars and pedestrians? These are the kinds of questions relating to spatial interactions about which urban designers should have objective knowledge and the insight of experience.

## The Elements

What follows is a description of the elements that make up the built world, a palette of what they are, why they're important, how they might get put together and why, and ideas about how their complexities might be managed. The chapter is organized in two parts. The first introduces consideration of the building blocks of places—the building, the lot, the block, and the street—and how these elements combine to define public space at the scale of local places. The second addresses how these various syntheses form neighborhoods, districts, corridors, towns and cities, and finally regions. You will see that the elements themselves are quite comparable across time, space, and society. Their interactions with each other and the resulting character of places created, however, vary as widely as do people and the environments in which they find themselves. These descriptions set up the following sections on principles and processes through which improvements may be realized.

### *Buildings*

From the earliest time, people have built structures to house their activities. Initially, the need for basic shelter generated building responses. Getting out of the rain, the snow, the heat, the cold, conserving tools, food, and other resources all advanced the quality of life for people. The needs for shelter have been broadening ever since. Examples of how buildings respond to human activities include sheltering family, supporting livelihood, providing defense, housing the exchange of goods and services, providing for recreation or entertainment, meeting learning and other functional needs, expressing societal hierarchies, and exalting spiritual beliefs.

Buildings all sit on the ground. Consequently they all must accommodate themselves to the natural conditions of that place. Over time better ways of

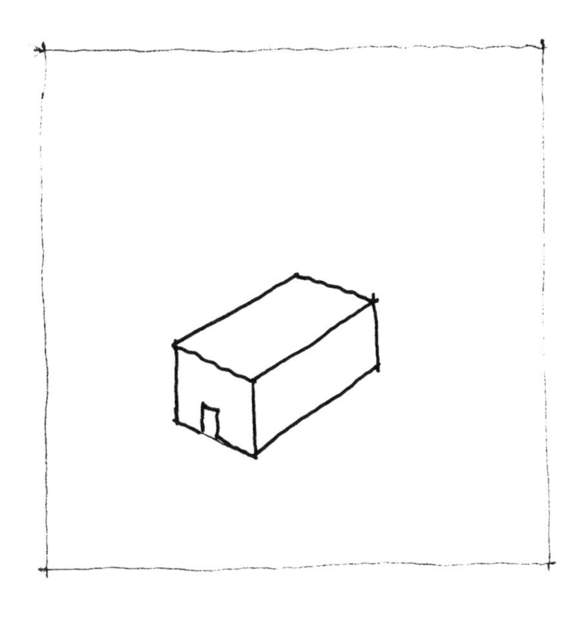

*Figure 3.11*
*Building—human shelter.*

fulfilling that goal emerge, through trial and error and through insights, both empirical and inspired. Buildings occupy a very specific spot of territory for an indeterminate span of time, based on their fulfilling a human need, their structural permanence, and their priority for that particular spot.

For urban designers, the innards and private functions of buildings are mainly of interest as they are accessible, visible, and usable in defining the interface between private space and public space. Together, buildings are significant in imparting the character and establishing the functionality of the public realm in ways that need the attention of urban designers. How they are used; how they are sited; how long, deep, and high they are; how they frame public ways; their ingress and egress; where to park the car; the way they meet the ground and are silhouetted against the sky; how they turn corners; their materials; their day and night light qualities; their bay spacing; their stairways; and their front yards are some of the main considerations in designing the public realm.

## *Lots*

In the United States the spots of land occupied by buildings and their associated front, side, or rear yards are most commonly referred to as lots, parcels, plots, or properties. Property is always owned, either by private or government entities. The right to property is a fundamental Constitutional tenet. The rights to use that property, however, are moderated by the rights of others affected by that use, most often in the forms of zoning and subdivision laws. Accordingly, while individual lots and whatever buildings may occupy them are the basic unit of built space, their arrangement and their use reflects a legal framework of socially accepted limits.

Lots come in all sizes and shapes, from grand estates to postage stamp urban lots and even slivers of leftover property. There is a range of ways to describe them legally. Subdivision laws or other publicly determined policies and laws usually control their arrangement relative to each other as well as often imposing other layout or design requirements. In current times, since the arrival of GPS technology, property descriptions and surveys have become quite precise, allowing a clearer datum for resolving disputes about boundaries. Going forward, expect to see fewer instances of people fencing over their neighbor's yard or building a garage that encroaches onto someone else's property. At the same time, GPS technology frees property description from the kinds of orthogonal geometries that proved so convenient in earlier eras. Accurate descriptions of curvilinear street patterns and block and lot shapes have become as easy to produce as rectilinear ones.

For urban designers the layout and arrangement of lots into blocks are critical for defining choices that may—or may not—make places better. For example, zoning, the dominant guidance for property development over the last 80 or so years, considers each property individually. In addition to permitted uses and sizes, it controls lot coverage and open space, front, side, and rear yard dimensions, sometimes referred to as setbacks, often requiring large front yard setbacks to accommodate parking for commercial strips, requiring separate driveways and service access for each property. While this elemental, lot-by-lot approach affords each property owner the ability to optimize the use of his or her particular lot, it effectively denies the ability for adjacent owners to come up with shared approaches to meet common needs. Or to paraphrase my colleague, Jim

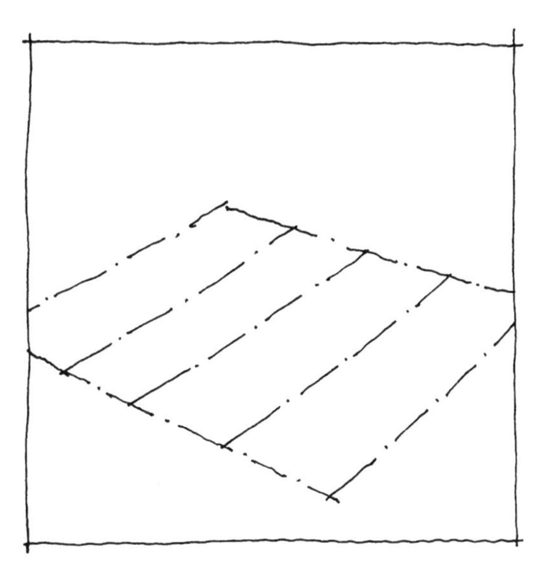

*Figure 3.12*
*Lot—the unit of private property ownership.*

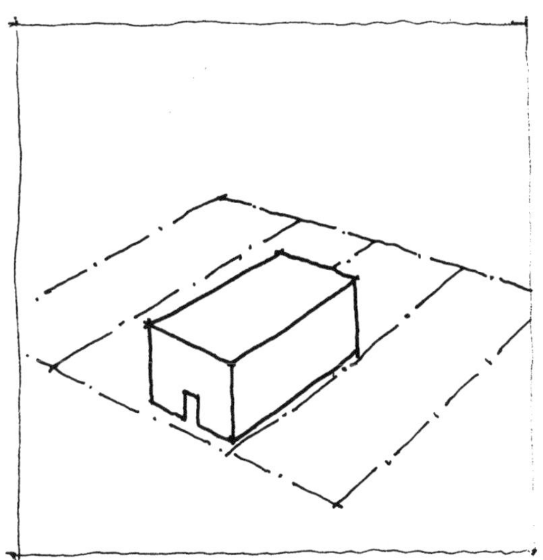

*Figure 3.13*
*Private building on private lot.*

Vaseff, "Zoning may optimize the use of each lot, but in doing so it suboptimizes the use of the blockfront as a whole."

## Blocks

Lots and the buildings that may sit on them are typically arranged in blocks. Blocks are groupings of lots whose size and configuration reflect the prevailing thinking of the time in which they are established. This thinking takes into account the natural setting, notions about the optimal sizes and shapes of blocks, and the best way to gain access to the lots and buildings. Further, block sizes and configurations tend to follow the traditions referred to through this book: organic blocks tend to be curvilinear, often larger, fitted into the landscape, highlighting or evoking a "natural" feeling; formalist or classic blocks tend to be orthogonal and regular, usually smaller, punctuated with axes focused on something important; and modernist blocks tend to be larger superblocks, often single use, reinforcing separation of roadways from sidewalks and both from the activities to which they

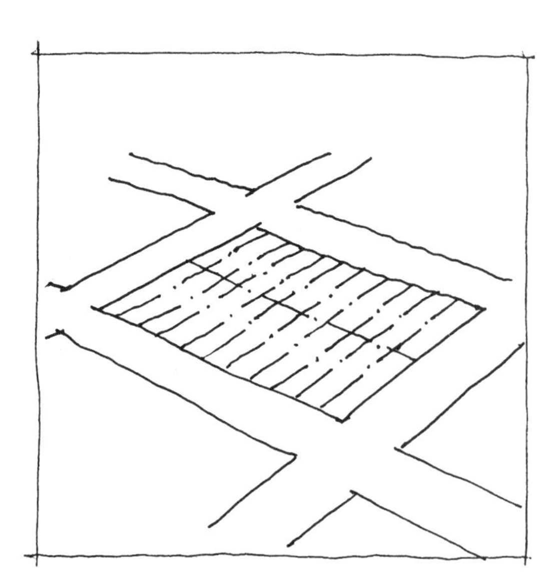

*Figure 3.14*
*Several lots create a block.*

are supposed to give access, hierarchizing streets, and in other ways bowing to the accommodation of the car as the inevitable city form-giver.

Block size, shape, and access characteristics should both meet current needs and allow flexibility for future reuse. Typically, the choices to be made in block design reflect the appropriate balance between access to the activities on the block and the demands for travel along it.

Blocks in suburban areas tend to be larger than in core towns and cities, reflecting the car as their dominant mode of access. Commercial strips depend on car access and by their length and layout their blocks don't lend themselves to pedestrian access. And the residential blocks in these suburban settings, also often very large, suffer in a different way as their disconnectedness and internal travel distances stymie retrofitting them for housing types that can accommodate the higher densities and greater income diversity that could support positive private reinvestment strategies. In short, large block sizes confound establishing the kinds of connectivity, reuse, and infill options that enable a diverse mix of activities and access choices to be established.

At the other end of the scale, smaller urban blocks in older towns and centers face challenges in accommodating large space–using activities, certain mixed-use buildings, and their off-street parking requirements. Getting block sizes and shapes right, then, is a central mission for urban design professionals, because blocks once built are likely to be around for a long time.

## Streets

Streets in all their permutations are fundamental shapers of urban form. At the larger scale, roadways connect towns and cities with each other and with the myriad of locations that produce the goods on which they depend, addressed in more detail in Chapter 5, Connections. At the scale of urban places, street design and its relationship to the activities that streets connect are in a state of flux, perhaps the most dynamic and affecting piece in the assemblage of buildings, lots, blocks, and streets that determine the quality and functionality of smaller-scale places. The general trend in this dynamic points toward rebalancing the diverse functions the street serves, generally lifting the priority given to the sidewalk, transit ac-

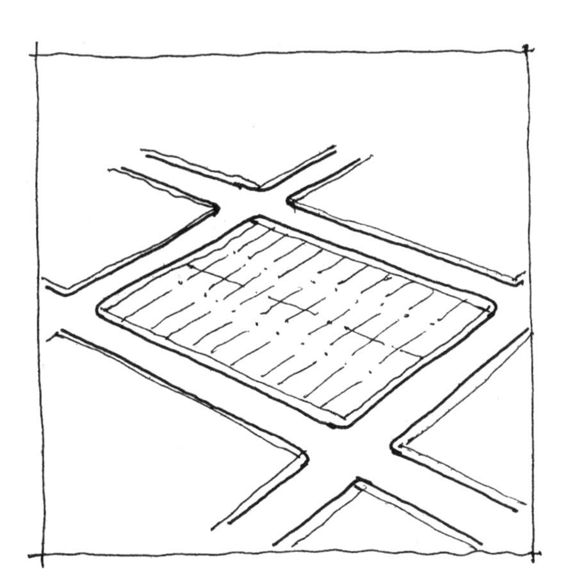

*Figure 3.15*
*Streets provide access to lots and buildings and shape block patterns.*

cess, bike ways, pedestrian access to buildings, landscape, and lighting, while still accommodating car travel and parking in ways that soften their negative impacts on the overall scene. The trend is driven by citizens who seek to improve their civic environment; urban designers and other professionals and markets increasingly favor this goal as well.

The advent of the car has dominated the design and functionality of the street over the last century, radically affecting the quality of the civic environment. The car's speeds and space requirements have utterly transformed notions of what constitutes an acceptable street. Mobility, being on the road, has been the primary focus of highway engineering, while getting to a destination continues to be the goal for everyone else. However the present trends play out, from the earliest times streets have given access to buildings and lots, arranged on blocks, and in so doing they tend to make lasting imprints on built territory.

Over the last 50 or so years, the fragmentation of the place-building disciplines has broken down the ability to conceptualize places as being whole and has had dramatic effects on roadway design. The emphasis on accommodation of cars essentially swamped all other considerations for what the roadway represented. The roadway occurs within what is commonly known as the public right-of-way, a significant term in civic design. Rights-of-way are the line of demarcation between public lands and private lands, between what the public owns and what private parties own. In the public realm, they make up the connective network of the built world. As public lands, they confer upon the public the right to use them for travel by all modes (walking, jogging, biking, transit, cars, trucks), for location of utilities of all kinds (water, sewer, and storm water lines, electric, gas, and telecommunication lines), for goods and services delivery and garbage pick-up, for public safety patrol and access, and for parades, marches, and demonstrations.

This diverse range of right-of-way purposes, as the network that connects human activity and to a great extent establishes the physical functionality and symbolic character of places, has been largely reduced and made subservient to the singular dimension of the car. To be sure, accommodation of the car in the travel way is usually the primary consideration in its proper use. The extension of freedom and choice enabled by the

Utilities are a prominent part of the built environment, which are discussed in detail in Chapter 5, Connections. Overhead utilities are the most visible intrusions into the built environment, typically lacing rights-of-way with poles and lines running every which way. Underground utilities, while less visible, are capital-intensive installations that make it difficult and expensive to realign the streets on top of them.

personal car has had a sweeping and generally positive impact on the march of society toward its aspirations for improvement. This accommodation must consider safety, car travel demand, capacity, travel speed, and all of the roadway design geometric criteria that come with the realities of car use. Without the resolute, single-minded, and effective response by the engineering world to the challenges that the car presented it is doubtful that the car would have so swiftly buried all other modes, beginning with transit, as the primary way to get around.

That very single-mindedness, however, so dominated the value system for designing places that it swept aside most of the other factors on which people judge the quality of their lives. Through the skewing of government policy and subsidy by monetary and fiscal programs, choices for how and where to live and work actually may have become narrowed by this dominance. People travel on a hierarchy of publicly built roads to houses subsidized by mortgage tax deductions and mortgage terms favoring newer homes in ever farther-flung subdivisions. While house construction costs are about the same, land is cheaper the farther out you go, and the opportunity for profit therefore high. These patterns have now reached the point where the costs of travel for many families in the median income range and below rival the cost of housing. Meanwhile, jobs remain more concentrated in clusters so that travel times to work continue to increase, for lack of viable closer-to-home choices.

Beyond the destruction of urban places that once housed lively street life, the single-mindedness of accommodating the car has blurred the reason for being in the car in the first place. Everyone starts out some place (like home) with the intention of getting to some other place (like work or shopping or school). The car is simply the means of traveling most of the distance in between. But every trip begins and ends walking—feet have not yet become vestigial—and the quality of the walking experience has markedly deteriorated under the prioritization of auto travel.

Think of the trip across acres of asphalt to get to the mall, or the trip through the parking deck to get to work, or the narrowed sidewalks and widened streets that degrade pedestrian safety and adequacy in so many neighborhood, town, and city centers. A compelling and ubiquitous example of car-think is the symbolism of freeway entrances and exits. You're only on the freeway to get from the place you started out to the place you are trying to get to. Yet you "exit" when you are arriving at your destination, and you "enter" when you are leaving. The message is that the freeway is the place to be, with the origin and destination as incidental afterthoughts in the minds of the old-time highway engineer.

I have tried to explain this exit-enter oxymoron to department of transportation officials in Alabama and Georgia, arguing that they wouldn't even have to make new signs, just switch out the ones they have. The conversations are at least entertaining for all. For such a change to occur, in fact, would take first acceptance of its premise and then a change at the federal level.

At the scale of the design of local places, roadway geometric considerations have widened lanes, narrowed sidewalks, emphasized speed over capacity, degraded transit options, widened turn radii, created acceleration and deceleration lanes at major crossings, placed lights to illuminate the roadway (not the sidewalk), and created signage systems whose scale addresses only the regulatory and wayfinding needs of people in vehicles. The effects on the quality and functionality of local places have been devastating. The pedestrian environment suffers from squeezed sidewalks; longer distances to cross the street; faster-moving cars; loss of the buffer that on-street parking provides; and removal of trees, plantings, and useful street furniture. These altogether diminish the attractiveness and accessibility of whatever buildings might line the blocks. These in turn may have been torn down to provide the parking lots required to replace on-street parking, less conveniently. All in all, it is roadway geometric design priorities that sacrifice access (the ability to get to the place you are trying to go) for mobility (traveling down the road, feeling sad).

Since transportation and specifically roadway system design is the dominant, most dynamic, and increasingly contentious of the elements that form our places at all scales, tracing its evolution and its relationship to citizen guidance is worth more attention.

Citizens and urban designers have played leading roles in seeking to redress the balance between the car and everything else in the urban environment. Now even the market is beginning to kick in on the side of providing the living and working choices that the era of car dominance has so narrowed. Resistance to the car's devastation of treasured urban places is not new. From the 1960s, ordinary citizens and the organizations they formed to save their iconic places have waged significant battles, some of which were mentioned earlier. These efforts are not always successful. San Antonio citizens battled all the way to the U.S. Supreme Court in an ultimately vain effort to divert the freeway proposed and ultimately built through the Olmos Basin. Yet even the defeats rallied citizens' efforts elsewhere to slowly but surely change policy and technical criteria for street location and design. Manhattanites redirected the replacement of the Westside Highway to a more boulevard-like street. Sacramento's citizens were able to replace a freeway widening with a transit system in the 1980s. Milwaukeeans tore down an elevated highway to reconnect the city to its riverfront. And, again, San Franciscans redirected the connection between the Bay Bridge and the Golden Gate Bridge from a limited access roadway to a network of surface streets. At the smaller scale, skirmishes are ongoing in most towns and cities over turning one-way streets back into two-ways; or pushing for on-street parking, or angled on-street parking, or pedestrian crossing traffic controls, or speed reduction measures; or removing acceleration or deceleration lanes on urban streets; or simply making sidewalks pleasant places to be.

As a positive example of private-public collaboration, when Atlanta won the opportunity to host the 1996 Olympics, one of its transformative achievements in bringing back the core city was the creation of networks of walkable streetscapes. The city, which 25 years earlier had dropped sidewalks off of its list of responsibilities in a cost-cutting measure, thus gave its citizens confidence that sidewalks were okay places to be, a lesson reinforced by tens of thousands of visitors. The consciousness, concern, and confidence that something could be done continues to accelerate and spread across the city—still, however, a long walk away from meeting its potential and the demand generated for a walkable city.

These kinds of stories are familiar to citizen activists all around the country. Each one is a difficult saga of persistence in the face of seemingly insuperable odds. Such blows for quality of life and quality of place, after all, rarely have been initiated by private or public sector interests, although public-private initiatives seem to be on the rise. Since these two spheres are in drivers' seats for most of what happens in the civic realm, they invariably look askance at some citizens' ideas about how to do it better. The battles, the strategies, and frequently the litigation may be titanic, and the David and Goliath aspect that accompanies most of them are further exaggerated by the great disparity of resources typically available to the community side for supporting "doing what's right."

At the smaller scale, sidewalks are coming back in cities all over the country, often at the expense of the very car lanes and narrowed lane widths that killed them in the first place. In a few places, like Portland's Chinatown "festival street," streets are beginning to share their vehicular travel surfaces with other activities such as pedestrian areas, fountains, public art, and the like—the Dutch *woonerf* providing the model.

Early experience with these experiments suggests that drivers are smart enough to make the necessary adjustments in their driving behavior, and that such concepts, carefully executed, might be just as safe as the

The *woonerf*, recalling the pre-bike, pre-car, pre-modernist era, proposes to function as a public gathering place, which could accommodate vendors, shoppers, gatherers, play spaces, and travelers in low-speed conveyances. It's the latter that causes the problem—whether in horse and carriage in the old days or cars and transit vehicles nowadays—of how to ensure reining in the car.

usual high-speed, highly regulated alternatives, producing a lot more balanced and pleasant places to be.

As citizens' organizations become ever more intent on fixing their car-damaged places, as the disciplines responsible for their design coordinate better, the effort to bring back quality and functionality (functionality here including social interaction) to street life shows more and more promise. These moves are interacting positively with changing retail markets to breathe hope back into the public right-of-way as a civic place.

## Synthesis—Building, Lot, Block and Street Put Together

As observed earlier, in urban design work the interactions between the pieces of the design palette are often more significant in determining both the functionality and character of places than any one piece. Each of the elements separately is relatively straightforward, but as each interacts with another a great range of possibilities emerges.

This synthesis tends to define our daily experience of places. The street, with travel lanes, maybe with a median, maybe edged by parking, sidewalks, street trees, and other vertical markers, maybe with buildings on the sidewalk or maybe set back behind yards or plazas, gives the context for the public realm. The street cross section, with the heights and uses of the nearest buildings, becomes a key shaper of people's experience: Is being on the street like being in a canyon or on an unbroken plain or the full range in between? These cross-sectional relationships engage and reflect our senses of the street as well as more tangible features, like sun and shade, accessibility of buildings, ranges of human activity to be expected, and so forth.

How might the assembly of parts—building, lot, block, street—better meet the quality of life and workability aspirations shared by most citizens for their own civic places? A useful way to begin is to visualize how these assemblages might occur within the framework of the three urban design traditions: the organic or garden suburb; the formalist or classical approach; and the modernist or technocratic approach. The value of understanding these traditions is that they provide both a handy context for reading, recognizing, and sorting pattern alternatives and a wellspring of tested concepts for judging the likely performance associated with each. While each tradition is generally recognizable, strategies for assembling the elements of the built world at the scale of local places may involve some degree of blending, yet usually with one of the traditions more evident.

An important consequence of the choices for block and street layout lies in their adaptability for accommodating different activities over time on the one hand, and on their accessibility for pedestrians on the other. Blocks with too great a perimeter discourage the establishment of pedestrian-friendly environments, while blocks that are too narrow may prevent large space–using activities and may limit other useful activities. Since on-the-ground conditions vary widely, there is no right answer to the block size question, though I have overheard colleagues debate the subject at length, with varying mixtures of certitude and passion.

While many cities in their earliest incarnations followed organic development patterns for a time, the centers of most U.S. cities and towns established and expanded in the nineteenth century are laid out in regular grids of blocks and streets, in the formalist tradition. In each formalist town and city, choices were made as to the sizes and shapes of blocks that the grid of streets circumscribed. They were usually rectangular or square, with widely varying dimensions depending on the town. Smallish blocks were 200 feet or so on a side (like in downtown Portland or the Fairlie Poplar district in Atlanta) with larger ones ranging up to blocks whose four sides added up to as much as 2,000 feet or more, with pedestrian accessibility favoring smaller blocks. Recently, in re-urbanization developments around the country, designers and developers are creating blocks that accommodate mixed use and medium residential densities where the cars fit in the middle, out of sight from the street (see Chapter 10, Tools). Blocks may have alleys running down the middle, providing rear access to the block's lots for parking and services and rights-of-way for utilities. Alleys save the street frontage from these visually and functionally disruptive kinds of activities.

The street rights-of-way may vary in size as well, ranging from as narrow as 40 feet up to 100 feet and wider, with newer formalist towns usually having wider norms. Major arterial or boulevard-type streets might be still wider. Within the right-of-way in quiet residential streets the width of the travel way, between the curbs, may be as narrow as 20 feet but more commonly ranges upward from about 32 feet, allowing for parking on both sides and two narrow travel lanes. Busier streets usually require 10-foot or wider travel lanes, sometimes with a left turn lane at busy intersections, sometimes protected by a median. Street widening within the right-of-way to accommodate growing car traffic reduces sidewalk width and increases pedestrian crossing distance. Four-lane streets typically require at least 40 feet for moving lanes; if parking is provided then the travel way is at least 54 feet wide, wider if a left turn lane is provided and wider still if bike lanes, usually 5 feet each, are installed. There seems to be increasing use of left turn lanes to ease congestion at intersections, which may turn a two-lane street to three-lane or a four-lane to a five-lane at that point, providing opportunities for medians or pedestrian crossing refuges. Roadway designers are moving away from the continuous fifth or "suicide" lane, trying to limit left turns and install medians for traffic control. Sometimes,

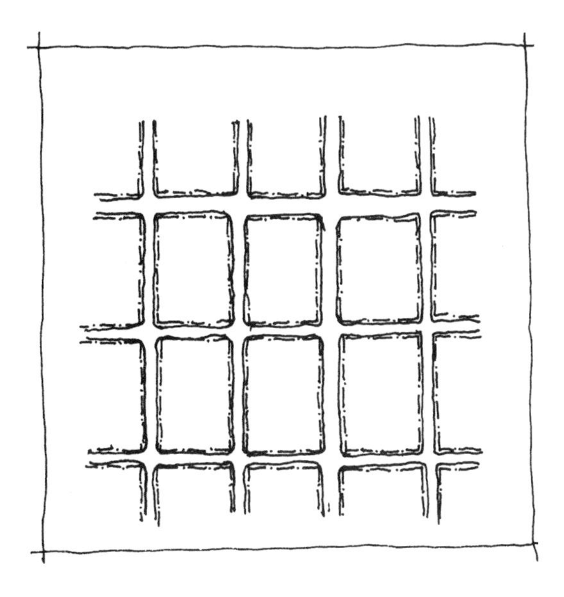

*Figure 3.16*
*Diagram of how streets, blocks, lots, and buildings might lay out in the formalist tradition.*

where excess capacity permits, a four-lane street can be reduced to a three-lane, or a six-lane can be reduced to five, where the left turn at intersections alleviates demand, and the middle lane can be used for various median purposes.

When widenings occur in existing rights-of-way, to compensate for reduced pedestrian space, additional sidewalk may be provided by zoning for it on private property, as has been done in Atlanta, or reversing the widening process within the right-of-way. (For additional information on street design, see Chapter 11, Techniques.)

These gridded block systems accommodate all kinds of buildings, from the single-family freestanding house on usually rectangular lots in a range of sizes to the multistory residential or office block or tower, sometimes taking up the whole block. The street system is logical and readable. You know where you are and have an idea of where you're going. If one travel path gets clogged up, a parallel one is likely to be available.

As cities were spreading out from their grid pattern centers, so was the organic, garden suburb tradition gaining ground. This tradition, launched by Olmsted and Vaux in Riverside, is flourishing today, represented by the work of countless subdivision builders.

This pattern is ubiquitous, existing in the newer parts and lower-density swaths of towns and cities as well as suburbs throughout the country. This building, lot, block, and street pattern, influenced by the modernist passion for separating uses at the scale of the superblock, suits individual, separated, freestanding structures, built by developers and homebuilders wherever they can extend roads and utility access. It does not contemplate providing for the mixes of uses, densities, and building types associated with the more flexible patterns possible in gridded urban places. Buildings tend to be set back farther from the curb, and most properties have their own driveways. In residential areas, block widths are usually a function of the local single-family-house market. The quarter-acre lot and smaller subdivision may produce block widths of 200 to 300 feet, while the acre lot and larger subdivision may result in block widths from 300 feet on up. Overall block lengths too are usually much greater than those in the grid tradition, and alleys are usually not included.

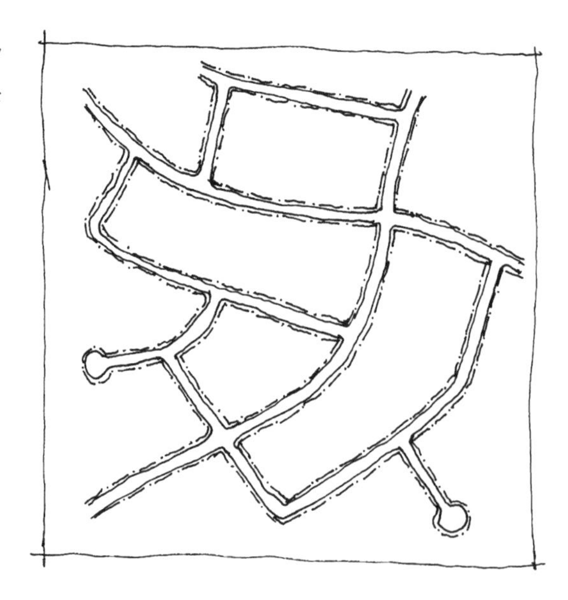

*Figure 3.17 Diagram of the organic tradition in subdivision design.*

The street patterns may be confusing, with changing directionality as they curve, discontinuity of cross streets, and reduced access caused by larger block sizes. Streets are often wider than in the grid pattern, accommodating and however unconsciously encouraging higher travel speeds in swooping travel paths. The street landscape is similarly informal, often lacking sidewalks altogether, sometimes managing storm water in valley rather than vertical curbs, with overhead utilities visible in lower-income areas, and incorporating trees in the right-of-way with yard trees to emphasize a kind of naturalistic look.

Finally, modernism laid the base for separated, single-use blocks that can be found both in urban renewal areas of core cities and in strip commercial street environments, shopping malls, business parks, and residential complexes—again a recognizable pattern throughout American urban and suburban landscapes. The rational, utilitarian efficiency that separated all of the formerly mixed-together urban activities into discrete parts could be replicated unendingly in large superblocks, controlling car access and parking.

Rationalism also imparted an economic meaning. Large blocks under single or unified ownership with single-purpose and often mass-producible structures meant less development cost and held the prospect for greater return on investment, as compared with the older traditions. There tended to be less land devoted to public rights-of-way, so that more net land was developable. The resulting patterns account for many of the problems experienced in both urban and suburban communities across the country today. Big developed blocks are hard to break up. Single-use complexes are resistant to diversification. The combination of big blocks and single-use complexes makes pedestrian travel and even some forms of transit untenable. The dendritic street patterns that in the 1950s seemed so rational now contribute mightily to the nightmare of suburban traffic and again don't lend themselves easily to retrofit. See Chapter 5, Connections, for additional analysis and discussion of these problems.

For the moment, in terms of building, lot, block, and street patterns at least, it seems that the tenets of modernism have left urban wastelands so memorable that whatever urbanist theory modernism has put forward has

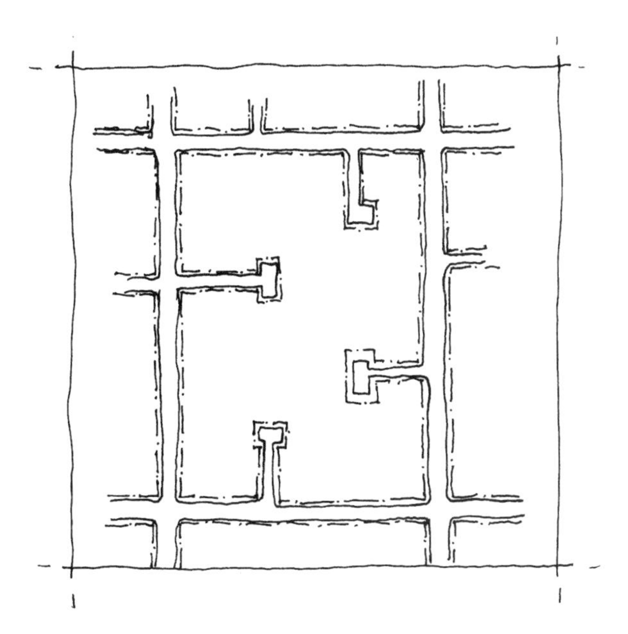

*Figure 3.18*
*Diagram of modernist approach to the building, street, block synthesis, usually favoring single uses within the superblock, like apartments or office parks.*

been discredited. Of the earlier models, the formalist models are regaining their appreciation in the form of new urbanism, and the organic are persisting in less dense areas, as well as providing for experimentation in more sustainable development models. What this all seems to mean is that Americans have come to realize that there are alternatives to the conventional subdivision way of assembling building, lot, block, and street, and there are choices for where and how to live and work as well as for how to travel in between.

## Parking and Utilities

Parking is always a consideration for designing places at every scale, though more so in higher-density areas. The needs for parking and often zoning, or lender requirements for parking, may directly conflict with the creation of a pedestrian-oriented civic environment. In older centers, surface parking has displaced buildings, replacing storefronts that provide visual enclosure to the street with seemingly limitless asphalt. In commercial strips and shopping centers, parking fields are the defining visual characteristic of the place, at least until you find your way inside. Parking for suburban apartment complexes and office parks creates an urbanscape that resolutely disconnects the building from the land or from adjacent buildings. The office component of this familiar suburban phenomenon has been aptly characterized as "single-family office buildings."

Yet parking is essential and will continue to be for decades to come. Surface parking is cheap. Structured parking is expensive. Many surface lots are held as low-maintenance, low-tax money machines, waiting to become the next high- or mid-rise complex. Most structured parking is good for one thing—parking—and so perhaps the least flexible structure in a downtown-type environment. But parking doesn't have to dominate the visual entries and seams of commercial destination. On-street parking, whether parallel or sometimes angled in lower-density areas, can actually improve the definition of the travel way while encouraging drivers to stop and providing a buffer for pedestrians. The right-of-way line, thus the other border of the pedestrian realm, can be defined any number of ways—by buildings, yards, plantings, low walls, and so forth. Parking lots can even be conceived as plazas that accommodate cars, prioritizing a kind of pedestrian-friendly civic order with rhythms of tree and other plantings and lighting fixtures. In centers that aspire to be high-density, mixed-use urban places, at some point parking needs to be restricted, become expensive, or be coupled with transit improvements to pick up some of the travel demand so that the place provides options to the car in order to continue its growth.

Utilities are dealt with in more detail in Chapter 5, Connections, yet I mention them here because of their direct and pervasive impact on the built world. Overhead utility lines, whether for electric power transmission or telecommunications, are part of the everyday environment, usually degrading the visual and to some extent the functional potential of the travel ways and places through which they pass. They stand as iconic symbols of the disjointedness with which our places are designed and developed, answering to a single set of corporate technical, cost, and profit criteria with no regard for their interactive visual impact on other pieces of their environment. There are choices, and whenever asked (not often by the utility companies who put them there), people say they generally prefer not to see the visual chaos these lines project into the environment nor suffer their periodic weather-caused outages.

## The Larger Territories

The foregoing discussion addresses the pieces whose patchwork makes up the urban quilt. Properties, buildings, blocks, and streets and their syntheses are always the elements out of which larger urban territories are assembled. Common among the larger territories of the built world are neighborhoods, districts, parks, towns, cities, and regions.

### *Neighborhoods*

Neighborhoods usually comprise more or less cohesive residential areas with reasonably definable borders. They may be mostly single-family, mostly multifamily, or various mixes of the two. Neighborhoods may be more or less distinguished by single demographic groups: white, black, Latino, Asian; rich, middle-class, or poor; even younger or older; or mixed in any number of the above combinations. The culture of neighborhoods varies widely as well, from proud to indifferent, from ethnic traditions or not, from well organized to not, from effective in articulating and acting on a vision to not. They often have a retail or commercial component, as small as a corner store on up to a cluster of shops and businesses, all of which are oriented toward meeting the needs of their immediate neighborhood setting. They may be larger or smaller by population and by geography and more or less dense.

A single street may be big enough to constitute a neighborhood, both spatially and socially, or a neighborhood may consist of a few hundred households. Spatially, they may follow any of the three traditions.

Densities may be very low, like one or less units to the acre, often associated with "exclusionary zoning" in high-end urbanized areas because the cost of land prevents major segments of the population from being able to live there. Mid-range densities for single-family detached house neighborhoods may fall in the range of four to six to the net acre (for example, lots of about 75 × 150 feet to 60 × 120 feet), with eight to ten to the acre approaching the high end (about 50 × 100 feet to 40 × 100 feet lots). Although a succession of theorists and practitioners have tried to suggest optimum size ranges for neighborhoods, in the end the people there, their social interactions, and physical layout determine neighborhood identity—there is no "right" size.

Still, it is useful to consider parameters that may describe a neighborhood, at least to get a sense of the relationship between measurement and neighborhood. Clarence Perry, for example, mentioned earlier as a proponent of the model established by Forest Hills Gardens about 90 years ago under the aegis of the Russell Sage Foundation, was an early such theorist. He defined neighborhoods into units of given sizes and characteristics. His "neighborhood units" were sized to be walkable, around 160 acres, so that one could walk from the center to the perimeter in about seven or eight minutes, with a mix of housing types and costs comprising densities sufficient to support convenience shopping, an elementary school, and amenities like small park spots to be shared by all. (See Figure 2.15 for a map of the neighborhood unit.)

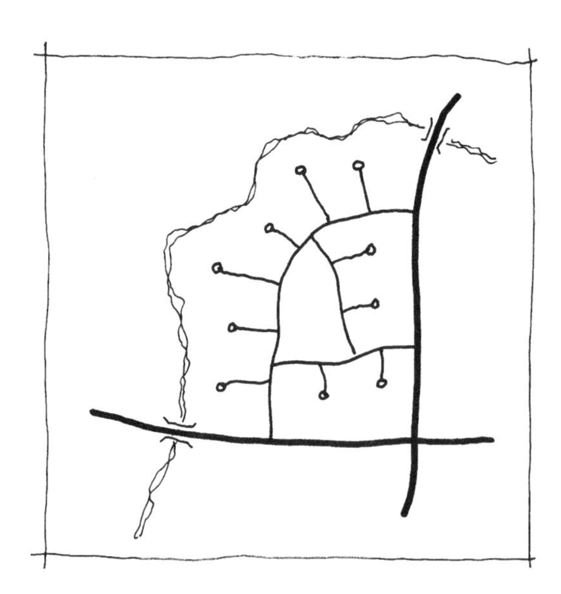

*Figure 3.19a*
*Organic-type neighborhood, usually single-family, detached housing, sometimes with multifamily or commercial activities along the principal streets.*

In the car-driven, less dense patterns of most of suburban America, though, neighborhoods may be much larger in area, smaller in population, less identified by their residents as "neighborhoods," and lacking in retail or service establishments. In these circumstances, it may take a handful of neighborhoods perhaps identifiable more as a community to support the shopping, school, and other amenities that Perry envisaged. As a way of getting a handle on neighborhood size and make-up, Perry's formula fairly well anticipates the neighborhoods promoted by "new urbanism," with such features as mixed uses, mixed housing types, park spots, and retail and civic structures, all arranged in a walkable setting where the presence of cars is downplayed.

It should be noted that until housing types reach multifamily densities, from townhouses on up, the increasingly relevant amenity of public transit generally cannot be supported. The block sizes above, however, are sufficiently flexible to meet those thresholds, generally from at least 15 housing units per acre on up. As densities increase, even with transit availability, parking becomes an issue. Townhouses can be designed with garage or tuck-under parking within the unit, often accessible from an alley of 20 feet or so. Two- or three-story garden apartments may accommodate pooled parking onsite. Five-story apartment blocks often locate their parking internally in two- or three-story parking decks. Mid- and high-rise blocks usually require multilayered decks. In districts that include significant amounts of office and retail space, parking can be shared to a certain extent, assuming that there will be some economies of scale from night users not being the same as day users.

The physical shape of the neighborhood interacts with its demographic and social dynamics and the development forces that create them. Physical form is rarely causal in neighborhood dynamics, but it certainly is a factor in how well or how quickly a neighborhood can undertake effective improvement strategies. Neighborhoods whose form promotes connectivity between residences are more likely to support the kinds of social contact necessary to organize cohesive positions on how to improve the neighborhood or on how to promote or respond to development initiatives. There are a number of ways physical connectivity can be assessed or

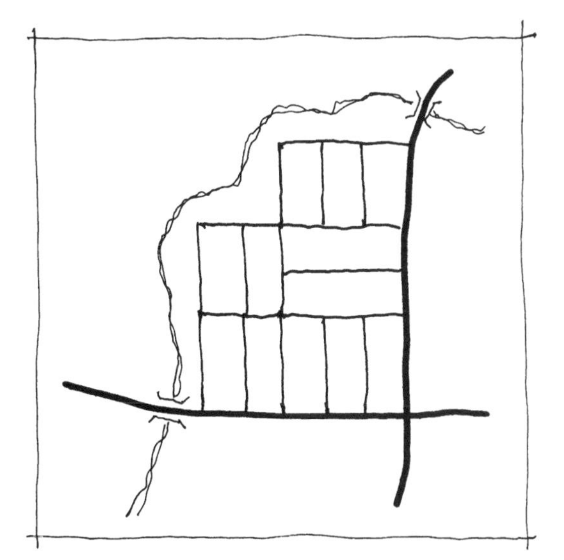

*Figure 3.19b*
*Formalist-type neighborhood, usually single-family, detached housing, but with the possibility of town homes, multifamily dwellings, and shops or civic activities toward the principal streets.*

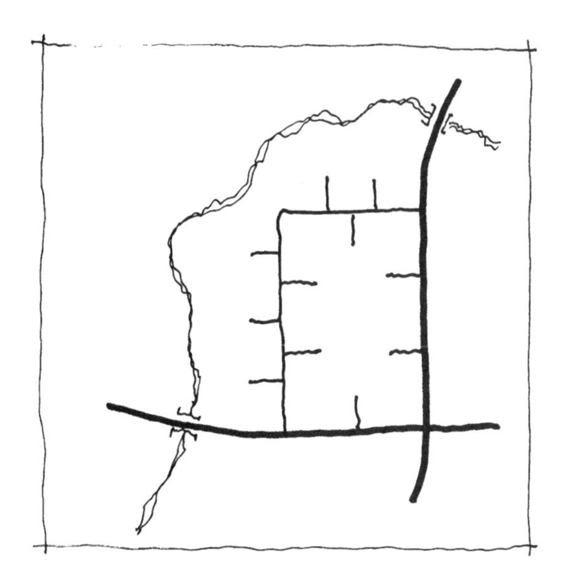

*Figure 3.19c*
*Modernist-type neighborhood, usually multifamily housing in repetitive units with commercial activities along the principal streets.*

designed. Block sizes and shapes, and the travel ways that give access to them, are fundamental. The techniques of space syntax theory being developed by my colleague at Georgia Tech, John Peponis, in the general parameters of the formalist tradition, for example, provide a clear objective framework for determining how well neighborhoods and districts are connected in physical terms. The theory further suggests the kinds of modifications desirable to improve connectivity, both in terms of travel and social interaction.

Other factors are important as well. The location of schools, libraries, and properly sized parks may serve to attract residents to places meeting common needs. The elementary school, for example, ideally within walking distance of the homes of the 500 or 700 pupils that it serves, remains a key institution around which neighborhoods form and organize themselves. This ideal works best when an even higher ideal is met: The school is first-rate, equal in quality to all other schools in the jurisdiction, and promotes diversity. The middle and particularly the high school becomes a center for the larger community, around which pride in training for the future can be instilled (or not). The travel paths to and from these community resources may further promote contact. Similarly, a corner store or cluster of shops and services may connect people to each other. Occasionally, a community center or religious institution may play this role.

Finally, density, the number of residences within a given area or neighborhood, may promote contact simply by increasing the number of opportunities for interaction among residents. As neighborhood densities increase, the tolerance or even embrace of diversity becomes a factor. If neighborhoods are accepting of a range of incomes, thus housing types and costs, ages, ethnicities, and household types, then social contact and social action can be very effective: In the political world such diversity spans multiple constituencies.

On the other hand, neighborhoods that are not physically well connected, perhaps with larger blocks and travel ways that limit visual contact and discourage pedestrian activity, may need to count on the car, the telephone, and perhaps a larger community-centered institution to provide social contact.

This kind of analysis of neighborhood form has served the new urbanist movement well, and the kinds of people attracted to new urbanist development projects are those for whom informal social contact is considered a plus. The market for social connectivity seems far deeper than the supply, and people all over the country, particularly in suburban or greenfield settings, are playing a pivotal role in securing their jurisdictions' support for the kinds of zoning and subdivision modifications to support this model, an alternative to what is likely to be all around them.

The most compelling issues for neighborhoods, though, may be only incidentally related to form. Issues like property values, stability, gentrification, diversity, improvement or decline, traffic, safety, children's walking access to school, park or neighborhood center, and adequate and reliable services are all day-to-day measures of functionality, satisfaction, and quality of life for neighborhood residents. Yet change forces often take a physical form, and the choices of how to respond in a way to protect or enhance fundamental values can quickly dominate the neighborhood agenda. A new development proposal, a deteriorating property, a traditional house replaced with a "McMansion," a new street or sewer project, all of these and a lot more changes to neighborhood form face neighborhood people everywhere with great frequency. How to respond in the context of fundamental values is a challenge for both neighborhood leaders and for urban design professionals, the latter of whom are just as likely to be associated with the change force (like a developer or a city agency) as with the neighborhood. With the advance in sophistication of citizen participation and availability of information, the opportunity is there to bend the change force to positively address neighborhood concerns or advance a neighborhood priority, to look for a win-win outcome.

Understanding the formal setting in terms of a building, lot, block, and street analysis can assist evaluation of the effects of changes occurring and provide better information about how to respond. The formalist, monumental, classical, or City Beautiful traditions tend to dominate the older parts of cities and towns, largely simply because of when they were originally laid out. The new urbanist model bases its approach on the positive aspects that this tradition provides, maybe incorporating some of the features of the garden suburb tradition, and typically applies them to new suburban settings, usually as single-developer projects. Understanding new urbanist principles, though, is helpful for guiding response to development proposals in older neighborhoods as well. Formalist and new urbanist principles are also useful to review for guiding infill development in core urban settings, like transit-oriented developments, abandoned industrial properties, or the effort to resurrect derelict urban renewal blocks. Still, the dominant pattern for developing new neighborhoods remains the garden suburb tucked into a dendritic street pattern, with largish unbroken apartment or strip commercial blocks as the streets become arterials, punctuated with the occasional mall. The demographics of these post-1940s neighborhoods tend to be more uniform with respect to age, ethnicity, income, and family structure than the older closer-in neighborhoods, although first-ring suburbs seem to be becoming more diverse (and maybe less stable).

In summary, neighborhoods are where most people live, accounting for about half of all urbanized private land, and they face change on a continuous basis. There are opportunities for neighborhood leaders to envision and then deal with the physical change forces in positive ways, and for urban designers to help them in the process. Understanding something of the make-up and forms of neighborhoods should improve the prospects for outcomes that make a neighborhood better than it was before.

## *Districts*

For the purpose of this analysis, districts are groupings of blocks and streets that contain commercial, recreational, or industrial activities, often including residential activity but where the nonresidential activity is likely dominant and gives the district its character. (Clusterings of neighborhoods, however, may be characterized as residential districts.) Downtowns, edge cities, town centers, community or larger neighborhood centers, mixed-use travel corridors, office and business parks, shopping malls, industrial areas, larger parks, hospitals, universities or research complexes, convention centers, or sports and other entertainment complexes are all types of districts. The discussion below identifies some typical characteristics of some of them, the kinds of forms they are likely to take, and urban design and community issues they commonly present.

Districts characterized by large employment concentrations tend to follow the application of one or a combination of the three urban design forms discussed above. These formal traditions are pretty easy to recognize as all three are likely to be found in towns and cities across the country. Older downtown districts are usually organized around a formalist grid of streets defining square or rectangular blocks with perimeters typically ranging from 800 to 1,600 feet. Suburban office park districts often show the picturesque garden suburb penchant for lush plantings and winding streets and cul-de-sacs, defining curving blocks typically much larger than grid-generated blocks. Many of these, as they attain greater dimensions as largely single-purpose blocks, take on the modernist character of very large superblocks with limited access and connection points. And concentrations of these along with shopping centers and malls form what are generally called "edge cities." These are often places where maximum land development overwhelms the connective system necessary to support them, resulting in congestion within and between single-use, property by property projects. Though difficult to retrofit to more workable

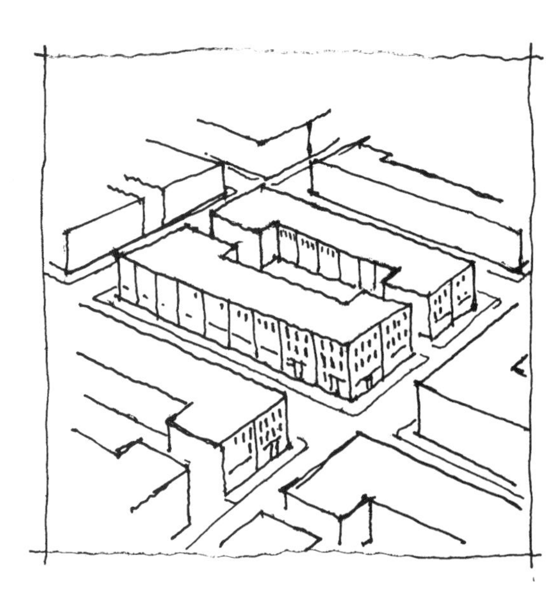

*Figure 3.20a*
*Diagram of viable downtown tenancy prior to over-optimistic zoning and vacuum sweeper effect.*

centers, many of these are nonetheless seeking to connect themselves better and to introduce both transit and street grids to overcome their original geometric limitations.

For each of these, meeting the ever-present challenge of providing for parking and the auto traffic that it generates shapes the overall civic environment. In older downtowns, the familiar pattern is blocks of asphalt ringing the remaining core areas, whose parking decks are insufficient and too expensive to provide for a parking demand that has grown geometrically since the downtown grid was first laid out. The garden suburb business parks and office parks tend to use a mix of structured parking and parking fields that at best are artfully landscaped so that the dominance of the parking necessity is shielded or filtered. In addition, this pattern must provide parking for all the daytime workers, since typically there are no transit or pedestrian alternatives for access (there could be a little carpooling), and the lack of any residential components preclude any day-night shared parking opportunities. The modernist-generated high employment district is likely to deal with parking in a manner similar functionally to the garden suburb–generated approach; that is, with a mix of parking fields and structures.

In the older downtown model, the interplay between land speculation, taxing policies, zoning, and the market tend to produce what I call the "vacuum sweeper effect." An older downtown that escaped urban renewal is likely to have each block lined by one- to four-story buildings housing a range of activities, most of them commercial. From the 1960s on, municipalities tended to over-zone their downtown properties, hoping that somehow if properties were zoned for mid- and high-rise commercial development, such development would actually happen. As the market for more intense concentrations of employment heats up, say for an office tower, a developer will assemble properties over a block or so and erect a mid- or high-rise structure, replacing maybe 400 jobs (and parking spaces) with maybe 2,000 and, absent transit, the need for almost as many parking spaces.

This kind of event launches a pattern where nearby property owners imagine that they will be able to put together the next big project, which

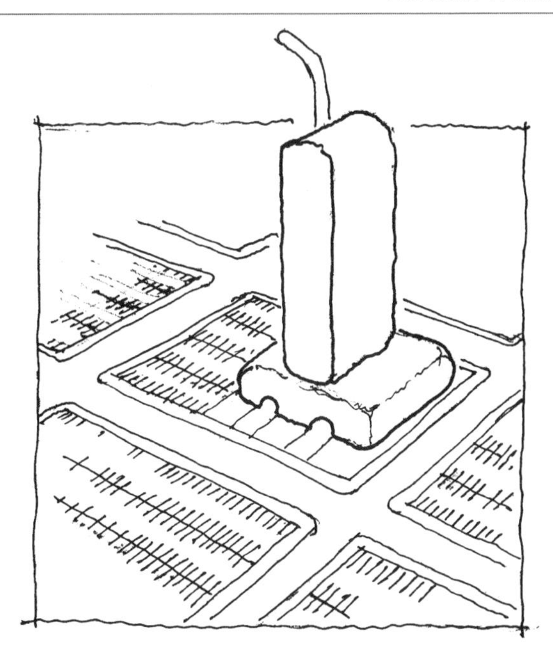

*Figure 3.20b*
*Cartoon of high-rise "vacuum sweeper" building sucking up tenancy from all around to fill its space, leaving wastelands of parking in its wake.*

the zoning probably allows, if they can just hang on, reduce their taxes, and wait for the market to catch up. Many of the tenants in these older nearby blocks are attracted into the newer "Class A" office space (businesspeople tend not to want to be in space that the market characterizes as "Class B" or "Class C"). The parking provided in the new project may not be sufficient or may cost too much for the new tenancy there, and so as nearby blocks are destabilized, buildings go vacant and are torn down and replaced with surface parking. This generates a reliable stream of income with much less overhead than the buildings that used to be there and a significantly reduced tax bill. In effect, the new mid- or high-rise has "vacuumed" out the nearby old business tenancies and left a vacuum in its wake—wastelands of asphalt.

Taking into account the core conditions of many districts, issues for urban designers in dealing with spatial patterns include a range of oft-experienced, finer-grained design characteristics and the challenges they pose. For example, establishing cohesiveness within the downtown or major center as a district is an elusive but essential goal. This usually means finding ways to bridge gaps caused by parking blocks or abandoned buildings, assuring a sufficient and distinguished streetscape environment for pedestrian and transit activities, keeping the lower floors of buildings at or near the sidewalk, presenting transparent glass fronts to the public, restricting driveways and service bays, providing focus for buildings or activities particularly symbolic of the district or the city, paying attention to skylines both for assuring light and air at the street level and symbolic possibilities at the sky, scrutinizing critically the occasional and usually misguided tendency to close streets and assemble bigger blocks in the modernist tradition, and so on.

At the level of the streetscape, it usually means assuring that taller buildings are broken in some way at the second or third level, like setting back upper floors or providing cornice lines that help pedestrians read the building at the scale of their view cone, which usually cuts off at 25 or 30 feet. It means paying attention to the penetrability of the building at the ground floor, either with windows or doors or both, and how the buildings turn corners, both considerations sharing the goal of feeling good walking

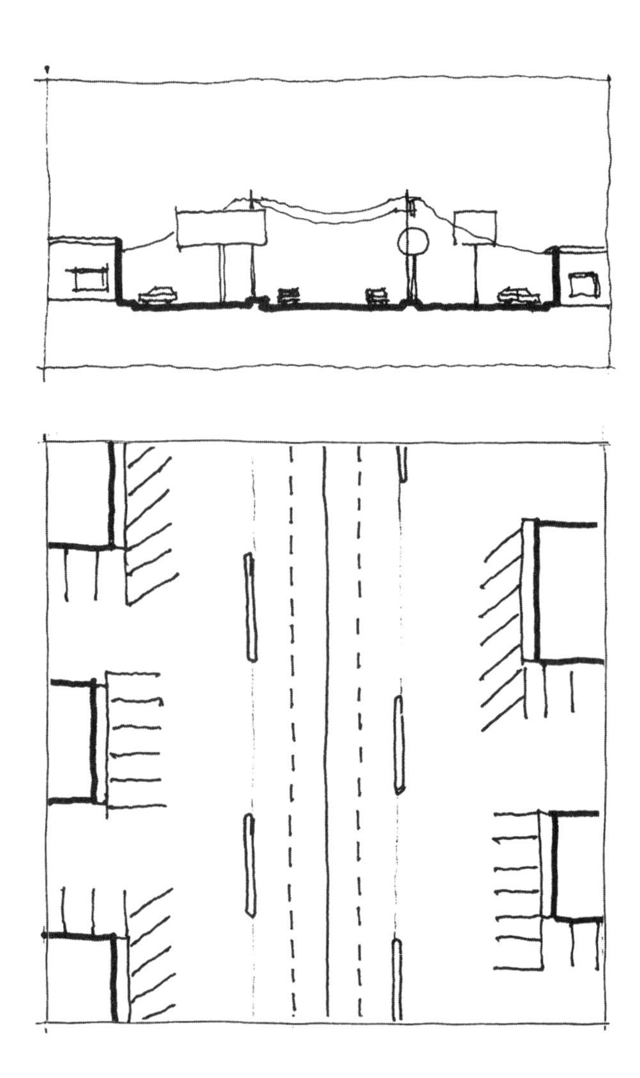

*Figure 3.21a–3.21b*
*Diagram of cross section and plan of typical strip commercial street condition.*

down the street. For leaders of surrounding communities and urban designers alike, the fringe of asphalt and disinvested properties that typically rings the downtown district creates a kind of no-man's-land that must be dealt with. The goals typically include preventing erosion into the edges of the nearest neighborhoods and at the same time assuring a properly respectful and ideally distinguished system of boulevards and roadways that buffer the neighborhood and connect to the district.

As interest increases in revisiting both older garden suburb and modernist-generated employment centers, urban designers are exploring ways to retrofit these forms into ones that might accommodate a mix of uses, including a range of housing types and costs and a greater mix of commercial and retail activities. Such strips and centers may be attractive either for upgrades or redevelopment, depending on the market cycle in which they find themselves. Emergent strategies include the introduction of more of a gridlike character, breaking up some of the larger blocks into smaller ones, increasing densities and rethinking the monolith of a single use, single look that makes these districts unable to flex with market shifts. Another, perhaps fresher approach has been advanced by Jude LeBlanc and Michael Gamble at Georgia Tech. More tolerant of the often cut-up ownership patterns that characterize many strips, they suggest going with

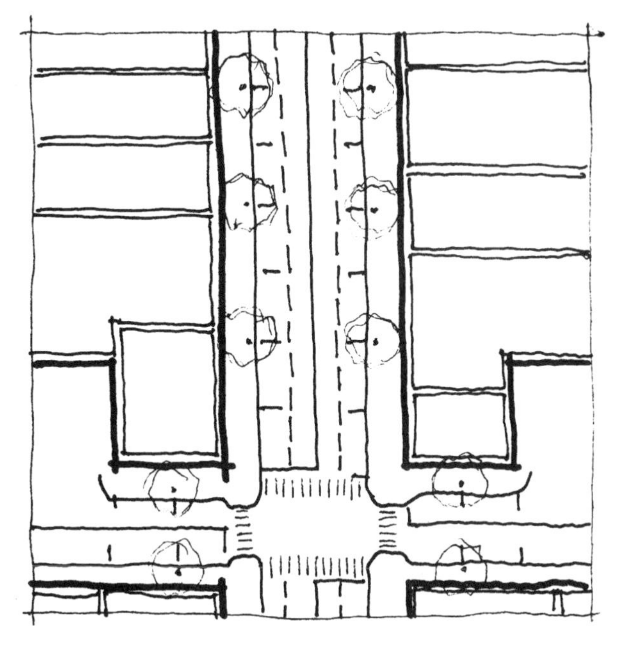

*Figure 3.22a–3.22b*
*Turning a typical strip into a metropolitan boulevard, in section and plan: incorporating the wide swaths of land resulting from zoning-required setbacks and parking to accommodate and support growing retail and residential space needs.*

the flow; that is, establishing streets that respond to ownership patterns and the informal driving paths that already occur between parcels and buildings. The result could be characterized as more in the vein of the organic tradition, incremental, informal, and more directly related to the interests of smaller property owners. These can continue in business and still allow their properties' activities to intensify, but in a much more ad hoc and casual way, over whatever time it takes. Again, how such retrofit strategies may affect surrounding neighborhoods, either positively or negatively, is a matter of concern for these nearby constituencies and for urban designers.

Larger employment districts present regional issues as well. At the present time, many are surrounded by higher-income neighborhoods, affordable only for higher-salaried employees, while the middle- and lower-income employees, the majority in employment centers, tend to have to travel greater distances to find housing that their wages and salaries can afford. This jobs-housing imbalance, as it is frequently called, beyond skewing up the cost of transportation for many workers compared to the cost of housing, has significant impacts on traffic congestion and travel times. Particularly nowadays in metro areas where the center city is being repopulated by gentrifiers and more affluent empty nesters and seniors, the watchword for housing growing numbers in the workforce is "Drive 'til you qualify." Around growing centers, another consequence is the likelihood that land costs reflecting commercial values may contribute to jobs-housing mismatch, with lower-income people having to drive farther, pay more for transportation, and contribute significantly to congestion, all because the choice to live near work is simply not available to them. One could imagine that as policy makers and investors come to understand this link between housing costs and the wage profile in employment centers, affirmative programs to support closing the distance gap between wage and housing cost could enter the mainstream of congestion mitigation strategies (with its attendant energy and air quality benefits).

So far, we have considered the characteristics of high density: increasingly mixed-use concentrations as centers, generally blob-shaped with typically radial connections in and out. The characteristics of the strip commercial corridor, a linear district if you will, may offer promising alternatives for focusing growth that is emerging in many areas. Such corridors proliferate in all metro areas, often connecting centers of the type described above. They provide "quick, convenient in and out" service for a wide range of usually low-density businesses, freestanding or in strip centers. Visually, they are usually dismal, confused, car-dominated, parking lot–flanked, utility line–afflicted barrens, often hard to get to off of clogged arteries. Yet their transformation into building-lined, streetscaped multimodal boulevards is not too hard to visualize. The great swaths of asphalt, combining perhaps 100 feet of travel asphalt and another 80 or so feet on either side for parking and service, in effect provides a 200- to 300-foot-wide resource, half public and half private, waiting for municipal and private sector design partners to transform.

Of the district types mentioned above, many include high concentrations of employment with accompanying diversities of daytime workers, yet their character may be dominated by a single type of enterprise. Centers of government often put their stamp on largish urban areas. The city hall, the county courthouse, state government complexes, and the like reflect the times in which they were built and express an attitude about the role of government and its employees, who typically make up a considerable portion of the local workforce. Universities, often with a workforce numbering a third of the student body that itself is "working" in learning during mostly daytime hours, have their own flavor. Similarly, hospitals are complexes with a wide-ranging workforce that put their own institutional stamp on a district. The same "territory marking" applies with research complexes or business parks.

In all of these there are compelling functional drivers that tend to give form to the complexes. Even so, there are choices to be made. One is the extent to which the institution considers housing and housing opportunity associated with the institution as a functional piece of its mix. Another, perhaps more fundamental, is whether to isolate itself from or integrate itself into the larger urban setting.

While there are examples of both approaches and everything in between, current trends support the notion that institutions that think of themselves as part of a bigger whole are likely to build better partnerships with their residential or business neighbors and ultimately better serve their own core purpose as a result. The balance that policy makers and administrators make between internal security and external hostility, between disengagement and contribution, increasingly reflects a consciousness that their workers, clients, and consumers are the same people as those across the street. Promoting continuity of community life with institutional life is often a more productive path than ignoring or barring it.

The three traditions are apparent in the forms these choices may take among different institutions, complexes, and campuses, creating widely different flavors. Government complexes have used all three traditions, singly and in various combinations. Thus during the City Beautiful movement many civic center complexes followed the formalist, monumental traditions as a way of asserting a clear and compelling presence, with axial order and classical architectural forms proclaiming a mix of pride and authority (see Figure 1.4). In the modernist era, the superblock, separation of use and supremacy of technocracy, asserts itself (see Figure 2.18). And many, mostly smaller, towns have used a folksier approach to integrate their local civic institutions into the landscape and culture of the people they represent.

The forms historically adopted for colleges and universities tend to include the familiar quadrangle or quad, usually with academic buildings surrounding pedestrian-only landscaped parks or squares, where bigger colleges may have one central or multiple quads. Other large institutions may adopt the quadrangle approach for their complexes as well. This form communicates a clear order, consistent with the traditions of formalism or classicism, where the more important or symbolic buildings tend to punctuate the vistas set up by geometric path systems. As an organizing device, the quadrangle is adaptable enough to either isolate or integrate the campus or complex into the surrounding environment, depending on how it connects to and through.

Other approaches evoke romantic traditions, creating in some instances a cloistered approach. Yale's campus, for example, uses both approaches, with its academic clusters and some of its residential colleges more classical and monumental and others almost medieval (even ones designed by Eero Saarinen in the 1960s), consciously seeking to evoke the mix of mystery and community of fifteenth-century centers of learning. Many of the newer campuses built after World War II follow the modernist approach, creating vast superblocks with buildings lost in the middle, widely separated, parking convenient to each, and producing environments that cannot foster pedestrian or even transit connectivity.

Colleges and universities typically occupy larger territories, with the potential of dividing communities, interacting positively with them around their seams, or even connecting them. Like residences and workplaces, they may be sited and designed on the one hand to awe and intimidate, or on the other to be comfortable and inviting. As learners, people make choices about where they seek knowledge, in which the physical aspect of one or another school, from bastion to "university of the streets," may attract or repel prospective students and faculty. Each expresses its position in how it arranges its interior campus spaces, quadrangles, squares, and pathways, and how those spaces connect to and interact with the neighborhoods and districts around them. These physical characteristics in turn are reflections of the will and the predilections of the administration, the trustees, and the faculty with respect to interacting with the nearby neighbors and the municipal government. Sometimes associated with universities, research complexes are institutions whose magnitude and growth (or shrinkage) may have significant impacts on nearby districts or neighborhoods as well, in ways similar to universities.

Issues for urban designers and nearby neighborhoods and districts focus on the seam: how the relatively private activity within the complex or campus connects or doesn't to the surrounding fabric. Whether universities, hospitals, or research campuses, these institutions may support and be supported by local businesses or not; may support a housing market for students, staff, and faculty or not; may connect to local transit or other travel way and parking strategies or not. The outcome enunciates the posture and attitude of the institution toward those environments that surround them. As the universities of the modernist tradition mature, for example, how they establish a clear identity for themselves, how they overcome their kind of car-driven disconnections, and how they position themselves in the larger community become compelling questions.

Industrial districts are a little different than others, though the distinctions have narrowed in recent years as technological production improvements have joined with environmental requirements to improve most industries' neighborliness. The business hours demographics are typically diverse, though because of the impacts of many industries on nearby neighborhoods, the distance gap between housing costs and wages paid is usually narrower. Here, how an industry addresses formal choices has a lot to do with respect—making sure that impacts of light, noise, air and water quality, traffic type, volume, routes, and time of day can be mitigated so that the activity is known for its positive job and economic benefit, not for its negative intrusions.

Larger parks are classified here as districts because, like other districts, they take up rather large, relatively uninterrupted territories, they put their stamp on the areas all around, they can be major traffic generators, and they tend to provide for a single clustering of activities, including recreation and entertainment or plain old relaxation. In some cities, there are cemeteries that fit in this category, as, yes, peaceful places of cultural richness and pleasing landscape. Parks' use patterns are quite different than the employment-centered districts insofar as their heaviest use tends to come before and after business hours and especially on weekends and holidays. Properly maintained and to the extent that they offer complementary activities and edge conditions, parks are usually considered highly desirable by neighborhoods and other kinds of districts. As federal and many states' and cities' funding support for these public amenities has declined, however, many cities and inner-ring suburbs are struggling to assure the appropriate level of maintenance, operations, and safety of their park resources. Many have turned to either nonprofit, "friends of the park" community organizations to build a civic support base for parks or to various types of privatization initiatives. The nonprofit, mostly volunteer route has the advantages of consciously rallying community enfranchisement in their parks, yet it tends to favor those communities with higher incomes and thus more resources and may leave poorer communities worse off. Operating park resources as for-profit enterprises is more problematic, since profitability depends on negotiating access to public resources that guarantee an attractive return and favors those in the community with the wherewithal to pay for services that should be publicly available to all on at least an equal basis.

Parks span the urban design traditions, and there are successful examples of all. Formalist or classical parks, or more often park parts, take their cue from the formal gardens of British and European parks and palaces, where geometrically derived layouts with strong axial views and functional links convey the order that kings and the wealthy asserted, of which the gardens at Fontainebleau or Versailles are notable progenitors. More frequently, however, the romantic, naturalistic traditions find their most comfortable expression in park design and layout. The work of Frederick Law Olmsted is the most familiar, but there have been a number of successful landscape architects and land planners from his time to the present who have enriched this tradition. Modernist park design examples are harder to come by, probably because the coolness of the modernist style and its emphasis on technological efficiency tend not to be consistent with the purposes of parks, although Parc de la Villette or Parc Citroën in Paris seem to have met with some success.

Along with landscape architects, urban designers are often involved directly in park design, since it is part of the public environment and the issues of design are familiar to urban design practitioners. The issues for this book, however, are less about how to design a park than how to integrate it into its larger environment, issues that are of concern to community leaders as well. Thus, the access points into the park, its continuity with neighborhood travel ways both vehicular and pedestrian, its presentation to the surrounding community, its lighting, its traffic generation, its parking provisions, the nature of its activities, the times of day and week when it will be most active, whether its range of offerings serve the immediate or much larger communities are central questions to be resolved.

Convention centers, sports complexes, and cultural and entertainment facilities often reach the scale of putting their own identity on urban settings and bring somewhat different challenges to urban designers and adjacent communities. Such districts are often event-driven and thus have wide swings in populations and traffic generation, from packed to empty. Since the people who participate are attracted by a single activity, the cross section so attracted is likely to be less diverse in income, age, and ethnicity than the overall population. A baseball crowd is different from a basketball crowd is different from a hip-hop crowd is different from a country music crowd is different from a hardware convention is different from a Baptist convention. As a whole, though, such districts are vital parts of city life, both for the events themselves and for all the spin-off economic activity they generate.

As it happens, these kinds of facilities usually house building-centered activities, and they find their formal comfort zone more in the modernist tradition than in the others. To be sure, the monumental or City Beautiful tradition may be found in cultural complexes from the early part of the twentieth century, as along the Chicago lakefront or museum complexes in other cities. The kinds of forms, though, that most of these large, sporadically used single-purpose installations take both functionally and stylistically are more compatible with modernist precepts both in architecture and urban design.

The challenge for urban designers is to assure that the interruption in the city fabric caused by the very size and monolithic character of such institutions can be accommodated so that surrounding districts or neighborhoods gain some benefits from their presence. This is most easily achieved with museums, whose structures are generally smaller and whose visitors are more evenly spaced than, for example, concert halls, amphitheaters, arenas, stadiums, convention centers, and the like. This

One could argue that Chicago's new Millennium Park, by virtue of stunning modernist pieces that find their home there, is an example of modernist park design. In fact, though, the mastermind for the park, and in my view the driver of its great success, is Edward Ulhir, himself a public servant parks planner, designer, and administrator whose 25 years in the Chicago Parks Department imbued him with the spirit of the people and their needs and desires for park space in that special environment.

means that special attention needs to be given to bounding streets and streetscapes, where pedestrian continuity is unlikely to make sense along such facilities' perimeters but can make access to major points of entry compatible with the travel paths generated by the activities in the larger community. In addition, urban designers and particularly community leaders need to resist the temptation among traffic consultants to design street systems that can empty these districts under their peak loading conditions. The alternative, far more palatable, is to count on operational plans that maximize the use of one-way entry and exit traffic, restoring access to two-way when the peaks are over. This more moderate and less expensive approach avoids the kind of freeway character that so typically isolates these centers of activity from their surroundings.

## *Towns and Cities*

In a way analogous to how buildings, lots, blocks, and travel ways are the built parts of neighborhoods, districts and travel corridors are the constituent parts of villages, towns, cities, and larger urbanized areas. Jumping the scale to this level, the focus of urban designers shifts appropriately to larger-scale concerns, like accommodation with all the relevant features of the natural world, how districts interface with neighborhoods and with other districts, the shape of the flows that connect urban concentrations together—the large-scale choices to be made, considering both short- and long-term consequences. This calls upon urban designers to study and absorb information from the regional planning, transportation engineering, real estate, and finance disciplines to a greater degree than necessary to work effectively at the neighborhood or district level.

Community leaders jump scale, too. Beyond political representation and public sector jurisdictional issues, ordinary citizens are daily affected by choices made at this scale, and increasingly their voices are gaining access to and influence on the larger-scale public and private sector forces making most of the policies and decisions about the now and future city. Obvious and ubiquitous examples are transportation and environmental quality issues. Others of the connection or infrastructure issues play a prominent role in design of cities as well. At this scale, too, the form of community leadership is likely to bring together related interest groups in ways to be able to generate the resources and continuity beyond the scope of issues affecting the neighborhood or the district. Thus coalitions of neighborhoods, environmental organizations, housing advocacy and consumer advocacy groups, and increasingly labor organizations are active in the affairs of the town, city, or region.

As with smaller-scale places, people are the front-line definers of cities. Who's there, where they came from, what they're doing, what they care about, how they make their living, how they deal with diversity or disparity, how they participate in civic life are all baseline characteristics of a city's identity, of its character. The mix and flow of people through time, the organizational forms that define their economies, and their political and social structures are the sources of the opportunities and problems identified and the choices made. How people carry on their activities at the scale of town or city and what kinds of physical accommodations will best support those activities are the markers of a city's physical presence. It is through their successions of people and the places they make that cities derive their meaning.

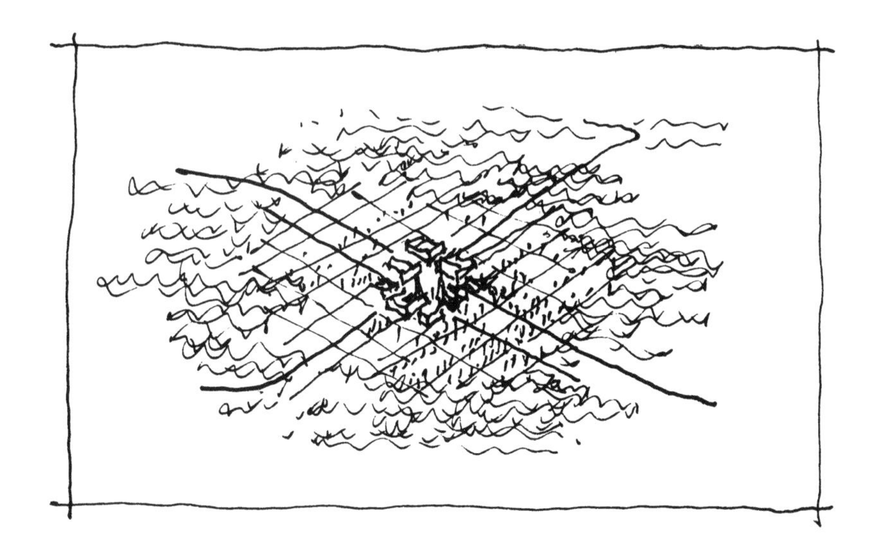

*Figure 3.23*
*Sketch of a town as a quiltwork of districts, neighborhoods, and travel ways.*

The natural environment is the canvas on which people make choices about how to house their activities. The classic generators of city form—defense, trade, religion, domination, manufacturing, and distribution—interact with the chosen physical setting. People have to arrange their particular combination of generators in ways that successfully deal with that setting as well as all of the factors described above, all across an unpredictable timeline. In our times, making these choices in ways that lighten the load on the environment has become critical. As in other times and places around the globe, there has been a succession of cities that have failed for lack of understanding the natural constraints or lack of acting effectively to adapt to the changing realities of nature. Done well, though, cities can be celebrations of human creativity and human spirit at its best, with a chance of advancing civilization for everyone.

The results of the interplay between people creating places for their activities and very particular natural settings are richly varied and continually fascinating (at least for people who cherish human settlements). Almost every town or city has its own distinctive character, much more as a whole place than, say, as a collection of subdivisions, which can be stultifyingly uniform. This identity is always reflected in the town or city's physical make-up, whose visual representation tends to pop up on postcards.

Beyond self-definition, interestingly, many towns and cities find themselves characterized by outsiders, and how the locals react to this phenomenon becomes yet another generational layer of the evolving identity and thus meaning of a place. On the other hand, visitors may see what locals don't because of their fresh eye for seeing the big picture or picking up on the unseen familiar.

Visitors, maybe with some generally informed knowledge of a place, don't bring the native, ingrained biases and thus expressive inhibitions about the place. While characterizations from beyond may be a helpful (or harmful) addition to the meaning of a place, it does not replace the local wisdom but instead at best joins it in further layering its dimensions.

Urban design at this scale concerns itself with the larger character-defining features of the town or city. Entries to the city; response to natural features like ridges, forests, waterways, orientation, and climate; treatment of the major travel and commercial corridors; skylines; what it

Kevin Lynch in his groundbreaking *Image of the City* set forth typologies for understanding cities' physical form. Still a good and straightforward reference for parsing physical elements of the city, he describes the city in terms of paths, edges (or seams), nodes, districts, and landmarks. These elements provide a way for "reading" the city, certainly valuable for outsiders and professionals, perhaps less helpful in connecting the people there with those of their problems and opportunities that include a physical component.

offers in terms of distinctive districts and neighborhoods; parks; whether there is anything to do; and how all of that comes together or not hold the keys to understanding and engaging the place at this scale. In these understandings, the dimensions of time and motion play important roles. Grasping the whole of a place invariably relies on how it is perceived traveling through it. How views are shaped, how a town's assets are sequenced, how legible is the place, do you know where you are and where you are going—all of these speak to understanding design as an in-motion discipline. These points are addressed in more detail in Part Three, Principles. Similarly, towns and cities read and function very differently at different times of day, week, and season. Designers must be conscious of these time factors at least as much as motion factors in understanding and conceptualizing choices for a place's future.

Often this kind of a reading of the physical attributes of a town or city may begin to answer other important questions in approaching city design. Is the town growing or shrinking? Is development favoring one area over another and why? Are conditions improving or deteriorating and where? Does it seem safe or risky and where? Even the extent to which people care about their city, the pride level, may be inferred from a careful reading of the physical place. These readings, though, must always be tested in interaction with fair representations of the people there.

One fairly predictable outcome of this interaction is that however positively or negatively people view their town or city they would all like it to be better. This common aspiration provides a starting point for designers and citizens to engage in the process of identifying how this "better" might come about. In my experience, too, it seems that people feel better about a bad place getting better than a good place getting worse.

One enduring measure of a city's success is to be found in how and whether it nurtures its middle- and lower-income residents, always the great majority of its citizens, in such spheres as the well-being of children, housing adequacy, economic opportunity, parks, public places and facilities, transit and sidewalk options, education, public safety, and overriding civility. All of these have urban design content and a physical, visible presence.

## *Regions*

Regions are the largest scale of urban settings where design has a direct role, yet where its potential is little realized. Regions are made up of many towns and cities of different size and character, usually sprinkled across unincorporated and lower-density suburban or suburbanizing counties. A region's towns and cities, as we have seen, are made up of neighborhoods, districts of various kinds, and a connective fabric of travel corridors punctuated by nodes and centers and other points of particular interest to the town. A region's cohesiveness or sense of the whole derives from its natural setting and its larger-scale infrastructure. Together, these describe its historical development trajectory and account for the location of the cities, towns, centers, and connective networks that are its distinguishing pieces.

This history in many instances reveals the tendency for regions, like towns, to grow concentrically, growing out from the first major crossroads that marked the center of town. In regions, however, the spread encompasses numerous such towns so that a bird's-eye view of a region would reveal larger and smaller concentrations of the kind of mixed-use,

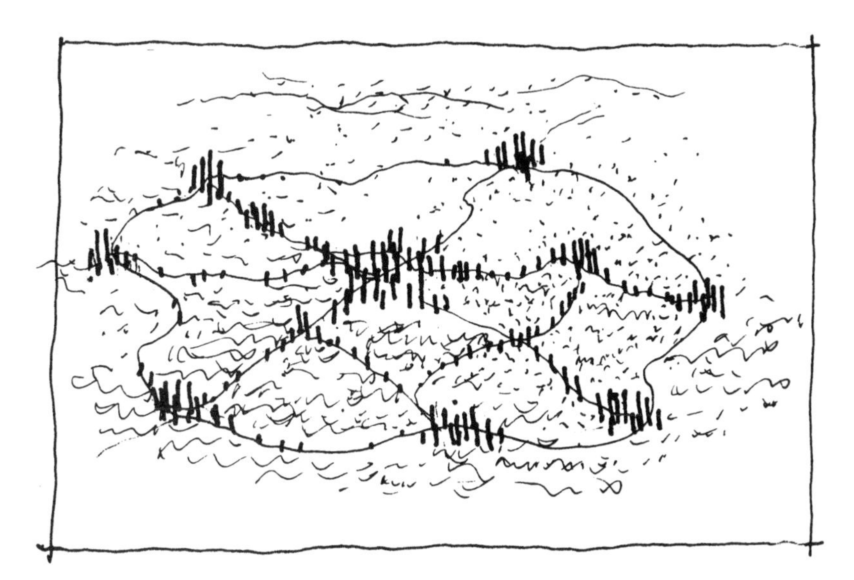

*Figure 3.24*
*Sketch showing the region as a number of centers and corridors.*

mixed-density development that commonly marked town and city patterns through the 1920s. These concentrations dot the spread of inner-ring suburb and then outer-ring suburban developments, which themselves are mostly single-family or low-density residential spreads. These rings in turn are laced with a hierarchy of travel ways, from commercial strips to freeways and, for the lucky, viable transit options. Most urban regions too have experienced the formation of "edge cities," places where through coincidence of travel infrastructure and real estate entrepreneurship employment and shopping centers have concentrated. Even more than for towns and cities, the main and sometimes only way to grasp regions as physical entities is to fly over them or drive through them, and so the design importance of experiencing them in motion is critical for understanding them and conceptualizing their futures.

To understand why regions take the shapes they do and the challenges these shapes pose, it is worth considering the evolution and trends in their organizational and conceptual frameworks. The growth of urbanized settlements and their melding into larger regional territories has called into being organizations for managing issues whose substance cannot be understood or addressed except at the regional scale. One of the earliest models for considering urban dynamics as a regional concern is the Regional Plan Association (RPA) centered in the New York City region. The RPA formed in 1922 and continues as a private, nonprofit advocacy group that seeks to synthesize the disparate activities carried on by dozens of different jurisdictions across interests and disciplines toward mutually beneficial purposes.

Since the 1920s, regional planning organizations and agencies have been forming, a region here or there, often enabled by state law and increasingly required at both the federal and state level. These typically concern themselves with comprehensive planning activities and have evolved from advisory bodies to carrying stronger mandates for planning and approval roles. Over the last 40 or so years, other fields of activity, like senior citizen and homeless services planning, water supply, sewer, solid waste management planning, libraries, parks, schools, and increasingly community health—in short, activities that cross town and county borders may characterize the agenda of regional agencies.

The most compelling mandates for metropolitan planning and coordination are connected to transportation planning and budgeting, stemming from the 1962 Federal-Aid Highway Act, which directed that states and localities were given until 1965 to synthesize and justify their proposed transportation projects from a regional perspective. These agencies, generically now called metropolitan planning organizations (MPOs) in most jurisdictions, joined with regional agencies that existed by then in one form or another, usually as purely advisory, with little influence or power and often viewed askance by urbanizing rural jurisdictions for whom private property rights were unqualifiedly sacred.

The federal act, however, established regional transportation planning as a prerequisite for receiving federal money for transportation projects. The MPO concept, further bolstered in 1969 by the National Environmental Policy Act (NEPA) and the amended Clean Air Act in 1970, finally established in the minds of most regional leaders that transportation was inherently a regional issue. Often reluctantly, they began to give up the old system—based on politicking and mutual back-rubbing—of evaluating and funding projects as stand-alones. They began to accept that to ignore larger network implications didn't make sense, even though the old way continues to boil up from time to time in most regions.

In Birmingham in the late 1970s, for example, a competent and committed regional planning director, Bill Bondarenko, was run off for suggesting to his six county board members the consideration of a regional land use plan as being in the common interest. The rural but urbanizing counties viewed such an idea as heretical, even Communist. It may not have helped, at that time, that he had a Russian name.

For decades, transportation planners, engineers, and departments of transportation have viewed mobility as a singular goal—get more cars moving longer distances safely and quickly—without studying how settlement patterns might make a big difference in the size of the problem they were trying to solve. Economic development advocates tended to support any promise of job and tax base growth, often competing with each other for providing government-supported incentives to achieve their short-term objective and with little consideration for collateral, comprehensive, and long-term effects. As regional planning got established, land use planners were in the thrall of modernist traditions of use-segregated neatness, mega solutions whose effects by now are being discredited as not meeting their promise for contributing to better living conditions. And environmentalists in the drive to protect precious natural assets—unspoiled forests or plains, topography, habitat, air and water quality—tended to become "no growth" advocates, denying or oblivious to population trends and forecasts.

The narrow spectrum of concern and focus reflected the rigidity of postwar theory, a remarkable reliance on such modernist precepts as there being "right" and lasting answers (for everyone!), the superiority of technology and technocracy as problem solvers, the omission of everyday people from the decision-making table, and a kind of overweening paternalism that presumed to "know best." And people bought it. But now, as we shall see, they're trying to widen the lens.

During this period, too, the very single-mindedness of the large economic interests so dominated the value system for designing places that it swept aside most of the other factors on which people judge the quality of their lives. Through the skewing of government policy and subsidy by monetary and fiscal programs to favor the suburban boom, choices for how and where to live and work actually may have become narrowed by this dominance. People travel on a hierarchy of publicly built roads to houses subsidized by mortgage tax deductions and mortgage terms favoring newer homes in ever farther-flung subdivisions. These patterns have now reached the point where the costs of travel for many families in the median income range and below rival the cost of housing. Meanwhile, jobs remain concentrated in clusters so that travel times to work continue to increase, for lack of viable closer-in living choices.

As the MPO system was getting established, concerns about sustainability heightened as groupings in the United States and elsewhere in the world began to face the fact that the earth's resources were limited. The U.N. subsequently adopted the definition from its Brundtland Commission report in 1987: that sustainable development "meets the needs of the present generation without compromising the ability of future generations to meet their own needs."

New ways of conceptualizing regional settlement patterns included shifting the balance of public and private development initiatives to approach the newly identified goals. Programs arose to use publicly financed, planned, and installed infrastructure to guide development in environmentally friendlier, less energy-consuming ways. In New Jersey in the late 1960s, the Ramapo plan was among the first to link development permissions to the adequacy of existing or publicly planned extensions of infrastructure.

Ian McHarg's *Design with Nature* proposed whole different ways of conceptualizing regional growth—how to go about planning new settlements in greater harmony with ecological values. Michael Corbett designed "Village Homes" west of Davis, California, where environmental sustainability, alternative energy, pipeless storm water management, and food growing strategies combined to show the possibilities of an alternative suburbia.

Along with a number of other experimental efforts, these responses to real, measurable environmental problems engendered what came to be known as growth management planning. Planners sought ways to bend short-term, ad hoc development initiatives into patterns, locations, and concentrations that would have fewer adverse impacts on the environment and that public jurisdictions could reasonably expect to support. Devices used included concurrent planning of infrastructure with private development, establishing growth boundaries, assuring funding for necessary infrastructure through controlling where development goes, and imposing impact fees.

An apparent lull in the oil supply and cost crisis together with the rapid ascendancy of the "market" as the leading edge economic theory slowed the underlying common sense of the growth management movement. Renewal of oil anxiety and the cascading woes accompanying the settlement patterns the 30-year lull produced have restored momentum to the idea of rebalancing the private gain–public benefit equation. Now debating what have come to be called "smart growth" alternatives, regions are actively looking for ways to overcome flaws in the patterns of the past, including environmental sustainability, providing better choices for changing housing and job markets and their transportation links.

There seems to be a growing realization that the shape of regional development patterns may need to shift, maybe in radical ways, in order to accommodate growth in urban areas that does not degrade quality of life. Major revisions in thinking are occurring across all of the place-building disciplines, partly driven or reinforced by market shifts that add up to the necessity to at least offer an alternative to the patterns that have so dominated post–World War II settlement. More and more these disciplines are advocating smart growth principles that seek to redirect new growth to already developed areas; create a mix of activities, densities, and hopefully incomes; and increase the viability of transit or pedestrian transportation alternatives to drive-alone trips.

Early advocates in the United States included Andy Euston, an architect and HUD official, and Sarah Harkness, a principal at The Architects Collaborative in Massachusetts, who joined with others to put forward analysis agendas and policy proposals to deal with the newly heightened sustainability concerns. Focusing on energy and environmental balance, these ideas made it into policy initiatives at HUD, and the AIA even declared energy as the Institute's yearlong focus for 1986.

Relaxation of the oil supply crisis and the Reagan administration's abandonment of tax credit incentives to support alternative energy initiatives sharply curtailed sustainability as a viable choice for how to grow the country.

Under the sway of the free market as the only acceptable way to conceptualize options, including growth patterns, the term "growth management," with all its implications that government might play a beneficial role in shaping the regions in its jurisdictions, got deep-sixed. Robert Yaro, now executive director of the Regional Plan Association, tells the story of how "smart growth" got positioned as a new and improved (and acceptable) growth management concept. When he was working for then Massachusetts Governor Mike Dukakis, faced with growing urgency for dealing with the problems created by that state's development practices, he suggested the need for more aggressive growth control or growth management policies and programs. Sensitive to overtones of anything akin to control or management, the governor asked Yaro to come up with a different name for any such initiative. When they hit upon "smart growth," the governor was satisfied—the term not only took away any threat to "growth," but it suggested that any opposition by definition would have to be for "dumb growth"—and who would stand for that?

The Atlanta Chamber of Commerce conducted a study in 2002 to find out what would happen to growing congestion woes if somehow the average daily trip length for Atlantans, then at 35 vehicle miles traveled per day, could be reduced to 31. That theoretical exercise confirmed that such a small reduction would actually reduce congestion, which under current plans is projected to continue to increase.

Transportation planners and engineers in more and more jurisdictions are looking harder for multimodal solutions as they understand that where people live and work and where economic development investments are made are choices that directly interact with travel choices. If you talk to a smart growth transportation planner (for whom an overriding goal is to reduce vehicle miles traveled), you will understand the term as the promotion of fully integrated transportation systems, favoring access over mobility, improving driving conditions but with emphasis on transit alternatives for heavily traveled areas, and walkable, bikeable local environments.

Economic planners are coming to realize that the reactive, ad hoc, deal-by-deal practices that have so characterized economic development may be damaging the long-term competitiveness of their region. With perhaps less consciousness of the wholeness of the forms of human settlement, the smart growth economic development professional will talk about the economic advantages and opportunities (and challenges) of "live, work, shop, play" communities.

Land use planners, urban designers, and architects are revisiting the functionality and forms of communities measured by how well they actually work for people. If you talk to a smart growth planning and design professional you are likely to get a form-based response, on the private side at least, advocacy for designed communities (usually single client–driven) with clearly identified, compact centers and some diversity of housing type and density, where the car is subjugated to more human scaled settings.

And environmental planners and advocates, recognizing that development will happen and will be profit-driven, are shifting their focus away from opposing what they don't like and toward advocating what they do like in the search for environmentally sustainable futures. The environmental planner or landscape architect is likely to talk about natural world responses with emphasis on the impacts of human development on a fragile planet and advocacy for creating sustainable communities. These models are now popularly measured by carbon footprint, where the goal in order to slow the pace of climate change is to curb emissions of carbon compounds into the air, water, or land.

The merging of these perspectives into integrated strategies seems to now be advancing in many regions and is likely to lead to decisions and choices different from what the single-minded juggernaut driving sprawl patterns achieved, one hopes for the better. Continued integration, together with growing market support, is essential to establish options for people to consider in choosing where and how to live, work, and travel. Urban designers in particular, as people trained, practiced, and committed to cross-disciplinary approaches and holistic problem-solving, have the opportunity and, I would say, the mission to facilitate this integration.

The issues facing regions are generally broader than the terms "sprawl" or "smart growth" address. The terms attach generally to physical settlement pattern alternatives and are thus useful for picturing what the regional debate may be about. The issues, though, extend beyond their scope to join with other planning, policy, and development issues that regions face, including where population is growing and declining, public education, conserving energy, conserving environmental assets, reflecting the particular physical and cultural patterns that differentiate one region from another, considering how trips are made, and offering a range of choices of how and where to live to its citizens. These issues interact with each other and with the settlement patterns they produce, and neither term encompasses their essence.

The other side of regional growth dynamics is decline. In every region, some areas are hot, where what sells is what's marketed in sync with larger market forces, like schools, services, amenities, mortgage availability, perceptions of good deals, and travel times. Other areas are not, where either in fact or in perception the reverse of the above attractants is creating stable or even declining markets. The people living in these areas, however, are as deserving of public policy and program support as those in hot areas. Urban planners, designers, and community leaders need to develop a positive consciousness of the dynamics creating these conditions, and there should always be corresponding guidances to address conditions of stasis or stability and shrinkage or decline. As it happens, all of these conditions hold opportunities for getting it right, smart no-growth or smart stabilization, or perhaps more elegantly retrofitting, if you will. Regional dynamics always include both sides of the growth coin, and both have their opportunities and challenges.

For several years the Environmental Protection Agency has supported and promulgated smart growth initiatives around the country and through a number of organizations that work nationally on various aspects of smart growth, all leading, one hopes, toward synthesis. The EPA website for their smart growth programs is http://www.epa.gov/livablecommunities. A nongovernment organization that provides an umbrella for and links to various initiatives is Smart Growth America, whose website is http://www.smartgrowthamerica.org.

While the resolution of these issues has profound impacts on settlement patterns—the large-scale design choices for the region—neither smart growth nor sprawl adequately frames the dialogue about what to do. Urban designers should use their cross-disciplinary visioning skills to join with the other place-building disciplines to understand the interrelatedness of the full range of issues and to help people picture the consequences of the choices.

Even so, smart growth in its more inclusive constructions has become a proxy for more government control, just as sprawl has become a proxy for the free market. The debate tends to push the two positions and philosophies toward a polarity that is more divisive than its objective basis, often frustrating any search for consensual visions or strategies. To begin with, there can never be an either-or, winner-loser resolution to the debate. Both positions depend utterly on public policy and public subsidy for their existence. Smart growth calls for introducing choices that are not presently supported by most market advocates (even though the market has clearly shifted to include smart growth options), choices that depend on government policy, legislation, and public finance. But the settlement patterns advocated by "market" forces are already dependent on government policy, support, and subsidy to maintain themselves. In many ways, then, it is not whether the market or smart growth is the way to go, but how much of the government pie each set of forces will be able to grab.

What seems clear is that there is a market demand for real choices that the pre–smart growth patterns did not offer, and consequently smart growth is reaching for a larger share and market forces are defending their traditional public resource base. As with many policy issues that translate into program and project realities, the direction the debate is trending may be more important than the nominal substance of the debate itself. And it seems clear by now that the smart growth momentum is here to stay, and that the market-generated patterns will continue to play a strong role in every region's settlement pattern mix.

In the suburban setting, projects billed as smart growth, or new urbanist or traditional neighborhoods, are almost always one-off developers' projects. Jurisdictions are reacting haphazardly to the phenomenon of market demand for smart growth developments. Whatever developer gets up a few acres of land and wants to risk market acceptance as a tradeoff for greater profit and can persuade local elected officials to give him license for the hunt is going to go forward. From the developer's perspective, acquiring property valued under current zoning for perhaps three or four houses per acre and getting permission to build maybe 12 to 16 units per acre represents a tantalizing potential windfall.

It seems reasonable to assume that reurbanization, with its higher density and closer-together patterns, will be joining the still dominant suburban pattern as a viable and strong option. The formal, design, and community fabric implications of this shift, as they are now emerging, are significant. This new regional settlement equation demands an attuned citizenry and focused, integrated design responses so that the search for a better way (at least the provision of a choice for how Americans want to live) establishes a new balance, both in the older urban and in the suburban settings.

Picking up on the market shifts that new urbanism has been able to achieve, jurisdictions at all scales are beginning to rework their regulatory frameworks to permit or encourage this new model as a potentially viable alternative to the old suburban subdivision standards, the problems of which are worsening. Without some integration of these individual development initiatives into larger infrastructure patterns, however, a smattering of perhaps by themselves attractive products, alternatives to the norm, could exacerbate all the problems already threatening outlying suburbs—more traffic, more school children to support from a primarily residential tax base, more strain on infrastructure, and so on.

Here is where citizen activists and responsible urban designers can begin to have an effect by influencing jurisdictions to identify where infrastructure will support such densification and where it won't. Densifying suburban areas exacerbates a whole set of problems that new urbanism is not solving. It adds to the traffic and other infrastructure loads that at their best were only designed to meet low-density needs. Yet, as mostly a developer-driven movement, the problem typically gets dumped on the suburban jurisdiction and maybe the region, even as the market to do more traditional neighborhood developments heats up. Private sector new urbanist practitioners may see these larger consequences of their developments as someone else's problem to solve.

People need to be able to picture the comparison between the traditional subdivision approach and the new urbanist approaches, not just in form as is now usually the case, but also in terms of the range of issues that will shape regional settlement pattern alternatives. In terms of physical form and functionality, the traditional subdivision approach is easy to picture—it's what's happening all around, with empirically confirmed consequences in terms of all issues, from transportation to social structures. The newer approaches are less easy for people to picture because there are still not examples in many jurisdictions (though this is changing rapidly), and the consequences of their patterns are still matters of speculation. Ultimately the people there need to guide the outcome, and so their grasp of the issues needs to be as comprehensive as any of the professionals, or developers, or public officials whose actions will build the future region.

For example, even the RPA membership with all its laudable commitments to regional betterment, was weighted toward powerful regional economic interests. The outcomes of its efforts naturally enough could not stray too far out of the bounds of those interests.

Fortunately, just as real choices are gaining market momentum, citizens are becoming more involved and active in entering the debate, with real opportunities to shape its outcome. At the same time, there has been a shift from collections of project-specific private initiatives accounting for regional growth patterns to acceptance that the public sector does have and should have more authority for them. While always fraught with huge jurisdictional complications, regions are becoming more and more identifiable entities.

Public health professionals are joining the dialogue, as they find direct relationships between the physical forms of the built world and a number of community health indicators. Settlement patterns directly affect walking and exercise patterns, basic indicators for any number of public health concerns (obesity, heart and lung conditions, and so on). And increasingly community development and housing advocates are extending their sense of equity and balance to the mix of what many consider intrinsic in the notion of sustainability.

Historically, activism at the regional level came mainly from the narrow interest groups who stood the most to gain: real estate, transportation, construction, commerce, and industrial interests whose members saw opportunity in advancing their interests in this larger setting. For most of the years of the growth of regionalism as a conscious concept, advocates for one or another of these large shaping issues as well as other less-physically-driven issues have strongly influenced the outcome, usually with little consciousness or regard for their interactive impacts on other challenges or opportunities—or their impacts on people's daily lives or a sustainable environment.

As we have seen in earlier examples, though, now other groupings are pressing to level the playing field with the traditional centers of power. They seek influence across a range of issues important for a region's overall quality of life, but historically kept in the shadows. Under this barrage of better and better informed grassroots-based advocacy, regional planning agencies are bending to calls for greater access and more transparency in their processes. In many regions, too, the expertise claimed by regional planners and their consultants has become debatable in the wake of successions of disappointment. Sometimes political and related economic forces override sensible recommendations, but sometimes the experts just don't get it right. Citizen leavening can improve both sets of circumstances.

At the macro scale, then, urban designers and community activists are becoming increasingly involved in the physical, spatial, morphological effects of urban settlement patterns. The interactive forces between home-to-work travel time and travel distance, the costs of housing and transportation, and the emerging awareness that the patterns we have are not necessarily either optimal or sustainable are driving a search for alternatives. At the same time the long run of the suburb, the strip, the mall, the spread across the landscape as the only feasible way for urban areas to meet their growth needs is giving way to both market and technical options. With changing demographics, the desirability and the demand for closer in, amenity-rich, mixed-use, mixed-density living environments is fueling urban rebirth in many cities. The market, including young people who grew up in suburbs, empty nesters who want to downsize, and the growing numbers of seniors who either can't or don't want to be car-dependent, seems far from sated.

# Summary

The built world provides the stage on which people's activities play out, at all scales from the neighborhood to the region. Its buildings house all of the more private and personal activities that people engage in, and its public spaces provide the common space that people share. Urban design is mainly about the latter but includes the former to the extent that the two interface. Altogether the syntheses of all this building and public environment that people share is infinitely varying, always complex. Yet, as we have seen, it is possible to break this complexity down into recognizable parts at the range of scales from neighborhood to region. Doing so, and further understanding how they come together to form patterns that fit within three comprehensible design traditions, urban designers and community leaders can begin to formulate ideas and priorities for "reading" their communities or the ones they are working in. The next chapter deals with how people carry on their activities in urbanized environments. Chapter 5 discusses how people and place connect to each other and to the infrastructure that sustains life and health. Together this content of urban design sets the basis for understanding how to act upon the civic environment to improve it.

# 4

# HUMAN ACTIVITY

## The Things People Do

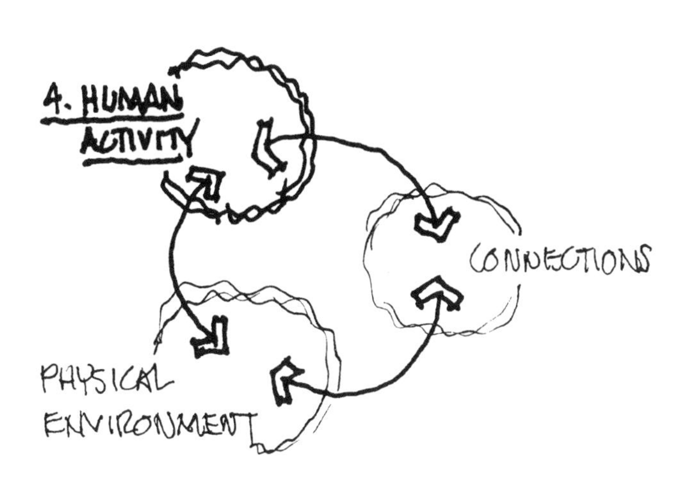


*Figure 4.1*
*Human activity interacting with the physical environment and connections to form the content of urban design.*

# What People Have to Do, Want to Do, and Where They Do It

## Introduction

The physical world wouldn't mean much to us if we weren't here (though I have run into folks who think that the natural world would be better off without us, and they're probably right, if impractical). Human activity, though, has girdled the earth, just here and there thousands of years ago, but ultimately spreading across the whole of it, if not to inhabit it certainly with impacts on it. The manifestations of human activity, the demands of human survival, and the quest for well-being, stretch from global settlement patterns to day-to-day living environments. These latter are the places where we regularly come into contact with each other, to share or to contest. Throughout time, people have sought to improve their lot—eat better, sleep better, feel better, live longer, work more easily and effectively, relate to each other better and, to support these aspirations, improve the physical environment in which they find themselves. People's activities shape these places, and the physical and symbolic features of these places in turn may shape our behavior. These are the focus of the discussion that follows.

Through this quest, which progresses unevenly, competition and cooperation vie in dynamic interaction as models for propelling civilization forward. Which way works best, or is there a constructive interaction between the two that is most effective in moving people forward? What is best for the most people, or is it about making things a lot better for a few and not much better or even worse for everyone else? How have people planned in their interactions with each other to achieve a better life? How have they dealt with issues of continuous, often massive change, in their social, economic, and political worlds? How have they tried to raise a bulwark against the ravages of nature through the millennia—in our times, for example, looming climate change? How do these dynamics interact with the civic environments people share? These kinds of questions are broader than our subject, yet how people create and use their civic environments is emblematic of their progress on larger life quests.

Martin Luther King Jr. expressed the sentiment and the hope on behalf of those who followed his teachings that the "arc of the moral universe is long, but it bends towards justice for all," a sentiment that this book shares. More to the point, people want to live in a better place, and understanding what that means and how to go about making it happen are the purposes here. In my experience, "better" or "worse" is largely a judgment of the people there, on the ground where the civic environment is, and where the judgment of the many outweighs the judgment of the few. A place doesn't work if no one is there. So what do people do, what are the activities that people routinely engage in, with special focus on how their shared activities shape and are shaped by public space?

Even though people tend to respond comparably to different spatial settings, conscious incorporation of evidence-based human behavior into urban design and other environment-shaping design practices is still in a primitive state. An early advocate for actually studying how people behave in typical urban spaces, sociologist William "Holly" Whyte, pioneered such an effort in *The Social Life of Small Urban Spaces* in 1980. He inspired Fred Kent and others to form Project for Public Spaces, a nonprofit (and that is important) think tank and design advisor for civic space improvement initiatives all across the country. His work and his thought is intertwined with that of Jane Jacobs; he exhorted design professionals to adopt more systematic efforts to actually understand how people behave in urban space and why, and then respond in ways to improve people's experience. Regrettably, however well-documented and compelling was his case, the design fields continue to assert their opinions of how people should or do respond with little study or effort to verify their impulses—public spaces are turned out everyday that neither function well nor feel good.

At about the time that Jacobs and Whyte were studying the effects of modernist-generated ravages on livable, walkable, sittable neighborhoods and districts, other movements were accelerating around issues of public access. First came the civil rights movement, where access was a cornerstone aspiration and ultimately a demand that began to be met. Then people with disabilities fought to overcome their denial of access to the public realm and its institutions, which their tax dollars supported. Issues of accessibility, the open use of all facilities in the public realm, have significantly altered the attitude and the forms of response to the larger society's gradual adoption and implementation of accessibility, with fundamental urban design implications. The blurring of public and private that comes with privatization should be carefully monitored for its impacts on this principle, as already the ability to pay is exacerbating a growing class divide all across the urban landscape.

Following in Whyte's footsteps, some research on human behavior and civic space is going on, and urban designers in particular should pay attention. The focus of this chapter is on what people do, why, and how, and on how these activities translate into the spaces we have built to accommodate or support the activities. In traditional city planning language, the focus of these activities is on their effects on the land—what is usually called "land use." Land use has been a convenient abstraction for designating how land is or may be used, but often prioritizes the two-dimensional over the three-dimensional, the static over the dynamic, the fixity of place over changingness of people, over time. Similarly, many are now focusing their attention on what is called "form based" design, incorporating the third dimension and thus considering space rather than maps as the base from which to engage the physical environment. Form-based codes are gradually joining with or supplanting use-based codes in many jurisdictions, producing for the most part more consciously designed and sometimes more fully thought-out physical development patterns and practices. Land use maps and use-based codes, as an example, typically ignore the public realm altogether, an omission that form-based coding is trying to correct. In fact, both approaches have merit, and urban designers should assist in finding and establishing their syntheses.

Consistent with the premises of this work, though, I emphasize what people do, the choices they make, and how those actions define places, with the physical world being the receiver of and responder to this impetus—activity-based design, if you will. Accordingly, below, I identify people's activities first, the kinds of spaces typically associated with the activities second, and land use designations third. Reviewing these major spheres of human activity, reflect on their "private" and "public" character: Those most public are those most associated with the design of places, the civic environment shared by all.

## Home

*"Be it ever so humble, there's no place like home."*
*"Home sweet home."*
*"Home is where one starts from."*
*"Home is where the heart is."*

The Activities: living, eating, sleeping, procreating, nurturing
The Spaces: the home, the house, the apartment, the condo, the townhouse, the homeless encampment, the hut, the mansion
The Land Use: residential, housing, single family at various densities, townhomes, multifamily at various densities, mixed-use

Home life, in its basic essence, is an activity shared by everybody to a remarkable extent across space, time, and shelter need. People all sleep somewhere, eat somewhere, lead their personal and private lives, create and nurture families. Out of the weather, a place to lay down the head, a place to prepare and eat food, a way for dealing with waste, and (more in the spirit of where people come from and where they're going) a place for loving, procreating, nurturing, hoping, and praying—or fighting and separating—but usually a refuge from an often hostile and challenging world outside.

People live and carry on the same basic functions, whether in homeless encampments or haciendas, favelas or fincas, caves or castles, with only a few living grandly and most living farther down the line. As class society and the will among some to differentiate or dominate has developed, the putative need to express class or status superiority has exponentially widened the way the "home" meets these basic needs. People on the make in all societies have used the shelter needs that all share for the purpose of expressing status, power, even dominance, flaunting purposefully the resources they have extracted from the society around them. Whether the "home" is a materially and psychologically driven expression of prowess and rank for some or simply a reasonably functioning shelter for survival for most, though, people still carry out the same core home-based functions described above, all pretty much the same way. (Even if you have a 10-bedroom, 5-bath house you still sleep about the same number of hours, put clothes on before you go out, and use the facilities about the same amount every day.)

For urban designers and community-minded people, beyond awareness of and commitment to the values of improving the quality of shelter for all, it is the interface between the civic setting and the private realm that commands attention. Thus how the public realm transitions to the home becomes critical, taking into account that these transitions are generally most focused in the early morning, after school, and after work. Is the privateness of the house honored, promoted, and graced, recognizing variations across time, place, and culture? Do people feel safe, comfortable, and pleased by the functionality and character of their approach to their homes? Their neighborhoods? Are the transitions to other activities of life convenient and clear? Do the connections people need to meet their daily requirements function well—getting to centers, jobs, shops, parks, schools, and other institutions? In short, does the public realm work for enhancing people's private lives? It is the urban designer's job to improve the functionality of this connective environment, to elevate pride in the civic values shared by whatever society as reflected in our commitment to that common place.

## Workplace

The Activities: making, working, earning, providing, investing
The Spaces: the workplace, office, shop, institution, factory, farm, construction site, the business district, the strip, the mall, the industrial district, mixed-use districts
The Land Use: commercial, industrial, retail, hospitality, institutional, mixed-use, agricultural

*"... a hell of a way to make a living."*
*"I need two jobs just to make ends meet."*
*"If my spouse didn't work, we'd never make it."*
*"I clip coupons..."*

The core of people's survival (as individuals, families, communities, cities, nations, humanity) depends on making a living. The economic conditions and structures under which this goal is sought are widely divergent, from slave, to feudal, to capitalist, to socialist models. In the present world all these forms exist, and, while most economies seem to have some mix of them represented in varying proportions, capitalism is presently the defining structure for the United States (and much of the rest of the world).

The range of job types varies widely, with pay usually associated with training, education, connections, diligence, accountability, hours of work and performance, and rewards tied to one's standing in the hierarchy for each type of work, depending on how the combination of performance factors are prioritized. What people do to make a living is all over the map, with about two-thirds employed in the private sector, a quarter in government, and the rest in nonprofit types of organizations. The work itself is usually a varyingly private endeavor, where in some settings the work requires a lot of social interaction and in others is essentially personal effort, all reporting to some sort of usually hierarchized management structure—the boss. Workplaces similarly range widely, with their relative concentrations directly reflecting the state and nature of the economy at any given location and point in time. Workplaces as buildings and their settings are expressed by their owners as widely as is shelter, from giddy, purposefully and flagrantly excessive opulence to workaday factories, hole-in-the-wall shops, hidden sweatshops, the garage, the backyard.

For urban designers and community people, the locational and connectivity factors of how individuals make a living along with the economic context and its trends are of great importance, from the regional or macro scale to the individual workplace. Like for living places, the environs, the interface between more or less private work activity and the public realm figures prominently. Here, though, typically the focus is on the daytime and on the public realm activities that support and interact with workplaces. How do people get there, at what time, how long does it take, how safe and comfortable is the surrounding environment? What are our access choices—cars and parking, transit, walking, or biking? Is the setting conducive to people feeling positive or at least okay with showing up? Workplaces all have settings, transitions from the public setting and its connections to the work itself. All of them could be better than they are, particularly from the perspective of the great numbers that characterize the workforce.

For example, a clerk or white collar worker in business attire sidling across an ornate plaza to enter a marble-faced, high-ceilinged corporate atrium on the way to a cubicle might feel about the same about his or her job as a booted, overalled worker slogging across a muddy work yard for eight hours at a production machine. Here again, just as housing expresses class and cultural status, so does the workplace. Depending on ownership, power, function, and self-image, it might exult, intimidate, wow, or be nondescript or careless, or isolate and keep out of sight. The workplace expresses the owner's values where for some hierarchy, control, or self-aggrandizement is more important; for others a productive, satisfied workforce; for others maybe a "who cares?" sentiment.

In any event, urban designers and community leaders have a stake in assuring that the workplace fits comfortably into its surroundings, that its travel, noise, light, and hours of operation characteristics are compatible with its neighbors and that its public environment respects both the people all around and the people working inside.

## Marketplace

*"Shop 'til we drop."*
*"Let's check it out."*
*"I'm gonna trade it in."*

The Activities: buying, selling, exchanging, trading, marketing, shopping, vending, hanging out
The Spaces: the plaza, the commons, the shops, the street, the markets, main street, commercial strips, malls, flea markets
The Land Use: commercial, retail, business, mixed-use

Among the first and most enduring activities people have undertaken, essential to their existence, is commerce, the exchange of goods and information through barter, money, or social interaction. Places from the earliest known settlements have been developed to facilitate this most necessary and fundamental function. The agora, the forum, the plaza, the commons, main street, the strip, the mall, the Wal-Mart have provided the exchange meeting ground for the diversity of people in the local society. Not just the exchange of goods for survival or enhancement, but the interactions of people, ideas, and cultures have their locus in the marketplace.

Here civic space is center stage, often the scene of social rituals, no longer the transition and seam to private activities. Locating and creating places suitable for the fullest range of such activities is a fundamental and ongoing mission of societies throughout time and across space—basic urban design, if you will. The triad of the physical world, human activities, and their interconnections plays directly into where and how such places may be established. At the same time, the marketplace of ideas has broadened infinitely with the Internet, "the space of flows" as Manuel Castells has suggested, in which the relative mix of eBay or Facebook and Face to Face is shifting to an unknown and not reliably predictable future.

Topography, orientation, climate, water, vista, landscape, where the products for trade are produced, where people live, the best travel paths, and other infrastructure connecting all these activities all come together to form places. Some of these work, and some don't, and some work in one time or climate or societal setting and not later on or elsewhere. Their forms reflect and express economic, social, and political structures that in the time of their creation organized human activity. For many towns and cities, the market in whatever form it takes is often the defining image of the place, not necessarily for the space itself as for how well that space responds to and supports the waves of activity that define civic life.

For urban designers, involvement in the creation of these civic places and institutions is of primary importance, almost definitional. To design, build, occupy, maintain, modify, and sustain this most basic, ubiquitous, and timeless activity in ways that elevate the functionality and experiential quality for all is a special challenge of urban design and of civic leadership. The integration of all skills and the inclusion of all with direct interest as well as representation from all likely to be affected by such a crucial place-making activity is essential, as will be discussed in more detail in Part Three, Principles. As with the urban designers' optimal role in other place-making activities, we should be particularly intent on listening to, absorbing, and reflecting the fullest of civic values in marketplace design, the physical world, the transportation and communications systems, and the full range of human activity to be accommodated and supported.

A special challenge in our time, but as a seam like other seams that urban design deals with, is tracking and understanding the interactions between physical space and cyberspace. How will Internet and cellular communications alter the character of and the needs for civic spaces? As with most dualities in this field, both spheres will continue on, but how will they affect each other, and what trends may emerge?

For lack of understanding of behavior, for lack of integration of relevant disciplines working toward a common whole, for lack of leadership that balances civic life with private life, creating the exchange place as a positive and defining urban environment and experience remains a struggle. Fortunately, going back to the spark supplied by William "Holly" Whyte, there are a few theorists and practitioners who are gaining ground on the problem.

Project for Public Spaces (www.pps.org) has been studying the characteristics of public spaces and marketplaces comprehensively for 30 years or so, and its work and the accessibility of its work to the public, as a dedicated nonprofit, provides insight, understanding, skills, and common sense to assist designers and community leaders to better shape these most central places in the civic environment. Private practitioners like Jan Gehl, a Danish architect; Anton Nelessen, Urban Design Associates; the Congress for New Urbanism; and others are building records of reasonable and growing success in public place design. These more recent theorists and practitioners have adopted more inclusive and interdisciplinary collaborations into their practices, and most make the effort to factor in human behavior into their approaches. What will draw people to the place, make it more appealing? What design and functional moves will encourage a more diverse meeting ground, usually a sure mark of vitality for a place? They know that the baseline criterion for a successful place is that there are people there, a result that depends on understanding, responding to, and supporting human behavior.

For community builders, whether in districts or neighborhoods, a place for exchange, at whatever scale, is critical for providing identity and a place for everyone in the community. Thus, in small neighborhoods, the crossroads, the mom-and-pop shop, the park, the school, the Laundromat, or a religious institution may provide the locus, however informally, for people to come together. At this scale perhaps the exchange is as much social as commercial, bringing the kids together, or meeting on community issues. Yet a defined place is almost a prerequisite for establishing the identity and the culture necessary for protecting and advancing locally held visions. Bigger neighborhoods and certainly districts and centers depend on this exchange even more centrally, and understanding how community leadership can support the development of such places is the mark of coalescing diverse populations around common purposes.

## Institutions

*"Got to get an education."*
*"Take care of yourself."*
*"Can't fight city hall."*
*"You'd better believe."*
*"Have faith."*
*"Be careful out there."*
*"Defend the borders."*

The Activities: learning, teaching, tending to health, administering government, believing, worshiping, policing, soldiering
The Spaces: the institution—schools and universities, hospitals and medical campuses, research complexes, "city hall" or government (with all of the associated public service facilities), religious buildings, outdoor institutions, police and fire training grounds, military bases, all with their associated outdoor spaces
The Land Uses: institutional, office/institutional, public facilities, or as included in other land uses

There are many activities that supplement, enhance, and improve people's ability to provide for themselves, engage in exchange, and meet their core eating, sleeping, shelter, and nurturing needs, each of which has its own way of fitting into the places we inhabit. These include activities listed above, to name a few of the more prevalent ancillary activities that are common among all peoples through all time. The generic adjective to describe the locus or land use of all these activities is "institutional." Broken down, this means spaces for agencies of government, the school, the library, the clinic, the hospital, the religious institution, the army base, the spaces of public safety. The activities that occur in these settings are for the most part analogous to workplaces. While their reason for being is to serve the needs of various constituencies, they are also workplaces for those rendering the services. They include activities that range from social, like in classrooms, to personal and private, like in the doctor's office. These institutions shape and occupy significant sites in the places we build, and each should be properly distinguished according to its function, its purpose, and its meaning.

The job for urban designers is to assure that the institution's mission of service carries through in its physical presence. Well-conceived, planned, and designed institutions reinforce rather than detract from other nearby activities; they support the public connective structure that ties them to their larger setting. Similarly, community leaders must involve themselves to accommodate necessary institutional activities in ways that acknowledge their essential nature without unduly assaulting community values. Seams again become very important. How institutions interface with their neighbors, whether residential, business, low density or higher density, become the focus of good urban design practice. The seams and connections don't need to be opulent to be inviting, and people approaching these centers of civic infrastructure, whether as workers or as clients, ought to be able to feel good about the experience.

Institutions and their siting and expansion are frequently the source of "NIMBYism" (not in my backyard) or "LULUs" (locally unwanted land uses), and so special care is required to involve everyone early in the choices that must be made. Site selection in particular is a crucially important step, functionally, spatially, and politically, and many of the most hotly contested institutional initiatives can be traced to really casual and slipshod site selection processes. The idea that an institution, public or private, can just put whatever they want wherever they want it because they are in some way a service provider, or because they don't have to adhere to local land development policies, is almost certain to lead to hostility and often time-consuming and embarrassing defeat. More importantly, short-sighted institutional decision-making likely will lead to a diminished overall civic environment.

The activities of local government employees span from maintenance to office work, and the spaces necessary to operate a government include utilities installations, police and fire stations and training facilities, fleet storage and maintenance, parklands, and a range of office-oriented service agencies. As suggested above, how sites are selected to provide the space necessary to render all these services and then how they are maintained are emblematic of the respect, perhaps the mutual respect, between the managers of government and the community.

A significant and visible part of the local government employee base is made up of people whose activities are preventing and fighting crime, preventing and fighting fires, otherwise providing security, and backing up these activities in court. "Police presence" is a divide word among those most concerned about crime, some advocating for a cop on every corner and comfortable with the associated symbolism, others with less trust in the even-handedness of police protection trying to dial it back. Some advocate "community policing," a partnership with the communities to identify, deter, and control crime.

Activities of learning and places of learning are the symbols and emblems of the status of knowledge for societies through the ages, sometimes exalted, sometimes in distress. Learning may extend to all or may be restricted and exclusionary, based on political structure, class, race, gender, or faith. Learning may be open, explorative, and questioning or limiting, catechistic, and indoctrinating. Learning may seek to develop the potential of everyone or it may serve to protect and promote the interests of the few. Places of learning reflect where in the above continuum a society may find itself at any given time, both in where they are located with respect to the activities of the larger society and in how they are designed.

The activities of health maintenance and treatment similarly evolve according to the values that guide health care from society to society. From indigenous, superstitious, and empirical to high tech, science-based, and test-based, from prevention to cure orientations, one can read the status and priority of human health in a society, and the extent to which those values spread over the whole of a society. The state, availability, and relative quality of health care can be read in their physical settings and conditions, echoing the ranges described above. Presently, too, public health professionals are incorporating standards of community health that favor prevention principles, like walking to combat obesity, and so they are much more interested in how their institutions engage the broader community.

Religious expression is a barometer of a society's institutionalized faith. Many societies define themselves as adhering to one or another faith, showing up in the prevalence and prominence of their physical institutions, maybe their dress and daily habits, their laws and governance. Others define themselves in terms of secular values, supporting freedom of (or even from) religion, showing up in diversities of physical expression in the form of churches, synagogues, mosques, or temples and the symbols that define each.

Religious institutions, like others, reflect and express the values and hierarchies in the broader society. Some integrate themselves in size, character, and impact with their surrounding neighborhood or district. Others, perhaps driven by shifts in demography, abandon the physical neighborhood that spawned them to follow their target populations. Some are humongous churches, usually centered in giant pools of asphalt, built in communities all across the country. Unlike the cathedrals that anchor villages and towns from an earlier day, they are often built, like shopping centers, at the fringes of encroaching subdivisions, with similar logic. They are positioning themselves to capture the market that will surely come, and they are recognizing that a growing church in an existing neighborhood will hit secular resistance as their building complex and parking lot footprint grows.

Finally among the major institutions that characterize people's reach for self-improvement are those dedicated to the activities of public safety and, on a larger scale, defense (or offense). A dramatic example is military bases, and their periodic closings (or expansions) having major impacts on their host communities. In the case of closings, they change the community's identity and put a dent in the local economy with the removal of so many primary and secondary jobs and the impacts on small businesses. Communities in growth cycles are better able to adjust than those where the base is the core industry. Expansions, on the other hand, raise all the issues that accompany other large space using activities.

Architects and landscape architects are inculcated with a culture that approaches every new societal wind as a "design opportunity" as well as a funding or client opportunity, usually not delving into the further implications or societal meanings of the latest tendencies.

In some ways, the presence of security forces, whether as uniforms, apparatus, barricades, or compounds, is a measure of the role, priority, and status of fear in a culture, which way the wind is blowing. Designing civic spaces around defense priorities became a subset for some in urban design in the wake of the unrest of the late 1960s and early 1970s. Its practitioners, most famously Oscar Newman, called for urban design measures driven by fear of crime in a book entitled *Defensible Space* in 1973.

Visible remnants of those times are near-windowless schools and banks, covered-over commercial storefronts, and office buildings and corporate headquarters set back behind walled landscaped plazas. The attitude toward law and order of that era led to Justice Department and HUD support and funding for what became known as "crime prevention through environmental design" (CPTED).

Since 9/11, activities focused on defense and security have taken a dramatic leap, and their manifestations have wrought palpable change in the civic environment. There has been a dramatic increase in design and construction technologies and devices to protect the civic realm from "evildoers." We have seen major physical changes in their interface with the public realm, federal buildings in particular, but other public buildings and "sensitive" private buildings as well. Some of these are blatant, taking the form of fortifications and redoubts that express fear, defiance, and defense; others, equally hardened in fact, show a friendlier face, covering their impregnability with landscape and "people places."

All of the above kinds of institutions house people's activities that support the prevailing structure, values, and organization of society. In so doing they define and communicate the character of the interface between their particular internalized activities and the public realm that positions them in and gives them access to the broader society. As suggested earlier, the choices for how to treat these interfaces seem to oscillate between two poles. Institutions may see themselves as separate, aloof, removed from and even hostile toward the surroundings in which they find themselves. Or they may view themselves as interactive with, part of, and giving and receiving benefits and resources from that interaction. More likely, given the ever-changing conditions in which institutions and their neighbors operate, they may be moving toward one pole and away from the other

Sometimes, particularly in the case of institutions of learning and religion, the public interface is central to supporting the activities their programs call for. This may take the form of playgrounds, "quads," church yards, or plazas, the purposes of which are to provide places for social learning or to support people's needs for rituals and pageantry that reinforce the message of the institution. These may be separated from or visible to the broader public, or they may be public spaces periodically expropriated for the activity's purpose.

For urban designers, the choices facing institutions define how to reflect and respond to the public spaces that they call for. Informed, interdisciplinary, and comprehensive guidance for institutions is especially important now. More and more of them are becoming more sophisticated in planning out their futures, understanding the larger contexts in which they are operating, and are developing broader views on the choices before them. The days of space planning when "just put the new building there" sufficed for most institutions no longer works, whether for internal reasons or because of community or government opposition. While there seems to be little formal academic training focusing on planning or designing for institutions (a little odd since institutions are such a prominent part of the urban scene), there are many consultant firms that as a matter of practice do focus on institutional planning and design, a number that is growing as the work opportunities grow.

Choices facing institutions as they experience changing circumstances are particularly important for the communities that interact with them, sometimes even with some dependency on the institution for their sustainability. As the community voice becomes more effective, it is incumbent on them to engage with institutions, in the same way that more and more are with developers, to assure that the institutional program takes into account the visions and values of nearby communities. The activities that the institution supports are in all likelihood essential to the overall well-being of the community. There is usually no reason why their provision cannot benefit both the aims of the institution and the needs and aspirations of their host community.

In Birmingham in the late 1980s, a major hospital sought zoning changes and variances to "harden" their perimeter against the "hostile" world beyond. Don Blankenship, our zoning administrator, an African American, and I suggested that they consider interacting with the surrounding neighborhoods, where many of their staff were living, in a more constructive way, programmatically and physically. The neighborhoods had shifted fairly rapidly from white to black; the hospital administration was all white, and their view of the world reflected that condition when they informed us that they used to involve the neighborhoods more actively but that "no one lives there any more."

On a happier note, in Atlanta, Carl Patton, recently retired president of Georgia State University, systematically led his campus from a blank-walled compound in the heart of downtown Atlanta to a fully interactive and open campus of the streets. And Wayne Clough, president of Georgia Tech, is leading a similar integration and engagement in its midtown location.

## Leisure

The Activities: hanging out, playing sports, walking the dog, running, biking, fishing, hunting, having a picnic, going to events, taking in a museum, shopping

The Spaces: parks, squares and plazas, sports fields and stadiums, civic centers, museums, entertainment venues (including concert halls and amphitheaters), shopping venues, nature preserves, rivers, lakes, waterfronts, fields, forests, hills, and mountains

The Land Uses: parks, public institutions, special designations for arenas, stadiums, commercial, agricultural, permanent open space

*"Let's go for a picnic; take the kids to the zoo; shoot a round of golf."*
*"Gone fishin'."*
*"Let's catch the new show at the museum; catch a ballgame; take in the concert; hang out at the park; go for a walk; go for a ride."*
*"Gimme a break."*

There is good evidence that throughout time and space humans have always sought for and treasured time to chill. The idea of a free day or a vacation or leave time, time away from the exigencies of making a living, appears to be as old as society itself. Many believe that this time and these activities are in fact integral to and essential for the effective functioning of human society: time for the body and mind to absorb, to prepare themselves, to think beyond the immediate, to divert, to work out, to fantasize, to hope, to aspire.

Our physical expressions of this need are wide-ranging and vary through time, space, and society. Hunting and fishing have evolved from their survival roots (still a necessity for many people) to become popular leisure-time activities, supporting major industries and engendering all manner of management procedures to balance their impacts. The coliseum, the stadium, the arena provide the nonparticipants the vicarious opportunity to go, observe, and ventilate. On the quieter side, walking, biking, picnicking, climbing, and bird-watching engage millions. Water for fishing, swimming, surfing, boating; air for hang gliding or parasailing. Football, baseball, and soccer engage millions on larger playing fields. In smaller settings, the basketball or tennis court, the billiards parlor, the poker table, the bocce ball, the ping pong table. All have a presence, more or less integrated into the other features of the urban place. In the present time, shopping for many has become a leisure time activity, for some a ritual, with the drawback that the wherewithal to consummate the activity requires more time at work, thus reducing net leisure time. Oh well.

The presence, make-up, and form of the spaces for leisure time activities are a marker for their importance to a society in place and time. They can range from completely informal, like the vacant lot on the corner, to highly organized recreational complexes, from nature experiences to grand arenas. They can be accessible for all, like public parks and waterfronts, or walled compounds reserved for the privileged few, like country clubs and polo grounds.

How the facility is integrated or not into the broader civic structure matters. Are there spaces within walking or biking distances or a transit ride that provide at least some leisure time outlet? Or can people only get there by car and then is adequate parking available? Does it support any other activities or is it a stand-alone? Does it express civic pride, or is it just an object on a parking lot? More broadly, does the provision of the opportunity to "take five" or take the day off actually attract people to the activity, make them feel like letting go? And is it safe? All of these factors and more are the concern not just of urban designers but of community leaders as well.

In the last few years, as mentioned earlier, health theorists and researchers have begun to focus on both leisure and community form as important links to community health, the physical forms of which either work or don't. The interaction between health professionals, urban designers, and community health advocates promises to provide better informed priorities and decisions for all those casual community leisure time needs, including the best ways to site and design the spaces necessary to support them.

Georgia Tech's Center for Quality Growth in the College of Architecture co-founded with Emory University's Rollins School of Public Health and the federal Centers for Disease Control and Prevention (CDC) a forum for engaging these questions and opportunities. Called the Healthy Places Research Group, it brings together planners, urban designers, architects, landscape architects, and public health professionals on a monthly basis to share research and experience and to advise on policy.

Presently, for example, maybe a little ahead of organized health organizations, communities have been successful in installing casual (as opposed to competitive) recreational facilities in towns and cities throughout the country. Barely a consideration until the 1970s, now most every city has supported and funded visible walking or jogging or biking or nature trail systems, together with strong advocacy from among citizens and increasingly community health organizations to multiply their support base.

These activities and responding to the demand to extend them further have become measures of community and civic leadership. They call upon urban design, particularly weighted toward landscape architecture, to engage in the process every step of the way. The impetus toward improving the quality of leisure time activities, especially those that are passive and nonprogrammed, has accounted for countless miles of walkable streetscapes and trails being built. The growth in urban parklands, reconnecting people to waterways and other natural features for leisure activities, connections formerly blocked by industries and highways, are happening pretty much in every city and town.

## Travel

The Activities: travel, walking, biking, riding, driving, getting about between places, communicating, connecting
The Spaces: streets, sidewalks, bikeways, transit ways, stations, airports, bus stops, cyberspace
The Land Uses: transportation, utilities, communication, parking lots and decks

*"On the road; stuck in traffic—getting there is half the fun."*
*"Every trip begins and ends on foot."*

As with all of the above activities, people have always traveled, have always needed to get from one place or another: sleeping place to working place; working place to trade place; between trading places; or just between. Except for people for whom it is the defining activity, travel is never an end in itself. Rather it is a means to facilitate ends. You start out some place to get to some other place, by whatever travel means. Being "there" is what matters. You pick up the phone or open up the computer to get to someone else or to an information source. Few people are on the road or online just for the fun of it (although the numbers online just to be there seem to be growing). In the case of travel, the time, expense, and behavioral impacts required to connect two points, the origin and the destination, are a growing portion of the day for people in urban areas. In reaction, there are signs that many people, both residents and employers, are acting to turn that trend around in their personal lives, driving growing reurbanization markets in urban and town centers.

This countertrend, gaining momentum over the last 10 or 15 years, has profound spatial implications for the future shape of cities and relationships between workplace, living place, and the other spaces that house human activity. Urban designers must be generally knowledgeable about the consequences of these trends and the travel behavior and technical responses that they engender. Community leaders too need to understand these broad and possibly sweeping trends, looking for the opportunities and issues of increasing demand for existing neighborhoods and districts to accommodate greater diversity of uses, densities, and people. The issues of travel and other connective infrastructure is dealt with in more detail elsewhere in this part, both in Chapters 3 and 5, and is addressed in Part Four, Processes, as well.

# Summary

Thus the physical world, natural and built, and the human activity that it engenders at various scales and across time and society coincide with the provision of civic space. Everyone is likely to carry on all or most of the above activities on a daily basis, and whether consciously or not integrate them together in the flow of daily choices and priorities. The spaces and flows that collect, attract, and facilitate people's activities and interactions with each other should be functional and pleasurable. If not, the physical environment may diminish, discourage, or even quell social interaction, which is a baseline measure of civil society.

The coming together of human activities that civic spaces should stimulate engages and commands a wide diversity of design capabilities and competencies. But it also commands the capability to synthesize, since people experience their world as places for integrating their daily activities, as wholes. In the present time, though, this work is too often parceled out among a variety of "experts" from different fields, who often don't think in terms of responding to the integrated needs of the people whose activities they are designing for. Accordingly, the experts tend to downplay the need and the potential of each other's contribution, or, worse, they compete for who or which discipline should dominate the others.

While we need the depth of knowledge and experience maintained by each discipline to solve the technical problems, we need cross-disciplinary integration even more. We have traffic engineers who would design places for the car—out of balance with pedestrians. We have the landscape architects who would design places for the tree and plant materials, maybe the fountains and plazas—obscuring activities that are the reasons for a place's being. We have civil engineers who would impose roadway, grade, and drainage designs that favor the car over the people or the natural environment. We have architects who would either design self-contained buildings without consideration of the places they are framing or design places as objects without consideration for the human activities and connections that make places work. We have public policies that favor the exploitation of private land over the civic purposes of public land. We have developers whose choices must be guided by maximization of profit to stay in business in a culture where such profit is single-mindedly equated with civic purpose. Urban designers have a duty to bridge the disciplines, to encourage integration, and to support links to community and other place-making forces. Community leaders must convey their integrated visions for better physical places to the design disciplines, must confidently inject the commonsense test into the technical work, and must fearlessly ask basic questions, sometimes over and over again, until they are answered and understood by all.

The important lessons of this element of the content of urban design are:

- Without human activity there are no places.
- The public environment provides the boundary and the seam with private activities.
- The civic realm provides the opportunity, maybe the obligation, to be the shared space for people's interchanges, whether material, conceptual, or cultural.
- The engagement of community representation and leadership with cross-disciplinary design and development professionals provides the best route to celebrate civic purpose in civic places.

# 5

# CONNECTIONS

## The Infrastructure That Ties People and Places Together

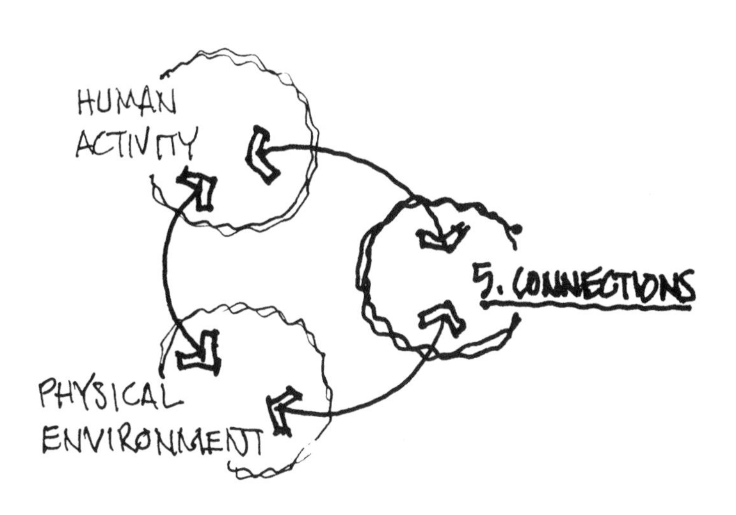


*Figure 5.1*
*Connections interacting with the physical environment and human activity to form the content of urban design.*

# Introduction

*"Let's hook up."*
*"You can't get there from here."*
*"Water runs downhill and finds its own level."*
*"What's on the tube?"*
*"Send me a text message."*

The connections between human activity and the physical world, often referred to as infrastructure, are the third in the interactive set of elements that make up the content of urban design. Together the three, the physical environment, human activity, and connections, describe how the urbanizing world develops. Over the last 150 years, and at an ever-accelerating rate, connections continue to radically shift the ways in which people connect—to each other and to the physical world. The shifts from sailing ships to steamships, from horses to trains to cars to airplanes, from pony express to telegraph to telephone and radio, to typewriter, to television to computer to cell phone and wireless connections, from chamber pots and open sewers to flush toilets and sewer lines and treatment plants, from water wells, cisterns and pails to central water supply and faucets are just a few of the radical shifts that utterly alter how people function and how places get planned and built.

Indeed, of the interactive relationships between connections, human activity, and the physical environment over this period, infrastructure changes have been and will continue to be the most dynamic. From the perspective of designing our present and future world, it is in the area of infrastructure problems, opportunities, and choices where the greatest changes are likely to occur.

How will the dynamic nature of these connections affect the relationships between people's activities and the places they frequent? How do they and will they connect to each other? What kinds of frameworks are necessary to facilitate the flows of people, goods, energy, communications, water, waste—all generated by people's activities? How do these systems relate to each other? How do they shape places from the neighborhood and district scale to the town, the city, the region? How may they either promote or threaten environmental sustainability? Who is responsible for and who designs and develops these systems? How can consciousness of the interrelatedness of these flows with each other and with serving their human activity purposes improve their effectiveness and the quality of life of people served by them? These are a few of the questions that this chapter addresses.

The infrastructure pieces that hook people together with each other and their places all have a direct impact on the shape and form of the world. The patterns that travel ways make are perhaps the most compelling, determining the form, shape, and character of built places at all scales. In addition, these travel ways define the public space people most commonly share, the most visible and most public elements in one's daily life. As public domain, making up about a quarter of all the land in a typical urbanized area, everyone is supposed to have the right of access and use of this domain. It connects people to the more private buildings that house most people's living, working, and leisure activities, and it is a place to share, to interact, to assemble, and to assert the right of access. This public right of access then too largely shapes the travel path of the other systems that people rely on to support their lives' activities.

In ways similar and just as important as travel ways, but not so visibly defining the built world, other connective strands are vital as well. The energy that lights and heats and cools homes and workplaces is generated at locations that serve that purpose and is then transmitted in networks,

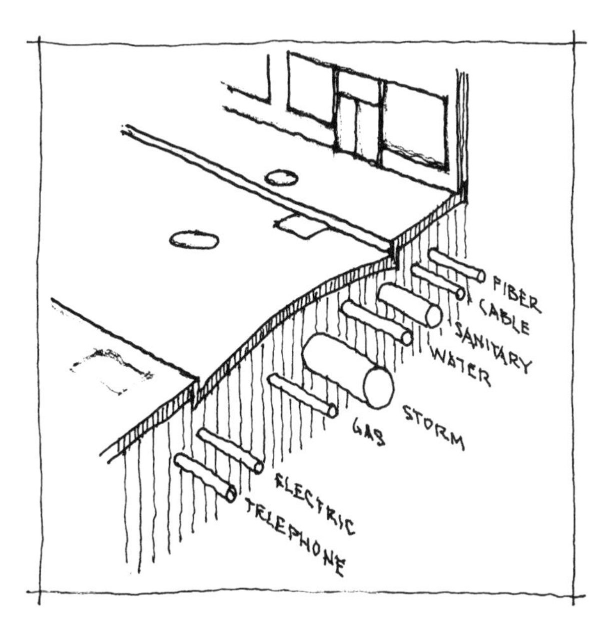


*Figure 5.2*
*Cutaway diagram of typical major street, showing all the other connections, beyond driving, riding, biking, and walking, that are made along its right-of-way.*

systems, or grids, designed to best assure reliable delivery. Thus electricity and natural gas overlay and underlay most built places, usually in wires on poles over, or pipes and tubes under, the travel ways, finally arriving at the duplex outlet or the pilot light. Usually, these systems follow the travel way pattern but, when faced with the typical suburban dendritic street pattern that often ends in a dead end, often create redundancy so that the energy transmitter has at least two ways of getting to its customer. Similarly, water distribution lines, telephone lines, cable TV, and computer access lines, as well as the means of solid waste disposal and public safety services, need to reach each building, on each lot, on each block, and the most effective way to do that is usually to follow the travel way.

Sewer and storm water run-off systems follow different laws than the supply side of utilities, since they want to do what water does, that is, run downhill. Whereas water supply is delivered under pressure, the best way to take water away, whether waste or storm, is by gravity, and so these lines may leave the travel ways and the convenience of their public access and run in easements across private property to find their most expeditious course to ultimate disposal, whether a treatment plant or a stream.

From a design perspective, how all these systems and networks lay out is fundamental in shaping the built world at all scales. Urban designers' focus is on the interaction between these systems and between the other elements of the built and natural world, not so much on any particular piece of the system. Their goal is to fulfill the purposes of each but to do it in ways that support the goal of improving both their functionality and the quality of the environment produced. Choices exist every step of the way and making these choices in ways that relate the systems to the other content of places opens new possibilities for making places work and feel better.

The planning, design, and installation of infrastructure has been a showplace for modern technology, with mostly good and some not-so-good outcomes. Among the elements of urban design content, technology has had its most profound impact on the connections people have established. Technology has aspired and in many ways succeeded in overcoming the natural and built world limitations that so defined the places of human civilization over the past three or four millennia. The technological progressions discussed in this chapter mainly flow from problem-solving innovators, most with backgrounds in the hard sciences and engineering fields. By defining the problems too narrowly, however, occasionally the wrong problem was solved, creating a new, worse set of problems. The problem-solving logic of straightening the drainage courses in south Louisiana to speed the evacuation of floodwaters, for example, scoured the fragile mesh of that state's estuary, destroying large areas of a vital ecosystem. In addition, having lost several square miles of this natural environment, the coastal plain lost its ability to buffer and attenuate storm surges, thus leaving New Orleans and other cities more vulnerable to Gulf storms, like Hurricane Katrina.

Less dramatic, but more pervasive and perhaps more threatening, the head-on, single-disciplinary approach to other infrastructure problems is now showing up in infrastructure failures large and small all over the country. The problem solved for invariably failed to consider linked issues and their impacts on the "solution," whether the corrosion of post-tensioned steel in parking decks at Berkeley (which then started to pop) or pigeon droppings on the bridge structure in Minneapolis (which among other factors caused structural collapse). In engineering for travel, storm drainage, or electrical distribution alike, the narrowly defined immediate fix-it approach works most of the time but risks not appreciating or incorporating larger contexts, both technical and social, with potentially damaging effects.

In the softer sciences of city building, modernist, technological, rational thinking decided, with little understanding of community, that slums were physical and social failures manifested in neighborhoods that upper-middle-class technologists wouldn't want to live in. And so well-meaning people launched urban renewal, ripping out decades-old physical and social infrastructure to create sanitized, rationalized environments in which the end goal of improving the lives of the people there was limited to what technology could provide—better water and utility supply, sanitation, minimum standards for window area, and outdoor air. These are all valuable contributions, but this top-down approach mostly missed the human, social, and cultural values that are fundamental to a stable and self-sustaining community. In fact, the rational, technical, standardized "solution" tends to generalize and marginalize people altogether—they aren't considered, consulted, or respected as individuals, families, or communities.

It is the people affected who judge whether their aspirations as individuals and communities are served by technological advances, the most prominent and problematic of which are to be found in the infrastructure that ties people together. In the 1920s, modernists in the place building design fields believed and acted on the premise that technologies would solve problems of scarcity, class divisions, poverty, need, and improved livability, most aiming at the whole population in their conceptualizations. The problem was that they geared their efforts toward solving the problems as they saw them and understood them, through a narrow lens. They made assumptions about what was best for people across the range of classes, cultures, and aspirations, as if everyone shared the same sense of needs and values and that simple, efficient, cost-effective, and repetitive physical solutions would take care of the problem. Thus people making decisions about these issues were persuaded that expertise, often self-styled, was in place and decisive in improving the urban environment.

So sits the dilemma of technology as the answer to the world's problems, or, more narrowly, the solver of infrastructure problems. Has technology created a sea change in how humans engage the earth? Without doubt. Has technology improved the overall quality of life for humans around the world? Probably, but not nearly as fundamentally as it has changed the field where life plays itself out. Look around your living room, your kitchen, your bedroom, your bathroom. Take away electricity, central heating and cooling, appliances, running water and sewers, and how different is what's left from what it might have been a couple of thousand years ago? Bigger probably, but still a place for the family to gather, maybe have some friends over, prepare food, sleep. The basic functions, the activities on which a fulfilling home life are grounded are about the same, some would say a little better, some a little worse.

Where real changes in quality of life can be measured is largely in the expansion of knowledge and to a lesser extent technologies affecting human health. Nutrition, sanitation, living patterns at the personal and community level are undeniably adding to and sometimes even doubling life expectancy, most of which reflects the expansion of knowledge more than the expansion of technology. People are facing accelerating changes in the natural world, many of which are caused or affected by the very technologies that mark the "advances." Those with a fundamental interest in the shape of the earth to come must deepen and broaden the knowledge links that can guide the development of technologies that will hold out hope that the coming changes can leave people better off than before.

Rising sea levels will call for both changes in settlement patterns and technological responses to anticipate and deal with impacts on coastal areas worldwide.

While infrastructure technology enables urbanization, its occasional failures seem to stem from two sources: lack of cross-disciplinary collaboration, and narrow problem definition. The theory, practice, and even culture of each of the infrastructure disciplines erects barriers to syntheses with the others. By not engaging each other in defining what the problem is, and even more fundamentally by not engaging the people affected by infrastructure decisions, there is a high risk that the problem "solved" will turn out to be the wrong problem. Passing every infrastructure policy, proposal, or project through a commonsense filter would seem to be a way to minimize problems. The accompanying disillusionment in technological solutions is dangerous, whether in infrastructure or other areas of the built world, since it is uninformed or misapplied technology—not technology itself—that has been the culprit in technological failures.

Like the other elements of the urban design whole, each of the infrastructure strands that connect people's activities and places by themselves is pretty straightforward. Travel paths, whether sidewalks, streets, transit, highways, and then water lines, sewer lines, storm water, electrical and gas lines, and communication lines all seek to achieve, from within the criteria of their separate goals and purposes, maximum functionality, efficiency, and in the private sector, profitability. The practice has been and largely still is, however, to plan, design, and construct these strands with little regard of how one system might fit with each other, with none particularly tied into overall settlement pattern strategies. It's serendipitous that most of these lines find it convenient to use public rights-of-way as their principal travel path, whose public ownership provides the path of least resistance for engineering the various systems that tie us all together. On the other hand, in spite of sharing the underground right-of-way, it is remarkable how little aware the various lines and their different disciplines are of each other. Ideas like shared duct ways still meet resistance from all concerned, and utilities continue to dig up and put down lines more or less willy-nilly, occasionally severing someone else's line in the process.

The integration of disciplines, the inclusion of all who can contribute, and the representation of all affected by the major urban settlement problems coming our way is essential to guide technology toward solving fully vetted problems. One of those discipline sets, often missing, is urban design. Its principles and methods at their best and fullest provide a cross-linking, three-dimensional, holistic problem-understanding capability that should always be at the table when large, complicated, unresolved infrastructure issues are taken up. In its current form, though, urban design, while broader than the other disciplines whose collective work results in urban places, needs to reach more broadly across disciplines and more deeply into communities. As defined by many, it does seek to integrate the overlapping aspects of architecture, city and regional planning, and landscape architecture. When it limits itself to these principal disciplines, though, urban design leaves out the most important place-shaping disciplines of all: the engineering fields involved in infrastructure planning and design, and especially transportation planning and engineering.

Civil engineering and its related urban infrastructure engineering subsets are more about solving the given problem than asking why or where the problem came from. Getting people, or their electricity or sewerage, from here to there is the focus, not why the problem exists in the first place or whether there are better ways, all things considered, to make these connections. Each discipline has its own culture, focused on the specific set of problems it sets about solving and as the solutions are developed any idea of trying to co-plan, co-locate, or even to co-think, are all too rare.

When the Georgia Aquarium was being sited and designed, streets and their utilities had to be relocated. There were opportunities to consolidate and relocate electrical utilities and to coordinate gas, water, sewer, and communications infrastructure in ways that would complement the vision of an especially well-connected and vibrant destination in the heart of downtown Atlanta. Software programs were put in place that allowed all agencies to communicate online, on-screen so that each could review the others' locational options. While not perfect, in this case communications technologies avoided the need to schedule and hold meetings as well as sending each idea back to headquarters for consideration at the next meeting—altogether an interactive breakthrough.

When engineering cultures collide with each other, each with certainty that their criteria override the other's, and then planning, architecture, and landscape criteria get thrown into the mix, and then economic and political factors are addressed, it is more surprising that things work out as well as they do than that screw-ups abound.

The irony, of course, is that wherever you look or travel, all of the disciplines are there—visible, evident, often seemingly haphazardly thrown together. Each item in the built world was put there intentionally, by someone, for some reason, following decision protocols that each by itself was entirely rational. The reason that the utility pole sits squarely in the middle of the wheelchair ramp is because it had spacing, structural, and cost-efficiency criteria that required it to be placed right there. Or the sewer grate inlets are aligned parallel to the curb instead of perpendicular—the better to catch bicycle tires. Or the spacing "norms" for trees, lights, parking meters, signs, and utility poles land them all in the same spot. Think of your own examples.

Urban design as an approach to solving holistic spatial problems must join the fray and seek to become a conscious point of integration for all the place-building disciplines. Why not take the steps necessary to bend their separateness into unity, their common sense–defying outcomes into places that reinforce, support, and assure places getting better? For this integration to occur, step one is to begin to understand where each is coming from, its goals, its purposes, and its internal cultures. The playing field needs to be level—integration will not occur as one or another of the subdisciplines of place design and development seeks to assert dominance over the others.

What follows is a more detailed description of these infrastructural elements, with most of the emphasis placed on transportation. Transportation is in a state of high tension, furious debate, and least resolution, and at the same time it plays perhaps the most fundamental role in shaping the built world. What the choices are, at all scales; how they interact with the natural world, with the make-up of the built world; how they meet people's needs in the existing economic, social, and political structures will largely define the future shape and quality of neighborhoods, districts, towns, cities, and regions. At the same time communications systems are having and will continue to have profound impacts on how future society operates as well as some impact on the future shape of the built world. Utilities will continue to follow their current path, responding and reacting to serious challenges driven by dualities such as energy sources and costs, conservation and waste, and privatization and equal access. At the scale of everyday neighborhoods and districts, who knows—perhaps we might even see a change in corporate attitude to reduce the afflictions of visual pollution and service vulnerability created by overhead wires.

# Transportation

## How People Get Themselves and Their Stuff from Here to There

Transportation is the dominant form giver to urban places, and at the present time perhaps the most volatile in terms of what problems it faces and the choices available to meet those challenges. This section will describe some of those challenges, their impacts on the functionality and attractiveness of future places, and what urban designers and citizens may do to shape better results.

Perhaps the most obvious among the various connective links is movement, travel, access, mobility. Transportation remains the most prominent of the connective structures—how to get from here to there most effectively. Providing for this connection is age-old, beginning with finding the simplest path. For millennia before the arrival of humans, indeed, animals faced the same problem: how to get from sleeping to eating, how to get from cold to warm as seasons change, how to get their goods transported. For people, the path, the trail, the way, then the road, the street, then the shipping lanes, the railroad, then the highway, the expressway, and finally the airways describe the evolution of this essential human need for connectivity. People must be able to get from where they live to where they make their livelihoods (though sometimes the same place), or to where they exchange their products for others that they need.

Walking is the base of all transportation, historically, across time and societies. Even though more and more societies walk fewer and fewer miles, every trip begins and ends walking. As the needs and motives for connectivity, for travel at all different scales, have multiplied, the webs of the connection of all the different modes and purposes of travel have become quite complicated. Returning to the traditional systems for understanding the built world may help to conceptualize the problems and decisions that lie ahead for improving transportation. All of these traditions of city form reflect the underlying and essential nature of transportation and the approaches for dealing with it and largely define the form and functionality of urban places, at all scales.

Mobility has progressed from walking to horseback, wagons, carriages, trains, biking, driving, and flying. The world has become successively more connected, or "smaller," at each stage of transportation improvement. This progression offers new opportunity and raises new challenges to the baseline premise of this book; that is, that people all want to live a little better than before. As with other human activity aimed at achieving improvement, in the case of the trajectory of travel technology, organization and practice is uneven, sometimes advancing, sometimes retreating, but overall leaving people perhaps a little better off than before.

Fundamental to understanding transportation both as a functional connector and an urban form giver, though, is that people do not live to travel. We always start out from a place with the intention of getting to another place, and transportation describes the time and the space between. In Chapters 2 and 3 we devoted considerable space to the history and present characteristics of streets as definers of public places. Here, we are more concerned with systems or networks.

In the earlier descriptions, we observed that as other modes accelerated people's mobility, travel began to be regarded as a thing unto itself, with the trip as primary, the origins and destinations as secondary. One of the enduring legacies of modernism on transportation design, stemming from touting the individual trip and the efficiency of the separate elements of a travel system, is the hierarchies of dendritic street layouts that began to replace the grid (see Figure 2.9). Street design, conceived as separated tree-like elements, created closed systems. Interconnectivity between each was neglected, severely limiting choices for whenever one piece of the rational dendritic pattern was interrupted, by crash, breakdown, or traffic glut.

This fundamental conceptual flaw figures prominently in the present growing dysfunctionality of regional transportation systems. It is a problem that is hard to fix because by the time the flaw is recognized, much of the land necessary to establish cross-connections has been developed, with built-in community opposition and crippling acquisition costs barring the necessary retrofits. It was during the transition from grid thinking to dendritic thinking, which took off after World War II, that the "experts" made the profound shift in their transportation emphasis from access to mobility. It was more important that the roads handled the traffic than that people's final destinations were adequately reached and served. This shift coincided with the flowering of suburbia, creating the patterns that characterize most suburban regions today. The shift, too, marked the leap in scale necessary to deal with enormous volumes of car traffic, the speeds at which they travel, and the safety concerns that this explosion engendered. Unfortunately, in seeking to optimize each piece of the roadway hierarchy puzzle, the system as a whole was neglected, not just roadways but alternative modes like transit, biking, and walking. The modernist mindset of efficiency, technology, and rationality coupled with individual, elemental market forces, prioritized the piece over the whole, relying on a belief that if each piece by itself met the technical and economic criteria the whole would work out just fine, too. The "solution," the car, defined the problem, leaving out all those pesky "externalities" like travel behavior, multimodal systems approaches, land use links, and settlement patterns that are the problems in fact.

Transportation presently faces many dilemmas, with the key to their resolution to be found in the problems and opportunities themselves. The motivating goal is to provide viable, functional, and positive quality of life choices for people whether in regions, cities, or towns. At the core of the dilemma is a mounting call for change from what is widely perceived and objectively documented as continuing deterioration of travel conditions in metro areas around the country.

Some jurisdictions, like Atlanta, have responded by focusing primarily on continuing roadway improvements and farther outward growth as that region's best hope. At the present time, business and political leaders leading the charge argue that the same strategies that grew Atlanta into the foremost city in the Southeast should continue to work: expansion ever outward, more and wider roads beefing up the dendritic pattern, with high occupancy vehicle (HOV) and high occupancy toll (HOT) lanes to handle bus and maybe truck traffic. Even so, continued deterioration is predicted in terms of travel times, vehicle miles traveled, congestion, and air quality degradation, and on top of that the models driving the region's transportation plan assume that energy will be as available and affordable in 2030 as it is now.

Other jurisdictions, like Denver, Charlotte, Houston, Dallas, San Diego, Portland, and others, are gradually moving toward a more integrated approach, viewing transportation as a system that provides choices for how to get there, recognizing a wider range of trip types and travel modes, and more interactive links between land use and transportation than the Atlanta approach.

On a positive note, there are signs that regional leadership, pushed by citizen activism, may look more seriously at transit alternatives, which might yet overcome legacies of suburban racism to finally become considered as an essential piece of the region's transportation future. Meanwhile, though, the base system, MARTA, alone among large metro transit systems, still receives virtually no state funding.

More fundamental than considering the choices within the transportation discipline is the review of transportation in the context of the other forces that build cities and regions. As noted above, at the regional scale there are dynamics underway that are pushing for greater conceptual integration of transportation with land use or settlement patterns, with environmental goals, with alternative economic development models, and with public policy and finance. A key subset in these dynamics is freight movement, presently a sometimes volatile mix that balances rail, road, ship, and air delivery systems, the outcomes of which directly affect design choices at the regional and often at the local scale. Out of these dynamics might come models that break with the patterns that have brought regions to their current state. These patterns were largely driven by the assumptions that cars and roads, as the dominant mode of travel, were the only dynamics worthy of attention, assumptions that worked pretty well into the 1980s but have begun to show increasing signs of disintegration over the last 20 years. These patterns objectively interacted with the larger land use, economic, environmental, and public policy, but these interactions were not considered as integral parts of transportation policy or strategy. Roads, real estate, the American dream of a single-family house, and public subsidy have brought us to this point, which more and more people, not just professionals, believe cannot continue to offer the advantages they once did.

One alternative model suggests that density should be increased where it already exists, that town and city centers would need to seek aggressive ways to bring housing costs closer into alignment with income profiles in their major employment centers. Presently, while the work force income profile in most major employment centers tracks the spectrum for the region as a whole, nearby housing costs are usually affordable only for

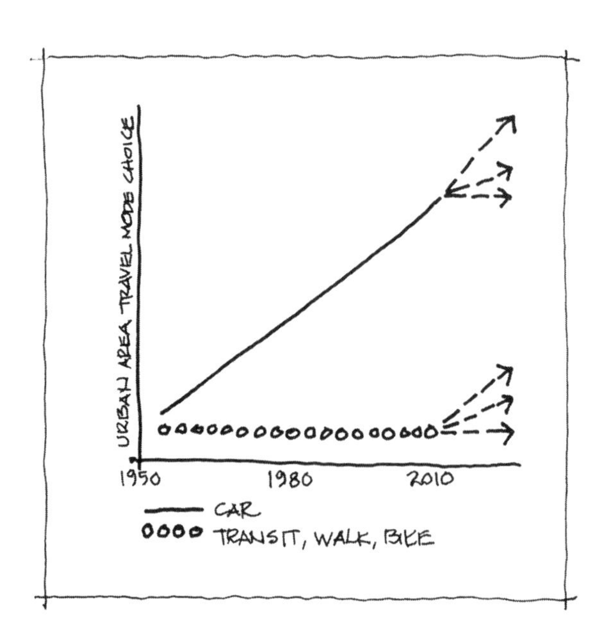


*Figure 5.3*
*The diagram characterizes how the different modes of travel have changed since 1950, with car travel accelerating rapidly and all other surface modes remaining essentially flat. The dotted line extensions show the options for projecting travel mode into the future—cars keep growing and other modes remain flat, or the growth in car use begins to slow and the other modes pick up, one of the goals of the smart growth movement.*

those higher up the income ladder. The transportation pay-off for bringing this gap closer together would be to provide the opportunity for lower-income families to shorten their journey-to-work trip, a benefit for all. For this model to work, too, transit internal to the center as well as transit between the center and other centers would have to be strengthened, and the quality of the walking environment would need to become a priority. If trip lengths and travel times could be shortened, numbers of drive-alone car trips reduced by the provision of transit, and walking choices made attractive, the result could at least stabilize and maybe begin to reverse the current deterioration. The result in the quality of places where most people are concentrated could be dramatic, a prospect for which urban designers and citizen activists alike should be working to achieve.

The economic development rationale is that existing centers and vested real estate values might be able to hold their percentages of overall economic activity, populations, and workforces. This is a seemingly modest goal but difficult to achieve as growth bleeds out across the regional landscape in growing regions. Conversely, holding focus on their centers as assets is an important strategy for turning around shrinking centers by offering the kind of diversity that is attracting younger generations to centers.

The environmental rationale is that by concentrating new growth where there is already substantial investment, less land would be necessary to sustain growth, preserving ecological values, and less traffic would mean fewer pollutants in the air. From the settlement pattern and public policy point of view, such a model would provide greater choice by balancing the current support structure for suburbanization with a corresponding structure of policy and financial support for strengthening centers.

An opposite model proposes further spreading development at lower densities, with less emphasis on distinct centers, and establishing new grids of widely spaced arterial roadways (a mile or so apart) to introduce better connectivity within the dendritic maze that characterizes most suburban territory. This model is entirely car-oriented and seeks to do whatever it takes to cure the current dilemmas with a singularly car-based set of solutions. The model assumes that the market's anointment of the car as the only supportable travel mode and the single-family subdivision as the overwhelming favorite living choice for people is final and fixed, thus the goal that must be met. It assumes that the petroleum–auto–real estate nexus that built most regions is stable, that energy will remain available and affordable, and that no constraints will limit the availability of new lands to build the model.

These two patterns represent poles of thought between which regions are making choices that trend toward either one or the other. In Atlanta again, for example, the Atlanta Regional Commission is traveling to some extent in both tracks: In terms of its actions and its approvals of the regional transportation plan and transportation improvement program (the projects that are supposed to go forward in support of achieving the plan's goals) in the name of mitigating road congestion, it is making choices that support the continued spread model. At the same time, however, it has established a growth management or smart growth strategy that encourages cities, towns, and centers to produce plans and establish supportive local legislation that would favor the centers- and corridors-focused models. Called the Livable Communities Initiative (LCI) program, it encourages and provides planning funding to jurisdictions that commit to completing plans and adopting land use, zoning, and subdivision measures that would support strengthening centers or defined corridors in support of transit travel options. These jurisdictions then become eligible for awards of capital funding to implement the corresponding transportation improvements, usually beefing up transit, improving intersections, and prioritizing pedestrian and bicycle access. This innovative program focuses growth management on strengthening centers instead of establishing infrastructure limitation boundaries. Aggressive and hostile pressures from development–real estate–construction combines, state transportation agencies, and current political leadership, however, have dogged the program, even though the market seems to be supporting it.

In the early 1990s, Mayor Richard Arrington Jr. of Birmingham, looking for ways to buoy flagging investment in the core of that city, suggested to the Alabama Conservancy that they adopt the slogan: "The best way to save the city is to save the countryside, and the best way to save the countryside is to save the city."

Many regions seem destined to muddle along toward crisis, settling for steady, gradual deterioration, and constrained by market forces that are heavily vested in past patterns and the public policies and subsidies that support them. These forces are joined with the professionals whose jobs depend on supporting the usual model and limit their consideration of other choices. Thus the professional community is discouraged from looking affirmatively for the new models that are probably necessary, as a practical matter, to solve the problems created by the old persistent ones.

At the scale of centers, corridors, and other focal places of urban environments, the prospect for creating better functioning and more satisfying civicscapes is more hopeful. Under mounting pressure from citizen and business organizations, many of the monolithic and suburban-oriented standards for roadway design are under review at national, state, and local levels across the country. These standards, which effectively have precluded walkable, shopable streetscape environments, were set up in the post–World War II era for the singular purpose of safe and efficient movement of cars. Since the main action during this period and for years to come was in developing suburban areas, the standards assumed this condition as the baseline on which all roadway design should be based. The standards apply to types of street identified by the roadway classification system, that is, major and minor arterials, collectors, and local streets. The classification determined the desired travel speed characteristics. These then provided an all-important threshold criterion: design speed. From design speed all kinds of design characteristics flow, like lane widths, horizontal and vertical curvature, turn lanes, intersecting street radii, driveway widths and radii, and so on. The various design characteristics are addressed in more detail in Chapter 3, The Physical Environment, and Chapter 11, Techniques.

To summarize, transportation has a profound impact on the form, desirability, and functionality of urban places, from the neighborhood center to the region. In many ways, from the perspective of creating public environments that people feel good being in, the truisms that have built our present transportation environment are failing at worst and being sharply questioned at best. Departments of transportation, public works departments, and civil and transportation engineering consultants and professionals have been responsible for planning and designing of transportation infrastructure. People from neighborhood to regional activists are increasingly effective in influencing the course, direction, and even the basic wisdom of many transportation projects. Urban design professionals are paying more attention to transportation planning and design processes, even as they are paying more attention to each others' subdisciplines. As the crises of transportation proliferate, great opportunities exist to probe truly new models, guided by broad-based citizen influence and better informed and better integrated teams of professionals, including those from the economic development and environmental communities.

# Utilities

Utilities as networks defining urban form for the moment rest in a fairly stable state. Their generation and distribution means and methods are fairly straightforward and predictable, and their visual presence is more or less in place. In the urban civic environment changes are likely to be fewer and much less dramatic than those buffeting transportation theory and practice. At the same time, though, while some urban designers like to point out that streets are more permanent than buildings (that is, harder to move and thus the primary urban design framework) it is often the utilities under the street that make changing street patterns difficult and expensive, not the streets themselves.

In the longer run though, and at the larger scale, issues loom for all utilities that rival those of transportation in their potential impact. Water supply and water quality will affect its stewardship and use, with choices to be made that will have spatial consequences. Storm water management similarly is facing sea changes in theory and practice. Energy sources are facing certain changes in how they are generated and distributed, as costs, availability, and the environmental consequences of fossil fuels continue along their volatile paths.

As with the transportation industry, the various segments of the utilities industry are dominated by sets of interests with sets of priorities embedded with technical design and support industries, none of whose cultures and ownerships is likely to initiate any meaningful change. The familiar pattern of citizens organizing initiatives for change around common sense and common interest, predictably resisted by vested private and linked government interests, will produce dynamics that will largely determine the shape and timing of the utilities' impacts on the future built environment.

In the meantime and at the smaller, day-to-day scale, utility decisions play pivotal roles in how, where, and with what impact places may take form, from the neighborhood to the regional scale. And failures in any of the utility categories may have disastrous consequences for life and property, let alone quality of life impacts. Integrating planning and design of utilities with others of the place-making disciplines can make big differences in whether places get better or worse and sometimes even mitigate the effects of failure.

Walk down any street and you see these utilities, though probably take them for granted. The ground below your feet is likely to be coursing with water, sewer, storm water, gas, electrical, or fiber optic communications lines. The signs of these under-the-street travel ways are everywhere. Manhole covers usually give you a clue as to what's there, who owns it, and where it is located, at least at that particular point. Those steel plates that make many streets bumpy as you clang your way over them probably cover fiber optic communications lines, vastly accelerating the speed of your computer to send and receive data (see Figure 5.2). And, of course, in most cities there is likely to be a maze of overhead utilities lines, casting a web that seems the work of a drunken spider from poles that are often leaning and spaced awkwardly along the street, both with connections to buildings and structures. Of all of these, each has its own implications for the design of places, regions, or both.

For example, dramatic improvements occur in the street corridor whenever overhead utilities are removed, either in easements behind street-fronting buildings or underground. Such improvements, however, come only from persistent, protracted community or citizen action, as utility companies typically do not consider overall aesthetic and property values or long-term functional advantages in their calculus of narrowly defined problems and short-term profits.

## Water, Storm Water, and Sewer

Water supply for the time being tends to be taken for granted at the local level. While there are always risks of service interruptions with the possibility of temporarily dropping water quality below potable levels, such interruptions are usually minor and of short duration. Larger issues, however, loom in many regions across the country. Parts of the Southwest and the Southeast are going through a drought cycle, with concern that climate change could protract and deepen the cycle. Cities like Los Angeles, Phoenix, Las Vegas, and Atlanta, the latter three growing at robust rates, could face long-term limitations on water sources that they have all worked hard and spent a lot of money to secure. Atlanta depends primarily on the Chattahoochee River for its water supply and is projecting that supply will not be able to sustain the growth curve for more than another 30 or so years. Denver depends on interbasin transfers, diverting major volumes of water from west of the Continental Divide to meet its needs, with ecological consequences of concern to many. Many cities depend on aquifers whose levels are declining. Most cities depend on trunk and distributor lines, many of them decades old, which require constant monitoring and maintenance.

These are all issues that the affected jurisdictions are dealing with, and strategies include the reduction of per person water use; changing rate structures to charge more for more water used instead of less, as was the pattern up to a couple of decades ago; curtailing or placing time of day limits on such activities as lawn watering or car washing; reducing the amount of water per flush in toilets; and so on. Water use is usually estimated at about 100 gallons per day per person. It seems likely that voluntary and mandatory measures will reduce that planning rule of thumb over the next 10 to 15 years. The changes required to accommodate these reductions may not be so dramatic, and they should make sense to most people.

Some of these will affect design at the local level. For example, xeriscape gardening, gardening that prioritizes plant materials that are native to that biome and so need little supplementary irrigation, are likely to replace lawns in many cities. Parks and golf courses may take on distinctly different looks as green turns to brown, lawn turns to mulch.

Taken together, people could be going through a profound shift in values, from a sense of abundance of water and even the flaunting of that abundance—which signified our attempts at the taming of nature—to a sense of conservation. These values reflect one of the great magnets that pulled people from Europe and elsewhere to the United States, the bending of all natural resources to support the good life, maybe even an extravagant life for some few. As the growth and maturation of the environmental movement signify, however, concerns about this stance of people in the natural world seems to be changing, many would argue none too soon.

New technologies over the next few decades could affect this picture and have significant impacts on settlement patterns. For example, what might be the impacts on urbanization of water purification tablet technology, which could make any water source potable without reliance on costly centralized treatment and distribution facilities? Could this technology, let's say along with solar, wind, and fuel cell technologies becoming alternative sources for the generation of energy, herald a new decentralization? And with what effects? Urban designers must be at the table when such scenarios are considered, since their potential impacts are in their essence comprehensive and connected to the functionality and quality of built space.

Sewer, like water supply, is in a reasonably stable state for the time being. Sewerage travels predictably from the toilet through ever larger pipes to treatment plants, where improving technologies filter out the toxins and discharge reasonably safe effluent into streams, rivers, or bays. As water supplies become constricted, alternatives to sewerage management are beginning to come forward, like separation of toilet discharges from "gray water" from sinks and showers, which requires much-less-intensive treatment and in many instances may be reused for irrigation purposes.

Many suburbs, however, continue to rely heavily on septic tanks and leaching fields to filter sewerage on a house-by-house basis, or on package treatment plants installed by developers with risks of unreliable long-term oversight and maintenance. These circumstances cannot be considered stable, since the risks of contaminating well, aquifer, or stream water supplies may become unacceptable. How sewerage is dealt with in suburban areas, then, could directly affect permissible densities and restrict the retrofitting of inner-ring suburbs without significant new public expenditure. As with many of the forces that develop places, the initiator (the developer) looks to get in and out of projects quickly, maximizing return on short-term investment, and government officials are under pressure to support this paradigm, even knowing that they (or more palatably, their successors) will end up holding the bag in the mid- and longer terms.

Storm water is an area where significant shifts are occurring. Run-off in urbanized areas has been found to be not much less polluted than sanitary sewerage. It picks up gasoline, oil and grease, pet poop, lawn care chemicals, battery acids, and so on, raising questions of whether it too needs some level of treatment before reentering water supply sources. Furthermore, as areas urbanize, their ability to absorb and naturally filter toxins from run-off water is reduced by the replacement of absorbent or permeable surfaces with impermeable ones.

The Clean Water Act Amendment of 1977 provided for planning and for awhile capital funding to properly build or retrofit sewer disposal sources, by and large an effective and essential program to safeguard long-term water quality. Its strategies prioritized "point sources" like sewage treatment plants or industries where discharges into water sources were concentrated. The act and funding initially anticipated providing support for dealing with "nonpoint sources" or storm water run-off, which proved to be much more complex, even as the quality of run-off water was deteriorating. Ideas have come forward about filtering run-off through ponds and wetlands and land applications, and many jurisdictions have taken active steps to implement such programs.

Many communities, too, have sought to "daylight" their historic water courses, seeking to reintroduce active streams that have been coursing through pipes, culverts, and concrete channels. These strategies, however, face problems in implementation. With the great increase in run-off caused by decades of replacing permeable surfaces like plains and forests with impermeable ones like roads, driveways, parking lots, and rooftops, the volumes such water courses must now accommodate tend to scour and deepen the streams to the point where their scenic or use values are severely compromised.

One may expect continued and probably growing attention given to this subject, taking the form of restricting development in active stream buffer zones, reworking how storm water discharge is managed, restrictions on percentages of impermeable surfaces, expansion of "green roofs" (where roofs are constructed to support plant material and thus filter rainwater) or modification of code requirements for paved parking lots and driveways.

These strategies also support other priorities in managing the urban microclimate, like mitigation of "urban heat islands," which beyond making already hot areas intolerable increase the demand for air conditioning and emission of pollutants into the atmosphere.

The spatial consequences of the choices to be made are significant. While the expertise necessary to assure stabilizing or improving overall water quality and quantity is essential, leaving the choice entirely to whatever may be the central technical discipline could lead to decisions that degrade the rest of the civic environment. Both urban designers and community leaders face these and related issues regularly, and both should be involved in policy and regulatory shifts to reduce run-off and better manage what's left, with the opportunity to improve the quality of the resulting environment.

## Energy Generation and Transmission

For the most part, the energy that heats, cools, and lights the urban world and that powers its machinery and appliances comes out of an electrical line above or below ground and out of underground gas pipes. And for the most part the points of generation and distribution are in power plants for electricity or separation plants for gas, whence the grids of distribution carry the energy source to our cities and buildings. Most travel modes are powered by gasoline or diesel fuels, which are distributed by rail or truck to the point of consumption. Propane and compressed natural gas (CNG), also distributed by truck, play a much smaller role, propane usually in more rural areas and CNG as a relatively clean fuel more and more powering bus and other fleet vehicles. Of all of these, electrical power distribution has the most immediate impact on the quality of the urban environment.

Most communities across the country are facing the issues swirling around how and where electrical power gets transmitted. Electric utilities' general ability to condemn right-of-way to run transmission and distribution lines wherever suits their cost and service models are well established but increasingly challenged. Once again, narrowly focused technical expertise focuses on a narrowly defined problem, albeit for the purpose of safely and effectively supplying power for the range of needs that characterize any urbanizing area and making a profit on shareholders' investments. The effects of this formula are evident in most places in the maze of poles and mesh of wires that they support, usually with little consideration of the visual impact that these choices have on the quality of the living environment.

Citizens' groups at all levels are raising a clamor about being at least consulted about some of these choices, and many in the more traveled civic places are seeking to place the distribution lines underground. As suggested above, for the most part, electric utilities don't want to listen, and brush aside these challenges as irrelevant to what matters to them, ignoring both the damage to community spirit and the economic opportunity loss from trashing up the appearance of an otherwise attractive place. Typically the utility's argument is that it costs too much to go underground, and taking a short-range stance they dispute the long-range maintenance and operation savings generally associated with storm- (and squirrel-) caused outages. While these protestations have merit, they reflect and perpetuate barriers to engaging in more holistic, better-thought-out designs for making places better overall. Often, for example, moving the lines from the street to the alley or to the back of property easements, while complicated, may produce a result nearly as attractive and probably less expensive. At a minimum, efforts to coordinate the users of utility lines along a better planned and more orderly system of structures can markedly improve the streetscape environment.

Important for all to know is that the right to use the public rights-of-way to transmit electricity is nominally controlled in most jurisdictions by local government. The agreements conferring these rights are generally called franchise agreements, and though usually long-term, it is worth finding and keeping track of their renewal dates, as one of the few opportunities short of litigation that are open to effect changes in the way these public rights-of-way are used.

Citizen organizations with the support of urban designers can work together to overcome utilities' opposition and little by little introduce changes in practice, either by persuasion or by regulatory action. In those relatively few jurisdictions where the local government is the electric utility provider, the opportunity and the will to cooperate with such ideas as phased undergrounding, or simply more orderly positioning and upkeep of overhead utilities, are generally much more productive. Interestingly, while these usually smaller cities and towns get harassed and challenged by acquisitive privately held utilities, they seem to be able and willing to listen to their citizens (who after all are "shareholders" as taxpayers). Accordingly, they may work out better solutions than the typically narrow, one-size-fits-all "efficiencies" that characterize bigger private industries, which also are more shielded from the public.

At the larger scale, electric power generation and distribution continue to grow, with the obvious impacts of where to put the next fossil fuel (or is nuclear coming back big time?) generator plants and how and where to transmit electricity, where to put the substations that break down the voltage into the distribution system, and how to muck up a well-traveled street or plaza by sticking some wires over them. It is conceivable, though, that rising frustration with our complex of energy dependencies might accelerate the shift toward more restraint in its use and viable options to ramp up supplementing this source with other strategies. The rapid advance of "green building" into the mainstream of designers' and developers' consciousness has just begun to scratch the surface of potential savings and redirection of electrical utilities' priorities. When one reflects that about 40 percent of energy consumption occurs in buildings, and another 40 percent fuels transportation (leaving industry to account for the balance), the opportunity for further reductions is exciting. Again, both designers of places, including the transportation designers, and citizen activists working together can generate a lot of influence over the future of electricity use and its placement in the civic environment.

Publicly owned utilities in Lafayette, Louisiana, and Newnan, Georgia, for example, are sustaining increasing pressure to privatize. So far this pressure has been resisted by local government on both cost and content grounds.

Of the other forms of energy distribution, most are more incidental to the character of places. Gasoline and diesel, stored underground for the most part and until the last 15 years or so in inferior storage tanks, have left a persistent stain on the soils in urban places across the country. They represent significant point-source pollutants of underground water, and under the 1987 amendments to the Clean Water Act, most of them have been remediated, usually at significant cost. These kinds of sites are joined by other brownfield sites, like old dry cleaners and other users of solvents, acids, and other polluting chemicals, to create real problems for urban designers and community activists. The corner gas station in centers at all scales in neighborhoods, villages, towns, and cities for years broke the continuity of cohesiveness that makes a retail or commercial center viable, first by introducing nonstop driveways interrupting pedestrian flow and then by preventing any effective redevelopment because of the cost of clean-up required to keep groundwater half-way clean.

Altogether as it affects the civic environment, one can assume that energy sources and transmission systems will not dramatically shift over the next 15 or 20 years, and the shifts that do occur will favor greater fuel use efficiency. Yet during this time the kinds of adjustments necessary to achieve a more sustainable environment will have begun, and designers should involve themselves in these processes, which could have a significant impact on the future design of cities. Otherwise, the risk of narrowly drawn and programmed technical solutions could either preclude opportunities for integrated enhancements or, worse, perpetrate some future degradation for lack of thinking holistically. At the everyday walking-around scale, one can hope to advance strategies to remove the tangle of distribution lines that are a plague on most cities. These will not come at the initiative of the power companies or the governments that they so effectively lobby. Only citizen action informed and assisted by urban designers and developers for whom the benefits in quality are evident will determine whether such a goal is worth fighting for.

## Communications

In recent years and for many more to come, communications is having an impact on people and their relations with each other and the places they inhabit that could come to rival that of transportation on the built world. Transportation's options are pretty well known, and it will be in their combinations, their syntheses, their systems integration, their co-planning with settlement patterns and economic development strategies that problems of mobility and access will be addressed. Energy generation and transmission and prioritizations and timing of one system over another may change, but again the technologies are pretty well known. Water use, distribution, and discharge—beyond the purification pill—again seem to have little in the way of technological breakthrough in the future. But right now at least the advance of technologies of communication and society's response to these technologies pose fundamental challenges to how people communicate, organize their societies, generate, edit, and share information, all having wildly different and volatile scenarios for the future.

Manuel Castells from the early 1990s anticipated the rapid rise of the "network society" and its impacts on the relationship between physical place and cyberspace, or as he called it, "the space of place and the space of flows." Earlier, Charles Dickens, with remarkable prescience, warned that "electric communication will never be a substitute for the face of someone who with their soul encourages another person to be brave and true."

Some have boldly predicted that information and communications technologies will break down the age-old patterns of people seeking each other out in person to interact, do business, socialize, and so on. While these musings on the power of the virtual over the real may go too far, there is no doubt that relations among people and structures of society will change and that the changes already happening are likely to accelerate. The potentials run to the poles of the imagination—from a "Big Brother" total central control styled either as "benevolent" or as "despotic" through virtual deception over the masses to democratic advances where decentralization of power is accompanied by unprecedented millions of people stepping up to exercise leadership, or to breakdown and anarchy.

The future will lie within these poles, with access to information for all, transparently available, being pivotal. The trend line, whether toward democratization or central control, will define the direction of society, with some societies more characterized by one or the other leaning.

Also prescient, perhaps, is pioneering rap musician Gil Scott-Heron with his 1970 hit assertion that "the revolution won't be televised."

In the built world in the meantime, beyond these wildly diverging possibilities, communications show up in all our towns and cities in the form of overhead lines or buried lines—the lines themselves running the gamut from the copper that has dominated communications since the late nineteenth century to fiberoptics whose capacities are multiples higher than copper. Fiber as an unspliceable material and more sensitive and expensive than copper typically goes underground, the evidence of which is the steel plate work that moves around the roadways whose underneaths are woven with this relatively new type of communications line. Cable TV, whose opulent lobbying allows them to get by with relatively little public regulatory oversight, and traditional phone lines using longstanding franchise rights join electrical distribution lines on their poles to further lace the skies with their visual pervasion. Another and newer significant intrusion into the urban viewshed is the cell tower. These towers, conceptually similar to most of the other separately engineered utility infrastructure, follow a logic that is based on spacing and topography that usually optimizes cost, profit, and communications efficiencies often with little or no regard to the towers' impacts on the context into which they are dropped. Every community has experienced this new arrival, where more affluent and resource-rich neighborhoods have been able to mitigate some of their effects and middle- and lower-income neighborhoods have not. The mitigations run from altering the location to be sensitive to preexisting vistas and landmarks (usually adding a little to the cost, and diminishing the engineering optimums and the profitability factor for that location) or creating towers that try to look like something else.

The management of the range of impacts possible is a fertile area for citizen involvement despite the telecommunications giants' obstruction of any such movement. Designers, for their part, must choose between going along and getting some modest concessions on aesthetic choices or working in support of citizens on the larger issues. It is important to keep in mind that the rapid rise in communications technologies has coincided with the period when large centralized corporate interests have rolled back regulation both practically and philosophically. Accordingly, since cable TV came along, citizens' access to oversight bodies like public utilities commissions for others of the infrastructure industries has not been so available—for cable TV and now for other digital communications technologies. People are stepping up their debate over how open and available communications networks should be, while the giants, their lobbyists, and like-minded legislators contemplate ways of charging for Internet access, for example, that so far has been close to free. Also in this balance is the regulation of content, the outcome of which will be a marker in the seesaw between democratization and central control. The inventor of the Internet in 1989, Tim Berners-Lee, an adamant advocate for the idea that the Internet should be as free as speech itself and who made no move to maximize his profits from his invention, nonetheless recognized and warned against what a powerful and profitable tool the Internet could be. From a spatial perspective, it is already quite apparent that the digital divide favors the rich over the poor in terms of access and that future costing of the system would further widen that divide. Communities of higher income are far more likely to have high-speed or wireless Internet access than those of lower income, further accentuating the information gap from which neighborhoods operate. These divides could affect communities at the regional scale, joining exclusionary zoning and other discriminatory bars to segments of the population on the basis of income or race.

In Atlanta's Buckhead neighborhood, for example, a rich, "wired" neighborhood was able to mask one of its cell towers as a "pine tree," a particularly tall and unbending pine tree at that.

# Summary

Of the elements making up the content of urban design, the coming together of forces that create the places where we share our lives, infrastructure is the most dynamic. Architects, landscape architects, and city planners, as the traditional fields out of which urban design has formed, have not sufficiently incorporated infrastructure design into their baseline planning and design models, either at the micro or macro levels. The engineering community for its part typically focuses its attention on solving problems assigned to it through developers, industry, economic development bodies, and political jurisdictions without getting too much into the policy bases from which the problem may have sprung. The effects of these disconnects, however, may and often do result in unintended consequences, like water quality and quantity problems; air quality problems; congestion; lack of choices in living, working, and traveling arrangements; and so on. Yet the biggest questions around whether people can make the world better or worse are more affected by infrastructure parameters and decisions than the other elements of the content of urban design. While the natural and built world and the human activity these support are completely interactive with infrastructure, both have more settled and predictable futures than their connections, infrastructure, which has a wide range of possible futures.

People, hopefully supported by the interdisciplinary synthesizing skills of urban designers, can have, have had, and must have a significant and decisive effect on the outcomes of these interactions. For these outcomes to improve life, the measures must value the whole of the people affected more than any particular segment.

# PART III

# *PRINCIPLES*

## Principles for Urban Design Theory and Practice

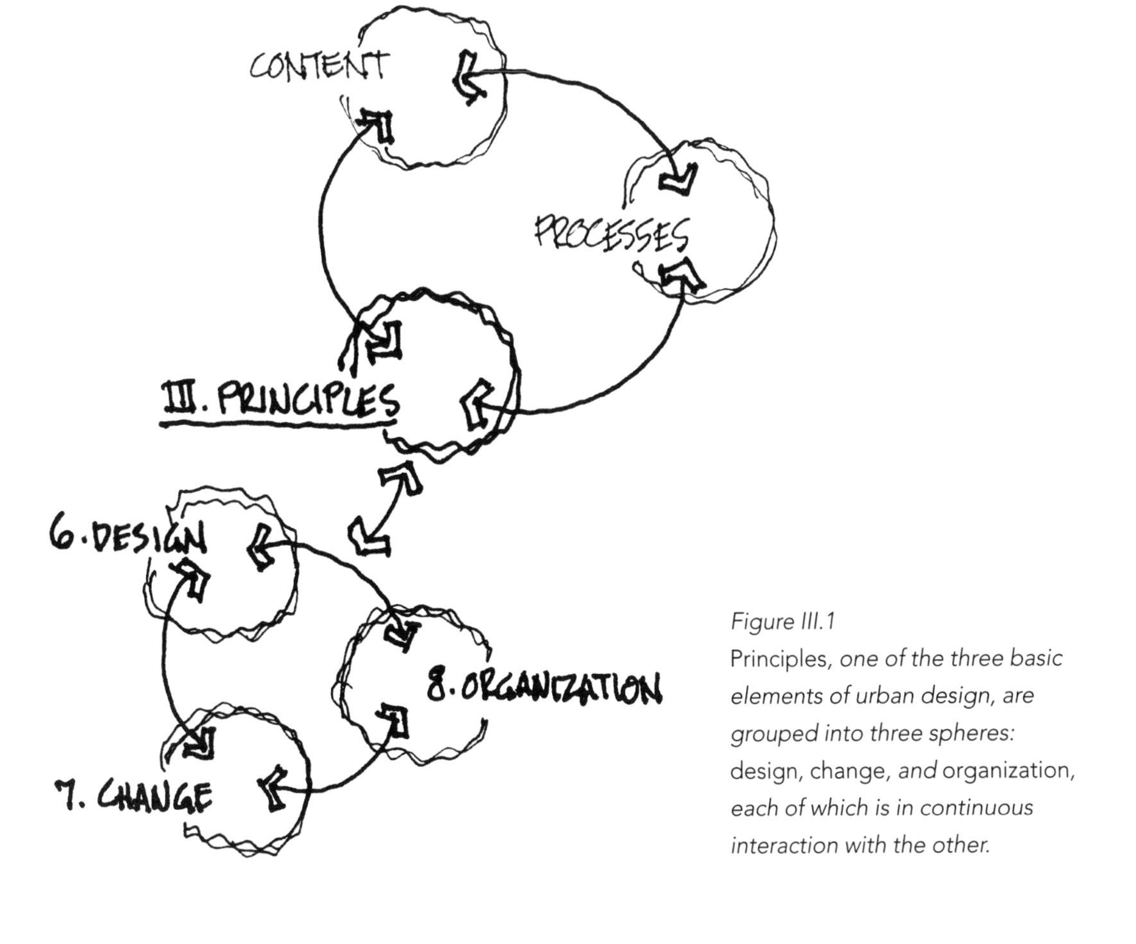


*Figure III.1*
Principles, *one of the three basic elements of urban design, are grouped into three spheres:* design, change, *and* organization, *each of which is in continuous interaction with the other.*

# Overview

We have reviewed the background of urban design and the roles played by societal structures, technical disciplines, and citizens in shaping today's urban design context. We have touched on principles that have guided that legacy. We have reviewed the content of urban design, the physical world, human activity, and infrastructure that connects these interactions. This section proposes and explores principles that are directed at shaping the **content** of urban design in ways that make places better and at the practices, methods, and conduct embodied in the **processes** necessary to get it done. The principles here guide both the conceptual side and the practice side of the work.

In approaching the myriad design and development opportunities and challenges that regularly face neighborhoods, districts, cities, and regions, what are the measures, the rules, the priorities, in short, the underlying principles, that should guide the work? How might these principles affect design, organizational, political, or economic strategies that have a chance of meeting the purpose of making things better? How do the substantive areas to which these principles apply interact with each other to provide guidance for making better decisions? These are some of the questions addressed in this section.

To place the principles below into their overall context, it is important to reiterate that the effective design and development of civic spaces always occurs in an interactive environment. Like civic spaces themselves, with their ever-changing mixtures of activities, physical attributes, connectivity, and development processes, the principles that guide their conceptualization and implementation must reflect the diversity of people and places as they are now, have been, and will be in the future.

Coming up with principles to guide people through these kinds of dynamics may seem complex, given the large number of moving parts at work in making places. Yet people all live in and experience complicated sets of interactions all the time and, however unconsciously, interact with the whole of their environment every day. The principles here, like people's experience, are dynamic, not static. They continue to evolve, they do not always all come into play in equal measure, yet places that work for people may always be described in their terms. They are interactive in fluid, often unpredictable, sometimes even chaotic ways. They do not necessarily follow a cause-and-effect model, typically neither linear nor sequential progressions. At the same time they are interactive with both the content of urban design and with the processes necessary to get it done. That is, based on the physical and human content of a particular situation, based on the particulars of its implementation path, the principles must be prioritized and applied flexibly.

Put simply, in urban spaces, everything acts on everything else over time. Interactivity means that the people, the physical environment, and all of the connections that make places are in continuous interaction in time and space. Any of the forces acting on any part of a place may affect any other in positive or negative ways. Urban design work calls upon its participants to understand and use to their advantage this nonlinear, often unpredictable, characteristic of the design, development, and maturation of places. Places that work allow for, indeed encourage, spontaneity, flexibility, and unforeseen opportunities (or adjustment for problems). Places aren't ever finished and shouldn't be conceived of or designed as finished sets.

To illustrate, imagine a fringe place down on its luck, on the ropes, at a neighborhood crossroads, or at an edge between a neighborhood and a business district. Its civic environment is a little sketchy, too much asphalt, unkempt, maybe dark, altogether uninviting. This picture can be turned around by a civic or business initiative, ideally both. A new popular business comes in, spruces up its sidewalk environment—the place starts to look good, cared for. Say it's a café or a shop that provides a needed service, engages the sidewalk with seating and landscape. It elicits first local community support, then local government support, which then results in sprucing up the rest of the street environment. This attracts the attention and then the investment of other business interests, and if all are supported by the community, in sync with its needs and culture, the place can turn around. Maybe this takes a couple of years, maybe sooner or later, and until the turnaround is consolidated, it's a fragile but hope-giving time.

My colleague at Georgia Tech, Richard Dagenhart, puts it a little differently: "Places are made, not designed," to which I might respond, "People make places, not designers."

Conversely, a place seems to be doing fine; then an anchor business closes down, looms as a dark and deteriorating gap in the space it occupied, business activity declines, causes other businesses to review their options, maybe one or two more sell out and move on; the surrounding community is not organized well enough to play a mitigating role, properties start looking unkempt, the local government doesn't enforce the property maintenance code, and the place loses its cachet, beginning a downward spiral.

Here, simple as they are, we have two examples of the interaction of change forces, organizational structures, and physical appearance resulting in the improvement or the decline of a place. There are principles underlying these interactive spheres or forces, and understanding them and then applying them should achieve positive results. To begin with, it doesn't matter which of these spheres of activity comes first. Maybe the business becomes unprofitable, maybe the civic space becomes shabby, maybe the community or the local government stops caring—or the opposite. It is the interaction among these spheres of activity that results in improvement or decline. And people's roles and actions, whether as individuals or groups, underlie the dynamic and may be pivotal in the outcome. For most, a bad place getting better feels better for the people there than a good place getting worse.

In addition to this overall interactivity principle, there are five other principles that apply to all aspects and phases of urban design and community improvement work. These address inclusion, information and communication, vision, building on strengths, and action.

Inclusion means that all affected by a proposed place improvement strategy should be included in the process. People determine the success of a civic environment by their knowledge, commitment, support, presence, and engagement with it. Designing with people—owners, developers, designers, public agencies, and a representation of the residents and businesses in the area—means all must contribute to the process from the beginning to assure a place's lasting success.

Include everybody, from the beginning—if everyone's in on it and up on it, it'll happen.

Information and communication means that all information that could bear on a place design process should be collected, analyzed, and communicated freely and openly among all participants. The work occurs in the public realm and so all relevant information should be publicly available. Lots of different people and data sources exist with useful informa-

Share and communicate all relevant information. Knowledge is power.

tion, and sharing all that across traditional, too often closed, disciplinary, jurisdictional, and cultural boundaries can only help to frame the fullness of the problems and to come together to discover solutions that will work.

Know where you're heading. If you don't care where you're going, it doesn't matter what road you take.

Vision means the consensual enunciation by all affected of the overall characteristics and values that a place should embody. The vision should set forth in general the people and activities the place will support, how it fits with and enhances built and natural surroundings, and how it is connected both with the buildings and activities that define it spatially and socially and with contiguous places and the larger civic fabric. The vision is a program, not a blueprint, for guiding design development and organizational activities.

Build on strengths. Is the glass half empty or is it half full?

Building on strengths means to approach all aspects and phases of the work emphasizing its positive attributes. Every neighborhood, every business district, every town and city has good things happening in it. It may be its physical setting, natural or built, its location, a business or neighborhood institution or amenity, or people, or even just a few individuals. In generating ideas and strategies for place improvement, it is important to identify what's already working and why. Understanding, analysis, and engagement of positive factors in a place improvement activity invariably supply the kinds of ideas, direction, and partnerships that work. While easy enough to do, focusing on what's wrong with a place, on the other hand, can only result in negative and likely ineffectual strategies. Addressing negatives, many of which in fact must be dealt with, is more likely to succeed if approached in the positive context of where the place is trying to go.

So, for example, in assessing a place design situation, look for those physical, spatial, and functional aspects in the area that are positive and contributive to design strategies for the place. Often, these are identified by people in the community, and they may be buildings, parks, places, streets, or they may be natural features, or both. Beyond the physical components that hold promise for conceptualizing a linking vision, often more important are other strengths, usually to be found in the character of organizations, institutions, or individuals whose leadership holds the key to discovering and building on sustainable renewal strategies. Remembering that the success of places ultimately depends on the people there embracing them, the special character of community leadership provides both the cues and the kinds of content that will reflect the community's aspirations.

Make something happen; otherwise, it's just talk.

Action means that every place-improvement initiative must build in action steps from the beginning. Too many civic planning efforts flounder for lack of the information, the understanding, or the orientation to actually; do something. Action needs to be at the top of every agenda. Practical, implementable actions that can get done set a realistic frame for sharpening the imagination and for committing to the process of achieving measurable results. Selecting action steps early, as soon as people can agree "we need to do this, whatever else happens," can demonstrate a visible, on-the-ground result. If chosen well and implemented in a timely fashion, the action step builds trust among the partnerships necessary to get it done, usually fuels the momentum to keep the process going, and even at worst leaves the place better than it was before. No place-improvement activity should begin without the commitment to get something done factored into the process of defining what could or should be done.

These overall principles show up throughout the text, and they apply in different ways and with different emphases to much of what urban design

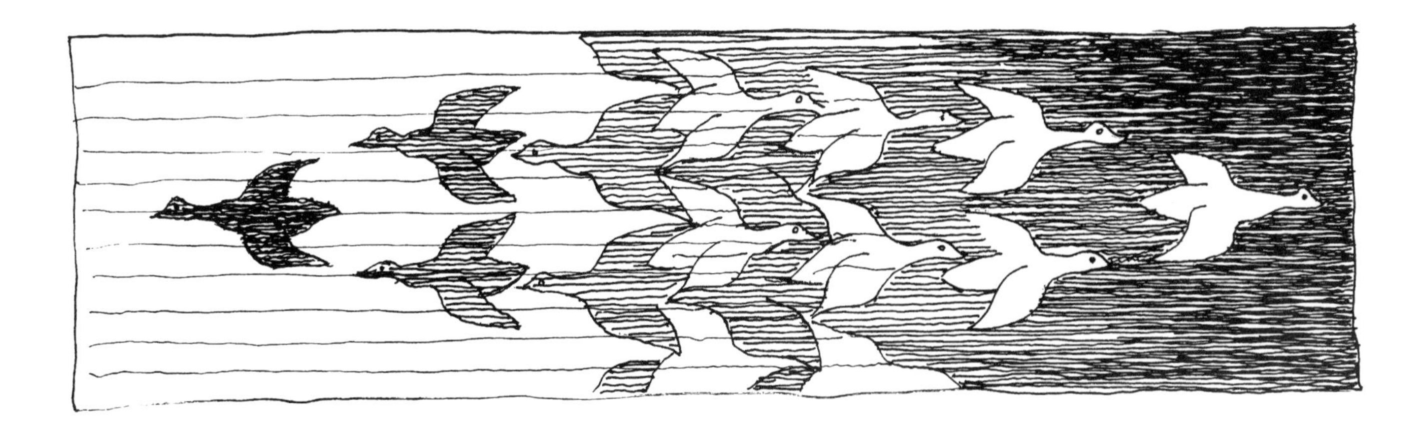

*Figure III.2*
*Many of Escher's works, like "Day and Night," build on the interplay between what was figure and what was ground, not just graphically but substantively as well.*
*After M. C. Escher: "Day and Night"*

is about and tries to do. As hinted at in the vignettes above, I have grouped the more specifically directed principles into three spheres, according to their most likely applications. Thus design-related principles apply most directly to the physical design and development choices that result in inhabited space. Change-oriented principles apply to understanding and managing the change forces always at work on the physical environment. And organization-oriented principles apply to how people organize themselves to act on their changing environment, for the purpose of improving it. The three spheres of activity to which the principles apply—***design, change,*** and ***organization***—are themselves in a state of continuous interaction, consistent with the overall principle of interactivity enunciated above. The principles are devised to recognize and support positive outcomes from these interactions.

The headings should be considered as permeable, as the principles may have applicability under other headings as well. Their interactive and permeable nature reflects the connective and comprehensive nature of urban design. It is not a single boundary-defined discipline, but rather one that reaches into aspects of all the place-making disciplines in the search for a comprehensive whole. In this search, it is important to understand that factors that may seem at first as contradictory or oppositional may and usually do end up being facets of the whole. They can be integrated as ingredients whose very difference enriches a place or over the timelines that always accompany place-building activities. A useful way to picture this characteristic of urban design is as a figure-ground relationship, stock in trade of urban design analysis. Such relationships have been famously portrayed in the works of M. C. Escher, but also in kids' sections of the newspaper, where the kinds of optical illusions produced allow the viewer to read images in two distinctly different ways. The "positives" or figures read one way, and the "negatives" or fields read entirely differently, and these readings can flip-flop. The emphasis in urban design should be on the "both-and" potentials of these dualities, not on the "either-or." Facing such dualities, urban design concerns itself with each and emphasizes the seams and synergies of both.

This kind of duality, however, is not just a visual phenomenon but applies to other aspects of the principles enunciated here. Their dualistic or dialectical nature is descriptive both of their essence and of their interactive relationships. As we shall see particularly in the change-related principles, change itself embodies an action-reaction essence. At the same time, the dynamics between action and reaction embody choices that affect both the understanding of change and the response to or management of change forces. Outcomes of these dynamics include such concepts as compromise or synthesis, in turn underscoring the importance of timelines and trends in design conceptualization and effective implementation.

Similarly, the organizational structures acting on the design and development of the civic environment are best understood through their interactions with each other, the pushes and pulls, authority and influence, and the status and cultures of the people who either put them together or experience their results. In all of these a key baseline measurement is whether the organizational structures and practices strengthen or threaten trust among all concerned. Characteristic of urban design, it is usually the building of seams between oppositional organizations that is more important than the organizations themselves.

Consistent with the dualistic or dialectical nature of principles is that for any principle enunciated below, there is an opposite principle implied. The merits of each principle that I espouse here therefore need to be measured against the system of values on which my experience and this work is based. The premise of this text is that the measure of making better places rests with the people who interact there, or in the case of new developments, those who will interact there. If the living environment for more of the people there is getting better as a result of a design or development action, then the place is getting better. If, on the other hand, the place is getting worse for more of the people there, it is getting worse. Similarly, if the place is getting better for a small number of people at the expense of the many, then it is getting worse.

The principles enunciated here, then, support the goal of improvement for the many. This is the measure that I apply in assessing public administration, at the local, regional, state, and federal level. At the scales of places, the measures become visible by community response and attitudes about the future. Behaviors either show satisfaction and pride in the form of objective measures, like new investment in homes or businesses, increasing community gatherings in places that work, visibly improved maintenance, or displeasure and resistance in the form of disinvestment, vandalism, people staying behind their doors, or moving on. The discussion of each principle will make reference to its opposite, which will be discussed and evaluated against the measure of improvement for the many. As suggested above, though, often the dynamic between opposites can produce a synthesis that is better than either position's starting place.

Together, the principles apply to the full range and scale of place-making activity, from the narrowest to the broadest, from the smallest to the largest. They will be referenced throughout Part Four, Processes, so that readers may understand how the principles apply to the range of actions necessary to implement better design.

I have come to these principles through my practice as an urban designer. Their sources are people across a wide spectrum: other practitioners or thinkers in one or another of the place-building disciplines for sure, but, at least as important, community people and their organizations, developers, and other businesspeople, elected officials, and civil servants. In sum, the full spectrum of people whose knowledge and energy build places have contributed. They reflect and seek to organize observation and experience to embody the purposes of urban design as a profession and citizen action as an aspiration for making better civic environments. They guide how to combine the various characteristics of the ***content*** of places with the ***processes*** of implementation in ways that generally result in making places better than they were before, or better than they might otherwise be. They apply to both the conceptual side and the practice side of the work. Finally, they should advance the understanding of the forces at work and the ability to act effectively on their improvement for students, professionals, developers, government officials, and citizens who are inclined to engage themselves in place-building activities. For me, careful consideration of this framework of principles has produced consistently positive and sometimes exhilarating results.

# 6

# DESIGN

## Design Matters (or There's No "There" There)

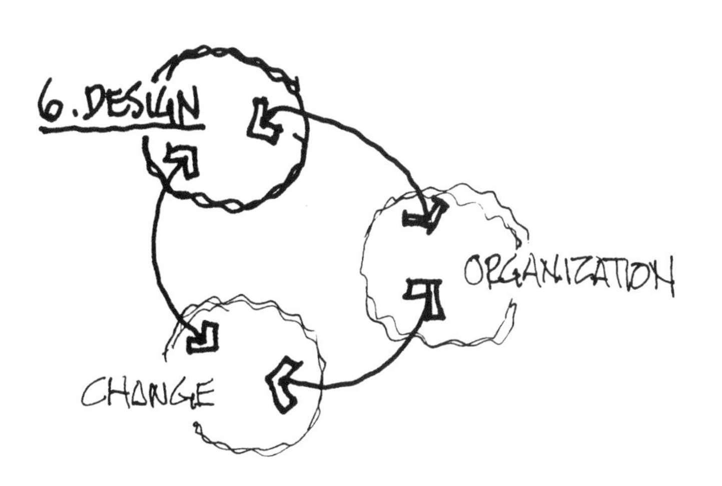


*Figure 6.1*
*Design principles interacting with change and organizational principles, together laying a base for urban design and development decision-making.*

# Introduction

The principles grouped under design are aimed both toward students and professionals in the civic design fields and toward community people interested in raising the design quality of their places. They are geared toward answering questions like: What role does design play in the functionality and quality of public space? How do the various design traditions inform design, development, and practice today? Who are the designers of public space; what skills should they have; how do they work together; and whom do they work for? How is design for places different than design for buildings, landscape, and infrastructure?

The design-oriented principles form the basis for approaching urban design situations, that is, the design of the public domain and its interface with the private activities that border it. Since private activities in fact dominate people's time and attention, the idea of how to design the spaces in between, whether for access or gathering, has tended to fall through the cracks. Architects foreground their buildings, transportation engineers put in streets and infrastructure, landscape architects try to soften and embellish what the architects and engineers do, and planners analyze for policy-making, prioritizing, and budgeting applications.

There are many ways of characterizing the "design" aspects of urban design. As the field began to take on its current form in the 1960s, some professionals in urban design, often architects, thought of it as just bigger-than-building design—that is, designing bigger, more complicated objects sometimes called "megastructures," of which shopping malls are the most familiar example. These showed little recognition that civic design occurs for the most part in the public realm, the field on which building objects are placed. A better starting place for all the disciplines and forces involved in building the public environment is consideration of the three traditions, an understanding of the frameworks and forms that typify most public space.

For architects, the shift in emphasis from private to public runs counter to most of their training, experience, and thus orientation, which is directed toward the design of buildings for private or institutional clients, typically to be privately used. But the design of civic places highlights the design of all the space that is left over after the design of objects is completed—space that is usually publicly owned and evaluated. To contribute, this calls upon architects to concentrate on the next larger context beyond the building and its lot, and to consider broad public values over narrow client interests.

Other approaches, often those of landscape architects, viewed urban design as discrete landscape problems, laying in streetscape or park and plaza treatments in response to client commissions. Now more and more landscape architects understand their design contributions as devices for giving the civic realm a cohesive and imageable presence. Still others are committed to conceptualizing more ecologically sustainable development models. For landscape architects, of the design professionals arguably the most central to the creation of livable civic spaces, urban design integration should mean continuing to expand beyond their traditional constraints as servants to the grand patrons—the kings, corporations, mansion builders, and office park developers that so dominated their earlier culture.

Still others, charged with designing the infrastructure that ties everything together, usually civil engineers, viewed urban design as the design of the infrastructure projects assigned to them as projects that happened to be in the urban environment. For these, who largely do work in the public realm for public clients, urban design should mean a shift toward viewing a successful larger spatial whole as the goal to which their technical piece contributes. Solving narrowly for the car, electrical distribution, water supply, or storm drainage as narrowly defined projects often comes at the expense of walking-around, everyday people, and their necessary or desired activities. This means working interactively both with other disciplines and with the larger visions, policies, and goals out of which projects get formulated.

Until recently, city planners have tended to view urban design as prettying up places here and there in the city—maybe a nice thing to do, but not the serious business of larger policy and equity issues that could actually make cities better. For them, urban design should mean thinking in spatial contexts, incorporating their own and other people's behavioral responses into the workings and feelings of places. The experience of place needs to be more consciously built into their information gathering and analysis practices, policy formulation, and regulatory activities.

A big boost for urban design came from nondesigners, people like Jane Jacobs, historic preservationists, and others who thought urban design should be interactive with preexisting civic form and supportive of community cultures and institutions. They put emphasis on "context" as providing important cues for how buildings should be incorporated into and contribute to the public realm. People who gravitated toward support of these views represented a cross section of citizens who were becoming jaded at the claims of improvement being made at the time, mostly by various strains of modernists whose design ideas by the late 1950s were devastating the physical and social fabric of cities all over the country. As such, activists and community leaders in these movements were challenging the "experts," and establishing a broad-based sentiment for civic improvement whose last flowering had occurred in the City Beautiful movement. For these, the principles should be focused on gaining sufficient design understanding so that they can confidently influence the discourse on design and development activities that immediately affect them. This will allow them to put into objective and communicable terms their sense and experience of familiar places—what works for them and what doesn't.

Finally, the people who actually build civic space, whether for itself or as the frame into which they place their buildings—the developers—need to join in the interactive swirl of forces that can make places better than they are. Necessarily constrained by the drive to maximize return on investment, developers nonetheless need to work in contexts where the civic outcome is considered in the approval process. The planning, urban design, and public works professionals who make recommendations to the elected officials on the approvals of development projects need to incorporate the larger community aspirations into that process and communicate it effectively to the development community.

It is in the interstices between these different perspectives, each of which has its own internal merit, where urban design lies. For the places we share to get better, all of these disciplines and forces need to consider and absorb the core principles laid out in Part Three's opening Overview, that is:

Include everybody, from the beginning
Share and communicate all relevant information
Know where you're heading
Build on strengths
Make something happen

As we move into those principles more directly associated with design, it is good to keep in mind the underlying interactivity between people and place; study and understand how people actually behave in civic environments; and think about how people can make places their own. The principles below, then, seek to clarify urban design's position in the weave of disciplines that design and make places as well as how to develop and employ urban design skills toward their betterment.

# Good Design Makes Better Places

*"Design shapes the way we live, so it ought to serve everyone."*
*—Eva Maddox*

The overall value of urban design in making places is guided by civic purpose and addresses these questions: Does the place attract people? Does the place reflect and serve the people there and their activities? Can people make the place their own? Is the place getting better or worse?

These questions and their answers can be measured objectively by such indicators as rising property values, business receipts, retail or office stability or growth, visitation, meeting diverse housing needs, and functioning efficiently. Just as important though, and more visible, are subjective measures, like whether people are coming to a place, using a place, enjoying themselves, feeling safe, inviting others to join them, hanging out, making it their own, keeping up the place, looking out for each other, and so on. You've probably all had these kinds of responses to places, and for our purposes thinking objectively about those responses is a key to participating actively in place improvements.

This kind of assessment has application not just for individual and local places but for towns and cities as a whole. If public places and street environments are working better and meeting needs better in just a handful of neighborhoods or districts, while they're deteriorating in most, then the community as a whole, the town, the city, or the region actually may be getting worse. The framework for assessing civic betterment, then, applies to the whole population. It is not enough to have chic, niche, gentrifying neighborhood centers that cater to and draw on the resources of the affluent. The same kind of improvement trend should be measurable in most, if not all, of the larger setting. The newly found market for urban living, if it is an indicator of prosperity, should work for everyone, not just a few, and should be judged accordingly. The good news is that good urban design is not necessarily expensive design. In fact, design that coordinates and synthesizes the various pieces that make up a public place may actually save money. Civic betterment is a shared professional/community activity, and urban design should reflect that purpose. How places work and look, how they become symbolic, how people can directly engage themselves in the processes of improvement, in my experience, is what successful urban design means.

# Design Places to Reflect the People Who Are or Will Be There

The source for this principle is the consideration of such questions as who places are for, who will use them, who will pay for them, who commissions them, who judges them, who gains and who loses from their development or modification. Unlike buildings or private landscapes, places are in the public, for the public, paid for in large part by the public, and ultimately judged by the public in their activities, with satisfaction or not. These characteristics throw urban design into a different category and set up different relationships between different designers, between design and owner, between client and user—different than one finds in individually commissioned design projects.

There are other designers in the public realm, like environmental graphics and lighting designers, who have much to offer technically but usually become part of highly patronized commissions, a circumstance that limits the range and scope of their potential contributions.

The design of buildings or spaces as objects, particularly for architects and landscape architects, is often approached as an expressive activity. The owner or client wants to make a statement, wants a certain look. The architect, especially the elite architects and landscape architects, want to express themselves, much as other visual artists do.

This patron-architect relationship is as old as formal architecture and probably inevitable for private buildings or landscapes for private owners, housing mostly private activities. In the public domain, though, these relationships are quite different. Places are mostly public, activities are mostly public, social, and in motion over time, and the "client" at one level is everybody and, at the other, is the public body that exercises authority over the place. In this setting, design should reflect this more diffuse set of participants. It serves broader but less specific purposes. It addresses shared space and the integration of time and motion factors into design. It focuses on knitting together a ground that satisfies people's diverse sets of needs, from functional to symbolic.

There are countless bits and pieces of public "urbanism" created by patrons and their designers that don't work and don't last, mostly because the exercise of their designers' skills comes from the expressive side of the design mind.

While there are successful urban spaces designed in the patron-architect tradition, insisting on consideration of the larger spatial and cultural context usually improves the quality of the design of places. Thus architects and landscape architects need to back off from looking at work in the public domain solely as a personal opportunity to express themselves. Rather, they should look for public guidance, willingly incorporate ideas they didn't think up, and interact with community leaders and other design disciplines. This approach is likely to produce more satisfying and enduring results.

Meanwhile, those who are not "designers" but nonetheless integral to the place-making process—engineers, planners, and developers—while keenly interested in functionality, tend to be oblivious to or shy away from the aesthetic values in their work. They thus finesse the issue of visual or spatial design quality. Engineers may wrap themselves within the narrow problem-solving palette that their profession and standards require. Planners may discount or underestimate the impact that design quality has on life quality. Developers are certainly sensitive to aesthetic values that may

*Figure 6.2*
*This well-known figure-ground cartoon is particularly apt for distinguishing reflective from expressive design, where people engaging each other is one interpretation and a trophy, or chalice, is the other.*

attract their target market, yet may be apathetic about how those values may or may not enhance the larger settings where their project is located.

There are other ways of illustrating and putting into action what is meant by "reflective" as opposed to "expressive" design. One way is to use figure-ground graphics to illustrate and analyze the relationships between buildings (the figures) and what's left over (the ground; see the city figure-ground maps in Chapter 2). Typically, architects, developers, or contractors design and build the spaces represented in black, mostly buildings housing private activities, while a hodgepodge of disciplines fail to design everything else, shown in white.

Urban designers use figure-ground relationships as a tool for assisting communities in looking at their physical space in new ways. For themselves, figure-ground diagrams provide a threshold device for reading the community fabric. The solids, or figures, usually depicting more private space, read one way, and the voids, or grounds, usually depicting more public activity, read entirely differently. Among a myriad of other such "both and" dualities, urban design seeks the seams between them and their synergistic potential. These diagrams show in often dramatic ways how urban space is organized, and they prompt a rough assessment and judgment about what seems to work or not work, based simply on this single level of graphic analysis applied to people's on-the-ground experience. In many jurisdictions, too, there are old maps, for example Sanborn maps, that were prepared to rate levels of premiums for insuring properties. Review of these, or successions of tax assessment maps, is useful for reading the history and evolution of formal space over time. Putting a succession of such maps into figure-ground graphic representations may reveal not just what happened, like when a disappeared neighborhood sustained the urban renewal wrecking ball, but also rediscover lost or newly relevant ideas about how territory might be better organized in the future.

By way of illustration, the three main design traditions for organizing urban space—the organic, the formalist, and the modernist—show up in every metro area as starkly contrasting diagrams, almost like Rorschach tests (see Figures 2.4a and b, 2.12a and b, 2.18a and b, and 2.20).

The two-dimensional plan view graphic immediately brings into our imagination corresponding three-dimensional images. Under this principle, the buildings (the figures) represent expressive design, each designed by someone, for someone, conceived as a complete object, and executed all at once (most of the time), symbolizing and expressing what the owner or the designer valued in the process. The ground, on the other hand, is reflective of all that is left over—the streets, plazas, parks, yards, parking lots, natural features, and the like. The ground is "designed," if you will, in bits and pieces, by different people at different times, for different purposes, usually with no thought about how the whole of the ground might hang together, either visually or functionally. It is in the interaction of the parts and the whole, the figures and the ground that the richness of understanding and conceptualizing better places can arise.

Another way to illustrate this principle is to imagine (or in practice to carry out) an exercise where all the people with interests in the outcome of a place are gathered together to visualize what the place could be, taking into consideration all of its strengths and challenges, opportunities and impediments. An expressively trained designer (most architects and landscape architects) would be inclined to formulate a concept or two and draw a picture of how he or she thought the design should be carried out and then try to persuade everyone to accept that single, limited picture as the right way to go. A reflectively trained or oriented designer would approach the situation differently. This designer through a variety of ways would elicit the group's thoughts, ideas, and images; identify and explore the possibilities; and try to record them all graphically, certainly on maps and probably with block models, sketches, and diagrams. Done effectively, it's almost as if the designer was holding up a mirror for the people to see their contributions reflected back at them. This way of designing focuses on the possibilities before teasing out alternatives and a workable design direction.

An early effort to employ this approach was undertaken by Chad Floyd and Charles Moore in Roanoke, Virginia, in 1974. Using local-access television, they showed base mapping for the center of town and opened up phone lines to citizens to call in suggestions. They recorded these as they came in, depicting them diagrammatically and with sketches so that other viewers could comment, add to, criticize, or change. The team was able to put together a rough consensual map by the end of the three-hour TV session—a good gut-check and contribution to the planning process they were charged with carrying out.

Design in this application plays the crucial role of communicating fairly, openly, and interactively the information that all bring to the effort. As a transparent, real-time experience, the tendency among various interests to hide or obfuscate private agendas is at least partly broken down. Reflective design, particularly as it may play out in public processes, can connect people with each other and their place of interest and can serve to coalesce divergent interests toward achieving those parts of goals that are found to be held in common.

All of the related and necessary place-making disciplines should be an integral part of these kinds of reflective visioning exercises. Each will contribute information that no one else in the room is likely to have, and, more important to a satisfactory outcome, each will hear the other disciplines' perspectives as well as the bigger picture aspirations of all concerned. With this information, urban designers may rethink how each particular discipline's skill set can flex toward achieving a unified bigger vision and purpose. Altogether, this kind of process is generally effective in generating most of the information and ideation necessary to frame a vision that people can recognize as their collective sense of where to head.

My wife characterizes this approach as being a "pencil in the hands of the people."

Yet another way to think about design as a reflective endeavor is to consciously seek out evidence for how people respond to the civic environment. The expressive designer may be inclined to assume how people

Perplexed with how many of the urban spaces designed by architects and landscape architects seemed to repel rather than attract people, William "Holly" Whyte, a sociologist with an eye for physical space, undertook a landmark study testing people's behavior in various urban settings—what attracted people and what didn't, and speculations about why. His work led to the establishment of the nonprofit Project for Public Places, a group that has dedicated itself to understanding how civic space works and helping jurisdictions all over the country to make improvements, large and small. Others involved in what still—remarkably, 40 years later—has to be called a pioneering quest include Clare Cooper Marcus, John Zeisel, and my colleague at Georgia Tech, Craig Zimring. There is yet much to be learned about behavior and the gap between feeling and reality and how that might be manipulated in designing public spaces. Earlier than Whyte's inquiries, and important for urban designers and community people to ponder, Westinghouse commissioned a series of behavioral studies to determine what kinds of features might be introduced into their work spaces to make their workers more productive. Interestingly, though there were responses to size, shape, color, and light, the most significant finding was that workers valued being consulted above any particular proposed intervention—very instructive for those of us who want to improve the civic environment.

*"How could they redo this street and leave all those ugly wires up there? Why is there a wheelchair ramp on this side of the street but not the other? Why is there no sidewalk to the bus stop? Who decided the street widening was more important than the sidewalk and street trees? "*

may behave, indeed presume to determine how people should behave in the presence of a design master work. The reflective one is more likely to actually want to find out how and why people behave they do in different spatial settings and base his or her work on the evidence obtained. The notion of basing design moves on evidence of human behavior is relatively new and problematic for most involved in practicing and teaching design in its usual forms. Traditionally, the design professions, while quick to respond to the owner or client, have been slow to understand and consider behavioral factors for the many who activate public spaces (or private spaces, for that matter). Even newer and probably even more resisted is the search for linkages between people's responses to space and how the brain is wired. Designers who care about how most people respond to their work, however, might do well to pay attention to these behavior and neuroscience explorations. If either the softer science of psychology or the harder neuroscience is able to predict behavioral responses that can make people's experience of place better, why not bring them into the palette?

Urban design is about the design of a place for the whole of the people who inhabit, traverse, and use it. Efforts must be made to both clarify and enrich the transition between the public realm and the workplace or home place in ways that add value, comfort, convenience, and amenity to these more private experiences. If the measure of successful places is people's satisfaction with them, measurable in both subjective and objective behavioral responses, then it is worth becoming more knowledgeable and better prepared to meet and exceed that criterion.

Remembering that places are about people—ones that work attract people, ones that don't repel them—design that reflects some cross section of how people see themselves in the picture, both the professionals and the community, will more likely succeed than those that are flown in out of a consultant's briefcase. This principle is directed at aiding this understanding, both as an attitude and a process. Designing reflectively considers the cross section of the people affected and the mix of design disciplines as the font for design. And it considers the ground more than the figure as the central design priority.

# Design Places Consciously and Holistically

## The Whole and the Parts, in Constant Interaction

Design and design quality should always be a consideration in any developmental process, whether in the private sector, the government, or the community, from the scale of the street or plaza to the scale of the town or region. All these places look like something, and they all function some kind of way. They all have features that urban design should be able to improve. No one getting ready to build a building or a road would think of proceeding without a design. Indeed, everything in the built environment was "designed" by somebody for a specific purpose, following rules, regulations, performance criteria, and other dictates that make it look and perform like it does. It is located where it is and managed according to its needs for specific reasons.

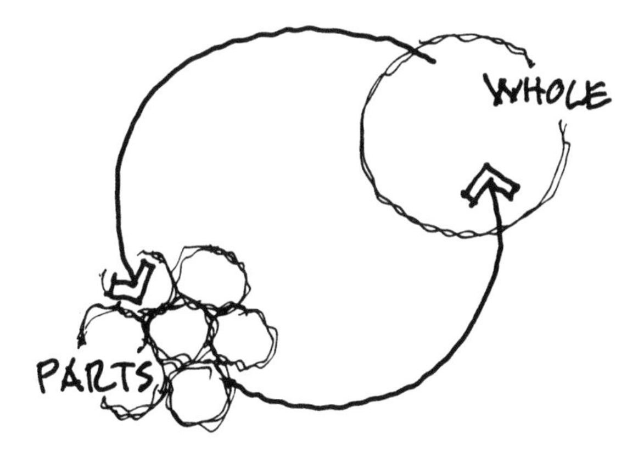


*Figure 6.3*
*The continuously interactive relationships between the parts and the whole.*

But places typically are not designed as wholes. They just happen. The traffic engineer, following traffic engineering codes and practices, takes care of lanes, stripes, signage, lights, signals, and on a good day, sidewalks. Other civil engineers, following public works codes and practices, take care of roadway design and water, sewer, and storm water structures, including locations, sizes, materials, and structural design. The utility companies, subject to franchise agreements with local government and technical and profit criteria, take care of where and how the energy and communication infrastructure is accommodated (usually with flagrant disregard for their visual or spatial impacts). The architect takes care of the building, its entrances, windows, structure, materials, its roofline, and its overall style. The landscape architect, if any, takes care of streetscape elements like sidewalk design, trees, shrubs, flowers, benches, and if the traffic engineer agrees, may have something to say about lighting and mounting structures. The city planner takes care of land use, zoning, and other regulatory requirements not already under the purview of engineering. And a range of others have their whisks in the soup as well, like the fire department, the postal service, the transit system, and other layers of government. Beyond all these different levels and priorities of the design actors, altogether the work takes place in a setting whose natural environment increasingly must be sustained and supported.

These are the pieces that make up place design, creating the environment for private activities to be located, connected, and developed. Yet not only is the place not designed as a whole, those involved in the design of the parts may or may not consult with each other beyond the minimum coordination (which itself is frequently omitted). With the lack of any overall guiding notion about how the place as a whole should look and function, it is no surprise that the places where we gather or travel through most frequently look so chaotic and function so haphazardly.

If, in furnishing your living room, you randomly picked people to each select an item of furniture of their choosing and place it in the room blindfolded, you would end up with a right-in-your-own-home example of why civic space looks the way it does.

This principle is directed at involving all of the above disciplines with interested citizens and organizations to imagine how the place should look and function, and then to identify the design elements, their interactions, and the coordination processes necessary to move toward a better overall outcome. This requires from the beginning coordination of all in the design disciplines as well as representation of all who use the place or street. This in turn requires not just a change in practice, but a change in attitude and behavior among all these parties in which the shared goal and purpose of the activity at least balances the insular, often distrustful, and sometimes arrogant cultures that have grown up within each.

*Figure 6.4*
*The typical urban commercial strip—a public space where each piece of the picture was consciously placed where it is, within the rational logic of its installer, creating...chaos. Courtesy of Dunn Foundation*

The absence of design is the reason why there is no "there" there.

At the same time, it is important to carefully consider the merits and possibilities of each of the parts, not just as freestanding and dissociated one from another but for their potential to interact with each other and to create a better whole. Well-designed pieces in a wholly designed place contribute mightily to its character, quality, and legibility, sometimes even its delight.

# Design Is an Essential Skill

Why does design matter in the making of civic places? What kinds of skills and attitudes does it take to be effective in place improvement processes? Civic space is that which people all share in their daily comings and goings. People either feel good or bad about their experiences and sensations in this common ground, or they simply take it for granted. There have been eras, that of the City Beautiful movement, for example, when the quality, functionality, and meaning of civic space commanded widespread attention, from ordinary citizens and from civic leaders. As countless visual preference exercises have demonstrated in charrettes or workshops around the country, people do respond negatively and positively to images of the civic spaces they encounter. There is a high level of agreement in these about the look and feel of environments that people prefer. Trusting one's own judgment about this experience of space is a reasonable starting point for engaging in its improvement. Moving civic design in the direction of these preferences is likely to make people feel better about their places, their cities, maybe themselves, which in turn may lead to commitment of time and resources to contribute to positive momentum or to resist deterioration. Design quality is central to these responses.

In order to be an urban designer, one must develop and hone urban design skills. The formal underpinning for these skills is taught primarily in architecture and landscape architecture schools. As it happens, many architecture and landscape architecture programs do not prioritize urban design in their curricula, though in most one can find relevant course and studio work. So, the fact that one studies in one of these studio-centered design training programs does not assure picking up the skill sets or the design orientation important for practicing urban design.

At the same time, people with city planning or engineering backgrounds, as well as community people dedicated to the purpose, can pick up the necessary skill sets to understand, participate in, and contribute to the dialogue and conceptualization of how to improve the places that they care about. The design of each of the separate elements that come together (or don't) to create a better place is not that complicated. Rather the complication flows from the sheer numbers of possible combinations of these elements in a dynamic social and political context.

The principal values in formal design training for urban design lie in learning to draw, to represent, to measure, and to solve holistic spatial problems, that is, to think in nonlinear ways. Drawing connects the eye, the brain, and the hand into a single perceptual and conceptual tool. This tool's application in urban design runs the gamut of value from observation, recordation, analysis, and conceptualization to representation. People all experience civic spaces more or less the same way, whether in a car or walking, pausing along the way, or sitting down. The eye picks up all kinds of cues, processed by the brain where such responses as comfort, ease, pleasure, safety, indifference, distaste, anxiety, fear, or anger are triggered by this visual information, however unconsciously. The other senses contribute significantly to these responses, and urban design should consider and incorporate them into analytic and conceptualization work as well. Much of what urban design is about is making conscious what everyone experiences every day so that both the pieces and the whole of a place can be noted and communicated, both to oneself and to others. Among the senses the eye-brain link is always there, but the ability to use this information consciously and actively depends on the hand. Thus drawing represents a step toward activating awareness and consciousness of what's going on spatially and provides a way to engage the physical world. Drawing in this application does not depend on talent but only on the desire to become active in urban design types of issues and the willingness to spend some time at it. If you can write your name, you can learn to draw well enough.

Drawing is important because so much of urban design is about visual communication. Being able to represent information and ideas graphically greatly assists bringing divergent information and ideas into the same sphere of consideration. Words in considering the world of spaces are not only cumbersome but also more likely to misrepresent than to clarify their speaker's intent, further confusing their listeners. Words apply a linear logic to the decidedly nonlinear subject of space with its range of problems and possibilities. Over and over again I have jumped up to the blackboard in the middle of a meeting about a place and rather quickly have been able to draw together disparate threads of lengthy sets of verbal communication into a diagram, a map, or a sketch and ask if this is what everyone is talking about. Even if it isn't, it shifts the focus from getting the words right to coming into the same picture. It's been reported that a picture's worth a thousand words—I agree.

Measuring is important because everything in the physical world has a size, and to design how the elements of place come together to make a whole you must know how big they are. The starting point for measuring is the human being. Everyone has a size, and everyone experiences the world in terms of that size. In fact, most everyone has two sizes, the one that measures the person and the one that measures the car, because most of how people experience public spaces is either walking or riding or driving. These two reference points, then, are the basis on which people experience, evaluate, respond to, and act on the world—everyone, everyday. The relationship between size and experience is often referred to as "scale," another word and concept that tends not to be addressed outside of studio design programs. So for each of us, scale is the relationship between one's size and one's experience of space. Scale is a factor in most of the range of responses people have in the physical world, whether a place "feels" good or right or comfortable or welcoming or forbidding. Other senses figure into these feelings as well. The sounds, smells, and touch and textures of places contribute significantly. Others of our feelings about place, just as important, derive from whether it works—that is, whether it functions to meet people's needs, and whether it fits with its natural setting, including topography and climate. Finally, does the place feel welcoming in terms of sociological and psychological responses? Who's there, who's not? Am I welcome, safe? Can I do what I need to do?

The first thing in measuring is to understand your size in relation to the elements and the whole of the physical world around you. This means using yourself as a measure of distances and heights, knowing how to pace off distances in a comfortable stride, measuring door heights and their multiples as a way of measuring heights, using dimensions of commonly known and recurring elements for estimating both distance and height. Measurement also applies to time, like the time it takes to go from here to there, and to materials, like becoming conscious of the materials that make up places as a factor in human response. The consciousness of self in a spatial setting or in approaching how to solve a spatial problem is a step toward gaining confidence in the validity of one's responses, both objective and intuitive.

Interestingly, human behavior in spatial situations, while varying according to the particular characteristics of the built world and social culture, seem overall to be reasonably comparable, and the scale of spaces seems to contribute to these crosscutting reactions. More work is being done on this notion, but empirical evidence as simple as what places around the world attract people the most for their physical qualities (and which postcards sell the most) is a crude but reasonable measure of places that people of all cultures and backgrounds seem to respond to. It's not an accident or a surprise that Paris is the most visited city in the world, in which the scale of its physical, spatial character is certainly part of its draw.

It is perhaps more interesting that places like Mesa Verde or Taos or similarly vernacular or indigenous settlements in other parts of the world have strong draws as well. This enduring popularity perhaps stems again from "a sense of scale," from a kind of deep, limbic association that people share and appreciate about others grappling with the challenges of their daily activities and creating places that both function well and reflect in their dimensions and relationships the important symbols and values of their culture. Part of this sense of satisfaction surely communicates itself through the places these other older cultures have created, bringing together living, working, exchanging, supporting, and celebrating a cultural life out of the materials and methods at hand, scaled to the natural setting of the physical environment in which they found themselves. Think of your own experiences.

In contrast, areas that seem to repel people have some comparability in physical terms (though again, social and cultural cues may play a more significant role). For example, an area is referred to as "scaleless" if it lacks connectedness to the human size or other positive visual cues—think of a couple of blocks of blank walls or a parking lot full of cars facing a sidewalk, or other similar and common urban settings.

Urban design problems always include a spatial character, and so that aspect of the problem requires spatial analytic and visioning skills. Studio design training teaches students to think, to analyze, and to conceptualize three-dimensionally, holistically, and simultaneously. That is, in architecture, for example, students learn to understand space as enclosures or volumes, where one must imagine not just what is before one's eyes but what is behind, above, below, and beyond, now and in the future. At the same time, they learn about the whole of the space and all its details, the overall building and all its parts, like structure, walls, roofs, foundations, doors, windows, light, mechanical and structural systems, and so on. The thinking skills associated with this kind of learning are nonlinear; they do not proceed along any particular step-by-step path. They tend to downplay cause-and-effect relationships and instead reflect the overall interactivity principle. Any one part of the architectural problem is likely to be linked to any other in patterns that defy any reliable linear sequencing.

This special kind of learning has applications to many other fields, obviously for urban design, city planning, and civil engineering, but for others far outside of the sphere of architecture. Architectural pedagogy, however, has seemed incurious about the value of training in spatial conceptualization as a broader skill and capability, even though less than half of architecture graduates end up pursuing architecture in their careers. Many programs are beginning to rethink old traditions, and perhaps the wider application of the skills associated with spatial problem solving, not to be found in most other mainstream fields, will become a greater focus in the future. As it is, these skill sets seem to propel those who learn them in a wide variety of directions, including digital and production industries, some of which by all accounts are as exciting as mainstream architectural practice and probably more remunerative.

In urban design, which has a reasonably bounded and describable set of components in its content, the level of design and technical complication and sophistication is generally simpler than in building or software design. This means that the parts and the wholes of urban design are neither mysterious nor beyond reach,  evidenced by the numbers of nonprofessional

It is worth noting that architects in particular manipulate scale for dramatic effect. For formalists like new urbanists this impulse might be directed to communicate through spatial order a sense of belonging or connectedness to the larger context. For organic-oriented practitioners, not counting typical subdivisions, the emphasis would be on the natural, the sustainable, the integration with the natural world. For modernists the impulse might be to impress, shock, or awe passers-by with an expression of technological bravura—buildings done because they could be done, for an owner who could pay. The last of these three tendencies tends to receive the most emphasis presently in teaching and in the mainstream architectural press and criticism. This priority may leave people trained in architecture out of touch with reflective, civic-oriented design, out of scale, or altogether scaleless.

I even had a conversation recently about whether this kind of holistic, simultaneous, four-dimensional problem-solving capability might provide a way to make sense of collapsing financial systems. It seems conceivable that apparent chaos might become understandable if people could add a spatial, temporal component to more conventional cause-and-effect and linear thinking.

people who have had direct and often positive impacts on urban design problems at all scales. Nonetheless, the ability to understand and communicate in the terms of each of the relevant design disciplines is essential to effectively participate in urban design and development activities.

All in all, the skills described above all come into play in the interactions out of which better places emerge. Attaining some capability in any or all of them will improve the chances that both practitioners and people in the community who care can engage and influence the civic design process for the better.

## Beware of "Solutionism"

Beware of the solution in search of a problem.

In another divergence from typical architecture and landscape architecture training and practice, where emphasis often is placed on the solution to a problem rather than on the problem itself, urban design happens in fluid, interactive, ever-changing circumstances. The process of making places that work and satisfy doesn't have a beginning and an end in the way that building projects or other time- and budget-specific projects might have. In addition, the context of community design must consider a much wider range of issues than normally found in a building design project. Urban design theory and practice emerges out of understanding and relating to issues of diversity of users and interests, out of public policies and regulations, out of shifting community values, out of time and budget uncertainties, and out of time and place ambiguities. While there may be a certain solution to a piece of the puzzle, the solution as a whole must itself be flexible so that it can attach itself to what is there and what might be coming. Otherwise, however it is crafted, the solution to one piece risks detracting from the success of the place as a whole. This risk may extend from the scale of a neighborhood center to a region.

Problem-driven design assures that the larger context, both spatially and temporally, and socially and culturally, and the interaction between parts and whole is kept in the forefront of any visioning or conceptualizing process. Solution-driven design, on the other hand, risks applying the "magic bullet" model to solve problems, reaching for the answer before the questions have been fully asked. The disconnect between problem and solution, always likely to be an issue, became exaggerated in the culture and practice of modernism in city design and planning, where problems were "dumbed down" to meet the solutions offered. For designers, a more fruitful approach focuses on the interaction between dynamic and comprehensive problem definition, identifying possibilities, coming up with conceptual alternatives, vetting these with representative constituencies, and then moving toward strategies that can be implemented and stand the test of time.

Again in Atlanta, citizens organizing themselves around community-held values, not local government and not corporate leadership, were the motive force for preventing cordons of freeways from lacing the city, and the motive force for preventing a combined sewer overflow facility to be placed in the middle of one of the city's few large parks.

Some designers rely on the "big idea," or three or four big ideas, as a way of synthesizing an urban design process into an actionable vision. If the big idea reflects a full vetting of the problem, a fully inclusive and citizen-guided process, or the flexibility to do so, there's a good chance this method might work—and it certainly assists in reaching an imageable and comprehendible vision. If, on the other hand, the big ideas simply come out of a consultant's medicine bag labeled "big ideas," then watch out. However persuasive and compelling, however unconsciously misleading, there's a fair chance that the purveyor of the big idea doesn't know why it has emerged as a generic solution in the first place, or whether its application to the particulars of a problem will make things better or worse.

This caution, though, is not aimed at discouraging the ideation process. It is vital to think of possibilities at all scales, to sketch or write them down to share in the process, but not to fall in love with them as "The Solution." Urban design contributes best when problem and solution interact with each other until each contributes to the synthesis that can improve the civic environment The territory of civic design missteps is littered with solutions that presumed rather than investigated the problems and then failed to make things better.

This is an area where civic leadership may succeed or fail. Proposals of development interests or politicians or even urban designers or other design professionals based on flawed information or lacking a full vetting of the problem often fail the commonsense test. The big idea may be so seductive, may get so imageable so fast that people are swept up in the process, potentially disastrous if the voice of reason or plain old common sense doesn't stand up. This risk becomes an even bigger problem as sophistication in marketing—in selling—becomes ever more compelling. Thus, lots of public energy and money may be spent on projects or strategies that are fatally flawed, but the flaws are adroitly "bandaided" so that the generating interest group prevails anyway. The local government may end up with the responsibility and the tab for fixing the problems that were ignored. Citizen activism can be effective in stopping or redirecting any number of such big ideas back to the drawing board, often bringing forward a better big idea that actually can be of benefit.

Where civic leadership is top-heavy with corporate leaders, the vulnerability to the "magic bullet" may be more pronounced. Successful corporate leadership depends on focusing on the core business, often a product line that is precisely definable, and turning out that product as efficiently and profitably as possible. The very narrowing of the agenda, together with metrics that end in the bottom line, often represents the antithesis of the civic agenda. Here the aspirations of a range of citizens often create less definable, amorphous, and somewhat ambiguous programs, where positive outcomes are measured in service values, making things better instead of worse, scratching out singles instead of hitting home runs.

The problem of solutionism shows up at various scales. Beginning in the 1960s, a "solution" to flagging main streets was to close them to auto traffic, as if that was their problem. Of course, that move, tried in countless towns and cities, accelerated the decline. Or, "festival markets," which worked for Baltimore's Inner Harbor and Boston's Faneuil Hall, tanked in most of the other places for which they were posited to be the "solution" to revitalize downtowns. In Atlanta, which has severe congestion issues, two transit "solutions" have emerged that commit billions of dollars to solutions that miss the problem. The problem is the need to provide transit options right now to get people to their workplaces in order to moderate the ever-upward growth curve of car travel. A regional authority, the Georgia Regional Transportation Authority (GRTA) (itself so far a dangerous example of failed "solutionism" at the organizational level), has instituted a far-flung commuter bus program that prioritizes miles traveled over riders served. Meanwhile, addressing the real problem, a simple shuttle between MARTA rail and a nearby major center, Atlantic Station, a trip of a couple of miles, carries more riders per month than the entire GRTA commuter bus system. Similarly, the City of Atlanta has committed a couple of billion dollars to a transit concept, the BeltLine, that can't be implemented for several decades and circles around rather than connects to its densest concentrations of residential and job populations. The first "solution" is offered as a way to entice a "better class of people" to transit. The second "solution" is a seductively presented and skillfully politicked "vision" of a nebulous future—"build it and they will come"—instead of an answer to the crying need of getting higher densities of residents to higher concentrations of jobs. The flaws in these examples stem from prioritizing the "solution" over understanding the problem.

# Design in the Context of Time (and Motion)

Why are some places so cheery in the morning, others so welcoming in the evening or okay all day long? Why do some work during the week, others on the weekend, and some only for special events? Some places are just outdoors, some flow between indoors and outdoors, and some are indoors. Some work in the fall and spring better than in the summer. Others attract in the winter.

Or, in wholly different aspects of time: How have places changed over time? How does a place reflect where it's coming from and where it's trying to go? Or, what does the timeline tell us: the past, the present, the future? And are things getting better or worse? Often it's better to be in a not-so-good place that's getting better, than in a great place that's declining. How do changing values change the assessment of a place or the pri-

*"Now you see it, now you don't."*
*"It went by in the blink of an eye."*
*"Why does it have to take so long?"*

orities for dealing with it? Or, who's in the game for the long haul or for the short turnaround—who's committed and for how long? Why does it take so long to get stuff done?

The element of time in design and development has many dimensions. Even though all don't always apply, all should be considered in any design strategy. The dimensions of time apply differently and at different scales—places, neighborhoods, towns and cities, and regions. Design and implementation responses to the dimensions of time will vary, yet maintaining a checklist will assure that the implications of time for design strategies at different scales are duly considered.

As suggested in the questions above, the dimensions of time at their most basic include time of day, time of week, and season. For understanding a place's and its people's context and status, key factors for informing design and development strategies, it is important to review historical maps, current policies, short- and long-term plans of all relevant agencies, and the timelines of capital improvement budgets. And for the more process-oriented dimensions of time, the time it takes for things to happen—for getting things done—needs to be understood and considered. Most urban design work benefits from being laid across a continuum, integrating all the steps that need to occur into a timeline, or maintaining a critical path analysis.

Time of day is a crucial factor in design at all scales. Not just where the sun rises, crests, and falls in different seasons, not just latitudinal or climate factors, but the pulsing of human activity through the course of the day play important roles in shaping better places. Places tend to focus people's public, civic, and social activities throughout the day. The intensity and nature of these activities respond to the rhythms of daily life.

Thus first-shift and construction workers, delivery people, early joggers, early risers, coffeehouses, bakeries, and breakfast places define the daybreak scene. As the day quickens, traffic picks up, often replacing on-street parking with travel lanes. Pedestrian activity picks up, breakfast and coffee pick up. Then other stores and shops open, and on-street parking returns; street life and place activity is more sporadic during the mid-morning. Then comes noontime—eating, shopping, socializing, heavy pedestrian traffic, more car and transit traffic. Then mid-afternoon, much like mid-morning except kids may start showing up to hang out, ride bikes, or skateboard. Then the evening rush picks up, returning pedestrians, cars, and transit activity to high levels—congestion of all kinds. At this point, places may take a fork in the road. Some pick up with happy hour, dining, and evening entertainment activities running late into the night with moderate levels of car and pedestrian traffic. Others wind down and join in the darkness of their surrounding neighborhoods or suburbs.

Just as time of day needs to be considered and reflected in design strategies, so do time of week and seasonal factors. In place design, the weekend is different. The work week is over, things typically start later, with less traffic; activity carries on at a steadier though usually reduced pace, with minor pulses around mealtimes, with these often attenuated beyond their weekday focus periods. Some places keep high loads of activity throughout the week, some come alive on the weekend when shopping might create congestion problems, and some go to sleep. Some come to life at night, even fairly late, some are locked up and dark. Most places take a breather on Sunday nights. Depending on the shared views of businesspeople, their customers, and others whom the place attracts, design strategies can join with other initiatives to support the "mix" that makes a place work, in terms of activities, business, and times of day and week.

Similarly, seasonal rhythms affect place activities, thus design. A place in the South in midsummer, or a place in the North in midwinter, needs to provide for indoor-outdoor flow of space that can work for the range of activities and people that make it viable. In the summer, kids are out of school, usually easing rush hour traffic. The period between Thanksgiving and Christmas is the time of year for which many retail-serving parking facilities are designed, which then blight their surroundings and travel corridors with blacktopped desolation the rest of the year.

Another dimension of time is motion. We first perceive places approaching them, passing through them, or, sometimes, after having passed through them. We might be walking, driving, on a bus, or riding a bike. We might have heard of a place and have it in mind as our destination. Or it may satisfy some need we have on a regular basis. However it is, getting there is a dynamic act, and it is important for designers to design for arriving, moving through, and even leaving places, which are the pause points that punctuate the physical sensing of daily life. The fixed world is not static—it changes by our changing location and speed, by the sun's or other light source's location, when it's raining or snowing. The buildings, the trees, the other elements in the streetscape may not move, but people see them differently based on their own motion through a place or by the forces of time, climate, and other changing forces. As with other design parameters, there is nothing that is a surprise about motion as part of experiencing a place. But its interactions with other parameters and consciousness of its possibilities and obstacles often causes motion to be overlooked in design decision-making. Thus motion should join with other parameters that allow a designer to employ this understanding to shape the dynamic experience of places.

Walking distance, for example, is a measure of time and motion; a currently popular rule of thumb suggests that a quarter of a mile (1,320 feet) or three or four blocks is a comfortable distance for most pedestrians to walk. Similarly, for drivers, sight distance is an important measure, relating the speed of travel to the distance where choices about driving behavior must be made.

At the larger scale, in Birmingham, motion in the form of deceleration from 60 mph to 30 mph was a key consideration in the redesign of freeway entrances to downtown (and later other) places. Overall, the design brief was directed at creating more welcoming entrances to the city, replacing a back-alley experience with a grand front-entry drive. This entailed eliminating bent chain link fences, broken concrete, weed- and glass-strewn dirt, and fast-food detritus and replacing it with sculpted, planted berms and tree screens, and an entrance pylon—all designed to shape decelerating car speed.

# Summary

The urban design principles here should guide both the technical and procedural work of both professionals in those fields who contribute to the making of places at all scales and those citizens who take a special interest in these kinds of issues. They will be referenced in Part Four, Processes, and Part Five, Strategies, where some of their applications will be illustrated. Urban design as a shared professional/community activity prioritizes substance over style. It introduces a public perspective on space design, very different from the private perspective, with which, however, it must be interactive. How places work and look, how they become symbolic, how people can directly engage themselves in the processes of improvement, in my experience, is what successful urban design means.

# 7

# CHANGE

## Change Happens

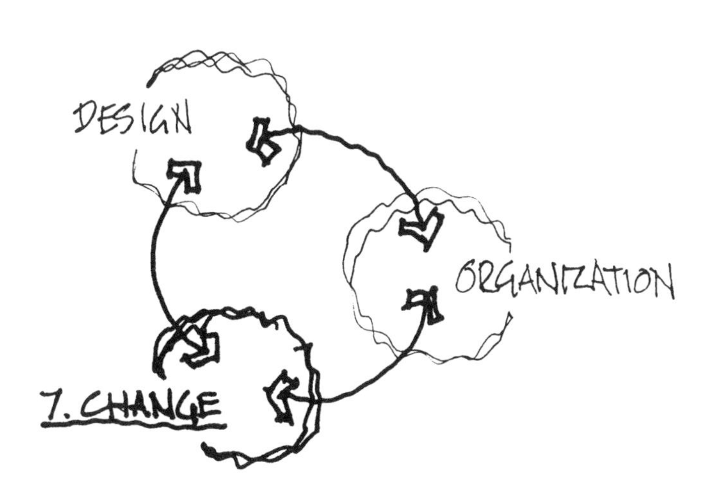


*Figure 7.1*
*The sphere of change in continuous interaction with design and organization.*

# Introduction

Places and the people who make them are in a state of continuous change, from barely perceptible to dramatic. Change is always a major force in community life, sometimes welcomed, more often resisted, as citizens and the people to whom they look for leadership come to grips with the forces of change. People can cope with change, resist it, or take advantage of it. Change affects everyone's daily life, whether as individuals, families, communities or cities, or states and nations.

This chapter is organized to first consider change itself—the circumstance of all urban places—with general understandings of what it is and how to formulate principles to share that understanding and to act effectively in change situations. The chapter then presents more specific change-related principles, highlighting those related to vision, information, action, choice, and readiness. Together, the goal is to prepare students, urban designers and development practitioners, as well as community leaders and government representatives, to approach change situations with a framework for guiding understanding and acting effectively.

The principles proposed here for understanding and dealing with change are discussed from both a conceptual and a practice perspective. And for our purposes, change principles are in constant interaction with design and organizational principles—each affects the other in the making of the civic environment.

We will address questions like: What kinds of changes does the civic environment commonly experience? What are the causes of such changes? What are the main constituencies that interact in the place-changing process? What principles underlie these change forces? How can urban designers, developers, and communities guide change processes to make places better than they were before?

People respond differently to change, both as a concept and as an occurrence. And they do not necessarily respond in a consistent way to a change event, the variation often being related to a perception of self-interest. In the physical setting people may deny that change is or should be happening, or they may embrace change as an opportunity for making their environment better—or anything in between. In the civic environment, a new building goes up or an old one gets torn down, maybe replaced with a parking lot. A street is widened (and the sidewalk narrowed). The neighbors paint their house, or another house gets boarded up. A fence gets built, or cars start showing up in the front yard. Trees are planted or chopped down. Private and public actions are constantly changing the frame of civic life, sometimes for the better, sometimes for the worse. In any event, change is a fundamental factor in any place-making endeavor.

In the stereotypical case, familiar to all interested in design and development matters, the change initiators are developers who have assembled some property and want to build a project that will be profitable for them. Depending on how the developer goes about it, the community where the development is proposed is the reactor, frequently resisting, occasionally embracing the proposal. Often the developer proposal requires approval from the municipal authority—"city hall," if you will.

This sets up an interaction dynamic that produces a change of some sort, regardless of the outcome. (Even if the proposal does not go forward, something happens to the property—maybe a lesser development, or a deterioration in its state, or it just hangs on, all for better or worse).

The premise of this book is that the outcome of this dynamic should leave more of the people affected by the change better off than they were before. At least it should do no harm.

Change principles directed at improving understanding and management of urban place-making activities need to be placed in a broader context. Change in any setting tends to challenge people. Meanwhile, stasis tends to be comfortable (even if it's uncomfortable). For better or worse, change happens along everyone's life path—birth, school, work, daily routines, marriage, moves, kids, higher income, lower income, care for aging parents, grand kids, retire, die. This general continuum, with infinite variations, is an understanding of change we all share, however unconsciously. Change, by definition overcoming inertia, embodies an effort that stasis does not. For many, there is a sequence of response when faced with a change situation: deny that change is happening or needs to happen; accept that change will happen, but resist it by all means; bend, moderate, or attenuate change to ease its burden of adjustment; or embrace change as an opportunity, a new vista over the horizon. People may find themselves in one or another of these categories, depending on the change circumstances that face them. And people go forward or backward along this progression of steps as they try to cope with or benefit from change.

My colleague from Atlanta City Hall days, Aaron Fortner, has a pithy way of describing this typical developer/community/government set of dynamics when faced with a zoning proposal: "The developer dreams up what *could* be done, the community tries to enunciate what *should* be done, and the government determines what *will* be done."

Communities, not unlike individuals, tend to follow similar patterns when faced with change situations, and any place improvement (or degradation) is, by definition, a change situation. Changes may be generated internally or driven by external forces, or both in interaction with each other. Similarly, our institutions change, go through cycles, are more or less effective, are more or less responsive to citizens, more or less friendly to developers and other concentrated private interests. In the planning and design of places, change is a factor with many dimensions, ramifications, and choices, challenging those seeking to manage a positive change process. Understanding and managing change positively and effectively is as important for communities who want to see improvements as it is for initiators and practitioners in the place-making business.

Through the continuous buffeting of change forces, differences may sharpen, even to the point of strife. People may feel these dynamics inside themselves—the self, coping, identity, confidence, the family, values, the job—and from the outside—the "them and us" tensions of class, race, gender, culture, belief systems. In this context, places are in flux, getting "better" or "worse," attracting new investment or being disinvested, improving in value or profitability or declining, getting their connective and community support infrastructure renewed or seeing it deteriorate. And what's going on around always affects places. Taken together, places are always subject to interactive, cascading, and cumulative impacts whose effects are not always predicted, nor predictable.

# Change Dynamics

Before moving on, it is important to review and provide some analysis for the recent history of change management in the evolution of places as I have experienced it. To begin with, momentum plays a big role in the good fortunes (or failings) of a community improvement initiative. Building positive momentum usually takes a series of positive actions. These may be small, almost unnoticeable at the time—steps taken by people

Now-deceased paleontologist and Red Sox fan Stephen J. Gould developed a theory that suggested that the process of evolution was not smooth and even, but rather marked by periods of relative stasis punctuated by major transformations, which could either internally build up or be caused by external forces, like what killed off the dinosaurs. He received a lot of criticism from colleagues, some anxious that such a concept smacked a little too much of the dialectics theories of Georg Hegel as further elaborated by Karl Marx. Self-deprecatingly, Gould was able to characterize his and his colleagues' work on "punctuated equilibrium" as "evolution by jerks" or "punk eke," at a time when "punk" was on the rise. Regrettably, Gould did not live to see his theory vindicated by recent Red Sox World Series successes.

turning the corner toward an emphasis on hope over despair. These may take on the form of physical, visually apparent improvements, like someone adding a room to a house, someone else planting a garden, someone else planting street trees or cleaning up the right-of-way. Public policy should support and reinforce these kinds of efforts through organizational recognition and funding priorities. What happens, then, is that a quantity of small, or with luck maybe not so small, actions build up to the point of triggering more significant and transformative actions, what some call reaching critical mass. Reaching the point where quantitative change morphs into qualitative change, like when water getting hotter and hotter turns suddenly into steam, is the marker for a neighborhood or district turning the corner, where more things go right than go wrong. Unfortunately, the same phenomenon of change dynamics can work in reverse—a little bad thing here, another there, and the neighborhood or district may descend into a downward spiral.

Even with growing enfranchisement of community leadership, the dominant change management strategies out there in place-making processes still typically aim at achieving success within the terms of the change initiator, not from the perspective of the community as a whole. As a result, we only occasionally find examples of a broadly shared vision for the future of a place or an inclusive process to implement such a vision. The values of those impacted are simply not held to be as important as the values of the "owner" of the change, whether private sector or local government. Time, money, and control of the outcome are the values of most change initiators, whether developers, businesses, institutions, or public agencies.

A typical or baseline change scenario, then, sets up a dynamic where the change initiator, a developer for example, has optioned (or sometimes even purchased) property, done a lot of work on the proposal, spent some real money, may have obligated a lot more money, has a timetable, and is certain that all has been done to move forward with the change (except maybe for securing a zoning or other public approval). Depending on how far downstream the community hears about it, the people there—where the change is proposed—then ask for more information, raise questions, raise objections, and make requests (or demands). The developer gets angry and frustrated, is put on the defensive, feels attacked, and seeks recourse. Before the progression of steps toward more democratic community enfranchisement since the 1960s legitimated the community's voice, community resistance didn't much matter. Whatever political will might be mustered to respond to people's concerns was routinely trumped by the power of money or status, and the project proceeded, occasionally with positive community benefit, but more often not.

While there is evidence of positive change, many developers (including public agencies) who find themselves in this dynamic, if they have the resources and stature to initiate change in places still take this traditional path. Take a little public relations abuse if you can't avoid it, but get what you want in the end. And, even now with greater lip service to community sensibilities, most "citizen engagement" or "citizen involvement" processes are set up by initiators' consultants for the purpose of achieving largely predetermined ends, including predetermined bones that may be tossed to the community if necessary. The persistent laments from the development community or other change initiators that have accompanied the progression of community empowerment include such comments as "they don't know what's good for them" or "we know better" or "this is costing us time and money, for what?" or "let the people who know how and have the wherewithal do their job—we'll all be better off," and so on. The logic of these arguments is that more can happen faster, maybe at less cost and thus higher profit. Any cost savings from an expedited process are not likely to find their way to the benefit of the community.

This line of argument, however, is becoming more and more suspect, as communities' access to information accelerates, the sophistication of skills in the community make-up grows, their font of local knowledge becomes harder to deny, and the progression of failed projects based on premises that defy common sense becomes more widely known. And the traditional path, of course, does not accept the premise underlying this book, that is, that ongoing citizen guidance and partnership in place-making activities is essential for their sustained improvement.

Thus community suspicion of new initiatives has a long and well-worn, grudgingly endured history. It is hard to find the kind of trust necessary to harness the capital and approval forces that might actually move toward fulfilling a broader community betterment vision. This pattern comports with the perception of most communities—disproportionately lower-income and minority communities that typically have little in common with most change initiators. From their perspective, the government and private interests work in tandem to ignore community aspiration and not hear legitimate issues, instead rolling over community objection and implementing the project anyway.

This picture anecdotally dominates the change dynamics of communities and their places, and thus engenders resistance or opposition to change as a community response pattern. This response is typically born of two sets of forces at work in most communities: the traditional lack of access to full information, powerlessness, and past experience on the one hand, and a relatively recent and growing democratizing trend and greater enfranchisement of the community's will on the other.

The first set of forces is quite predictable and represents the dominant community experience with change, and thus resistance to it. The start-up presumption is that any change that "they" may be seeking, for whatever reasons, is likely to make things worse and therefore should be resisted at all costs. This is the well-established "NIMBY" pattern (the acronym for "not in my backyard," generally used as a pejorative by those who don't want to hear from the people there). In terms of making places better, the logic in this pattern holds this flaw: If any change is bad change, yet change is inevitable, community dynamics can only be negative. Denying that change happens, resisting change, can only result, at best, in things getting no worse.

Much of the tension that accompanies a development proposal or a public infrastructure initiative derives from community experiences that have been negative or performed well short of their promises, either in that community or one nearby. The easiest thing for a would-be community activist to do is to stand up in a community meeting and oppose a change initiative. Community leadership at all scales and in most American communities has been dominated by leadership forged in defense; just saying no is easy, sometimes effective, but more often not. What too often underlies the occasional defensive victory is a presumption that "what is" is surely better than what might come. While this hunkered-down representation of community leadership with respect to the usual change initiators may seem overly dour, in its own maturation the community leadership picture is beginning to change, bringing with it the possibility of more hopeful futures for civic environments.

This leads to the second set of forces. Not too long ago, before Model Cities, the National Environmental Policy Act (NEPA), and the Community Development Block Grant program (CDBG) in the late 1960s and early 1970s, most communities lacked any institutional sanction to effectively question or block place-altering activities in their communities. To be sure, community activism has a much longer history, but until the civil rights/women's rights/anti-war era sea changes in institutional empowerment, effective community activists were usually disaffected people of privilege, acting on behalf of their own community betterment or, through a sense of noblesse oblige, on behalf of others less fortunate. In response to a general community clamor for democratizing review and approval processes for federally funded programs, however, Model Cities, NEPA, CDBG, and other federal acts required, for the first time and however tentatively, community involvement in the project decision-making process.

Initially, this newly enfranchised voice was lifted in opposition to whatever "they" were getting ready to do to the community, reflecting the time-tested presumptions of community resistance, but with a new and more powerful effect. Yet little by little, as community involvement in change matures, there are growing instances of increasingly positive responses to change forces. In these, communities at all levels, incomes, and ethnicities are beginning to view change initiatives from the perspective of the opportunity to step forward to realize their own visions for a better place.

Over a relatively short 40 or so years, then, community leadership for stewardship and enhancement of place has progressed from not being officially recognized at all in the place-making process (developer, lender, and city council basically determining the outcome) to being increasingly an effective and recognized voice, and now to openness to partnership with government and the private sector for place improvement.

Power exercised in support of "design" may have topped the charts when CBS built its headquarters in Manhattan in the mid-1960s, designed by Eero Saarinen and Kevin Roche. William Paley, CEO and chairman, is alleged to have ordered that employees adhere to a design code right down to their cubicles, where even their kids' art was suppressed. On the other hand, Paley put in place the delightful little respite park farther west on 53rd Street that bears his name. And he chaired a blue-ribbon panel that studied the state of civic design in the city and advised incoming mayor John Lindsay, among other things, to establish a design-trained unit in city government that later became the Urban Design Group in the City Planning Department—my first public sector employment.

All of these progressions, from usually hopeless resistance to the recent continuum of community leadership maturation, reflect one common thread: the will of people to exercise some control, some power to act to improve their places. By their own actions, whether stopping threats or supporting opportunities, they can and do bring forth their visions of what improvement means. People, as individuals, families, or groups, generally want to assert some control over their lives. Thus, at the most basic level, how one dresses, how one organizes one's possessions, how one parts one's hair, are expressions of that self which even in the harshest conditions are hard to take away.

The extent to which the basic humanity of all is recognized, respected, and included is the extent to which consonance with a society's economic and political institutions can be measured. If people's control over their environment ends at arranging bric-a-brac on a shelf, however, they are not likely to have much of a stake in the world beyond. The place where they live will show it. Where people have sufficient authority to assert some degree of control over their lives, their consonance with the political, economic, and social institutions is much higher, their stake in the larger community is higher, and their places show that.

Lifting the community voice into a semblance of parity with the private sector and the government represents a rebalancing of interests from traditional patterns. It stems from what can only be called demands for democratization that grew out of other democratization and equity movements that peaked in the 1960s and early 1970s. The processes then set in place lifted the bar on criteria and expectations that communities could legitimately look to in their interactions with government and the private sector. Looked at objectively, communities to be affected by a major new private or public development initiative almost always have a higher share of their collective net worth bound up in a place's future than any developer that wants in. And as a practical matter, processes that lift the prospect of meaningful community guidance bring with them the carrots and sticks involved in project approval. Communities don't have and I think should not have authority over these approvals, but their engagement and voice may gain influence through time and money saved through consensual processes.

In any event, the changing role of community leadership has now become much more important in the planning and design of places. If it's fair to say that places are continuously changing and that the power of the people there to affect this change is on the rise, then understanding and managing change is essential, for both practitioners and community activists who want to support positive results.

# Framework for Understanding and Managing Change

The change process must understand and respect the divergent forces that cause it. Change management must constantly reach for common ground as a basis for building trust. Further, participants in a change process must adopt a "both-and," not an "either-or," approach, so that the strengths of contending forces can be incorporated positively into the place-changing strategy. Trust, often lacking in present practice, is a crucial goal in this quest. The simple yet sincere willingness for divergent interests to reach toward each other is a positive first step.

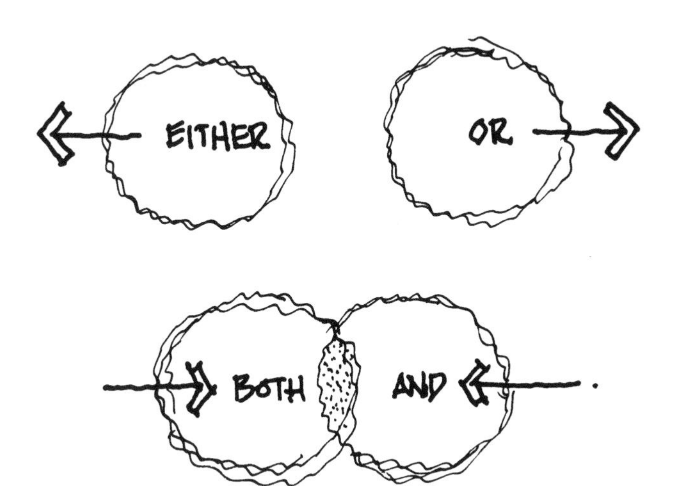


*Figure 7.2*
*The diagram pictures two outcomes for oppositional positions—toward resolution through "both-and" dynamics or toward greater conflict through "either-or" dynamics.*

Both the societal and physical dynamics of any place include dualities or polarities. These are nominally opposing forces that, left on their own, don't resolve themselves. Yet for a place to get better they must be resolved, and in a positive manner. There are three ways of viewing the relationship between the polar opposites in a duality. The first considers the opposites to be in a static relationship, along a continuum or axis. This is the dominant characterization of the dynamics between opposites in current place-making practice. The usual and predictive resolution of opposites so conceptualized (unless the power balance significantly favors one over the other, in which case the powerful side wins anyway) is to search for compromise. With compromise, some degree of loss and an accompanying sense of loss for both positions is the measure of the outcome. The referee's admonition is: Pain accompanies mediation, and the goal is to have a reasonably equitable sharing of the pain. The process of resolving dualities through compromise, while better than no resolution at all, nonetheless deprives the opposite positions from a different outcome, one in which both ends of the duality gain.

The search for compromise is the normal model that comes into play for opposing positions faced with a place-changing situation. It reflects the differences of interests and perceptions of those involved. The developer wants to build something that doesn't complement the neighborhood's or district's vision, that puts a strain on infrastructure, like road capacity, or wants to build more or higher than the community is willing to accept. The local government wants investment but in a way that is consistent with its overall plans and zoning regulations or is subject to due process if any change in those is sought. The community wants its scale and character respected, usually wants to keep its taxes stable, and wants its infrastructure to work for them. The compromise model is based on finding things that all three parties typical in this ubiquitous scenario are willing to give up so that something better than nothing can happen.

Second, a variant and frequently an improvement on the compromise approach for resolving a duality is to conceptualize the dynamic of differing positions along a timeline, where today's resolution may bend toward one pole, but the element of time might bend toward the other. Since place-making is never completed, an understanding of the continuum of some foreseeable timeframe may result in gains for one pole within its time priorities and gains for the other in its. It's remarkable how many times I have encountered circumstances where divergent interests lack any sense of the time implications of the issue that divides them, like "right now" is in the forefront of both parties' minds. Stepping back and viewing the issue from the perspective of time often reveals that the "right now" is in fact a multiyear continuum, across which their real interests are spread and may often end up dovetailing and not conflicting.

The third way, for me the one to seek as the most effective framework for managing a place-development duality, relies on an interactive, progressive approach. Here, the relation between opposites is dynamic, in which the strengths of the two positions are acknowledged, then structured or posed to interact positively. Often, these dynamics begin with a position, say that of the initiator, that engenders a counter-position, say that of the community, and that interaction opens up the possibility for a new third position that may be above and beyond what either start-up position contemplated—a new synthesis, if you will. Positioning the duality in such a way depends on fostering a search for any common ground, or "both-and," between the two start-up positions, however small that overlap might be. Right away, proponents of opposing forces find their position validated, which may allow progress on the shared purpose of project success and community improvement, making the place better. The value of affirming the validity of both positions in a duality is that the creative and potentially contributive force that leads their proponents to the position in the first place is allowed to flow forth, untrammeled by the need to doggedly defend the position from the onset of the process. Opposing forces can be engaged interactively to achieve outcomes beyond the starting positions of either, bringing new conceptual and often material resources and partnerships to bear on the job of improvement.

A short way to summarize these approaches to resolving dualities is that the compromise approach stems from an "either-or" attitude, which can be moderated by recognizing the timeline as a mediator, and the synthesis approach reflects a "both-and" attitude. In my experience, the latter is the most effective and satisfying, the one I aspire to, followed by the time-tempered approach to compromise and, if necessary, compromise. It should be noted at this point, as the sidebar example suggests, that the duality may in fact involve more than two poles. Nonetheless, the rationale for managing the change process as described for the duality applies to situations with multiple poles—they're just a little more complicated.

In the business world, the reach for outcomes positive for two or more parties is often described as "win-wins" or even "win-win-wins," depending on how many poles actually exist in the nominal "duality." Here, though, the main measure of "win" is usually profit, while in place-improvement activities the measures include a wider range of both quantitative and qualitative values, of which profit for the developer or investor is but one.

These ways of conceptualizing how to manage dualities in a place-changing process assume a number of shared baseline conditions: First, the parties engaged in the process, representing different positions in the place-changing duality (e.g., a developer and a community leadership) at some level want to make the place better. Second, the parties care a lot about their stake in the place that is subject to the change forces. And third, they are sincere in the positions that they espouse, not just working hidden agendas. It is not so important if others of their goals are divergent like, for example, the developer having to make a profit or the community leadership having to gain positive note for its actions.

In repeated interactions of this kind, I have found that it is not such a reach to uncover these baseline conditions, at all scales of place and with all demographic make-ups. To be sure, some circumstances are more difficult than others, usually depending on how long and how deeply the community side of the equation has been ignored, lied to, or violated. However worthwhile pursuing these change-management strategies may be, it is important for practitioners to keep in mind two key aspects of the place-making dynamic: First, listen to and respect the dualities expressed in the start-up positions, and induce those participating in the process to do the same. People don't believe what they believe for no reason, and the kernel for positive resolution lies in respect for the two positions, if for no other reason than the intensity of the expressed position itself. Second, no place gets better unless the people there, at least a few of them, care. Anyone who cares deeply about a place's future, no matter how at variance with other positions that may be out there, must be respected. Thus

In one place-building effort, in Five Points South in Birmingham, after a few months of unproductive back and forth around four or five different positions held by property owners, retailers, renters, neighborhood residents, city traffic engineers, and other institutional participants, one of those most entrenched in his position unlocked the process by asking: "Can't we all just agree that it can be better than it is now?" This motion, by Gordon Cleage, who operated the hardware store, was approved unanimously, and the common ground had been struck. About the same number of months later, construction began on a very successful place-improvement process that continues today, 25 years later.

Urban design practitioners often find themselves to be the nexus in a diversity of zealots. Our job is to stretch ourselves to include these zealots, however much consternation they may cause, so that the power of their commitment can be bent to the common purpose of making the place better. This challenges us to check our own egos at the door, to realign our thinking, and to redefine our own views to merge both with the citizen-driven vision of place improvement and the change initiator's measures of success. Meeting this challenge may alter our own learned or believed predispositions, ensuring that diverse and special places reflect diverse and special people.

In downtown and midtown Atlanta, together the central core of the city, there are numerous examples of how such a dynamic plays out. Both overseen by development review committees, for example, civic values are represented by inclusion of the district leadership, the government, and particularly in the case of midtown, neighborhood representatives. Both areas have undergone substantial modification to their zoning rules, and both have received significant infrastructure improvement funding and regulatory support. A specific result of these partnerships has resulted in consistent and gracious sidewalk and streetscape improvements, which often encroach on the adjacent private property. The agreement by the city to acknowledge that ownership in calculating the permissible floor area ratio, coupled with the recognition by developers that the resulting public environment significantly enhances their projects, create a win for each. The city gains a superior public environment, the developer gains a more marketable and prideful project, and the general public has a really nice place to walk—not always the case in sidewalk-challenged Atlanta.

an overriding priority for improving change management is to find a reliable basis of trust between the change initiator, the community affected, and the apparatus of government to ensure a fair and positive outcome.

While compromise remains the dominant and usual approach to managing change forces, the more productive approaches are beginning to show up in practice here and there. The context for their advance will be the gradual incorporation of communities and their interests as real partners in making better civic decisions. As it stands, without an acknowledged advisory voice, communities may continue to be the source of much of the friction that accompanies design and development initiatives.

# Trends in Change Management

The good news is that there are signs in both the development sector and in the community that the advantages of a partnership approach may outweigh the disadvantages. The climate of change is beginning to alter the development community viewpoint (and in general I include here large institutions and government agencies like parks, public works, and highway departments). The traditional default position of "just let us do it" is evolving, as the duality of private gain and public benefit has become energized with citizen empowerment. Little by little, the development community is willing to offer a hand in partnership to at least review the possibility of common purpose. Early results of such processes are promising: Both community and developer goals are advanced and sharpened as communities get a better understanding of what's doable and developers tap ideas and impulses that improve their projects, both in connectivity with their larger context and within their own cost-revenue measures. And usually developers would just as soon support community-held place-improvement goals, since they could enhance property values and diminish the hostility associated with cross-purposes (unless the development is an old-time block-busting strategy, or the placement of a landfill).

And in communities, with the drive toward greater equity gaining ground, new forms of community leadership are developing. The strident naysayers are still out there, and they need to be until the forces they react against begin to actually listen. But I am encountering and am involved with more and more community leaders who are reaching to actually get stuff done in their communities that represents steps toward their vision of a better future. They recognize that the private sector holds most of the resources and the know-how to actually build things and that gaining community-defined improvements as part of developers' projects leads them to form partnership relations. Instead of just saying "stop," this changing form of community leadership is saying "maybe," provided that community goals are respected and advanced in the process. Most exciting in this new trend is that communities subscribing to this form of leadership are actively engaged in envisioning what they want their communities to become, and how their communities can change for the better, not just trying to stop whatever in order to hang on to what they had.

It may be too early to suggest that this new model of seeking a synthesis for mutual benefit might replace the old and still dominant default compromise position, but if it works better and advances both poles of the duality's position beyond their starting positions, then it has a chance to become more pervasive. These relatively new yet growing examples of partnership could signal erecting a stile over the wall of distrusts that has for so long separated community from change initiators, a shift that would bode well for continued place-making improvements. In larger contexts, similar change-management processes could be useful in advancing more equitable outcomes from divergent interests.

Beyond the principles that address the evolving dynamics between the private sector, the community, and the government, there are other change-related principles that can help the place-improvement process no matter where in the continuum of change a community might find itself. These address key elements of any change-management process under the topics of vision, information, and action; choice; and readiness.

In one community in Atlanta, under the leadership of a group including a retired labor official, the community engaged in a deliberate partnership-forming process with a local developer that resulted in support for the first underground Wal-Mart in the country. The store is at the base and out of sight of the community, with a layer of parking above and a shopping square at the level of the community. The project also includes a significant component of rental housing. (The labor official had sought out different big-box tenants with more balanced positions on the labor-management duality, but reluctantly acceded to the group's successful negotiation.) The partnership approach, representing a synthesis of divergent opinions, transformed a challenged approval process into a speedier one, worth time and money to the developer, and good public relations for the PR-challenged Wal-Mart organization.

# The Triad of Vision, Information, and Action

Vision, information, and action are change-oriented principles that are dealt with as a dynamic, interactive triad, or set. All of the activities for which principles are advanced here are in continuous, nonlinear interaction with each other in any civic environment. A vision for a place is affected by the information on which it is based and actions that have shaped it, or are underway or contemplated. Similarly, actions are always happening, both planned and random, from small to major initiatives, changing both the information base and the vision of what's possible. And information is constantly updated both in general and in the particulars that define places, sometimes stimulating the vision-setting process or guiding action. Within this tri-polar context, there are principles that apply to each that are useful for understanding and interacting effectively to achieve positive change.

## Work Toward a Unifying Vision

There's an old saw that goes: "If you don't know where you're going, it doesn't matter what road you take." This applies as well to communities as to individuals: communities (or districts, towns, cities, or regions) serve their interests by developing some shared sense of their future, and the more inclusive of the ranges of interests in the population, the more achievable and sustainable that vision will be. The idea of working toward a shared vision is itself an acknowledgment of changing circumstances. Often the trigger for bringing people together is a change initiative, either from inside, like dealing with some challenge, threat, or opportunity facing the community, or from outside, like a new development or infrastructure proposal.

Similarly, the convener for a visioning process can come from within or outside of the affected community. In the latter case, a growing phenomenon associated with larger development initiatives, whether by a private developer or a government entity, is that the "visioning" process comes with and is part of the initiative. Consultants are hired to manage the "citizen engagement" process, bringing with them techniques that facilitate the process of reaching some kind of consensus. Communities should be on the alert that these processes can range from open-ended and genuine to tactics to achieve support, or at least nonopposition, to the sponsor's project. Using the resources provided to obtain the broader purpose

Building on examples of projects here and there in place in Atlanta, a community-based organization, Georgia Standup, has established a more general nomenclature for these kinds of partnerships to work on such projects: Community Benefit Agreements. The concept, as they are promulgating it, draws from other such initiatives around the country. The organization has been successful, for example, in getting the City Council to include the principle in a major tax increment financing authorization. Their goal is to assure that community people will benefit from development supported by these public funds, whether in development that helps build neighborhood visions or in job opportunities for local citizens.

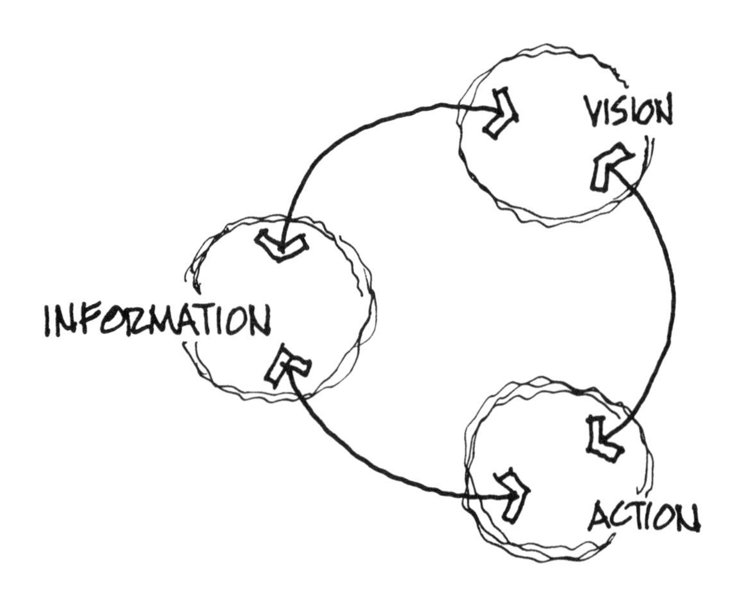


*Figure 7.3*
*The spheres of vision, information, and action together represent a key component of managing change to produce better places.*

of understanding each other and coalescing around what path to take, however, is an opening to processes that traditionally have been more closed, an opportunity worth considering.

A "vision" sets what direction to go. In the context of improving the civic realm, a vision seeks a shared general picture of how the place can look and function better than before. It is not a "blueprint" or in any way a detailed plan for the future. In fact, since coming together with others with different views, reaching for a shared vision almost by definition is a search for the most basic commonality. Detractors might complain that such a reach might be settling for "the least common denominator," a phrase used particularly by some to describe social or politically driven impediments to their quest for their own perceived maximum gain. And they could be right, but their gain is in a dualistic or dialectical relationship with the values and aspirations of the larger community, the resolution for which, as we have seen, could draw on the strengths of both positions. In the civic environment, maybe in civic life, finding where values are shared is the starting place, not the final destination, for civic design—the foundation for building the civic environment.

The example cited earlier of agreeing that "it can be better than it is" is an example of the most basic kind of "vision," yet one that establishes a positive consensus on which more concrete ideas can be considered and against which they can be measured. Several years ago, to cite another example, Portland, Oregon, engaged in a publicly convened and broadly inclusive visioning exercise in which the consensus was synopsized as: "We want a city where everyone can see Mount Hood and every child can walk to a library." Still general, this vision nonetheless speaks to that city's values of environmental respect, workable transportation, and care for its future generations.

While a unifying vision may be as brief and pithy as Portland's, it may just as well include a little more detail. Typically, successful visions build on strengths already evident in the community, both in its people and in its physical assets. Yet it should be manageable in length, since it will stand for a time as the metric against which more detailed plans, designs, and strategies will be gauged. Approaching the visioning effort from the perspective of fixing what's wrong, on the other hand, does not lead toward the best of what could be—the negative is limiting conceptually and downbeat psychologically. Just as important, since the vision is of an improved physical and social place, it should be visually imageable. People should be able to readily imagine the picture they create for their future. At the same time, people should create their vision with an open mind, with the flexibility to bend their course a few degrees as the other interactive parts of this change-management process are engaged. Information may come to light that either crimps aspects of the vision or that enlarges its possibilities. Actions may be underway, known or unexpected, that can change both the information base and the vision, again with impacts that may enhance or bend the vision.

## Find and Put to Use All Relevant Information

Information is crucial in any change-management process. Without good, relevant, full, and useful information, the best intentions and most broadly supported vision or aspiration can be dashed. This is a problem for individuals, communities, towns, regions, and even nations. We are living in a time when raw information is expanding geometrically, yet too often the manipulation of information to attain the focused purposes of concentrations of narrow interests is expanding even faster: spin. The very sophistication of the information explosion lends itself to manipulation by those with best access to the tools to do so. The widening gap between haves and have-nots is magnified in the information world, a circumstance some call the "digital divide."

At the same time, particularly at the level of community and civic space design, the availability of useful and relevant information affords people the opportunity to lift their information base to a level that enables them to take a much more prominent role in any place-improvement process. The broad parameters and the mix of disciplines necessary for effective place-improvement efforts are not so complicated, and websites are proliferating in ways that legitimately offer citizens a guiding role in their places of interest. Thus the mystique of superior information that used to intimidate citizens from asking questions or enunciating views at variance with the "experts" has given way, allowing the process of place design to become more collaborative.

Any place-changing dynamic, regardless of sophisticated or detailed information sources, should always begin with interacting with the citizens there, usually the most useful database, often overlooked or downplayed by professional practitioners. Who's there, what are they doing, what do they care about? How do they view their trends, positive and negative? What are their assets, what are their challenges? How do they represent their places? What are their priorities? In addition to lots of important factual, historical, and cultural data, community-generated information includes a commonsense factor that threads people together on the reliable ground of shared experience. Information from the community about itself, about what matters, about its values and patterns is the pivotal information base on which successful place-improvement strategies can be built. This is true at the neighborhood level, the district level, and though more complicated, at the larger urban scales as well.

Across this range of scales the people there usually know much of what needs to be known to make their place better, but they do need the help

In the growing and diffuse field called urban design, it should be noted that many practitioners put their emphasis on form as the pivotal and lasting criterion of what makes a good place. I have even heard such practitioners dismiss the people there or who will come as unimportant in the quest for ideal form, that the form is what will last, and that there are timeless design principles to whom all people "should" respond positively. Needless to say, this book asserts a different position—that is, that people make the form, interact with the form, and ultimately judge whether the form is successful, from both a workability and an aesthetic satisfaction point of view.

In preparing a "neighborhood strategy area" plan—a HUD program at the end of the 1970s—for the Mason City neighborhood in Birmingham, we engaged a civil engineer, Joe Miller, to prepare a new storm and sanitary sewer plan to better serve this very low-income and long-neglected neighborhood. Using the best available technical base information, topographic maps, and development history, he presented his preliminary plans to the neighborhood. The people there, through their observation and experience, knew that significant parts of the information of record was simply wrong—"the drainage flows down this street, not that street" kind of information. To his credit, Joe readily accepted and welcomed the neighborhood's data and changed his design, and we implemented an effective drainage-improvement project. I have had to argue with others who are sure that their "scientific" information had to be right, that the neighborhood couldn't know about such matters. Fortunately, I have been in the position to win a lot of these arguments for including serious consideration of neighborhood data in any design deliberation.

*"A popular government without popular information or the means of acquiring it is but a prologue to a farce, or a tragedy, or perhaps both."*
*—James Madison*

that technical information and other people's experience can lend them. They need the more in-depth information that they likely don't have. This may include various technical reports, public resource and regulatory information, information on comparable precedents, private sector real estate and development economics information, and process information—how to get stuff done. This kind of information in community improvement situations should be accessible to all involved. Armed with common sense and reliable and relevant information, people are likely to be able to interact with each other not just to come to a shared vision but to move down the road toward useful and sustainable actions to improve their places.

Unlimited access to information—transparency—has been enunciated as a goal for a trusting and trustworthy democracy, the premise being that people with fully shared information can figure it out. And certainly access to information is an important piece of formulating a vision for a place and devising actions to progress toward that vision. Yet, both in the public and private sectors, this access, information transparency, remains elusive and when available, is often selectively disclosed. There are various reasons for these information gaps, ranging from sinister to silly, from reprehensible to understandable, as the examples below suggest.

Developers are not likely to share their bottom line, not just to protect their projected profit margin but also to not tip off the competition. Yet developers invariably approach communities with their proposal represented as what they must have to "make the project pencil out," or build the project at its projected return on investment. Most communities with experience in these skits by now know that that representation is the starting point in a negotiation where some amount of community benefit is still realizable.

Government agencies are leery about sharing too much information too freely, for what in my experience seems to be some blend of turf protection and fear of revealing internal processes (making them "too accessible" to the interested public, anxiety about some inadequacy being revealed, covering for not having information that they should have, or an exaggerated sense of duty to protect higher-ups' or private sector interests—or in the worst situations, both).

Meantime, the Freedom of Information Act (FOIA) has clearly advanced the goal of information access. People who care, with enough persistence can usually get at least some of what they need to inform themselves about the public policy side of development management. (People so inclined, too, should persist, pleasantly, in getting past the occasional public employee practice of providing the narrowest response to the broadest question; that is, prepare to ask follow-on questions.) The media, the ultimate information processor and disseminator, has used FOIA to good advantage in revealing how government works and how its "partnerships" with the private sector may or may not be a good deal for the public. At the same time the media may select and bend information to tell the story that its higher-ups expect or sometimes require. Access to information through the media is further constrained by the concentration of its ownership into fewer and fewer hands, which regardless of intent almost automatically limits the breadth of news and information available (unless you really want to follow O. J. Simpson or Paris Hilton).

At the same time, the continuing explosion of alternative information sources through the Internet to some extent compensates for the truncation of news and information from the major and mainstream media sources. The issue in this hopeful countertrend is moves by media monopolization forces to control and ultimately profit from these "free" sources of information and its infrastructure. Such threats could further penalize lower-income communities' ability to take an active and informed hand in shaping their future—people who are already experiencing a resources gap to gain access.

This picture of access to good, reliable information reflects my experience as well as that of my colleagues, developers, practitioners, and community people in different cities around the country. Its focus here is to aid in making good decisions about what, when, and how to improve the places we live and work in. The state of access to reliable information is what it is, and understanding that is important for formulating working principles for dealing with it. Recognizing the importance of access to information for community people to be able to have a voice in their democracy and the gaps and obstacles that they presently face, there are a number of positive initiatives underway to improve access to information. These promise to benefit communities and districts as well as professionals, developers, and public servants.

Among the websites dedicated to getting neighborhood information out on the Internet are the Center for Neighborhood Technology in Chicago, www.cnt.org; the UCLA Neighborhood Knowledge Project, www.nkca.edu; the Local Government Commission (California), www.lgc.org; or the Orton Family Foundation Data Center, www.dataplace.org; as well as many more local governments.

Beyond access, there are other challenges to developing and using information for the purpose of improving places. The various technical disciplines that engage themselves in the urban design and development process are often not forthcoming about the criteria that they use in making their judgments—often, I have found, for reasons similar to those of government workers. These disciplines include a wide diversity of information bases and rarely does any one have much of a grasp of the others. The information needs to be synthesized—part of what urban design should seek to provide. The gap between theory and practice within disciplines is wide enough. The gap between the disciplines themselves may lead to really poor decisions, often confounding common sense.

On a streetscape–public building interface project in Birmingham, for example, the traffic engineer had one spacing for streetlights and another for parking meters, the landscape architect had a different spacing for street trees (including removing the only mature, healthy oak along the block), and the architect had ideas about where the building entrance should be that related to neither. The result could have been trees and lights occupying the same holes, obscuring the building's entrances in the process. This kind of thing happens all the time and requires some kind of synthesis and resolution, often overcoming the "truths" that each discipline defends—the job of an urban designer and sometimes a commonsense citizen activist.

Between planners, civil engineers, landscape architects, architects, developers, public agencies, lawyers, and contractors, to mention a typical mélange, information that is useful to shaping the vision and action aspects of change management is hard to bring together. Each discipline has its own professional culture, values, and information priorities that don't necessarily line up with the others. Each is inclined to stress levels of detail that may not be important to arrive at a synthesized whole.

The urban designer's job is to develop levels and topics of information that are useful and relevant to the task at hand at the time when it is most needed. Keeping in mind that the information base necessary to approach an urban design and development task is always interacting with actions and a unifying vision, information should be sought out, analyzed, and applied to maintain these interactions in a constructive way. Put another way, the information effort should be developed as needed. Typically, beyond the first step of listening to the people there and hearing their sense of assets, challenges, and priorities, the start-up data should include information that is pretty well fixed in time, like census information; data about the physical environment, both natural and built; history, identifying areas more or less susceptible to change; and the local jurisdiction's regulatory guidance, like comprehensive plans, zoning and subdivision ordinances, property ownership data, transportation plans, and the like.

Some practitioners approaching a challenging project, however, take refuge in mountains of data, including time-sensitive data whose application may not be relevant to the unfolding project or may be outdated by the time the project planning period is completed. To guard against this tendency, it is important to list all of the data that the community and technical disciplines think might be important. Then step back and prioritize, developing the information only to the level needed to feed into the process. Indeed, a good way to identify and assemble relevant data is to characterize the database as permeable and frankly invite comment and criticism on what has been put together so far. In this way, community leaders and practitioners may discover new sources or new combinations that draw them more closely into the culture of a place.

These kinds of data problems may stem from practitioners thinking in a linear fashion; they may stem from an insecurity in getting into the middle of a project with a lot of community people, developers, or practitioners from other disciplines; or they may reflect a lack of understanding that the urban design and development visioning and programming processes are live, happening affairs where no one wants to wait for a linear set of steps to unfold. Finally, as the process moves along, needs for information and kinds of information not initially identified or thought of invariably pop up, as the interaction with vision and possible action scenarios are developed. This calls upon the partners in a planning and design exercise to keep flexible and to understand that the book on injecting new information into an ongoing process is never closed.

## Identify Action Steps

The remaining sphere of activity to consider in the vision/information/action dynamic is action. Action is almost synonymous with change. Stuff is always happening—little, big, of slight or major consequence. Planning and urban design practice used to frustrate itself by trying to stop or slow down actions that were going to happen anyway, hoping to get the "plan" in place first. This sort of insistence on following a linear process in the face of major forces beyond the control of that process is a major contributor to the frequent lament: "Plans? We've got plenty of plans, all sitting up there on the shelf gathering dust." Current practice is clearly improving, but too often the action or implementation parts of the planning process are left to the end, for someone else to worry about, disconnected from the realities of process in the jurisdiction and thus essentially unimplementable—plans on the shelf.

In my practice, whether or not an urban design initiative can be implemented has always been a key criterion for my commitment—I like to work on things that can actually happen. The point here is that action as a concept and a set of steps should always be part and parcel of any place-improvement process. After all, it may be an action or actions that precipitate the need for an organized change-management strategy. Similarly, actions that occur along the way may bend the visioning process or call for additional information in order to bring the interactive process to a useful point. Finally, thinking about what actions should be or can be taken from the beginning is more likely to assure that action will be taken along the way and in the end.

Incorporating the sphere of action often provides insights that can result in both a better and a more realistic improvement scenario. It's more likely to engage the practical people who actually build change initiatives, developers or agencies that have a job to do and know how to get it done. While it may be a strain for these action-oriented partners in the planning and design process to step beyond the narrow context of their "project," if their knowledge and purpose are respected all are likely to find the outcome superior to the initial proposal. This infusion of get-it-done perspective usually enhances and helps to focus the process, improving it qualitatively and realistically.

As the change-management process moves along, incorporating the three interactive spheres as described, there usually emerges early in the process an agreement about some things that could be done right away that would improve on the current situation. These might be fixing a dangerous intersection; replacing or installing a missing sidewalk; taking care of a property maintenance issue, a too-wide roadway, a too-narrow sidewalk; landscaping a left-over piece of public property; and so on. When this occurs, it represents a special opportunity to demonstrate the value of the process underway. If the process includes the community, the government, and private sector interests (as it should), the nexus is in place to define a project, identify the resources, and follow the approval path necessary to get it done.

The values of moving forward on such a consensual project while the planning and design process is underway are many. The focus and the resources to inform the action steps are in place. The ability to move forward builds trust among interests that don't necessarily see eye to eye, with the chance of cementing the kind of partnership understandings that will be necessary to sustain the improvement strategy. A well-chosen action step will provide visual and physical evidence that the process can be productive, building confidence in its continuation. And, in any event, even if nothing else happens, the action leaves the place better off than it was before. My colleague in Birmingham, Victor Blackledge, termed this process "stand-alone phasing," a good and clear way of characterizing the process. In fact, what usually happens is that such an action builds momentum, even a certain impatience to keep the ball rolling.

It is important for practitioners involved in such a process to be careful with the detailed planning, design, budgeting, and scheduling of the agreed-on work. As a framework, it is important to vet the details with all involved and openly receive design guidance. Often a good strategy is to assume the real cost will be about double the estimate, and that the time frame will likely be twice as long as reason would indicate. In this way, the chances are good of coming in with a well-understood and accepted design, built within the budget and time schedule. Such performance makes it almost a lock that the process will be supported and sustained, well beyond its nominal end date (and of course in the real world of the civic environment, there are no end dates).

Professionals are usually involved in place-improvement planning and design activities, all along or at different points along the way. These may be private consultants with various professional backgrounds, or local government planning, urban design, and civil engineering staff or professionals who may be living or working in the community of interest. While they typically bring a solid base of general knowledge, it is important to push them to listen carefully to the particulars of the situation at hand. Community people, too, need to remind themselves that to stay in business, consultants need to deliver what their clients expect—that's what they're paid to do. In fact, in terms of planning what to do, private professional consultants may be the least vested in the ongoing implementation of an improvement scenario—they don't own the project like the developer or

In Atlanta's Old Fourth Ward neighborhood, for example, a particularly energetic and intrepid neighborhood activist, Mtamanika Youngblood, set out to turn around her neighborhood by first rehabbing and then building new infill housing along a downtrodden block in a disinvested neighborhood. The first action step was rehabbing, beginning with her own house, and then another and then another. The action showed neighbors, and eventually sources of city and private sector support, that something could happen; that if nothing else happened things were better off than they were before, but in fact the momentum had begun. Lessons from each step informed the next, in vision, in information base, altogether interacting with design and organizational principles. She got a group together to form the Historic District Development Corporation—the district being the district encompassing Dr. Martin Luther King Jr.'s birth home—and then house by house, lot by lot, she was able to galvanize a transformation of an entire neighborhood that spilled over into others.

public agency, and its outcome usually doesn't directly affect them. No matter how well crafted, the job of getting it done falls to the developer and the community, the most vested, and the approval of the local government, which also carries the ongoing responsibility to monitor and manage the result.

This is not a reflection on the competence or commitment of any set of private consultants, simply recognition that consultants participate in these efforts to make a living, that their commitments are not open-ended, that the process always takes more money than anyone anticipates (threatening the consultants' profit margin), and that consultants are rarely responsible for actually implementing the program. As suggested above, this effort usually falls to vested private development interests and the local government, with community oversight to assure that the work stays on track and that it is carried out as it has been represented and agreed to.

In my practice as a public servant, I have found it more effective and efficient, in time, money, and outcome, to build the core staff capability in-house to do the basic work that needs to be done and to engage consultants as more specialized and in-depth work tasks are required. I came to this practice fairly early in my career, after receiving materials that looked good, that may even have had community support, but that lacked an understanding of how to take the next step, along with a reluctance to make the necessary modifications to make the product usable.

The present drive toward privatization may modify the roles in place-making activities, possibly tilting them toward more responsibility given over to consultants, particularly in smaller jurisdictions. Government's use of the privatization model is showing up frequently in public works kinds of activities, not so much yet in planning, zoning, and urban design areas. Communities, civic organizations, and governments should keep in mind, however, that the drive toward privatization is itself a private initiative, where profitability is more important than service, and where in any event it is public money that pays the freight.

The key principle to keep in mind from the above discussion, however, is that vision, information, and action are interactive and dynamic spheres of activity. Each is continuously affecting the other, in no particular order, and effective change management needs to be sure to incorporate these dynamics.

# Provide for Choice

Intrinsic in any change process is choice: Whether to even embark on a change of direction, in this case a place-improvement process, is a choice. Then the process offers forks in the road all the way along. Should we go this way or that way? What are the likely consequences of making this set of choices instead of that? The interactive set of vision, information, and action sets up the choice-making context for developing a place-improvement strategy. Alternate visions, the emphasis placed on various information sets, and action options all set up a key part of a process; that is, the development of alternatives.

Fortunately, stemming from the democratic reforms in planning processes launched in the 1960s, many planning processes, particularly for larger or publicly funded projects, are now more or less formally obligated to consider alternative ways of approaching a place-improvement initiative. Included in this construct usually is what is called the "no-build" option; that is, no change from the current circumstances or practices. While the need for a formalized process for considering alternatives is somewhat incorporated in the more interactive change processes described above, it is still important to provide people, stakeholders if you will, the detail and the analysis on what the choices are. The reality usually is that all alternatives, including the no-build, have pros and cons. The complexity of interactive elements in any place-improvement effort and the challenges of grasping them as wholes made up of a variety of interacting parts require careful and inclusive consideration of the tradeoffs.

Not surprisingly, given the opportunity and necessary information, people are pretty well able to interact with each other to consider choices about their places and their consequences. One of the pioneers of urban design and development visioning techniques, Anton Nelessen, uses a process he calls the "visual preference survey" (which he trademarked) to tease out people's shared values (at least in terms of what looks good). The core of this process is to give a roomful of people a slide show full of choices: Do you like this image or that image better, and by how much? Variations of these kinds of exercises have proliferated through the practice of both consultant and government professionals, and they are a useful part of any change management strategy. Interestingly, people in almost any given place seem to show a pretty strong consensus on what images they like and don't like, setting a basis for at least the visual choices preferred by the community, which often symbolize more complex values.

While the visual images carry meaning beyond the picture, it is important in formulating choices, alternatives, to consciously frame these choices, both quantitatively and qualitatively. In this way the full meaning of substantive changes can be worked through. Choices about transportation and other infrastructure; environmental sustainability; civic space and institutions; mix of housing, retail, and commercial space and their affordability and densities; and other issues are important in arriving at a place-improvement scenario. All of these, of course, have consequences that extend beyond visual satisfaction to the workability and overall quality of a place, all the business of urban design and community betterment.

As people empower themselves to play more active roles in making their choices for future civic environments, the role of the market is worth a few words. As noted in the information discussion above, the power to manipulate choice through marketing means may be at a zenith, or on its way thereto. The technology of marketing communications; the concentration of artistic, musical, dramatic, and writing talent in marketing; and its application to satiate the relentless profit demands of competition in every sector—all color consumer choice. This condition in many sectors can switch the calculus from selling what people actually want or need to selling what generates the highest bottom line. While perhaps less well-formed in the diffuse area of place improvement than in other consumer fields, it is nonetheless advisable for the community to assert what it has determined as beneficial from its perspective, not necessarily to "buy" the current place "product" without close scrutiny. Fortunately, as people become engaged in their places and their access to useful information proliferates, the range of choices available for consideration is broad—though some are more heavily marketed than others.

# Be Ready

Often, the conditions for positive change are missing. Resources are lacking, development interest doesn't exist, communities or districts have not organized themselves, public policy and funding priorities don't support needed changes, no crisis demanding attention exists—these are all common circumstances where change opportunities or possibilities are not there.

In these circumstances, discouraging as they may be, it is nonetheless important for communities and professionals to anticipate and prepare for change conditions that will inevitably arrive, sooner or later. At the large scale, for example, a federal change with respect to transit or environmental regulation policies and resources could reset the table for regional and local government. Best be ready so that your jurisdiction can be at the front of the line. At the smaller scale, a change in elected officials could focus on community-based economic development and affordable housing as priorities, or the private sector sees opportunity in a long disinvested area. Again, best be ready. Of course, it takes time and resources to plan for such speculative and hypothetical possibilities of change. Yet in the process of developing and evaluating alternative courses of action, one of these should usually contemplate what would happen if such shifts occur and what steps could be considered to take advantage of—or minimize any negative impacts of—such a change. Often, putting oneself through these "what if" exercises spawns ideas for the short term that wouldn't otherwise have been thought of. Even more constructively, sometimes planning for change actually helps to precipitate the process.

Highlighting being ready was impressed upon me by Allan Jacobs at a Mayors Institute for City Design workshop in Berkeley in the mid-1990s. He described an initiative from years earlier when, as San Francisco's planning director, concerned with the billboard industry's growing visual assault on the city, he directed his staff to prepare a stricter billboard ordinance. The billboard industry, being what it is and always able to marshal great resources to protect and advance its cause, was able to beat back this effort. A few months later, though, with visual clutter being a campaign issue in municipal elections that sought reforms, the new mayor asked how long it would take to put together a new, stricter billboard ordinance. Music to the planning director's ears.

Urban designers and planners in the public sector are usually in the best position to exercise the positive aspects of being ready on behalf of the public environment. They have a better overall grasp of development activity in their jurisdictions than anyone else. They are able to see the connectedness between private development and public policy and infrastructure projects. They can create partnerships between their sister agencies, private developers, and communities that may positively leverage both private resources and community vision to achieve improvements—when not having the information, not being ready, would blow the opportunity.

# Summary

Change and community response to change are windows into the state of a place. Through these windows one can gauge the consonance between community and the larger civic and private forces that impact their place. Consonance, in turn, may predict trust, and levels of trust may predict attitudes toward change forces. The more a community is comfortable with the civic and private "establishment" (which can only occur when there is some shared sense of purpose), the more likely they will be to trust both external and internal change initiatives that reinforce their sense of consonance with the places that mark their community identity. People will be open-minded toward change if they view the change as advancing quality, within the terms of the particular place where the change is occurring.

Conversely, people will resist change if they see it as a negative and a threat to the quality of place, again within the terms of the place.

Trust is the basis on which positive change management can go forward. It is possible to forge this trust, using the above principles and examples, yet it takes hard and committed work on the part of the community, the private sector, and the government, in which urban designers can play a helpful role, to make it happen. Even so, trust is fragile and subject to continuous renewal if the best can be made out of the change forces out there. Finally, as a reminder, change and its manifestations and principles are in continuous trinary interaction with both the design principles of the last chapter and the organizational principles of the next.

# 8

# ORGANIZATION

## Coordination and Partnership

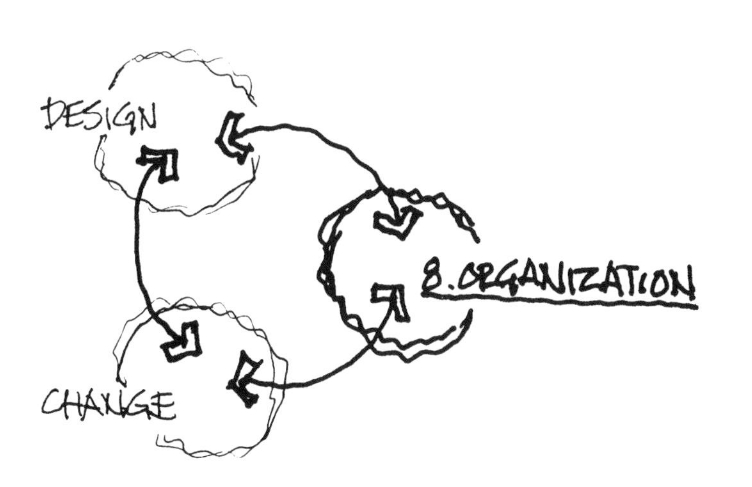


*Figure 8.1*
*Organization as the third of the interacting spheres of principles that together guide urban design theory and practice.*

# Introduction

*"Never doubt that a small group of thoughtful, committed citizens can change the world."*
*—Margaret Mead*

This chapter deals with the organizational entities that typically involve themselves in urban design and development. It proposes principles that urban designers and community leaders may consider to improve the quality and workability of civic environments working through such organizations. These entities are in continuous interaction with each other, and they are interactive with the design processes and with the forces of change that, all together, set the framework of principles for guiding how to improve places. Accordingly, the principles arranged here in the sphere of organizations, like those in the spheres of design and change, may reinforce or overlap with principles in the other spheres.

As a physical place, the civic environment is the manifestation of a complicated interplay between social, community, cultural, economic, professional, institutional, political, and government organizations. People arrange themselves into these organizational forms for the purpose of improving their lot as opportunities and circumstances arise, either to benefit or to cope. They try to figure out what to do and how to get it done. There is an unlimited variety of these arrangements and responses, depending on the structure of society and the tasks perceived as necessary to advance that society. These general impulses and responses encompass and reflect all human social activity, and the focus here is on the organizational forms that together produce the civic environment where people share their lives.

What kinds of organizations are involved in shaping the civic environment? What roles do they play and how do they view their roles in making civic places? How do they structure themselves, and why? What kinds of principles for working with various organizations might best advance the cause of making places better? These are a few of the questions discussed below, with my sense of the forms and principles that seem to work.

Over the last 40 years, I have interacted with all of the forms of organization outlined below, from the neighborhood to the regional scale. The observations and the principles for engaging organizations in the quest to improve the civic environment reflect and incorporate the views of the full range of people involved, from the streets to the suites, from the workaday to the wonk.

The overall themes of inclusion, information, vision, building on strengths, and action underpin the principles that are more focused here for putting together and guiding the organizational structures necessary to achieve civic space improvements. All of the forms of organization that together conceive and implement urban design and development activities should share this underpinning. I have framed these forms here in the spheres of community, private sector, and government.

This organizational framework is based on the premise that successful places depend on the government's policies and processes to support building better places, the private sector's positive participation to build the place, and the community's acceptance and embrace of the place. That outcome is more likely when the people there are involved from the beginning, the better organized the better, in whatever state or transformation the place may find itself. Similarly, the private sector, mainly represented by development, real estate, attorneys, finance, and design consultants, benefits from integrating its various phases of work. A seamless, interdisciplinary, and interactive design and delivery process usually produces a more time- and cost-effective project. And government invari-

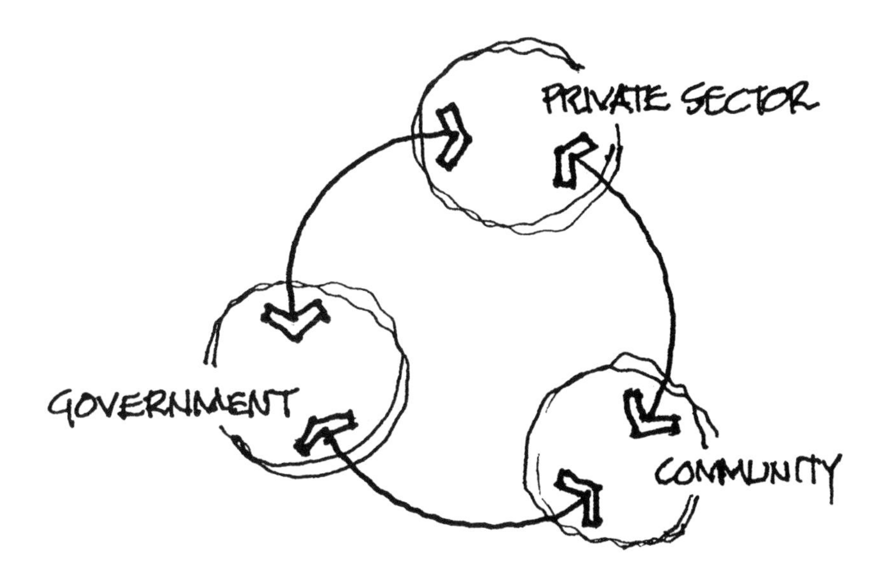


*Figure 8.2*
*However unconsciously, however cooperatively, every place involves and reflects the interactions between the private sector, the government, and the community.*

ably distinguishes itself when it plays an inclusive, open, and transparent role in guiding or directing how processes and projects get formulated, approved, and implemented. Government effort better meets its underlying service purpose when it works cooperatively across disciplinary and agency lines and, when called for, across jurisdictional lines. All of these windows into successful organizational structure depend on developing an inclusive, interactive, and collaborative attitude.

Similarly, these interacting organizational spheres function better when they individually and collectively gather and share information relevant to the purpose at hand, bend it toward teasing out a shared vision about where to go, base their strategies on building on strengths (not correcting weaknesses), and keep action steps in the foreground.

Before looking at the finer-grained principles that provide insight into how the various organizational forms operate, it is worth considering leadership models that are in place across the range of organizational form, mission, and performance.

# Leadership

*"Who's on first?"*

For each organizational form there are leadership and accountability models that range from autocracy to hierarchies of varying steepness to horizontal. Having a handle on what to expect from the leadership found in these organizational forms, what might work and what might not, how to measure and assure accountability are all important for urban designers and citizen activists wishing to influence the organizational side of place improvement. The evaluation of success for various leadership models uses quite different criteria, depending on which organizational form is being evaluated.

Thus community leadership, usually in a volunteer setting, should emphasize listening, building trust, building the organization, seeking consensus, and developing partnerships and alliances, all geared toward effectiveness in achieving community goals. Community leadership tends to be fluid and evolves across a usually wide, diffuse, and attenuated agenda and is measured in accomplishment of positive change, however vaguely or precisely the goal is defined.

Private sector leadership in place-building activities, as it must under the economic system, emphasizes profit on a focused project-by-project basis. It tends to be hierarchical, task-specific, and time-defined. It is measured in effectiveness in overcoming obstacles with a minimum of time and cost and ultimately producing a lease-up or sale that is profitable for the developers and their investors.

Government leadership is charged with mediating and facilitating fair outcomes, in which both communities and the private sector benefit equitably, and the public policy goal of an improved civic environment (and the pride that builds) is achieved. Also likely to be hierarchical, government leaders must focus at least as much on programs as projects. They work in a continuum of time punctuated by projects and events that are often unpredictable, all further qualified by the sine curves of electoral seasons. Ultimately, the measure of government leadership is public service rendered and public confidence built.

These are times when people's confidence in leaders in both the private sector and the government generally seems pretty low. In these circumstances, locally based leadership can, in some instances does, and probably should, challenge the dominant models, most of which, whether private sector or government, are ultimately driven by the influence of money, not by community improvement or service. Community leaders, as part of and closest to their immediate constituency, might be in a position to assert more responsive and effective leadership than can or will what seem to be less and less trusted private sector and central government leaders. Greater democratization through more inclusive, decentralized, and responsive models might alleviate the growing restiveness over the failures of leadership in the same old institutions at all levels that don't always leave places better than they found them.

Intriguing new thoughts in leadership models, related to rolling leadership discussed later on, identify the group—pejoratively, the "mob"—as having a certain ability to respond to and initiate actions without defined leadership. This tendency among social groups to be able to move one way or another based on a semi-conscious sense of common purpose has been increasingly exploited in the marketing of products. There is no reason, except anxiety over loss of control, that organizations should not consider tapping the energy of the whole more effectively in structuring their positions to gain improved influence. The potential for such a "leaderless" model—really shared, rolling, or less hierarchical leadership—seems to be growing at a rapid rate with the explosion of digital communications. Think "rave." Or another mass model with a clearer leader: the Barack Obama campaign.

The discussion of principles for each of the major organizational forms below includes more detail on leadership issues and how urban designers and community activists might engage them.

# Principles for Guiding Community Organizations

*"Stop? Or go?"*

As we are using the term "community" throughout this work, community organizations here encompass a broad and disparate group. Place-based community organizations include neighborhood associations, community development corporations, and business district associations as those most prominently involved in the activities necessary to improve their civic places. Issues-based community organizations, like advocacy groups for housing, civil rights, community development, labor, the environment, transportation, historic preservation, and consumer rights, are often involved as well, depending on the make-up and priorities of the place-improvement effort. Place-based organizations are the main focus of this discussion, although the principles may have direct applicability to more issue-specific groups as well.

Consistent with the premise that the people there determine whether a place is working or not, community organizations are often the decisive factor in the success of the civic environment. One project or another might meet its initiator's goals, yet still leave the larger civic environment in which it sits an unpleasant or unworkable place to be. Its chances of contributing to a larger whole go way up when the community organization takes an active role in the development of the program and design of the project. This involvement can save the initiator time and money as well. Communities are able to assert what they want for a better future and to establish how they want to be treated in that effort. Whether for a clean-up project or a landscape improvement project, at one end of the scale, or for shaping a larger-scale development project into a broader community or even regional vision at the other, communities can succeed in advancing their visions.

In my experience, those communities that actively elicit and encourage open and inclusive participation are best able to develop a shared vision and the steps and priorities to move along that path. Such communities seem to be more likely to coalesce behind similarly inclined leaders to mount and sustain programs of self-improvement. On the other hand, communities that form around the interests of a few or that support leadership that is narrowly focused seem less likely to achieve goals and to maintain support over the long haul, critical for sustaining improvements over changing circumstances.

Similarly, neighborhoods or business districts that find themselves in a terrain of multiple, de facto competing organizations, each purporting to represent the "real" interests of the community, usually are not effective, as neither the government nor potential private sector partners can figure out whom to work with or who really does represent the larger community interest.

Interestingly, the phenomenon of multiple competing groups and organizations is not one in my experience that correlates with income or race. In Atlanta, for example, I have experienced fragmentation that has diminished effectiveness in the poorest, blackest as well as the richest, whitest neighborhoods. In neither circumstance have such neighborhoods been as effective as their neighbors in gaining public support, though of course the private sector always invests more where there is more to be gained.

For dealing with the kinds of circumstances facing community-based organizations outlined above and focused on applications of the overall principles noted above, I suggest the following principles. Each has implications for selecting, supporting, and sustaining the kinds of leadership models and styles briefly discussed above.

**Include all:** Make sure to represent the range of viewpoints in the community organization, typically owners and renters, residents and businesses, customers and employees, and support leadership that encourages and respects the cross section of views.

**Shape a vision:** Move from reacting—stopping bad things from happening—to shaping and agreeing on shorter- and longer-range priorities for neighborhood or district improvement; identify the steps necessary to move in that direction and the resources for carrying out place-building initiatives.

**Get formal recognition:** Neighborhoods and districts should encourage local governments to formally recognize their organizations' standing to provide a voice and to render advisory opinions for both public and private initiatives that impact the quality and functionality of neighborhoods. This standing should apply at least to major infrastructure projects, zoning, public works, and related land use code activities. Such organizations, however, should not have formal approval authority, which is properly a jurisdiction-wide function of government.

**Form a legal entity:** Neighborhoods and districts should form themselves as, or associate themselves with, legally recognized entities so that they can enter into mutual benefit agreements and covenants with private sector entities and local government.

**Form alliances and partnerships:** Neighborhoods and districts should try to bring together different tendencies and organizations functioning in the same area to identify and unite behind what they can agree on—respecting differences outside of agreed-on tenets—and similarly look for mutual benefit alliances with issue-based community organizations, like housing, environmental, or transportation-focused organizations, or with private sector or government organizations.

**Track performance:** Measure progress and leadership based on effectiveness in advancing the agreed-on agenda.

Community organizations form around community interests, either to resist a proposed change that is perceived to be harmful or to promote opportunities that are beneficial. Community motivation may reflect the sentiment that the government is not protecting or promoting the community's interest or that some private sector entity is proposing a project that either poses a threat against or holds broader opportunity for community advancement. The community organizations directly involved with improving their civic environment may be wholly voluntary (usually the case with neighborhood associations and small merchant associations) or have a staff component usually responsive to a volunteer board (usually the case with community development corporations and larger business associations). In either case, such organizations depend largely for their success on broadening their base of voluntary support, building constituencies whose resources and initiative can reach throughout the community and into private sector and government resources to build functioning partnerships.

Since so much of community work is voluntary, the distribution of income across communities is a good predictor of community effectiveness. Richer communities have both more time and resources (both money and people) than poorer ones, where the time and resources commanded by survival priorities leaves little for community organizing. In any event, understanding the voluntary nature of community involvement should be taken into account by both government and private sector development representatives, both of which get paid for the time and effort they put into getting their respective jobs done. Community work isn't easy, doesn't pay, and can't be counted on to be always rewarding, but it is the pivotal part of the support structure necessary to assure the improvement and quality of the civic environment. The discussion below focuses more specifically on three kinds of organizations whose activities directly affect the civic environment.

## Neighborhood-Based Organizations

Neighborhood-based organizations are key building blocks on which cities' social, cultural, and political structures are formed. This is where people live, where most of their assets are tied up, where they vote, where they raise families, go to school, hang out, face problems of public maintenance and security, where there are daily reminders of whether things are getting better or worse. The strength of neighborhoods is a measure of the health and quality of their cities overall. It is in recognition of these realities that towns and cities should accord to neighborhoods and their organizations formal standing for consideration of the affairs of the town or city including the chance for influence on projects within their area. Thus zoning and other initiatives that may impact the land use quality or transportation and other infrastructure functionality should be formally considered by neighborhoods to render an advisory opinion to the approval bodies. Such recognition encourages neighborhood involvement, responsibility, and civic pride; without it, neighborhoods find it difficult to convince themselves that their voice will be heard.

The formation of neighborhood organizations more often than not is in reaction to threats, proposals from outside that portend change whose impacts are perceived as deleterious to the civic environment that defines neighborhoods' sense of place. The ability to organize to resist a focused, here-and-now "enemy" is easier than organizing around a more generally defined, longer-range vision. But in order to achieve goals the community can agree would advance its quality and workability, a longer-range, more broadly defined agenda is essential. The principle to apply in this situation is to bend the energy mounted to stop something toward figuring out what to support—converting STOP to GO. Many neighborhoods have successfully resisted one assault or another only to see all of their energy dissipate and recede, awaiting the next "crisis."

More and more, though, neighborhoods are learning to use today's crisis to build tomorrow's sustaining organizations to figure out what they want to be and where they want to go. As these moves accelerate, they lay the base for engaging the next change threat as an opportunity for positive partnership, or at least to be better able, better informed, and better connected to affect its outcome. It is at this stage that the principles enunciated above come into play. Their application, in no particular order, should guide neighborhoods to more effective engagement with their de facto partners, the government and the developers.

This kind of transformation requires a transition in leadership—those best able to stir up resistance may not be the best to sustain a more measured self-improvement strategy. Sometimes, the initial leaders can make the change themselves from opposer to proposer; other times there may need to be a transition in leadership. Often it is good to anticipate the need for a kind of rolling leadership, since community needs are likely to include passionate advocacy, reasoned management, and implementation single-mindedness at one point or another. As suggested above, sensing the potential for a group to think and act in concert could be a dimension worth exploring for its potential to gain influence.

Steps for applying the principles for making these kinds of changes include putting in place an ongoing structure for planning, designing, and implementing a future that all can subscribe to. This structure does not

Policy and practice debates about neighborhoods' roles in planning, design, and development processes often focus on "NIMBY," the acronym for "not in my backyard." The term evolved to describe private and public sector planners' and developers' frustrations with neighborhoods and citizen activists who stood up to resist initiatives perceived not to be in the neighborhood or community interest. While some look for ways to take the negative, even pejorative, implications of NIMBYism and turn it to positive ends, many look for ways to dodge, bypass, or "get over on" the NIMBY phenomenon. The reality is that the NIMBY position represents a high level of mistrust by neighborhoods, often justified by a history of experience wherein private or public sector initiatives have ignored or even attacked neighborhood values, organizations, or interests. The principles here suggest respecting and engaging neighborhood interests from the beginning as a way of creating a process that recognizes the clear interests of neighborhoods in parallel with the normal private sector and government initiators. This means that planners and urban designers need to bend their attitudes away from the modernist predilection for technologically couched notions of "right answers" and expertise toward more interactive, shared, and partnering approaches.

Anyone who has attended a public hearing on a contentious matter, or participated in demonstrations, or in religious expressions of various types for that matter, has experienced the force of the collective. It seems possible to glean from this force ways to build leadership models that could enhance the group's influence over its future.

require numbers so much as commitment to work for a better future. Consistent with the underlying inclusion principle, representation is essential from most viewpoints within the community, at least including owners, renters, and local business. In this way the vision will be richer, the support broader, and consensus around priorities easier to achieve. What keeps people's attention is the hope that their voluntary effort will mean something, will make a difference. And it can. But it won't be easy.

Another step is the active pursuit of opportunities—looking for and building on strengths; sharing experience; with others similarly situated, to gain access to expertise and forming planning and development partnerships with government, community, and private sector developers to realize projects at all scales. Finally, maintaining contact with the base, fully sharing relevant information with the neighborhood as a whole and including its range of perspectives, is the surest way to steer the process in fruitful directions and build the trust necessary for any leader to be effective. These forms and shifts in neighborhood organization and leadership are all around us, some more effective, some less, but generally growing and greatly aided by the rapid proliferation of useful information available to inform, research, respond to, and influence just about any proposal that might come forward.

The opportunities that neighborhood activism affords are many, beginning with evolving downward and pushing forward the democratic experiment. Neighborhood organizations become a testing and training ground for decentralized civic leadership, grassroots initiative, and accountability. This means, of course, that mistakes will happen, just as in the school boards and city councils on which neighborhood organizations frequently pattern themselves (sometimes a mistake). Neighborhood organizations, particularly as they seek any kind of formalized recognition by their local governments, may expect resistance from their elected officials, who will correctly see the advance of neighborhood organizations as democracy imposing inconvenient standards of accountability. These processes prepare new leaders who may bring a challenge for the incumbent's seat.

Gaining ground for neighborhood recognition faces internal challenges as well. The legacies of mistrust born of historic mistreatment, particularly for lower-income and minority neighborhoods, tend to restrain the reach for partnership so essential to corral the resources necessary for real community improvement. Agenda-dominating ego pursuits of some in neighborhood politics may discourage others from participation. Occasionally, people involve themselves in community organizational settings for the singular purpose of personal gain, either as bona fide residents or as plants for some outside development interest. In all these circumstances it is important to assert the primacy of the community-improvement goals and measure the participation of all against those criteria. In this way, the influence of the jaded and self-serving is minimized while their associated energy may be turned to constructive purposes.

There are fundamental public policy implications in the dynamics of the advance of neighborhood organizations and their presence in the public forum. To begin with, irrespective of the income or the power of their residents, equitable public policy should accord all neighborhoods equal formal standing and influence. For lower-income neighborhoods to actually be able to assert their equal right to participate, public and nonprofit priorities should be given to level the playing field for those neighborhoods with less time and resources available to organize themselves, based on some income criterion.

On the other end of the scale, much has been made of neighborhoods that adopt frankly and blatantly exclusionary policies, often aimed at barring lower-income or minority populations or renters. Such neighborhoods may even assert their positions from a base of broad and consensual support, consistent with the underlying principles espoused here, yet in the context of democratic values of the larger society, they may be out of line—in violation of the larger consensus.

There are laws and codes of ethics that can be enforced to attack both of these kinds of problems, such as the Fair Housing Act. Yet from a strategic point of view there may be other policy initiatives that can prove effective as well from the local to the national level. Public policy priorities can be established that channel attention, both regulatory and financial, toward supporting and rewarding neighborhoods whose positions and practices are consonant with policies of fairness and equity, while simply not responding to those that do not. Typically, the resources available to local government to support neighborhoods under any circumstances are well short of what's needed, yet the targeting of resources, including guiding private sector involvement, can be an effective way of getting the fairness message across. If exclusionary policies and practices extend to a whole jurisdiction, then the issue may need to be addressed at the state or even federal level. Strategies that combine fair housing laws with local-level policies and practices are likely to be most effective in asserting democratic rights.

However neighborhoods deal with the nitty-gritty issues they face, internally and in interaction with their jurisdiction and private sector forces, their organizations are invariably involved with and committed to the improvement of both the quality and functionality of the neighborhood. Its civic environment—the streets, sidewalks, transit access, parks, landscape, topography, public facilities, gathering places, entrances and exits, seams with adjacent neighborhoods and districts—is the physical place that identifies and is identified by the people who live there and care enough about it to pitch in for its improvement. People's motivation to consider and commit to civic betterment depends on believing that action is possible, that it can happen.

## Community Development Corporations

Community development corporations (CDCs) are another form of neighborhood-based organization, or community-based organizations as they are sometimes called, usually put in place as an action arm for neighborhood goals, most often in housing rehab and development and various other services in lower-income and minority neighborhoods.

They have their antecedents in Model Cities organizations, reshaped and supported to varying extents in successive Community Development Block Grant authorizations as well as other public and foundation support sources. Their roots in the "Great Society" aftermath of civil rights and its broader unrest represented recognition of the need for additional resources and the commitment to build planning and development capability in disinvested neighborhoods. In most places the recognition flowed from federal mandates, programs, and funding, picked up and reflected unevenly at state and local levels.

A board and paid staff—usually underpaid and overworked—typically oversee and operate such organizations. They are usually nonprofits, a prerequisite for large portions of their funding base, which usually includes a

Partly in response to the Community Reinvestment Act (CRA), which was put in place in 1977 to try to oblige at least a token effort on the part of commercial banks to invest in areas they'd rather not, banks have established what they also call community development corporations that are mainly set up to loan money to neighborhoods and other ventures in low-income neighborhoods as a way of meeting their CRA obligations in which neighborhood CDCs are sometimes the borrower or otherwise partners.

blend of federal or other public sources and private foundation and other private philanthropy sources. They are accountable to these sources as well as more generally to the broader neighborhood in which they operate.

They face special challenges. The job of the director is usually a greater challenge than a comparable job in the private sector. Administrators need to cobble together both technical and financial resources from myriad sources, public and private, each with their own reporting and accountability standards. They work in challenging physical environments, reflecting deterioration of infrastructure and public and private disinvestment. Their client base is always on the edge of qualifying or not qualifying for mortgage money, being able to meet the rent levels, or developing employable skills. Usually brought into being on a wave of hope for self-help capacity, they face unrealistic community expectations, with little reward for their successes and sharp criticism for any missteps. It usually takes time and patience for the seeds planted to sprout and lots of skill, commitment, and nurturing for the CDC to leaf out and flower. Finally, even if really effective, directors earn less money for more headaches than their counterparts in the private sector. What this takes then is a special dedication and commitment to the premise that people deserve service and a shot at improving themselves whether or not the process will profit someone else. Needless to say, the pool of qualified applicants for this kind of job is not deep.

Where they exist and sustain themselves, though, they can be important allies in the process of achieving civic improvements. They combine both community knowledge and technical know-how that is invaluable for shaping and prioritizing an improvement plan. And they begin without the trust barrier that outside development resources might face. Like any development corporation, these organizations have had successes and failures, often reflecting the kinds of dynamics described above for neighborhood organizations in general.

At their best and most effective, they have blossomed into full-blown affordable housing development and economic development corporations, with wider than single neighborhood effect, producing housing and building employable skill sets for people whom the mainstream development community ignores. At their worst, they usually do at least more good than harm, and at least seek to address issues and problems that don't attract the normal development and investment markets' interest. They usually are active in areas and circumstances where the need is high, yet little or no profit is to be made from meeting it.

In my experience, however unconsciously, the more successful CDCs adhere to the same principles identified for other neighborhood-based organizations, and less successful ones have been able to improve through application of the principles.

## Business District Organizations

I treat business district organizations as community-based organizations because, even though they are usually better funded and their membership is made up of enterprises whose bottom line is profit, they share many of the circumstances and issues that face neighborhoods. For the most part they represent a diverse mix of constituents with varying interests, they are usually nonprofit organizations, and their coming together reflects a common desire to improve the quality and functionality of the civic environment that they share. In small jurisdictions they may overlap or even be cast as chambers of commerce. As places dominated by commerce, they provide settings for much more human interaction than most neighborhoods and thus are properly a major focus for any urban design and development attention. At the same time, as the markets for living nearer to jobs and shopping continue to grow, these organizations increasingly have the opportunity to include their residential constituencies.

As a matter of practice, I encourage their formation as the surest way of developing a shared vision and a set of priorities that can focus the attention of the local jurisdiction and the investment of private capital to advance an improvement agenda. Again, the principles above provide a useful guide and checklist for forming and sustaining effective organizations. The focus here applies to existing business districts, whether strips or centers, whether relatively new or old, where there is multiple ownership, lot-by-lot parking (or not), and where change forces are evident, either for better or worse.

The usual starting point for business organizations is either the threat of changes that may diminish their viability as a district or, conversely, the opportunity for enhancing their position. The impetus can range from a Wal-Mart sucking up the main street's business at one end of the scale or on the other a renewed market interest in that main street, capitalizing on historic fabric to create a vibrant mixed-use urban environment. The formative leadership is usually made up of people who understand that there is a relationship between the success of their individual business and the larger civic environment in which they work. This perspective often carries with it the recognition of the need for inclusion, the underlying principle for organizational development, certainly from among those doing business in the district and sometimes to partner with surrounding neighborhoods as well. Without this kind of perspective, districts that contain businesses are just that—each business is looking out for itself, focused on weekly or monthly revenues and expenses, marketing itself in a vacuum and either doing okay or not.

It has been my experience that three or four businesses getting together can begin a process where their commitment to the effort of the improvement of their shared place can persuade others to join in. There are always a few at the other end of the scale who don't want to be bothered, and the fortunes of a fledgling or sustaining organization may depend on the many in between, not leaders but interested. For their part, these in-betweeners may swing one way or the other on the question of forming and supporting an association, depending on how persuasively the case is made for seeking common purpose. A typical sequence of events includes the small group, a steering committee if you will, planning for how to engage their fellows in exploring the effort.

In some jurisdictions, business support organizations, like a chamber of commerce or a larger-scaled business improvement organization, may already exist to support a new initiative. Since the businesses that make up the prospective initiative are usually bottom-line-oriented, they are more focused on time, structure, and practicality than a neighborhood organization might be. The structure chosen is usually more formal and often more hierarchical than for neighborhood organizations, reflecting business models more than democratic ones. As long as the principle of inclusion guides the affairs of the organization, including nearby residential

In the North Birmingham business district, where the surrounding population had shifted from 90 percent white to 90 percent black during the 1970s, many of the merchants, most of whom were white, tried to hang on to their historic customer base. Their denial or reluctance to embrace the changes that had occurred in the surrounding neighborhoods set up a widespread decline and closing of many businesses, sapping away a center for the neighborhoods. A few merchants, led by Jack Sellers, who had a furniture store, recognized the change and sought to adjust to it by coming together to develop a plan and strategy. Retooling their operations to serve the neighborhoods as they had evolved was at the base of their strategic planning process. Supportive merchants and property owners then formed the nucleus that partnered with the city and neighborhoods to complete the plans and garner funding necessary to implement the plan from federal, local, and private sources. Early on, the merchants were somewhat resistant to including the neighborhoods' leadership in the process, but under the city's urging—tied too to the extent of its support—inclusive organizations and forums greatly strengthened the plan and funding strategies, both substantively and politically. At the same time the city encouraged and achieved merchant participation in the neighborhood associations, thus setting up a dialogue that spanned both business-neighborhood and white-black issues.

participation, and as long as access to information and the opportunity to voice diverse opinions are provided, these organizations can function perfectly well and succeed in creating places that positively reflect the richness of their diversity.

While business culture often resists it, the principle of inclusion invariably serves the business organization well. To begin with, the question of who should be members must be addressed. Often, the business interests who identify themselves as the "movers and shakers" see themselves as the convening group and are inclined to leave out the smaller businesses, tenants, residents, or other interests. As the trend toward mixed-use development and diverse business offerings gains ground, however, the wisdom of including all affected to create an actionable vision becomes even more compelling. Many organizations structure their membership dues to reflect the varying stakes of its participants. Similarly, the first impulse among many may be that the work to be done is their business, and that including nearby neighborhoods, government, or nonprofit organizations will slow things down, or complicate them, or bring in issues they may see as irrelevant. Again, though, particularly with the growing encouragement of a strong residential component in many districts' planning agendas, along with the resources that may be available through government sources and nonprofits, the potential for gain tends to overshadow the parochial.

A large business-based organization in central Atlanta, the Midtown Alliance, in the wake of the 1996 Olympics, launched a "blueprint" planning effort that sought to galvanize the languishing north side of the city's central core. Members of its leadership considered what structure would best propel such an effort and adopted a more inclusionary approach than was typical for Atlanta's business organizations. The city planning and development department, which oversees the comprehensive development planning and zoning processes, had indicated that the extent of its interest and partnership in the process would be tied to the organization's commitment to undertake an inclusive process. The Alliance selected a consultant team led by Anton Nelessen, whose processes similarly encourage broad participation throughout visioning, planning, and program development. Midtown has enjoyed a remarkable turnaround and is anchoring its resurgence as the center for amenity-rich, high-density mixed-use development in the region. I am asked from time to time why it is that Atlanta's other large place-based business organizations have not seemed to be as successful, and the answer is clear: The others have not as thoroughly embraced the inclusionary model in their purposes, board make-up, or agendas, or some combination of the three.

Most states by now have legislation in place that enables districts to form self-taxing districts, often called community or business improvement districts (CIDs or BIDs), that in partnership with local government may serve such purposes as supplementing maintenance and security, undertaking capital projects, and collectively promoting themselves. In addition, districts can help to focus tax increment financing projects, usually in blighted areas at their fringes, where typically the improvement of the civic environment can be financed through bonds anticipating future increases in tax value as the source for paying off the bonds.

In an urbanizing world that has been dominated by cars, endless suburbs, and the commercial strips and malls that support them, a demand for another choice is now rising rapidly. This demand is fueled by changing demographics, where the nuclear families that fueled suburbanization have shrunk, young people who grew up in suburbs may not want to stay there, empty nesters don't want or need the bigger house and yard and want to be closer to amenities, and seniors can't or don't want to be car-dependent to have access to their needs and pleasures. Public policies that have supported strengthening closer-in centers or modifying suburban commercial strips and malls for more diverse and more accessible uses are finally gaining ground, with an apparent depth of markets that seem to be a long way from being satisfied. Districts that get their acts together, then, may find a favorable public policy climate and increasingly interested investors to support their moves toward self-improvement—good for business, good for service to diverse constituencies, good for tax revenue.

Once engaged, with a base membership in place, the organization moves through stages of visioning and planning, identifying priorities for implementing planned capital or operational projects, private and public; striking the necessary partnerships within the organization, with the local jurisdiction, and with neighborhoods; identifying and marshalling the resources to take the next step; getting projects done; maintaining high levels of upkeep and security; and marketing themselves as a place with a distinctive, particular, and action-oriented identity.

The measure of success of such initiatives is whether people come. Urban design quality and skill of the kinds promulgated here become paramount in assuring this positive outcome. A place that is attractive and that works well to serve the myriad needs of myriad customers, that provides for living opportunities in mixed-use buildings or close by, that accommodates the car while prioritizing the pedestrian environment has the essential ingredients for sustaining success. For the vision to be formed, though, the principle of inclusivity, a fair representation of the real and prospective participants in the place to become, has to provide the base on which to shape, represent, and prioritize the vision. From this point, gaining recognition, creating strategic partnerships, and tracking performance mark steps likely to result in an ongoing civic improvement program.

# Principles for Guiding Private Sector Organizations

*"It's my money."*
*"It's my property."*

Private sector organizations involved in place-improvement activities usually include those companies and firms whose business it is to deal in real estate, initiate and carry out building projects, finance development, and provide the range of professional services necessary to plan, design, assist in legal and approval matters, construct, and market development projects. With the underlying principles as a base, the emphasis here is on principles tailored to help urban designers and community leaders to interact with project-driven organizations like developers, although business district associations may find value in the discussion as well. These principles may seem a little quixotic in the experience of many in the place-building game, yet I have had many experiences where their application in various combinations has achieved positive results for all concerned.

**Private sector organizations build most of what gets built:** Remember that private developers, private contractors, private consultants, and private finance are the agents that actually build stuff, even in the case of government-initiated infrastructure and building projects; therefore if communities want to see any building occur, they must be sensitive and somewhat knowledgeable about the initiative, investment, risk, and return factors that make development happen.

**The ultimate measure is the bottom line:** Improving the civic environment might be a nice to-do, but the project is what the developer really cares about; if improving the civic environment shortens the approval process or if public support induces projects that connect better to the larger whole, the developer may become a willing and resourceful partner.

**The project's the thing:** The private sector approaches city building on a project-by-project basis. Any sense of the values or possibilities of the larger context is incidental at best and immaterial at worst. Only if these values or possibilities can demonstrate promise in increasing the bottom line do they have much of a chance of happening.

**Be sensitive to time and timing:** "Time is money" goes the old saw, and urban designers by stressing holistic interdisciplinary processes and communities with the ability to shorten or lengthen approval times can influence the making of better civic environments.

**Partner on infrastructure:** Know what infrastructure improvements will improve the civic environment and look for opportunities to incorporate these into responding to development proposals.
**Assure accountability:** Make sure that what is promised actually happens; in the approval process establish some kind of reporting and updating process, keeping in mind that many projects encounter obstacles that may legitimately require changes in scope, siting, or budget. Formal agreements between legally constituted entities are the best way to track progress.

## Private, For-Profit Entities

The following discussion places the principles' application into the private sector context. To begin with, the constellation of private sector interests grouped around a private development project tends to be more inclusive, multidisciplinary, and strategic in organizational structure than one finds in communities or even government. The singular focus of getting a complex job done requires putting together structures that integrate all those skills, knowledge bases, and practices that can plan, finance, design, build, sell, and operate a project. Urban designers have become increasingly involved in these processes, understanding both the multidisciplinary, holistic, and crosscutting problem-solving skills required to get them accomplished, and sensing and taking advantage of the opportunities their special integrative skills offer. Community organizations, after years of skepticism and mistrust born of the private sector's penchant for stealth, misrepresentation, and often less-than-satisfactory outcomes from the community perspective, are beginning to realize and accept that developers will develop, that development is a necessary activity for community self-improvement, and that their engagement in the process from as soon as they find out about it can bend the outcome to better community-building purposes.

For their part, while inclusivity of skills and resources is an essential grounding for any development project, developers are only now beginning to show a willingness to explore the values of partnership with groups they have historically tried to avoid or ignore, like communities and often local governments. This is an encouraging trend—urban designers' practices are growing, public facilitation or community engagement consultants are springing up and growing, mostly in acknowledgment of the growing role of community involvement in approval processes. Usually the motivation on the developers' part has not changed a whole lot—"get me my approvals to do what I have set upon to do"; "it takes what it takes"—and their private consultancy choices reflect that drive to get the project done.

For their part, consultants are usually every bit as much driven by the bottom line as their private sector clients (a drive that carries over to their public sector clients as well). The competition for projects is intense. Responding to requests for proposals to compete for work may cost in the thousands of dollars. Big overhead money is at risk, absolutely requiring winning a contract from time to time to cover. Getting a consultant to adopt inclusive attitudes and practices into the scope of a planning and urban design agreement, then, may pose problems. Inclusive processes and information-sharing practices usually translate into lots of time, time that is difficult to estimate. They need to plan carefully, cover their upside costs, and still be competitive.

In recognition of the widening range of skills necessary to pull off projects, consultant firms are diversifying—the more the skills can be kept in-house, the more revenues can be kept there too. More to the point of urban design and community improvement, this diversification increasingly includes urban design capability, people who can focus on how the disciplines must come together to effectively and efficiently create a successful place-improvement strategy. The market for urban designers in planning, architecture, landscape architecture, and civil engineering firms, as well as in development companies, is at the moment, way short of being filled. Interestingly, even though the place-designing consultancies are going through major merger and acquisition activity, some even going into exchange-traded public ownership models, there remains a discipline-bound resistance to diversification. An engineer-based architecture and engineering firm, or a planning, landscape architecture, or architecture-based firm will likely remain close to their base, just bigger. Even law firms and lenders that support development and developers are more inclined to hire applicants in their profession who have planning or urban design backgrounds. So even with recognition of the need and the potential effectiveness of integrating all the requisite place design skills under one roof, inclusivity is still hard to achieve.

The Georgia Conservancy supports neighborhood-guided planning and urban design efforts through a steering committee whose membership includes architects, landscape architects, city planners, urban designers, civil engineers, developers, home builders, and green building advocates. In recent years, with the Conservancy's support, I have been able to structure urban design studios that usually include graduate students from the above disciplines to listen to the client neighborhood and each other, generally with good outcomes and certainly preparing them for a future of cross-disciplinary respect and collaboration.

Even so, many developers are much more conscious of the connectedness of their projects with larger community issues and aspirations and may be willing to partner up for specific project improvements, usually in the form of public infrastructure. Most would rather be liked and supported than having to duke it out. There is tangible value in gaining community support, both in approval facilitation and in the bottom line of a project that contributes to the quality of the larger place. Developers are showing a growing tendency to use public involvement meetings, workshops, or charrettes managed by urban design or community engagement consultants to get their projects expedited. Unless these reveal themselves as just another way to get over on a community, they offer the opportunity for communities to take advantage of the forum provided. They can thus organize themselves, focus their perspective of the pros and cons of a project, and inject infrastructure or other project modification proposals into the process that will benefit the community.

The next step in applying the inclusivity principle in dealing with the private sector, then, is an earlier, more forthright engagement in shaping projects that the community will welcome. For the community, recognizing that stuff doesn't usually happen unless the private sector is fully involved—and that profit is the motive—the next step is to organize around civic visions, identify realistic, implementable steps and, if the project contributes positively to the civic environment, to support the public approval processes that most development projects require.

A few years back, I participated in an Urban Land Institute study to focus attention on what was by then a clearly emerging market trend toward infill housing development. Originally billed as a "market rate" infill housing study, after comments from public officials and community-based development organizations, the study morphed into an "affordable" or "workforce" infill housing study, in recognition by the more progressive developers that dealing with housing issues in older cities benefits from a holistic, inclusive approach.

## Private, Nonprofit Organizations

Except for the neighborhood-generated nonprofit community development corporations (CDCs) dealt with under neighborhood-based organizations above, most nonprofits involved with the improvement of the civic environment are best understood under the heading of private sector organizations. Private nonprofits, foundations, and service organizations, sometimes referred to as nongovernmental organizations (NGOs), represent a very significant, often vital resource for improving places. Their funding sources, essentially donations from people and private entities that have the wherewithal to donate, both reflect the fruits of private gain and project a private vision of how the funds should be distributed or invested. Private nonprofits represent a vehicle that reroutes the payment of income taxes to tax-deductible worthy causes as defined by the donors, whose wealth might otherwise be allocated according to government-set public policy priorities through greater tax revenues. To limit the tendency among some such organizations to engage in self-dealing, that is, using the tax exemption as an alternate path to personal gain, the Internal Revenue Service has instituted tax code provisions to govern NGOs.

Fortunately, some of the very wealthy have the desire to "give back" where, in varying degrees, they get to pick the recipients. Others use their capital accumulations in ways less contributive to the improvement of the civic environment. Many foundations are active in putting forth their priorities on how the civic environment should be improved, most with positive results. In Atlanta, for example, private nonprofits are active in preserving and increasing tree cover; protecting the quality of watersheds; supporting the expansion and operation of green space; building greenway trails; financing, building, and operating below-market-rate housing (both in support of and in addition to neighborhood-based CDCs); and sprucing up downtowns, to mention a few. Most of these are affiliated with or supported by powerful foundations, like in Atlanta the Woodruff Foundation, founded on Coke money; or the Blank Family Foundation, founded on Home Depot money; or the Turner Foundation, founded on money from the various enterprises of Ted Turner; the Annie Casey Foundation, founded on United Parcel Service money; or, nationally, the Enterprise Foundation, founded on money from the various enterprises of Jim Rouse; or the Local Initiatives Support Corporation, the Ford Foundation, and many others.

It should be noted that there are a number of issues-based nonprofits that have proven vital for advancing quality of life for Americans as well as internationally across the full range of issues facing human society. Many of these, while structured as private nonprofits, undertake research, communications, educational, and outreach programs that shine light into the seamier tunnels of both for-profit and government enterprises. While not "advocating" (so as to remain in compliance with the IRS code), these nonprofits lift the level of knowledge and understanding for the interested public, sometimes the whole public, that neither private nor public enterprise wants to let be known. These kinds of nonprofits struggle constantly to gain sufficient resources to carry on their missions, usually from foundations or government agencies that recognize that change may be necessary and that good information and its dissemination are crucial to achieve that end.

The culture of private foundations and thus the principles for understanding and engaging them are more closely aligned with private sector values and behavior than with either government or community organizations. It is a culture of wealth whose characteristics reflect the single-mindedness that created disposable profits in the first place, often carrying over to the purposes on which such funds are focused. Like other funding sources, securing and applying these resources to improvements that integrate physical and social purpose may be a challenge.

The bottom line for foundations is to see their resources productively used. If organizations benefiting from their largesse achieve the purposes for which it was solicited in the first place, the foundation is likely to see the initiative through to its best outcome. In addition, these organizations tend to be supportive of strategies that leverage their assets. "If so-and-so is supporting this initiative, I guess we can or should too." Or, "We will support your initiative to such and such an extent, provided that you match our support with other resources."

On the other hand, gaining nonprofit funding support for the ongoing maintenance and operation necessary to sustain a successful place is usually very difficult to obtain, since there's no place in operations to display the benefactor's name or lasting presence. "We gave you the money to build it, now it's your job to keep it up." This outcome often ends up falling to local government, likely diverting its always stretched resources to an installation that would not otherwise have commanded its priority in the larger scope of municipal needs.

# Principles for Guiding Government Organizations

Most of the government organizations involved with the development of places are at the local level, including typically the planning, permitting and inspection, community and economic development functions, the public works functions, as well as often the parks, law, and finance functions. Regional and state agencies also relate significantly to local planning, design, and development activities, particularly metropolitan planning organizations at the regional level and at the state and occasionally federal level, with the departments of transportation and environmental protection being among the more prominent. The discussion of principles for guiding public organizations, again based on the overarching principles of inclusion, information sharing, vision, building on strengths, and action, here focuses on the planning, design, public works, and approval functions but includes the other functions as well. In all cases, beyond their value for practitioners in the place-making fields, the principles may also be helpful for citizen activists, public servants, and private sector participants in the place-building fields who are trying to make a difference.

**The government—the people—own most of the civic space:** The opportunity, some might say the responsibility, lies with citizens through government to improve the functional and visual quality of their property.

**The measure of government is service—to all citizens:** Each administration should leave things better than it found them, not just for some people but for everyone.

**Include all disciplines:** Press for synthesis among the various place-making disciplines, from both outside and inside government, to make places better.

**Include all agencies and jurisdictions:** Press the establishment of inter-agency, inter-jurisdictional teams or task forces to coordinate planning, urban design, and development processes—at a minimum the left hand should know what the right hand is doing.

**Break down "turf":** Press for the breakdown of "turf" within government—it interferes with access to information, coordination between disciplines and agencies, and ultimately accountability and effectiveness.

**Beware of "privatization":** While privatizing government services may, or may not, yield short-term improvements, remember that the first and unavoidable measure for success of the private enterprise is to make a profit, more important than providing service, and that public funds are the source of that profit.

**Praise good service:** Whenever civil servants provide responsive service, praise them, especially in this era when pundits and politicians routinely, often vehemently, malign government and its workers as the cause for all that's wrong. The stunned look on the praised person's face may give way to motivation to keep going—and to remember someone who appreciated their effort next time.

The structure of most local governments is comprehensive. It includes administrative functions like overall management, finance, and

*"The government owns the public space."*

law; operational functions like running the water, sewer, parks, or traffic systems; public safety functions like police and fire protection; and shaping the physical environment, like planning and building the civic realm and shaping private development through zoning and building codes. Altogether, then, local government provides the framework for and is the seam between all aspects of development projects' interface with the public realm, which typically makes up about 30 percent of a jurisdiction's land area.

*"The measure of government is service."*

The principle that should distinguish government's role and purpose in the quality and functionality of its civic environment is that the places over which it has authority should get better—for the citizens who use and share the place and for the well-being of the town or city as a whole. Each administration should leave the places with which it was entrusted better than it found them. Or, to think in the terms of the Hippocratic Oath, at least do no harm. This principle is the special province of government, especially local government, in the context of place design. The community is looking to improve itself, make the quality of their places better than they were before, yet not necessarily as judged by its impacts on neighboring communities. The private sector is primarily concerned with making a profit on a project-by-project basis, in which any impact on the overall environment which they share is tangential—fine if the project makes things better, too bad if it doesn't.

The standard of making things better than they were before sounds modest and reasonable, but it is a tough measure nonetheless. It calls into play the principle of always considering the whole and the parts—even as the quality and functionality of neighborhoods and districts must improve, so must the jurisdiction as a whole. The principle to which governments should be held accountable has to apply inclusively to all of its constituents, discouraging the money-driven favoritism that so often infuses the political process.

Beyond including and considering the needs of all of its constituents in discharging its responsibilities of public trust, the inclusivity principle applies at the very practical, day-to-day level as well. All the built stuff in a place (buildings, streets, sidewalks, sewers, and so on) gets built, all the operations and maintenance happens, and it all flows through offices of local government, one way or the other. As it relates to building and maintaining civic places, though, governments have a hard time in focusing their disparate agencies into unified development processing practices, either with respect to the community where a development is proposed or with respect to the developer who is proposing it. Smaller towns or counties usually have an easier time than larger ones, yet for all integrating development support functions is a challenge.

*"Include all disciplines."*

An obstacle within local government that echoes to some extent a problem in private sector consulting is what one might call professional chauvinism. Each of the professions or disciplines is mainly focused on itself, sometimes to the extent of wondering why the others matter. Yet they must—and one way or another do—come together to build the civic realm and the private building frames that define it. In the case of any given development project, the civil engineer in the public works department is satisfied once the roads, grades, water, and sewers are taken care of. The traffic engineer is satisfied once the lanes, parking, signals, traffic control devices, and lights are taken care of. The planner is satisfied once the comprehensive plan is adopted and the zoning and subdivision approval processes are established and working. The building official is satisfied once the plans have been checked and corrected, a building permit issued, and inspections proceed smoothly. These separate disciplines and their agencies need to come together and become more aware and respectful of their contributions to their larger public purpose.

*"Include all agencies."*

One theory holds that if each agency simply does what the rules and good practices within its own discipline call for, their job is done, and everything should turn out alright. Yet as we shall see in more detail in Part Four, Processes, these rules and practices come from within disparate disciplinary traditions, and when it all comes together on the ground, disjointedness, cross-purposes, the lack of a unifying vision for a place or even common sense, often become evident. Adopting and asserting inclusiveness, cooperation, and interdisciplinary collaboration as a core principle begins the process of better integration of the development services functions of government.

*"Break down 'turf.'"*

Beyond the disciplinary splits within a government, turf often becomes an issue. That is, the many agencies and subagencies of local governments may develop a certain protectiveness of their unit, born partly of making sure their function is done "right," and partly of wanting to control their work flow and priorities. On the darker side, agencies might want to cloak their doings from public or even peer agency scrutiny, for one reason or another. In addition, the tendency to build and protect turf stems from the problems of different professional cultures noted above. In any event, turf seems almost endemic in many government settings and large private organizations as well. Turf contradicts the underlying principle of inclusivity in many ways, always hampering the smooth functioning of government. Turf interferes with information sharing; it discounts, or is even oblivious to, the importance of many interrelated functions; it defines problems more narrowly than reality or common sense might call for; it snags approval processes; and it fosters other difficulties, not the least of which may be a kind of interpersonal animosity that may further diminish the ability to provide service and build trust.

For a period of time in Atlanta, we established what we called a "development council," where on a regular basis representatives from the place-building city departments; the development authority; the housing authority; the school board; the transit agency; community development corporations; representatives of relevant county, state, and federal agencies; and others, depending on the nature of the development programs and projects on the agenda, came together to share information and look for mutually supportive planning, design, and funding strategies. These sessions produced consistently useful results. Beyond many projects and approval strategies identified through the process, the simple sharing of information in an informal atmosphere worked toward establishing relationships and building trust.

In my experience, the best way to overcome the difficulties that turf may pose is to hold steadfastly to the principles enunciated here and as further described in Part Four. It is important to understand the setting in which public servants function and the trends that are presently affecting that setting, often confounding any search for common purpose within government. The government, in our case usually the local government, largely owns and controls the public realm. Its decisions, its priorities, its purpose directly shape the quality and the functionality of our places. Not just the streets, sidewalks, parks, plazas, and public institutions, but how private buildings engage, connect to (or don't) that public realm are to an extent controlled through government, usually through zoning, subdivision, public works codes, building permitting, or sometimes design review authority. So the agencies that have responsibility for managing the processes for any number of private sector initiatives under the best of circumstances have a big job.

Under these pressures, civil servants are likely to take on the culture and attitude of their most closely allied private sector discipline as they perceive and experience it, and turfs invariably arise. "Knowledge is power" thwarts any service-oriented impetus to information sharing that might enhance the service. "I know what I'm doing, leave me alone" denies and frustrates the essential service value of working cooperatively and collaboratively with other essential disciplines. "My judgment in the process is the one that matters most" denies awareness or concern about the larger issues and opportunities that might arise, often against the measure of common sense. "Your application is in my stack—I'll get to it when I get to it" slows down any process and denies the existence of any legitimate priorities. And all of this is overlaid with a kind of struggle to establish some sense of self-worth in a national culture that ridicules government service, leading to often destructive interpersonal one-upmanship.

The political discovery (most famously by Ronald Reagan) that deriding government gives a candidate a leg up has ravaged the balance between democracy and capital, leading to a vicious cycle where the calculated erosion of public trust in civic institutions leads to diminished government capacity and performance. The current drive toward privatization, toward "running government like a business," reflects the ascendancy of the so-called free market model, touted among other features for its promise to shrink the government. But try to think of some significant sector of the "free market" economy that addresses the needs of the whole people or that is not substantially intertwined with the government through public funding, regulation, subsidy, tax policy, or contracts. Then remember what motivates the private sector.

*"Beware of 'privatization.'"*

Of course, privatization has not shrunk the government. It has only found new ways to divert public money into private hands, where the private sector identifies services that might make a profit and then structures deals to assure that profit. The movement leaves services with less promise for profit in the hands of government, with reduced resources and flexibility to meet those obligations. Or, as several commentators have noted, the movement seeks to privatize public assets and to socialize private risk. In place making, privatization is making its greatest inroads in infrastructure projects, like roads and water supply, where taking over a "sure thing" with tantalizingly promising short-term budget relief for government may seem irresistible. The bottom line for all of these is profit, and the idea of neighborhoods, districts, or other community interests having input is anathema. Realizing civic spaces whose goals and purposes do not coincide with a healthy return on investment thus becomes difficult to imagine—maybe Rockefeller Center (private) or Central Park (public) should set up toll booths for entry to these civic spaces?

*"Praise good service."*

On the other hand, shared private-public planning, design, development, and operations of crucial civic spaces holds more promise. Here, as in park conservancies, for example, the private face is usually the nonprofit foundation. While these partnerships may be testy, as the prospective partners sort out who gains and who loses—and often whose name gets affixed to effort—they may be very positive, or even essential in these times of erosion of public resources for maintaining public assets.

The urban designer's interest in the principles that apply to understanding how government works is to figure out where and how to fit into the processes through which projects must pass, whether in public or private practice. This understanding should support both looking for ways to expedite project design and approval and supporting internally generated improvements that civil servants often seek to make.

The community's interest is to seek ways to build constructive and reliable partnerships with agencies and individuals who can help them with information and procedural guidance—different than attacking civil servants for not performing. In addition, civil servants in their home life are just as likely to espouse community-supported visions as any other active neighborhood leader—another basis for common cause and possible support for improving government process. Appreciating the civil servant who responds well, who is both civil and provides service, is a great way to begin to form government-community or government–urban design alliances.

# Summary

Urban designers and community activists, while playing different roles, are able to advance their purposes when they understand the essential and universal interactions between community, private sector, and government. These interactions account for how civic environments come to be and then evolve. While these interactions may not always seem or feel like a "partnership"—sometimes far from it—the three organizational spheres always leave their fingerprints on the outcomes. Every built environment, at whatever scale, reveals the presence of the community, the government, and the private sector. The principles above provide a fuller understanding of these relationships and ways of nudging them toward common purposes. Without their consideration, urban designers and community leaders alike can only partially fulfill their aspirations to participate in the process of making places better.

# PART IV

# PROCESSES

## What It Takes to Get It Done

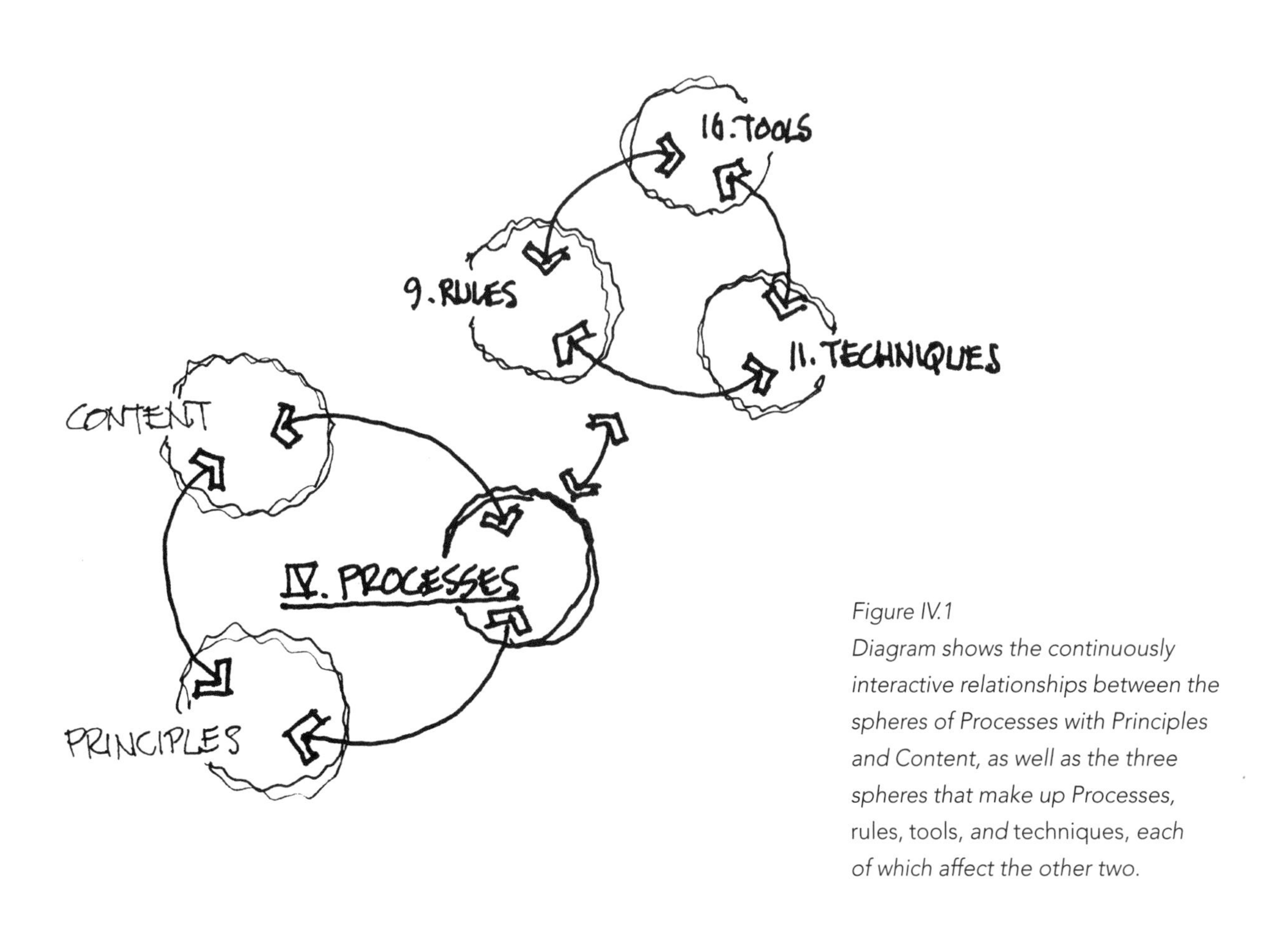


*Figure IV.1*
*Diagram shows the continuously interactive relationships between the spheres of Processes with Principles and Content, as well as the three spheres that make up Processes,* rules, tools, *and* techniques, *each of which affect the other two.*

# Overview

Processes are all about getting it done. Planning and design for the public realm actually must get built to materially improve people's quality of life, to make their places better. Part Four, Processes, describes how the **principles** of urban design applied to designing its **content** can be transformed by actions to develop places that have a reasonable chance of success; that is, places that attract and meet more people's needs over time.

Processes in some ways become principles in action. Processes reflect and interact both with the content, the elements out of which places are designed and developed, and with the design, change, and organizational principles for shaping that content to produce a positive outcome. How and in what sequence principles and processes together may interact with the content of places varies widely, yet out of these interactions better places may be made.

Over a career dedicated to achieving positive outcomes, I have created, collected from multiple colleagues, neighborhood and business leaders, and assimilated and tested these processes in various combinations for their applicability, effectiveness, and timeliness. Like the principles, these processes represent a working synthesis of both my own and other people's experiences and insights. The processes described here are interactive, dynamic, and in flux. They address the frequent disconnect between idea and action and offer ways of thinking and acting that have proven to be at least somewhat successful in closing that gap. They should provide students, design and development professionals, and community leaders information, approaches, and strategies for getting community-serving or community-generated improvement initiatives into motion.

Part Four has three chapters, covering most of the processes that in interaction with each other describe how to approach implementation problems in ways that can produce positive results: Rules, Tools, and Techniques. These in turn play into Part Five, Strategies, which suggests ways that all of the parts of the book might come together to launch a place-improvement program.

Rules describe those policies, laws, and regulations and standards that to a large extent "design" the world we live in. Understanding their origins, purposes, and shortcomings is key to changing things for the better. It's pretty much always been that way, more or less formally, and future urban places too will be shaped by rules. Why this is, what the rules entail, and how to deal with them are all dealt with in Chapter 9, Rules. Chapter 10, Tools, describes tools to support urban and community design and place-making processes and shows how the rules can be refashioned to enable better planning, design, and citizen guidance practices. Chapter 11, Techniques, focuses on techniques for understanding, supporting, designing, communicating, and finally carrying out agreed-on initiatives, including technical and organizational tools, and attitudinal and behavioral considerations for acting positively in community-improvement settings.

Common to the substance of all of the chapters in this Part are underlying circumstances, conditions, and premises that lay the basis for applying the suggested measures. To begin with, it is worth reminding ourselves of the larger context and baseline parameters under which design and development happen in the urban setting. Economic development purposes generate much of what happens in the built world. Most economic development activity, beyond all its other manifestations, takes on a physical form, from the factory to the bank, from the housing complex to the retail strip. The U.S. economy is often described as a market economy; that is, the principal driving incentive in the private sector is to make a profit. In fact, private enterprises of all kinds only stay in business if they do make a profit and, in a food chain where the larger eats the smaller, the best safeguard to staying in business is to maximize profit.

The structural, philosophical, or theoretical obstacles to getting things done that flow from these realities reflect a complicated picture that is embedded in the contradictions, fluctuations, and interactions between our economic system and our political system. The former is based on market capitalism and the profit motive, while the latter is based on democracy, equality, and the rule of law. The state of these relationships directly affects settlement patterns at the larger scale and the prospects for getting things done at the smaller.

Presently, the widening gap in incomes between the rich, say the top quintile of incomes, and the middle- and lower-income communities, everyone else, produces widening gaps in education, culture, and access to services and resources. When it comes to improving the civic environment, these gaps tend to favor the "have" communities over the "have nots." Out of these dynamics and the widening disparities that they are propelling come ideas and efforts to rebalance the playing field, to work for social equity. One example has been a growing sensitivity for "environmental justice," a concept that seeks to mitigate the historical tendency to stick dirty industry or dirty municipal functions into low-income and usually minority neighborhoods.

As it relates to getting things done, affluent neighborhoods or business districts are more likely to have the time and the resources to gain access to public funding and public approval processes to accelerate their aspiration for improvement. This advantage in gaining access to resources both directly and indirectly blocks access to the same pot to neighborhoods or business areas that are not so fortunate. This aspect of the market economy becomes an obstacle that actively constrains people in the larger society from being able to make their places better.

This book is aimed at improving all places, and so from the very local to the regional level the goal is to seek processes that may result in improvements across the board, which requires a better sharing of the resources out there, both public and private. Accordingly, the processes offered seek for everyone a better way to get on in the world—a decent place to live, a job, a way to get back and forth, all with some sense of safety and satisfaction. The physical setting that nurtures these basic human functions should be okay and getting better. The resources to achieve this modest goal exist, and better distribution could go a long way toward achieving ongoing civic improvements everywhere.

Most of what gets built in the United States is built by the private sector—developers, homebuilders, corporations, large institutions, and the like. Government and nonprofit development is mostly designed by private sector consultants of various kinds and built by private sector contractors. The processes for making places better, then, need to take into account that the development vehicles will be mostly private (though usually mixed with a public regulatory, monetary, or fiscal component). While meeting the public space needs for human activity may be important, for the private sector making money is usually more important. Accordingly, rarely does any one private sector entity initiate civic-improvement processes unless the goal of profit has a good chance of being realized. This is probably just as well, since spaces driven by that singular requirement are unlikely to meet the broader palette of needs and desires that an effective public space fulfills.

There have been recurrent patterns that characterize successful outcomes, all navigating between the economic and the political side, the private sector where most of the money is and the public sector where most of the regulatory authority lies, where the role of the broad public, or the specifically interested public, is gradually increasing its voice and influence over the outcome.

Under these circumstances, the planning and design of civic spaces ultimately falls to the government to accomplish. Yet, while government has the authority and usually owns the space where civic improvements take place, it does not usually initiate them. Making places better, then, presents an underlying challenge to community leadership to marshal enough public support to induce the government to enable or even take a lead in the place-improvement process. Its motive must be civic improvement, only a part of which may be business development and the taxes that may generate. Many cities are stepping up to meet this challenge, mostly at the initiative of communities, whether neighborhood or district based. Tracking the resurgence of interest in living and working in core areas, cities and towns are beginning to express a new civic pride in physical and visual ways. The current downturn in financing and development activity alleviates the constant pressure to react. This lull may actually provide the opportunity to plan proactively, to get community and civic visions in place, and to identify priority projects to begin to implement the vision when public infrastructure and private development projects pick up steam.

It is perhaps too soon to compare these stirrings with other great placemaking eras, like the City Beautiful movement, but perhaps to its advantage the current organizing is more extensive and diverse in its base. Increasingly, broader-based civic and community groups are organizing themselves to launch, design, build, and sometimes even maintain civic-improvement programs. Business organizations, too, representing a number of interests within an area or district, are quite likely to undertake civic-improvement initiatives, usually with the overall goal and purpose of improving business, cognizant of the appeal that well-executed places have for their customers and employees.

Processes necessary to implement place improvements begin with this baseline understanding of the players, their motives, their relationships, and the trends in the times we find ourselves. Understanding the participants, their interests, purposes, and motives, and then finding the overlaps, the bases for cooperation and collaboration, is some of what this Part is about.

The good news is that, like most everything else about urban design, each piece of the puzzle by itself is usually not too difficult to understand. The knowledge base is what it is, and making places that people like to be for the most part does not depend on science or technology. The content of the problems is mostly familiar in everyday experience, and open-minded observation of the range of responses reasonably predicts people's behavior to various spatial features. What complicates the design and implementation of improved places is the sheer numbers of elements that must be considered and the potential complexity of their interactions.

As we approach the all important how-to-get-it-done material in this Part, then, it is important to not let the quantity of material described cloud the relative simplicity of each piece. In fact, both urban designers and community leaders are likelier to appreciate how the different pieces interlock than specialized "experts." Often it is in the daily experienced synthesis, the putting together of the pieces, where the commonsense factor overrides the specialization bias of those who focus on separate components. In addition, specific ways of getting things done just a few years ago in one particular setting might not work today. So the emphasis here is not on detailed steps but rather on overall understandings of process approaches and phases for completing a course of action.

# 9

# RULES

## That Make Places What They Are

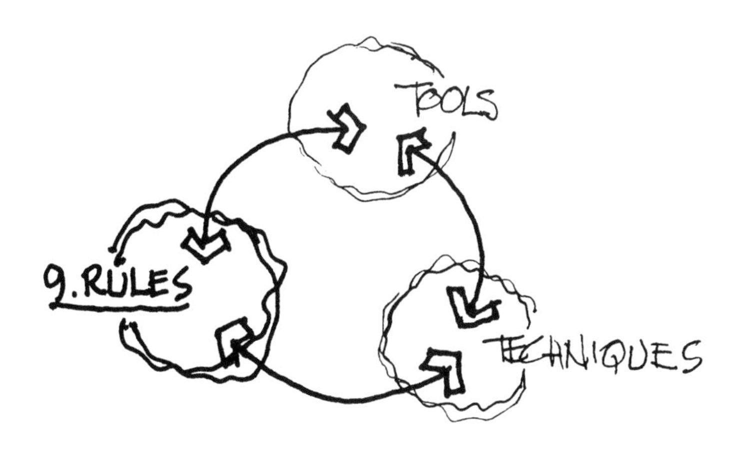


*Figure 9.1*
*The rules sphere in its interactions with* tools *and* techniques.

# Introduction

*"There ought to be a law..."*
*"Like it or not, you've got to play by the rules."*
*"Rules are made to be broken."*

Drive down almost any commercial street in the United States and what do you see? Except in dense older centers, you see multiple traffic lanes, driveways everywhere, signs of all sorts and descriptions, utility poles and lines running every which way, parking lots—one for each disconnected building. In short, a cacophony of confusion that has to be sorted out to find the place you're looking for and then get there safely.

In urbanized areas this scene dominates the most heavily traveled routes—where people travel the most looks the worst and functions poorly in providing clear, safe, and certain access. Yet what you see is the product of codes and rules that have accreted reactively and disconnectedly to address travel, property rights, utilities, and the "market" since World War II. In my classes, after recalling this and other familiar scenes, I make a point of taking a "code walk" with my students, showing how virtually everything they see is required, shaped, or at the least influenced by codes or standards of one kind or another. What are the major rules that dictate the quality and functionality of the civic environment? Where do the rules come from? Who makes them? Who enforces them? And how can people concerned with making better places influence them, turn them to better outcomes than the present rules produce? This chapter addresses these kinds of questions.

Design professionals want to conceptualize and create, developers want to build and sell, and communities want voice and influence to improve their places, but place making is to a large degree constrained or mandated by rules. The rules governing how and where things get built for what purpose didn't spring out of nowhere. Virtually every rule, in fact, was put in place either to perpetuate experience with how to do the necessary better; how to fairly balance the interests of the individual and the larger community; or how to safeguard health, safety, and welfare against ignorance or profit-driven corner-cutting impulses. When the roof collapses, or the all-night club locates down the street from your house, or a crash occurs at the unsignalized intersection, or someone gets electrocuted plugging into a faulty wall socket, people rise up and proclaim, "There ought to be a law!"—and by now, by golly, there usually is.

Rule making for the most part has been a remarkably elemental, linear, trial-and-error sort of a process. Something bad happens, and a rule gets put in place to try to prevent it in the future. Or some good practice emerges, and people want to assure that this practice becomes the new baseline standard. When one ponders all of the disciplines and subdisciplines that claim jurisdiction over this or that rule, it seems a wonder that the thicket of rules that accounts for how places get built works as well as it does.

## Context

The origin and evolution of rule making as it relates to the design and development of the civic environment pose major challenges to designing places functionally and attractively, not to mention inclusively and comprehensively. Underlying the challenges are tensions in policy and law that are dynamic, tensions that will always be in play as codes relating to design and development swing back and forth between individual and community rights and values.

In legal terms, this tension plays out in constitutional requirements for equal protection and fair compensation for land that may be condemned for public purposes among other provisions. Laying a code over a territory requires that all affected parties are treated equally. As interests become more and more fine-grained and diverse, codes and their applications get more complicated, harder to understand and manage. Even when people agree, for example, that an area is suitable for commercial activity, it isn't enough to simply use a single commercial classification or form. The kind, size, shape, amount of activity, and related parking requirements that may make a commercial activity acceptable in some districts may make it unacceptable in others. Then more classifications may be added, with more provisions, until the next time the underlying tension pops up.

In a similar vein, the tension between private property rights and community rights frustrates viewing a neighborhood or even a block holistically. Each property owner along the block has a "right" to build whatever the zoning permits, usually a uniform right along the block front, and each property owner has the "right" of access to their property. These "rights" among others must be equally applied on a property-by-property basis up and down the block, up and down the street. The effect is there for all to see, for example, along the strip commercial streets cited at the beginning of the chapter as typical of major travel ways in every city. Individual buildings are lined up according to common setback, use category, height, parking, loading, sign requirements, each with its own utility line drop and its own driveway. People have all experienced entering the wrong driveway and finding curbs barring them from simply going next door, requiring driving back out into the street instead. From the perspective of each owner (assuming the business is successful), the system works—"I've got mine, and you've got yours." But from the perspective of the block or the street and the public that travels the street, occasionally to gain access to one or another business, the scene is confusing, chaotic, and may be even a little dangerous.

What's happening here illustrates two points. On the public side, while codes in their formulation and administration address the separate pieces, they do not address the situation as a whole. On the private side, while the typical set of rules may seem to optimize rights and opportunities for each separate property owner, it suboptimizes the functionality, not to mention the clarity and attractiveness, of the strip as a whole, for both the public and arguably the interests of the owners themselves. Responses to these conundrums are beginning to gain ground here and there in the various professions and jurisdictions that bear the responsibility for the current state of affairs. Over the last few years, for example, state DOTs have been moving to cooperate with local jurisdictions to establish what they call "access control" or "access management." The goal of these efforts is to group access to a string of properties into a single driveway, or at least as few driveways as possible, thus reducing vehicular and pedestrian conflict points and clarifying how to get to all the businesses along the block. But for this to happen requires a communitarian commitment on the part of adjacent small business owners (never easy) or a law.

These conditions are a good illustration of the need for the application of the principles that call for considering the whole and the parts together and then seeking to synthesize the polarized values.

For all the issues they raise, for all the problems they present, though, rules are necessary, and the emphasis here is to improve their framework. Without them the unfettered market, as it tends to do whenever there aren't rules, would tilt toward the individual profiteer, creating buildings, places, and cities whose primary criterion would be profitability for the few at the expense of health, safety, welfare, and just plain functionality and civility for the many. Market apologists argue that excesses in the market are self-correcting, but there is little evidence in the public domain to support that claim. The growing disparity in access to participate in the market economy is reflecting the growing gap between what the market provides and what people need. The poor quality of most civic environments manifests this gap in our subject matter. Reflecting back on the principles for a moment, the dynamic that bring rules into being is the duality of individual and community; what may be good for any particular individual may not be the best for the community as a whole, especially if profit is the primary measure of "good."

My very first meeting with an Atlanta developer, about the second day I was there, underscored for me how business is done in the city. The team consisted of the developer, two attorneys, and one architect, who filed into my conference room in that order. The developer wanted to impress upon me that his project, which the attorneys presented, would be a great addition to the Buckhead area of the city and that accordingly I should certainly support the comprehensive development plan and zoning applications that the project required to go forward.

It was a large-scale project, I was new and not yet too familiar with the location, and so I assured him I would give his proposal my most thorough consideration. He thanked me for that and then let me know that whatever the outcome of my analysis, the Neighborhood Planning Unit recommendation, the staff recommendation, the Zoning Review Board recommendation, and the City Council's final action, if the project was not approved he would sue and he would win. This position was reinforced by his attorneys, who gave me a short lesson on development law as practiced in Georgia. Welcome to Atlanta.

As it happened, the City Council did not approve the project; the developer sued and won in lower court. The city appealed, and armed with clear policies stated in the Comprehensive Development Plan, was able to win on appeal, and the project, which was flawed in many ways, did not go forward. So, better know your law and hope for good legal representation on your side (in which the city's legal staff on the case was superlative) if you want to make sure that your actions are making the civic environment better instead of worse.

## The Various Disciplines

Aside from balancing of community and individual rights and responsibilities, at the practical and operational level rules have become parsed into the various disciplines that hold the technical jurisdiction to understand, formulate, and oversee them. Over time new rules get added or old ones changed so that at any point in time there are rules that conflict with other rules, even within each discipline, and when taken together many rules in one discipline are likely to contradict rules of another. Fire codes, public works codes, and traditional neighborhood development codes, for example, are almost certain to call for different street widths and corner radii, with the former two wanting bigger numbers (but not necessarily in agreement with each other) and the latter wanting smaller.

The keepers of the different sets of rules each put their priority on the unique criteria of their particular discipline, either not interested in or not aware of the impacts their rules may have on other pieces of the big picture. Communities seeking better places are as active in stimulating moves for a better integration and cross-disciplinary approach for improving rules as are professionals in the disciplines, government, or developers. Rules are not so easy to change, though, and so without a sustained effort that joins progressive-minded practitioners with community political pressure, the status quo will die hard.

Most of the technical place-building disciplines do have rule-making oversight bodies, though, which do the best they can to continually synthesize and update their discipline's rules, periodically issuing new codes or addenda to old ones. Yet even these good intentions result in processes that are ponderous, confusing, and frustrating for all concerned.

Finally, the legal profession plays a fundamental and pervasive role in all rule-making and rule-enforcing activity. Not unlike the disconnectedness between the various technical design disciplines, lawyers tend to specialize in one or another of the subdisciplines of urban design. Most people active in neighborhood and district design initiatives have encountered land use and zoning attorneys, in some cases hiring them to represent their interests. In most larger jurisdictions, indeed, almost any significant development initiative is represented by the initiator's attorney, a person fully versed and experienced in all the ins and outs of what it takes to make the initiative successful.

On the other end of the stick, attorneys are in the forefront of any litigation that might arise out of disputes over actions or inactions that may occur in property or public infrastructure development. Again reflecting the fragmentation of interests and disciplines involved in creating the public environment, attorneys only occasionally reflect any consciousness of the big picture—they are usually too focused on the narrow interests of individual project-specific details to relate to larger implications, beyond the context they must follow from case law.

## The Authority

For the most part, the local governments administer the rules. While there are state and federal rules that shape land development design and practice, local government oversees most of the rules that give form to the places we live, work, and travel in. These most prominently include comprehensive development plans, zoning regulations, subdivision regulations, public works codes, utilities franchise agreements, building codes, fire codes, and health codes. Many jurisdictions also include design review requirements; historic preservation codes; sign codes; environmental codes like tree codes, stream bank, wetlands, or shoreline buffer codes; and housing and property maintenance codes.

Sometimes communities initiate more specialized codes, like for preserving natural or historic assets in a neighborhood or district, often targeted to forestall or prevent what people view as destructive incursions into the values they have embraced. These kinds of initiatives may be disjointed, sometimes inconsistent with other municipal policies, difficult to administer, or even contrary to the best interests of the jurisdictions as a whole. Such community-improvement initiatives, however, have been on the rise for many years, and I consider them generally as markers of commitment and pride, cornerstones of civic betterment. In most cases with which I am familiar, these kind of special code initiatives do more good than harm. Urban designers should pay close attention to these community-driven aspirations to make their places better and at the same time look for ways to synthesize these efforts with other, more comprehensive rule sets.

Planning, building, and public works departments generally have the primary staff responsibility to administer the rules, with oversight by the executive branch and code approval by the legislative branch, usually the city council, board of aldermen, or county commission. In theory and often in practice, the comprehensive plan governs the policy framework for enacting and enforcing the more specific rules. The plan is supposed to be the process and the document that points local government toward realizing its citizens' collective aspirations.

In fact, governments, partly because of the often haphazard and ad hoc ways that codes come to be and partly because of the technical difficulties and costs associated with administering such codes, often have difficulty applying and enforcing codes in a consistent manner. It is fair to say that few jurisdictions have the resources or the commitment to enforce all the laws and codes on their books in any event, a circumstance where individuals or organizations with sufficient resources and sharp lawyers can gain an edge in achieving their purposes. Although theoretically most of the actions taken to establish or administer codes are matters of public record, access to these processes for interested citizens varies according to local law and practice, from easy to hard.

The rules that shape the living environment in various combinations and forms are likely to be in place for most jurisdictions. Below we synopsize some of the most prominent rules by category, outlining what they are, why they're important, and how urban designers and community leaders might lay the groundwork to make positive changes. Urban designers as well as community leaders have a clear and obvious stake in jumping into this fray. How to recast the rules we have into the tools we need to address the needs is the subject of Chapter 10, Tools, whose purpose is to arm both professionals and citizen leaders with enough information to get started making transformations from rule to tool.

# Zoning

## Provisions

*"World Peace through Zoning!" —a bumper sticker observed in Telluride, Colorado*

The regulatory framework established through zoning joins street layout and design as the most powerful shapers of the urbanized United States. While the comprehensive plan, itself a rule of sorts, is supposed to provide overarching jurisdictional policy for guiding development, in most jurisdictions zoning gets the most attention. Zoning lies at the seam between private and public property. Zoning directs how a property can be used, what can be built, the size, height, placement, often the shape and sometimes even the materials of any building provided for that use, as well as requirements for open space, parking, and loading. These provisions are typically found in a zoning ordinance or land use code, where a text describes in detail the provisions for each zoning classification and a map describes where all the different classifications are located.

In most of the older ordinances, there is a range of use types, densities, and siting requirements, where single-family residential, itself usually gradated by lot size, is the more restrictive and less dense, up through commercial classifications that at their densest usually describe major centers and then industrial classifications, with the most intense usually located at a distance from population centers. These classifications are usually designated as "R" districts for residential, "C" districts for commercial, and "M" or "I" districts for manufacturing or industrial, with more particular zoning classifications that vary according to locality. The letter code is usually followed with a number designation in which the lower the number, the more restrictive the use and density.

As in the modernist era separation of use and density precepts have fallen away, more and more ordinances are introducing mixed-use and mixed-density provisions to encourage more diverse development patterns, in some ways not unlike those that predated zoning. These recent reform initiatives take many forms, from systematic modification of existing ordinances to include new provisions, to classifications for new forms, like "traditional neighborhood development," or, usually in smaller communities or new development projects, "smart codes" or "form-based codes."

The provisions of all zoning ordinances largely account for the forms of the buildings they produce, at least in broad strokes like placement on the lot, density, height, and permitted activities or uses. Consciousness of that link has grown rapidly in recent years as more and more people actually trained in design become active in the process. Zoning codes have gone through successive modifications to better align them with desired form and use outcomes. Their prescriptions have become more detailed and fine-grained (resulting in fatter ordinances). In some cases their intent is more defined by performance than prescriptions, sometimes a problem for maintaining consistency of interpretation. Many codes provide for conditions that may be imposed to account for particular site or contextual conditions. Sometimes even more detailed design guidelines direct how buildings look and perform, usually in specific geographic settings. Mixed-use codes have increasingly replaced single-use code constructions.

This growth in activism presently underlies "form-based coding," a term of art that has come into use to emphasize the form or appearance of the development to be regulated over the substance of the activities it houses. The rationale here is that activities that may not have been considered to be compatible because of their form or environmental impacts, if designed properly might enrich rather than detract from the civic environment. Some of the new initiatives, too, recognize the relationship between street and sidewalk design and the buildings to which these give access and suggest or mandate streetscape and sidewalk treatment in addition to private property provisions. In so doing, they recognize the importance of the civic environment as a whole and begin the process of breaking down the separation of disciplines that has frustrated this integration in older codes.

One new contribution to the vocabulary of zoning regulation comes in the form of what is known as the "transect." This way of conceptualizing development controls, promulgated by the consultant firm Duany, Plater-Zyberk, arranges permitted development activities by density, use, and street type. In this system, "T-1" is the less dense, mostly residential and more restrictive, from which the transect ranges up in logical steps to "T-6" where the densities are projected to be the highest and the activities permitted are the most diverse, like a town or district center. In the ideal case, the transect includes designing streets to reflect the progression of densities and diversity of uses in terms of access, walkability, and streetscape treatment.

Overall, the transect approach, like traditional zoning, recognizes a need for a range of densities and uses depending on infrastructure availability, environmental conditions, and larger market-driven development patterns. But the transect approach is simpler, easier to visualize, and can be more flexible than some of the older codes. Like other form-based coding initiatives, the system tends to prioritize form over content in shaping development. In underscoring the importance of form, provisions are clearly illustrated as graphic codes, where people can actually see what the prospective development might look like. Altogether, these initiatives, now being promulgated as "smart codes," make a contribution to both understanding development choices and showing the way to better practice. At the same time, reflecting on the "both-and" principle, it is important for community leaders and urban designers to not lose sight of the importance of the content of development—both the form and the substance. And reflecting on the dangers of "solutionism," they need to understand that none of the new initiatives in any way represent a "final solution" to zoning problems, since those will continue to pop up as change continues to occur.

The importance of the cross-sectional relationship of building-street-building, however, is not a new discovery. Among many examples, Louis XIII of France placed height to street-width relationships along many of Paris's boulevards, while successive New York City zoning ordinances required setbacks for buildings that wanted to exceed established street-wall heights, resulting in what some call the "wedding cake" look along Park Avenue. Both recognized the importance of allowing light and air to penetrate to the sidewalk level, for the benefit of pedestrians, the public-at-large that shared the common space so regulated.

## Public Process

Beyond its obvious and immediate impacts on a specific property and neighboring sites as well as its role in shaping the larger urban landscape,

*Figures 9.2a, b, c*
*The diagram shows typical zoning provisions, including yards or setbacks from property lines and heights in single-family residential districts (a), provisions for typical strip commercial (b), bulk or density controls and (c), often expressed in terms of floor area ratios, or FAR. A FAR of 1, for example, nominally permits the floor area of a permitted building to equal the area of the lot on which it sits, 1 to 1; an FAR of 0.5 would allow half as much floor area as lot area, while an FAR of 2.0 would allow twice as much.*

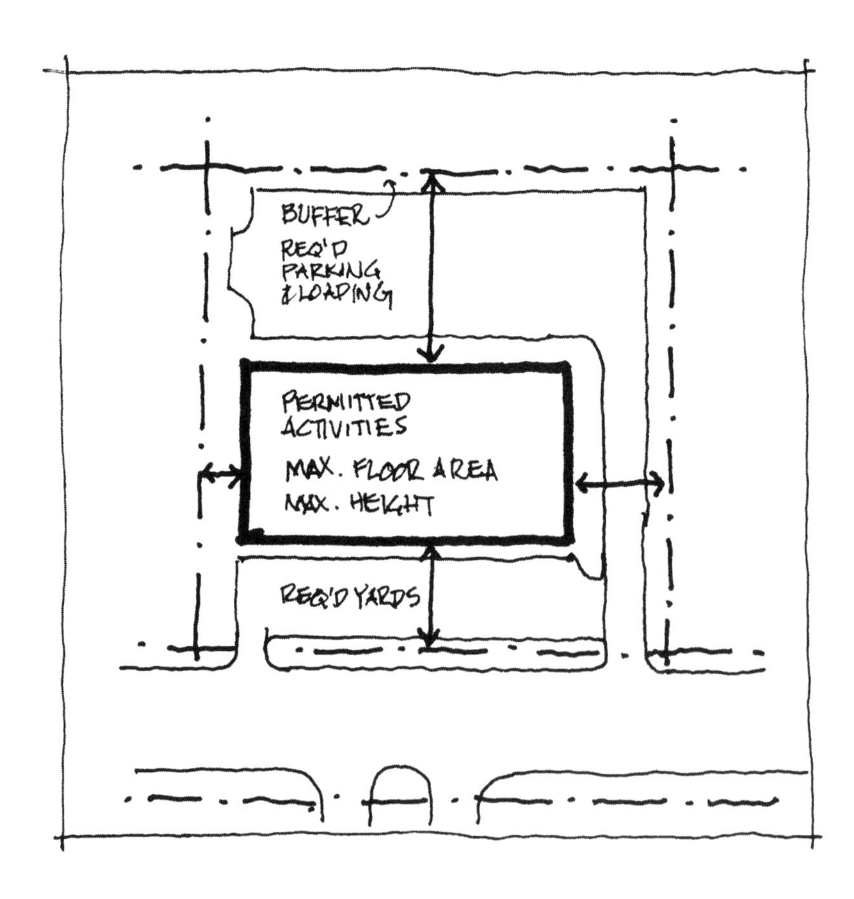

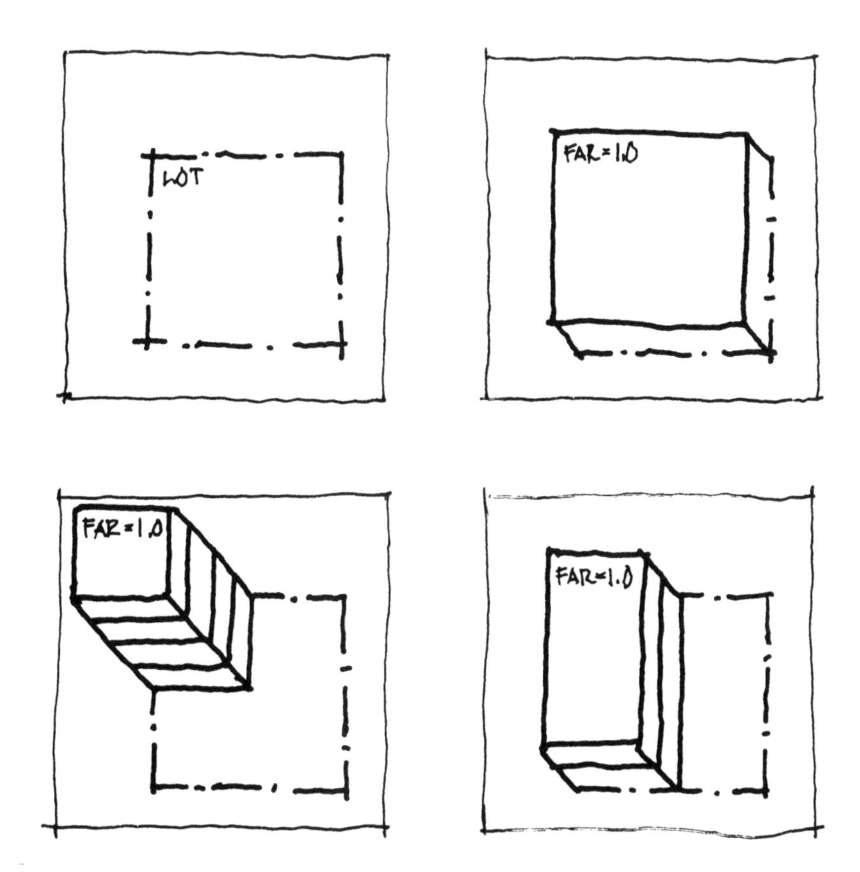


zoning is the most accessible of the codes for everyday people. In recognition of the fundamental community values and rights at stake, most zoning actions require an open and public review process before the legislative body can create or amend ordinances or render other zoning-related decisions. So people come to zoning hearings, at the neighborhood, district, and city-wide levels to exercise their civic right and even responsibility to state their views and ask questions, like a common one that shows up in various forms: "Why shouldn't a new development leave the area around it better than it was before?"

Zoning, in fact, is the action expression of a jurisdiction's development policy, and as such, interacting with market demand, a significant determinant of real estate values. So land owners, sellers, speculators, and developers have a key stake in any zoning activity that affects their interests. For them, their capital, their equity, or their potential or real profit is at stake. For the community, their values and their future as a place is at stake. Indeed, community residents typically have a much higher portion of their net worth bound up in their property than do the developers and speculators who typically initiate most zoning activity.

In many ways, then, zoning hearings are the front lines of engagement in the back-and-forth dialogue seeking to balance community and individual values in terms of the built environment. All across the country, from small towns to cities and counties, there are hundreds if not thousands of zoning hearings going on every month. Indeed, many citizens who emerge as neighborhood leaders and go on to elective office cut their teeth on localized zoning issues. Zoning's ability to bring up close and personal issues of vital concern to all affected, its de facto challenge to the

Zoning ordinances generally provide for minor adjustments to be made by a quasi-judicial body, usually called a Board of Zoning Adjustment or something similar. Such adjustments are usually occasioned by on-the-ground circumstances that make the strict provisions of the applicable classification unworkable, infeasible, or impossible, or otherwise cause a documented hardship beyond what the classification intended. Such actions, often called variances or special exceptions, typically have little impact on the larger civic environment but may be pivotal for the effective use of a particular parcel of land.

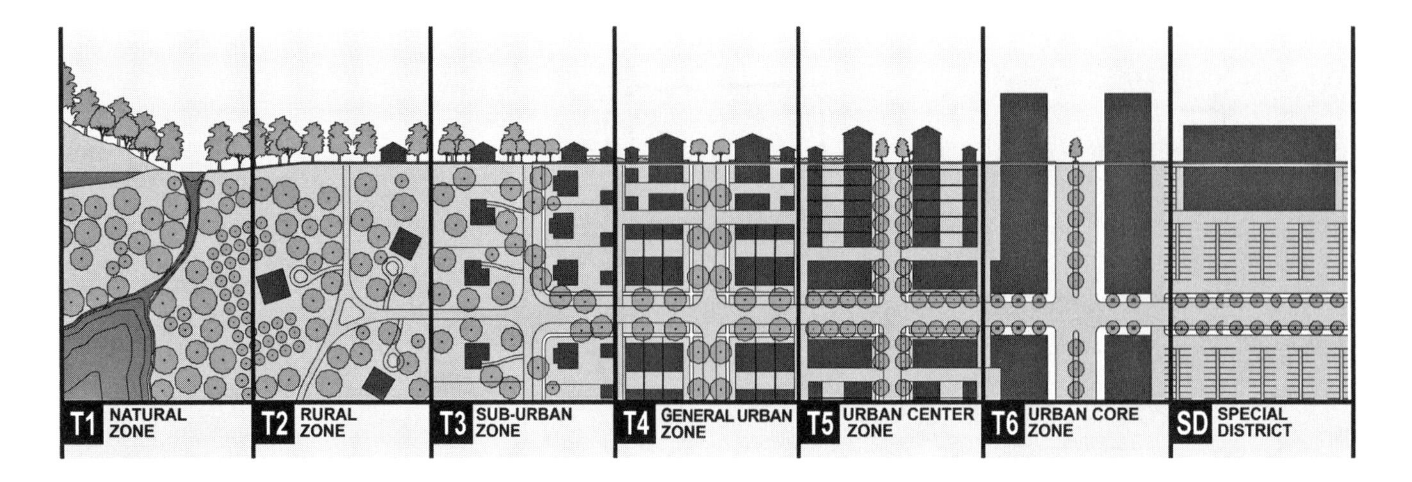


*Figure 9.3*
*Illustration of the "transect" concept of development regulation as promulgated by the Duany, Plater-Zyberk firm, showing a progression of densities and uses from low-density areas to centers. Courtesy of Duany Plater-Zyberk and Company*

"Zoning," in its currently understood meaning was by no means a new concept when New York City adopted its ordinance. The balancing of interests between the individual's right to do whatever on his or her property and the rights of the larger community impacted is an issue that dates all the way back in history. One notable example occurred in sixth-century Constantinople, when the emperor Justinian decreed that people building closer to the Bosporus were not allowed to block the views of those farther back.

status quo, and its multilayered public process that provides direct access to a jurisdiction's elected officials all make it a quick entrée into the workings of government at a personal and graspable scale.

## Zoning History

Zoning's history in this country dates formally to the New York City zoning ordinance of 1916. Recognizing the importance of advancing community standards and values in the land development process, jurisdictions across the country followed suit, spurred on by federal legislation, the Standard State Zoning Enabling Act in 1926. This legislation and two years later the Standard City Planning Enabling Act, championed by Commerce Secretary Herbert Hoover in the Coolidge administration, are arguably the most comprehensive urban planning and development laws ever passed at the federal level. Among other provisions, they provided to states a federal blessing to regulate land use and development practices and processes. Inevitably, as most Americans subscribe to either the tradition or the aspiration of private property as a near-sacred right, challenges to this assertion of a community's interest in how private property is developed wound up in court. Most famously, the Supreme Court ruled in *Ambler Realty v. The Town of Euclid, Ohio* in 1926 that zoning was constitutional, relying primarily on the legitimacy of the government's role to protect the health, safety, and welfare of the larger community.

Zoning as a concept, as a set of rules, and as an ongoing process is subject to constant modification. It seeks to mediate between conferring rights to property owners to develop their property and placing obligations on that development to safeguard or advance the broader community interest. As initially conceived, zoning was relatively simple, specifying broad categories of permissible development activities and fairly minimum constraints on where and how one might build on their property. As it became entrenched as the major land development control, however, it inevitably became more and more complex. As suggested above, both the conditions which zoning could control and rising community demand to exercise that control have become codified in ordinances and administrative procedure in almost every urbanized jurisdiction.

Under the influence of modernist planning precepts, zoning was the tool available to carry out ideas like the separation of uses and the controls of density that were supposed to buffer single-family neighborhoods from multifamily neighborhoods, buffer people in their home life from their work life, or buffer them from the pollutions of industry. Jurisdictions used the separation of uses and densities to separate people in residential communities not just from commercial and industrial activities but by income, and in the South by race as well. The modernist "experts" seem to have held the view that the practice of separation of uses and densities would help people function better and be happier.

The planners of the day, from the 1920s into the 1970s, typically did not engage the public in open and meaningful ways in the process, rather deciding for them their needs, aspirations, and even behavior. Under the guise of "rational" planning and narrowly conceived architectural applications of form over whole societies, separation of uses into exclusive functional categories must have just seemed "better," or "cleaner," or more "rational," or more "aesthetic." The power of these ideas gained momentum across the United States and even across the world as they dominated not just zoning but urban renewal and suburban development in the United States, rebuilt postwar Europe, and Asia.

Once entrenched, these precepts of city building, with zoning along with transportation investments as the chief implementation tools, have been very difficult to change. Discriminatory applications of zoning restrictions continue to separate people by income and often de facto by race as well. The idea of reestablishing mixed-use communities or more generally providing for broader choices in living and working environments, while gaining momentum, still faces major obstacles in many areas.

Reactions to the failures of this earlier era of land development controls multiplied, however, to the extent that over the last 25 years most jurisdictions have been in the process of overhauling and weeding out many of the more clearly dysfunctional aspects of their codes. In looking for models, many people—planners, urban designers, and community leaders—are wondering what was wrong with the way neighborhoods were developed before zoning took on its increasingly discredited forms. Most cities have communities that were built before zoning, or before zoning became so directive. These reflected the ideas collected by Clarence Perry in his formulation of a "neighborhood unit," a walkable area that combined housing types, densities, and neighborhood-serving shops and parks. Such neighborhoods, developed from the turn of the century into the 1930s, often combined single-family and multifamily housing, with the multifamily usually ranged along main streets. At strategic locations, often crossroads, shops or other places of employment were located, along with sometimes small parks, public plazas, or comfortable streetscape environments.

These "traditional neighborhoods" began to reemerge as models to form the basis for reactions to separation of use and density rules that zoning increasingly promoted from the 1920s into the 1970s. Jane Jacobs' 1961 book, *The Life and Death of Great American Cities*, represents a milestone for opposition to the spread of modernist environments. It focused on the destruction of and threats to neighborhoods in dense settings, in New York, and especially her Greenwich Village neighborhood. Her lament called attention to the positive values of the social and cultural content in the older forms, so missing in the modernist urban renewal conceptualizations of her day.

## Current Trends

When we established these kinds of code alternatives in Atlanta from the late 1990s, we called them "quality of life" zoning codes or we incorporated their features into "special public interest" zoning districts. It's often better to use nomenclature that fits into the context of broader community improvement initiatives.

In the 1960s, cities like New York, Chicago, San Francisco, and others began to modify their zoning ordinances to be more conscious of and supportive of achieving forms and mixtures of uses that countered the modernist effects of uniformities. That process has gained momentum, and over the last 15 or so years most cities have begun to modify their ordinances to support at least some modicum of mixed-use and mixed-density development. Now most prominently represented by the new urbanist or traditional neighborhood development movements, as noted in the beginning of this zoning discussion, these modifications increasingly use nomenclature like "smart code" or "form-based code," often projected across a "transect" to describe the densities and diversities of uses from lower to higher.

Growing popular appeal, a kind of nostalgia for real or mythic neighborhoods and districts of yore, and profitability in the marketplace are presently fueling the traditional neighborhood development and new urbanist movements. The current interest in reviewing and in many cases modifying zoning rules is a healthy development. The process itself engages people in shaping their futures. Affirmatively providing for mixed-use, mixed-density, pedestrian- and transit-friendly environments offers a choice different than what many of the longstanding ordinances permit. Perhaps most notably, these kinds of codes can support "smart growth" strategies—the common sense and fairness of development scenarios that offer choices in living and working locations that can reduce travel demand, energy consumption, and air pollution.

Urban designers and community-improvement leaders, either one or both, have played a big and sometimes decisive role in both the pace and the direction of what has become a national zoning reform movement, played out differently in every locality. Probably the most important contributions from the professional side have been to show that design really does matter and that design of the civic environment must be interdisciplinary and must be adopted into the code. From the community side, the growing consciousness that communities can make a difference has fueled a drive for identity, recognition, and improvement whose sophistication and influence is growing rapidly. Together, these two forces for change offer a lot of hope that the civic environment will continue to improve and that the improvements will reflect the culture of the rich variety of places where the movement has taken hold.

# Comprehensive Plans

*"If you don't care where you're going, it doesn't matter what road you take."*
*—words of an A.M.E. preacher*

Reflecting the priority of individual private property rights over community vision, the federal government, as noted above, provided for the regulation of the development of private property through zoning two years before doing the same for comprehensive planning with the enactment of the Standard City Planning Enabling Act. Having some idea about how the community as a whole wanted to see itself in the future, though, was a concept that gained ground quickly. If it made sense for there to be a balancing of community and private values in the development of individual properties, then it made sense to establish some vision about how all these properties and their connective infrastructure were laid out for guiding growth toward realizing that vision.

Typically, the comprehensive plan, which may have a variety of local names, like general plan, master plan, regulating plan, comprehensive development plan, and so on, projects a long-range overall vision for how an area should develop. It covers the whole of a jurisdiction's area and includes all of the elements of its built environment. The core elements usually include land use, transportation, housing, economic development, the environment, public facilities, public safety, parks and recreation, and increasingly, urban design. It suggests how all of these elements affect each other and which of them should proceed in what order in which location to move toward achieving the overall vision. It often includes a public improvements plan that projects costs and funding sources to build prioritized streets, sewers, parks, and other infrastructure that will advance the plan. Policies beyond those directly manifested in the physical place are sometimes included as well, like public education or equity policies.

In practice, advocates for good government and rational process are always trying, with mixed success, to put the policy and the desired direction for future development out front and then apply zoning, subdivision, and capital improvement plans as tools for moving forward in the planned direction. Such plans, however, are often overly general and not quickly responsive to conditions or initiatives that may pop up at any time, some positive, some not, usually reflecting changes in economic strategies or political shifts. Zoning is where the action is. Zoning interacts with real projects, developments that will become visible in a year or two, for better or worse, within the timeframe of election cycles. Accordingly, most jurisdictions that buy into the nexus between a comprehensive plan and zoning as an implementing tool have ways to consider zoning applications more or less at the same time that they are considering amending the plan to accommodate the zoning. Many other jurisdictions in practice may dispense with adherence to the plan as an inconvenient nicety in the face of a zoning proposal that has momentum. Courts, however, are generally much more likely to uphold a jurisdiction's zoning actions if they are carried out in pursuance of an adopted plan.

The idea of planning the city was not new. Notable examples in seventeenth-century America include Savannah, Philadelphia, and New Haven. In 1791, George Washington hired Charles Pierre L'Enfant, a French veteran of the American Revolution, to lay out the future nation's capital on the Potomac. L'Enfant borrowed from French and English formal, monumental models in crafting the framework that became and continues to be Washington. In Chicago, following the Columbian Exposition of 1893, which marked the coming of age of the City Beautiful movement, powerful civic leaders hired George Burnham and Edward Bennett to lay out their plan of "make no small plans" fame. Burnham and Bennett borrowed from French Second Empire ideas of the monumental city to put in place the framework that continues to guide and provide the touchstone for Chicago's development and redevelopment. Another early formal model for thinking forward about a community's opportunities and problems was the privately formed Regional Plan Association centered in New York City. More comprehensive in its scope, its plans and processes are often credited as a milestone in comprehensive planning as well as a source for the provisions of the Standard City Planning Enabling Act.

Like zoning actions, the comprehensive development planning process potentially offers broad access to the citizenry. Different jurisdictions approach this opportunity differently, however. Depending on state law—many states require the adoption and regular update of the plan by jurisdictions over a certain size—and local practice and who's in office, citizens may have anywhere from very significant to next to no influence in shaping the plan for their collective futures. Here again, the duality of community and individual is in play. All jurisdictions must face some balancing between what is more broadly needed and what is more quickly salable. Some tilt toward the idea that "market forces"—usually investors, speculators, and developers with ready access to government processes and resources—should determine their future, while others favor broader representation in setting and enforcing land development priorities.

The comprehensive plan is the place where urban designers and citizen activists must press for the inclusion and articulation of standards for both the quality and the functionality of the civic environment. Such provisions should spell out how streets, sidewalks, and parks define the framework within which urban development occurs, and how development, controlled through zoning and subdivision policy, should engage that framework. Establishing policies aimed at improving the civic environment lays the basis on which ensuing private and public development initiatives can be judged. Dealing with the comprehensive plan is just the first step, but it is a crucial step for improving places.

# Public Improvement Plans

*"Put the public's money where the public's need is greatest."*
*—community activist*

In many jurisdictions, comprehensive plans lay the basis for public improvement plans that both define public project priorities and shape the capital budget. These plans (which may have different names in different jurisdictions) are listings of capital projects, sometimes just listing the jurisdiction's capital funding sources, sometimes listing matching funding sources (like county, state, federal, or private). Here a jurisdiction may develop a fully vetted strategy for prioritizing public-improvement projects in support of implementing the comprehensive plan. The public improvement plan reveals where, how, and when streets, sidewalks, and storm and sanitary sewer facilities get built; which public facilities (like parks, libraries, and schools) will be built or improved; how these priorities stack up against stated policy or new policy initiatives; how public improvements track (or don't) private, district, or neighborhood development strategies. In many jurisdictions this information may be held in different agencies, using different criteria and formats. Occasionally, agencies, unaware of each others' initiatives, may launch projects that conflict with each other. Here in particular community awareness of what your government is doing for you can be helpful in sorting out these kinds of contradictions.

To the extent that the jurisdiction allows this to be an open and equitable process, the public improvement plan can be a way for underserved communities to rebalance in their favor the use of the revenues collected or generated centrally. From the urban designer's perspective it is important to understand how and from what sources infrastructure projects may be funded. From the community perspective it is important to learn how capital improvement projects come to be, to gain a sense of how they may be prioritized and to figure out how project proposals may be influenced. In reality, one quickly finds out that the gap between capital needs and available funding is discouragingly large, and with widespread and growing tax freezes and reductions, the competition among neighborhoods for scant funds can be vicious. In these competitions, those with the best understanding, the most resources, and the strongest commitment—usually the most affluent—are most likely to come out on top.

## Subdivisions

*"But I thought my lot fronted on a street with water and sewer, and I didn't know it was going to be under water half the year."*
*—disgruntled 1921 Florida property owner*

Subdivision regulations arose in the wake of wild and scurrilous land speculation practices dating from the nineteenth century and still a threat in many areas. People thought they were buying a parcel of land to put their house on, or their farm, and found out that the paper they were sold conveyed nothing, or conveyed property that was below water or inaccessible. The sellers got their money and skipped town, the richer for it, and moved on to the next territory. So there had to be a law, again to protect the many from the few.

Subdivision regulations nowadays have their widest application in residential properties, from single-family homes to condos (which have their own covenants, codes, and restrictions in addition), and in the land assembly or disposal process they may apply to commercial or industrial properties as well. Normally, they set forth how and where land can be subdivided, or parceled out for the sale and the construction of whatever kinds of structures are allowed under zoning. The subdivision process usually begins with the requirement for a preliminary plat. This map shows topography, natural features, and how streets will be laid out; where utilities will go; and what easements may be required for public purposes, all in accordance with public works design standards. In addition, the plat shows lot lines with the size of lot and some indication of what part of the lot can be built upon. Once the preliminary plat is approved, the subdivider, usually a developer or home builder, may proceed to the construction of infrastructure, subject to posting a bond that guarantees construction consistent with the jurisdiction's regulations. Before any lots can be conveyed to prospective buyers, the plat needs to be finalized and certified by the appropriate jurisdictional authority, usually the planning commission, and recorded in the tax assessor's office (usually county) so that all can see in clear detail who owns what and what the conditions of that ownership may be.

Subdivision laws have gone a long way to clarify and rationalize the processes of land ownership and exchange, as well to as assure compliance with community-adopted standards for development. Subdivision regulations continue to evolve. The standards that most jurisdictions have been applying may be very destructive of natural resources, may be "overdesigned" in the sense of requiring civil engineering design measures that are unnecessary, inconsistent with broader community design objectives, or just plain outmoded. Such standards, for example, may apply the same roadway and side slope requirements that could accommodate relatively high volumes of 35-mile-per-hour traffic on streets that serve only a few houses, design parameters that neither would nor should happen. Yet their application makes what should be a quiet, walkable, kids-play-in-the-street kind of neighborhood look like a thoroughfare. The one-size-fits-all approach that accounts for most roadway and drainage design is finally beginning to break down and flex up as public works agencies are recognizing more of the values that need to be honored for the prospective subdivision as a whole.

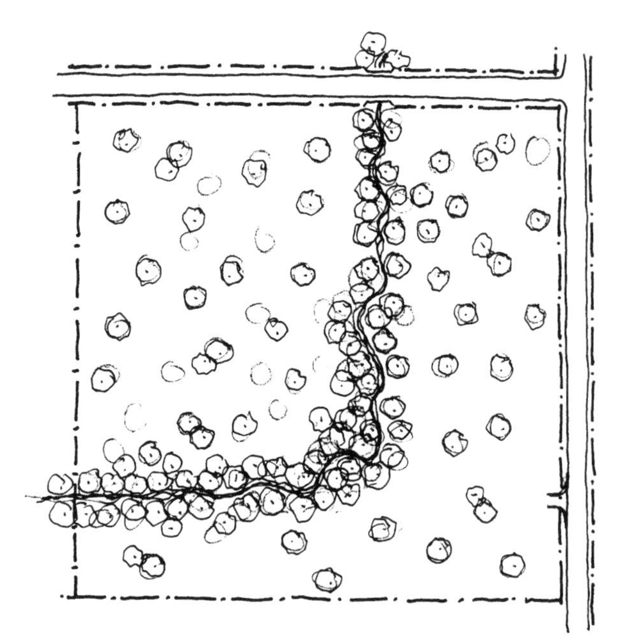

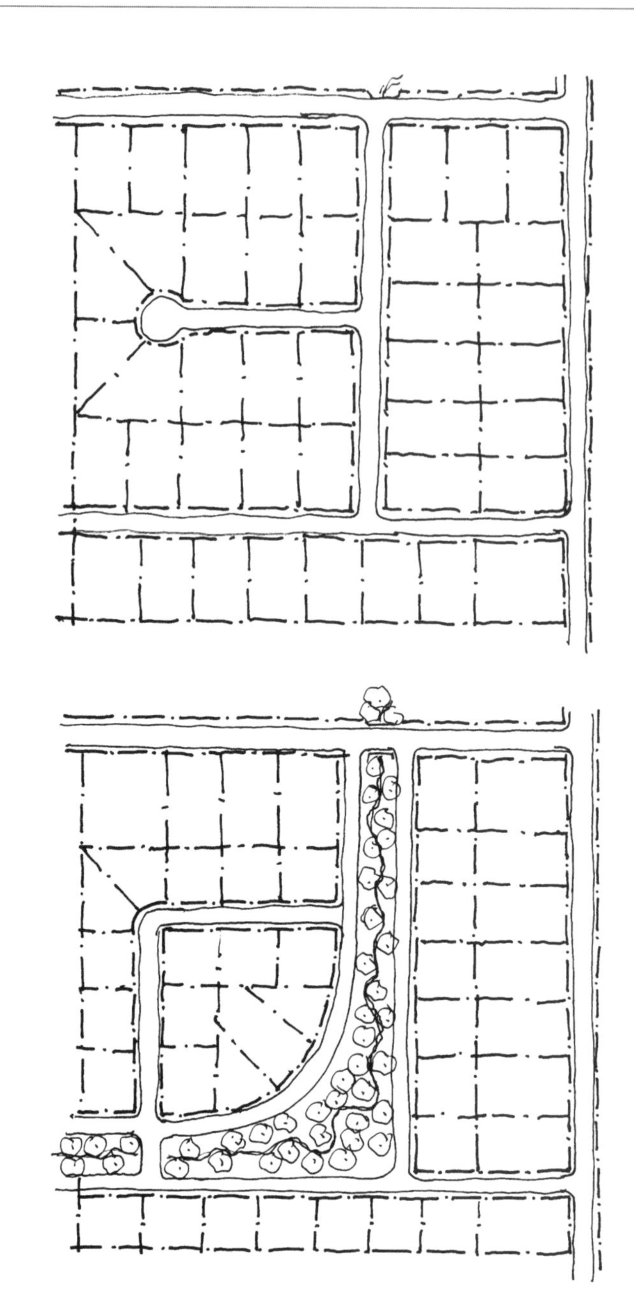

*Figure 9.4a, b, c*
*In many jurisdictions, the standard approach to subdivision design limited itself to maximizing lots within the permitted zoning provisions, in which natural features and their accommodation were trumped by engineering design standards that were narrowly drawn and one-size-fits-all oriented. Here, a typical undeveloped lot is shown (a), a conventional subdivision adheres to minimum lot sizes required by zoning, piping storm water under the street (b), and growing in popularity, a conservation subdivision approach (c), with its roots in planned unit development zoning ordinances, seeks to preserve and accommodate natural features as assets that can reduce environmental impacts and increase aesthetic values, while at the same time maintaining the same density of development overall by making some lots smaller.*

Subdivision design has been primarily the province of civil engineering over the last few decades and so has given short shrift both to the ecological and spatial design expertise of landscape architects and urban designers and to the comprehensive community design expertise of planners. Again, we have another in the long string of examples of the limitations of approaching a holistic urban design problem from the perspective of any single discipline—what the civil engineer knows and does in putting together the subdivision plat is essential, but it's way short of everything that should be considered.

One response to the rigidity of engineering standards has been the proliferation of private streets, and not just in gated communities. Developers trying to create an overall ambience that reduces the impact of the street in the community may seek approval for the streets as public, yet when turned down will build them as private streets, still subject to public works approval but not nearly as restrictive (or as expensive) as for public streets. It is generally not good public policy to allow such practices, since some developers take advantage, both in building streets and sewers that won't stand up over time and in being too casual about informing buyers that they are on the hook for the maintenance of this infrastructure within the project. The end result 10 years or so down the road may be that the project's owners petition the city to take over the streets, with no recourse to the original developer, who's probably a few states over by then.

A better example is the new trend toward integrating disciplines in subdivision design commonly called the "conservation subdivision." Here right-of-way and roadway widths may be narrowed, turn radii tightened, side slope ratios modified, grades steepened, and storm water run-off put in swales or ponds instead of pipes, to name a few features. All of these measures are designed to save values in the natural world, like stands of old growth trees, rock outcroppings, steep slopes, streams, and ponds, which typically have been lost under the standard practices of the last 50 or so years. Often these ventures into more holistic approaches to land development must be accompanied by equally flexible zoning standards. These may take the form of "planned unit developments" or "cluster housing provisions," where densities over the whole of a property may remain the same (or even come with a density bonus) to encourage more sustainable and sensitive results or even to enable or encourage patterns of social interaction among residents.

Urban designers are more involved in subdivision design than they used to be, yet they should press forward to hook up with the civil engineers who dominate and landscape architects who, like urban designers, are trying to broaden the criteria for subdivision practice. The point to apply pressure is generally the planning commission and the local elected officials. Community activists are less involved, since except in multiphased projects, no one lives there during the critical planning period. They get involved later, when they suffer the results.

# Public Works Standards

*"What do you mean, you have to remove that row of 100-year-old oaks to widen the road? We don't have any traffic here!"*
*—community leader to public works field engineer*

Public works codes come in different forms and have different names across jurisdictions, but together they lay down a set of rules every bit as defining of civic space as any of the other codes. Typically, beyond subdivision design which we have just reviewed, they address the design of streets, sidewalks, signs, street lights, traffic signals, sewers, and storm water runoff, and they set the parameters for utility location. In the rush to accommodate the oncoming car as efficiently and safely as possible in the wake of World War II, standards were set in which this accommodation was the dominant driver. Many of the standards were set by the American Association of State Highway and Transportation Officials (AASHTO), as it is presently called. Rules for roadway design, generally put in place for higher volume, higher speed, or suburban or rural environments, dominated many of the key provisions of public works road, drainage, and sidewalk design standards. At the same time, the Manual on Uniform Traffic Control Devices became the bible for signs and signals.

As a result, most public works codes reflect one-size-fits-all standards that prioritize the car and its movements over all other considerations in designing the public right-of-way. If traffic in built-up areas is too fast, if there aren't enough crosswalks for pedestrians, if driveways are too wide, if adjacent topography or tree lines are decimated by road design or widening, if street lights light the roadway but not the sidewalk, if traffic signal housings are all bilious yellow, it is neither an accident nor an intentional assault on community values. It flows from a rational and linear thought process that prioritizes a single problem over all others: Move the car quickly and safely.

At last there is growing philosophical and practical debate about the drift of public works standards since World War II. The Institute of Transportation Engineering (ITE), AASHTO, and many state and city DOTs are questioning whether their old ways are the best or only ways to approach the problem. Transportation and traffic engineering is largely empirically based, and so the straight-ahead, trial-and-error, linear body of information on which so many of these fundamentally place-shaping decisions have been based has not reflected the systematic considerations of researched alternatives. The "how to get it done" questions have eclipsed the "why do it that way in the first place" questions.

Times are changing, though, as the persistent community- and market-driven search for better ways is forcing the transportation and traffic engineering disciplines to reconsider their standards and the bases on which they have been promulgated. Just as with architecture, landscape architecture, and city planning, engineering as an isolated discipline often defies the logic of common sense. Engineering practice often shies away from optimum design solutions for whole systems and instead seeks to optimize only its part. As for all the place-building disciplines and processes, the job is not to discount the design and technological expertise that has built up through the years but rather to incorporate it to serve more integrated and holistic community design and building purposes.

## Land Development Rules at the State and Federal Levels

*"If there's not a federal law and enforcement, it ain't going to happen."*
*—1960s civil rights activist*

While local jurisdictions control most of the rules affecting how places look and function, it is worth mentioning a few of the federally or state-mandated rules that also shape the built environment. Beyond what we have already covered, these may govern to varying extents transportation, environmental protection, and housing and urban development issues, among others. States often have more focused rules in the same categories and are often responsible for enforcing federal regulations as well.

In addition, many states have gone from enabling to requiring local jurisdictions, usually graded by size, to prepare and adopt comprehensive plans. Often this requirement is linked to their eligibility for state or state-controlled federal funding for a variety of capital programs. While more difficult to access for citizen groups, as much for the scale on which the state has to work as by bureaucratic impenetrability, these processes are open to the public and an avenue for exerting influence. Usually there is an agency with statewide planning oversight authority, with its power and effectiveness controlled through the political process, the most important piece of which is the budget. With respect to some kinds of programs and their funding, like federal Community Development Block Grants, smaller jurisdictions may have direct relations to state planning agencies, since the sums involved are too small to warrant locally borne overhead.

The state's willingness to promulgate and enforce provisions for improved growth patterns and environmental stewardship can be a powerful motivator for local government to improve its practices. This works better when the state is more enlightened than local jurisdictions and tends to have the opposite effect when it is the local jurisdiction seeking more progressive directions.

## Transportation

The most powerful form-giving agency at the state level is the Department of Transportation. Out of the state transportation planning process, which typically includes roads, transit, and freight planning and management, flow the priorities and the project funding that reflects the power structure of the moment. Typically, these agencies operate under a politically selected board structure, which often means that their memberships are more likely to reflect politics than any particular technical expertise. The engineers that administer and staff such agencies then use their superior knowledge and experience to advance agendas of the director and top staff leadership through the board approval processes. As long as the political or personal interests of the board members are not terribly compromised, this system has allowed many DOTs to operate relatively freely within traditional power structures. These are heavily influenced by real estate, finance, auto, trucking, petroleum, road-building, and rural political interests, with the weighting of interests varying according to how urbanized the state may be.

In recent years, though, many state DOTs have begun to grow beyond the road-building activities and interests that dominated their origins. Before, even though transportation agencies began changing their names from "Highway Department" to "Department of Transportation" in the late 1960s, for many the changes were in name only and did not reflect any substantive reorientation toward creative and interdisciplinary planning and project-development systems. Even now, not all DOTs understand the linkage between land use and transportation or the choices for how transportation policy and funding priority can interact with economic development strategies. Many remain comfortable in the old wisdom of "if you build the road, people will come." This adage is fine if it doesn't matter what kind or how much or when such development would be beneficial from a statewide perspective. Such an approach fits in well with other narrowly cast and understudied economic development practices, like where and how much taxpayer money to spend to attract or maintain a large corporate job generator.

Even so, the transformation from "highway department" to "department of transportation" represented yet another of the progressive victories for citizen drives for better, more accessible, and more accountable government coming out of the 1960s. Through these reform years, the requirements for vetting transportation programs and projects through a metropolitan planning organization, or MPO, were strengthened, potentially affecting priorities of projects that included federal funding. MPOs began to emerge in the mid-1960s in response to the call in the Federal Aid Highway Act of 1962 for comprehensive, coordinated, and continuous planning (the "3C" process), reflecting the commonsense logic that transportation systems transcended local jurisdictional boundaries. The MPO established that elected officials, agencies, and citizens in adjoining jurisdictions should have a role in coordinating, planning, and approving transportation infrastructure projects and funding. By way of example, in its simplest terms, the MPO sought to put an end to the phenomenon of one jurisdiction through political or economic suasion six-laning a roadway up to its boundary with an adjacent jurisdiction's two-lane continuation of the road. This kind of disjuncture, however, even with better systems planning still pops up from time to time, usually reflecting differentials in political or economic clout, or narrowly focused community resistance to road widening generally.

Newly organized MPOs began by meeting their citizen participation requirements in the most minimal of ways, chary of opening the windows on the often musty processes by which transportation systems—and by extension settlement patterns, however unconsciously—were decided. Requirements that transportation projects (mostly roadways) provide for some minimum public review process as stipulated under the National Environmental Policy Act, adopted in 1969, was a signal shift in processes and practices. Thus the process progressed from the fine print ad in the legal section to public hearings (which tended to favor long-winded citizen activists over others) to public-involvement processes that are more informal and dispersed. These latter sap the ability for citizens to stir up people, but on the other hand they impart more information in less charged ways.

From the urban designers' perspective, familiarity with these organizations and their processes holds the key to the regional or large-scale choices for how and where people will live in the future. Citizens' access to these kinds of decisions find some of their best outlets in the forum of the MPO, often part of regional planning agencies with purposes and duties beyond transportation, where questions like job-housing balance, land use patterns, environmental stewardship, transit priority, suitability of overall infrastructure and economic development strategies can be debated. Decisions made by the MPO over systems futures determine what the regional transportation plan for 25 years out will look like. Closer to real time, transportation funding priorities are usually set through shorter-term transportation improvement programs, decisions that measure the pulse of political and economic power on one hand and on the other, the priority accorded to place-improvement projects like sidewalks, bikeways, medians, or transit shelters at the local level. It is at this scale, too, where design standards may be addressed. The rules that are usually cited to preclude the improvements to the streetscape environment, like trees close to the curb, narrower lanes, and tighter turn radii, for example, flow down from the federal level when federal money figures into a project. Typically too, state DOTs use the federal guidelines for projects that include state funding sources, again with the effect of confounding the desire to create walkable, low-speed streetscape environments.

The most effective influence for countering the usual vested interests, hard though it may be to organize, is citizens who inform themselves of the options and make choices about how, where, and how much they want their region to grow. They can call attention to what changes in the split between car, transit, and other trips it will take to set up a transportation vision and network to support those choices. If holistically oriented city and urban designers and citizens who dedicate themselves to seeing things done better than they have been in the past don't do it, no one will. These changes will not come from within the vested real estate, finance, petroleum, road-building, and car-based interests, nor from government agencies whose appointing authorities are likely to be all too beholden to the financial support of those larger status quo–oriented power brokers.

## Environmental Protection

Most states have environmental protection regulations that mirror those of their federal counterparts. In some cases states establish more detailed or more intensive provisions where the goals of environmental protection warrant them. In addition, states have environmental and health agencies whose reach extends into local jurisdictions for issues the state considers to be of statewide importance.

The National Environmental Policy Act (NEPA) put in place a framework for considering environmental values across a wide range of development activities. These include consideration of such issues as clean air, clean water, brownfields, of habitat protection, and in development activities that receive federal or in some cases state funding. The framework sets up an evaluation system in a checklist format that assesses the potential for environmental degradation associated with various types of development activities. The framework includes a grading system in which activities range from being exempt, to requiring environmental assessment to requiring an environmental impact statement, where each stage may impose more stringent measures for mitigating the proposed activity's impacts on the environment. Meant to be comprehensive and interactive (that is, various checklist provisions interact with others), the framework launched processes that recognized the connectedness of development initiatives to all aspects of the physical environment, consistent with the overall interactivity principle cited in Part Three.

More at the scale of individual developments, rules governing the treatment of wetlands or providing for stream bank buffers continue to provide for lively debate at the federal, state, and local levels. Real estate and development interests generally push for their relaxation so that they can develop more and cheaper, while environmentalists, both citizens and technical experts in agencies charged with environmental duties, push for more stringent provisions.

Looking more closely, for example, at wetlands protection as another of the rules that environmentalism and democratization generated in the 1960s, these rules give communities the opportunity to satisfy themselves that their water quality and ecological values are protected. Any construction that encroaches on a wetland requires approval by the Army Corps of Engineers, commonly referred to as a Section 404 wetland permit. Designers should be aware of the criteria governing this provision and the procedures required for mitigating its effects, usually ranging from "don't do it at all" to "build an equally effective new wetland somewhere else." Within this range, it is possible to positively incorporate the overriding need to protect wetlands as the genesis of so many life forms into design and developments that meet the standard of leaving the place better than it was before. All of this takes time, first to design an acceptable strategy, then to secure the necessary approvals, and finally to get the project built and operating successfully. There are many instances where community action has been essential in redirecting or mitigating the adverse consequences of a development to assure its contribution toward achieving a more satisfying, comprehensive, and sustainable community vision.

The government response to the tug of war between the private project-friendly position and the community benefit position, likely to continue indefinitely, is a direct measure of the balance of influence between private development forces and community-wide safeguards in executive and legislative branches at all levels. As concerns about environmental sustainability mount, one might expect to see the balance tipping toward values that favor community well-being, but without sustained organizing efforts don't count on it.

The playing field that has now allowed the community to field a team is directly attributable to NEPA's stepped-up requirements for citizen participation in development activities conducted within its purview. This reflected the federal government's response to the growing unrest and calls for citizen activism that characterized its era. Once setting a new standard at the federal level, citizens are obliging governments down the line to provide similar access and influence down to the very local level. For the old guard, these developments are a direct threat to the old ways of doing business, both in the public and the private sectors, letting the cat out of the bag in a way. For people motivated to take a more active citizenship role, however, they represent a great leap forward, opening doors to information and processes that were only guessed at before. Much of what was guessed at proved to be more or less accurate as the doors were set ajar.

For urban designers and citizen activists, the provisions of NEPA and other related environmental protection and enhancement legislation, like for transportation, applies to design activities from the scale of the region to the most local places. Looking for new ways to deal with water supply, sewerage and storm water, air quality, brownfield redevelopment, and habitat protection, among others, greatly widens the palette for improving places. Together these kinds of explorations push older paradigms about, for example, whether places "are a part of nature or apart from nature" to new levels of understanding and opportunity, stimulating and supporting what some call "landscape urbanism."

It now appears that sustainability and the environmental responsibility required to attain that goal have become an unstoppable wave. The surge of adoption of green building standards and the rapid advance of green community design, the Bali agreement, the acceptance of the crucial nature of climate change with its associated need to reduce carbon footprints all signal a turning point, every aspect of which has direct, still-evolving design implications. Those trained in design, those who care about what the incipient technologies look like, how they really work from the level of neighborhood to the regional scale, must engage themselves in deliberative processes occurring all over the country. Left to environmental scientists and their technologies, there is no guarantee that responses to environmental challenges might not wreak as much havoc on the social and physical fabric of society as urban renewal did.

## Housing and Urban Development

The combination of road-dominated federal transportation and suburban development housing policies, programs and funding have largely created the settlement patterns for towns and metro areas all across the country.

Road building and car dependence join with lending and tax policies and programs to create a momentum that is far from running its course. It isn't clear that this one-two punch of federal policies intended to produce the patterns it did, since the federal government has largely ducked comprehensive urban policy as a matter of concern or attention since the halcyon days of Calvin Coolidge. Now some of this probable lack of forethought is creating problems at every level, from congestion to the environment, from social stratification to financial sustainability.

On the housing side, easy credit and tax deductions have fueled a great wave of home building and home ownership, a signature characteristic of the American way. It is apparent now, though, that changing demographics and some of the emerging downside aspects of this pattern are mounting a drive for another option. People, at least enough people to make a mark, given the choice are opting for living in more compact communities, closer to work, shopping, and services. These show a tolerance, sometimes even an embrace of diversity in who are their neighbors, in class, age, race, and culture. The idea of mixed-use, mixed-density, mixed-income, mixed-age communities has been around for decades, and after taking a hit from modernist precepts about how people ought to be happy living, has revived as an option and is promoted effectively by advocates for "traditional neighborhoods" or "new urbanism." Federal, state, and local jurisdictions have embraced this revived settlement pattern option unevenly, with some moving to lift the movement to parity with the dominant suburbanizing pattern, many ignoring it, and some discouraging it.

At the federal level, during the Clinton administration and under the leadership of Secretary Andrew Cuomo at the Department of Housing and Urban Development (HUD), for example, the HOPE VI program enabled and encouraged federally supported housing authorities to rebuild their complexes as mixed-income communities. Deconcentration of poverty was a primary goal of this program. The idea was that dispersing the poorest citizens into neighborhoods with federal housing program Section 8 vouchers that promised affordability in alternate housing, coupled with bringing market rate housing into formerly ghettoized compounds, would begin to reconnect people in cities across income and race lines. Cuomo put design of these new facilities on the front burner, and, recognizing that design quality would be critical to attracting middle-income people to the new developments, he embraced the design ideas of architects who were active in creating mixed-use, more compact community development models. While HOPE VI had its detractors, in many cities it was accomplishing what it set out to do until the Bush administration killed it.

However one views the program, though, it clearly made conscious the importance of design in housing models. Other HUD programs, like the longstanding Community Development Block Grant (CDBG) program, have been seeking to direct relatively small amounts of money into propping up or revitalizing lower-income neighborhoods ever since enacted in 1974 under the Nixon administration. In addition, other programs, like support for the provision of shelter for the homeless and Empowerment Zones have represented a modicum of federal support for leveling the playing field between the haves and the have-nots. While mixed in their success rates, at least as much for the wide gap between the needs and the resources provided as for any other reason, these programs have usually done more good than harm.

All of these initiatives, including from the state level in some states, end up creating a physical presence, not just in the provision of any individual housing unit, but for establishing a community character through the treatment of the public realm. In most cases, trained urban designers and supportive community advocates have been missing from the processes that create these environments. Yet, particularly as cities and towns continue in their renaissance, the quality of design, functionality, and connectedness of efforts to improve people's lives and to lower the barriers to full participation in the community as a whole demand design and community support attention.

# Special Purpose Rules

*"If there's not a rule, we'd better make one up."*
*—beleaguered bureaucrat*

The above rules have pervasive and fundamental impacts on how the built environment looks and works. There are other rules, however, that may have significant impacts as well, but are targeted to limited situations or to specific districts in the world we experience. These include codes designed to protect or advance special interests or design review provisions that supplement the blunt instrument of zoning with a finer grain and more subtle guidance for places of special community concern.

## Historic Preservation

Historic preservation codes, which may be distinct or incorporated into zoning ordinances, are directed at preservation of districts whose historic character represents clear and commonly held values for the larger community. Rules are put in place to safeguard such areas against the threat of out-of-character new development. Initially, the historic preservation movement had a distinct class bias to it—preservation of the buildings, neighborhoods, and culture of the upper classes as valued messages in the preservation of the hierarchy of community structure. Over the last couple of decades, however, many lower-income and minority communities have embraced the movement as values of pride of origin and social structure with their physical manifestations extend the enduring cultural values of history to those often forgotten in the past.

Another prime source for the rapid rise and spread of the historic preservation movement was the alarm caused by many of the modernist plans and practices that were wiping out historic community fabric. Historic preservation codes are usually directed at the "look" of the neighborhood or district and sometimes its social or political significance. They restrict the size, shape, architectural detail, materials, and often colors to assure that what is new or added meets standards of complementarity. The baseline reference for the application of such codes is national, stemming from the National Historic Preservation Act of 1966, which placed enforcement in the Interior Department. The ruling document is the Secretary of the Interior's Standards for the Treatment of Historic Properties, and the state structure to assure compliance is typically housed in the State Historic Preservation Office, or SHPO.

Historic preservation codes have obvious and not-so-obvious implications for both urban designers and neighborhoods and districts. For designers working in historic areas, comfort with moving forward with complementary, or in the terms of art in the interior secretary's Standards, "contemporary compatible" design, represents an important value to maintain. More broadly though, historic preservation symbolizes the pride and cultural meaning not just of neighborhoods that are old but of people asserting the right and the priority of knowing how they want their places to look and insisting that these values be respected.

## Design Guidelines and Design Review

Often in conjunction with historic preservation, zoning codes, design guidelines, or private homeowner associations and sometimes related to revitalization programs, people call for design review processes to ensure that what is intended for the improvement of the physical place is actually achieved. Usually there is a committee of some sort that reviews proposals in the designated area for their consistency with design guidelines set up to contribute to and be compatible with the values that the jurisdiction or community has established. The features of these kinds of rules can range from quite general to remarkably particular. Design review processes can cover all of the baseline provisions of the zoning ordinance, which themselves cannot be weakened, and they may add more detail, like scale relationships to other nearby buildings, materials, percentage of window to solid along façade walls, treatment of parking and loading, sidewalk, lighting, landscaping provisions, and the like.

In going beyond the generally accepted provisions of zoning or even historic preservation, design review regulations, procedures and approval authorities raise the hackles of many property owners and architects, eliciting such characterizations as "taste police" and "design Nazis." Indeed, there is the risk of overzealous or even personalized application of these rules; and urban designers, who generally favor the more particularized, finer grain–shaping that design review affords, and citizen leaders must be on guard against the reach for power that can corrupt any in authority. Effective design review processes depend on well-crafted, clear, and consistent guidelines that derive their legal authority from umbrella zoning provisions so that they will be defensible if challenged in a court of law. The positive side of design review processes is their ability to work with collections of buildings in detail sufficient to ensure that the quality of the desired civic space is improved through design measures that are usually sensible and easy to achieve.

## Signs

Many jurisdictions have sign codes, again either in the zoning ordinance or freestanding or both. Community sentiment for improving the appearance of their main travel ways and district often drive the establishment of sign codes, although governments have been known to take the lead as well. Signs along the commercial strip, often blocking out neighboring signs, compounded by overhead utility lines, present a scene of chaos and confusion that often confounds the purpose of the signs' presence in the first place—that is, to announce the presence of a business or a product. Because of their generating purpose, their composite effect is to make the most heavily trafficked travel ways, where the city should look its best, instead look the worst.

But the sign industry is always in the top five of slathering money around at the local, state, and federal level, lobbying incessantly to protect their interests, sanctimoniously invoking their right of free speech to force their presence into the public way, and thus very effectively preventing regulations that would establish better-functioning and more attractive corridors and districts. Generally, the industry falls into two more or less equally cacophonous subsets: the outdoor advertising industry and the business sign industry. The outdoor people pursue their interests with special zeal, taking advantage of their right (except in Vermont and Hawaii) to profit from expropriating public air space to impose whatever message will pay them the most to do so. Periodically, in the effort to tout themselves as good citizens, the industry will display messages that do communicate information of community value, like warning against teen pregnancy or promoting United Way. These tax-deductible messages usually manage to get positive stories in the local media, another prong in the strategy to protect this most profitable enterprise. As a relative handful of national or regional corporations, the outdoor industry puts itself into a singular position to win its way.

Opposition forces speaking on behalf of larger community values at the local level are not paid, not well-organized, and busy with their lives and a myriad of other civic issues and so not often effective in combating the assault. The industry can deploy its forces to meet local-level challenges with massive force, using campaign contributions, intensive lobbying, or sometimes even seduction to protect and advance their interests.

The other wing of the industry, the on-premise or business sign people, are much more localized and so as an industry lack the ability to bring laser focus and wads of instant cash to arm their efforts. In addition, as for the most part local businesses are eager to be part of the trends for civic improvement, they usually are much more understanding and supportive of sign pollution clean-up efforts. In most cases holistically conceived sign ordinances actually improve rather than harm their business. This happens through upgrading the economic climate conveyed by a community that cares and looks like it, and it reestablishes information as the base purpose through well-ordered and rationally located sign structures and messages. Indeed, a well-thought-out sign strategy can make urban places lively and vibrant, from the neighborhood corner to the central business district. Typically, business signs are controlled as provisions of the zoning ordinance, with restrictions more or less tailored to the character of the commercial district or strip in which they are located. Perhaps the most predictable area of possible conflict is in the area of rooftop signs or signs that penetrate above the roof plane. Here the "look at me-ness" of business can't resist the impulse to sing it from the rooftops, regardless of how that assertion might affect the look and the cohesiveness of the skyline as a whole.

From a regulatory point of view, these two classes of signs are often classified as "on-premise" and "off-premise," where the first identify businesses located on the lot or block and the second hawk products to the general public. The outdoor industry usually flashes large corporations or businesses, like airlines, cars, casinos, or attractions in the next town, on big signs along the freeway and messages touting liquor and payday loans on smaller signs along streets in lower-income neighborhoods. Jurisdictions usually have some success with the spacing, sizing, and height of these signs as well as the kinds of zoning districts in which they may be located, but any effort to restrict any of the provisions beyond what presently exists is always met with virulent and usually successful resistance from the industry—even in small towns. There's probably a reasonably profitable way to provide useful information along the roadway, but with their concentrated power, high profits, and widely strewn lobbying money it is not likely that the industry would step up to look for better ways.

Signs and their incorporation in the civic environment are often pivotal in conveying the values of a community. As with utility lines, signs can obliterate in a heartbeat the positive contributions the best designed building façades, sidewalks, street furniture, trees, lights, and landscape. The point is not to get rid of signs, but simply to incorporate them in a properly balanced way with the other values that the community wants to advance, usually focusing on their informational values, sometimes their graphics, only rarely (as in Times Square) their dominance.

## Overhead Utilities

Overhead utilities join with signs, zoning, and public works or highway design codes to create the typical experience along any highly traveled collector or arterial street. Of the three, utilities are the hardest for the public—or the developer, for that matter—to deal with. In most jurisdictions, utility companies are is the least accessible through public processes, the most technically inflexible, and altogether the most resistant to considering their piece of the civic environment as part of a more important whole. They wrap their status and posture in the sanctimony of their two-pronged purpose: deliver the service and maximize return on their shareholders' investment. The power of their position is hard to engage, since in fact urban life as we know it does depend on their service. Yet there are ways to safeguard the exigencies of provision of that service and still improve their presence in the public environment; and figuring out a way to gain their partnership is essential for this outcome.

The electric utility is usually the big player in the overhead utility game in urban areas, with telephone and cable or other providers piggybacking onto their infrastructure of poles for their separate transmission and distribution lines. The electric utility sets its standards for pole locations, spacing, height, and structures, as well as mounting and separation requirements for lines of various voltages. The other pole line users, with much lower-voltage transmissions, then negotiate where and how their lines can be accommodated. In addition, the electric utility locates substations for breaking down higher-voltage transmissions into lower distribution lines and transformers for local service.

Typically the electric utility has the power of eminent domain for locating its infrastructure, and typically its oversight body is a state-level public utilities commission, usually an elective body. At long intervals, local governments have a crack at the problem through the franchise agreements that allow the utilities to do their thing in the public's right-of-way. These moments usually provide the best entrée for influence over their policies and practices. The cable and other communications utilities are typically less accountable to public oversight, partly the result of the deregulation binge accelerated in the Reagan administration.

## Environmental Rules

Aside from federal and state environmental rules and subdivision codes, there are often locally enacted environmental protection codes, usually focusing on preservation of one or another of a community's environmental assets. Tree protection ordinances exist in many jurisdictions to restrict clear-cutting, or sometimes any cutting outside the buildable area of a lot, usually with provisions for penalties or payment into a tree-replanting fund. These ordinances may also set forth provisions applicable to tree cutting and trimming in the public way. A typical goal for such ordinances, for example, is to ensure no net loss of trees as a policy under which the regulations are promulgated and enforced.

Local jurisdictions may also strengthen state or federal laws, for example, to increase stream bank buffers, to divert storm water runoff, to use reflective or green roofs to reduce the heat island effect, to further restrict dumping or disposal of toxic or polluting materials into the storm water system, to limit disturbance of valuable ecological assets, or to protect visual assets or viewsheds. For stream bank buffers, for example, the rules may stipulate minimum distances from the edge that must be maintained for construction. For storm water management, the rules may require minimum open space or permeable surface areas or stipulate materials that must be used to prevent water quality degradation. All of these and others join with the larger and growing framework for environmental protection rules to have a direct bearing on the design of the community and its civic spaces. For the most part, these represent design opportunities more than design problems for urban designers, and heightened consciousness among community leaders affords another tack from which to improve proposed development initiatives in their communities.

## Other Rules of Note

There are other special interest rules, like those for schools and parks, that directly affect the shape, character, and functionality of places. Most states, for example, mandate local school boards to follow standards setting minimum acreages for schools at different grade levels and for different sizes. The effect of these codes is to make it all but impossible to build new public schools in town or city centers or in already built-up areas that are now gaining back population or increasing their densities. Perhaps without intending to do so, these standards represent another bit of social policy that pushes new development into greenfields, where land is cheaper because of its undeveloped and low-density condition, which, however, virtually ensures that the only way for kids to get to such schools is in cars or school buses.

Park standards-setting organizations, too, while usually not carrying any particular legislative mandate, tend to set standards for park sizes and accoutrements based on acreages for different levels of populations served (for example, neighborhood, community, and city or regional), in which size is cast as the main target to be reached in park planning. In fact, recent research (along with common sense) suggests that having a park nearby, even a small park or play spot, is more important than having a bigger park that one has to drive to get to. And in our era of safety concerns, parks that are more linear than blob-shaped are more likely to both seem and be safer, following Jane Jacobs's "eyes on the street" criterion. And reinforcing that concept, parks generally should be bounded by public streets, both to clearly delineate public from private and to ensure their visibility. People looking out for their children, for example, don't have to penetrate deep forests or scale tall hills in order to see what's going on—at best the eyes can see right through the park to the other side.

The conceptual problem with these standards, as with most that end up shaping the places we live in, is that they have been abstractly formulated and indiscriminately applied, usually with no serious vetting process against the realities of people's behavior or preferences or within the context of real physical circumstances or more comprehensive policy goals.

## Federal Special Purpose Rules

Another pervasive shaper of the everyday environment that comes from the federal government is the Americans with Disabilities Act (ADA), enacted in 1990. Yet another in the series of citizen-driven movements to level the playing field for all Americans, the ADA, among other provisions, has significantly altered how access to public facilities must be provided.

The ADA has a significant impact on the design of private structures as well, but these tend to not have such a pervasive shaping effect on the civic realm.

The ubiquitous wheelchair ramps provided for any new sidewalk as well as retrofits of older ones, the handicap spot nearest the door at every parking lot, the ramp alternative for access for public structures or parks, the numbers of buildings, parks, and places that have abandoned multi-level design concepts or dispensed with raised first floors are all familiar examples of how fully the ADA has directed the shaping of choices and options for how to design. Providing compliant access, whether for new or retrofitted facilities, comes at a cost—both in terms of dollars and design options, yet, like most rules, there are ways to turn these into tools for improving places for everyone.

Provisions of the federal Title VI of the Civil Rights Act may provide parameters for how many regional policies are formulated and carried out. Practices that discriminate against minority neighborhoods, like bank or insurance redlining, or discriminatory zoning practices, or financing practices that disproportionately favor higher-income areas over lower-income ones, or the siting of noxious facilities (like landfills) in minority, lower-income neighborhoods (reaction to which led to the environmental justice movement), or structuring regional governance bodies like MPOs in a way in which minority populations are not fairly represented can all be causes of action against the offending authority.

Finally, as in federal environmental legislation and its effects on place design, over the horizon may come too legislation creating community design rules safeguarding public health. Professionals and citizens more and more frequently are raising concerns over physical factors that threaten community health, like the lack of sidewalks to connect people to parks or shops or transit or kids to schools or libraries, or development practices that separate people from their support services and amenities or from the natural or social world. Since there may be a lot of overlap between environmental and human health rules affecting the civic environment, it is important to try to systematically synthesize the two to ensure that they do not put forth duplicative or, worse, conflicting provisions. Already in Britain, and at the threshold in a few American cities, momentum is building to require health impact analyses of development initiatives, where it is not clear whether people are considering their provision in the context of other codes that already exist.

# Building and Life Safety Codes

For the most part, building and life safety codes are directed at buildings or practices in which there is a clear health and safety purpose. Building

As told to me by Norman Koplon, longtime chief building official for the City of Atlanta, a milestone in the return of atrium space occurred in the 1960s when architect John Portman sought approval for a grand atrium for the downtown Hyatt Hotel. Working with the building and fire departments and national fire protection professionals, Portman demonstrated that pressurizing enclosed stairwells prevented the potential chimney effect of an atrium fire from compromising the safety of the stairwell as an escape route. He did this by setting a controlled burn in an older building he owned and planned to destroy anyway that had a sufficiently high atrium to prove his hypothesis. This event predated the rise of historic preservationism, and so there was no outcry. The Hyatt with its grand atrium is now approaching the age necessary for its designation as a national historic landmark.

codes, fire protection codes, and health codes are examples. Yet these codes may have a direct bearing on the quality of civic spaces resulting from their requirements. The requirement for at least two code-compliant stairways from buildings got rid of fire escapes, once distinctive features along streetscapes in older cities, which themselves weren't required until people trapped in single-exit buildings died in fires. Requirements for spacing new buildings a distance away from adjacent buildings the walls of which have window penetrations affects the character of the street wall, not to mention the access to light, air, and some kind of view for inhabitants of the older building. Interior lobby space options dramatically improved when it was determined, after a 40-year or so ban under fire protection codes, that it was okay to have multistory atrium-style lobbies, provided that the exit stairs were sealed and pressurized so that smoke could not chimney up them. The idea of building lobbies as distinguished public spaces, prominent in the early 1900s, returned as a tool that among others of their attributes dramatically improves the palette of tools for mediating the seam between public and private, the flow of outdoors to indoors.

Most fire protection codes address building design, ingress, and egress, like accounting for the demise of old-time fire escapes. Yet the fire-fighting community may have a profound effect on public works codes, for example, dramatically affecting such key community-shaping elements as roadway widths, turn radii, and cul-de-sac dimensions. A general practice is to defer to the dimensions of the fire truck (or sometimes the garbage truck) in setting these standards. While civil engineers and fire protection professionals may reach agreement on what these should be, overall community design may suffer if others in the design and development disciplines are not involved in the process. Without more holistic consideration, the relationships of car and service vehicle measurements to those conducive for social and civic environments may be out of whack.

Health codes, too, affect how the urban built environment looks and works. Perhaps the most familiar example is outdoor dining or dining in the public right-of-way. Many local health codes discourage or prohibit serving food outside along or in the public right-of-way, where flies might be flying or roaches scurrying or birds dropping. Liquor service is even more problematic, usually controlled through liquor licensing laws and usually a real problem in the public right-of-way. While these potentially health- or morals-compromising issues are a concern, many jurisdictions have altered the rules to permit such activities—legally (it's one of those areas where the charm of outdoor dining has not always waited on permission to be implemented—easier to get forgiveness than permission).

# Financing Rules

Beyond routine, tax-based funding sources for public infrastructure or other civic improvement projects, local governments may have access to other funding that may be available to assist projects deemed to be in the public interest, usually in support of revitalization of blighted or disinvested areas or lower-income neighborhoods or affordable housing. The sources of these funds may be local, state, or federal, and they may be used to leverage each other for private or foundation funding. Common examples are Community Development Block Grants (CDBG), HOPE VI funds, or other HUD program funds for public housing redevelopment, housing rehab, housing for people with AIDS, or homeless shelters. There may be tax increment financing bonds available for certain projects, a source of capital funds that depends on the proposed development generating sufficient increases in property taxes in a designated area over time to pay off the bonds. There may be vehicles to provide financing through municipally constituted development authorities that may offer financing at municipal bond rates. There may be community improvement district funding available, financing where property owners and businesses agree to tax themselves beyond what the jurisdiction requires to be able to carry out improvements or manage programs in their common interest.

Understanding something of how private finance works is likewise essential for crafting realistic proposals in terms of feasibility, priority, and staging. Private finance and the internal rules governing its underwriting criteria have discouraged projects that mix uses, densities, and cost structures, although that picture is beginning to change as markets for such projects are clearly on the rise.

Lenders instead have tended to be as specialized in their activities as design disciplines are in theirs. A residential lender looks at deals that are purely residential, an office building lender the same, and so with retail and other single-use projects. When compounded with the single-use mandates of many zoning ordinances, the ability to plan, design, and develop places that respond to the growing market demand for more diverse places understandably can be quite difficult. As both public jurisdictions and lenders see political and market demand for providing these kinds of choices in living and working environments, one can only hope that both will be expeditious in providing the flexibility and support necessary to do so.

Christopher Leinberger wrote a piece for *Urban Land* in the fall of 2003 titled "Financing Mixed Use Development," which detailed the fragmentation in the lending industry as a significant obstacle facing policy makers or developers who want to make mixed-use development work.

Private lending also may be affected by the Community Reinvestment Act of 1977, put in place to discourage redlining, the pattern among many lending institutions and insurance companies to resist advancing credit or offering equitably priced insurance in lower-income, often minority, areas. The CRA is overseen by the Federal Reserve and other federal banking regulatory agencies and obligates some portion of a commercial lending portfolio to be invested in historically low-income, disinvested neighborhoods and districts, an opportunity for better serving the need for better places where resources remain scarce.

# Summary

We have grazed our ways through a field of rules that directly shape the nature, character, functionality, and attractiveness of our daily world. It is important to remember that community concern generates many of the rules, academic research some as well, and occasionally government or the private sector takes the lead. These kinds of rule-making initiatives may be disjointed, sometimes inconsistent with other municipal policies, difficult to administer, or even contrary to the best interests of the jurisdiction as a whole. Community-generated code initiatives, a growing phenomenon, tend to reflect the desire to fix something that's not working, preserve values that are threatened, or otherwise contribute to the quality of life and place. In most cases I am familiar with, they do more good than harm. Government code initiatives generally stem from response to community agitation or budgetary constraints, or to provide smoother, more efficient operations. Private sector initiatives are invariably put forward to either enhance the chance or prevent the erosion of some profit-making venture, usually without regard to broader community impact—at least until they hit the political process.

Urban designers should pay close attention to the community-driven aspirations that lead to rules whose intent is to make their places better. At the same time, urban design professionals and citizen leaders should always be on the lookout for ways to synthesize these efforts into more comprehensive and complementary rule sets. They should be wary of the rapid increase in marketing sophistication used to sell development projects. Many of the very techniques that can elicit community guidance and coalesce unifying visions in positive ways can be used to trick people to support rules or rule changes that may not be in their interest. The advances of digital imaging and community involvement processes, especially Internet communication, may be real assists along the path of community improvement, or they may be seductive devices for gaining approval for predetermined outcomes benefiting narrow interests.

As with so many of the urban design and community design issues, knowing that there are processes and how to gain access to them, and being sufficiently organized to persist in seeking better ways and better outcomes is far more important than being an "expert" in any one aspect of the process. Knowing how to get past the first level of questions, knowing how to persist in the face of private interests or even bureaucrats hiding behind niceties of terminology to hide information are skills that both urban designers and community leaders must develop if real community improvement is to occur. Finally, one must develop an attitude about rules that acknowledges their essential nature while at the same time developing strategies to convert them from restraints to enablers—rules to tools, the subject of the next chapter.

# 10

# TOOLS

## Using the Right Tool Makes the Job Easier

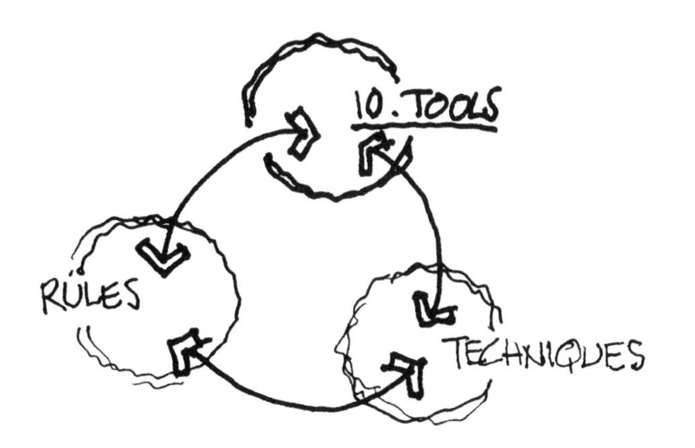


*Figure 10.1*
*Diagram of* tools *in the context of* rules *and* techniques.

# Introduction

*"Without the proper tools, it's hard to build."*
*"Use of tools distinguishes humans from other species."*

In the course of making places better, just like for any other building project, getting the job done means knowing what the right tools are and how to use them. This chapter describes many of these tools, why they're important and how urban designers and community leaders can find them and use them. It places the tools into their interactive context with the rules and techniques that together infuse successful place-improvement strategies. It describes process tools that are available to assist communities, private sector, and government participants in coming together to understand and envision a better future and to agree on travel paths toward that goal. It describes ways to transform rules, which will always exist, into tools that may improve their application to better serve civic and urban design purposes.

This chapter reflects my experience with virtually all of the suggested, distilled, and synopsized tools as a representation of what it takes to get civic improvements done. In this sense, it is one person's take on how to get stuff done and so is open-ended and flexible, inviting the experience of others to enrich the palette. It builds on the material covered thus far on content and principles, and it leads toward the last chapter, which describes the strategies that must be engaged to make positive change actually happen.

# Process Tools and Resources

*"Is that how it's done?"*

We have established that rules determine what the civic environment looks like and how it works. We have suggested that among the forces that build this environment—developers, local governments, and communities—many desire to change these codes to produce better results, or at least to enable choices beyond what practices over the last 50 years have produced. Now it is worth discussing some of the organizational and technical tools available for moving that transformation along. What kinds of organizational and institutional support systems exist? What has been the progression of the growing emphasis on creating better places to live and work in? What's going on now and where do trends point? What tools are available to assist community leaders and urban design professionals to succeed in the process of overall civic improvement endeavor? This chapter provides an overview of the answers to these kinds of questions.

The run-up to the present interest in civic quality and related code reform activity began when design-trained individuals in the 1960s began to wake up first to the power of zoning and then to the opportunities of others of the key planning and design rules for shaping places. In New York, San Francisco, and Chicago, people with architectural design training, knowledge, and experience started showing up in municipal agencies, tantalized by the opportunity either of applying their design skills to the larger scale that urban design represents or of meeting the needs of larger populations than just the normal single-client model of practice.

Over the years, other jurisdictions have been bringing urban designers on staff to work on the whole spectrum of the improvement of the civic environment, in which reconsideration of codes' purposes and effects has been a central focus. Similarly, private sector practitioners, mostly coming from architecture or landscape architecture backgrounds, have been stepping up their venture into "urban design" as a field willing to explore the seams between the various place-building disciplines.

## Urban Design and Citizen-Guided Visioning Processes

To begin with, consciousness of the need for integrating government, the private sector, and the community into an integrated place-based, problem-analysis and problem-solving structure began its big leap forward in the mid-1960s. One response to the need came from a handful of architects who organized a way to address the place-design aspects of the integration. As described in Chapter 1, they established the Regional/Urban Design Assistance Team (R/UDAT) program, housed at the American Institute of Architects (AIA). Their purpose was to assist local jurisdictions in sorting out the planning, design, and development issues to achieve a consensual vision and action priorities. The idea was to put a team of people knowledgeable of the kinds of issues faced by the community on the ground for a short, intense charrette exercise with the goal of producing a report that encapsulated the community's goals and the team's knowledge and experience into a vision that the community could then act on.

They recognized that their local area clients needed to create an organizational structure to guide the R/UDAT and that in advance of the team visit this steering committee had to be well organized, committed, able to share all the relevant base information, and inclusive and representative of all the local interests. They recognized that architects were not the sole font of knowledge necessary to deal with complex urban spatial—and occasionally societal—problems. And so, depending on the nature of the inviting community's problem definition, they scrupulously formed teams drawn from transportation engineers, planners, economists, sociologists, public officials, academics, developers, environmentalists, landscape architects, or others of the place-building disciplines.

With a solid base of well-organized and inclusive local leadership and a team of professionals with diverse skills, the R/UDAT event is ready to take place. The event, a charrette, is a five-day intensive immersion of all parties into the locally identified problem. The team, often assisted by students from the nearest architecture (or landscape architecture or planning) school, goes through the process. Over the five days, it takes oral testimony from any citizens or groups who want to speak; collects, synthesizes, and analyzes information; checks out the analysis with the local steering committee, public agencies, and the public; conceptualizes alternative scenarios for how the future might go down; and then produces, publishes, and presents its findings on the fifth day. (Then they rest, both on the sixth and seventh days.) Many of these efforts have produced the basis in consensual vision and practical actions that jurisdictions large and small have adapted to local practices, adopted, and implemented.

An even older program, the Urban Land Institute's (ULI) panel advisory, has similarities with the R/UDAT program, but most panel advisories begin a little downstream from R/UDATs. They start with the impetus and the premise that a local area's problem is a development problem, leading inevitably to a development solution. After all, the ULI is made up of

In the Urban Design Group in New York City Planning Department, beginning in 1967, we found our way to using zoning to shape both formal and functional improvements to the continuous churning of the city's development. Among many other applications of these tools, we reestablished the importance of the street wall on the east side of Broadway in the Lincoln Square district (countering the anti-urban plaza bonus installed in the 1961 zoning ordinance); we provided density bonuses for building theaters in the theater district at a time when Broadway theaters were being demolished for higher-density, higher-return development; and we established a Planned Unit Development ordinance to encourage environmentally responsible subdivision practices in the outer boroughs.

AIA's R/UDAT website is http://www.aia.org/liv_rudat.

ULI's panel advisory website is http://www.uli.org

developers. The make-up of panel advisory team members is accordingly more developer- and designer–weighted and less sociological, public official, and community represented. Nonetheless the basic format and structure of the two programs, centering on a well-informed and prepared charrette process, have provided the framework for more and more consultant teams and local governments to adapt as ways to focus on a particular problem or opportunity and to get a jump start on what to do about it.

Among the growing number of private consultants who offer this approach as a service, Urban Design Associates was among the first. Their founder, David Lewis, a regular participant in R/UDATs and enthusiastic supporter of the AIA's Regional and Urban Design Committee, experienced firsthand the value of the R/UDAT approach and realized that it could be valuable to both public and private clients seeking to flesh out an overall approach to a planning, design, or development problem.

It should be noted that there were other place-based initiatives underway during the 1960s that sought improvements for the local community as well. Some of these, like the Model Cities initiative or the Architects Renewal Committee of Harlem, or ARCH, led by Richard Hatch, were ongoing efforts at building and sustaining grassroots empowerment, mostly in lower-income and minority communities. Like the advocacy planning of Paul Davidoff or the focused community organizing of Saul Alinsky, though, these efforts sought to build capacity from within the community, focused on economic and community-development priorities more than on the character and functionality of the civic environment. These initiatives' suspicion of "the establishment," however well-grounded, led them away from an inclusive approach to community improvement. Yet these efforts clearly laid the basis for sustained community-directed improvement strategies in general, and their passion accounts in some ways for the general drive toward citizen empowerment that persists and grows. It is probably no accident that some involved in the R/UDAT program later on were also adherents of Architects, Designers, and Planners for Social Responsibility (ADPSR) or Architecture for Humanity, people who are concerned about the social consequences of city-development strategies.

ARCH may have been the first "community design center." It formed in 1963 and was dedicated to offering architectural and planning services to help community residents revitalize their neighborhoods. Many of the architects and planners involved in ARCH were largely influenced by Paul Davidoff's work, "Advocacy and Pluralism in Planning." Max Bond Jr., architect of the King Center in Atlanta and the Civil Rights Institute in Birmingham, was one of ARCH's founders. The Community Design Center movement grew during the 1960s and into the 1970s, times when the AIA supported both the initiative and the architects dedicated to community improvement. The AIA phased out its support in the late 1970s.

Organizing around the inequities of resources available among neighborhoods and classes spawned a number of sustaining community-driven efforts to improve the civic environment. As referenced in Chapter 1, Bridge Housing is one of California's leading affordable housing development partners, which decided in 1983 that building was more important than studying or advocating for affordability. Since then it has developed over 13,000 homes in the San Francisco Bay area. The Association of Community Organizations for Reform Now, or ACORN, is the United States' largest umbrella organization for low- to moderate-income groups working together for social justice, for which affordable housing is a longstanding priority. In addition, other organizations with nationally relevant information, particularly focusing on neighborhood issues, are Neighborhoods, USA, and the National Association of Neighborhoods. One that is not so much involved in spatial issues but worth being aware of, especially if food prices and availability continue to be an issue, is the Food Research and Action Center. And in a similar vein, Bioneers is an activist organization that annually brings together transdisciplinary teams to explore innovative possibilities for joining environmental sustainability with social equity.

These different responses to the drive for broader representation in civic-improvement strategies charged up and supported the development of more community-driven approaches. The idea of bringing diverse people together to share ideas, experience, and aspirations to improve their places was not occurring in a vacuum. Consciousness-raising groups that trace to the 1950s and 1960s in the civil rights, women's, and anti-war movements, or therapy groups dealing with social or psychological concerns, or even focus groups figuring out how to market products or politicians, all shared in various ways and for diverse purposes these community-involvement features. All recognized that people together are a source of energy, a collection of knowledge and experience that is hard to replicate in theoretical models. This was at once an advance for broadening the influence of citizens and, conversely, an advance for figuring out how to manipulate people. The establishment and dissemination of cross-disciplinary and broadly representative structures for managing the change and growth of civic places had begun.

Later, in the 1970s, the National Trust for Historic Preservation (NTHP), interested in averting the rampant destruction of older towns' and neighborhoods' main shopping streets, launched a different kind of place-improvement strategy. The retooling of America for the car, suburbanization, and disdain for anything old under the tenets of modernism combined to eviscerate older centers, relocating businesses out to surrounding suburban strips. The National Trust Main Street Center program, organized and led for many years by Mary Means, put a national face on the values of old town centers and brought national resources to bear to deal with their problems. The program features a four-point approach as a comprehensive and tailored strategy to address all of a commercial district's needs, focusing on design, economic restructuring, promotion, and organization. Behind this approach are eight guiding principles: a comprehensive approach, incremental changes, self-help, partnerships, identifying and capitalizing on existing assets, design quality, change, and implementation. Seed funding was sometimes provided to pay for a coordinator for a period of time, but local area funding is essential and pivotal in successful programs, of which over the years there have been many hundreds across the country.

Main Street coordinators might come to their positions from a variety of backgrounds—planning, marketing, business administration, historic preservation, architecture, sociology, and so on—but through the integration of the disciplines necessary to do their jobs, they became de facto urban designers. The program, like the R/UDAT and panel advisory programs, has had widespread success in communities across the country, in consensus building, visioning, designing, and setting in motion preservation, rehabilitation, and compatible new development initiatives that have markedly improved the civic environment.

The early forays into community- or district-based planning generated many creative spin-offs, adding new tools and techniques to work at levels and scales for which few tools—and little interest—had existed before. Chad Floyd, along with Charles Moore and others who founded Centerbrook Architects, conducted a call-in local access video visioning program for Roanoke, Virginia, in 1974, where callers could identify their ideas of all kinds for community improvement. Floyd and his staff would busily draw up their understanding of the input and display it back over the TV screen to see if they got it right.

Another approach to injecting better quality and functionality into the civic environment is the Mayors' institute on City Design. Lacking any community-involvement process, this approach assumes the mayor's position as the highest elected official in local government is a reasonable proxy for community sentiment. The brain child of Mayor Joseph Riley of Charleston, South Carolina, the institute started operation in 1986, with technical assistance from Jaquelin Robertson, then dean of architecture at the University of Virginia, and Jonathan Barnett, colleagues from the New

---

Probably the best way to contact ADPSR is the website http://www.forum@adpsr.org. Architecture for Humanity's website is: http://www.ArchitectureforHumanity.org Bridge's website is http://www.bridgehousing.com/. ACORN's website is http://www.acorn.org. Neighborhoods, USA's website is http://www.nusa.org. National Association of Neighborhoods' website is http://www.nanworld.org. Food Research and Action Center's website is http://www.frac.org. Bioneers' website is http://bioneers.org.

---

The website for the National Trust's Main Street Center program is http://www.mainstreet.org.

In the same timeframe, Baltimore and Birmingham at the local government level were putting together commercial revitalization programs that shared many of the characteristics of the Main Street program. In Birmingham, our program was geared more toward revitalization than preservation, yet the design guidelines that the city administered reflected historic values. Its four key components included generating a consensual vision or plan for revitalization, both for the civic environment and organizationally; building the community, business, political, and marketing support necessary to function as a unified entity (like a shopping center under single ownership can); coming up with detailed plans of action for how to induce and require businesses and property owners to rehab structures to common design standards; and identifying, designing, budgeting, and gaining public support and approval for public improvements necessary to connect and reinforce the vitality and viability of the business district.

York City Urban Design Group days. Mayor Riley's insight was the fact that during their terms of office mayors are cities' de facto chief urban designers. They hold the reins of power, are in the middle of about every issue facing the city, have either the bully pulpit or executive authority, face any number of crucial physical development decisions in the course of a term or two, and might benefit from advice of "experts" from a range of relevant disciplines. The National Endowment of the Arts liked the idea and has provided all or some of the program's funding ever since, presently co-funded by the U.S. Conference of Mayors and the AIA-affiliated Architecture Foundation.

Here, the format is different, providing direct support to the mayor to work through the implications for the civic environment of various choices in making decisions about a key current physical design problem that his or her jurisdiction is or will soon be facing. This program is explicitly not inclusive, discouraging or even barring the mayor from bringing any staff or planning director on the grounds that such a presence could limit the range of possibilities considered. The technical panel members, serving pro bono like for the R/UDATs and panel advisories, act more like advisers to the king than facilitators of consensual visioning. They focus on the problem with each other, the mayor and fellow mayors in the program, and hopefully impart some useful wisdom and guidance to arm the mayor to both understand the design implications of the alternatives and to do the right thing.

It works like this: The program selects and invites the mayors. Mayors are busy people and getting three days off to focus on a single problem is not always easy. So mayors tend to self-select based on whether the urban form purpose of the retreat is a priority, usually a judgment made both on the technical and the political merits, as well as scheduling availability. In short, the mayor has to want to participate. A typical institute has six to eight mayors. A national institute, usually pitched to larger cities, occurs annually, often at the University of Virginia in Charlottesville. Typically, institutes for regional or smaller cities occur annually at other geographically distributed universities, like The University of California–Berkeley, Tulane, Georgia Tech, University of Minnesota, MIT, or other campuses.

The mayor and his staff identify the problem or opportunity that they would like the institute to consider, and they prepare background information to communicate the situation to the team and to their fellow mayors. The institute staff culls this material into a briefing book that can be shared in advance so that all parties will show up prepared. The mayors arrive at the university on the evening of day one, and have a nice banquet, orientation, and inspirational speech (Mayor Riley delivers a good one).

The next morning the institute leader presents the purpose and overview of the session. Then, technical team members and mayors alternate presenting information about the problems to be dealt with, the technical resource speaking from precedents and experience, and the mayor speaking specifically to the problem facing his or her city. The institute tries to group cities sharing problems along a loosely defined common theme. The discussion is focused on each mayor's issue, so that each has about an hour and a half to two hours of direct and interactive feedback from the technical team members and their fellow mayors.

These go on for two days and into the third, with everyone departing in the afternoon. Like charrettes in the sense of being an intense immersion for a short period of time, institutes have the value of an interactive exchange of high-level information, but they lack and indeed are not interested in community-driven consensual outcomes. Having worked for two mayors who have participated and having participated in several as a resource team member, I find the institutes to have been quite successful. They inculcate mayors with the consciousness that design matters, and they underscore the realities of getting things done for practitioners, who may learn more than the mayors do. They stretch both the understanding and the consequences of what's possible. In many cases they have assisted mayors in finding a clear path for exercising leadership that makes for a more positive outcome on the real-time issue than would have happened otherwise.

Still another model to consider for place-improvement strategies is that represented most effectively by the Project for Public Spaces (PPS). Inspired by sociologist William "Holly" Whyte and founded in 1975 by Fred Kent and with a cross section of professionals from all the relevant disciplines, PPS has been offering place-making technical assistance that has mounting successes all over the country and now internationally as well.

Project for Public Spaces is a nonprofit organization—this status distinguishes it from most practitioners in this field, which are for-profits—that seeks to help people create and sustain public spaces that build communities. The organization began a place-making movement built around nurturing people's health, happiness, and well-being. The program areas of focus have included parks, transportation, civic centers, public markets, downtowns, mixed-use developments, campuses, squares, and waterfronts. Its expertise is interdisciplinary, including environmental design, architecture, urban planning, urban geography, environmental psychology, landscape architecture, arts administration, and information management. Its recent activities increasingly recognize the importance of community-driven processes and ideas as holding the key to successful civic-improvement outcomes.

For urban designers, the various community charrette models, the Mayors' Institute, and the PPS approaches are right down the alley of professional development. To begin with, the nature of the problems always includes visual and functional dimensions, invariably cutting across all disciplines. Then, members of the technical team are likely already to have been identified as people with transdisciplinary interests and experience, and so everyone comes with a sense of achieving a shared result, not the affirmation of any one team member's personal vision or perspective. Indeed, there have been teams where an ego problem crops up, and these naturally are not successful—in fact "me-first" team members have been known to have been sent home. In the charrette models, the interaction among team members, local leaders, and activists—whose make-up is similarly cross-disciplinary—and the community at large is highly stimulating. The likelihood of viewing problems differently than any team member might have before is high. So, skills can advance quickly, ideas can be tested in real time against a fair proxy for the interactions that happen back home, and the taste for improving places as a necessarily comprehensive effort is heightened.

Unlike in Great Britain and Europe, where urban design has a wider and older critical history, journals dedicated to the subject in the United States have been limited. *Places,* a journal spearheaded by architect Donlyn Lyndon, has dedicated itself to tracing the evolution of urban design and the progress in creating places for people. The journal consistently reports on trends, successes, and processes that professionals are engaged in across

Like David Lewis, many of the members of the AIA's Regional and Urban Design Committee, with their links and experience to the R/UDAT program, developed variants on the R/UDAT. Grey Plosser, a Birmingham architect, with others set up a state-based R/UDAT-like program in Alabama and led district-based programs like one for downtown Atlanta that was called a D/UDAT. Jim Vaseff carried similar visioning ideas and processes to smaller towns all over Georgia as a program of Georgia Power to refocus communities on their historic cores (and sell more electricity). Ball State University's architecture program, in what came to be known as the "community-based projects" program, took the show on the road, buying and outfitting a Winnebago with drawing and mapping equipment and setting it up on main streets in smaller towns all over Indiana, so that town leaders and ordinary citizens could engage in a community-improvement dialogue and see their ideas mapped and sketched right there on Main Street.

The website for the Mayors' Institute on City Design is http://www.micd.org.

Richard Arrington Jr. Birmingham mayor at the time, brought the myriad issues around his resolve to go forward with the Civil Rights Institute as part of the Civil Rights District as the problem for the Mayors' Institute to consider. While he and I were returning to Birmingham, he hit upon a theme that guided him—and me—through the political, cultural, organizational, financial, and technical thickets in the way of realizing the project.

The park space around which the district would continue to be built, with the Civil Rights Institute as a major frontage addition, carried the historic name of Kelley Ingram, to memorialize the first Birmingham casualty of World War I, a white man. The park, however, was also the foreground of the Sixteenth Street Baptist Church, where four little girls had lost their lives in 1963, in one of a series of church bombings that tipped national outrage in favor of the passage of a succession of civil rights laws. The park was also the battleground of a succession of civil rights demonstrations in the early 1960s, repeatedly turned back by water cannons and police dogs. A lot of people in the community, not surprisingly, thought the park's name should be changed.

Arrington, however, having been able to focus his attention on the matter at the institute (a special value of the institute, since mayors rarely have the time necessary to focus on the rush of issues that face them daily) came to a different route. He would keep the Kelley Ingram name, but he would prominently subtitle it "Place of Revolution and Reconciliation." This conceptualization, and the guidance it provided to all involved, began to transcend the nasty polarities that had for so long defined Birmingham and helped to smooth the way for the Civil Rights Institute's construction and the complementary improvements to

the spectrum of disciplines necessary to create places. Lacking the support base of any professional organization, *Places* has been a testimony to the perseverance of a few cross-disciplinary theorists and practitioners who know that places matter. Recently it has expanded from its historic home at UC Berkeley and Pratt Institute to engage other campuses' architecture programs, like Georgia Tech, MIT, the University of Miami, the University of Michigan, the University of Maryland, and the University of Washington, tapping the resources from these institutions that can help the cause along. A newer effort in the United States is the *Journal of Urbanism*, housed at Arizona State University and published by Routledge, which also covers urban design issues.

The recognition side of urban design remains pretty slim. Still, most of the single-disciplinary professional associations have established award programs that recognize urban design achievement. The ULI established an urban design student competition, largely underwritten by developer Gerald Hines, that requires student teams of no more than five representing no less than three different academic fields to compete. The competition project is a large-scale urban design and development problem that requires a range of disciplines to come together to solve. The site and program is made known to the competitors ten days before the final project is due. It has been a great assist to those of us in academia who try to underscore the vital nature of cross-disciplinary collaboration. One of the earliest organizations to recognize the importance of urban-oriented programs and projects is the Bruner Foundation, whose Rudy Bruner Award for Urban Excellence gives major awards every other year to a fascinating cross section of urban improvement initiatives.

Countless iterations of these processes, initiated from different professional bases, have pointed in one general direction. Most of the results have validated Jane Jacobs's notions about what it takes to make places successful—that is, compact, mixed-use, walkable, legible neighborhoods and districts where the quality of the civic environment is decisive in attracting people and meeting civic needs. In so doing, this body of experience generally rejects the modernist precepts that so dominated urban policy and practice from the 1920s into the 1980s. From the perspective of this book, the placement of people as the judge of the quality and functionality of places rises above any particular formalistic tendency that may make places more people-friendly.

## Emerging Organizational Tools to Support Civic Improvement

Among other constructive responses to the growing interest in the rediscovery of old urbanist ideas was the formation of the Congress of New Urbanism (CNU) in 1993. Launched mainly by architects with larger-than-building-scale design experience and interests, the CNU has emerged as more diverse than most design-centered professional organizations. Over its brief life as an advocacy organization for new urbanist principles, it has recognized the essential interdisciplinary nature of civic design. It has added to its architectural core landscape architecture, city planning, transportation, economic development, environmental sustainability, and other place-building disciplines.

While tending toward the propensity among architects who venture into urbanism—not unlike the modernist architects—to want to tell people how they should want to live and other professions how they should practice, the CNU is nonetheless making a useful and significant contribution. The focus on interdisciplinary collaboration, the consideration of the public realm as a whole, the importance of design quality in making successful civic environments are all testimony to the advances the movement has made. If the CNU movement doesn't listen carefully to different potential constituencies, though, it risks—and in some ways already is—becoming a style, a product, or a commodity instead of a set of process tools that people can use flexibly to improve their communities. In short, "new urbanism" is no more a one-size-fits-all answer for improving the civic environment than is modernism. It would be a shame if attitude compromises the organization's ability to listen and, finally, to genuinely commit itself to the principles and practices of inclusiveness on which the success of places in the civic environment depends. This evolution in attitude is important if the organization wants to tap the widespread community and market malaise that is pushing for positive alternatives to the modernist legacies of urban renewal and sprawl.

As it stands, though, its conventions, its members, its energy, and its publications, like *New Urban News*, provide a wide-ranging palette of tools, techniques, and precedents for community-improvement work, particularly directed at carrying out its principles, which project a strong, mainly formalist design position. As we shall see, too, the new urbanist movement has aggressively adopted code reform as a central priority.

In approximately the same timeframe that CNU was forming and organizing itself, the Urban Land Institute (ULI) was reinventing itself as a leader in studying, understanding, and promulgating to its membership the merits of smart growth. This movement, which was the heir to "growth management" as a growth-shaping strategy, depends on holistic approaches to development, from the project to the region, and aims at environmentally sustainable practices and the structuring of government policy guidance and funding to produce better results. The State of Maryland under the governorship of Parris Glendenning came closest to asserting government leadership to advance smart growth, and other states have moved in this direction as well.

From a ULI perspective, smart growth as a process is akin to what developers have to do at the project level anyway, and extending the thinking to the district, city, or regional level from a technical process point of view is not too much of a stretch. To get projects done, developers must synthesize a range of disciplines, gain approvals from government, and gain financing from investors. The same skills apply to understanding and implementing smart growth strategies, and many members were already beginning to focus on urban opportunities, wanting to get out in front of emerging markets for alternatives to the suburban patterns that had been such a meal ticket for so many years.

Under the leadership of its board and its chief executive, Rick Rosan (also an alumnus of New York City's Urban Design Group), the ULI has moved rapidly to adapt itself to ideas of sustainable development, green building, mixed use, and mixed density, with even some acknowledgment of the need for mixed-income development. On the one hand this seems like a huge swing for an organization that represents a development community more known for following rather than leading design and marketing trends. On the other, however, developers are the only ones (except for an occasional public official) among those responsible for actually

the park and the district as a whole. It was a great advance for the choice of "both-and" over "either-or" thinking, a great advance for projecting a synthesis for a trenchant polarity that moved the issue to a new and in this case a healing level.

---

The website for Project for Public Spaces is http://www.pps.org.

---

The website for *Places* is http://www.places_journal.org.
The contact for the *Journal of Urbanism* is journalofurbanism@asu.edu.
The website for the Rudy Bruner Award is http://www.brunerfoundation.org.

---

The website for the Congress of New Urbanism is http://www.cnu.org.

---

The *New Urban News* website is http://www.newurbannews.com.

building places who must put the full range of disciplines together to get the job done. Developers must deal with real estate, finance, codes, architects, engineers, landscape architects (on a good day), approval processes, contractors, marketers, and property managers—in short, the full range that none of the others involved in the process have to deal with. Through their very practice, then, doing what it takes to get a project built, developers experience firsthand and daily the inefficiencies, the cross-purposes, and the contradictions that make their life difficult (and threaten their profits). Nirvana for a developer is to hire one outfit to do the full cross section of work that goes into a typical development project and then go to one place to get all the approvals necessary to build it.

Beyond its panel advisories, the ULI puts out a continuous stream of technical reports that tap the theory and practice of its multidisciplinary membership; its journal, *Urban Land*, covers many place-building activities, usually from the developer perspective; and the organization is active in disseminating information and providing technical assistance in a number of its larger metro markets.

There is value in both of these two organizational initiatives, CNU and ULI, and indeed there is a good amount of cross-membership. At this point it would appear that the ULI approach, while perhaps less focused on the civic environment, may have more impact. The ULI, after all, is the home for the people who are predominately responsible for building buildings and places.

And they among all of the organizations whose memberships are involved in place building are the most integrated in their make-up, stemming from the reality that to develop something, you have to bring all the relevant disciplines together in order to orchestrate a program that produces buildings on the ground that make money. And developers seem to be moving rapidly toward the notion that the quality of the environment in which they build directly affects their success, in terms of profit, long-term gain, and ultimately, satisfaction.

The National Association of Homebuilders is home for those who build single-family and low-density residential development, and the Association of General Contractors is the membership organization for most commercial builders. While these organizations are picking up rapidly on the new trends, particularly in the area of "green" building practices, neither is in the forefront of conceptualizing how to build a better public environment.

Private practitioners for whom urban design services are a central offering have been growing and proliferating so that virtually all metro areas have competent consultants to contribute to improved visioning and urban design strategies. The business card ads of private practitioners that list urban design as a service have multiplied in trade journals of all the place-design disciplines, from just a few to dozens over the last several years.

The design of places, where design and holistic, integrative approaches are fundamental, is getting more attention in the conventions, journals, and participation from other professional organizations as well. The Institute for Urban Design, formed in 1979 by Ann Ferebee, continues to maintain a presence in the urban design dialogue. The American Planning Association (APA) has had for several years an Urban Design committee (presently it has a separate "new urbanism" committee!) and regularly features place design and community process articles in its journal *Planning*. The AIA, with its longstanding Regional and Urban Design Committee and its Communities by Design program, presently the home for the R/UDAT and SDAT programs, has a sustaining (though not very large) constituency of members who are dedicated to improving the public realm. The Institute of Transportation Engineers (ITE) has recently collaborated with CNU to produce a manual of standards for improving the quality of the civic environment, titled *Context Sensitive Solutions in Designing*

*Major Urban Thoroughfares for Walkable Communities: An ITE Proposed Recommended Practice*, a title that says it all. The American Society of Landscape Architects (ASLA), the American Public Works Association (APWA), and the American Society of Civil Engineers (ASCE) are among the venerable organizations whose agendas have begun to include place and urban design (though not so much about community process).

Beyond being directly involved with the design of places at the walking-around or district scale, there are a number organizations and agencies that address urban design at the scale from town to state to nation. Usually associated with some aspect of the smart growth movement, these include the Environmental Protection Agency's smart growth program, which awards grants to analyze, promulgate, and support smart growth initiatives, and at least one national nongovernmental umbrella organization, Smart Growth America. Since transit—for many, *rail* transit—is so closely associated with and interactive with effective smart growth concepts, there are a number of transit-centered organizations representing the integrated transportation aspect of the movement. These include the American Public Transit Association (APTA), the Surface Transportation Policy Project (STPP), Reconnecting America, and Rail-Volution, among others.

Foundations and other nonprofits have been picking up the call as well. Partners for Livable Communities, PlaceMatters, International Making Cities Livable, the Seaside Institute, and New Partners for Smart Growth have for years been convening people from the range of disciplines that make places to probe the intersection of people and disciplines that can improve the civic environment. The Lincoln Institute of Land Policy is a research organization that studies the dynamics of land policy applications comprehensively. The Local Government Commission, the brainchild of Judith Corbett, while California-based and focused, generates much that has applicability for place improvements at all scales around the country.

More tilted to the people side of the equation, the Orton Family Foundation, the Annie E. Casey Foundation, and the Wallace Foundation have been seeking ways to step up community involvement and build grassroots capacity to improve places where people live. The AFL-CIO has added to their community development interests the Partnership for Working Families, whose emphasis is on the places where working people live and how to improve them.

In addition, there are numerous organizations at state and local levels forming around these kinds of issues, from the specifics of place design to regional growth strategies. In the 1990s, for example, the Georgia Conservancy decided that it made more sense for them to pursue their goal of environmental preservation by figuring out what it took to foster sustainable communities and to develop and support best practices instead of simply opposing anything that threatened the environment. Its leadership became highly skilled at eliciting responses from the widest range of interests that was civil, mutually informing, and leading to the Conservancy's goal. They established a program called "Blueprints for Better Communities," which paired their staff; their partners, representing all the disciplines in the place-building business; and academic planning and architecture programs, to assist neighborhoods and communities to develop actionable visions. As a participant in these efforts, earlier as a public official and now as a teacher, I have been struck by the organization's commitment to ensuring the community's leading role and the support they provide to make that so. The Conservancy's website is http://www.gaconservancy.org. Other Atlanta

The website for the Institute for Urban Design is http://www.instituteforurbandesign.org.
The website for the American Planning Association is http://www.apa.org.
The website for the Institute of Transportation Engineers is http://www.ite.org.
The website for the American Society of Landscape Architects is http://www.asla.org.
The website for the American Public Works Association is http://www.apwa.net.
The website for the American Society of Civil Engineers is http://www.asce.org.

The website for the EPA program is http://www.epa.gov/livablecommunities.
The website for Smart Growth America is http://www.smartgrowthamerica.org.
The website for APTA is http://www.apta.com.
The website for STPP is http://www.transit.org.
The website for Reconnecting America is http://www.reconnectingamerica.org.
The website for Rail-Volution is http://www.railvolution.com.

organizations focusing on one or another part of the city's infrastructure include PEDS, a pedestrian advocacy group; the PATH Foundation, builder of greenway trails for walkers, joggers, and bikers; and Trees Atlanta, which has installed thousands of trees around the city. All of these have been very effective both in advocating for the inclusion of their interest in ongoing development, and in literally building and maintaining the infrastructure to which they are committed.

The website for Partners for Livable Communities is http://www.livable.com.
The website for PlaceMatters is http://www.placematters.org.
The contact for Making Cities Livable is Suzanne.Lennard@LivableCities.org.
The website for the Seaside Institute is http://seasideinstitute.org.
The website for New Partners for Smart Growth is http://www.newpartners.org/.
The website for the Lincoln Institute of Land Policy is http://www.lincolninst.edu.
The contact for the Local Government Commission is info@lgc.org.

## Current Practices

One tool that has continued as particularly effective from the R/UDAT and panel advisory and their successor approaches has been the charrette. This brings people together in one place and fosters and promotes interaction among participants with varying agendas and different skills and experience. The tool has value at the small scale, for private development initiatives, as well as for large-scale community applications. There is now a national nonprofit that advises on charrette techniques and options, The Charrette Institute. Private consultant teams often start their processes for dealing with new assignments by pulling together the key team members and outside resources to brainstorm their way into the project, a half day, full day, sometimes two or more day process, depending on the complexity and commitment to the project. In some cases, firms may set up role-playing exercises as a way of teasing out the perspectives of the range of likely participants in a community improvement initiative.

The website for the Orton Family Foundation is http://www.orton.org.
The website for the Annie E. Casey Foundation is http://www.aecf.org.
The website for the Wallace Foundation is http://www.wallacefoundation.org.
The website for the Partnership for Working Families is http://www.communitybenefits.org.

On the public side, the practice of grouping people around tables of 8 or 10 people, either self-selecting or matched for diversity, to talk, listen, draw, and write their ideas developmentally, table by table, has become almost standard. This basic format can either support a short, intense charrette or a more measured process, conducted over three, four, or more sessions with time in between for the participants and the technical staff to absorb and reflect the input in subsequent meetings.

Such sessions usually begin by convening the participating group as a whole to present baseline information and perhaps to carry out a visual preference survey. This survey typically selects images analogous to those that characterize the area under study, in which studiedly "good" and "bad" examples are shown and the participants asked to react to them. It gives the convener a sense of who makes up the audience and some sense of their place consciousness and proclivities. Then the group divides into separate tables, with maps, tracing paper, and markers or Lego®-type blocks, and is set by the conveners and their consulting team. They lay out the range and scope of the problem as they understand it and ask for participants to identify assets and challenges in the area under study—its opportunities. Typically, they arrange the issues under three or four different categories in which may be grouped transportation, land use, urban design character, the environment, properties' susceptibility to change, and housing and economic development problems or opportunities.

The website for the Charrette Institute is http://www.charretteinstitute.org.

This is the kind of program in which everyone with an interest should be able to participate. Everybody has places they like and places they don't like, places they want to go to, not just for whatever functional need might be provided, but for the character and workability of the place. Is it easy to get to and get around in? Do the people there satisfy practical business needs or the human need for interaction and connectedness? Is it comfortable, pleasant to look at? Do you feel welcome? Indeed, through countless workshop and charrette-type exercises in recent years around the country, place by place, when shown images of typical places it is remarkable how much consensus there appears to be around what people like and don't like in their developed places and why.

In these sessions, people are usually given the opportunity to simply identify what they particularly like or don't like in the course of the exercises, often reinforcing the visual preference survey, perhaps prompting their memories with aerial photo wall maps and street level images on which they can mark their subjective feelings.

Subsequent meetings present back findings from the earlier ones to the group. Typically the meetings flow sequentially, presenting updated base information, findings from the analysis process, and possibilities for combining the issues into alternative development scenarios, and then making recommendations based on a consensually determined common vision. Visual preference surveys may be used as the focus and detail of the effort sharpen. GIS and imaging software provide bases on which to track, modify, and portray the work in process.

In this way groups from 20 or 30 all the way up to 150 or 200, dealing with discrete neighborhoods or their centers and downtown or pieces of downtown, have a pretty good shot at quickly building up their base of knowledge and understanding, learning as much from each other as from the orchestrators of the charrette or workshop process. In these exercises, it is good to keep the time focus on any one topic fairly short, like 30 to 45 minutes for each of four or so topics, introducing breaks so that people can refresh and recharge themselves, but disciplining the length of breaks so that the momentum and intensity of the table sessions is maintained.

It is good to hold such efforts in spaces where there is some visual access to the area being studied so that people can either look out or go outside to add the reality of the place to their input and feedback. In a typical exercise of this sort, it is important for the participants, the convener, and the consultant team to all be open to each other's input—each brings information the other doesn't have, and a genuine visioning effort needs to be open and flexible enough to entertain new ideas from all. Trust in the process and trust built among parties whose interests may be divergent is critical for this kind of openness and respect to flow toward the most positive outcome. Application of virtually all of the principles suggested in this book—relating to change, design, and organization—come into play in putting together and following up on this kind of visioning exercise to ensure its success.

For community leaders, whether representing residential neighborhoods or mixed use or business districts, the experience is likely to be highly stimulating and rewarding. People not involved in any of the city design disciplines are likely to find nonetheless that their observations about their places and their hunches about what to do about them overlap considerably with what the "experts" say. This overlap merges the experts' knowledge with citizens' day-to-day experience of the place as a whole place, an experience that necessarily integrates all aspects of its content and application of commonsense judgments about what works and what could work better.

Paralleling the development of more inclusive techniques and practices, technologies able to support these more inclusive and richer processes have been developing and expanding rapidly. The sequence from public access cable television, to computerized information systems,

---

Role playing, incidentally, is also especially useful in classroom settings. In teaching a class in the city planning program at Columbia in 1970 in the heady months following the Columbia strike, I set up roles by lot for students to contemplate a large-scale development initiative proposed for across the East River from Manhattan. The student who was most stridently anti-establishment in an energized classroom setting happened to draw the role of developer. It turned out that he was able to persuade the others, most of them initially in oppositional roles, to support his project with minimum conditions.

---

Urban design practitioner Anton Nelessen actually trademarked the phrase "visual preference survey" to stake his proprietary claim to the process of showing people pictures of common urban or suburban scenes and recording their responses on an immediate reaction, like–don't like scale. Since then—and before then—the technique has been used in various formats to elicit citizen feedback on choices that might be made to improve places. We discuss this in Chapter 11, Techniques.

Akin to these kinds of efforts, through the years as a public official, I often made use of the old technology of the overhead projector to flash maps and then mark on them what people thought were key issues and ideas across various subject areas. This provided a way to assure them that I was listening; related information to a geographic base so that all could put themselves in the picture; and provided a way to get at needs, aspirations, and priorities for community improvement. My wife, an activist, termed this technique "putting a pencil in the hands of the people."

I have had students who, stimulated by this kind of experience, decided to quit their "real" job and take up urban design, planning, or architecture, after becoming directly and intensely involved in their neighborhood. They were sure that working on the community and its improvement was more interesting, stimulating, and challenging than whatever they were doing before (though likely less remunerative).

The website for the Center for Neighborhood Technology is http://www.cnt.org.
The website for the DataCenter is http://www.datacenter.org.
The website for the UCLA neighborhood knowledge sites are, for Los Angeles, http://www.nkla.ucla.edu, and for California, http://www.nkca.ucla.edu.

to breakthroughs in mapping, like geographic information systems, to visualization software, like Google SketchUp, and now blogs and cell phones with visual capabilities have geometrically expanded information access and the graphic means to portray it legibly to anyone interested, not just in the formally convened sessions but remotely. Such digitally aided processes continue to expand and deepen, and such programs as the Center for Neighborhood Technology in Chicago, the DataCenter in Oakland, or the UCLA-originated community knowledge network tools are working to put the information at the disposal of the full spectrum of citizenry, piercing through information sumps that until recently were simply not accessible.

For all the advances in techniques for engaging the public more effectively, the old model still abounds. That is, clients at all levels—private, public and institutional—continue to commission planning and urban design and planning studies to guide them without any particular interest in or commitment to hearing what the affected public might think. This approach to securing planning, design, and predevelopment technical support remains the dominant model and is probably appropriate for many projects or for new developments. If the project affects broad community interests, however, there should be a process for assessing and if necessary mitigating its impacts.

In the Atlanta region, for example, projects over a certain size, whether or not they require NEPA reviews, require review under what is called a Development of Regional Impact requirement imposed from the state level. Many other jurisdictions have similar review requirements. Even if the review thresholds are not reached (and developers have been known to phase their projects to avoid this review), community acceptance is becoming an increasingly important factor since its lack can portend a rocky approval process. Neighborhood or district organizing can improve projects so conceived should they threaten or undercut neighborhood or district values, particularly if they require prebuilding permit approvals and the legislative body is attentive to the community voice. Projects that are conceived in the context of a larger neighborhood or district planning and urban design framework, on the other hand, can gain support for whatever approvals may be needed.

Both neighborhoods and business districts have benefited from charrette-type visioning processes. Their use has multiplied over the last few years, reflecting both their efficacy and the rise of place-based advocacy. Business district organizations in particular have been able to discover and project their strengths to attract the growing markets for mixed-use and walkable civic environments where design quality is so important. These district-driven efforts usually have the advantage of being better funded and more focused than most neighborhood-driven efforts, and their constituencies usually include scions of the larger community, accustomed to access to the political and economic structures that hold the reins of power. Even so, these organizations have found that broadening their base and including a wider range of interests in their strategizing can be effective in consolidating the support necessary to support their core agenda.

For all their potential for democratizing and enriching the visioning process, a word of caution to community leaders is in order about these charrette-type visioning processes. If the effort is initiated by someone outside the community, either a developer or local government (or sometimes both), there is a good chance that the initiators have a good idea about where they want to come out before they launch the process. They may be seeking input or feedback to a plan that is already in motion, and they may use the charrette-type process as a way of getting over on the community in the guise of seeking that feedback. In this model, increasingly prevalent as project sponsors see how happy a community might be to be invited to participate, the developer or local government may be very selective about how the process is framed, emphasizing known-to-be-popular assets of a proposal and obscuring any information that might lead away from a positive outcome. The sponsors may even be a little prickly and nonresponsive if a community member happens on a weak point—an indicator of true motives. They may try to pick up on a few ideas, make a few tweaks that don't compromise their first purpose, and show the community how responsive they've been. Then they walk away with the prize, their approvals—the price to be paid later by the duped community. This pattern, of course, is not unlike the old days of developers doing what they had to do to get the project approved, community-be-damned in the result. Conceding the appearance or "sense" of participation may be just as cynical and no more community responsive than older patterns—old agenda, new style.

And know thy urban designer. People gravitating toward urban design careers share common understandings of what is involved, yet they tend to fall into two broad camps, reflecting the dialectic that is intrinsic to the field. They either work in the private sector, or they are oriented toward public or academic settings. The former typically work as consultants for clients, both private and government, while the latter are usually government employees or teachers. This split in emphasis and motivation is likely to cause a split in attitude.

The private consultant, like all enterprise, must make a profit, a reality that obliges consultants to streamline or minimize process or to cushion themselves with fees adequate to accommodate the big unknown of how much time and iteration is involved in an urban design visioning and approval process. This in no way means that great competence is not to be had in private sector urban design consultants, whose very private organizational structure allows them to reward that competence in ways that are not available to government employees.

Public sector urban designers, on the other hand, are usually motivated primarily by the hope of a steadily improving environment for all in their jurisdiction. Their measure is the services necessary to achieve that outcome, not the profit that may be derived from it. They recognize process in and of itself as essential to positive outcomes, yet the budget and priority necessary to achieve the best outcome is a constant challenge. Inadequate municipal budgets, impatience or disinterest on the part of the elected officials, and pushiness on the part of project-driven developers are among their principal threats. Both as private consultants and as government officials, however, urban design–trained people have become central to the effort to improve the civic environment.

The other side of the coin for community leadership, though, is to remember that getting stuff built in the neighborhood, like it or not, depends on developers and private sector investment. That is where most of the money and most of the actual skills and experience to build things is lodged. A public program might be able to catalyze or jump-start a new development trend, but a market where profitability for the developer

I suggest to my students early in their careers that they consider following a zigzag pattern between three career poles: government, private sector, and academic or nonprofit. That is, work first in one sector and then in another and then maybe back again. This approach not only holds the advantages of understanding the various perspectives and value sets, but also may be a path to career advancement. When one's career path looks to be slowing, the skills and knowledge developed in one sector may actually provide a boost over a comparably placed practitioner in another—and vice versa—not unlike attorneys who flip back and forth between the three sectors.

and his or her investors is the baseline measure will determine its sustainability. There truly is such a thing as project feasibility, and there are limits beyond which a project may crater. Gauging the difference is somewhere between chess and poker—where the pieces are on the table for all to see, but where what's behind or under the pieces is subject to the bluff or the poker face. Remember that rarely does a developer expect or need to reach his first ask—some may be pretty close, others may be shooting for the moon. Neighborhood people would do well to do a little research on the developer and his or her principal investors. What have they done before? How have they worked with neighborhoods or districts? Have they been straight shooters? Have they honored their commitments?

Another concern in engaging in development approval processes may apply to both neighborhood organizations and to developers. Be wary of the neighborhood activist who has all the answers—and is all too willing to dominate neighborhood, planning commission, or city council meetings with those answers. The fact that a person is willing to put in long hours and lots of energy on a neighborhood issue is not the only measure of his or her commitment to better outcomes for the neighborhood. Sometimes the motivation is purely for ego gratification, in which both the neighborhood and the developer can be misled. More ominously, sometimes the motivation is for personal gain, possibly to the extent of being bought off. Perhaps the best way to gauge the potential for positive effect in the neighborhood interest is transparency: Is the neighborhood leader or leadership willing to share information? Absorb new information? Reach out for information from new sources? Work in a leadership structure that is itself open and accessible without dominating it?

## Action...Along with Vision and Information

The visions that emerge from charrette-type efforts are usually just that. They enunciate a reasonably comprehensive snapshot of a better future from the perspective of all involved, based on the information available, a tribute to community commitment, and dedication. And thanks to the skills of the urban design team, the results are portrayed in visible, communicable form so that everyone can put himself or herself into the picture of that future. They point toward a direction to pursue. But they are not a "blueprint" or a detailed plan of action. They may identify priorities and broad general descriptions of the kinds of steps that somebody is going to have to take to stride out in the right direction—a good thing.

They usually do not represent, however, a complete analysis or detailing of the kinds of actions that will need to be taken to carry the vision forward, usually a process that develops interactively with other factors over time. At best, they may identify an early action step or two, in which case these should be geared toward being manifestly doable, fairly simple, not too expensive, and able to be seen and experienced rather quickly. Following the action principle, such actions show participants that projects can happen, validating the trust and confidence the process has promised. A visible result that leaves the place better off than it was before can stand on its own or, better, generate momentum to keep the process going and its ensuing projects coming.

We have seen how community-involved visioning processes have enabled many community and district planning efforts to get started and gain momentum, fairly consensually and fairly expeditiously, the two being related after all. In addition, these charrette approaches at their best enable lots of information to be exchanged and through the process new information generated. The third leg in the vision-information-action principles trinity, action, is always messier, less predictable, and sometimes contradictory to the best-laid plans. If the charrette is the quick hit, it is action that requires commitment over the long haul, essential if anything tangible is to come out of the charrette. Without action the visioning process is at risk of lying on the shelf of history, by now sagging badly under the weight of so many other plan documents. That's why both designers and community leaders on the one hand need to be thinking of actions and priorities and resources even as the visioning process is being put together, and on the other, positioning themselves to respond to actions that may already be in the works that may or may not have benefited from being on the same page as the vision-setting exercise.

The real work, then, begins after the charrette (some of which could be aided by future, more focused charrette or workshop processes). Following the organizational principles, the work invariably depends on flexible partnerships that include the community, like a neighborhood or business organization; the private sector stakeholders, like property owners, businesses, and developers; and the government. To act on the vision almost always means changing the rules. The current ones probably at least partly account for what's wrong with the area in the first place, yet changing them is not easy and requires close coordination. For example, the government, usually the planning department and the public works department, must go through the detail of analyzing the code structure to enable, encourage, or require the changes called for in the charrette vision. This has to be closely coordinated with the property owners whose present rights will change and with developers who must scrutinize the process for its financial and marketing feasibility. While such a process will probably lie at the core of what needs to be done, other actions requiring such partnerships need to happen as well, like project definition and financing strategies.

As we have seen in Part Three, Principles, actions always affect the information base and may put a turn in the road toward the vision as well. In many cases, these happenings should be seen more as new data rather than as spoiling the plan in place before the actions were taken. Actions for the most part are de facto feasible occurrences, since presumably if they weren't feasible they wouldn't have happened. The job of the community guidance system and urban design and planning professionals is to shape actions generally in the direction of the consensual vision, or at worst to look for ways to mitigate any negative impacts arising from actions that occur outside of the sphere of the vision.

Actions imply change, and we have discussed the range of rules that may need to be changed into the tools for carrying out the new vision. We have described the kinds of interactions between the private sector, government, and the community that either facilitate or obstruct the rules-changing process. We have noted the difference between exhilaration at finding the way to a shared vision and the hard work that it takes to implement that vision. Here, it is important to discuss the models for changing rules that are out there for moving forward and to review their advantages and disadvantages as action processes.

# Rules to Tools

*"Like going from night to day."*
*"Fix it!"*

Rules will always be with us in one form or another. Why not try to thoughtfully and systematically reshape the rules we have into tools that come closer to producing places that people can all agree would be better than what they have now? Changes in knowledge, purpose, attitude, partnership relations, and resource allocation are all necessary to take advantage of the opportunities to reshape the rules to a better purpose. Questions addressed here include: Why should and how can rules be turned into tools? Which rules are more likely to lend themselves to this kind of transformation? What are key provisions for considering changes of the rules? What are the processes available? Who is involved in these processes? What are the longer-term prospects for improving the rules?

By now, bound by the desire to make their places better and the knowledge that the code structure largely determines the character and quality of their daily environment, more and more people are involving themselves in the processes of land development code reform—rules to tools. These include academics, public officials, consultants, developers, and other private interests as well as neighborhood and district activists.

In the last chapter we described most of the existing baseline rules that, taken together, account for how the civic environment looks and functions. We used the example of the strip commercial street to describe one such picture. The rules in place in most communities do not serve to provide for the range of places people want to live in, work in, or travel through, nor do they even accommodate the demand for choices that has become apparent in the market. Yet the rules are largely responsible for what people see and experience in the physical world. The failures of the rules are manifold. People trained in the design disciplines have been notably absent in most of the older code-making processes, so that how places might actually look under the code provisions has been largely ignored. Most codes fail to take into account places as a whole—their overall workability and attractiveness—instead considering urban land on a parcel-by-parcel basis. They tend to be disjointed and often in conflict across purposes, disciplines, and jurisdictions. Rules tend to be inflexible and hard to update, and they often stunt creativity or block useful innovation.

The key to rethinking the frameworks of rules that build places begins with creating and agreeing on an overall and consensual vision as to the kinds of places the rules as tools are supposed to help create. Planners and designers must develop the understandings, partnerships, and tools to enrich the dialogue of reform and point the way toward getting the job done. Developers and lenders need to step beyond the traditional tried and true to provide for the choices that markets are increasingly demanding. Communities need to recognize that the private sector accounts for most development, and that they can influence the course of this development. The rule-making institutions need to be flexible and proactive in reviewing and updating the rules, discipline by discipline, and more importantly trying to recast the rules into a synthesized, integrated framework. Toward this end, the relevant disciplines must come together in the uniting purpose of sustaining and improving the living environment. They increasingly find themselves having to do this anyway just to get the job done, and it would help if they could change their cultures to embrace this kind of integration more positively.

The possibilities and processes for bringing rules into closer alignment with the tools necessary to achieve desired gains are full of promise and indeed underway in many jurisdictions. The demand marked by growing markets for more choices and better civic environments is combining with the private market, government will, and technological capabilities to accelerate the change process. The rules that most designers simply grumble about can become the "tools" for shaping better places. Below is an exposition of some of the more prominent and focused initiatives in what has become a countrywide effort, along with some of the antecedents that together are full of hope and, increasingly, results.

## Approaches to Code Reform

Overall, the recognition for the need and the beginnings of changing rules to create more satisfactory design results started to gain momentum maybe 40 years ago with urban designers in New York, Chicago, and San Francisco city governments. Since then, the various visioning exercises have continuously focused on outcomes that need changes in the rules as we have identified them in the last chapter. Organizationally, the APA and the CNU have been active in zoning code reform activities, the former mainly working within the framework of existing comprehensive planning, zoning, and subdivision codes and the latter putting forward a more integrative model that builds on the emerging priority on urban form.

It should be noted that land use law has played a hugely significant role in the evolution of zoning from its earliest days, and lawyers have their own organizations that focus primarily on the subject of land use codes. The law, as interpreted by the courts, has been the arena for determining the balance that society strikes between private property and community rights. Courts, and thus the law, have tended to swing—somewhat—one way or the other in this dialectic, depending on the era and the location, and land use attorneys take their cue from this series of precedents. The APA too has based most of its code reform activity within the framework of case law thus established, recognizing that its guidance to its members should ultimately stand the legal test. Accordingly, code reform within the framework of typical ordinance structures tends to be conservative. Furthermore, so much of that structure is built on the rights not just of private property in general, but on particular individual circumstances, where case law deals for the most part with one individual entity, often a landowner, against another, often a local government, or vice versa. This makes the goals stated here of a holistically conceived, cross-disciplinary set of codes much harder to move forward, since zoning is the code that frames the civic environment.

Architects Andreas Duany and Elizabeth Plater-Zyberk ("DPZ") recognized this dilemma when they designed for Robert Davis the now iconic 80-acre resort village of Seaside in Florida. In the course of setting up the rules, having created a plan that espoused the values of "traditional" neighborhoods, they established a more holistic code structure. In some ways like Clarence Perry's neighborhood unit concepts of the 1920s and certainly responsive to ideas of Jane Jacobs, the plan and the code put in place to implement it featured a walkable mixed-use, mixed-density village, with a clearly defined center and a formalist street structure whose dimensions and focal points downplay the presence of cars. This was all carried out in a county where laissez-faire policies allowed a lot of freedom to prospective developers. (Most developers used this latitude to produce the "same old same old" of the day.) Thus out of this simple code that relied on descriptive graphics to establish the desired forms for the new village, which included street design, was born what has now evolved into the "SmartCode" and more generally "form-based coding." DPZ has continued working on its SmartCode as a way to replace current zoning ordinances with ones that are more design-based and more simply communicated. Their effort has fed directly into the CNU's code reform initiatives and is being adapted and tested by other new urbanist practitioners in many areas.

The Form Based Codes Institute, http://www.formbasedcodes.org, offers courses for professionals or jurisdictions who are interested in the possibilities of this approach.

Aside from the CNU initiatives, other jurisdictions and practitioners already working on code reform have continued their efforts, in which design and integration of other key factors figure prominently. Altogether, these approaches to code reform suggest with some validity that design quality can mitigate and even make desirable some of the functional conflicts that may otherwise arise in a mixed-use environment. Where modernist era codes sought to deal with conflicts by barring them, present-day approaches seek to overcome potential incompatibilities through design. Thus disparate activities can be made to look, seem, and even function in complementary ways through the scaling and materials of buildings, their relationships to the street, and such functional factors as control of location of parking and delivery, light sources, sound, and so on. The viability of this approach has lots of workable and even charming precedents in town and city development throughout time, but it flies in the face of the separate-at-all-costs mentality on which most zoning codes cut their teeth. It enables the by now well-documented interest among many people to live in environments that concentrate and encourage the range of activities necessary or desirable to meet daily needs without having to drive.

In some ways the new code approaches are simply a rediscovery of commonsense communities of earlier eras, the kinds Jane Jacobs and others held out as enduringly successful alternatives to some of the more crazed tendencies in modernism. Yet in other ways, these moves have signaled a profound shift in what more and more in the development community as well as local jurisdictions consider "cutting edge." "Mixed use" was a term that sent chills up the spine of the real estate development and investment sectors, local government, and most communities as recently as 10 years ago. Now, live-work-shop-play communities are moving up the scale of what mainstream developers and real estate professionals are touting, building, selling, and profiting from, and local governments are scrambling to facilitate. If the sequence underway is true to the principles espoused in this text, then mixed use needs to extend to mixed densities, mixed income, and mixed travel mode in order to create truly sustainable alternatives.

At the larger scale, it is important to remember that the codes taken as a whole describe and prescribe the systems that underlie city form and function. Thus infrastructure systems, transportation systems, and underlying environmental systems, as well as the activities, forms, and relationships that make up a region's or town's settlement patterns all follow code provisions of some kind or other. As the people responsible for these systems come to understand their interdependence, the prospect for their complementarities begins to come into focus, which can only serve to improve the quality of the civic environment.

Many jurisdictions are undertaking code reform initiatives. Some of them—mostly new ones, single projects, smaller ones, or defined areas in larger ones—have adopted various forms of the SmartCode or more generally amendments that incorporate some of the provisions of form-based codes. Many more are at least considering these factors more seriously in their code reform processes.

Beyond reforming and integrating the content of codes, with the accelerating access to and utility of Geographic Information Systems (GIS), there is hope for streamlining and rationalizing the structure and management of both intra-disciplinary and cross-disciplinary rules. Such a tool could also expeditiously incorporate changes as the need arises, whether from changes in vision, new knowledge, or technological advances.

It is technically conceivable, for example, to load up all the codes enumerated above in some detail and then overlay them selectively to check both for consistency and common sense as well as to analyze and evaluate them according to evidence of their performance, both technically and behaviorally. Out of such an effort could come a whole new way of conceptualizing a model code, perhaps an integrated code system that enabled the kinds of systems integration noted above, whose impacts would stretch beyond the civic to the whole of the built environment. Perhaps someday, someone with the resources, the time, and the technical expertise will be motivated to undertake such an effort, which would be neither quick nor easy. Once accomplished for any one jurisdiction, though, such integration would likely spread rather quickly, in the same way that jurisdictions' use of GIS or the proliferation of green building codes has done. At the scale of individual buildings and projects, for example, rapid advances are occurring in holistic integration of all elements under programs generally called Building Information Modeling (BIM). These bring together all the relevant disciplines into a single dialogue that facilitates and streamlines all of the myriad of technical information that eventually creates and then operates buildings.

When I was the planning director for Birmingham, Alabama (1987–1993), we were among the first cities in the nation to install a full-blown GIS capability, ultimately linking the full range of planning and engineering data into a common spatial database. Under the technical leadership of Vince Spraul in planning and Ellen Cowles in engineering, the system enabled us to systematically, efficiently, and accurately update the city's land use plans and zoning maps in nine sectors over a couple of years. The major drive for carrying out the updates came from neighborhoods that were beginning to experience growth or change pressures that were not accounted for in the existing maps and regulations.

Communities are increasingly demanding changes in the rules that can better support improving their communities. Community awareness of the shortcomings of existing code structures coupled with a growing consciousness of communities' ability to influence change are providing major impetus for reform, putting pressure on governments, developers, and design professionals to respond. This growing popular base, armed with better and more accessible information about choices, ultimately can provide strong support for change and improvement initiatives among the planning, design, and development professions. Neighborhood and business district activists become advocates for code changes they recognize as necessary to better guide private and public development initiatives to support neighborhood and district visions.

In Atlanta, for example, in dialogue with several neighborhoods and business district leaders, we introduced a set of "quality of life" zoning classifications that enabled and encouraged mixed use, mixed density, and either transit-centered or neighborhood-centered development; it was the neighborhoods, through Atlanta's Neighborhood Planning Unit (NPU) system, that were decisive in securing their approval.

Recalling the "both-and" and the "solutionism" principles, urban designers and community leaders would do well to approach code change opportunities holistically and with some caution. There is no "right" answer to the issues that zoning presents. Instead, the way to develop zoning strategies and ultimately ordinances is to consider the strengths and the interactions between the old and the new as both adding value and to recognize that zoning will always be dynamic and on the move—and thus not fixable with any particular magic bullet. While it is clear that form counts for more than the older, more traditional codes recognize, the goal is to incorporate the rich mix of physical, social, and functional possibilities that are more likely to produce places that really work for people over time.

For both urban designers and community activists, then, familiarizing oneself with all the possibilities, like incremental or form-based or SmartCode alternatives, is worth the trouble. Probably more important is to familiarize oneself with the codes already in place. In larger, older, more complicated jurisdictions, code modifications need to be approached, as always, with a vision of what sort of places one wants the code to enable, encourage, or require and then pick from the tools available to achieve those changes. One thing is for sure: Codes that are in sync with each other, particularly zoning, subdivision, and public works codes, are going to move closer to the mark than disjointed ones. The result will probably be a blend of provisions, incorporating what activities are encouraged, what kinds of densities are appropriate where, what kinds and designs of access and other infrastructure provisions are necessary, together with a more conscious visual picture of what the results might look like (form-based) and how the place should function as properties develop or redevelop.

Community activists and public officials should be wary of consultants hawking zoning or code expertise. Maybe, maybe not. Stock in trade for consultants is to blow into town and make the seductive pitch that for a couple of years and a few hundred thousand dollars they can fix all the code problems. Champions for some of the new approaches, for example, may represent them as the cure-all for current zoning shortcomings. Most consultants, though, have never administered zoning, subdivision, or public works codes. Some may not bother to conduct a detailed analysis of the existing code or the processes and procedures necessary to modify it. They may carry a single baseline package that can be wrapped in different colors, provide a few locally sensitive tweaks, and once delivered it falls back on the government and the community to figure out how to adopt and administer it. Then everyone wonders what happened when the proposed new code fails to address any number of old issues, or it doesn't anticipate all the new ones. Communities cry foul, politicians get sanctimonious, and public servant planners take the brunt for trying to make the thing work. And the consultants skip merrily away to their next target with easy dismissals aimed at the ineptness of government or the backwardness of communities—"We did our job, now you do yours."

Jurisdictions thinking of doing a major code upgrade need to consider the appropriate balance between consultant technical assistance and in-house staff capability. In any event, they will likely need to beef up their planning staff since the inclusion of design criteria into codes requires design-trained people to interpret and administer them. To some extent sending existing staff to training sessions or building training into consultant contracts can meet this additional need. In striking the balance, limiting consultant involvement to just the specific and narrower technical issues may be a good strategy, while ensuring that staff stays on top of the process, since they will have to anyway as the new code is adopted and enforced.

It is also important to involve the jurisdiction's legal counsel every step of the way, since some code purveyors may be a little breezy about how their package meets local legal requirements. The likelihood is that there are many aspects of the old code that are important and useful to incorporate. The interactive dynamic between the old and proposals for update are likely to produce a sounder basis for going forward toward the community vision than chucking the old and installing the new, untested. In this way, the code gets upgraded, the transition is likely to be more attenuated and seamless, routine business goes on, only better in quality, and the staff in place—including the legal staff, which may need to be prodded to embrace the change—has become skilled in both the conceptual opportunities and the operational requirements to carry out the improvements. In fact, as times and markets change, jurisdictions should plan on regular reviews and updates of their codes and not expect that any code fix is somehow permanent. The rules, tools, and resources of implementation are always in flux, just as the vision is fleshed out by successive actions and new information.

As people have become more aware of the significance of zoning, subdivision, and public works codes and standards and their interactive effects on the future quality of their neighborhoods, they have become more and more active, sophisticated, and effective at bending these rules to support their neighborhood or district vision and goals. Similarly, urban design professionals are growing in their understanding and ability to influence these codes to achieve their purposes, either as consultants to private development clients or as officials or consultants serving the broader public interest.

In most jurisdictions around the country these codes are locally administered laws, and moves toward their reform have been uneven, episodic, and mixed in their intentions. This range of responses reflects the relative balance of influence among the three main interest groupings at work in every jurisdiction: the government, the private sector, and communities. Since almost all jurisdictions in urban areas have zoning, subdivision, and public works codes, though, change lies within the power of the local government to accomplish. Strategies can range from incremental tweaks to each of the different sets of rules to wholesale replacement of all of them. As a practical matter, the size and age of the jurisdiction will probably have a lot to do with which strategies and their combinations will be most effective, with larger, older ones likely to be more incremental and the small or new ones better able to be more sweeping in their approaches. The codes that dictate the functionality and quality of the civic environment are never written in stone, and good governance should expect changes periodically to positively accommodate the full range of dynamic factors that mark a place's evolution and development.

As it relates to the regulation of development of private land, zoning, whether "Euclidean"—separating land uses into hierarchies by type of activity and density, as with most of the earliest codes—or "smart"—favoring mixed use, compactness, and environmental sustainability provisions with some attention to form—still deals with the same basic issues and regulates the same basic ingredients out of which places are built. Fundamental is the appropriate balance between private property rights and community health, safety, and welfare. Where the balance is struck is subject to continuous change, and presently community values—both property values and character values—are increasing their weight in the mix.

Philosophical, physical, and ultimately legal issues are implicit in this individual–society dynamic: Should zoning rules apply solely on a lot-by-lot basis or should they consider the design of the environment as a whole? The premise of the former approach, still dominant in most zoning codes, is to afford each lot development rights as if it exists in a vacuum, with the often unintended consequence of creating larger stretches or blocks of development that may be suboptimum or even dysfunctional—

and markedly unattractive, like the strip. Optimizing the subsystem sub-optimizes the whole system.

The premise of the latter approach, now steadily gaining ground, is to conceive of zoning as operating at at least two levels: the individual parcel level, for sure, but also with respect to how the parcels might add up to a more effective whole—and sometimes with consideration for larger issues, like optimizing transportation access, improving the jobs–housing balance, providing for affordable housing, or developing in environmentally more sustainable ways.

The first set of premises is simpler to grasp and to legislate: It applies to private property only, and it simply requires a text that describes common characteristics for each zoning classification and a map that shows where each set of characteristics apply. The second set of premises begin to apply to private and to public property, insofar as the code mediates the space shared by private and public ownership, and so it begins to imply or require synthesis or at least complementarity between zoning, subdivision, and public works codes. If working within the framework of the existing zoning is the preferred approach, then to achieve the result of being able to provide the option of more compact, walkable environments likely will require changes in the subdivision and public works codes that complement changes in zoning. Either way, as the need arises jurisdictions can change their codes to allow for steady improvement, whether along their strip commercial corridors, in their centers, around transit stops, in key nodes, or in neighborhood places.

## Doing It

The process begins with understanding what the code structure presently prescribes, considering what works and what doesn't from that framework and then acting to improve both the codes themselves and the processes necessary to accelerate and synthesize the necessary tasks. Traditionally, the motivations and initiatives for changing the code come from three different general directions: the private sector, the community, and the government. Private development interests, like developers, homebuilders, real estate companies, corporations, and individual businesses or institutions dominate the action in numbers of initiatives and transactions. Their activity is almost entirely limited to project-by-project efforts to provide for themselves a more remunerative or otherwise better outcome than the existing codes provide. While not disinterested in the quality of what surrounds and connects to their project, their focus is, as it must be to ensure profitability, on the particulars of their deal. They are likely to be a little chary of overall code modification because it takes them out of their comfort zone—they, their lawyers, and consultants know how to work within the code that is, and major changes sound like time, money, and uncertainty for them.

Citizens, on the other hand, including neighborhood, business, academic, civic, and special focus groupings and their coalitions, take these kinds of initiatives out of motivation to improve the functionality and quality of larger places and contexts. These may range from streetscapes, to mixed use, to affordable housing, to environmental sustainability—in short, any part of the environment they care most about, from neighborhood to town square to region. This second group may become so area- or issue-specific that they push for codes with little regard for their impacts, or consistency or lack thereof with other codes.

The government is the third and ultimately decisive source for code change initiatives since city councils approve and city staff administers all local codes. Usually elected officials or planning staff, responding either to best practices they have heard of, or their communities, or the development sector, or consultant solicitation, or simply to improve on what they already have may launch the change process. Planners and urban designers managing the code reform process, usually public employees, sometimes guided by or trying to implement consultants' recommendations, must be careful to place each new broadly conceived code change initiative into the larger context. It inevitably falls to government to bring the whole process to closure and then manage the result. Code change should always be seen as an opportunity for advancing code synthesis, for establishing and maintaining consistency and mutually complementary outcomes for the range of code provisions that in essence dictate the places we live in and travel through.

Below is a brief summary of the options for shifting existing rules that by consensus need changing into tools that may improve the civic environment, with examples both of what the changes might be and the processes for initiating them.

Step one, for virtually all of the rules that dictate how places look and function, the overall policy document—the comprehensive plan, or however else it may be named—provides the framework for crafting the rules. Its umbrella covers all the rules that at the local level determine how places—public and private—end up being developed. What is the public policy? Which directions do people and their governments want to take? What should be the code choices available for carrying out the vision? It is often difficult for many jurisdictions to put the comprehensive plan in place, since it must by definition include widely divergent interests and political power bases, where consensus is hard to reach. In theory too and often in practice, the comprehensive plan provides the framework for prioritizing capital improvement funding, like whose districts get what projects, which parks or roads or sewers are more important, and whether there is fairness in the distribution of funds. Once in place, it is often difficult to update. And so, even where states mandate local adoption of a comprehensive or general plan, many localities fall back to what they last adopted, perhaps a little uneasy in their vulnerability to legal challenge in the more tangible world of zoning and other land development codes.

In the practical, day-to-day world of zoning, other codes, and legislative and operational functions, however, dominated by real-life, project-by-project proposals, all parties manage to find the ability to act. In simple terms, the relevant codes deal in the permitted sizes, placements, relationships, and activities that occur in physical space, both fixed and in motion. Actions on projects put the question of what they might add up to, their comprehensive impact and meaning, off into the philosophical realm—nice to think about, but don't hold off my approval. Yet to change the codes, jurisdictions must be prepared to change their guiding visions and show how the code changes can implement that vision. Areas in need of improvement, then, at whatever scale need an overall guiding policy document and then typically depend on combinations of codes covering zoning, subdivision, public works, and utilities location and design, as well as other codes identified in Chapter 9, Rules, and discussed below.

In Chapter 9 we dealt with the status of these codes, how they got to be how they are, why they are important for urban designers and citizen leaders alike, and some of the moves underway to rethink them. Here it is worth outlining the technical steps necessary to analyze and modify the codes that are likely to apply across a range of jurisdictional sizes and practices. The suggestions below come from within a context of aiming toward integration and synthesis as desirable for effective code updating. More specifically, zoning, subdivision, and public works codes in particular are addressed with a view toward how they may be synchronized, not just as separate, disconnected code sections.

## Changing the Zoning

How does one go about changing the zoning, either fixing the existing or introducing the new? Who can change the code? How is it done? How can urban designers support that process toward the goal of achieving better places? How do urban design values get inserted into zoning codes where the principal application is directed at private properties? How does a community go about upgrading its code base to provide the tools to better meet its vision for the future?

As the consciousness of access to the zoning codes and their modification processes spreads through communities and urban design practice, both are increasingly active in their efforts to influence the process. As emphasized above, the starting place for changing zoning comprehensively or on a single-property basis is the comprehensive plan. It describes the vision for how citizens want their place to be and sets the policy framework for how to get there. Within its framework, property owners or local jurisdictions may initiate the change process, and it is through the latter that communities have their best shot.

City councils by whatever name are very conscious of the comprehensive planning and zoning processes, since hardly a meeting goes by in which something related to the zoning code isn't on the agenda. Most of their zoning business is typically private property owner–initiated, where land law attorneys most often make the case for change. Many council members, however, completely familiar with the processes and the kinds of issues that zoning raises, are interested in the idea of being proactive in their zoning strategies to achieve better communities, or at least forestall predictable frictions between developers and neighborhoods.

While the city council usually has the last word, zoning initiatives, whether for a single parcel of land or for the whole of the jurisdiction, usually pass through a city planning commission or other form of zoning board. These are usually made up of volunteer citizens, usually appointed by the city council or other legislative body, and often with a membership that includes representatives of the various land planning and development interests at stake. These are truly remarkable bodies: Their work is grueling, time-consuming, and often singularly unappreciated (and often outright attacked by angry parties on whatever side of an issue). Yet their members' only discernible incentive, since there's no pay in it and they are prohibited from using their position for personal gain, is to work for the improvement of their town or city. People with this level of commitment, coupled with the considerable knowledge they pick up, are invaluable allies in any place improvement initiative.

In this context, council members or planning departments may initiate or citizens may petition on behalf of a neighborhood or district to rezone an area. In this way the rules can be changed to a set of tools for achieving a longer-term vision for a place. These kinds of initiatives take lots of time and commitment from the government, the property owners, and the community and usually organizational structures to keep up with and guide the effort. The success of such initiatives depends on support by the community, usually a majority of the affected property owners and finally endorsement and adoption by the jurisdiction.

As with most matters governmental or financial, the formal rezoning process invariably involves filling out forms. Typically, the form requests all the details necessary to consider the application, and the process describes what will happen as the application moves its way along toward approval—or denial. In more and more jurisdictions, applicants are encouraged—in some required—to consult with neighbors and the local leadership structure. In all cases applicants, either through local government or by their own action, must confirm that property owners within a certain radius have been informed of the pending action, since these adjacent or nearby property owners may have a direct economic stake in its outcome. In most jurisdictions, the travel path for an application then goes to planning department staff review, analysis, and recommendation, and then on to a planning commission or similarly constituted body for its consideration. In some jurisdictions, this body may approve or deny applications, but in most the commission recommendation goes to the legislative body—a town, city, or county council or commission—for final action. Both the applicant and affected property owners may appeal the governing authority's decision, usually in a court of appropriate jurisdiction.

When the City of Atlanta worked with the Midtown Alliance to rezone its entire district, some two square miles in the middle of town, the two had done such a good job of communicating the purpose and the process to the Neighborhood Planning Unit and to the private and the public sectors that signs started listing properties under their proposed new zoning weeks before it was actually adopted. Similarly, developers started designing their proposals to conform with what was coming, even when it meant needing variances from the existing outmoded zoning to do so.

As it happens, zoning and the issues constantly swirling around it gain lots of attention from all parties to any proposed action—the applicant, the affected neighborhood, the staff, the planning commission, and the elected officials of the authorizing jurisdiction. Intense interaction among neighbors, between neighbors and applicants, meetings, hearings late into the night, negotiations, sometimes spikes in campaign contributions—and occasionally darker forays into the ethical thicket—and modifications to original proposals or initial opposition all wind up with a final action. This often launches the development for which the zoning was necessary, or occasionally it makes the property more attractive for resale.

Dialing back to the beginning of the process, though, in most cases it is possible for all parties to contemplate changes in zoning and ensuing development that tend to merge rather than divide the interests at stake. Beyond the minor changes that make up a significant part of any jurisdiction's zoning agenda, larger initiatives may be managed in such a way as to bring together rather than separate the affected parties. For this to occur, the developer and the neighborhood or district must be open enough to each other to probe mutually positive outcomes. The government's planning staff or the council member is usually best positioned to facilitate the necessary dialogue.

In this scenario, a prospective development company has decided to risk its—or more likely its investors'—money on a project for which its analyses show a sufficient market demand to be able to make a satisfactory return on its investment. This means that new private investment will come to the community, usually a sign of confidence in the community and usually—but not always—increasing property values accordingly.

The community, if not blindsided, can usually imagine that new development could be a good thing, provided that the proposal does not degrade values that it collectively holds. A tool that is growing in use, increasingly called the "community benefit agreement," or CBA, provides a basis for communities to enter into a formal agreement with developers to ensure that commitments made by both parties are honored. Such agreements may provide for needed developer support for public improvements, like streetscapes, sidewalks, or parks and are strictly an agreement between two private parties, usually the developer and a legally constituted neighborhood or community organization, usually a 501(c)3. The neighborhood in turn works to facilitate the development approval process.

The term "community benefit agreement" has come to describe an initiative of the Partnership for Working Families, which seeks to unite community, labor, and faith leaders in community-improvement activities, an alliance that could be very effective in bringing about improvements to the civic environment. Full information on that organization's use of CBAs is available at www.communitybenefits.org.

Legally barred from such private agreements, the government is usually in the middle, on the one hand favoring activities that mark "progress" and raise the tax base, thus operating revenues, while on the other, wanting to serve its constituents and to support their aspirations for an improved environment. Many jurisdictions too, depending on state and case law, may impose conditions to zoning approvals that fine-tune expected outcomes within the framework of the provisions of the zoning ordinance. Thus, issues like hours of operation, light spillage, or favoring carpooling or transit can find their ways into a final zoning approval. Many states and local jurisdictions have established laws that seek to rationalize and constrain excesses that a local jurisdiction may try to burden a development with. Under such laws, these excesses, which may be called "exactions," are barred and replaced with systematically calculated impact fees. These provide for the reality that developments are likely to impose impacts on the jurisdiction, like traffic, water or sewer capacity, and the need for more public safety or for parks, and that developers should contribute toward offsetting the expenses of the additional impacts. In these jurisdictions, the conditions that may attach to zoning approvals must be consistent with the laws that establish the impact fee.

The threats to conceiving of such a development and rezoning process are myriad. The level of trust necessary to accept the premise that a new development initiative could be a good thing is usually lacking in the community, a mistrust usually grounded in prior experience. The parties to such a scenario have not typically thought of themselves as partners in a larger venture. The transparency required for a partnership approach runs counter to private sector and sometimes even public sector culture. The community has a hard time accepting that nothing much will happen if private investment doesn't come in. The developer has a hard time accepting that community values are important and must be honored to achieve a successful outcome. The government is usually more comfortable reacting than stepping up as facilitator.

The government, though, can be effective in setting the stage for a fruitful developmental dialogue if it balances its support for both parties. It can assure the developer an expedited process once community agreement is reached, committing to the kinds of zoning and other public actions necessary to support the development. At the same time, it can counsel the community on the legal and procedural matters that are in its interest, it can set conditions on zoning that ameliorate its impacts on the neighborhood, and it can provide tacit support for any covenants that the neighborhood may want to negotiate with the developer that are beyond the purview of municipal authority. Given the choice, developers would all rather have their development supported by the community than opposed—it saves time, it saves money, it brings forth a project into a friendly neighborhood or district setting—no pickets, for example—and it feels better to be thought of as a good guy. For this to happen, however, it is important for the community to remind itself that without a shot at the developer's reaching his or her projected return on investment the whole deal might tank.

As suggested above, the interactive processes that are brought into play in this choreography invariably lead to and are supported by transparency. Information sharing is crucial. It is important to remember that no prospective development deal is a "sure thing." Most communities won't fault a developer and his or her investors from aspiring to a target return—they're just more tolerant of a reasonable return than an obscene one. Digital analysis tools are both increasingly sophisticated and increasingly accessible, lifting the level of dialogue. Among these, pro formas that outline the bones of a development deal enable urban designers and community leaders to at least understand the interactive relationships that a developer must consider. Figures sufficiently in the ballpark to understand the ranges of risks and returns associated with a proposal can focus the dialogue between developer, community, and the government without revealing proprietary detail or the hidden additional percent or two or three hoped for by the developer.

In all my years of conceptualizing, interacting, and administering land development processes, only once did I run into a developer who, given the choice, would rather stick it to the neighborhood than be ultimately embraced for his hard work.

Little by little jurisdictions, communities, and developers are waking up to the idea of seeking common ground and looking for mutually beneficial outcomes. Indeed, without this kind of approach, the possibilities of making the civic environment better are limited. Private investment is essential. Bending it to work for community benefit in addition to return on investment is a benchmark of mutual success. Such a success actually helps the developer's project and builds toward opportunity for additional fruitful investment in an area where some kind of working partnership has been established.

The world's first underground Wal-Mart, in Atlanta, came about through such a partnership. And the partnerships established continue to lift the quality of other development that requires zoning or other municipal approvals.

## Changing Subdivision and Public Works Codes

Subdivision and public works codes at this point in time are less open to citizen influence or integrated design guidance. Subdivision codes, for example, have for so long been narrowly focused on meeting single-minded and unholistic civil engineering criteria on the one hand, and by the incontestable rights ascribed to property ownership on the other, that many ordinances do not afford formal public access to the consideration of subdivision approvals. This practice, like all the others relating to land development codes, is beginning to break down, as stronger interactive links between zoning and subdivision form, community values, and environmental values come forward, and as the comprehensive aspects of the impacts of narrowly defined subdivision practices continue to produce less than satisfactory or sustainable results.

We noted in Chapter 9, for example, the rapid rise of "conservation subdivisions" as a kind of counterpart to older "planned unit development" zoning codes, both aimed at the same target—that is, flexibility to better shape development to the land. Both are examples of recasting necessary rules into tools that produce more sustainable, attractive, and functional results. When one considers that most of the urbanized land is residential—typically more than 60 percent—most of which is relatively low-density subdivisions built according to what are increasingly viewed as outmoded standards, the need for cross-disciplinary thinking is essential to push along subdivision reform. Like most code revisions and updates, though, the process is neither quick nor easy. For starters, in most jurisdictions, subdivision and zoning codes operate separately from each other, with subdivision and the civil engineering discipline laying out the street and other site development rules according to mainly public works code types of considerations, and zoning and the city planning discipline stipulating the yards, height, size, parking, and lot coverage requirements for the structures according to the private development stipulations in the land use or zoning codes.

As the conservation subdivision concept gains momentum, some jurisdictions are now improving the integration of the street layout and subdivision design, with the zoning rules governing house type and configuration into a single picture where the connectivity and character of neighborhoods are addressed as wholes, and not just within themselves but as they may connect to adjacent neighborhoods or collector streets, either existing or future. For example, the width of the street, both its right-of-way and its curb-to-curb dimensions bears a relationship to the scale, height, and location of residential properties, whether single-family detached, townhouses, or multifamily (condos or rental). Thus streets with little traffic and low design speeds may be designed with narrower roadways, tighter turn radii, or steeper grades. These kinds of features in turn can produce more favorable environmental results, like less cutting and filling; preservation of natural character like tree stands and topographic or geological features; higher percentages of permeable surfaces (like for on-street parking and sidewalks); swales instead of curbs, gutters, and storm sewers, and so on. These rule-to-tool shifts are especially important for the growing market of those who favor living in more compact, more intimate, and more environmentally conscious neighborhoods, but they have benefits for those who prefer the traditional suburban neighborhood as well.

Public works standards or codes, comparable to subdivision codes, are likewise resistant to direct community, or even other design disciplines', "meddling." This veil was put in place in the 1950s when great attention to roadway and other infrastructure design was needed and civil engineering seemed to be the discipline with the most expertise to set standards and manage processes for designing and building the public environment. Now, the engineering profession, along with other design professions and people in the community who have experienced the results, is looking for better ways.

While from a narrowly technical perspective public works standards have addressed most of the problems facing development of the public realm to accommodate cars and storm drainage for subdivisions, key provisions of both practice and process need updating. Environmental sustainability considerations as well as shifting markets that stress human-scale livability are driving these needs. These together seek to suppress the in-your-face presence of the car—its wide streets, its parking pad and garage door frontages, its too-fast travel speeds, its rescaling of neighborhoods from the people who live there to the cars that drive there. Just as for subdivisions, public works codes need retooling to support more livable and diverse centers and corridors, with new emphasis on the pedestrian and transit environments, where the access purpose of the roadway comes into better balance with its throughput purpose.

Urban designers, as they grow in number and broaden in scope from hip urban centers to the whole of the metropolitan environment, have the opportunity, and again I would say the obligation, to apply their transdisciplinary skills and attitudes toward assisting subdivision and public works codes to better practice and process. These codes should be plainly more interdisciplinary and the public should have better access to the change

The Institute for Transportation Engineering (ITE), the American Association of State Highway and Transportation Officials (AASHTO), the Transportation Research Board (TRB), and the Federal Highway Administration (FHWA) are all actively reviewing, revising, and expanding their theory and standards activities to reflect what amounts to a sea change in thinking about the relationships between transportation, land use, economic development, and livable, higher-density urban places. The websites for these agencies and associations are as follows:
ITE: http://www.ite.org
AASHTO:
http://www.transportation.org
TRB: http://www.trb.org
FHWA: http://www.fhwa.dot.gov

process. The good news here is that the engineering community is moving steadily toward incorporating the message into its theory and increasingly its practice: first, by the emergence of "context sensitive design," focusing on re-conceptualizing roadway design to recognize that access, getting there, should be a key concern; and now by "context sensitive solutions," which place an even larger context around the design of roadways than the simple interface between travel way and destination.

## Changing Other Codes That Determine the Quality of Places

Beyond the zoning, subdivision, and public works codes changes that largely determine what places look like, with zoning particularly dominating the municipal or county agenda, citizen groupings have been effective in establishing or changing other land development codes, at the neighborhood, district, and city-wide level. Preferably always in the context of the comprehensive plan, in addition to area-wide rezoning initiatives, these may include district-focused design review provisions; historic preservation designations; environmental sustainability-driven codes; rules governing location of community facilities, jurisdiction-wide sign codes; utilities, building, and life safety codes; and the rules governing financing. These codes may show up as chapters or sections in the zoning ordinance, public works or building codes; they may be freestanding pieces in the municipal or county code; or as in the case of financing, they show up in private sector underwriting criteria as well.

### *Environmental Sustainability Tools*

In this era of growing concern for environmental values, buzz words and "solutions" are coming fast and furious. Based in citizen-driven reforms from the 1960s, the National Environmental Policy Act set forth policies and enabled regulations that sought holistic approaches to managing environmental issues. Thus, for example, environmental review was structured to reflect levels of potential impact and to increase the required levels of analysis and mitigation as environmental risks increased. In addition, these reviews crossed disciplines, so that historic and cultural values, for example, required attention in the same way that preservation of habitat or risk of contamination did. This early venture into codes synthesis of a sort, however, doesn't always fit with others of a jurisdiction's place-making codes, like zoning, subdivision, and public works codes. Now many local jurisdictions have lost track of the intrinsic connectedness of all things environmental and are dropping codes into their ordinances wherever it seems convenient, responding to the environmental buzz of the day, like reflective or green roof codes, permeable surface requirements, stream or shoreline buffer codes, and tree conservation codes.

Indeed, each such initiative is worthy and more than likely needs to happen. Each represents creating or re-crafting a rule into a tool that can produce a place-ameliorating outcome. It shouldn't have to fall to the citizen activists to construct the appropriate code structure into which to insert a needed new provision directed at overall improvement of the civic environment. Yet planners and urban designers, particularly those in academia and in public service positions, would do well to create the framework upon which each new hot code item can be hung. This need for synthesis, perhaps beginning with coherence, will become more pressing as moves for health impact codes gain momentum. Citizen activists, though, should not wait; they should continue to press for measures to maintain or clean up the natural world. The rapid advance of the green building movement, codified as LEED (for Leadership in Energy and Environmental Design), shows that jurisdictions and professions can amend their codes to allow and then encourage green building practices if sustained public pressure and creditable science support it.

Picking up on the rapid and generally positive rise of LEED and its scorecard-based standards for building and site design, dedicated professionals, academics, and community leaders are formulating standards that could apply to larger contexts. This LEED-ND (for neighborhood development) momentum is detailed in Douglas Farr's new book, *Sustainable Urbanism: Urban Design with Nature*, published by Wiley (2008). Akin to the SmartCode movement for modifying zoning, this still-in-progress effort seeks to establish a scorecard for evaluating and then favoring development projects that meet the criteria over those that don't.

While certainly a step forward in understanding the issues at stake, the proposals and their applications still need a lot of vetting as well as strategies for introducing their provisions into the ongoing evolution of land development policies and codes. One thing is sure: governments, communities, and private sector partners will have to continue to find better ways and places to develop in the face of environmental sustainability and climate change challenges.

## *Design Guidelines and Design Review*

Design guidelines and design review are tools that provide a finer-grain, more interactive process for ensuring design quality. Usually put in place for downtowns, centers, corridors, or historic districts that are prominent visual features in an urban area, these kinds of rules can play a major role in preserving or enhancing places whose values are widely held to be central to an area's definition. They usually address such issues as building setbacks, heights, window and door location and treatment, signs, awnings, bay spacing and articulation, horizontal banding, sidewalk and streetscape design, lighting, location and treatment of parking and loading, and the like. As more broadly targeted codes, beyond their risk of conflict with other codes, design guidelines generally should incorporate safeguards for their larger, shared civic purpose. The interactivity and inclusivity principles provide a framework for ensuring that proponents for different codes' shifts from rules to tools do not divide into camps. Thus, for example, design review provisions applied to a district should probably focus on outcomes more than details, so that the overall area-wide look and functionality takes precedence over whether the window trim is mauve or puce.

Design review in the public arena usually accompanies some significant public investment in a particular area, like where streetscape improvements have public funding, or where public funds support rehabilitation and upgrading of structures, or where there is a major public park or perhaps transit or other transportation investment. The organizational structures put in place to oversee design quality and complementarity usually have some authority, most often advisory to planning staff or commissions but sometimes vested with the last word. Board memberships should probably represent an inclusive and diverse set of citizens, steering clear of individuals with obvious conflict of interest questions as much as possible. While designers of one kind or another are important board members because of their professional capabilities to review and communicate issues that are design-centered, they should probably be in the minority when it comes to voting. If the design merits of a particular proposal are so compelling to them, they should be able to tell their fellow "lay" members why.

Privately constituted design review rules and oversight are ubiquitous in the form of condominium associations, whose covenants, codes, and restrictions (CC&Rs) can themselves mark battlegrounds among those experimenting in this form of mini-democracy. CC&Rs as they relate to the design quality and functionality of the common areas may include such issues as color, materials, landscape and fencing treatment, exterior lighting, and treatment of pedestrian, park, and parking and loading. Whether private or public, the larger goals should be careful to favor consensus positions over any particular individual's tastes or proclivities.

When we put together the design review committee structure to oversee Birmingham's commercial revitalization program, we created an interdisciplinary and inclusive body, in which the dialogue over design issues became a two-way street. The designers, a minority, had to persuade the majority nondesigners of design merits, in which the limitations of taste-based design sometimes swayed even designers away from their first impulses.

## *Historic Preservation as a Tool*

Historic preservation was one of the first sets of rules that provided the tools for the preservation and enhancement of the character of vital or promising urban places. Such places were often targets of urban renewal or new, sweeping development initiatives, the kinds of phenomena that Jane Jacobs's book railed against. Historic preservation thereby found itself one of the parents of urban design. Its rules, beyond those aimed at individual buildings, are directed at particular, usually rather smallish districts where citizens and then government decide that the building fabric of the place is so compelling in shaping the public domain that it is worthy of formal, publicly sanctioned preservation.

To turn this stand for quality into tools that advance the overall vision and identity of a place usually requires action by the local jurisdiction to put in place the tools necessary to carry out the intent. Citizen movements to designate such areas often bring forth opponents from the same area. Some don't want their property to undergo further scrutiny than zoning already requires as a condition for, say adding a room or a porch or painting the house a nonapproved color. Others don't agree that the proposed historic preservation provisions are the right ones for carrying out the intent of preservation and maintenance appropriate to the area.

In the Grant Park neighborhood in Atlanta, the division of the pros and cons over a prospective historic district designation was about even, where taste seemed to be a divide issue. The antis, who eventually lost—the district was established—parodied the pros by hanging pink plastic flamingos in their front yards.

For all the good that historic preservation movements have done to protect the character and even the existence of important swaths of urban America, there are cautions that should apply to their practices, particularly engaging the principles relating to holistic and inclusive representation. The interior secretary's standards, the guiding federal bible for the administration of the movement, approval of districts, and eligibility of incentives like tax credits, tend to create an "either-or" framework, beginning with a 50-year rule. This rule stipulates that once a building or a district reaches 50 years plus one day, it is nominally eligible for designation, with whatever protections that provides. However intended, this rule tends to freeze places, interrupting the decennial flows that more realistically account for a place's ongoing development and vitality.

The "either-or" character may spill into others of historic preservation code provisions, risking setting up a kind of "them and us" dynamic where

In Birmingham, we were able to persuade local historic preservation groups and the State Historic Preservation Officer (SHPO) that in our Five Points South commercial revitalization program the historic values were developmental; that is, that the area's special charm did not rest with any particular period or style of architecture but rather with its eclectic accretions over the years. This sort of "living history" character both provided protection to the older building fabric and loosened up standards for what might come so as not to mummify the area.

the preservationists are the righteous and legitimate questioners are the unwashed. To some extent the "either-orness" is perhaps a shadow of one set of the movement's historic society roots, where preservation of class and cultural supremacy was as important as its physical manifestations. The overall positive goals of preservation need constant yet flexible and inclusive participation. Carried out in the name of improvement of the civic environment, the movement needs to insist on even-handedness and then combinations of persuasion and the use of various historic preservation incentives, like tax credits or locally devised subsidies, to accomplish truly successful rehab or preservation outcomes.

The website for the National Trust for Historic Preservation is http://www.nthp.org.

## Schools and Other Public Facility Tools

The rules governing the siting, size, and design of the full range of public facilities directly affect the functionality and quality of neighborhoods and districts at all scales, from regional settlement patterns to neighborhood viability. Yet it is unusual to find these criteria cast into contexts beyond agency considerations of geometric spacing, land size and characteristics, land cost, and narrow jurisdictional priorities. When the opportunity for new facilities arises, community activists and urban designers alike should take an active role in analyzing alternatives and, where necessary, arguing for flexibility in standards to serve more holistic community-wide goals. For example, while many cities and towns are experiencing growing populations, opportunities for families with children may be restricted by the inability to build new schools or expand existing ones in urban infill areas because of minimum property size requirements. Often these size requirements are imposed at the state level and they reflect both the great wave of suburbanization that is now slowing and the one-size-fits-all modernist ideal that were in vogue from the 1950s and 1960s on.

Bringing the school board, or for that matter the library board, the parks department, the fire department, or the police department into the conversation can only strengthen the decision-making process for overall neighborhood or district improvement. Site selection for public facilities of all kinds should be viewed as a cornerstone opportunity for shaping civic quality and functionality. Once the comfortable insularity of agency prerogative is replaced with the reach for comprehensive improvement as a motivating factor, the responsible agency is likely to better fulfill its ultimate mission and purpose—that is, contributing to stronger communities.

The conversation itself is useful if for no other reason than information exchange. In the course of routinely conducting such conversations in Atlanta, for example, the school board reversed its preliminary decision to close a middle school because of falling attendance. The conversation revealed that the housing community that accounted for much of that attendance was in the process of being vacated to make way for a new larger residential community under a mixed-income HOPE VI program. Instead, the board decided to rehabilitate and expand the middle school.

## Dealing with Sign Codes

With signs, as discussed in Chapter 9, it is important to understand that the source of the rules is always citizen-driven and that there are two distinctly different industries and thus sets of interests in play. On the first point, it is clear that left to their own devices both sets of industries would never initiate regulation, although now one finds industry proposals for regulation whenever the issue comes up—better to put the fox in the henhouse than to risk it to the hounds. On the second, strategies and timing for engaging the two industries should be different.

The outdoor or off-premise industry is national, well-heeled, centrally represented and able to deploy massive and concentrated lobbying power to any local or state jurisdiction whenever the idea pops up that billboards may not provide the best presentation of the community's values to the traveling public. Beyond the obvious forays against a reform strategy via campaign contributions at their disposal, look for an increase in "pro bono" and "public interest" messages—all of a sudden the art museum or teen pregnancy prevention and whatever else the industry can project to gain sympathy for their public service "generosity" shows up as a way of blunting any challenge. Now, for example, in an effort to gain support for mass deployment of their flashing digital electronic product, Clear Channel is trying to gain support by playing to the terrorism market in the form of posting FBI "most wanted" information, a great way to herald one's community to the public.

The business sign or on-premise industry is usually much more localized, made up of usually smallish sign shops competing for business among usually smaller business clients—and maybe a few iconic corporations. As local businesses they are easier to engage and may be easier to persuade to improve their overall presentations if part of a strategy that their clients and business organizations are part of and endorse. For these reasons, undertaking to improve the rules for the two industries should not occur at the same time.

Whether for billboards or business signs, the beginning point is to find out what the existing rules require—usually by zoning district, size, height, spacing, illumination levels, and so on—whether the rules are enforced; who is involved from both the government and from the industry; and whether there have been citizen-mounted improvement efforts before, who was involved, and what were the outcomes. Based on this information, citizen activists or urban designers can assess the possibilities for mounting the effort to change the codes. These kinds of campaigns are never easy, yet they can result in improvement, and they usually fare better in the context of larger civic improvement efforts. The organization Scenic America has been active for many years in trying to and succeeding in cleaning up billboard clutter. The key is always an organized, committed, inclusive citizen base, where usually six or eight people with an open-minded government can make the difference.

In Birmingham, perhaps overzealously responding to general citizen concern about a growing visual cacophony of signboard litter, we elected to take on both the on-premise and off-premise industries at once. Wow. While we were ultimately successful in making things better than they were, including some cleaning up of downtown freeway entrance ways, stirring up both industries at once was probably not the best strategy. Were it not for representatives of 80 of the city's 100 neighborhoods showing up at a crucial city council vote (a showing organized by a particularly committed and energetic community resource officer, Ann Adams), I doubt the vote would have succeeded—as it was, it passed by a one-vote margin. Some campaign war chests surely had to find other, probably harder sources of support.

## *Dealing with Utilities Rules*

With utilities, as noted in Chapter 9, the effort to change usual practice—that is, to brush off any efforts to clean up the visual environment—is even harder than with signs. Utility companies at best are regulated at the state level through public utilities commissions, whose main interest is usually auditing and rate setting, not beautification. Again, though, sustained citizen activism can bring about some gains. Specific steps are suggested in the case of the strip commercial corridor at the beginning of this chapter. The effort has to figure out ways to engage the local government and the development industry to have much of a chance. The only "rule" at the local level that has a chance of modification for the better is the electric utility franchise agreement. The first thing to do is to find out from the government's legal counsel when is the next opportunity to have a voice on the renewal, keeping in mind that these are long-term agreements. Should such an opportunity present itself, start very early, and expect fierce opposition.

The website for Scenic America is http://www.scenic.org.

Some communities have publicly owned utilities, and in these cases, the concept of contemplating how to better integrate the problem of overhead utilities into larger community betterment strategies may be easier to engage. Such communities, usually smaller, often have difficulty resisting private industry strategies to take them over, and so citizens concerned about the effects of putting utilities a step farther away from their opportunity for oversight need to take heed—the visual nuisance of overhead utilities is just one of the issues at stake.

Local jurisdictions in response to citizen activism occasionally try to influence others of the utility industries, like for example, the location, size, and design of cell towers, but organized citizen suasion is likely to be more effective, so limited is the legal authority of local jurisdictions. All of these utilities are notorious for their lobbying power, which functions at all levels of government to market their position and to block interference to their effectively self-regulating purposes.

Obviously, urban designers in any commercial district setting must consider such a pervasive and usually detrimental intrusion into the public viewshed as a high priority in any civic improvement strategy. While never easy to deal with, any mitigation of this condition will improve the outcome. For citizen activists, many of whom are veterans in dealing with utility line, substation, or cell tower battles, the subject commands attention as well.

## *Building and Fire Codes as Tools*

For the most part, building and fire codes focus on building safety and thus are usually not so much a factor in the quality or functionality of the civic environment. As noted in Chapter 9, though, fire departments' insistence on road width and turn radii requirements, generated by assuming the worst case event, may for all other times—24/7, year in, year out—directly diminish the livability, walkability, and sociability of countless neighborhoods. While the stakes are bigger, the effect parallels designing commercial strip and mall parking lots to accommodate day-after-Thanksgiving demand, leaving bleak deserts of asphalt for most all other times.

Firefighters legitimately ride a pretty high horse when it comes to setting standards, human life being a hard place to argue for flexibility. But to design community character solely around events that one hopes never happen may be, as with other single-disciplinary commands, going too far. In fact, progress has been made on all fronts in the interests of protecting and preserving street environments that are more pedestrian friendly without compromising fire and emergency accessibility.

As an example of a stratagem that comes out of a holistic design approach, one of the problems is the provision of an adequate turn radius when one narrower street meets another—how to make the turn without having to back and forth your way around. Since these narrower streets are typically built within rights-of-way of at least 50 feet, there are two possibilities. The optimal solution is to provide for bulb-outs or curb extensions at the corners, which provide refuge for parallel-parked cars and shorten pedestrian crossing distances. These can accommodate the 25 feet or so turning radius required, keeping larger vehicles a little honest in where they begin their turning movement. The other possibility is to provide curbs at the corner that are designed so that they may easily be rolled over: The turning radius problem goes away. So what if an emergency vehicle with its siren screaming and lights flashing rolls up onto sidewalk space once every few years or so? People can understand, and they will get out of the way. Similarly, the cul-de-sac is usually designed with at least a 60-foot diameter so that the emergency vehicle can leave the scene as quickly as it got there by not having to back up. It turns out that many fire departments acknowledge that backing up is no big problem, since the urgency to leave the fire scene is much less than the urgency to get there. Altogether, you have lots of square feet saved to provide the possibility for a walkable neighborhood or district character that will sustain peoples' commitment and investment over the long haul, without compromising emergency access.

As is usually the case, these kinds of breakthroughs can occur if the disciplines and community leaders get together and pledge to work for the goal of a holistically designed community. It turns out that most older communities have a lot of narrow streets already and that fire trucks historically can make it down them, maybe by driving more carefully but not necessarily costing in valuable seconds to get to the fire. So, yes, narrower streets than most current public works codes permit can be accommodated. The key, though, is not whether these particular suggestions work but whether the range of interests and disciplines can come together with an open mind toward a larger vision that will then fine-tune the dimensions and other provisions.

Portland, Oregon's "skinny streets" program is one example of moderating single purpose–generated rules. In Atlanta, we put in place a traditional neighborhood development zoning code for infill projects over a certain acreage that integrated street design with zoning provisions to accommodate projects like Glenwood Park, a new urbanist type of community.

## Financing Tools

While issues around financing public improvement programs and projects can get pretty technical pretty fast, both urban design professionals and community leaders wanting to create improvement strategies should include in the mix an understanding and concept of financing. Public project financing or even financing of private or nonprofit projects that serve some public purpose usually involves leveraging—that is, mixes of funds from a variety of sources, which might include public, private, or foundation sources, each with its own internal set of rules. In short, financing may be cast as an incentive for local jurisdictions to adopt policies and rules that support a greater good as determined by a higher authority.

Community people should familiarize themselves with the various financing vehicles, at least to the point of finding out their eligibility for consideration for financing structures for community projects layered from these sources. Urban designers responsible for having an idea about how to implement program or project proposals, should likewise be familiar and in touch with the managers of these various fund sources. Learning at least the framework and key features of the financing rules and requirements will allow both community leaders and urban designers to carry on conversations with local governing bodies and managers as well as private lenders or foundations so that they will be able to think strategically about how to structure the kinds of deals necessary to get projects financed. Since few projects occurring in the civic environment find their funding from a single source, understanding that different sources can be brought to bear on a project, with some idea as to how that might happen, is crucial information for influencing community improvement initiatives.

As with other aspects of urban design practice and implementation activities, the urban designer doesn't need to nor is likely to be able to structure the details of any such deals, only to know their overall framework with a view toward identifying possible resources and strategies that can make a project happen. Toward this end, the ability to put together a simple development pro forma, at least for the purpose of scrutinizing a developer's pro forma with some confidence, is worth learning, especially now when understandable software packages are widely available. Financing,

Still another barrier to holistically conceived neighborhoods or districts comes from the fire protection equipment industry in the form of ever larger trucks. As with all vehicles American, bigger is better, and, as competitive as fire departments typically are within and across jurisdictions, the perfectly swift and serviceable truck is not good enough once the manufacturers come out with the latest and greatest—and usually larger—product. It is easy to see that if street width and turn radius have a direct bearing on the walkability and human scale of neighborhoods, having to accommodate ever larger vehicles, even with acrobatic turning capability, doesn't help. These are the kinds of dynamics between problems and solutions that can only find happier outcomes if professionals from different disciplines get together with community leaders to support each others' individual aspirations to achieve a better whole.

obviously, is a critical step in moving a project forward and knowing whom to contact and how to bring people together to make it happen can help the process along. With such an understanding, financing may be cast as an incentive for local jurisdictions to adopt policies and rules that support a greater good as determined by a higher authority.

# Summary

We have reviewed a number of the key rules that determine how the civic environment looks and functions and suggested measures or strategies to consider for turning the rules we have into the tools we need to improve places. We have described ways that both urban designers and committed citizen leaders can engage themselves in codes and code modification. By analyzing the separateness of the various codes we have identified the high desirability and even the need to work toward synthesizing codes or in any event to improve their cross-disciplinary, cross-jurisdictional coherence and consistency. From a technical perspective, urban designers are in a good position to support this kind of effort or at least to place the various codes they encounter into an overall contextual framework. With this knowledge, urban designers can both help to conceptualize the components of public space as integrated systems and communicate that to their citizen and client constituents. Community leaders help themselves when they too become knowledgeable about how the codes work, and I have interacted with many who are more knowledgeable than many of the staff. At a minimum, they should be aware that there is a thicket of rules out there and that awareness of its make-up will assist finding a path through it. For both, consideration of the principles—change, design, and organizational—will assist navigating both the technical and the process content of the codes and their modification. Overall, the trends are positive for reshaping the regulatory framework to become an aid and not an impediment to making better places.

# 11

# TECHNIQUES

## Putting the Tools to Use

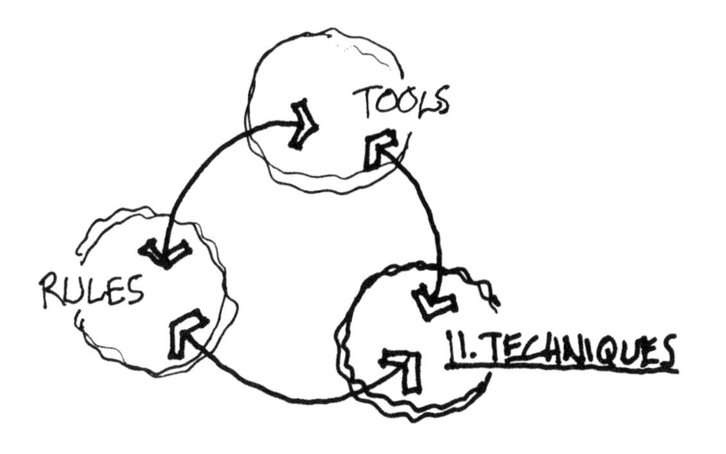


*Figure 11.1*
*Diagram portraying the interactive relationships between the rules, the tools, and the techniques for accomplishing place-improvement work.*

# Introduction

This chapter describes baseline considerations for approaching community design settings—how to apply design principles and tools to think about and conceptualize typical lot, building, block, street, neighborhood, district, town, city, and region configurations. Then it describes techniques for approaching community and urban design and development work, including managing technical materials on one hand, and on the other, behavioral and attitudinal considerations for interacting effectively with others in the place-making partnership. As has been the case with each of the main spheres of urban design methodology, the Process spheres—Rules, Tools, and Techniques—are all in continuous interaction; that is, what happens in one sphere might affect the nature and application of one or both of the others. For example, a new information technique, like the ability to synthesize codes using a GIS tool, could and probably would rather quickly change the ways in which the rules are crafted and bring forth a new set of tools for managing development rules.

The following guidance addresses considerations for street, block, lot, and building design in some detail, all oriented toward the improvement of the public realm. Then it deals with methodological skills and organizational techniques to assist in urban design and community engagement work. Finally, it considers attitudinal and behavioral factors that affect the processes for getting civic improvements done.

# The Pieces

*"A quilt of many colors..."*

The following design elements and measures are a sampling of the palette available to urban designers and citizen leaders to consider in creating or modifying the civic environment, particularly in mixed-use, mixed-density centers or corridors. They focus on the seams between the private and public realm. They are likely to figure in much of the content of community visioning processes for such places. All of the situations they address already have a presence in the codes and procedures of local government, and the suggestions here may prove useful in approaching code reforms. They span the rules of zoning, design guidelines, subdivision, public works, and others of the more specialized code provisions that account for how places are created and modified over time. In one way or another, rules addressing such issues are on the books in virtually every urbanized local jurisdiction.

For designers, the following guidance is offered as at least the beginning of conceptualizing the elements of places in terms that are measurable or quantifiable in some way. Designers and community leaders may want to think of them as a sort of place design checklist, particularly as a guide for how the rules might be better written to become positive tools for place improvement.

## Elements and Measures of Street, Block, Lot, and Building Patterns

Both for conceiving of new places and for stitching sites into an existing city or town fabric, urban designers should understand in functional and dimensional terms how to modify or design for sensible street, block, and ownership patterns, and building locations. They need to delineate the predictive street hierarchy, use, priority, and treatment. They should begin by considering the physical environment, reviewing its natural world characteristics first. Then, in considering the built world context, they should consider what the dominant patterns are in the place where they are working. They may follow the formalist, classic traditions where grids of streets take the lead in shaping block structure. They may choose to follow the organic, informal traditions where buildings and blocks they sit on may take the lead in shaping street patterns. Or for certain kinds of activities they may choose to follow the modernist tradition, where street and building may be dissociated from each other. Or they may choose some combination of the three.

In any event, they need to understand the environment they're working in, in terms of these basic elements. They should then aim toward setting forth a reasonable array of block types and sizes to support the anticipated range of activities, to provide access to these activities, and to create a walkable, pleasant civic environment as the seam between public and private. They need to encourage ownership patterns that will complement the underlying structure as well as provide for some flexibility of use over time.

Every urban territory, whether urban infill or a new urbanizing area, is different from every other, yet their elements—buildings, lots, blocks, and streets—are comparable. The starting place for urban designers is full consideration of all of the defining natural world characteristics, like topography, climate, hydrology, site drainage, green space, tree cover, other natural and biotic features, orientation, viewsheds, and the like. Such analyses, even where natural world features may have been obscured or obliterated, often reveal possibilities and values not necessarily obvious in the world you see before you. Then, thinking in terms of the three traditions, how properties, buildings, blocks, and street patterns lay out becomes the designer's focus. Natural features, human activities, and the built forms that accommodate and connect those activities are what give places their special identity.

In the "Built World" section of Chapter 3, we laid out several models that exist for defining the relationships between building, lot, block, and street, both functionally and dimensionally. Together, these form the palette from which community leaders can assess place-improvement alternatives for their neighborhood or district and urban designers can formulate initiatives for modifying existing or creating new urban territories. On the physical side, their analyses should always include the cross-sectional relationships across and along streets as they relate to the underlying natural topography. On the functional side, they should always consider the kinds of human activities and interactions that the civic environment is supposed to accommodate and support. From these analyses, the character, mix, and scope of a place can inform the dimensions, relationships, and accessibility requirements for street, block, lot, and building combinations.

## *Street Layout and Measurement*

Streets are the most obvious and ubiquitous shapers of urban form and more particularly the public realm. In urban areas they come in various hierarchies, carrying high, medium, or low volumes of vehicular traffic and providing access to the range of private property activities that flank them. In the organic or naturalistic pattern, streets are usually organized in a loose mesh of curving streets, usually not as predictably connected, following natural contours or other features or stylistically evoking such features, usually enclosing larger block sizes. In the formalist or classic pattern, streets usually are arrayed in grids, occasionally cut through by a preexisting historic travel way or by diagonal streets that may highlight points of interest in the grid. In the modernist tradition, street design theory supports the idea of dendritic street patterns at the larger scale and "superblocks" at the smaller, all requiring less land to be given over to auto travel and access and putting more emphasis on hierarchies of street type, from high to low volume, in which sidewalks are often disconnected from the vehicular travel way.

Organic, curvilinear, or naturalistic street patterns, with less predictable interconnectivity and larger blocks, tend to make alternative travel paths less certain or clear and as a result tend to favor some blockfronts over others. Grids of streets provide the greatest flexibility for both travel flow and blockfront development, since alternate travel paths are always available and all blockfronts have more or less equal access. And modernist street patterns with their emphasis on hierarchy and very large blocks tend to break down as travel paths when any part of the hierarchy is blocked, and they tend to limit street-fronting development only to those blockfronts designated for the purpose. With a few notable formalist exceptions, like Philadelphia, New Haven, and Savannah, older cities in the United States began their block and street patterns in the organic or naturalistic traditions. As they developed and as new towns and cities were established, they joined the "railroad cities" with more regular grids of streets and blocks. City and suburb development over the last 50 years shows the influence of modernist tradition, with its dendritic and usually disconnected street hierarchies and large blocks and the organic tradition with its winding, would-be picturesque streets.

"Railroad cities" is the term often given to the numerous towns laid out along transcontinental rail lines in the nineteenth century, in anticipation of their development potential stemming from railroad access (see Figure 2.13).

Transportation engineers grade streets in urbanized areas according to their network and traffic purposes into four categories, from the most heavily traveled and regionally significant to the most local, as follows: principal arterials, minor arterials, collectors, and local streets. These categories best describe the dendritic pattern, where cul-de-sacs flow into local streets, local streets flow into collectors, collectors into minor arterials, and minor arterials into principal arterials. Local streets are usually two-lane, mainly residential streets, while the rest serve progressively denser residential and commercial purposes, ranging from two-lane to four or more lanes. For the purposes of improving the civic environment, the main focus here is on the latter three and especially on principal arterials, with the rationale that where the most people are traveling should both look and function the best.

Principal arterial streets by definition carry high volumes of traffic and are often highways, with four or more moving lanes. In urban settings, they may also provide access to the myriad of commercial and higher-density housing that typically lines them. Minor arterials are like major arterials but serving lower traffic volumes and typically with two to four or sometimes more moving lanes, with mixes of commercial and residential activities. Collectors tend to be more weighted toward residential environments, often multifamily with occasional strips or nodes of commercial activity. For all three (except highways) in urban areas, it is essential to beef up the access function and slow down the through-traffic function, to rebalance the right-of-way use to favor the pedestrian over the car. It is possible, over time, to reconfigure such streets where they go through centers or for defined stretches along their corridors to become more like "boulevards" or "main streets."

For citizen activists and urban designers alike, incursions into what has been the province of the highway engineer may seem radical, calling into question both the travel speed and the behavioral assumptions that have accounted for so much of the anti-pedestrian, anti-bike effects of their earlier work. With little evidence-based research to support the roadway design assumptions as they have been applied to denser urban roadways, most highway engineering rests on the core premise that people don't possess the common sense to alter their driving behavior under urban driving conditions. Consequently, roadway design is significantly guided by the presumption that the crash will happen, and standards emphasize mitigating the damage, personal and property, mainly considering the car and driver.

While driver safety is certainly an important concern, many other factors are just as important, like the safety of other users of the right-of-way, reducing design speeds in congested areas, and prioritizing access over mobility. Designing only for the worst, drunkest, or the most distracted driver ignores the emerging realization that many of the roadway design rules actually exacerbate the very safety conditions they were assumed to improve.

The import of the shifts that are beginning to occur in highway engineering circles is profound. What happens in a right-of-way directly interacts with the size and distribution of activities along the block. Over the last 50 years, these interactions have tended to produce long stretches of higher-speed, unbroken car corridors, with building access and uses circumscribed by the demands of the roadway. This pattern is entirely familiar and describes countless miles of urban and suburban strips built under highway and traffic engineering standards. Popular and market demand is increasing, and new research is supporting, a sharply different approach, particularly for both existing and new centers and corridors that have a mixed-use and higher-density future. This approach utterly shifts long-term design strategies to support an activity-rich, higher-density frontage of buildings that requires wider sidewalks, landscape, better sidewalk lighting, bike and transit accommodations, narrower travel lanes, on-street parking, more traffic signals, and slower travel speeds.

If there is a single metric that can control the difference in these two radically different visions for the street, it is "design speed." Design speed, usually associated with a hierarchical street classification system, controls all kinds of design characteristics, like lane widths, horizontal and vertical curvature, turn lanes, acceleration and deceleration lanes, intersecting street radii, driveway widths and radii, on-street parking, and so on. These characteristics can make a street slow and walkable, not to mention bikeable and transit friendly, or not. They can enable or prevent a desirable urban environment, whether for a node at a crossroads, a village or town center, or a business or mixed-use district.

Recent research by Texas A&M professor Eric Dumbaugh and others, for example, suggests that lining an arterial street with trees set back three or four feet from the curb actually has the effect of slowing traffic and reducing accident rates, contrary to the prevailing assumptions over the last 50 years or so. (Design standards for years have required an eight-foot setback for street trees; that is, trees with greater than about a three-inch trunk diameter. One effect of this requirement has been to build curbside sidewalks with no buffer for pedestrians. This means placing soft objects—pedestrians in the curbside sidewalk—into the "vehicular recovery zone" instead of fixed objects such as trees. This rationale, giving the car and driver more time to correct the inevitable run-off-the-road impulse that we're all supposed to possess, prioritizes the potential crash damage to car and driver over the chance pedestrian who might otherwise be protected by trees or light standards.

For decades their application has degraded the quality and even the purpose of centers at all scales. Think of the sweeping curves at intersections that widen the pedestrian crossing distance and encourage higher turning speeds. Think of the acceleration and deceleration lanes that even further widen the street and reduce consciousness that a pedestrian might be present. Think of the absence of parallel parking and the treeless environment that eliminate any sense of buffering from the whizzing cars. All of these stem from imposing a 35 mph or higher design speed onto streets in high-density places where no one should be traveling faster than 20. In short, too-high design speeds account in large part for the anti-pedestrian, anti-frontage use character of most such streets. For starters, then, design criteria should consider a context that begins with lower design speeds, like 30 mph on denser, mixed use–serving urban arterials, with 20 or 25 mph more desirable for any street that anticipates or wants to attract pedestrian traffic.

Now, under mounting pressure, and with the increasing evidence emerging from the science noted above, the roadway design discipline is cracking the door on accommodating and even supporting an urbanist agenda. After all, from the point of view of the resident or daytime worker, there is rarely any reason for the travel speed to exceed 20 mph in urbanized, denser, mixed-use environments (except in the case of controlled access arteries or boulevards). From the point of view of the commuter, until now the singular focus of most highway systems and roadway design, higher speeds have seemed desirable, even though roadway capacity peaks between 25 and 30 miles per hour (a finding based on closer vehicle spacing at lower speeds). Another way to picture the dichotomy is to understand that the standards in place work pretty well for most of the country's lane miles, but they don't work for where most of the people are concentrated—city centers, town centers, suburban centers trying to retrofit, or urban corridors seeking to densify, diversify, and incorporate transit and a pedestrian-friendly environment.

One of the effects of separatism among the design disciplines responsible for the public environment has been a kind of schism between roadway design, design for transit and bikes, and sidewalk design. Together, these functions constitute the use of the public right-of-way. The right-of-way boundary establishes the edge between the private and public realms. Urban design and its collaborative disciplines, working together, can do a lot to create more effective use of the interface between curb and private property, both functionally and aesthetically. As suggested throughout, designers should consider the whole of the right-of-way as well as its access, seams, and interfaces with flanking property in approaching any urban design setting. A recent step in this direction characterizes itself as the "complete streets" movement, another welcome addition to the dialogue to broaden the synthesis of skills necessary to make places better.

The sidewalk piece of this wider weave of the public way has its own geometric, functional, and civic design characteristics, often taken for granted but important for urban designers to consider. The sidewalk, itself rarely considered holistically, serves a number of functions and puts a definitive stamp on the civic environment. It should contain, facilitate, and make safe the flow of pedestrian traffic; it should be attractive; and overall, it should make pedestrians glad to be there. The flow includes walking along, providing access to the street side and private property destinations that flank it, and pausing and maybe changing directions at corners and crossings. Beyond these pedestrian purposes, which should make people comfortable to use them, sidewalks are the key seam between public and private, where the transition from public life in the right-of-way to where the private activities behind the doors, windows, and walls occur. Finally, sidewalks are the repositories for all manner of necessary artifacts of urban living, like light poles, utility poles, traffic signal poles, signal control boxes, parking meters, regulatory signage, fire hydrants, newspaper boxes, vendors, bus shelters, bike racks, mailboxes, gas and water meters, grates, manhole covers, and standpipes, as well as amenities like trees, flower boxes, shrubs, grass, awnings, and benches.

A way to picture the sidewalk is to think of it as a stream or river. Its main current is the walking-along portion, where people just want to make it down the street with as little friction as possible. Its eddies are on either side of the main current. On the street side, the eddies may contain many of the above artifacts and provide access to parked cars, delivery trucks, or transit vehicles, or provide a buffer against moving traffic. This transition zone is a place for plugging meters, picking up a newspaper before proceeding into the main current—more a place to traverse than to walk along. On the private property side, the eddies may contain others of the artifacts and provide access to doorways and windows. Sidewalks that lack eddies are likely to be neither as pleasant nor as safe as those that have them. On the street side, walking alongside moving traffic or where people or goods are being discharged doesn't fulfill the design mission for a good sidewalk. On the private property side, without eddies the ability to pause to look in a window or pass through a door conflicts with the main stream of traffic.

The main current doesn't need to be fancy—its priorities should be to make the walking surface smooth and uninterrupted. It should not be a place where toes or high heels can catch. It may be useful to introduce a cross-pattern at regular intervals so that pedestrians can sense the progress they are making—and this sense of progress can be reinforced on the street side by the spacing of trees and light poles and on the private side by spacing of building bays. The eddies provide the best opportunities for incorporating the necessary artifacts with the amenities to create pausing places that are pleasant and work well—like for window shopping, going into and out of buildings, and getting into and out of vehicles without interrupting the main current.

While the river analogy helps to describe the sidewalk along the faces of blocks, it is not so effective at the confluences—when the sidewalk reaches the corner. Here, the flow slows down and the pedestrian has to make choices about where and when to go next—turning the corner, crossing the cross-street or the parallel street, waiting for a signal, buying a newspaper, or avoiding bumping into others making similar choices. The corner, then, is a place with a slower pace, where urban designers have the opportunity to reflect this change in experience and purpose in its visual cues. For example, is it a place where pausing is encouraged or where facilitating crossing traffic is more important?

The pedestrian corner zone can become plaza-like, converging people and activities. This is often where pedestrian-activated walk signals are located; higher levels of light may be found to better illuminate the mix of activities and choices that distinguish any intersection from blockfront travel paths. Intersections in many activity-focusing places are further enhanced

*Figure 11.2*
*A typical stretch of sidewalk along a blockfront, showing the main walking zone flanked by the transition or "eddy" zones that give access to parked cars or transit stops on the curb side or building entrances or window shopping on the building side.*

by pushing the curb line out, sometimes called "bulb-outs," "neckdowns," or "curb extensions," creating more space for the mix of activities that the corner plaza accommodates. If the pedestrian corners are so enhanced, there may be room for benches, news boxes, or plantings to further accentuate the corner's pedestrian character and reflect the higher traffic levels that intersections experience over blockfronting sidewalks.

A checklist for approaching street and sidewalk design functional problems, then, might include the following:

- Safe and effective flow of both vehicular and pedestrian traffic
- Transit access—a clear delineation of where transit goes and stops, sidewalk accommodation of the stops, and a distinctive design vocabulary to signal its presence
- Pedestrian safety and quality, including pedestrian crossing frequency, distances, comfort, and safety
- Appropriately spaced and configured intersections
- The geometry of the traveled way; that is, lane widths, turn radii, medians, discouraging acceleration and deceleration lanes, consideration of off-peak on-street parking, access control (minimizing driveways)
- The role each particular civic improvement plays in the larger urban context, like a rhythm of nodes or punctuation points or continuums, like avenues or boulevards
- Community landmarks, focal points, and gateways
- Careful thought about how frontages will look and function traveling along them, both from vehicles and on foot; for example, the massing, rhythm, pulse, flow, materials, transparency, and scale (vertical

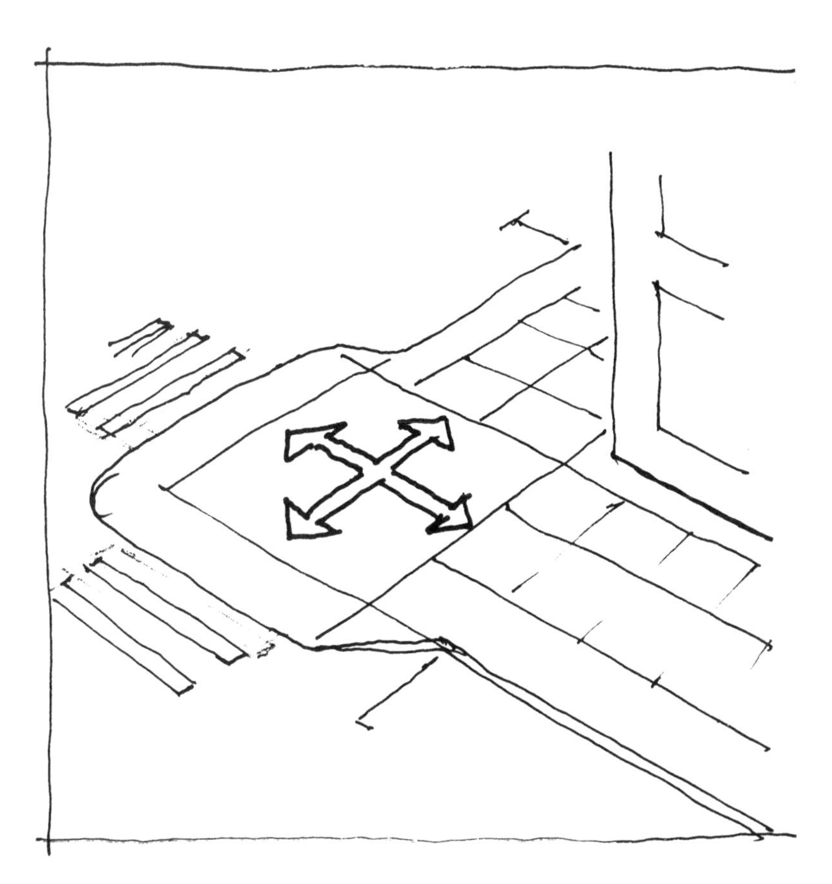

*Figure 11.3*
*The corner is a place for slowing down, pausing, changing direction, crossing the street, or buying a newspaper. This diagram shows the "bulb out" or curb extension as a way of providing a more gracious mini-plaza to favor diverse pedestrian needs—at the same time, parked cars are buffered from turning cars, which in turn have more generous turn radii and a disincentive to cut the corner.*

and horizontal) of the buildings, as well as the streetscape and pedestrian environment, including the vertical ordering devices of lights, trees, sign structures, and meters, and the horizontal ordering devices of sidewalks, plazas, landscaping, street furniture, parking, and the like

- In short, thinking of the public right-of-way and its flanking activities as an integrated, holistic design problem

There are standards that more particularly describe the dimensional and operational goals for streets in these urban settings, mainly from those put forward in the AASHTO "Green Book." While most of these set forth recommendations, not strict rules, many public works departments are inclined to incorporate them into their standards, where the balance between pedestrian and car tilts heavily toward the car. I suggest, therefore, some dimensions below and in the accompanying diagrams to bear in mind when negotiating design standards issues that inevitably arise in civic improvement efforts. Support for some of these may be found in the ITE's *Context Sensitive Solutions in Designing Major Urban Thoroughfares for Walkable Communities: An ITE Proposed Recommended Practice*, a more flexible and place-friendly set of standards worked out in dialogue with the CNU.

The guidance below is suggestive and flexible, and its applications should be considered in the larger context of the whole of the public right-of-way, according to varying local practice. As such it is not definitive (nor should be others' proposed standards), but a starting point for considering common dimensions associated with pleasant and functional streetscapes.

As noted earlier, the reevaluation of the rationale behind right-of-way design rules is actually beginning to take the form of proposed—and even in a few jurisdictions adopted—guidelines and standards. Oregon's Department of Transportation and Portland Metro have been in the forefront of such modifications, going back several years. The USDOT's Federal Highway Administration (FHWA) has recently promulgated a new guidance titled "Flexibility in Highway Design." Massachusetts has issued a new design guide based on CSS principles, and the Texas DOT is considering adopting the ITE/CNU proposed standards referenced here.

- Lane widths: try for 10 to 11 feet, where 10 feet (or an inch or two less) is associated with slower travel speeds and more pedestrian-friendly places; where transit lines exist or are likely, the outside lanes should be about 11 feet (many public works departments will press for 12 feet as optimal for moving traffic safely and swiftly, but keep in mind that this calculus tilts heavily toward the car, not all the other traffic).
- Turn radii: try for 10 to 15 feet in areas with high pedestrian traffic and no corner curb extensions or "bulb-outs"—shorter turn radii mean slower turning traffic and shorter pedestrian crossing distances, improving pedestrian safety and quality.
- Corner curb extensions or "bulb-outs": try to get them considered at high-pedestrian intersections—they afford greater turn radii for trucks or transit while reducing pedestrian crossing distances by projecting the curb line farther into the traveled way; they can improve the quality of the pause that occurs at corners; typically they embay parallel parking spaces, but they should generally not extend to the full 7 foot width of the parking space—5 feet or so is fine—so that it is easy to maneuver the car and so that bike lanes at intersections are more flexible.
- On-street parking: try for on-street parking on all streets lined with attracting destinations, thus pedestrian traffic; and for streets that carry significant vehicular traffic, try for on-street parking during the off-peak hours (many public works departments will discourage this on heavily traveled streets on the grounds that it impedes peak traffic, may be unsafe, and/or that enforcement is too difficult—again a

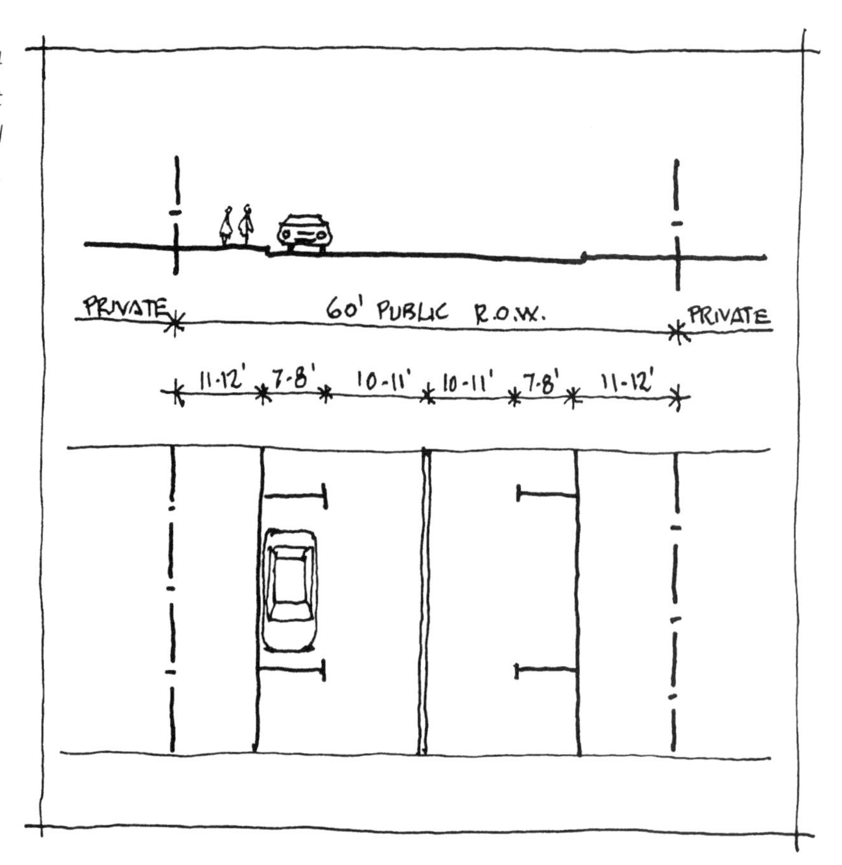


*Figure 11.4*
*Diagram of typical street characteristics in section and plan with nominal dimensions.*

question of balancing the interests according to a holistic vision of how people want their civic environment to work and look).
- Sidewalks: travel path, the "main current," should never be less than 5 feet wide (generally even in residential neighborhoods) and should be wider depending on the pedestrian traffic flow; street side band or "eddy" should be at least 3 feet and more depending on all the stuff it has to accommodate; private property side band or "eddy" should be at least 2 feet, again depending on how much stuff the building side of the sidewalk has to accommodate (usually not applicable to lower-density residential blocks).
- Lighting: try for a lighting system that works both for the traveled way and for the sidewalk; this is important for both residential and mixed-use high-traffic areas, although the latter need higher-intensity lighting. Typical spacing for roadway lighting ranges up from 60 feet, often staggered from one side of the street to the other, with mounting heights ranging up from 25 feet. Pedestrian lights, usually spaced more closely, are about 12 feet high so that they are not shaded by tree foliage.
- Trees: in general, street trees should be selected in ways that consider positive visual impact, growth rate, suitability for a constrained urban environment, shape, seasonal performance, and shedding characteristics, among other features; my experience, mostly in the South, suggests that street trees should be at least 3 inches caliper measured at breast height and either vase-shaped or limb-upable, so that clearances for pedestrians, awnings, and curbside trucks and buses are sufficient—usually a minimum of an 8-foot vertical clearance or more

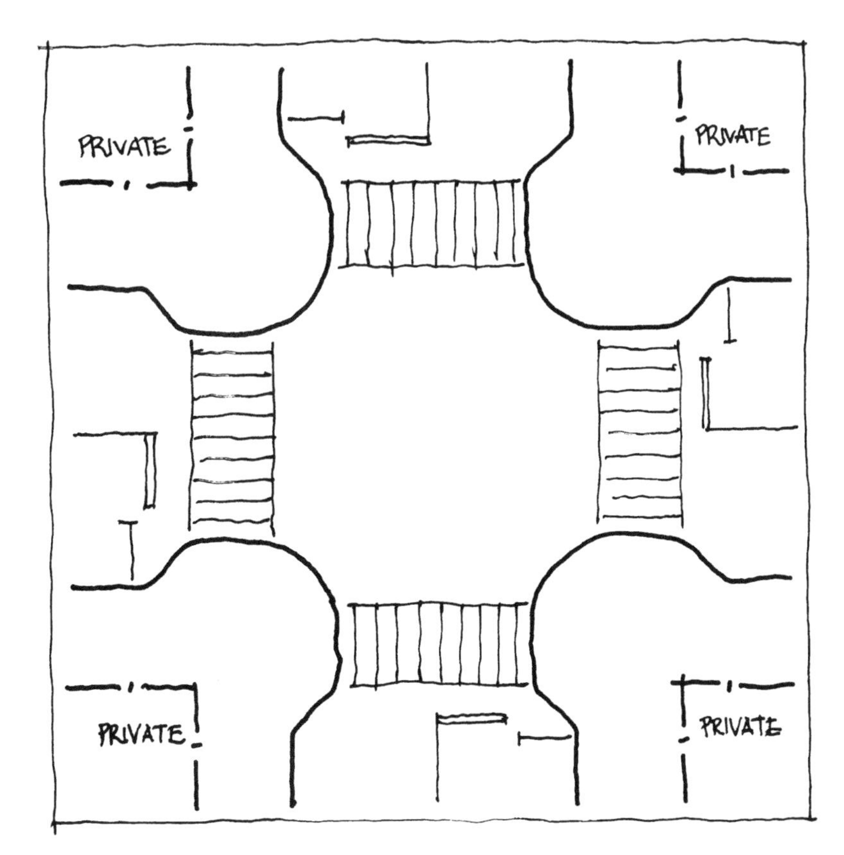


*Figure 11.5*
*Diagram of corner characteristics with bulb-outs or curb extensions, which shorten pedestrian crossing distance while still affording adequate turn radii for large vehicles.*

is desirable; trees' root structures typically need at least 25 cubic feet of planting room in a suitable planting medium, with 25 square feet of permeable surface area, to have a good chance of making it (and these numbers may vary according to geographic location); planting details should provide for root growth in ways that do not cause sidewalks to heave or underground infrastructure to rupture.

- Materials and detailing: so varied is the cast of characters, in this case the artifacts or objects, that need or want to be in the streetscape, that any aim for uniformity of design is probably quixotic and even if successful potentially stultifying; it should be enough to be conscious of all the stuff that needs to be accommodated and aim for some degree of complementarity, both functionally and aesthetically.

The important thing to remember about standards, whatever their sources, is that they come laden with the values—and the authority—of their authors. Urban designers should familiarize themselves with all of them but should always keep the longer-term holistic vision, the bigger picture, in mind in selecting them for design applications. In the context of the code modifications necessary to fulfill the larger vision, they should also expect resistance from whichever authority is responsible for interpreting and administering the codes.

Despite whatever problems the process throws up, a positive and graphically portrayed view of the desired bigger picture can become a useful motivator, from citizen or district organizations through their elected officials and professional planning and urban design staff to the agencies whose cooperation is ultimately essential. Using Adobe Photoshop or Google SketchUp software, an example of such a picture could show the transformation over time of the typical arterial street into an urban boulevard: narrower travel lanes, perhaps medians, more frequent intersections, tighter turn radii, slower travel speeds, on-street parking, shorter pedestrian crossing distances, wider sidewalks (reclaimed from the usual big setback, surface parking frontages), street trees, pedestrian-oriented lighting and signage, lined with two- or three-story or higher buildings with windows and doors opening onto the sidewalk and parking and utilities behind, beside, or at least neatened up.

Community leaders and urban designers can join forces to proclaim such an outcome as a policy goal, get that adopted into the jurisdiction's comprehensive plan, and then set about changing the code structure to make it happen—over time. For both current practice and each and every one of the above alternatives is subject to the rules—the codes and standards that create the places we live in. Such transformations, even with a single block so treated, can catalyze others up and down the way. The change can also support and accommodate commercial and residential densification, thus property value, through attractive, walkable, and workable civic environments.

## *Block and Lot Layout and Measurement*

The streets, mostly public, provide the connective fabric for the blocks, mostly private, that accommodate the full array of human activities that make up urban life. Block, lot, and building patterns both reflect and promote the relationships among these activities, from accounting for necessities to proclaiming the latest style. In current times, low-density residential blocks remain pretty much like they have been over the last hundred years; that is, either gridded as in the formalist tradition or curvilinear as in the organic tradition. The push and pull between optimal block sizes reflects the interplay between land cost, marketing, and bottom line. Except in the most affluent neighborhoods, the more "product" a developer can place on a block structure, the higher is likely to be his profit margin, since cost of construction does not vary as greatly as cost of land.

In the more mixed-use and higher-density environments, there has emerged a kind of pattern and set of dimensions that accommodates retail, residential, and parking requirements, where the residential and retail activities wrap around a central core of parking and maybe community space. I call the ordering device for these kinds of patterns and blocks "the magic number 60, plus or minus 10." Sixty feet and its multiples more or less accommodate a range of current mixes of uses pretty comfortably, though all the above activities can be accommodated in other modules as well.

*"The magic number 60, plus or minus 10..."*

Street-level retail activities tend to favor depths of at least 60 feet. The most efficient parking bays are those with perpendicular parking on either side of a central driveway, and 60 feet is about the minimum that can accommodate such bays. For circulation between bays to work, there should be two or more such bays, so that 120 feet becomes a convenient dimension for accommodating parking internal to the block.

As seen in Figure 11.6, 60 feet also describes an approximate depth for residential bars—that is, linearly arranged apartment or condominium units that might occur along a blockfront or above retail space. Sixty feet allows for a double-loaded interior corridor and residential units on either side whose interior dimensions allow for good light and view penetration from the exterior wall. Often, though, depending on the density of units and parking requirements, lower floor bars are likely to be single loaded, or perhaps 35 feet deep, since the view into a parking deck is undesirable except for the most car-addicted.

Putting this all together, block widths of 240 to 250 feet can accommodate internal parking with residential and retail activities that can face onto the street. The length of such blocks is less sensitive, though subdivisions or multiples of 60 feet again have advantages in terms of logical retail and residential structural bay spacing, so that block lengths of up to about 420 feet are pretty flexible and still sensitive to the walking distance along the blockfront. For reference, the circumference of a 240 by 420 foot block is a quarter mile, about as big as blocks should be to accommodate mixed uses and densities in a good walking environment.

Picturing multiples of such blocks corresponds to rules of thumb of about five minutes, or one quarter mile as a comfortable walking distance for most people. Twelve such blocks arranged in a rectangle of four blocks wide and three blocks long describes a near 40-acre square of one half mile on a side.

Parallel-parked cars tend to be definable in 60-foot modules as well, since three spaces add up to about 60 feet (really about 63 feet, since the target dimensions for parallel spaces are about 7½ by 21 feet). Finally, street rights-of-way with all the elements noted earlier tend to be definable around the 60-foot dimension, a kind of minimum for a two-lane collector street with parking on both sides. and about 80 feet being a kind of minimum for a four-lane street with on-street parking.

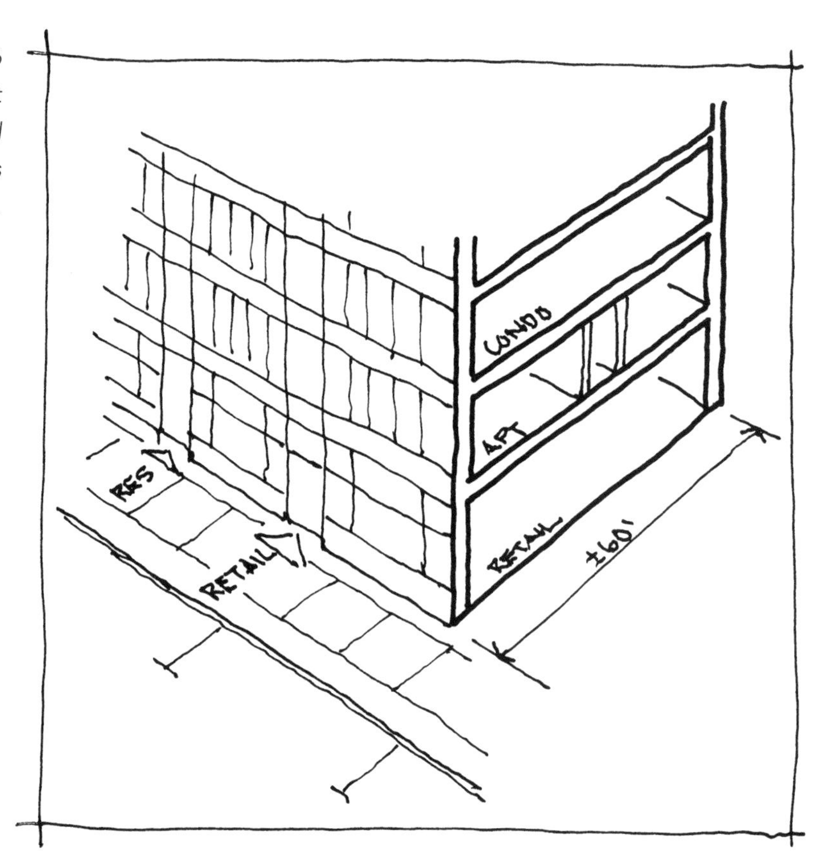


*Figure 11.6*
*A 60-foot nominal depth is sufficient to accommodate many retail and commercial activities, as well as residential or office activities above.*

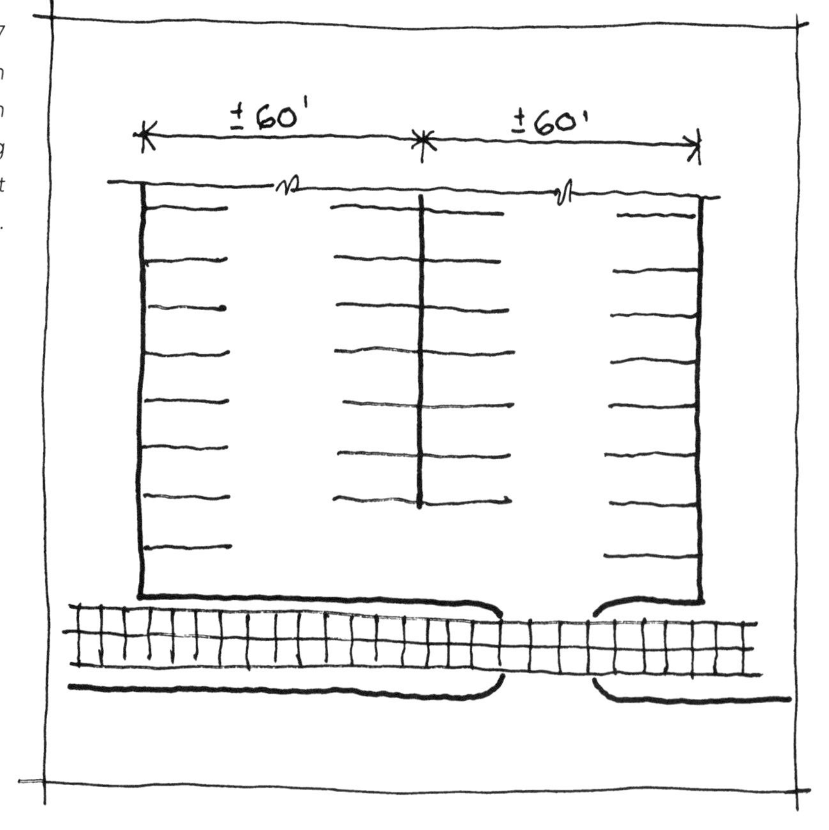


*Figure 11.7*
*A 60-foot width is about the minimum to accommodate parking bays, with cars parked perpendicularly along a central aisle—the most efficient configuration for off-street parking.*

For urban designers and community leaders, the "magic number 60" and its applications should not be taken as standards or directions but simply as convenient touchstones for assessing and comparing the values of various approaches to street and block design and the possibilities for various multiples or subdivisions of that number. Developers are usually not particularly conscious or interested in such relational parameters, since their frame of reference is the project and making the project work in whatever framework it has to. Government planning departments are more likely to conceive of their tasks in such terms, since comprehensive planning is always a baseline of their activity. Even so, because of the property-by-property application of zoning rules and the continued disconnect

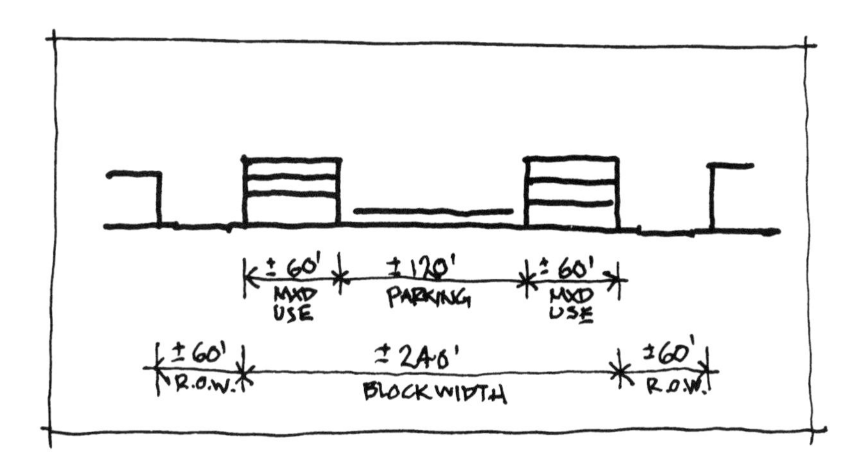


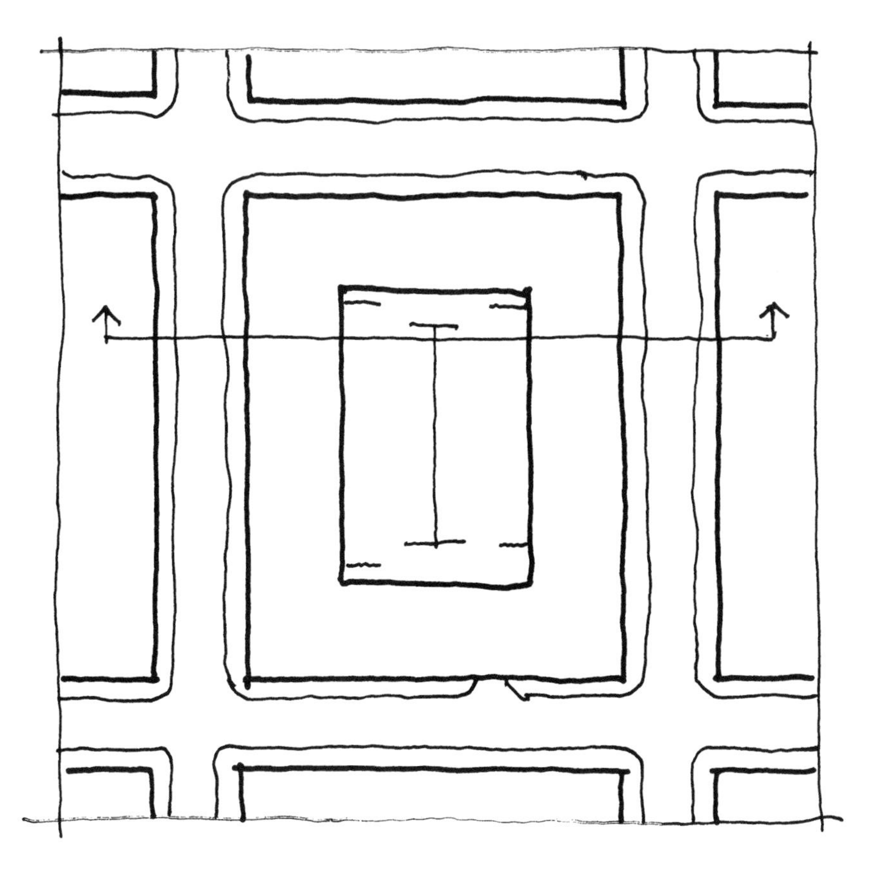

*Figure 11.8a, b*
*Diagram showing the make-up of an urban mixed-use block in section (a) and plan (b), with parking and community open space in the middle surrounded by retail and residential activities with public pedestrian entrances off of the street.*

between zoning, subdivision, and public works standards, grasping pieces of urban territory holistically remains a challenge for many.

Finally, at the scale of the activities that line the blockfront, zoning and design guidelines have a decisive impact on the quality of the civic environment. Such issues as building setbacks, heights, window and door location and treatment, signs, awnings, bay spacing and articulation, horizontal banding, materials, ornamentation, sidewalk and streetscape design, lighting, location and treatment of open space and of parking and loading altogether define a place, visually and functionally. Zoning provisions and design guidelines provide the palette of what's possible, which should be tailored to the particular character that exists or is desired.

## *Private Property Interface Considerations*

Beyond any particular area's zoning or design guidelines, which are usually pitched toward individual private buildings, urban designers should consider some of the larger-scale implications of private property and building design that may define places within the context of the block. These may address such issues as building and activity adjacencies—what's next to or across from what. Mediating the changes that new, higher-density and mixed-use developments bring to urbanizing or infill environments requires careful analysis of what surrounds the site to ensure that the change works, contributes to, and gains the support of the existing community.

Both in terms of compatibility of activities or land uses and in terms of scale and access, do the proposed adjacencies make sense? What does one see across the way from the front door, the parked car, the second or third story (or higher) window, and is that what one wants to see? What is the spatial and functional experiencing of arriving at the place, whether on foot or in a vehicle? This analysis process applies equally within the place and between the place and the communities around it, both horizontally and vertically, especially for vertically integrated, mixed-use proposals. Whether in high-density or neighborhood-oriented centers, urban designers need to pay attention to the issues of adjacencies.

Mixed-use development, increasingly accepted as contributing to the lively character of urban places, has its own set of issues. Where are the front doors, the public face, and back doors, the private or service space? Where are the residential entrances (private), the office entrances (semi-private), and the shopping entrances (public)? How are parking, service, and delivery for these mixes accommodated? What is across the street or down the street from what, and how does the character of streets and streetscapes and public plazas or park spaces contribute toward the accommodation of the range of activities, from private and low volume to public and high volume? For residential mixed-use structures, this means identifying where and how the general public gets in and out and where residents and their visitors get in and out. For retail structures this means addressing the "two front door" dilemma caused by providing a walkable streetscape on the one hand and sufficient parking for auto access on the other—often on opposite sides of the building.

Considerations for putting together design guidelines or for creating or reviewing building designs should include all the ways that buildings frame, shape, activate, and interact with the civic environment. Guidance about these relationships could include:

How the building meets the ground;
How the building engages the pedestrian realm;
How buildings frame the street (or park or plaza);
How the building turns the corner;
How the building meets the sky;
How the building announces itself—in the vista, at the scale of the site and the front door;
How, where, and for whom is open space provided;
What is the building made of—what are its exterior materials;
How is the building ordered—its vertical bay spacing and its horizontal banding to reinforce pedestrian travel patterns and view cones;
How and where is service provided; and
How and where parking is provided and connected to the building.

Parking needs to escape its parasitic site-by-site framework and find more holistically conceived strategies, addressing its spatial and connectivity challenges and opportunities. Shared parking can obviate the need for every block, or worse every lot, to be broken up by parking and driveways. Parking design should provide a clear, safe, and encouraging pedestrian travel path from the parked car to the intended front door, whether on surface lots or in decks. The design elements to achieve this end may include such features as sidewalk delineation and treatments, light and light structures, trees and other landscape devices, wayfinding devices, topographic ordering techniques (e.g., terracing to break up large expanses of pavement), vertical circulation structures (in decks), and adjacent activities or land uses.

## *Larger Considerations*

Design considerations for larger agglomerations include some of the following factors. The activities that make up mixed-use areas, for example, whether a center, a corridor, or a transit stop, include retail, residential, office, and civic space. Where retail is a significant component of a mixed-use development, consideration must be given to the full range of retail types, sizes, and markets. Concepts that affirmatively address public policy goals, community aspirations, and design values, while not always turning the quickest profit, may better meet with sustained success. Again, the issue of adjacencies, both horizontal and vertical, need to be addressed, such as the kind of retail that should face the arterial street; whether, how, and where to locate "big boxes"; where and how retail can be stacked, how parking and structured parking can support rather than detract from the environment; what kinds of retail activities complement each other; what kinds of retail activities serve the three- to five-mile (or farther) radius around the site; and what kinds of retail serve the nearby, more walkable neighborhoods.

Streetscape design considerations, which should be conceived in both transverse and longitudinal section as well as in plan, begin with the recognition of the street as the public access for all of the private uses that flank it. The goal is to properly frame an attractive, walkable environment and to create a rhythm of activities that celebrates the connectivity that the streetscape provides. Pedestrian and/or bike connectivity within and to and from the place—both its civic spaces and its mixed-use activities—should be clearly delineated. The discussion above on streets addresses many of the elements to consider.

Public policy priorities are increasingly calling for mixes of housing types in higher-density centers and corridors, including single-family, townhouses, and multifamily; either freestanding or mixed use (over retail or office or surrounding parking); or adaptive reuse of existing structures. Similarly, public policy is gravitating toward support of a range of price points that, to the extent possible, provide housing choice for the range of incomes to be found in the employment of the centers and nearby areas. These should consider flexibility in how housing can interact with retail, community space, and existing neighborhoods, in the context of proposed street and block patterns.

Office space tends to concentrate in or near major commercial centers or corridors and is usually not a major activity in smaller or more neighborhood-oriented areas. In the more suburban or modernist separation-of-use environments, offices may cluster in their own campuses, usually with no residential activity and minimum retail services or eating establishments beyond the company cafeteria. Even in mixed-use centers, though, those responsible for creating large office buildings, whether corporations or developers, are usually intent on making their mark. This means a presence unsullied by coffee shops or residential components, often a grand plaza or a grand entrance lobby, shiny expensive materials, and the space of civic interface carefully patrolled. In smaller mixed-use areas, convenience office space is a good contributor for meeting neighborhood and wider community need, often providing continuity in street-fronting activities where insufficient retail demand might otherwise leave blanks.

Civic spaces in mixed-use urban environments take many forms, responding to and reflecting the range of human activities that require or desire them. These are the places where people mix. Maybe in a little square or plaza; maybe along a street with a wide enough sidewalk for trees, benches, or kiosks; maybe in a coffee shop or bookstore, which some have termed "third space"; maybe in a park. The activities that civic spaces support line up pretty well with the design goals for civic environments. They make places where people want to be with others, whether friends and family or strangers—people who are drawn to the same place for reasons that perhaps signal a certain compatibility. Shops, restaurants, and building lobbies all provide the interpenetration of public and private that encompasses that seam, and the suggestions above about how to make that seam work all apply to this type of civic space. The suggestions about streetscape treatments similarly apply to the character of the public space that connects private activities and their seams.

Another kind of civic space is that which incorporates elements of the natural world into the shared space—"green" space in its full range of interpretations. The ability to connect people in their places with traces of the natural world usually enhances the goal of creating an attractive and workable civic environment. Thus trees, plants, flowers, water, topography, landscape views, natural features, and links to park spaces all figure into the design palette for civic space. Any place-improvement strategy should generate an affirmative position toward the green space environment, both in the immediate site area and in its connections to adjacent neighborhoods. Urban designers and community leaders should put community-serving purposes first and design civic space to achieve that end.

Designers are finally coming out of a dismal period of park and plaza designs where they have created an unacceptable number of failures, perhaps for lack of a holistic understanding of what draws and serves people or perhaps for too much deference to the monumental design traditions of landscapes for the rich and royal.

Akin to the "green" content of civic space are always the larger environmental issues: the air, the water, the land, the earth, the climate, the orientation. It has become clear that the sustainability of the environment, from urban to wilderness, is a front and center issue for now and the generations to come. Urban designers have had a kind of two steps forward, one step backward history of recognizing and incorporating this reality into their theory and practice over the last 40 years, with landscape architects being perhaps the most forward-looking over that time. By now, all involved in civic design, from civil engineers to building architects, should be designing spaces and structures that consciously and integrally incorporate approaches that mitigate or enhance the environmental consequences of project proposals. The consciousness and integration should run the gamut from details of how storm water run-off will be handled or how site and building designs respond to the path of the sun to how the civic space design encourages use of other modes of transportation than the drive-alone car, among others.

The framework for considering the range of environmental issues came into being with NEPA and its multiple state and local spin-offs. Now on the horizon and moving toward front and center are issues of human health, like how does the design for the workability and pleasure of the civic environment affect individual and community health? Issues including many environmental factors, like microclimate and air and water quality, are being joined by connectivity patterns, which run from walkability and its impact on physical health to civic space as described above and its impacts on social health. We have described the potential impacts this confluence of human impact and environmental impact might have on rule making, and we pointed out how vital it is to have design-trained people in the middle of any such conversations. Without such a presence, the legal, scientific, and public policy participants who usually dominate such activities, however unintentionally, are certain to create outcomes that don't work spatially, either from a functional or attractiveness point of view.

Altogether, these elements of built space in urban centers and corridors, the streets and the block, lot, and building configurations they define, make up the palette for creating better civic environments, both functionally and aesthetically. Keeping in mind both the pieces and their holistic possibilities will aid both urban designers and civic activists in engaging the change processes that are always underway. They have application both at the policy or comprehensive plan level and at the more focused zoning, subdivision, and public works standards level and at the design guideline level. The ultimate success of design choices is likely determined by the extent to which they reflect the values and aspirations of those in whose name they were conceived.

# Navigational Techniques

*"Let me count the ways..."*

In addition to the elements and measures available for managing visioning and information sharing processes, there are many methodological techniques that urban designers and community people may find useful. I include here those that I have come to over the years, incorporating the work of others similarly involved along the way, as well as others that are in common practice. The first set relates to skills, and the second set focuses on organizing the work. Many of these particularly support and encourage community-involved planning, design, and development, while others may facilitate more centrally directed processes. We urge their use here for overcoming commonly accepted truisms that seem to or do block the way toward success, like "you can't fight city hall" or "I couldn't get a loan" or "if I do that, my project won't pencil out," or any number of other cliché obstacles that may face the process. Finally, we consider attitudinal and behavioral postures that may affect attaining success in improving places.

## Methodological Techniques

### *Placemaking Checklist*

As a way to pinpoint characteristics of good urban design, various theorists and practitioners have promulgated lists that serve here as useful references or checklists. In forming the Congress for the New Urbanism, its founders proclaimed a charter, in which they grouped their principles or observations into three sets of 9 each: one for the region, city, and town; one for the neighborhood, district, and corridor; and one for the block, street, and building. The full language of the resulting 27 is available on their website, noted earlier. Others follow the Letterman "top tens" format. The AIA's Center for Communities by Design suggests:

Design on a human scale
Provide choices
Encourage mixed-use development
Preserve urban centers
Vary transportation options
Build vibrant public places
Create a neighborhood identity
Protect environmental resources
Conserve landscapes
Design matters

My colleague Richard Dagenhart places a primary emphasis on the subdivision of territory, listing it first in his 10, which I have paraphrased below:

Subdivision of territory takes precedence over design or land use
Streets are primary in determining urban form
Boundaries create places, buffers destroy them
Pay attention to what is the "front" and what is the "back" in organizing blocks and buildings
Focus on type, not style
Design for incremental change
Mix uses
Places are made, not designed
Architects should think like landscape architects, and landscape architects should think like architects
Invent with vigor

Jeff Speck, when he was the director of design for the National Endowment of the Arts, put forth his 10, as reported in Planetizen in January 2005:

Design streets for people
Overrule the specialists
Mix the uses
Hide the parking
Small is beautiful

Save that building
Build normal (affordable) housing
Build green/grow green
Question your codes
Don't forget beauty

The Urban Land Institute has put out a number of pamphlets and books that tailor their checklists to specific place typologies, many of them using the "top 10" format as well. Project for Public Spaces has developed sets of principles over a long practice of providing place improvement services. These and many others available in the websites noted earlier are all useful examples for those involved in place improvement initiatives, both as ways for organizing the work and to make sure that important considerations are not omitted. All of them, though, are subject to selective application according to priorities that emerge from processes specific to each place, its people, and its set of circumstances.

## *Rules of Thumb*

We identified a number of dimensional characteristics of streets and blocks in the foregoing discussion. These can be thought of as "rules of thumb," or predictive and recurring information that is useful for designing the civic environment. As one gains more experience in all of the various phases of place planning, design, and development, one comes across a whole treasure chest of rules of thumb that the people involved have come up with as shorthand ways to inform their thought and decision-making processes. While the computer has certainly upstaged the back of the envelope for all of the different actors in the development business, most still carry with them a handful of facts and relationships that they have found to be reliable in understanding, shaping, analyzing, checking, or testing assumptions about what to do, and how and whether to do it.

For urban designers, these rules of thumb, either of necessity or by definition range across all the place-building disciplines. As with others of the cross-cutting information datasets that an effective urban designer needs to know, the idea is not to be an expert in any one aspect of the endeavor but rather to know enough to have a feel for the interactive forces and criteria that are likely to guide one's or another's position or decision on some aspect of the process.

For my students (and before them my staff) I encourage absorbing, picking up, and recording these kinds of measurements and other useful bits of information as they proceed along on particular improvement initiatives as they encounter them. The list here is a starter kit, spanning both design and development criteria. The values are always approximate, in which consciousness of the existence of such criteria with some sense of their rational ranges and relationships is more important than any particular number. They describe many of the elements present in places. Observing, understanding, and becoming facile in using these measures and terms will enhance one's ability to generate urban design and development concepts. Many of them derive, logically enough, from our sizes, capabilities, and comforts as humans seeking to act effectively in our physical world. Knowing them from the small to the large scale will contribute to reasonable and accurate proposals, as well as establishing credibility and effectiveness in interacting with people from other disciplines engaged in the place-making business. In compiling such a booklet or file,

I encourage the use of graphic means, even simple sketches, so that one has in mind a picture of these key and recurrent facts about our physical world, not just a number.

## *RULES OF THUMB (for the reader to fill in and supplement):*

### Typical Dimensions

#### *People-related dimensions:*

Person size (typical range)
Seating height, width
Table height and width (typical)
Door size (typical)
Handrail height
Americans with Disabilities Act (typical dimensional standards)

#### *Vehicle-related dimensions:*

Car size (typical range)
Lane widths
Parking space (parallel)
Parking space (angled)
Parking bays (typical widths)
Vertical clearance (parking decks, roadways, railroads)
Bike lanes
Bus dimensions and capacities (typical range)
Rail transit dimensions and capacities (typical range, e.g., light rail, street car, heavy rail)
Travel design speeds and related lane widths, grades, turn radii, horizontal and vertical curves, and shoulder and curbside requirements

#### *Street, block, lot, and streetscape-related dimensions:*

Street widths (one-way, two-way, parking one side, parking both sides, two-lane, four-lane, five-lane, and more)
Right-of-way considerations and typical widths (sidewalks, building setbacks, etc.)
Block sizes (blocks whose typical dimensions seem comfortable for a pedestrian to walk along)
Comfortable walking distances, including comfortable vertical walking conditions, like hills and stairs
Lot sizes (typical dimensions related to the types of activities or land uses that occur on them)
Streetlight mounting heights (pedestrian, roadway)
Setback distances from face of curb or back of curb to trees, lights, parking meters, signs, and other street furniture
Tree heights, caliper, and placement (typical range for new trees of different species in the streetscape)
Sidewalk width and placement (typical range)
Crosswalk width and placement
Tree well size and placement (typical)
Benches and seat wall dimensions and placement
Bus shelter dimension, L × W × H, and placement

Phone booth dimensions and placement
Mailbox dimensions and placement
Vendor cart or booth dimensions and placement
Trash basket dimensions and placement
Street signs (names, regulatory, and informational), size and placement
Parking meter size and placement
Signal control boxes
Utility poles—heights and placement of transmission and distribution lines as well as communications
Sewer inlets—size, location, design, and apparent direction of flow

### *Building and mixed use–related dimensions:*

Floor area ratios (FAR)
Building setbacks or yards
Building heights (one story, two story, etc.)
Window heights and spacing for storefronts
Entrance setbacks, doors, and lobbies
Residential unit sizes (single-family house—range; multifamily residential—approximate square footage ranges, for studio, one-bedroom, two-bedroom, three-bedroom, and four-bedroom; ceiling and floor-to-floor heights)
Retail space considerations, e.g., frontage dimensions, depths, heights, loading requirements, and locational considerations for various types of retail
Office building—floor plate area ranges and ceiling and floor-to-floor heights, square-foot-per-person ranges, and the like
Other building type typical-sized generators, e.g., big boxes, sports facilities, educational space requirements, research facilities
Densities required for transit of various kinds to be viable
Densities, FARs, and parking ratio ranges in areas where new initiatives are proposed

### *Characteristics of the natural environment:*

Latitude, longitude, altitude
Acre, township, and range dimensions (also hectares)
Sun angles (through the day, through the seasons)
Shade and shadow
Prevailing winds
Microclimate (heat islands, surface winds, sun, and shadow)
Percentage of impermeable surfaces
Topography (slopes, grades)
Land/water/sky interface

### *Typical cost ranges:*

Rent rate retail (typical ranges)
Rent rate office (typical ranges)
Rent rate residential (typical ranges)
Residential cost ranges, pegged to HUD affordability criteria
Travel cost ranges, pegged to vehicle miles traveled per day and fuel costs

Development costs (typical ranges and elements)
Housing construction costs (typical range by type)
Office construction costs (typical range by type)
Retail construction costs (typical range by type)
Land costs (typical in various settings)
Streetscape costs (typical for sidewalk, trees, lights, underground and aboveground utilities, street furniture, other common elements)
Basic elements of a standard development pro forma

## *Self as Measure*

Perhaps one of the more heartening aspects of urban design and community leadership is that activities related to place improvement tend to validate one's own responses and reactions to places. If you like or don't like something about the physical or functional character of your neighborhood or your business district, there's a high probability that lots of other people agree with your assessment. This general consensus has been borne out in countless visual preference exercises and charrette table exercises over the last 15 or 20 years. What this means is that people can approach the tasks of place improvement with pretty high confidence in the relevance and validity of their own responses, reactions, and ideas, at least to the point of laying them on the table. People are all the time moving through their civic spaces, pausing, stopping, driving, arriving by transit, walking, biking, feeling the place through its daily and seasonal cycles, finding it easy or not so easy to find one's way, to navigate, irritated by some aspects, pleased by others.

This daily constant immersion into the regular places of one's life is a way of understanding "scale"—how a place feels in the context of one's own size, shape, movement patterns, access, and comfort. The issue is not the validity of one's experience or any special knowledge required to interact with that spatial experience; rather it is the degree of consciousness that one brings to the experience. One can trust his or her reactions and responses, both objective and subjective, but to enhance the positive or reduce the negative in those daily experiences, one needs to become ever more conscious of the materiality of that experience. Knowledge or consciousness of place can be thought of as a sort of three-dimensional matrix, where intersections represent bits of information to be connected. All of us have many of those bits of information stored up through our daily experience of space, but without consciousness—which takes interest more than intellect—of how these bits might hook-up or of how they might hook up more effectively, the bits just sit there.

Examples that pop out in conversation or more formal settings are rife. There's not enough signal time to walk across the street. Or, it's great since they extended the curb out and put in a median. The sidewalk is too narrow to comfortably walk down it. Or, the setbacks on those new buildings sure make for a nice walk. There's dog poop in the tree well. Or, I'm glad people have started picking up after their dogs. There's no tree in the tree well. Or, it's good to have those new trees. There's newspaper or fast-food wrapping blowing across the sidewalk. Or, I saw someone picking up the litter, I think I'll do the same. The building's 300 feet long and only has one entrance and no windows into the inside; or the ground floor windows have reflective glass in them, and I can't see in. Or, those show windows really look nice. The parking deck is dark, dismal, dirty, and smelly. Or, ever since they painted the deck white and installed those bright lights, I feel safe; I know where I am and where the elevators and stairs are. The parking lot is hot and a long way to the sidewalk or building. Or, it really makes a difference since they broke up that lot with trees to provide shade. It's raining or snowing and there's no cover. Or, I like this street because of the awnings and canopies that shelter me from the elements. Here it is, our main street, and look how shabby it is. Or, those banners and flower boxes make me feel like someone cares. Why can't they do something about that old weedlot in the middle of our business area? Or, that's such a pleasant little pocket of greenery in the bustle of the city. There's graffiti on the bus shelter and a bottle in a bag on the bench. Or, since they got rid of that old advertising contract for a new one, so far the bus shelter is clean and pleasant. That burned-out house down the block casts a pall on the whole neighborhood. Or, that new code enforcement guy has really been able to keep things neat in the neighborhood. I have to walk in the street because there's no sidewalk or where there is one it's all broken up. Or, I'm glad the city found the funds to provide sidewalks since so many of us walk. Why do they have to park their car in the front yard? Or, one thing I like about this old neighborhood is the alleys: keeps the street looking nice—no power lines, no cars in the yards.

These are all daily and valid experiences, where most but not all would agree on the importance and on the pros and cons of the experience. It should be noted, though, that even if there is a general consensus about the merits of a physical attribute in the civic space, that doesn't mean that a minority view might not also be valid and important to consider in determining a course of action. Sometimes it is the minority view whose inclusion in the planning and design for a place is what enriches it.

We live in a cultural world these days where much is made of the virtual, the appearance of things being more real than the reality, making decisions based on appearance alone. Reliance on illusions is an often compelling way to sell products or ideas, or to divert people from realities that may be depressing or advertised as unfixable. Periodically, people can be dazzled with a big lie, unmoved by a little one, and disinterested in the cold truth. If using oneself is to be a reliable measure for assessing the civic environment, invoking change principles, perhaps people should not be too resistant to the power of the immaterial in inducing them to behave one way or another. Instead, they should insist that the whole picture be contemplated—it's not either the material or the immaterial, it's both of them interacting with each other that has more likelihood of uniting people around common action.

One day when I was railing on about utility lines trashing up an otherwise perfectly good streetscape, my colleague Dot Matthews demurred that such lines provide good roosts for birds on a wire.

## Communication

Fundamental to appreciating and understanding the nature of a place and what to do about it is sharing information in ways that are efficient and as unambiguous as possible. Talking works okay, but as a linear expression that only works when only one person talks at a time, it may be inefficient for communicating holistic characteristics or ideas, and no matter how descriptive or even eloquent one may be, lots of different pictures are elicited in different people by the same words. So it is good to use graphic means to describe and conceptualize places. Urban designers in particular must have an effective set of graphic communication tools in their kit, ones that are flexible, descriptive, and attractive.

Some of the software programs with good representational and conceptual capabilities that are reasonably user-friendly include:

PowerPoint—allows one to organize photographic, graphic, and text information into simple presentations

Photoshop—allows one to manipulate photographic or other graphic images to show how different modifications might look; a good "before" and "after" tool

SketchUp—allows one to picture structures and the spaces they define in three dimensions

Google Earth—allows one to download aerial photography of just about anywhere at whatever scale one wants and to create bird's-eye views of the selected territory, as well as ground level photography for many places

ArcGIS—allows one to map all manner of critical information into a visual relational database, so that, for example, building outlines, property lines, ownership, zoning, tree cover, and demographic characteristics may be displayed and compared in all possible combinations

Nationally relevant websites that may provide images and techniques useful for urban design communication were identified in Chapter 10, and most regional and local planning agencies, as well as chambers of commerce, utility corporations, and larger business district organizations are likely to have a wealth of usable information on which to build a communications database.

Huge advances have and are being made in technologies to fulfill this mandate for anyone who expects to be effective as an urban design professional. Mapping, photography, animation, websites, and computer or physical modeling are just some of the techniques that have become pervasive, accessible, and relatively easy to use to improve on the age-old "a picture's worth a thousand words" truism. As it happens, these tools are no longer held in the special province of any particular discipline but are more and more accessible to anyone with the interest and Internet access.

The goal of communications graphics for urban designers is to be able to put people into the picture. Being able to see yourself in the picture cuts through all kinds of ambiguities and uncertainties that texts or the spoken word can't overcome. At the same time you can share that experience with your fellow conceptualizers. The more closely you are able to replicate your daily experience and then imagine various alterations to that experience, the more effective will be the process. After all, our experience of places is never linear. Even walking down the street is not a linear experience, since you are aware of and experience what is all around you and all your senses are at work, so that even daily public space routines are immersions into the whole of the environment, for better or worse. The desired goal is to capture and to be able to communicate that wholeness in a report or meeting setting in order to identify the objective aspects of the experience for shared analysis.

For all the "gee whiz" graphic packages available and in use, it is still important for urban designers to be able to improvise by hand—drawing, ideally sketching but at least diagramming—so that all one needs to communicate a set of circumstances is a chalkboard and chalk or a flip chart and marker. Low tech; if you can write your name you have the ability to draw—not make art, but draw. The skill of linking the eye to the brain to the hand to the paper is one that is learnable, and anyone wanting to be effective in urban design should take the time to learn that skill. Drawing and diagramming are not just useful skills for being able to put people around the room into the picture. They also provide a way for urban designers to make objective the sensations of their experience. In ways similar to the rules of thumb or using oneself as a measure, drawing is a way to record, measure, and consider all of the content of urban design for the purpose of exploring alternative models for how to make places better.

There are inherent drawbacks to most of the computer-based graphic design and representational tools. Computer images often look "finished" or "fixed," conveying a "done deal" message on the one hand, and discouraging interaction on the other. Their graphics too are often cold and abstract, even the three-dimensional ones, so that the very regularity and precision of the medium in fact misrepresents the places so pictured. Freehand graphics, on the other hand, even fairly crude ones, share with the real world a kind of unfinished, work-in-progress presence, and they lend themselves to depicting the character of a territory as we experience it. For example, cross sections that are scale accurate through an area may not represent the experience of the place, where modest topographic contours might actually be a pretty steep hill to climb on foot or on a bike. Or a single large tree in an otherwise barren urban landscape might seem insignificant on a scale-accurate map, but the most important event in the actual experience of that landscape.

Sometimes, simply marking up a computer-generated map with freehand enhancement or text notations might make the map or image much more approachable by people who feel comfortable putting their mark on the image instead of fearing to sully the polished computer image. Some users of computer packages to portray their proposals, in fact, are quite aware of trying to represent their work as much further along than it is, and they do so in the hopes that people will be inclined to accept their representation as "finished." The ability to change the picture, to absorb, incorporate, and reflect legitimate feedback of the group is a way of building trust and team spirit. It is also a way of ensuring that valuable information and values are picked up and incorporated into the project as it moves forward.

While on the general topic, it is worth a few lines to underscore the importance of the onrush of digital communications means and capabilities. The opportunities for community activists to engage this resource seem boundless. Their applications are in no way limited to tapping information sources as discussed above. The ability to communicate with constituencies and support groups whenever and wherever is a great resource for advancing a thought-out position on all manner of activities that may enhance or afflict the public realm. The better informed and more consensually understood and supported community positions are, the more likely they will gain support and possible approval and implementation.

Where the tools of mass personal and direct communications media will take the enterprise of improving the civic environment is hard to predict, except that the prospects for broad-based community influence can only improve. Like others of the new technological advances in this field, however, people should be alert to the potential abuses from the usual suspects and even from within one's own constituency where personal agendas may be lurking.

For city planning students interested in the physical environment and urban design, I have come to offer a one-unit freehand drawing course. Its principal purpose is to break down inhibitions and build the confidence to be able to draw or diagram commonly recurring images and relationships that people in the field regularly encounter. More substantively, my colleagues and I have developed an urban design methods lab that familiarizes students without any design background, as well as architecture students lacking any urban design background, to consider, absorb, and apply much of the content outlined thus far in this chapter.

My first eye opening on the subject came a few years back when a bank headquarters had purchased an adjacent block with the intention of tearing down the few remaining buildings and installing a nice asphalt parking lot. Few though they were, the buildings housed activities that had a wide base of support in the adjacent neighborhood and among the people who worked in the area, one of which was a decades-old and treasured restaurant. Within hours of discovery of these intentions, the CEO of the bank had received hundreds of emails, temporarily overwhelming his computer. He backed off the proposal.

## *Organizing the Work*

Here we deal with ways to organize the work and to keep track of the myriad moving parts that go into a place-improvement process. There are lots of different techniques for carrying out these kinds of tasks, and I have found the ones summarized below as effective in dealing with a range of place-improvement endeavors, often in various combinations or at different stages of the process.

### The Caterpillar

For all the emphasis on the interactive and holistic sets of relationships that are pervasive in urban design and community design and improvement, this technique may appear quite linear and deterministic. Instead, the "caterpillar" is a simple way to remember all of the types of action steps that invariably happen to get a project done in a place-building process.

While the caterpillar may be a convenient mnemonic and organizational device, it is important to bear in mind that the actions its segments represent may occur in any order, seemingly later ones sometimes fundamentally altering seemingly earlier ones. With this prelude to this technique, as the diagram shows, the actions may typically occur, however, more or less in the order shown below:

Vision—sets the broad framework and general direction for an urban design and development initiative

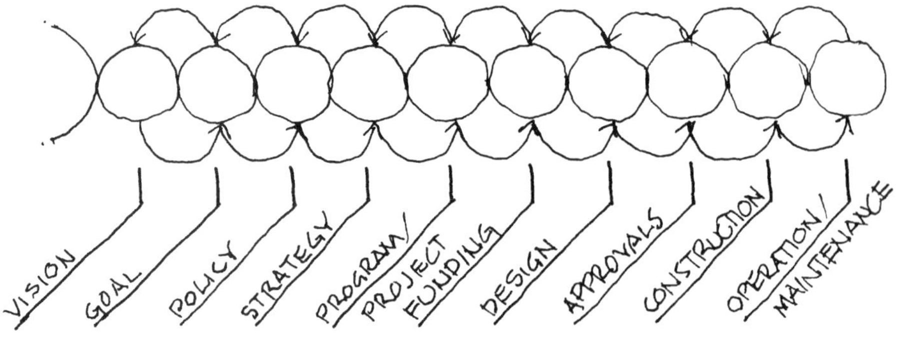

*Figure 11.9*
*This diagram, dubbed the "caterpillar," describes the range of activities that generally make up the flow of work for an urban design and development project; following the overall interactivity principle, however, any one phase along the continuum may affect any other, at any time; thus the forward and backward arrows that give the caterpillar its form.*

Indeed, the project development process is so interactive and dynamic that I considered using a roly-poly as the right image to portray it, but one of my students, Chirayu Bhatt, pointed out that a caterpillar properly nurtured turns into a butterfly, while a roly-poly or pill bug just goes downhill.

Goal—identifies in detail what the initiative is supposed to achieve
Policy—identifies or establishes the formal and legal framework within which the initiative will be carried out
Strategy—charts the course of actions, priorities, and milestones necessary to carry projects forward
Program or project—spells out the elements, location, timeline, and outline pro forma of the project
Funding—identifies the budget, sources, and uses of funding necessary to build
Design—details what the project will look like and how it will work, verifies the budget
Approvals—secures the rights to build the project from whatever are the approving bodies
Construction documents—translate the design into the form (plans and specifications) necessary for a contractor to bid on and build the project; verify the budget
Bid and award—receiving bids and awarding contract based on price, schedule, and other project delivery criteria
Contract—provides the legal agreement between the owner of the project and the builder, the basis for moving forward to construction
Construction—builds the project
Operation and maintenance—completing, commissioning, operating, and maintaining the project over its life

Over the last several years both public and private project sponsors and developers are gravitating toward various forms of "design-build" delivery strategies, where the elements above from Design to Construction become more closely integrated, usually saving time and money; this trend represents commonsense integration of disciplines, in which the standard bearers for design quality need to be particularly active.

As Figure 11.9 shows, while the actions necessary to get a project built generally follow something like the above sequence, new information may be discovered or developed at any point in the process that may call for a review and possible adjustment of earlier action steps. Obviously, the farther downstream toward construction a project reaches, the more cumbersome, costly, and inconvenient such new information may be to absorb and reflect in the project.

The realities of project development place a priority on getting it right the first time and on coming up with strategies where new feedback can be anticipated and accommodated with minimum disruption to the flow of events. Where a jurisdiction anticipates and recognizes a formal community input process, it should be clear that this input should be occurring in the caterpillar's head, not in his midsection where approvals are to be found.

These steps apply to any project in the civic realm, not just good ones. Yet it is important for any urban design professional to be clear on the whole of this framework and bear it in mind all the way along—know where he or she is in the continuum and always be aware of the steps taken and the steps to come. Community leaders similarly need to be aware of the steps and sensitive to their time requirements and cost impacts if the community is to be a constructive partner in the place-building process.

In Atlanta, the Ansley Park neighborhood took advantage of the project timeline for the Atlantic Station development to interject monetary demands at a time when the project was so committed that its developer and state agencies essentially had to negotiate to keep the project going.

## Timelines

It is important to develop and maintain time tables, critical path charts, or some other time and task management device for any initiative. Such a structure identifies and monitors all work tasks and their interrelationships with each other across the anticipated timeline, and it provides a way to communicate with all involved the status of the work as it proceeds. The timeline should be structured in a way that the work is broken down into understandable and digestible chunks so that anyone can see and understand the work program and its progress as a whole.

In setting up the timeline, it is important to build in time for each task and the project as a whole to account for unknowns that invariably pop up. A lot of impatience develops over this issue, yet it is critical to be up-front and to resist the insistent impulse to commit to dates that cannot be met. If the time pressure demands are too great, then at least commit with clear conditions so that when the inevitable delay, like a need for new information or additional work effort, happens the urban designer can absorb the ensuing frustration with as good grace as possible. Rarely does something happen as quickly as everyone would like. Completing work on time and in budget, a cliché goal, is still valued by nearly all. Design and implementation responses to the dimensions of time will vary, yet maintaining a timeline checklist will ensure that the implications of time for design strategies at different scales are duly considered.

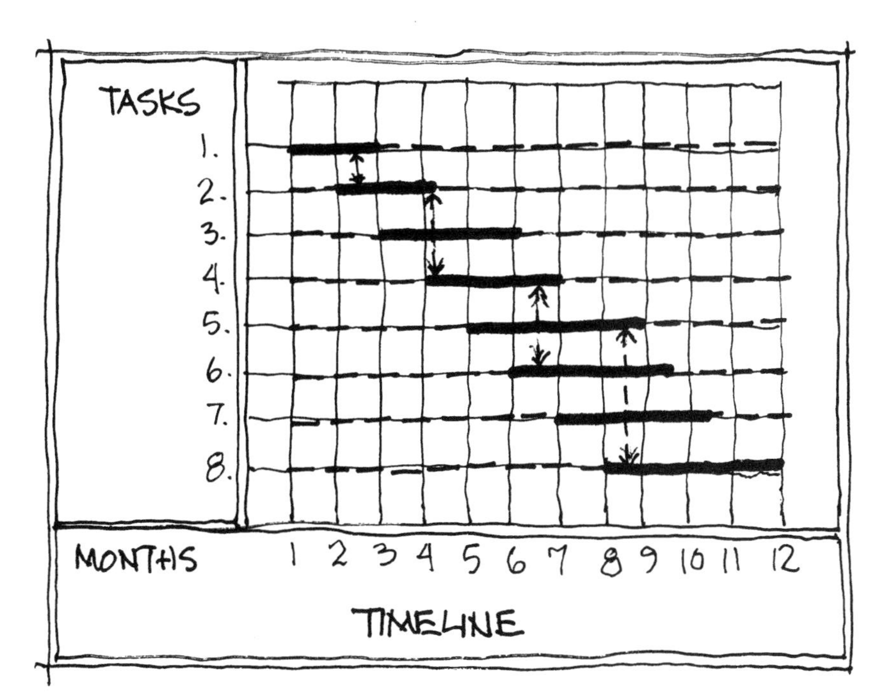


*Figure 11.10*
*It's always a good idea to at least rough out a schedule that identifies all of the tasks necessary to get from the beginning to the end of a project and the timelines when they may be expected to be completed. Note that the activities may interact with each other across the timeline at various points.*

Another dimension of the timeline to bear in mind applies to design and implementation effectiveness. Where does a place come from? What have been its strengths? What are its lasting salient characteristics? Its ups and downs? Its demographic history? Its access or connectedness to surrounding communities? What is it now? What's been working? What hasn't been working? What are the views of the people who live in the place? Make their livelihood there? Why does a place attract people? Same people? New people? And how do all these different groupings of people view the future? Are they in it for the long haul? Are they quick-buck artists? Looking to build or sustain a place as a community anchor? Or ready to move on? What is and for how long is their interest or investment in the place likely to remain? Only with some understanding of the people's and the place's history and potential future can a designer come up with strategies that can realistically be met.

Applying the design and change principles to project initiatives will address this set of considerations.

## TOPIC

I use the acronym TOPIC to remind myself of the range of factors that usually affect the analysis of an initiative or a proposal for changing the public realm:

T stands for technical
O stands for organizational
P stands for political
I stands for investment (financing)
C stands for cultural

Together they define the range of issues to resolve to move projects forward. (I use *I* instead of *F* for financing because TOPFC is hard to pronounce and remember.)

There are always technical issues, the nuts and bolts of designing for a physical problem at whatever scale. This is where the premises of the desired outcome get tested for fatal flaws, whether they may be conceptual or material. The technical analysis, for example, is a good way to guard against "solutionism," where the ache to launch a big idea may get ahead of its realistic groundings. Or it may be a good way to test alternate ways to solve a solvable problem, compare costs and timelines, establish priorities, and pick a way to proceed. The principles in Part Three, and especially the design principles in Chapter 6, provide a good framework for dealing with technical issues.

The ideas for the kinds of cooperative partnerships it takes to get work done in the public realm often falter over organizational issues that invariably arise between and within the private and public organizations that share the responsibilities for action. The principles and especially the organizational principles are useful for navigating through these often troubled waters.

Since everything that happens in the civic environment requires approval and often other forms of support from the jurisdictions where it is happening, urban designers and community leaders should understand the political issues that could arise and be ready to craft an approval strategy that can gain political approval. This is where the change principles may be particularly helpful to understand what's going on politically and how to deal with it.

Whatever the vision, the program, or the project, it will cost money. Developing a financing strategy is fundamental to getting anything done, and the sooner financing approaches are integrated with other aspects of a developing project the more likely it can get done. As pointed out in the discussion on financing rules and tools, much of the work done to improve places requires or calls for mixed financing, from multiple public, often private, and foundation funding sources.

Finally, urban designers and community leaders should pay special attention to the culture of the place that is calling out for improvement. Recalling the change and design principles, places work best if they reflect the existing or intended users, their culture, their vision, and their sense of priorities. This means not flying in some "solution" that worked somewhere else and assuming it will work anywhere. Usually, some of the base premises and measurable attributes of urban design that works will carry the designer into a project, but only listening and an attentive reading of the community will produce a truly satisfactory result.

Like the relationships between other elements of urban design, the TOPIC elements predictably all interact with each other, but in unpredictable ways. A change in assumptions in any of the five is likely to change the definition of the problem for the other four. Thus, for example, if the technical, organizational, financing, and cultural issues seem to be coming together, a political problem can cause the need to shift or adjust some or all of the other sets of issues. Or substitute any of the elements for any of the others, and you will get a sense of their interactive nature. I have experienced all the combinations.

## SWOT Analysis

Another acronym, SWOT stands for Strengths, Weaknesses, Opportunities, and Threats. This method derives from strategic planning practices from the 1980s in both city planning and business management theory, which I mark as an early recognition of the interactive nature of planning and urban design practice. The idea is to approach situations with the recognition that the factors that, in our case, act on the civic environment are already in play and to figure out how to engage them in ways that can generate strategies for improving them. Associated with the somewhat puckish characterization of "disjointed incrementalism," strategic planning contrasts with the more linear, "rational" planning methods that date from the modernist ascendancy. Like other methods and techniques, the SWOT analysis is a useful framework that needs to be joined with others as appropriate to engage place-improvement initiatives.

The idea is to research and analyze an ongoing situation in the framework of its strengths, its weaknesses, its opportunities, and the threats that may compromise an effective outcome. Consistent with the "build on strengths" principle, the logic of beginning with strengths is that effective strategies are built around positive, not negative factors. Even so, every situation has its weaknesses, and these need to be understood as well for creating a workable strategy. These understandings and analyses when placed in a larger context can be counted to reveal opportunities that may not have been apparent, both internal to the situation and external from its surrounding conditions. Correspondingly, threats may become apparent that could diminish or even thwart the effort to improve the situation.

Imagine, for example, an inner-ring suburb where strip commercial properties have been vacated as the demographics have changed from middle-class white to lower-middle-class minority populations. The former merchants, white dominated, moved farther out to stay associated with their perceived customer base, and the new population has yet to prove its customer potential to the usually white-dominated retailing and investment base. The strengths in such a situation are likely to be a large, close customer base and the superior access afforded by the arterial street. The weaknesses are the perception or perhaps the reality of limited buying power and the bleak aspect of the largely abandoned strip. The opportunities are to recast the real estate into a more vital and more attractive node along an otherwise undifferentiated travel corridor, probably requiring the impetus of neighborhood organizing and minority entrepreneurs to recast the market to reflect its new demographic. The threats could be difficulty of access to private investment capital, disinterest on the part of local government, or inability to maintain the persistence necessary to organize and proceed through the daunting obstacles.

As generalized as such an example is, in broad strokes it describes a methodological approach to improving a situation in the civic environment, and such improvements are occurring all over the country, both in inner cities and inner-ring suburbs. The people involved may or may not be conscious of any particular formulaic construct within which the necessary activities are taking place. Yet what happens is describable in terms of the SWOT analysis, and the applicability of the caterpillar, timeline, and TOPIC analyses and action strategies should be evident as well. The premise here is that urban designers and community leaders may be more effective if they relate what needs to be done to achieve a positive result to frameworks that will help keep track of their progress and plan for follow-on steps. The importance of design cannot be overemphasized, for if the work that gets done either doesn't function well or doesn't visibly proclaim an attractive transformation, it will not attain its full market potential and may not be sustainable.

## PEA

Professor Ellin's book, *Incremental Urbanism*, provides a full discourse on this way of approaching urban design situations.

More specific than SWOT analysis but related to it is PEA, where *P* stands for Preserve, or as its formulator puts it, "protect what is valued"; *E* stands for Enhance; and *A* stands for Add, or "address what is missing," which could mean adding new development. This mnemonic comes courtesy of Nan Ellin, an urban designer and teacher at Arizona State. Particularly applicable to dealing with existing community situations, practitioners necessarily must proceed respectfully to follow its guidance. It rather neatly incorporates the principles of building on strengths; reflecting the culture, values, and priorities of the people there; and coming up with action steps that grow out of a citizen-driven process. It is a device which guards against "solutionism" or the one-size-fits-all approaches that too many consultants and theorists are likely to espouse.

The positive nature of the PEA approach begins with *preserve*. Thus the urban designer or the community leader defines a situation with the assumption that much of what exists is likely to contribute toward an improvement strategy—drastically different, for example, from the modernist inclination to blow it all up and start over. *Enhance* means to build on the contributing elements, looking for opportunities to bend them toward a cohesive vision that is likely not evident in the current situation. Finally, *add* means identify missing pieces whose inclusion can complete the cohesive vision. As an attitude, the PEA methodological technique conveys respect and a commitment to listening from the beginning. It provides a basis for teaming with local stakeholders to discover and honor what's already working and building the improvement strategy from that base. Needless to say, such an approach is more likely to build the trust necessary for successful outcomes than any number of more top-down or "expert" approaches.

## The Dummy

In undertaking improvement endeavors that require an organized work product, it is often useful to prepare a "dummy" of the expected product on day one or at least early on in the process. Even though most of the pages will be blank, the scope of the work to be done takes on a tangible form, and the dummy provides both an electronic and hard copy organizing and filing tool. Thus the broad stroke content of the work may include such sections as:

- Introduction and summary
- Background research (which may include history, demographics, policy framework, the physical, social, cultural, and political environment)
- Testimony (which may include the information and ideas of the stakeholders, ideally including a fair representation of citizens, leaders, businesspeople, professionals in the various disciplines, prospective investors, and government officials)
- Analysis and prioritization of all of the above
- Alternative scenarios
- Feedback
- Recommendations
- Appendices

Relating back to the interactivity principles, the caterpillar, the timeline, and other devices, the urban designer may find pieces of information flowing into such a system seemingly randomly. A citizen has a good idea—it may go into the alternate scenario section. A longstanding opportunity to make a quick, consensual improvement pops up—it may go into the recommendations section, or even be taken as an early action activity that is doable and can build trust and confidence that improvements can happen. The important thing is to be able to contribute to, see, flip through, and assess a document that looks like a product. It gives confidence that the work can and will be done, while not committing to what the content of the work might end up being.

The dummy has equally effective application for organizing the graphic content of any report. Corresponding to each content section, there should be rough sketches that will picture what the graphic images are likely to be. Thus the background and history might include historic maps or images of the place; a figure-ground map that focuses on the built/unbuilt or private/public patterns; mapped and sketch representations of the natural world checklist; and dot maps of demographic data, like population, income, age, and race. Here too might be images of precedents—other places that have dealt with comparable problems and their results.

Analysis maps may include various layerings of the data, like patterns caused by overlaying population maps with transit lines, schools, parks,

This device is used widely in the R/UDAT program, where participants benefit from the focus and urgency that the dummy provides for producing a finished document in five days for client towns and cities, often published as a supplement in the local newspaper.

and job concentrations, or topography, transportation, and density patterns. Or, at the finer-grained scale, parking lots, on-street parking, sidewalks, driveways, utilities, building footprints, and property line boundaries. Or whatever may be relevant to teasing out an emergent vision for how people want the place to become. Manipulation of such spatial and graphic data in any number of ways has become both accessible and quick through GIS, and identifying in sketch form the kinds of graphic data useful to the purpose is a good way to think through what will be necessary or useful before going high-tech. Picturing alternative scenarios follows a similar process, where at the beginning you know there will be alternatives without knowing much about what they're likely to be.

All in all, making and keeping up the dummy is a way of thinking through and picturing the work before it happens and as it is happening. It's a way of figuring out what format options there might be for both graphics and text. It's a way for organizing materials for electronic or hard copy presentations. It's a way to prioritize what's more important than what, like, for example, a brake against getting bogged down in data collection or research that isn't likely to contribute to a vision or its interactive actions. The emphasis on visual representation too should shorten and focus text, usually reaching a more communicable balance, since the pictures are worth a thousand—or more—words.

### Journalistic Device

What I call a journalistic device is the simple framework that is characteristic of news reporting—covering the what, who, where, when, why, and how, and how much—questions that any work flow needs to answer. As obvious as these questions are, it is remarkable to me how often one or more of these considerations is omitted from documents or presentations. In particular, the why question seems to get short shrift, especially in technically dominated work efforts. Civil engineers often call the why question the "need and purpose" statement, others may wrap something like it into a goals statement. Yet many reports and presentations simply take the project or work as a given, without examining its motives or motivators, important information for a process that intends to involve all the participants who will ultimately determine the successful outcome of the project. My concern with inadequate consideration of the why question is that it may mask political or financial gain motives that could run counter to the broader civic purpose to which projects in the public domain aspire.

## *Dealing with the Media*

In the course of any civic improvement synthesis-seeking process, particularly if in a business district or in a prominent or controversial neighborhood setting, the press usually gets wind that something's going down. How to deal with it? Usually if synthesis is the goal and possible, especially if a development initiative proposal or neighborhood position is particularly aggressive, the best news coverage is usually no news coverage. The problem with both the print and video media is that they are there to write a story that will capture the attention of their readers or viewers, where conflict and polarization are the best attractors. The reporter is unlikely to know much about the development process or the background of the situation and consequently will fall back on premises or understandings that are untested stereotypes. The story pitch will reflect what the reporter brings to the story (often not much), not what the story brings to the reporter (for which the reporter hasn't the time nor often the interest). Through this inevitable distortion, if the story sounds good to one side it will sound bad to the other, with the wider exposure further driving the wedge of difference between the parties and leading them closer to a winner-take-all kind of attitude, in which no one is likely to be the winner.

The real shame of all this is that the opportunity that almost always exists for the win-win outcome dims, the parties start playing to the media, and the media, whether through hubris or to sell newspapers or advertising, becomes a player. Thus any news is bad news.

Only when the media makes it a priority to really understand and report the fullness of the substance and all of the positions on a topic of importance can it play its information-sharing role in a way that may contribute to a reasoned and acceptable outcome. I have had the good experience from time to time to work with reporters or editorial writers who are interested and willing to give a civic improvement initiative its due. Such coverage can serve to defuse a hot issue and contribute to reaching a workable synthesis. But it may not sell newspapers or attract TV advertising.

Press relations, an industry in itself for large private sector organizations and political leaders, is important for civic improvement efforts, though planners and urban designers working in the public interest, lacking the PR resources, pretty much have to wing it on their own. In these circumstances I offer a couple of suggestions. First, keep in mind that usually the media motive is to flesh out a story that can vie for the front page or the top of the news. This invariably draws them to controversy, even to the extent of fueling controversy. They will want to get a brief sound bite or pithy quote that can serve that purpose. They may even suggest a "fact" or two from some other source as a way to elicit a confirmation or denial that will reveal more than they knew before. I have found the best way to deal with these situations, unless the reporter has shown himself or herself to be serious, thorough, and responsible (in which case I feel comfortable sharing full information), is to begin at the beginning and lay the fullest of policy background and base, in a way that monotonizes—but fully elucidates—the story. Planners are usually good at lots of detail, and I find that the reporter interested mainly in the brief, pithy, and controversial, either chokes or nods off when given the whole story—often the roots are a couple of years old and the options for the future are many. Halfway through, I often get a "thank you" and I give a hurt look that I can't finish.

Another approach to engaging the press in these kinds of situations is to turn their tactic back around on them. The reality is that they have probably talked to some or most of the parties involved in the situation and that as a result they may be more up on who thinks what than anyone else. Since the planner or urban designer is likely to need to know any new information or where people stand on any given development initiative, one of the best ways to find out is to ask. Sometimes a reporter is disarmed to hear that an "expert" is interested in hearing their opinion and will provide both information and perspective on the issues of the moment. This approach can actually contribute toward a positive outcome. Another way to start is the way a reporter might try to ask, "I hear that so-and-so has taken the position that..." If caught off-guard, the reporter may divulge important and timely information that can be used to support a synthesis among opposing positions. In any event, it is important to be

Among many examples, I attribute the successful approval of two very high-impact programs in Atlanta to the absence of press coverage. In one, city voters approved a city-wide quality of life bond initiative of $150 million dedicated to sidewalks, parks, plazas, bike lanes, streetscape, and other infrastructure improvements covering all city council districts. The campaign was waged through council members, Neighborhood Planning Units, and neighborhoods, mainly a word-of-mouth kind of strategy. This occurred halfway through the second term of a mayor whom the mainstream media regularly demonized, yet for whatever reason they chose not to cover the bond election story until the last few days, by which time support was well established. Had they started earlier and placed the bond initiative into the context of an administration that could do no right, the referendum might well have failed. Instead, it passed by 85 to 15.

In the same timeframe, the city and a major business and community association, the Midtown Alliance, brought forward a major rezoning initiative to reshape the area's future. Both the city and the Alliance had done their homework, and most active property owners and neighborhoods knew what was happening and had participated widely in the process. Again, the local media ignored the story and the initiative gained approval with little difficulty. Had they highlighted the pending sea change afoot in a core city business and emerging mixed-use center, it is likely that many of the several hundred properties affected would have awakened and possibly stalled the process, depending on the slant the media might have taken, again in the context of an administration they didn't like.

conscious of the role that the media plays and to look for positive ways to engage their information and communication bank as a resource.

My most dramatic and fulfilling experience with positive media coverage occurred during the effort to locate a new bridge across the Mississippi River in New Orleans in 1971–1972, along with other major transportation proposals. Ferrell Guillory from the *Times Picayune* and Alan Katz from the *States Item* took a keen and deep interest in the project, whose range of possible outcomes ran from devastating to positive for the future city and region. We ran a storefront study process, media and everyone else welcome. Over the course of the study, substantive stories appeared about twice weekly in both newspapers, supporting a citizen-guided process that produced a positive outcome.

## Attitudinal and Behavioral Considerations

Finally, one's attitude and behavior may profoundly affect the outcome of place-improvement endeavors. I share ideas here for how to evaluate and improve one's interactions with others in the process. These dovetail and are consistent with the principles and premises of this book. They flow from my own experience as well as observations of others who have been effective in supporting civic-improvement processes that last.

## *LAURA C*

In preparing for community interaction environments, whether engaging people in regular community meetings, considering substantive business like zoning changes and the like, or in preparation for charrette-type visioning processes, I always try to carry the acronym "LAURA C" around in my head. Since almost anyone not a regular at a community process meeting is an outsider, if you want to be helpful in that setting plus learn a thing or two yourself, remember:

L—Listen
A—Accept
U—Understand
R—Respect
A—Appreciate
and if you're lucky,
C—Celebrate!

While these steps are fairly self-explanatory, it is worth a sentence or two for each to describe their meaning and intent. *Listen* means open your ears to what people are actually saying or trying to say. It does *not* mean fit what you are hearing into your prejudgment of the situation or the people in it. *Accept* means let it sink in and spark your mind's ability to open itself up to new ideas, not conclude that people can't mean what you are hearing. Nor does it mean that you personally have to agree with the view presented. *Understand* means absorb what you're hearing and accepting, sometimes requiring more research about the people or place or both. *Respect* means honoring people's rights to their beliefs and holding them in your esteem for doing so. *Appreciate* means actually gaining some enjoyment or pleasure from having made yourself get this far to welcome and to try to find a way to support a different set of perspectives and their roots. Finally, *celebrate* means being able to join in with the culture and its values to the extent that you are able to synthesize them into a strategy that moves the place forward in the terms of the people there.

Following these steps, more or less in order, prepares the urban designer or community activist to find ways to bring disparate parties together, beginning with oneself. It reflects the role that an urban designer often finds oneself in; that is, as the nexus in a diversity of zealots. One must understand that above all, zealots are people who care, and better communities don't happen if people don't care. In adopting the acronym as an attitude for approaching the community process, one is more or less gravitating toward the view that has come to me; that is, that the best way to make places better for me is to make them better for everyone.

One can apply this attitudinal framework to physical places to some extent as well, though only to places that citizens view as positive models for extension or replication. Thus, "listening," accepting, understanding, respecting, and appreciating the strengths of civic environments may be an avenue for creating or improving places that people will celebrate.

## *The Three Ps*

In the course of trying to manage your way through a process to get something positive done, there are always bumps or turns in the road that have to be navigated, no matter how inane or unnecessary some of them might seem. In these circumstances, it is easy to feel frustration—in fact, it's hard not to—yet communicating frustration is rarely effective in getting past the blockage. The more experience one gains, either as an urban designer or a community leader, the greater one's ability to see beyond any particular impediment one encounters along the way. Over my years of being on all sides of the processes required to get things done, I have developed the concept of "the three Ps," and when I have obstacles in front of me (often) I remind myself in the shower to remember them. The three Ps are:

P—Persistent
P—Patient
P—Pleasant

The three Ps are a shorthand way of remembering that you can't get anything done unless you stay at it, that nothing in the complicated place-building world happens fast, and that people you encounter along the way, no matter how oppositional they may be, must always remember you as being pleasant. It might be worth recounting how this trinity has come into focus for me through the years. Persistence and patience are process traits taught me by the veterans of the civil rights movement in Birmingham, where no other explanation should be necessary. Being pleasant was taught me in the first year of my civil service career by Don Ciampi, a Queens homebuilder who wanted an expedited review of his Planned Unit Development application under the new PUD zoning provisions we had put in place. He showed up in my doorway, frequently, unexpectedly but always pleasantly. It was hard to get mad at him. He probably got through the review process quicker than some others (in retrospect, he was persistent and patient, too).

## *Habit Thinking*

I had the good fortune to study basic art under the tutelage of Josef Albers, a special artist, teacher, and individual who came to the United States out of the Bauhaus in Dessau, Germany, in a Nazi-induced scattering of that remarkable collection of modernist artists, architects, and thinkers. Aside from all that I learned and experienced with my classmates, one lesson comes to mind nearly daily, and it seems to have special application in urban design or community-building activities. Mr. Albers, whether in teaching us how to see or how to represent what we saw in various media, continuously railed against what he called "habit thinking." Ultimately, this admonition has made its way to my checklist for

---

In the 1990s in Berkeley, I was called upon to manage communications between the UC Berkeley campus, the city, and the community for a new "hazardous materials handling facility" slated for construction in Strawberry Canyon, at the foot of Panorama Hill (often dubbed "Pandemonium Hill" for its consistent and noisy defense of its quality of life). In the course of meeting city and community leaders, I invited a neighborhood woman named Ann Slaby to join me for coffee at Strada (still the best coffee anywhere). For a lot of reasons, some of them entirely valid in my view, she hated the campus for its arrogance and occasionally dumb decisions that did in fact diminish the quality of life for some of its neighbors. She displayed her attitude and expectations for the hazmat facility with barely contained rage. She raised a number of important questions, though, ones that the consultants either had not considered or had dismissed too lightly. I listened. Her parting pronouncement was that she would find it difficult to hate me, and I left feeling that I would be able to engage the campus, the community, and the city in the kind of dialogue necessary to produce a workable result. In the end, for both purely technical and for community and city responsive reasons, the campus relocated the site to one that was much more workable, aesthetic, and environmentally acceptable.

---

A student with a lot of public service experience suggested that there should perhaps be a fourth "P" for funny, apparently spelled "pfunny," noting that humor is often the factor that breaks through the impasse to communication. This reminded me of my old boss and mentor, architect Paul Rudolph. He was given to bold and sometimes outrageous ideas. He had a way of tossing them out there as if he was joking. When the laughter subsided, though, people realized he might be serious. The humor broke down resistance, allowing the idea to pass through a keyhole into the consciousness where it had a chance to gain a footing.

how to think, how to act, and even how to experience the world. The idea is, we all fall into habits, beginning as infants, and adopting new habits as we move along through life. Some of these may be coded in our DNA, many are learned from parents, siblings, peers or authority figures, and all provide a pretty important set of tools for getting on with our lives. We have "good" habits, and we have "bad" habits. We sort of know which are which, largely determined in the culture of the larger world that we share. Of course, a good habit in one culture may be a bad habit in another, and some of those disparities are in contest every day on the world stage.

Yet, I have found it to be a good "habit" to be conscious of my habitual responses and behavior and to subject them to ritual challenge. This exercise I have found to have two different kinds of value. First, I make conscious why I do what I do and either then affirm or alter my behavior whether in planning and design, or in understanding people who walk in different shoes, or in other aspects of my life. Second, I often find out things about the world (or myself, or others close to me) that I would never have discovered without a bent toward challenging my habits and habitual responses. Carrying this habit around with me over and over again has enabled me to see beyond the immediate, the obvious, the habitual.

The applications of this guidance can range from changing the order in which one carries out one's ablutions, to changing which leg you put through your pants first, to changing the route you travel to work or school, to talking to someone you might not ordinarily want to talk to, and so on. In this line of work, intentionally pulling yourself out of your comfort zone both stretches your ability to see your world and prepares you for the likelihood that you will in fact be pulled out of your comfort zone frequently and unpredictably. Occasional forays into the unfamiliar, however, should in no way replace or diminish the daily life and work routines that allow people to function efficiently. Going back to the change principles, it is in the dialectic, dynamic, and interactive relationship between the routine and the conscious step into the unfamiliar where deeper understanding and new insights may be found.

## *Surviving*

There is a lot of stress associated with urban design and community engagement work. For all the different kinds of situations one encounters, the work often requires meetings of all kinds, levels, and participants. Sudden shifts in schedules or work priorities are the norm, such as pressure for accelerated work production sometimes interrupted with slow-downs—the hurry up and wait phenomenon. Ambiguity infuses many processes. Hostility may pepper the course of the work. The tips below for how to deal with these kinds of stresses are mainly geared to urban designers in public sector environments. These may be public servants or officials, or they may be consultants to a government or represent clients seeking approvals through a public sector–mandated process. But I expect that community leaders will relate to the advice and it may aid them in understanding how to be effective in public arena activities.

To set the stage for the drama that swirls around development initiatives, lack of trust is probably the single biggest obstacle to achieving a consensual approach for improving the community among citizens, developers, and government in any place-building endeavor. The project initiator, sometimes the government but usually a developer or other private sector business, seeks approval from the local government. Developers are steeped in cultural traditions that trumpet the unfettered market, profit, and entrepreneurship as values not to be questioned. They may have a hard time understanding why the community may not hail whatever they bring forth. After all, they are the ones who do the building, put together the financing, take the risks, create jobs, and build the tax base—why shouldn't they be able to maximize their return on investment? Public policy, though, reflecting the contradictions between gain for the few and the broader values of the many, often calls for some degree of balance, often taking the form of zoning or other rules of the game. Developers may view the effort to balance as at best a necessary evil, and they may distrust the system that seeks to impose the balance. They are inclined to try to duck contact with the community, manipulate political processes, and do whatever it takes to get around any potentially time consuming or costly approval processes.

Indeed, this approach has dominated and, even in these times of greater recognition of the value or the requirement of public participation, continues to dominate how private development goes down. In these circumstances, naturally enough, communities have long experience of being cut out of the process and often victimized by the results—the development left the community worse off than before. They are not likely to be in the mood to interact with or trust private developers enough to enter into dialogue, instead more likely to call on their elected officials to kill, mitigate adverse consequences, or incorporate community-serving features into the project. This call is sometimes heard, often not. In such a dynamic, representations may be made that one party or the other has no intention of honoring, further exacerbating the climate of distrust that swirls around so much of what gets built.

The government tends to be, as it should be, cast in between developer and community. Planning and urban design staff, those who usually are in the middle of any of these development approval processes, are likely to be distrusted by both sides. The developer feels the planner is siding with the community, the community feels the planner is siding with the developer. In fact, the public sector planner or urban designer is in the unique position of being able to see the merits of both sides and has no personal stake in the outcome. Thus, with the judicious application of principles, visioning, and process skills, such staff members have the chance to support new positions that can synthesize a positive outcome out of oppositional positions. They can both incorporate the developer's need for profit to do the project in the first place, and build the good ideas into a result that supports improvements, mitigates impacts, and leaves the community better off than if nothing had happened.

Involvement in these situations is often stressful, whether the venue is the conference room, the city council chamber, or the public meeting. The battle lines have been drawn on either side of a public policy or law that the planner or public official must assert, from the broad policy to the minute detail. In preparing for what I know will be a hostile situation, I have two devices that serve to take my persona out of the picture and thus free me up to have a chance to contribute to a hopefully productive outcome.

One is to project my mind a couple of hours beyond the end of the stressful meeting that has not yet taken place. There are two positive outcomes from this kind of preparation, one substantive, the other soothing.

First, from a substantive point of view, you can look back on the meeting (that hasn't happened yet) and "see" how things went. You can prospectively see the sticking points and the possible areas for overlap that could lead toward synthesis. You can see what could have been presented and in a way that would have been more effective to reaching a forward step. Insights might emerge that couldn't have if the only preparation were in the anticipation of dread. Second, the soothing benefit of this tip, of course, is that with your mind focused on two hours after the meeting (that hasn't yet happened), you've gotten out of your presentation outfit, you're leaning back on the sofa, eating, drinking, watching TV, or enjoying your mate. The anticipation of the relaxation that awaits puts the impending disaster into a more tolerable light—whatever happens it will be over by then.

Another useful tip for coping in a stressful meeting environment as it is happening is to imagine that your eyes and ears are actually watching a TV drama or sit-com, where the parties, including yourself, are all playing roles and your eyes and ears are TV screen and speaker. This device has, again, two beneficial effects. If you see the event unfolding in the context of it being a widely shared experience, reasonably predictable, often kind of funny, sometimes kind of dramatic, then you will be able to understand your role and the roles of others in the context of the thousands of such meetings that play themselves out monthly across the country. In addition, by placing yourself into the choreography of a stage drama, you will understand that any comments or attacks that otherwise might be personally hurtful are not really a comment on your personal persona. You will see them for what they are: an attack on the system, the "establishment," or on the role that you are representing—an expression of distrust born of bad experience or failed earlier efforts. The urban designer or planner in this situation should bear in mind that his or her role is in fact exciting, calling for improvisation and quick thinking, often jumping back and forth between splitting hairs (like in whether a development should have 100 or 105 parking spaces) and catching spears (like "you're just here to destroy our community").

Related to these two coping skills, it is important if you are in the middle—the mediating and ideally the synthesizing position—to try not to be anyone's hero. That is, if one side tries to get too close, becomes too laudatory, then perhaps you are not maintaining your balance. One side's hero quickly becomes the other side's villain, regardless of the merits. Maintaining this balance should not be confused with neutrality. Neutrality suggests that it is all the same to you what position prevails, while in fact if the goal is to make things better than they were before, the urban designer (and often community leader) must work toward and then assert a position that, if it includes the strengths of the two oppositional positions, can provide a basis for positive resolution.

## *Having Fun*

No one gets involved with urban design or community-improvement activities because they have to. Something that urban designers share with neighborhood or district-oriented citizen activists is the nature of the problems they face. These problems have to do with the whole place. They are made up of several interacting components, none of which by itself is usually hard to understand but whose complexity arises from the numbers and interactions of the components. Urban designers and community leaders share in the desire to improve the quality, functionality, and attractiveness of the whole place, for designers by whatever accepted criteria, for community people for the people there, their neighbors, fellow businesspeople, constituencies. And because the nature of the problem is dynamic, closure on any part is temporal—no sooner is one advance made than the new set of conditions it enables lead to the next problem. Finally, because of the intensely human and diverse nature of the processes involved in getting anything done, the uncertainty of the paths for getting there and the activities involved require of its participants a high tolerance for ambiguity.

For people so inclined, though, these activities should end up by being fun—or rewarding, stimulating, challenging, fulfilling, amusing, diverting, engaging, or whatever other ways "fun" might be defined. There come times when it is helpful to remind oneself of the upside—it helps to see over the horizon and to recalibrate one's perspective.

If the quantities of information or participants or the ambiguities or the processes required end up being too frustrating, maybe it's time to ratchet down the scale and scope of one's activity to more predictable definable and simpler goals. One thing this kind of work is *not* is repetitive or routine. If it seems that it is reaching such a point, then perhaps the product is dominating the process, as can happen when either the drive for profit on the private side, politics on the public side, or fatigue on the community side call for a timeout. In addition, there are subfields within and contributive to larger urban design and civic-improvement processes that may not require public rough-and-tumble or whose information bases and procedures are more predictable. These might include focus on some of the comprehensive development plan's constituent parts, like a subset of transportation or environmental planning, housing, or historic preservation. If at its most comprehensive or in its constituent parts the material palls, then it is time to reassess—perhaps zigging or zagging along the career path as suggested earlier.

These attitudinal and behavioral observations may or may not be helpful to all those involved in making our civic places better. Regrettably, they may lend themselves to co-optation by people whose interests and purposes are narrower. Remember that many of the people involved in the planning, design, and development process are driven by goals that are short range, usually measurable in profit or reelection, and it takes a steady hand to keep the focus on improving the larger environment.

# Summary

This chapter has suggested a number of techniques for applying the ***principles*** of urban design to its ***content*** in order to get improvements to the public environment accomplished. The first part focuses on the pieces that make up any urban environment—typical public spaces, private spaces, and the interfaces between. These discussions provide the kind of information that is crucial for urban designers and citizen activists in conceptualizing place-improvement strategies. While information like dimensions and other hard data vary widely from case to case, the point is that the pieces must all be considered even if their priority and make-up are different. The pieces are knowable, and each by itself is pretty straightforward. The task is to integrate and synthesize these different pieces so that they make a place better or create a place that at a minimum is conceived as a whole interacting with its parts. The role of urban designers and citizen activists is to assure that the particular disciplines responsible for each piece are in touch with each other and working toward a common vision.

The second part of the chapter focuses on techniques that are likely to ensure that any urban design or development initiative is thorough, complete, and responsive to the premise that people's involvement is the likely indicator of an improvement strategy's ultimate success. In addition, people involved in these kinds of initiatives should be conscious of the kinds of forces likely to come into play as an initiative is launched and how to look for positive opportunities as well as deal with issues that are likely to come up. The interactions between rules, tools, and techniques provide the basis on which to devise strategies to make things happen, the subject of the next chapter.

# PART V

# STRATEGIES

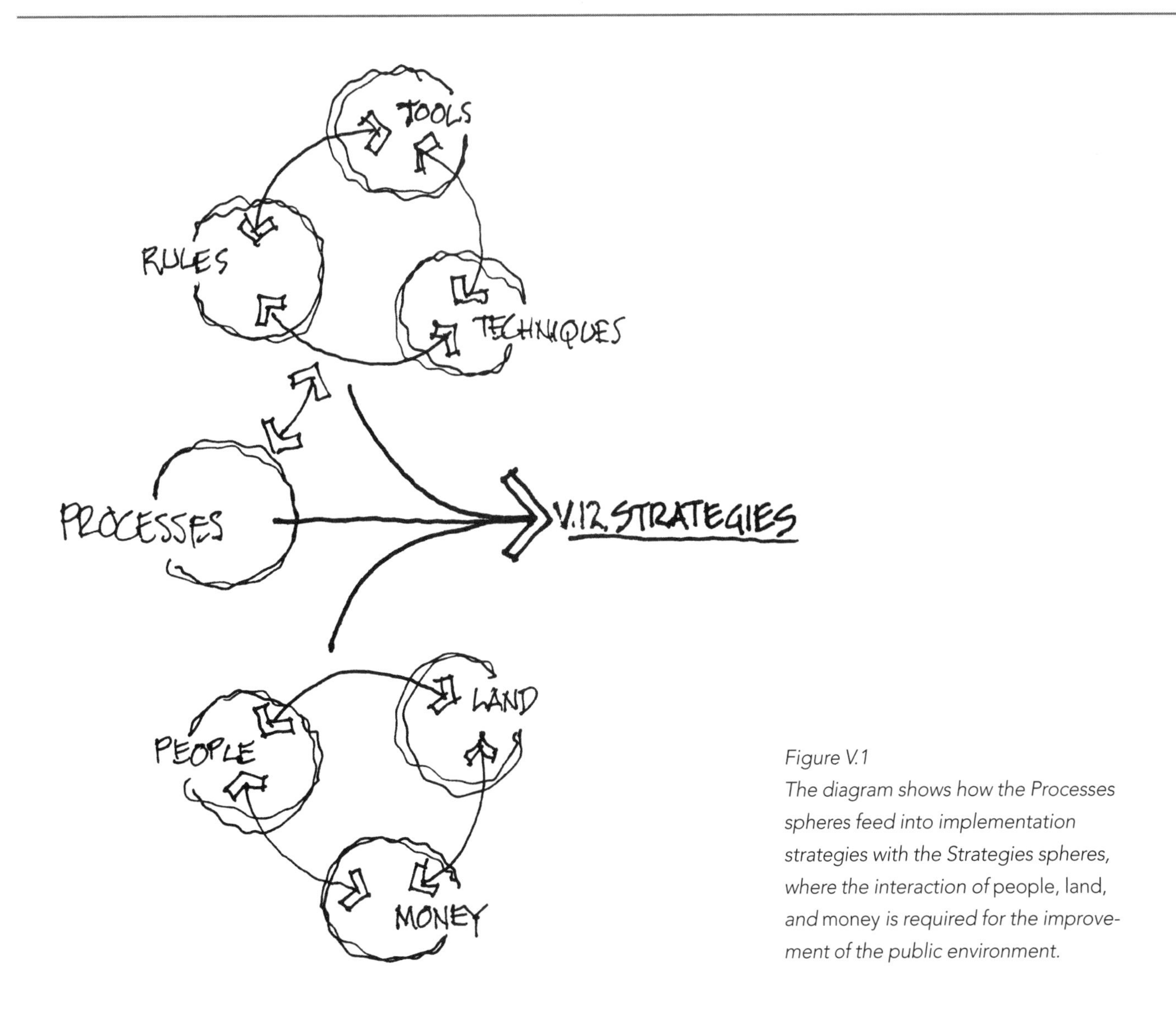


*Figure V.1*
*The diagram shows how the Processes spheres feed into implementation strategies with the Strategies spheres, where the interaction of people, land, and money is required for the improvement of the public environment.*

# Overview

Part V, Strategies, describes the bases on which citizens and urban designers may carry forward many of the strategies suggested in the foregoing chapters, that is, the resources and the strategic orientation necessary to implement a place improvement initiative. It seeks to broaden the framework of understanding necessary to seek better ways for integrating the place-building forces in times of economic uncertainty. Its purpose is to prepare community leaders and urban design professionals to take a more active role in the planning and decision-making, whose intensity is likely to rise even as actual economic growth and development falter.

# 12

# STRATEGIES

## Merger of Processes and Resources

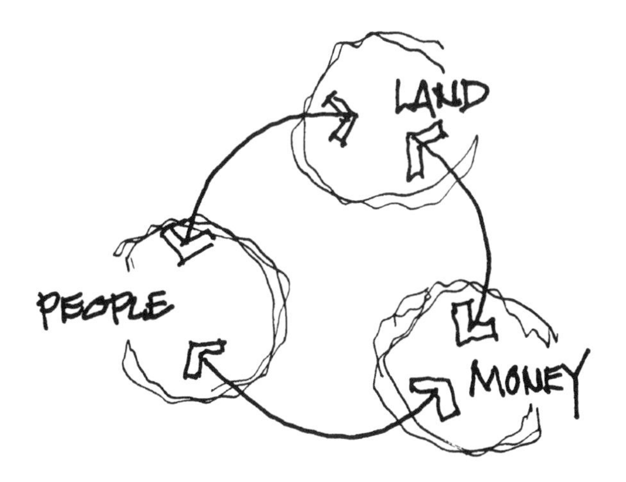


*Figure 12.1*
*The resources required for the improvement of the public environment: people, land, and money and their continuous interactions.*

# Overview

*"Every journey begins with the first step."*
*"If you find yourself in a hole, the first thing to do is stop digging."*
*"The foolish old man who moved mountains…"*

Part V, Strategies, describes the bases on which citizens and urban designers may carry forward many of the strategies suggested in the foregoing chapters, that is, the resources and the strategic orientation necessary to implement a place improvement initiative. It seeks to broaden the framework of understanding necessary to seek better ways for integrating the place-building forces in times of economic uncertainty. Its purpose is to prepare community leaders and urban design professionals to take a more active role in the planning and decision-making, whose intensity is likely to rise even as actual economic growth and development falter.

# Introduction

This chapter draws together material from the foregoing chapters to illustrate how their various combinations may apply in addressing a few commonly recurring challenges to improving the civic environment. It reviews the triad of people, land, and money as the resources that must come together to create a properly thought out, staged, and technically and financially viable place improvement. It considers both geographically and topically defined challenges, all from the primary perspective of the quality and functionality of the public realm. It identifies how urban design professionals and citizen leaders can be effective in generating or participating in place-improvement strategies. It seeks to answer such questions as: How can community leaders and urban designers chart a course for making things better? How might the various tools and techniques be applied to get things started and then keep them going? How do the principles assist in guiding the work; for example, how can the change forces always at work be harnessed to improve conditions for the full citizenry, whether in the region, the town or city, the district or the neighborhood?

*"Can you make a silk purse out of a sow's ear?"*

To begin with, the chapter discusses the resources that must be tapped and assembled to launch a place-improvement activity. Here, reflecting the organizational principles, the community, private, and government interests and capabilities are explored as a triad of people, land, and money. True to the overall interactivity principle, these three spheres interact continuously, and no public-improvement project happens without their conscious application.

# Resources

The initiators of civic-improvement strategies may be citizens or the government or the private sector, but to be successful the resources and organizational commitment of all three are necessary to reach reliable and lasting success. Increasingly, the surest way to secure and sustain approval for necessary changes is for broad-based constituencies to embrace them. While the big power approach to decision-making in the civic realm persists and perhaps still dominates, its success in getting things done right and even in getting things done at all seems to be dwindling. The premise here then is that formulating effective urban design and development strategies depends on private-public-community partnerships. Their substance lies in the interactions between the content of the problem to be addressed; the application of change, design, and organizational principles for guiding the work; and the processes that synthesize the applicable rules, tools, and techniques, and identify the resources necessary to develop effective strategies.

To begin with, the partnerships, as we have seen, invariably include, however unconscious of their role, the private sector, the government, and the community, as described in Chapter 8, Organization. Each of these three has different motives and different measures affecting their role and mission, and from a strategic perspective, urban designers and community leaders need to search for overlaps to tease out at least some shred of common ground. So in seeking to find common ground, it is important here to remember some distinctions among the would-be partners. The private sector must profit from its activities, either sooner or later. The community seeks tangible and measurable improvements, at least preventing harm. The government, in the middle, is measured by the service and even-handedness of its performance.

Similarly, the behavior of each sphere is likely to be different according to their different cultures, habits, and sense of right and wrong. The private sector, in its profit-driven culture, reaches for an "anything goes" ethic, the theory being that the market will correct any egregious excesses. In fact, as borne out once again in the recent credit crisis, when the excesses of a few damage the vital interests of the many, government, however reluctantly as in the recent case, must step in. Meanwhile, since their ultimate measure is service provided, neither government nor community-based leadership shares the "anything goes" culture. Instead, at different scales perhaps, at their best they take their service mission seriously and measure their performance by whether their actions made things better or at least not worse for their constituencies. Under our market democracy electoral system, this edge may get blurred for elected officials through campaign finance practices, yet for civil servants the line should be maintained.

A simple, common comparative illustration: For a businessperson to treat another to a sporting event, a round of golf, or a trip to the tropics is perfectly alright and normal for doing business in the private sector, where both parties are angling for personal gain. Government workers, on the other hand, are usually held to a higher standard—perks are barred, since any quid pro quo between private largesse and government action represents a violation of the premise of government as the even-handed provider of services to all its constituents. (Of course, here and there, particularly at the higher levels where the private-public revolving door has been spinning in recent years, the private sector has succeeded in corroding this ethical and cultural buffer.) And a community leader who gets too much attention and perhaps more from a prospective developer is likely to quickly lose his or her stature among peers for violation of the same profit-versus-service ethical boundary.

With these baseline understandings, then, below are selected examples of how people, land, and money can interact with each other and come together to fuel public realm development initiatives.

## People

*"The city is the people."*

People are who make place improvements happen. How do people come together to build their world? People make places, not the other way around (although a special place may affect a person's perception of the world, for better or worse). Examples range from barn raisings to community playgrounds, from imperial grounds and palaces to corporate plazas. All involve people working together, whether by obligation or by cooperation, since the job of building usually tests the limits of human technical and organizational capability. However unconsciously or however formally, physical improvements always occur in the form of partnerships, and so the people who have to be rallied to get involved will always be doing so in a de facto cooperative setting (even though there may be a lot of finger-pointing and nay-saying along the way).

I often marvel that anything ever gets built, considering the array of competing interests that somehow have to make it all work. Developers routinely have to secure land; line up financing; hire lawyers, architects, engineers and other consultants; oversee design; get approvals; get bids;

line up contractors and subcontractors; enter into contracts; oversee construction; market the result; and make a profit. Except from the government and the community, which are mostly involved only in the approval process, everyone involved every step of the way also has to make a profit, and so there is no end of cross-purposes that must be worked through. Yet development happens, and those who contribute to it end up cooperating to get it done (even if they don't always feel that way).

Profit drives the private-development equation, and so what does it take to initiate improvements in the public environment, projects motivated by civic purpose? Who takes the lead? How are the necessary skills marshaled? Who puts the resources together? For the most part, as we have seen, the civic environment falls under the purview of government, usually local government. Streets, plazas, parks, civic buildings, and grounds are all subject to improvement as markers of a place in time and the will of the people then and there.

Often the initiative to make these kinds of improvements comes from community organizations, either neighborhood or district based. The people who take the lead in organizing for a better place get a lot of credit in my book. They are civic minded, have a bigger-picture view of the world, usually take the time and trouble over and above however it is they make their living (unless they are paid by an organization), and show the kind of persistence it takes to achieve some result. They represent a starting point, a strength to build on if you will, and almost every community has people like this. The job of community people and urban designers is to sense who these people are and reinforce their best tendencies to become involved and perhaps take leadership roles in making the place better.

The skills, experience, creativity, and will normally associated with private sector developers, as well as their supporting cast of consultants, are also a necessary resource for making civic space improvements. These capabilities are often scarce to find since they are lodged and honed mainly in the for-profit world. Occasionally though, seasoned developers can be induced into the quest to fulfill a broader public purpose. Most communities, in fact, have developers working in nonprofit settings, usually around affordable housing or other community-development work, and this may be a good place to start looking.

These developers have eschewed the profit route (though they still have to finish in the black), and in so doing are likely to already have a broader view of the world, or neighborhood, and what to do and how to make improvements in the public interest. Sometimes a for-profit developer can be induced into a community-based improvement strategy, particularly if there are problematic approvals facing his or her project, the reason to become engaged with the community in the first place. These kinds of engagements often result in what are increasingly being called "community benefit agreements," in which development proposals that exceed what the current rules permit may be traded off for community-enhancing improvements, like sidewalks, parks, lighting, street and signalization improvements, community-based hiring, and the like. (See Chapter 10, Tools.)

The supporting cast skills, essentially the same array required for the private developer, may be found in the community, or there may be professional organizations or individuals that are willing to take on some pro bono role (though be a little wary, since some of these could be angling for future remuneration, which is alright as long as it's upfront). Sometimes the supporting cast skills can be found in the local government, usually in the planning department and its urban design section, sometimes in the public works or parks departments. In any event, the local government should be engaged early and positively since, beyond the possibility of offering resources to help whatever gets envisioned, the government will need to approve a project to get it built.

Remember, the same sequence of activities identified above and in the caterpillar (see Figure 11.9) for any private sector development will apply to community-driven development as well. Identifying the people who can and will play a role in the usually less formal, less remunerative work of community improvement is a challenge, but there is a long record of really remarkable community-initiated civic-improvement programs that have left a lasting and positive stamp on places all over the country. Think of one or two in your community.

*"They're not making any new land."*

## Land

Land (here including water) is where places happen. Usually public places are built on publicly owned land, although since the civic environment often forms the seam between private and public activities, private and public ownership often dovetail. Public ownership of places supporting public activities is an important principle, both for the quality and functionality of the places and for the exercise of rights as citizens. Private ownership or control brings with it a compromise of purpose, since proprietary rights are likely to bring with them the ultimate aim of private gain. Furthermore, freedoms afforded citizens in the public realm, like free speech and assembly, are not assured on private grounds—main street versus the mall.

Most civic space, though, is dedicated to streets, publicly owned and freely accessible to all. Streets, or more properly street rights-of-way, typically take up about a quarter of the land in urbanized areas, more than half of which is usually taken up by vehicular travel ways. It's the rest of the right-of-way, though, where the greatest improvements in the quality of civic space can be achieved. This is where decent walking environments, suitable transitions between public and private activities, landscaping, lighting, signs, and shelters can create spaces that are memorable both for their functionality and their appeal. In so doing, they enhance the private activities that frame them, creating inviting foregrounds for residential activities and enhancing business activities' commercial and retail success. As pointed out in Chapter 11, Techniques, the approach to right-of-way design should be holistic and inclusive of flanking private development that interfaces with the public realm.

The bits and pieces of other public land, plazas, grounds of public buildings, re-appropriation of overly generous travel ways, or unkempt right-of-way lands all offer promise and potential for beneficial public use. In the course of private-development processes too, lands for schools, parks, or plazas may be provided to soften the developmental impact on the public environment, either as part of the subdivision approval process or in the form of impact fees or both. Urban designers can use their creative spirit to help identify and conceptualize the possibilities for such lands. Communities can take the lead in formulating their desired uses for public lands or even misused private land.

It must be said, though, that with the present onslaught of private appropriation of public resources, highways are beginning to be given over to private combines to design, build, operate, and maintain, all paid for by the public through anticipated toll or other revenue. This may work for awhile until the pressures of maintenance mount when—don't be surprised—the highway is dumped back into the public realm, after all of the upside profit has been drained away through the privatization and the public sector is called upon to absorb what's left after the facility has deteriorated. Think savings and loans crisis, airline industry crisis, disaster insurance crisis, credit crisis, auto industry crisis, and so on. To use transportation terminology, think of the government as a collector-distributor system, where it collects from all and distributes to a few, privatizing public assets and "public-izing" private risk.

A droll example in my experience was occurring in southeast Atlanta when I arrived in 1996. The school board, the parks department, and the library board, three separate government jurisdictions, had each in about the same timeframe separately purchased adjacent properties along a minor arterial street. Even though the possibilities for synergies were manifest, each went about planning and building their separate facilities, each with its own driveway and parking, with no thought about how one might relate to the other, either programmatically or physically.

Another area of land-based concern for communities and urban designers is the whole issue of site selection. Where to put what kinds of facilities is a key factor in shaping the quality of urban space. A properly located school, library, park, fire station, police precinct, or post office can reinforce and enhance the way the neighborhood or district lays out—or it can result in really dumb and dysfunctional decisions. Regrettably, neither design nor community input very often plays a role in this process. The sponsoring agency identifies a general area to be served by the new facility, often with little or no reference to the community's or even the city's plan—testimony to characteristic fragmentation—and with little internal investigation into the possible synergies with other public uses or other activities going on in the area. They then solicit proposals from the area, either for land or as a complete land and building package; evaluate the proposals from the two perspectives of their operational needs and what's cheapest; then make a decision and take it to the council or school board for approval.

Often, this is when the community first hears about it, with little time or standing to respond, since the deal's already in the works. The process is often further bowdlerized by property owners who are eager to unload a property undesirable for their optimum development purposes. (Ever wonder why so many housing projects, Section 8s, and even schools are in hard-to-get-to or environmentally challenged locations? Or why so many of necessary but unpleasant public facilities end up in poor people's neighborhoods?) Site selection, in short, has the potential to really advance the workability and desirability of the civic environment or to really screw it up.

Some lands may become available because they are not "developable" in the private market sense. They are too steep, they are in wetlands or marshes, they are the wrong size or shape—all features that could make special public places, where their natural condition actually shapes their use, context, and connectedness to the rest of the public realm. There are countless examples of how the natural character of land has given people their most treasured urban places. Think of one in your community.

Land is becoming an increasingly sensitive issue and not just for its provision to support urban quality of life. Land is a limited resource, a commodity for some, sustenance for others. There won't be any new land (except maybe for some palm tree-shaped islands created in the seas of the fabulously rich). The quality and condition of the land (including the dirt below, the air above, and the water around) may be deteriorating, the climate is changing, presently built-on land may not remain above sea level in the not-too-distant future. The kinds of initiatives being taken now by many countries, states, and cities to stabilize and hopefully reverse the damage are essential to safeguard the future quality of places and the natural areas that supplement them.

The growing realization of the scarcity and fragility of land has prompted a variety of responses in both the public and nonprofit sectors. Beginning with the formation of various environmental organizations through the last century and their spawning of sweeping environmental protection legislation from the 1960s, conservation, preservation, and sustainability measures have become more and more a central part of the U.S. culture.

The context for securing lands in urban areas for the range of uses from conservation to recreation has become more supportive. Through such organizations as the Trust for Public Land, The Nature Conservancy, and even some local communities and local governments, lands are being bought up to be held or conveyed to the public for conservation purposes. The tax codes presently support these kinds of activities by considering the donation of some or all of the values of these lands as charitable contributions. These can take the form of full-value donations or a combination of donation plus sale at a discounted price, sometimes called a "bargain sale." In some states, like Colorado, the values given up can be taken as a tax credit against state taxes. Countering these moves to conserve special natural lands, though, current federal policy is bent on enabling the private sector to recover resources off of considerable portions of federally owned lands, in the form of gas and oil field development, harvesting timber, or outright sales of public lands to the highest private bidder.

In Atlanta, for example, with the coalescing of green space acquisition funding put in place by Governor Roy Barnes, impact fee monies collected from development in the city, a citywide quality-of-life bond referendum and dollars the city committed for creekway acquisition under a consent decree, the city elicited from all its neighborhoods ideas and priorities about unbuilt space, private or public, that might meet some of the neighborhood's or larger community's green space needs and aspirations. The city then purchased some of these lands pursuant to an overall green space plan, part of the comprehensive development plan, often with the intermediary assistance of the Trust for Public Land or The Nature Conservancy.

Finally, when contemplating land as a resource for making our places serve people's objective and subjective needs better, it is important to remember how fundamental the cost of land is in shaping cities and regions. Land is a limited resource, and it is priced accordingly in the marketplace. While taxes factor into land pricing and availability, overwhelmingly the calculus is how much development can a developer place on the land to come out with the best profit possible. Development costs, while somewhat sensitive to codes and labor and material costs, do not vary that much by category between one area of an urban region and another. The bigger variable is land cost. Thus housing costs far out from centers are mainly lower because the land is cheaper, not that the building is so much cheaper. Similarly, in a town or city that is stable or growing, building on or even maintaining the stock of "affordable" housing becomes difficult, because of rising land values, costs, and property taxes, factors exacerbated by gentrification.

Land cost, then, plays a significant role in the shapes our urban areas take, and communities, urban designers, and public policy formulation should consider whether this factor is facilitating or hindering shaping the area the way the community would like. Right now, for example, many suburban communities are dealing with increasingly concerted pressures from developers flying under the banner of "new urbanism." This approach to suburban development touts the advantages of mixing housing types, providing some level of commercial activity, and community open space or other facilities, all in a higher-density "walkable" environment. While many of these features may be desirable, and they certainly offer an alternative to the "same old same old" suburban pattern, what they for sure do is provide the developer a huge prospective bonus. If a developer can buy land that only permits a couple of single-family houses per acre and then gets approvals to put, say, 12 units per acre on the same land, well, what a windfall.

*"Money isn't everything, but it sure helps."*

From a regional perspective, too, these pockets of high-density clusters are often not well-located in relation to their necessary support infrastructure, most notably transportation. Without access to transit, the same already overburdened road network now has to pick up significant new trips generated by "new urbanist villages." As long as the market for this kind of product holds, though (as it probably will because the normal suburban alternative is so one-dimensional and vapid), cashing in on low land costs is likely to continue to generate these developments haphazardly across the landscape.

## Money

The third component of the resources necessary to build good quality public spaces is—surprise—money. Ultimately, lining up the people to form the partnership to conceptualize and the organization to follow through and identifying the land appropriate to carry out the improvement are necessary and good, but someone's got to pony up the dollars to pay for the sequence of steps necessary to get it done. Urban designers and community leaders need to catch up to the ways of public and private sector finance sufficiently to develop a financial strategy and plan. As with most of the other components involved in crafting successful design and implementation strategies, one does not need to be an expert in the various ins and outs of the sources and uses of funds, though as a process gets formed it is extremely useful to have such an expert available to the partnership.

The discussion below provides a brief overview of various funding sources and their combinations that I have encountered most commonly in my place-improvement practices as a public official, with emphasis on more recent programs. The hope is that it will provide a starting place for searching out more specifically tailored finance strategies and provide some insight into the cultures and attitudes about finance that urban designers and community leaders may encounter.

### *Public Funding*

Since urban design mainly applies to design and development in the public realm, it is reasonable to consider what funds may be available from public programs or agencies to design and build a civic improvement. Typically, a town, city, or county has capital fund sources derived from taxes and bonded indebtedness to cover infrastructure and place enhancements. The taxes are usually made up of property taxes, sales taxes, and various fees. The bonds are usually secured by anticipated revenues, often in the form of municipally approved bond initiatives put in place for specific purposes.

The place to begin to look for the amounts and the projected uses of these funds is in the jurisdiction's capital budget, a public document adopted annually. In many jurisdictions, too, the comprehensive plan or general plan (which may be found under a variety of other names) should be a valuable source of information. In addition to portraying land use and other adopted policies, these plans may identify capital projects by name, rough cost estimate, and approximate timeline. Sometimes this information shows up in a separate capital improvement program, which is linked to the comprehensive plan. If the jurisdiction denies having this information or balks at sharing it freely, listen carefully and ask questions before getting upset. It may be that the jurisdiction maintains this information in a different form, requiring the requester to find the right question before getting to the right answer (an occasional problem with public agencies generally). Check first with the planning department, since they are the ones, along with finance and budget, that usually put it together.

If the jurisdiction is simply not forthcoming, citizens can at least raise consciousness of the need for a program that outlines how its jurisdiction plans to use the money people pay to operate their government. Sometimes, a jurisdiction simply doesn't want to share the information, for whatever political or cultural reasons. Often the reason is no more sinister than workload. In these cases, it is important to be able to identify oneself as representing a group, like a neighborhood or a business district, and then to employ "the three Ps" to follow the trail to the information. Keep in mind that the people being asked are probably the same as the ones your organization will need to partner with later. Attack politics, while perhaps heady and satisfying in the short term, may actually impede getting to the starting point for improving the civic environment.

The public works department and the parks department are usually the implementing agencies for civic improvement projects already identified and in some state of implementation. In addition, the planning department is often the department that initiates new projects, whether infrastructure, parks, housing, or other community-development work. The planning department, too, is usually where to look for projects that are in the formative stage, perhaps not yet listed in the capital budget.

From a staff perspective, the planning department, as the one that routinely engages the public in all manner of development activities, is where one can usually find someone who carries something of a public service perspective in their work. From an elected official perspective, the district council member or the mayor, depending on the size and formality of the jurisdiction, is a good contact to make, perhaps introducing the idea of a needed civic improvement before formulating any "asks." If a jurisdiction doesn't have this kind of information or refuses to share it, it is time to try to reform the situation.

Through a steady draining away of public resources dedicated to public spaces, most notably parks, many towns and cities have been obliged to partner with nonprofits or even for-profit franchisees for necessary funding. Their superior fundraising talents and capabilities are tapped to enhance capital improvement and maintenance needs to keep parks current and well-maintained. While these kinds of partnerships may raise issues of citizen and government oversight, they seem to be becoming increasingly necessary, and many such arrangements do in fact deliver better results for the public. Most towns and cities do have public space support groups of one kind or another, in the form of beautification organizations, park support groups, conservancies, committees of planning commissions, city councils, or nonprofits whose donors have prioritized the civic environment. These trace their roots to the municipal arts and City Beautiful societies that marked the heyday of commitment to the public realm from the turn of the last century. They seem to be on the upswing now in many cities because of the realization that neither the private market nor the government is likely to initiate such improvements on its own, the former because they're not profitable and the latter because they lack the resources.

It should be said that such moves toward civic betterment have been widely reported as contributing in substantive ways to the local economy. Private sector support, if only moral support, accordingly, is gaining as is government support, since both recognize that public investment and the show of pride it represents enhance nearby private property values.

In addition, many jurisdictions have other programs or have the opportunity to implement financing programs for consensually agreed-on public purpose initiatives. Bond referendums are most common, and communities through their elective representatives are often the initiators of these, seeking better infrastructure, parks, streetscapes, pedestrian and bicycle improvements, and other civic spaces. These efforts require identifying a reliable stream of funds to pay off the bonds, which may be a property tax, sales tax, or other revenue source, like real estate transfer taxes. Most states by now enable local jurisdictions to use tax increment financing or business improvement districts to fund civic improvement infrastructure. Tax increment financing allows a jurisdiction to identify an area, usually a disinvested area, where proposed improvements are anticipated to substantially lift the value of the real estate and sometimes sales, hence taxes, and the increment between today's taxes and future higher annual taxes is dedicated to pay off the debt—all limited to the designated area. Business-improvement districts allow property owners in a designated area to tax themselves beyond baseline property taxes and to use that increase for civic-improvement purposes whose make-up and priority they are able to direct.

Finally, often the most complicated yet with persistence rewarding, are various federal and state funding programs that can support infrastructure improvements. Federal transportation funds typically flow through state departments of transportation, and in urban areas their programming is typically run through what is called the metropolitan planning organization (MPO), which usually has a more place–specific name (like the Atlanta Regional Commission or the Denver Council of Governments or the Association of Bay Area Governments in San Francisco). These organizations are required by law to conduct extensive public review of transportation policy and project proposals, and in many jurisdictions concerned citizens have played active and effective roles, often struggling uphill in a highway-dominated atmosphere. In fact, without consistent and unrelenting pressure from communities, professional organizations, academics, environmentalists, and others, it is unlikely that some of the recent reforms for balancing support for transportation modes, for conceiving of transportation as a system for access instead of the road to mobility, could have begun. Funds are also available directly from various state transportation sources and from local governments as well, usually located in public works departments.

When I first got to Berkeley in 1993, I raised the possibility of the university and the city partnering to secure a "TEA" grant for the purpose of enhancing and improving the streetscape between the downtown BART station and the campus. The TEA grant (acronym for Transportation Enhancement Activity) was available through a set-aside of funds first put in place in the Intermodal Surface Transportation Efficiency Act of 1991. I had been able to work with my colleagues in Birmingham and the state highway department to partner on this funding source to accomplish freeway entrance and streetscape improvement work.

So historically and habitually strained were the relations between the campus and city that the idea of such a partnership produced some great guffaws. I persisted (patiently and pleasantly) and got the city planning director, Gil Kelley, to join me in an appeal to the Caltrans TEA funding committee in Sacramento. The city and the university appearing arm in arm with a common request was a shocker in light of our notoriously fractious relationship, probably enough in itself to secure the grant. Donlyn Lyndon was selected to design the project, which was reasonably expeditiously executed and has now become a hot restaurant row—in addition to a clear and gracious pedestrian link.

Two things to bear in mind in going after state and federal funding sources: First, they may be among the most "political"; that is, a whole lot of deal-making is likely to cloud access and cloak information about how these various funds are spent, usually involving local and state elected officials, large property and real estate interests, highway contractors and consultants, and so on. Second, they all require a local match, which means hard cash from local government coffers or foundations or both.

It is often productive in support of transportation-related place improvements, like sidewalks and bikeways and other right-of-way improvements, to engage these agencies and foundations. To begin with, go to MPO meetings, state highway board meetings, or local government public works oversight committees, not to propose a project but to figure out what's going on, to talk to people, to ask questions, and to get information on budgets and policies. Daunting as all this may seem, it is your government. With any luck, there will be people in the community partnership necessary for improving places who are already familiar with and maybe connected to these processes.

An important consideration in devising strategies for using transportation money for place-improvement activities is the time and baseline requirements for using these funds. State DOT processes usually require levels of documentation that may render their funds too cumbersome to use for small projects. Requirements for surveys, environmental clearance, levels of detail for construction documents, and the like might overwhelm the budget and time of delivery for a couple of blocks of sidewalk.

In Atlanta, for example, the documentation required to do sidewalk projects cost more than the capital cost of construction—and took months. We didn't try that again.

Public funding that may be available to support housing and community-development initiatives, particularly for low- and moderate-income communities, includes sources administered through HUD like community-development block grant funds (available through states for smaller jurisdictions), HOPE VI funds for leveraging other sources to rebuild public housing and their civic environments, and funds for housing homeless people and people with AIDS. The planning and/or community development department is the likely place to look for housing and other community-development activities funding, much of which is likely to be passed through from federal or state sources. These funds are income-limited and purpose-specific, and they may be combined with other sources to improve not just the immediate housing need but to create a civic environment that may enhance the sustainability and success of the core housing mission.

Low-income housing tax credits, a federal tax incentive program administered through states, may provide equity investors for housing developments that the conventional private market can't address. These may also leverage place-improvement initiatives in conjunction with the core purpose. Many states have affordable housing support funding programs as well. The point with these kinds of programs is that while most of them are strict about limiting their use to the core purpose, that very strictness calls for additional support to make sure that the quality of the development and the improvement of the setting in which it is located are addressed. A lot of money is being spent, why not do it right? Housing for lower-income people should not equate to low-quality housing. Otherwise, as has often happened, the mean-spirited social statement made by sub-par practice adds to the stigma and burden of people who are trying to reach for the next rung on the economic ladder. Also in the housing area, which should never be dissociated from the quality of its setting, many cities and towns have affordable housing support programs, including housing trust funds, bond set-asides, land bank programs, and the like.

## *Private Funding*

The primary application of private development dollars to civic places comes mostly from two sources: foundations and developers. Foundation funding has long played a pivotal role in the improvement of the public environment in many cities and towns across the country. Many of the beautification movements, dating back to the era of the "City Beautiful," have sustained themselves through the aid of private nonprofit foundations. These organizations are typically endowed by the wealthiest families in the area, or even nationally, who donate some portion of their income to an entity set up to support the causes and purposes that they favor. For them, it provides an attractive tax-avoidance mechanism, allowing them to fund what they deem to be worthy causes as an alternative to taxes that would be more generally spread across the public agenda. For community activists and urban designers in search of funding strategies for community improvements, foundations represent the potential of adding their support both technically and financially.

The first step is to identify foundations with a history of supporting community-improvement initiatives, and finding out what values have the best chance of pushing their buttons. If there is a good overlap between the civic-improvement goal and the foundation, then finding out how to make a proposal is the next step. There tends to be a social and cultural character to many such foundations that should be researched as well. One is likely to find more foundations and higher levels of support for improvements in principal business districts and their surrounding neighborhoods, where their largesse will be visible and prominent, than for smaller districts and modest or lower-income or minority-dominated neighborhoods. The donors and the administrators of foundations are less likely to have direct experience with the conditions in such neighborhoods and districts, thus less comfort. If they have any interest at all, they may require a higher bar of accountability than for organizations whose leaders share a common background, and may live in the same neighborhood and golf at the same clubs. In addition, foundations are likely to put special emphasis on who else is lined up to support the civic venture.

Many foundations, too, don't like to be alone in their support, partly because the more organizations whose stature they respect are lined up, the more comfortable they are in lining up too. In addition, of course, they like to stretch their charitable donations to other worthy causes, and using their resources to leverage others is a good way to achieve that goal. Finally, since most of the funding that flows through the nonprofit foundation channel is supplied by wealthy individuals or their foundations to accomplish purposes that they determine, the voice of the broader public tends to become muted in determining the priorities for such "public" improvement expenditures.

The second source of possible private funding for place improvements may come in association with private development projects. Since profit cannot usually be realized off of civic space directly, private involvement is likely only if it is required by regulations, if the expenditure is certain to improve the marketability of the development product, or sometimes as a civic gesture. In this last case, the donation often expresses the giver's personal view of what civic space should look like, not necessarily what a civic visioning process might call for. Many private developments, in the course of boosting their business, do provide "civic" spaces, like arcades and food courts at the mall, the atrium at the hotel, or grand lobbies in corporate headquarters—but as noted above, these spaces do not permit the freedoms and flexibility of use that true civic spaces do.

For private development to fund improvement of its civic interface with the public environment, then, the most promising source comes in association with the approval process. Zoning ordinances may require certain civic space improvements carried out in accordance with a plan and a process for the neighborhood or district where the development is located. It is normal practice, for example, for a new development to provide the sidewalks, curbs, and gutters and street repairs that get torn up in the course of development. It is better for the jurisdiction in conjunction with its district and neighborhood partners to have an adopted plan to specify how these improvements will be installed to complement and enhance its surroundings. The result might include streetscapes, lighting, landscaping, and plazas that are cohesively designed to both work effectively and to highlight a civic presence. These provisions can be further enhanced if there is any public funding support for the project, like, for example, tax increment financing for the public-serving parts of the project.

Finally, if the project requires approvals for development beyond what the existing regulations provide, conditions can be attached to the zoning approval. Increasingly, too, as neighborhoods or districts become better organized and clearer on their improvement priorities, separate agreements can be struck that are directly between the community organization (which must be a legal entity) and developers to either mitigate impacts or partner on improvements. These are increasingly referred to as "community benefit agreements." Typically the local government is not a party to such agreements, but its approvals can be complementary to and supportive of such agreements if a clear public purpose is served.

Despite increasing community sensitivities on the part of developers, these kinds of initiatives and provisions are not always welcome. In the same ways that other aspects of urban design benefit from inclusion, though, the first step is to invite the developer to community meetings and listen to his or her perspective, if possible before he or she has settled on the scope and program for the development. Always keep in mind, too, that no development at all is likely to happen unless there is profit to be made. In these circumstances, even modest benefits stemming from the resources and skills that the developer brings may offset any adverse impacts, either real or perceived.

Finally, it is unlikely that any civic-improvement activity will find a single source of funds. Virtually any one funding source will likely require other funds to match theirs, whether it is public funding, private, or foundation funding. In fact, potential funders will expect potential applicants to know this and will be looking for this kind of commitment, likely beginning with what the neighborhood or district is willing and able to put in to the project. Of course, these expectations tend to favor organizations that already have resources and to discourage those that don't, once again reminding us that as a society we have a long way to go to reach equity. Nonetheless, active, eager, together, and well-organized community organizations, even if of lower income and resources, have been able to persist to achieve the goal of making things better than they were—but it might take longer.

Summarizing, in the current setting, there appear to be two trends running in opposite directions in terms of resources for civic involvement and civic improvement. The trend noted in the earlier discussions of citizen participation seems positive. People in communities are becoming more conscious that to make their world better, they may well have to pitch in, organize themselves, and figure out how to do it themselves; those who are doing this are succeeding. The countertrend to which communities are reacting finds private sector real estate and development interests increasingly focused on maximizing profit for survival or gain, and governments less able to pay for what used to be core services. This circumstance is further exacerbated by the increasing infusion into government of privatization initiatives that prioritize those services that realize profits for their private sector partners, often not those that are most needed. One can only hope that the forces for civic purpose can be effective in balancing those seeking personal gain.

# Strategic Considerations for Communities

The strategies should have applicability for all community-based organizations, whether neighborhoods, districts, or issue-based. Chapters 10 and 11 identified a number of ways for addressing the physical attributes that make up the civic environment; strategies for applying them to selected situations and scales are addressed in this chapter. Just as important as these are policy and process strategies that can carry a community forward toward reaching its aspirations. Often, the biggest impediments toward making positive change lie in hidebound private sector, government, or even community structures, habits, cultures, and practices. It is possible, though, to motivate any of the three to listen, and with luck come to allow or even initiate positive change and achieve positive results, though often needing to overcome skepticism or opposition from one or the other that doesn't get it yet.

Threshold questions for community activists will reveal the status that their organizations and their constituencies hold in the current balance with government and private sector organizations. Answers to such questions should also point toward trends and priorities for advancing their interests. For starters, does your jurisdiction's charter or policy formally recognize its neighborhoods' right to consider and advise on prospective developments? On zoning applications? Or liquor license permits? Or the capital budget? Or the comprehensive plan? Are applicants encouraged to review their proposals with neighborhood organizations? Are they required to? Does the jurisdiction freely share its information with neighborhoods or districts about pending development actions? Or is it hard to get such information? Has the jurisdiction put all relevant physical, property ownership, zoning, and other regulatory information online? Do the elected or appointed officials routinely ask in their public deliberations for the neighborhood's or district's perspective on a pending proposal? Does the governing body pay attention to a duly constituted neighborhood organization in forming their own position and vote? Or does the local governing body simply allow individuals to speak at required public hearings? What does the record show on how well the jurisdiction sticks to its own adopted policies in taking formal actions?

The bodies that usually most reliably provide the arena for engaging the public on these kinds of questions are the planning commission; the zoning review committee which may be part of the planning commission; and the city council, by whatever name. Planning commissioners and zoning review bodies themselves are usually made up of citizens who, like community activists and leaders, are people willing to step forward in a volunteer capacity to spend time, often lots of time, for the betterment of the community. They are usually appointed by councils or mayors or both, and while one assumes in this process a certain alignment of viewpoint with their appointers they can and are supposed to act independently. They are under constant pressure from those who come before them asking for something, usually from developers or businesses and their attorneys and consultants—who are paid—with a focus and intensity that is often daunting. The better informed is the community position, the more likely their voice will be heard.

Historically, the community's influence in these processes has favored those areas that already have the most resources, assets and wealth, the higher-income neighborhood and business districts. Lower-income communities have lacked the technical and institutional support to go head to head with the system. The advance of citizen empowerment—enfranchisement, better access to information, the right to speak out, and ultimately the right to vote—seems to be narrowing the gap in many jurisdictions. The traditional "have" neighborhoods may complain about having to increasingly share access to the seats of power with the "have nots," arguing that their higher property taxes, thus support for the government, should entitle them to superior access. While perhaps accurate in terms of dollars per property, this perception may not be accurate in terms of percentage of household resources going to government, especially when factoring in sales taxes.

As it stands, though, in the absence of well-organized and aggressive advocacy for leveling the playing field and the formal adoption of policies to support equitable distribution of scarce resources, poorer neighborhoods will continue to get the short end of the stick. In these circumstances, it is even more important to figure out ways to induce private investment into such areas, knowing that profit is the bottom line and guarding against the kinds of disruptions and dislocations against which lower-income neighborhoods have few defenses. In the context of the economic system, the goal might be to figure out how to make the market work for everyone, not just for those who already have theirs.

All these and more such questions provide the context that community organizations need to understand in order to act effectively in influencing official actions of their government. As implied in the questions, jurisdictions are all over the map in their policies and practices. In Atlanta, neighborhoods are formally recognized in the city charter, and they are afforded an advisory opinion on most of the kinds of actions that can affect the quality of a place.

In other places lacking such a formalized entitlement, perhaps a strategy to consider is how to get to that point. The acknowledgment and encouragement of neighborhood- or district-based organizations as a policy covering all of a jurisdiction's citizens, if not already afforded, is a good place for community leaders to start. The steps needed to gain such formal recognition necessarily brings together widely disparate groupings of people—rich, poor, white, black, Hispanic, Asian, younger, older, and so on.

Without the necessary legal framework and processes within which to exercise their right to speak, neighborhoods are subject to the variable whims of the politics of the day. The process of gaining recognition for a defined role in the public actions that determine the quality of a place is an exercise in democracy that elected officials may have a hard time resisting. For their part, though, the devolving or sharing of power or the risk of challenge for their seat by particularly effective community activists may not be so palatable, and so expect resistance.

The very process puts people in touch with others who may otherwise have little in common, yet the formalized structure only advances the ability for those most affected by pending actions to actually have the opportunity, ideally the encouragement, to influence the outcome. Such organizing effort too prepares neighborhoods or communities to identify or form legally constituted entities that may enter into agreements with prospective developers to partner on related community improvements. In the course of building support for having a seat at the table, neighborhood-centered organizations should consider hooking up with other broader issue-based citizen organizations, like housing, environmental, consumer, jobs, and labor advocacy organizations. While each has its interest area–centered agenda, program, and goals, finding an overlap of interests can bring mu-

---

In the Atlanta zoning process, for example, the developer typically presents his or her proposal to the Neighborhood Planning Unit (NPU), often after presenting to the particular neighborhood where the proposal is located. The NPU makes a formal recommendation to the Zoning Review Board, which that body considers along with the staff report developer and neighborhood presentations, and makes its recommendation to the City Council. The City Council's Zoning Committee then considers all the input and makes its recommendation to the Council as a whole, which then either approves, approves with conditions, or disapproves the application. This sequence of public meetings usually results in an outcome that is better than what was proposed to begin with.

---

tually valuable resources and broaden constituencies necessary to push forward toward meeting a community goal. At the same time, even a simple dialogue may serve to minimize possible conflicts and shift priorities toward greater shared purpose.

Common to most urban design and development strategies is the early step of coming together to develop the shared vision of what could be, written into policy, often a comprehensive plan. The various charrettes, workshops, or other visioning tools and techniques may help in taking this step. The "TOPIC" and "the caterpillar" techniques, for example, provide an overall view of the issues to be faced: TOPIC because all of the issues it stands for must be addressed, and the caterpillar because it provides a checklist for all of the steps that come into play. All of the tools and techniques identified in Chapters 10 and 11 should be periodically reviewed for conceptualizing strategies along the way, just as anyone with a toolbox or a kitchen drawer looks over which tools might be helpful to do which task at what point.

# Strategic Considerations for Urban Designers

Overarching place design principles cut across design of all typologies and all scales. In going through the discovery and analytic processes to approach any urban design and development situation, unifying themes emerge that help summarize and encapsulate the guiding vision. These will point the direction and provide measures for maintaining consistency and consensus with the vision as the work gets detailed into action items and project level work. Urban designers may refer to the themes embodied in the vision as the "big ideas" or the "overall direction" or the "unified vision."

When Portland was conducting its 2040 visioning plan in the early 1990s with the consulting assistance of Peter Calthorpe, for example, unifying overarching themes included that everyone should be able to see Mount Hood, and that every child should be able to walk to a library. One speaks to the natural environmental value of a region-defining icon, the other speaks to walkability, connectedness, and neighborhood quality. Reaching such a point is very valuable, since it represents physical images that almost everyone can agree with, begins to suggest the kinds of action steps that need to be taken to head in that direction, and provides a sufficiently imageable picture that those not involved in the details of the process nonetheless can begin to relate to it at whatever level they choose. Big ideas with physical and readily imageable representations can carry a lot of power in both giving form and communicating more abstract visions, and they figure in the vignette strategies described below.

One caution: Make sure the "big idea" actually addresses a real problem and is not an exercise in "solutionism." It should pass through the TOPIC and other evaluative screens. It should be technically sound. Organizations should be able to come together to support it. The politics should work. Its potential costs and funding sources should be in the ballpark. It should be able to be doable within an acceptable timeframe. And it should represent a nexus of the cultures where it is proposed. Make sure that it is not someone's (watch out for designers) personal agenda. In short, make sure that it has some chance of actually working, or at least pointing in a direction that can be made to be workable. Regions, districts, and neighborhoods are rife with examples of the failed "big idea," usually because the "solution" did not address the problems, a typical failure of "solutionism." Keen design ideas, even if they're doable, are an important part but usually a lesser part in making places better.

At all scales, incorporation of the principles associated with change, design, and organizational structure lies behind strategies for improvement. Recognition that change happens and being ready, positively oriented toward the possible opportunities it might bring, are essential. Committing to some kind of visioning, information sharing, prioritization, and action agenda process is the next step. Being sure to include choices and some sense of their pros and cons will help guide the change process to positive outcomes. In going from visioning all the way through to project definition, the design principles provide a set of slalom poles through which the physical possibilities must pass. Finally, following the organizational principles, structures that are inclusive of all jurisdictions, all disciplines, and all interests are likely to produce a fruitful process.

*"We're against density."*
*"We're against sprawl."*
*"We need more roads."*
*"We want transit."*
*"I'm entitled to my little piece of green."*
*"Our habitat is threatened."*
*"Buy the neighborhood, not the house."*
*"There goes the neighborhood."*

# Strategic Approaches for Recurring Development Problems

A sampling of strategies for dealing with some of the more prevalent issues facing urban designers is outlined here. It is beyond the scope of this book to detail them, yet both tested responses and interesting possibilities suggest themselves as the country moves into a whole new phase under a new administration that many believe could radically alter the approaches for managing America's continued urbanization. The interactive triad of principles related to design, change, and organization will be at work as the country enters this new and unpredictable stage. They are: design for making decisions that both function well holistically and improve quality of life; change for finding ways to glean the positives from nominally oppositional positions and create new syntheses; and organizational arrangements that can represent the broadest of citizens' interests in shaping the inclusive, interdisciplinary, and consultative collaborations necessary to manage the opportunities—or problems—before us.

At the scale of regions' futures, choices need to include consideration for growth and settlement patterns in the face of climate change; carbon footprint implications; jobs, housing, and income disparities; transportation sufficiency; and economic development prospects. At the broadest scale, one choice lies in the balance between the extent to which policy and resources continue to support "sprawl," where land availability and cost drives an ever-outward uniformly low density pattern, or concentration, where places with sufficient infrastructure absorb much of new population and job growth in compact, connected centers, corridors, and transit-oriented development patterns. While there is much to argue for in the concentration model, not least of which are the market shifts that are now supporting it, the likelihood is that regions will experience both patterns. The question will be how much of each fits with citizens' best sense of their desired future and their ability to influence the traditionally dominant forces of real estate, development, transportation, finance, and their political support structures.

Urban designers' opportunity and obligation in this dynamic is to generate and share information about the functional and quality consequences of the two models in the context of shared visions about how people want to see and prioritize their future lives. The interactive set of Vision, Information, and Action as a way of tapping and synthesizing change forces should be useful in both assessing and picturing the consequences of the balances to be struck.

Subsets of this example of regional choice incorporate reading and understanding the region's change forces, its strengths and opportunities, and its relationships with its towns and cities and the transportation networks that tie it all together. For example, most regions retain historic cores, have spawned edge cities, have engulfed older town centers, and have extended strip commercial corridors—almost all of which patterns depend overwhelmingly on the car as the way to get about. Alternative models could include continuing the current dominant pattern, one that everyone knows; revitalizing and intensifying historical city centers; retrofitting edge cities for residential concentrations and transit connectivity; rediscovering the engulfed older towns as major activity centers; and retrofitting strips as mixed-use, higher-density multimodal boulevards.

Continuing with current patterns, while enjoying the inertia of decades-long development relationships and public policy and resource support, is showing the strain of shifting demographics, travel time and cost, and energy and other natural resource excesses. Few urban designers endorse the continuation of these patterns as beneficial or even sustainable, either from an environmental or social sustainability perspective. Yet, millions of families presently enjoy this pattern, and so the job of urban designers is to serve it better with strategies that can prepare for transitions that seem by now inevitable over time.

While the forces at work in the growth dynamics of regions are many and complex, transportation choices seem to provide the best proxy for predicting their future form and functionality. They interact with environmental goals and consequences, with the relationships between housing affordability and job availability, with economic competitiveness, and with cultural and political boundaries. They affect regions as a whole, and they affect regions' subparts: city centers, edge cities, older towns, and the corridors that connect them all together. The following growth management alternative strategies, therefore, all have transportation as a central feature.

These strategies fit within the general rubric of growth management, or how to shape growth more consciously to best meet the needs and aspirations of a region's citizens. Clearly urban designers have a significant role to play in sorting out these dynamics, partly because their holistic workability is crucial and partly because their ability to foster pride by picturing future physical places is essential for rallying citizens' will. In the past, too often these dynamics have not included this role.

Atlanta has become a pioneer in the growth-shaping strategies that support the settlement pattern alternatives. The region was stunned in 1999 by an air quality conformity lapse that denied federal funds to build transportation projects, a circumstance that threatened to paralyze the region's vaunted growth curve. Casting about for a better way to focus growth, the Atlanta Regional Commission (ARC) convened a representation of the region's planning directors to look for solutions. Most growth management precedents depended on such devices as urban growth boundaries (if you are within the boundary you can develop, if you're outside it's harder) or infrastructure concurrency requirements (if you don't have the infrastructure, you can't develop there). Atlanta's planners hit upon a new strategy that supported intensification and reinvestment in existing centers and strips by the simple-seeming device of redirecting 20 percent of projected growth into these and restricting by 20 percent growth in "environmentally sensitive" areas. Modeling the result proved to bring the region within its air quality thresholds and thus lift the federal funding ban.

But how to make the theoretical redirection of growth actually happen? The planners crafted a strategy and then a program that held promise for achieving the goal. Fundamentally different than growth boundaries or infrastructure concurrency, the strategy put more emphasis on the carrot than the stick. Called the Livable Centers Initiative (LCI), the ARC offered centers in towns and cities, and later major travel corridors, funding to prepare plans to strengthen and densify these and to advance their transit and pedestrian access priorities. Then, when the jurisdictions receiving the planning grants followed up with the necessary code changes, transportation priorities, and match funding, the ARC was able to offer capital funds to build key supporting projects. The program didn't force itself on any jurisdiction, rather counting on evolving sentiment favoring the densification goal from both lifestyle and environmental sustainability perspectives to promote its use. Put density where it's wanted, not where it's not.

The EPA recognized the innovation and the major effect of the LCI program on the Atlanta region by giving the ARC its 2008 Smart Growth Achievement Award.

The program has funded dozens of LCIs, which in turn have spawned hundreds of projects that support the goal of shifting policy and financial support away from the next roadway project and toward support of more compact, mixed-use, and ideally mixed-income formations. Importantly, citizen groups, not just local governments, have initiated a significant portion of all the LCI activity, underscoring the potential and the reality of the force of community influence.

Not just Atlanta, but many regions in different ways are engaged in advancing centers and corridors strategies. At the largest scale of consideration are major centers, like downtowns and edge cities. Most such centers already concentrate a significant percentage of a region's jobs and retailing activity. Some have significant housing components, and others are moving to beef up their housing markets. Most have some form of transit. These combinations, coupled with the renewed interest in these kinds of markets, put such centers in position to compete to increase their regional market share. For while employment may have been growing, employment in the sprawl-generated pattern has often grown faster.

The keys to taking full advantage of the combined strengths at this scale are improving housing affordability and increasing the transit and walking share of trips. The range of incomes in these larger centers pretty closely mirrors income distribution for their regions as a whole. Ideally, housing would be available for a significant portion of the centers' workers, ideally with costs that mirrored the income profile. In fact, typically neither ideal is approached, with the result that most workers live at some distance from the workplace, and many of lower income have to travel long distances to their job. While many prefer it that way, many simply don't have the opportunity to live close affordably. One could even imagine that transportation dollars to subsidize land costs necessary to provide affordable housing would be a more efficient way of using the funds than widening rights-of-way and building more lane miles.

On the transit front, many of these larger centers have significant inventories of underdeveloped land, like parking lots and scattered nondescript buildings. Their ability to realize their full development potential is constrained unless the percentage of new trips gets tilted in favor of greater transit and walking share. Particularly where the transit system is based on a rail or other fixed guideway system, transit-oriented development (TOD), or as ULI prefers "development around transit," becomes a way of further heightening the potential for accommodating high densities in existing centers, whether in the core or at the edges. Vehicle miles traveled is a key indicator of travel cost, time, congestion, and air quality, and beefing up major centers is a good strategy for reducing VMT.

A strategy for stitching subdivisions better together and with their region is to reconsider the older, mostly bypassed towns that got swept up in the wave of suburbanization as points of connection. While the retail and office vitality that used to characterize these older centers got sapped with the advent of the roadway strip, many of them retain the good bones of their historic fabric and character. Indeed, many such towns are experiencing a resurgence in which historic character and pedestrian scale are joining with shifting markets that favor such distinctive places. They provide the kinds of mixed density and housing types, and the kinds of retail and office activities that more and more people in the market are seeking. Many are not density-resistant. In some places, like Atlanta, such older towns are finding common cause as places that share features that argue for policy and investment priority. By their history, they tend to be denser, more mixed in population and income, and more focused in their retail and service centers than the subdivisions and strips that surround them. These are the very attributes that attract the shifting markets of young adults who don't choose to live in the subdivision of their childhood, the empty nesters who grew tired of the yard, and seniors who want to be closer to their needs and not so car dependent. Older towns also share the problems of age, and so they need to prioritize public and private infrastructure resources to fix and maintain what have become assets in the emerging markets for urban quality.

In Atlanta, towns including the City of Atlanta banded together and formed the Metropolitan Atlanta Mayors' Association or "MAMA." One of its first successes was to impress on the state DOT the need for treating the state routes that often pass through their historic cores with design treatments more sensitive to their contexts. Or, as one of the mayors put it, "mind your mama."

Strategies focused on strip commercial corridors provide ways for preparing the vast swaths of subdivisions for a more potentially energy efficient and socially democratic pattern. The strips can be pulsed at major crossroads with four corners concentrations of mixed use, mixed income, and mixed housing type development. The ensuing density can support concentrations of amenities and services that provide jobs and serve both the immediate and nearby communities. Such crossroads can become principal stops along transit routes. The streets and roads themselves can pick up decent sidewalk, streetscape, and median treatments to further emphasize punctuations along the travel continuum. In between the crossroads or nodes, the street can take on a boulevard character, with street trees, sign control, utility burial, and controlled access to flanking properties. In this way, what are often dismal and chaotic low-density strips can become distinctive avenues that support a wider range of housing choices and higher levels of shops and jobs, as well as transit alternatives to the car; all together connecting subdivisions better with each other and the wider region.

Older urban neighborhoods have increasingly become "hot" as places where the benefits of proximity match with the fabric and tolerance of diversity that the market is now anointing. This phenomenon brings mixed blessings. In terms of advancing the goal of greater concentrations and densities where infrastructure is in place, it has beneficial settlement pattern effects. In many instances, it is heartening for older neighborhoods to see the confidence that comes with new investment in the form of fixing up, painting, gardening, engagement in neighborhood groupings, and increasing property values. In many others, though, stable lower-income neighborhoods, while encouraged by new investors' commitment, may experience both cultural friction and the tax bill increases that threaten their families' ability to sustain themselves in the old neighborhood.

This effect is referred to as gentrification, and community leaders, local governments, and urban designers should be attuned to both its upside and its downside in order to assure quality of life improvements for all concerned. Taking advantage of the market strength that gentrification indicates, there are strategies that may be helpful in sharing its benefits with the people already there. These include attenuating the period over which transformation occurs, mounting education and outreach campaigns to warn of real estate shysters and predatory lenders, and assuring that new development proposals be considered from the perspective of what values they can impart to the neighborhoods around them. Now, with the collapse of credit and dropping house values, both the positives and negatives of gentrification are likely to go into remission, allowing community people, local government, and developers to reconsider goals and programs. Urban designers can help assess both the likely physical outcomes of various mediation strategies and their workability, as well as picture their physical impacts.

Density is another two-pronged issue that faces many neighborhoods, both in urban and suburban settings. We have dealt with the subject in earlier chapters in discussions of smart growth and new urbanism. More generally, in and around existing neighborhoods, population density is an indicator of the levels of amenities and services available, the feasibility of workable transit, and to some extent, income, age, and ethnic diversity. On the other hand, though, density without the infrastructure to support it, and density driven by developers without regard to its impacts, can detract from neighborhood quality. The likeliest candidate areas for introducing or supporting densification strategies are in underdeveloped fringe areas, like in parking lot–laden centers and along strip corridors, where the development can be properly buffered by scaling down density or otherwise respecting the nearby neighborhoods.

From a strategic point of view, city policies should favor those neighborhood situations where the people there support density and discourage it where it is not wanted. As described earlier, development initiatives that need zoning changes provide affected neighborhoods the opportunity to negotiate for mitigations or amenities that leave them better off after the development than they were before. An example would be to condition the zoning provisions parallel with the use of community benefit agreements. The stability and well-being of settled neighborhoods is likely to be more important than abstract or one-size-fits-all density propositions. There are no cities where the need for growth is so great that encroaching on unwilling neighborhoods is necessary.

# Summary

The dual focus of strategic effort for this book is on strengthening the community sphere in the interactive dynamic with the private sector and the government, and heightening the importance of design and the involvement of urban designers to improve the quality of the civic environment. What community-based leaders and urban designers share is a history of episodic prominence dotting an otherwise peripheral presence in the dynamics that create the urban landscape. What the two groupings can aspire to and how they can support each other in that aspiration is to extend and broaden their impact to make better places for everyday citizens everywhere to conduct their lives. Communities, generally not directly motivated by profit, have the numbers that are necessary to build increasing influence over investment and development decisions that affect their interests, specifically their civic space. Urban designers can reach beyond either their profit-driven private practices or their time-intensive public practices to provide the technical assistance necessary to show what civic improvement alternatives might look like and how they might happen.

Communities gain technical capability that cuts across the separate disciplines, one or another of which usually dominates the outcome of conventional project-by-project development. Urban designers gain a constituency that can be pivotal in advancing better patterns of development and higher quality, better functioning day in–day out environments.

Based on the premise of this text that things only get better to the extent that they get at least a little better for everyone, and that winners and losers is not an acceptable urban design outcome, the strategies here aim toward leveling the playing field. Their context is making the places where we carry on our daily life activities better, at the walking-around scale of places or the getting-around scale of regions. Making places better for everyone, not just a few, is the goal, which suggests that recognizing and accepting that a place getting better for everyone is getting better for me. A place getting better for some few, on the other hand, may not be getting better for me.

It takes a lot of commitment, a lot of work, a lot of time and tolerance for a lot of frustration to figure out and then carry out strategies that will work for the improvement of places everyday people live in. Much of the necessary work goes uncompensated in money, whether neighborhood or district volunteers or people in the design disciplines working beyond the scope of their paid jobs. People, though, are putting themselves through this process in increasing numbers in places all over the country for the overriding purpose of improving the environment that supports their daily lives. People in search of a world where they matter started to push open doors in the 1960s that are still a long way from fully open. The forces inside, whether consciously or not, continue to resist the necessary changes.

The trends are positive, though. People are using increased access to government and private sector development processes to put themselves into the game. They are using increased access to information to inform themselves of what's possible, to find models for how development affecting the civic realm can be done better. They are getting together, organizing with their close neighbors and broader groupings to foment for change and then follow through on the opportunities that open up.

Urban designers for their part are still a new, small but growing force. They are putting the understanding and the integration of disciplines and general knowledge of the whole of the civic environment over any one subpart. They are gravitating toward engaging in and contributing to the larger civic processes that ultimately produce places that work better for people, both in attraction and functionality. Some of them, frustrated with the one-dimensional requirement of private practice and eager to redirect government priorities, are taking back their government by going to work for it.

The strategies suggested here are just smatterings of the kinds of processes that are multiplying around the country, where the common goal is making places better for everyday people's everyday lives, to provide a leadership role for those people in determining the outcomes. Especially now, with the drum roll for development interrupted by the credit crisis and broader economic downturn, citizens, governments, and developers can catch their breath and plan for a better future. Such plans can take into account mounting pressures for better environmental stewardship, energy diversification and efficiency, climate change, crumbling infrastructure, and the widening, deepening gulf between haves and have nots—all issues fundamental to the quality of life of all citizens. As people's widely separated initiatives to improve their places gain momentum, one can look forward to pushing the agenda into rearrangements of all the forces that have generally resisted the new and people's role in it. Local, state, regional, and federal policies, comprehensive plans, rules, tools, and requirements can change, and private investment priorities and measures can adjust to support a more progressive dialectic in the ongoing dance between profit and people.

# BIBLIOGRAPHY

## Introduction

This book is the product of experience, mine and others'. The principal value of the books listed below lies in their provision of an overall framework for comparative analysis. In that context, I find them to represent a useful and valuable compendium for further reading on the subject. In addition to the titles and authors below, for currency in the fast-changing field of urban design, I recommend keeping up with and at least scanning articles on the subject in all the journals and websites listed in Chapter 10, Tools.

One of my challenges in undertaking this effort has been the dialectic between practice and theory. Practice in urban design is all over the map, and, consistent with its intrinsic interactive, multidisciplinary nature, new experience may significantly alter older ideas. Research and publication on any subject lags behind what is actually happening. It focuses instead on what already has happened for the purpose of understanding and projecting the lessons and the meaning of past experience, hopefully into useful future applications. In many fields, this process is able to focus on discreet, definable, and circumscribed topics within the larger field, with the goal of searching out reliable truths. This is not so easy for urban design, partly because it is relatively early in its conceptual and research life and partly because by its nature it is not a discrete field and puts more emphasis on links between its associated disciplines than on itself.

Nonetheless, this book seeks to provide a way of framing and acting on urban design and development issues that recur and can be counted on to continue to recur, even though their particulars might vary widely. In my view, the books listed below generally share this aspiration.


Alexander, C. (1977). *A pattern language.* Oxford, UK: Oxford University Press.

Alexander, C. (1987). *A new theory of urban design.* New York: Oxford University Press.

American Association of State Highway and Transportation Officials (AASHTO). (2004). *A policy on geometric design of highways and streets* (5th ed). (The "Green Book.") Washington, DC: AASHTO.

Appleyard, D. M., Gerson, S., & Lintell, M. (1981). *Livable streets.* Berkeley: University of California Press.

Banerjee, T., & Southworth, M. (eds.) (1990). *City sense and city design: Writings and projects of Kevin Lynch.* Cambridge: MIT Press.

Barnett, J. (1982). *An introduction to urban design.* New York: Harper and Row.

Barnett, J. (1986). *Elusive city: Five centuries of design, ambitions, and miscalculations.* New York: Harper and Row.

Barnett, J. (2003). *Redesigning cities: Principles, practice, implementation.* Chicago: APA Planners Press.

Barnett, J., Benfield, F. K., Farmer, P., & Poticha, S. (2007). *Smart growth in a changing world.* Chicago: APA Planners Press.

Ben-Joseph, E. (2005). *The code of the city: Standards and the hidden language of place making.* Cambridge, MA: MIT Press.

Bruegmann, R. (2005). *Sprawl: A compact history.* Chicago: University of Chicago Press.

Calthorpe, P. (1993). *The new American metropolis: Ecology, community, and the American dream*. New York: Princeton Architectural Press.

Calthorpe, P., & Fulton, W. (2001). *The regional city*. Washington, DC: Island Press.

Carson, R. (1962). *Silent spring*. New York: Houghton Mifflin.

Castells, M. (2000). *The information age: Economy, society, and culture*. New York: Blackwell.

Chase, John, Crawford, Margaret & Kaliski, John (eds.) (1999). *Everyday urbanism*. New York, NY: Monacelli Press.

Chaskin, R. J. (2005). Democracy and bureaucracy in a community planning process. *Journal of Planning Education and Research, 24*, 408–419.

Clay, G. (1973). *Close-up: How to read the American city*. New York: Praeger Publishers.

LeCorbusier. (1973). *The Athens Charter* (A. Eardley, Trans.). New York: Grossman Publishers.

Davis, M. (1992). *City of quartz*. New York: Vintage Books.

Doxiades, K. A. (1968). Ekistics: *An introduction to the science of human settlements*. New York: Oxford University Press.

Duany, A., & Plater-Zyberk, E. (2008). Smart Code, Version 9.2. www.dpz.com.

Duany, A., Plater-Zyberk, E., & Speck, J. (2001). *Suburban nation: The rise of sprawl and the decline of the American dream*. New York: Farrar, Straus and Giroux.

Duany, A., & Talen, E. (2002). Transect planning. *Journal of the American Planning Association, 68(3)*, 245–266.

Ellin, N. (2006). *Integral urbanism*. New York: Routledge.

Faga, B. (2007). *Designing public consensus: The civic theater of civic participation for architects, landscape architects, planners and urban designers*. Hoboken, NJ: John Wiley & Sons.

Farr, D. (2007). *Sustainable urbanism: Urban design with nature*. Hoboken, NJ: John Wiley & Sons.

Garvin, A. (2002). *The American city: What works, what doesn't* (2d ed). New York: McGraw-Hill.

Gindroz, R., Levine, K., et al. (2003). *The urban design handbook: Techniques and working methods*. New York: W.W. Norton.

Glazer, N., & Lilla, N. (eds.) (1987). *The public face of architecture: Civic culture and public spaces*. New York: Free Press.

Hall, P. G. (2002). *Cities of tomorrow: An intellectual history of urban planning and design in the twentieth century* (3d ed.). Oxford, UK: Blackwell Publishing.

Hayden, D. (1995). *The power of place: Urban landscapes as public history*. Cambridge, MA: MIT Press.

Hess, P. M., Moudon, A. V., & Logsdon, M. G. (2001). Measuring land use patterns for transportation research. *Transportation Research Record* (1780), 17–24.

Hester, R. (1985). Subconscious landscapes of the heart. *Places 2(3)*, 10–22.

Hillier, B. (1996). *Space is the machine: A configurational theory of architecture*. Cambridge, UK: Cambridge University Press.

Howard, Sir E. (1902; pub. 1946). *Garden cities of tomorrow*. London, UK: Faber and Faber.

Institute of Transportation Engineers (ITE). (2006). *Context Sensitive Solutions in Designing Major Urban Thoroughfares for Walkable Communities: An ITE Proposed Recommended Practice*. Washington, DC: ITE.

Jackson, J. B. (1994). *A sense of place, a sense of time.* New Haven, CT: Yale University Press.

Jacobs, A. B. (1996). *Great streets.* Cambridge, MA: MIT Press.

Jacobs, A. B. (1985). *Looking at cities.* Cambridge, MA: Harvard University Press.

Jacobs, A. B. (2006). The state of city planning today and its relation to city planning education. *Places 18(2).*

Jacobs, J. (1961). *The death and life of great American cities.* New York: Random House.

Koolhaus, R. (1998). *Small, medium, large, extra-large.* New York: Monacelli Press.

Kostof, S. (1992). *The city assembled: The elements of urban form through history.* Boston: Bullfinch Press.

Kostof, S. (1991). *The city shaped: Urban patterns and meanings through history.* Boston: Little, Brown.

Krier, L. (1998). *Architecture: Choice or fate.* Windsor, UK: Andreas Papadakis.

Krieger, A., & Lennertz, W. (1991). *Towns and town-making principles.* New York: Rizzoli.

Kunstler, J. H. (1993). *The geography of nowhere: The rise and decline of America's man-made landscape.* New York: Simon and Schuster.

Leccese, M., & McCormick, K. (eds.) (2000). *Charter of the new urbanism.* New York: McGraw-Hill.

Litman, T. (2008). *Use impacts on transport: How use factors affect transportation behavior.* Victoria, BC: Victoria Transportation Policy Institute.

Lynch, K. (1984). *Good city form* (2d ed.). Cambridge, MA: MIT Press.

Lynch, K. (1960). *The image of the city.* Cambridge, MA: MIT Press.

Lynch, K. (1976). *Managing the sense of a region.* Cambridge, MA: MIT Press.

Lynch, K. (1971). *Site planning* (2d ed.). Cambridge, MA: MIT Press.

Lynch, K. (1972). *What time is this place?* Cambridge, MA: MIT Press.

Madanipour, A. (2006). Roles and challenges of urban design. *Journal of Urban Design, 11(2),* 173–193.

McHarg, I. (1967; pub. 1992). *Design with nature.* New York: Doubleday.

Meyer, M., & Miller, E. (2006). *Urban transportation planning: A decision-oriented approach.* New York: McGraw Hill.

Morris, A. E. J. (1996). *History of urban form: Before the Industrial Revolution* (3d ed.). London, UK: Prentice Hall.

Moudon, A. V. (ed.) (1987). *Public streets for public use.* New York: Van Nostrand Reinhold.

Mumford, L. (1961). *The city in history: Its origins, its transformations, and its prospects.* New York: Harcourt, Brace & World.

Newman, O. (1972). Defensible space; crime prevention through urban design. New York, NY: Macmillan.

Peponis, J., Bafna, S., & Zhang, Z. (2006). *The connectivity of street: Reach and directional distance.* Atlanta: College of Architecture, Georgia Institute of Technology.

Rowe, C., & Koetter, F. (1984). *Collage city.* Cambridge, MA: MIT Press.

Sorkin, M. (2001). *Some assembly required.* Minneapolis: University of Minnesota Press.

Southworth, M., & Ben-Joseph, E. (2003). *Streets and the shaping of towns and cities.* Washington, DC: Island Press.

Talen, E. (2008). New urbanism, social equity, and the challenge of post-Katrina rebuilding in Mississippi. *Journal of Planning Education and Research, 27(3),* 277–293.

Trancik, R. (1986). *Finding lost space: Theories of urban design.* New York: Van Nostrand Reinhold.
Van der Ryn, S. & Calthorpe, P. (1991). *Sustainable communities: A new design synthesis for cities, suburbs and towns.* Jackson, CA: Sierra Publishing Co.
Venturi, R., Scott Brown, D. & Izenour, S. (1977). *Learning from las vegas.* Cambridge, MA: MIT Press.
Whyte, W. H. (1980). *The social life of small urban spaces.* Washington, DC: Conservation Foundation.
Whyte, W. H. (1984). *Learning from the field: A guide from experience.* Beverly Hills, CA: Sage.
Whyte, W. H. (1988). *City: Rediscovering the center.* New York: Doubleday.
Wright, F. L. (1935). Broadacre city: A new community plan. *Architectural Record, LXXVII,* 243–254.
Zeisel, J. (1981). Inquiry by design: Tools for environment-behavior research. Monterey, CA: Brooks/Cole.
Zube, Ervin H. (ed.) (1970). *Landscapes: Selected writings of J. B. Jackson.* Amherst, MA: University of Massachusetts Press.
Zukin, S. (1996). *The culture of cities.* Cambridge, MA: Blackwell.

# INDEX